D1230543

BOUND *for the* PROMISED LAND

BOUND *for the* PROMISED LAND

—

Harriet Tubman,

PORTRAIT OF AN AMERICAN HERO

KATE CLIFFORD LARSON

BALLANTINE BOOKS

NEW YORK

A BALLANTINE BOOK

Published by

THE RANDOM HOUSE PUBLISHING GROUP

Copyright © 2004 by Katherine Clifford Larson

All rights reserved under International and Pan-American Copyright Conventions.
Published in the United States by The Random House Publishing Group,
a division of Random House, Inc., New York, and simultaneously in
Canada by Random House of Canada Limited, Toronto.

Epigraphs on pages 55 and 85 are from "Runagate Runagate" by Robert Hayden in
The Norton Anthology of African American Literature, edited by Henry Louis Gates, Jr.,
published by W. W. Norton & Company, Inc., in 1997.

PHOTO CREDITS

Opposite title page: Harriet Tubman, circa 1905. Courtesy Cayuga Museum of History and Art,
Auburn, N.Y.   *Page 28:* The Maryland Historical Society, Baltimore, Md.   *Page 77: Cambridge
Democrat,* September 5, 1849. Courtesy Jay Meredith.   *Page 79: Cambridge Democrat,* October 3,
1849. Courtesy Jay Meredith.   *Page 118:* Photo courtesy Judith Bryant.   *Page 147: Cambridge
Democrat,* October 28, 1857. Courtesy Jay Meredith.   *Page 164:* Courtesy the National Park
Service.   *Page 215: Harper's Weekly,* July 4, 1863.   *Page 223: Scenes in the Life of
Harriet Tubman,* Sarah H. Bradford. Auburn, N.Y.: W. J. Moses, Printer, 1869.
INSERT: *Frederick Douglass, William Still,* and *Thomas Garrett:* Courtesy Chester County Historical
Society, West Chester, Pa. *Lucretia Coffin Mott* and *Martha Coffin Wright:* Courtesy Sophia Smith
Collection, Smith College, Northampton, Mass. *Gerrit Smith* and *Sarah Hopkins Bradford:*
Courtesy Jim McGowan. *John Brown:* Private collection. *Colonel James Montgomery: Recollections of
Seventy Years,* Franklin B. Sanborn. Boston: The Gorham Press, 1909. *Franklin B. Sanborn:*
Courtesy Concord Free Public Library. *Taken in 1887 or 1888:* Courtesy Division of Rare &
Manuscript Collection, Cornell University Library. *Harriet Tubman, date unknown:* Courtesy
Norman F. Bourke Memorial Library, Cayuga Community College, Auburn, N.Y. *Harriet Tubman,
circa 1896–1898, Harriet Tubman Home for the Aged,* and *John Brown Hall: Tribute to Harriet Tubman,
the Modern Amazon* by James E. Mason and Edward U.A. Brooks. 1915. *Margaret Stewart Lucas* and
Harriet Tubman, circa 1908: Courtesy Schomburg Center for Research in Black Culture, The New
York Public Library. *Harriet Tubman in her last year:* Courtesy Norman F. Bourke
Memorial Library, Cayuga Community College, Auburn, N.Y.

Ballantine and colophon are registered trademarks of Random House, Inc.

www.ballantinebooks.com

Library of Congress Cataloging-in-Publication Data
is available from the publisher upon request.
ISBN 0-345-45627-0

Maps by William L. Nelson, Accomac, Va.

Manufactured in the United States of America

FIRST EDITION: JANUARY 2004

1 3 5 7 9 10 8 6 4 2

Book design by Barbara M. Bachman

To Spencer, Rebecca, and Trevor

ACKNOWLEDGMENTS

—

THIS BIOGRAPHY WOULD NOT HAVE BEEN POSSIBLE WITHOUT THE contributions of many individuals and institutions. I am particularly indebted to my dissertation committee members, J. William Harris, Ellen Fitzpatrick, W. Jeffrey Bolster, and John Ernest, all from the University of New Hampshire, and Jacqueline Jones, from Brandeis University. Thank you for your amazing efforts in guiding this biography to completion. I am also indebted to numerous institutions that provided me with financial support, including a University Dissertation Fellowship and a Summer Fellowship for Graduate Students from the University of New Hampshire; a Mary Catherine Mooney Fellowship from the Boston Athenaeum; a Margaret Storrs Grierson Scholar-in-Residence Fellowship from the Sophia Smith Collection at Smith College; a Research Fellowship from the John Nicholas Brown Center for the Study of American Civilization at Brown University; a Price Research Fellowship from the William L. Clements Library at the University of Michigan, Ann Arbor; and a Legacy Fellowship from the American Antiquarian Society.

There have been many, many other people along the path of research for this biography to whom I am also greatly indebted. The librarians, archivists, and staffs at the following institutions deserve special acknowledgment for their patience and diligence in helping me find records and documents. Many of them are working with limited staff and funding, and I appreciate the efforts they expended on behalf of my work. Thanks to the Maryland State Archives, Maryland Historical Society, Sophia Smith Collection at Smith College Library, Cornell Special Collections Department, Boston Public Library Rare Book Room, Boston Athenaeum, American Antiquarian Society, John Nicholas Brown Center, William L. Clements Library, Dorchester County Public Library, Seymore Public Library (Auburn, New York), Houghton Library and Schlesinger Library at Harvard, Syracuse University Special Collections Library, Troy (New York) Public Library, Special Collections Department at the University of Rochester, St. Catharines Museum, Historical Society of Pennsylvania, National Archives, Library of Congress, Swarthmore College Special Collections Department, Schomburg Library, Winchester Public Library, Harriet Tubman Home (Auburn, New York), Harriet Tubman Organization (Cambridge, Maryland), University of New Hampshire Library, Dorchester County Register of Wills, Cayuga County Clerk's Office (Auburn, New York), and Lambton County Library (Sarnia, Ontario, Canada). There are also many others around the country who graciously and professionally tracked down references, often very obscure, in their collections. I am indebted to the untold numbers of genealogists around the country who post their research on the Internet's numerous genealogy Web sites; this has made much of my detailed research into family histories far easier and more accurate. I am also deeply grateful to the Harriet Tubman relatives I have met, particularly Judith Bryant, whose early support and enthusiasm carried me through many a difficult day. There are other individuals I would like to acknowledge and thank as well, including Jean Humez, Jim McGowan, Milt Sernett, John Creighton, Barbara Mackey, Bonnie Ryan, Vicki Sandstead, Beth Crawford, Dennis Gannon, Susan and Jay Meredith, Kay McKelvey, Charles Blockson, Mark Solomon, Nell Painter, Harriet Alonzo, Paul Hutchinson, Pauline Copes Johnson, Pat Lewis, Bradley Skelcher, Gary Broadus, Robert Stewart, Helen Maddox, Gwen Robinson, Brian Prince, Harriet Price, Arden Phair, Don Schaefer, Mike Long, Ward DeWitt, Stephanie Bryant, Rachel Bryant, Peggy Brooks-Bertram, Frank Newton, Harold Ruark, J. O. K. Walsh, Pat Guida, Vivian Abdur-Rahim, Paul and Mary Liz Stewart, Scott Christianson, Sid Taylor, and Mariline Wilkins.

Thank you all. I would also like to thank my friends for their kindness and helpfulness while I worked on my dissertation, and then as I re-crafted that work into this book. Gretchen Adams deserves special note for listening and advising so well over the years. I thank also my agent, Doe Coover, for having such faith in me and this work, and my editor, Elisabeth Dyssegaard, whose expert guidance and patience helped bring this biography to print.

The most important acknowledgments go to my family, and in par-ticular my husband, Spencer, and children, Rebecca and Trevor, who embraced Harriet as another member of our family. They gave up vaca-tions, weekends, and evenings while I spent all my time researching and writing this biography. I do not know where they found the patience to continue to support me with love and enthusiasm. Thank you for everything.

C O N T E N T S

—

INTRODUCTION

—

*T*HEY LITTER THE FOREST FLOOR, SOMETIMES INCHES DEEP, NATURE'S bed of nails. The seedpods of the sweet gum tree, common in the forests of the Eastern Shore of Maryland, are large, round, and covered with spiny, prickly burrs. The spines pierce the calloused, unprotected feet of terrified runaway slaves. Struggling to contain the involuntary impulse to wince in pain, the fugitive slaves hesitate, knowing that a moment taken to pause or cry out could end their dream of freedom. The lucky ones had shoes. The children never did, and they suffered the most. How ironic that the sweet gum would be so cruel.

For many of these slaves, the sweet gum tree had provided for them since birth. A hollowed-out trunk would be fashioned into a cradle, affectionately referred to as "the gum," for generations of slave children. The sweet gum's bright green star-shaped leaves, which turn a magnificent scarlet in the fall, emit an aromatic fragrance, a subtle hint of its therapeutic properties. A cut in its bark reveals a yellowish resin used in making folk treatments for skin irritations, wounds, and dysentery. Yet for these runaways the burrs of the sweet gum tree would be among the first of many barriers—whether natural or human—on the road to freedom. Harriet Tubman knew this was where the weakest would turn back. For the faint of heart she carried a pistol, telling her charges to go on or die, for a dead fugitive slave could tell no tales. Not all the tracks on the Underground Railroad were smooth.

It was late November 1860, and Harriet Tubman had returned to Dorchester County, on the Eastern Shore of Maryland, to rescue her sister Rachel and Rachel's children, Ben and Angerine, from slavery. Tubman had spent ten years trying to bring them to freedom. Time and time again, Rachel had been unable to join Harriet; separated from her children, Rachel had been unwilling to leave them behind, and Harriet had been unsuccessful in retrieving them. This attempt would end in failure, too. Unbeknownst to Harriet, Rachel had died some months before. To compound the tragedy, her nephew Ben and niece Angerine remained out of Tubman's grasp. Overcoming deep anguish and profound sadness, Tubman turned her attention instead to rescuing another family from slavery: Stephen and Maria Ennals and their three children.

The weather was bitter cold, and the unexpected driving snow and icy rain made this trip with children particularly dangerous and tense. With little planning and no additional clothing or food, the Ennalses trusted Tubman to bring them through to freedom. They suffered terribly. The baby had to be drugged with opium to keep it from crying and revealing their hiding place as slave patrols passed by. They starved and froze, but they eventually celebrated Christmas in freedom. Though this was another successful trip for Harriet, the loss of her sister and the debilitating effects on her health from the difficult trip were almost too much for her to bear. A decade of bringing family and friends to the North and freedom had taken a great toll. This would be Tubman's last rescue mission.

WE ALL BELIEVE that we know Harriet Tubman, who lived from 1822 to 1913; referred to as "Moses" in her time, Tubman is best known for her role as a conductor on the Underground Railroad. Her secret journeys into the slave states to rescue women, men, and children have immortalized her in the minds of Americans for 130 years. These accomplishments, however, have also served to create a mythological image of a woman about whose actual life we know little. Though she is one of the most famous women in our nation's history, most of us have come to know the narrative of her life through biographies written for young people. In fact, the last adult biography of Tubman, Earl Conrad's *Harriet Tubman*, was published in 1943.

In 1863 Franklin B. Sanborn, editor of the *Boston Commonwealth*, an antislavery newspaper, published the first biographical sketch of Harriet Tubman. "The true romance of America," he wrote, could be found "in the story of the fugitive slaves." Setting the stage for future biographies, Sanborn claimed that the drama of Tubman's life story had the "power to shake the nation that so long was deaf to her cries."[1] Two years later, Ednah Dow Cheney added to Sanborn's sketch, describing Tubman as "probably the most remarkable woman of this age," who "has performed more wonderful deeds by the native power of her own spirit than any other."[2] A more detailed biography by Sarah Bradford appeared a few years later; released in 1869 as *Scenes in the Life of Harriet Tubman*, it set Tubman's early life permanently in the historical record. By the time William Still's famous 1871 documentary volume, *The Underground Railroad*, was published, Tubman's status as a heroine without equal was established.[3]

In elementary schools across America, children now learn of Tubman's heroic deeds. Relegated to the dustbin of history before the civil rights movement of the 1950s and 1960s, Tubman reemerged during the 1970s and 1980s as one of the ten most famous Americans in history, after Betsy Ross (number one) and Paul Revere (number two).[4] Harriet Tubman has become part of the core American historical memory. But incredibly, what children learn about Tubman is largely all that we as a nation know of her.

The reality of Harriet Tubman's life is far more compelling than the partly fictionalized biography so familiar to schoolchildren. Why have we been satisfied with the mythical Tubman and why has her biography remained within the province of children's literature? Although the myths are rooted in actual achievements and serve to enhance the legend of Harriet Tubman, they do so at the expense of her real life story. The true facts of Tubman's long life, including her years under slavery, her family life, her profound spirituality, her accomplishments as a freedom fighter from her Underground Railroad days to her Civil War exploits and then later her suffrage and community activism, reveal a remarkably powerful and influential life endured during some of the darkest days in American history. Motivated by a deep love of family, Tubman struggled against great odds to bring scores of relatives and friends to freedom in the North. Necessarily shrouded in secrecy at the time, the details of her escape missions have been buried in the historical record for generations. There is, therefore, a need to rediscover Harriet Tubman, to separate reality from myth and to reconstruct a richer and far more accurate historical account of her life.

HARRIET TUBMAN WAS BORN Araminta "Minty" Ross on the plantation of Anthony Thompson, south of Madison in the Parsons Creek district of Dorchester County, Maryland, probably in late February or early March 1822. She was the fifth of nine children born to Harriet "Rit" Green and Ben Ross.[5] Both slaves, Rit and Ben were owned by different masters: Rit was enslaved by Edward Brodess, Anthony Thompson's stepson, and Ben, a highly skilled timber man, belonged to Thompson, who was a wealthy and prominent landowner. The Ross family's relatively stable life on Thompson's plantation came to an abrupt end sometime in late 1823 or early 1824, when Edward Brodess claimed ownership of Rit and her children through the estate of his mother, Mary Pattison Brodess Thompson. He took Rit and her five children, including Minty, away from Ben to his own farm in Bucktown, ten miles to the east. Brodess often hired Minty out to temporary masters, some of whom were cruel and negligent, while selling some of her siblings and their children illegally to out-of-state buyers, permanently fracturing the Ross family.

Working as a field hand while a young teen, Minty was nearly killed by a blow to the head from an iron weight thrown by an angry overseer at another fleeing slave. She suffered from headaches, seizures, and sleeping spells (probably symptoms of temporal lobe epilepsy) for the rest of her life. During the late 1830s and early 1840s Tubman worked for John T. Stewart, a Madison merchant and shipbuilder, bringing her back to the community near where her father lived and where she had been born. About 1844 she married a local free black named John Tubman, shedding her childhood name, Minty, in favor of Harriet, possibly in honor of her mother.

When Edward Brodess died at the age of forty-seven in 1849, his many debts left Harriet and her siblings at risk of being sold. To avoid an unknown fate on the auction block, Tubman took her own liberty in the late fall of 1849. She tapped into an underground organization that was already functioning well on the Eastern Shore. Traveling by night, using the North Star and instructions from black and white helpers, she found her way to freedom in Philadelphia.

Over the next eleven years Tubman returned to the Eastern Shore of Maryland approximately thirteen times to liberate family and friends; in all, she personally brought away about seventy former slaves, including her brothers and other family and friends. She also gave instructions to approximately fifty more slaves who found their way to freedom independently. When Sarah Bradford published her first biography of Tubman in 1869, she flagrantly exaggerated those numbers to nineteen trips and three hundred rescued. Tubman herself claimed to have made only eight or nine trips and rescued approximately fifty people by the summer of 1859.[6] Even this, however, was enough to earn her the byname Moses. Her monumental and dangerous efforts to bring away her enslaved family and friends elevated her status to that of a heroine without equal. Long obscured in the historical record, the details of these escape missions reveal intricate planning involving complex networks of black and white supporters who risked their own lives to help Tubman achieve her goals. Compelling and moving, these stories testify to multiple acts of heroism inspired by the pursuit of freedom.

Tubman relied heavily upon a long-established, intricate, and secretive web of communication and support among African Americans to effect her rescues. The collective efforts of free and enslaved African Americans operating beyond the scrutiny of whites along the various routes to freedom were crucial to her success. Though white Quaker and abolitionist support was vital to Tubman's survival and success, it was the African American community from the Eastern Shore of Maryland and the Chesapeake Bay to Delaware, Pennsylvania, New York, New England, and Canada that provided the protection, communication, and sustenance she required during the darkest and most dangerous days of fighting for freedom.

Tubman's father, Ben Ross, who had been freed in 1840, greatly influenced her. An Underground Railroad agent himself, Ross faced arrest after he was exposed in 1857. At enormous risk, Tubman returned to the Eastern Shore to rescue him and her mother, and bring them to safety in Canada. There never was a $40,000 reward for Tubman's capture, a figure that became grossly exaggerated through the retelling of her story. It was not until eight or nine years after Tubman had run away and had made several trips back to rescue family and friends in late 1857 and early 1858, that slaveholders on the Eastern Shore became aware that someone was likely helping slaves run away from their masters. Even then, they did not know the identity of the culprit, or whether that person was a man or woman, black or white.

Tubman's remarkable ability to travel undetected in slave territory piqued the interest of John Brown, a radical abolitionist and fiery freedom fighter. Tubman became a devoted supporter and confidante, helping Brown plan for his ultimately flawed attack on Harpers Ferry, Virginia, in 1859. Her total commitment to destroying the slave system eventually led her to South Carolina during the Civil War, where she alternated roles as nurse and scout, cook and spy, in the service of the Union army. Eventually she became the first American woman ever to lead an armed raid into enemy territory.

Settling in Fleming, New York, outside the city of Auburn, after the Civil War, Tubman became an active member of the local African American community. She welcomed scores of orphaned children, destitute and sick former slaves, and others in need into her home, and was often reduced to begging for food, money, and clothing. Maintaining her relationships with a multitude of former white abolitionists, Tubman moved between two very different and highly segregated worlds. Through them, however, she remained an active presence in the woman suffrage movement that struggled, foundered, and renewed itself in the latter part of the nineteenth century. Though destitute and frail, she continued her campaign for civil rights until her death in 1913.

IN 1907 AN ARTICLE about Harriet's life appeared in the *New York Herald*. "There is not a trace in her countenance of intelligence or courage, but seldom has there been placed in any woman's hide a soul moved by a higher impulse, a purer benevolence, a more dauntless resolution, a more passionate love of freedom. This poor, ignorant, common looking black woman was fully capable of acting the part of Joan d'Arc."[7] This imagery of a "poor, ignorant, common looking black woman" belies Tubman's intellectual development and her evolving confidence in her own abilities, and it demonstrates the journalist's failure to grasp the substance of Tubman. While enslavement itself was certainly motivation enough for Tubman to seek freedom, ignoring the other aspects of her life and times makes it impossible to fully explore her rich and productive intellectual and spiritual life. This is a reflection of the limited potential identities available to black women as historical actors.

In the years following Tubman's death in 1913, the black community maintained Tubman's memory, mostly in segregated classrooms. With her story shortened and simplified, she entered the pantheon of black achievers, where her narrative became part of a usable past for African Americans. Highly fictionalized accounts of her life started appearing in the late 1920s and early 1930s, specifically works for children and young adults that highlighted the history of the Underground Railroad, which had caught the interest of the nation.[8] In 1938 a reporter named Earl Conrad began researching a full-length biography of Tubman. In the age of Jim Crow, Conrad's efforts to shed light on certain aspects of Tubman's life were thwarted repeatedly by uninterested archivists, librarians, and publishers who found no value in the biography of a black woman. Conrad's book, *Harriet Tubman*, did help lay the foundation for the scores of juvenile biographies published over the last six decades.

Harriet Tubman was unable to read and write for herself, and so her narrative has come down to us as a series of mediated images created and exploited by others. Tubman's life story has been reduced to a simple account of a courageous mother figure rather than the complex story of an intelligent, crafty woman, with flaws and needs of her own, who transcended negative assumptions about black women's abilities and achieved what very few men or women, black or white, have accomplished. We may never know how selective or creative Tubman was when she revealed her life story to her friends, but she ultimately played a significant role in the crafting of her image as one of the most famous Underground Railroad conductors of her time.

Nevertheless, in the absence of a written personal record we are left with accounts of her life that reflect a variety of contrived and incomplete portraits. The significance of a new biography of Tubman lies not only in its detail but also in the way it illuminates the patterns of neglect and complacency expressed in the racial stereotypes that have minimized, if not erased, her many contributions. Based on new information and fresh sources from hidden and long-forgotten private and public records, a more accurate life story of the real Harriet Tubman is finally possible.

TUBMAN WAS GUIDED by an interior life shaped by a particular slave experience. Suffering under the lash, disabled by a near-fatal head injury, Tubman rose above horrific childhood adversity to emerge with a will of steel. Refusing to be bound by the chains of slavery or by the low expectations limiting the lives of women and African Americans, Tubman struggled against amazing odds to pursue her lifelong commitment to liberty, equal rights, justice, and self-determination. Owing her success to unique survival techniques, Tubman managed to transcend victimization to achieve emotional and physical freedom from her oppressors. Supported by a deep spiritual faith and a lifelong humanitarian passion for family and community, Tubman demonstrated an unyielding and seemingly fearless resolve to secure liberty and equality for others.

She died a free woman, surrounded by family and friends in the home for aged African Americans she had dreamed of for decades. Although she did not live long enough to witness the granting of the vote to women, Harriet Tubman's role as an ardent suffragist and political activist, fighting for the rights of African Americans, has inspired generations of Americans who have been deeply moved by her lifelong quest. Like the biblical Moses who led the Jews out of Egypt, Tubman

sprang from an unlikely background—uneducated, female, and black—
to emerge as a leader among men. It is this tale of physical and spiritual
struggle that has resonated with Americans of many backgrounds into
the twenty-first century. Tubman's remarkable life, more powerful and
extraordinary in its reality, is the stuff of legend and, ultimately, of a
true American hero.

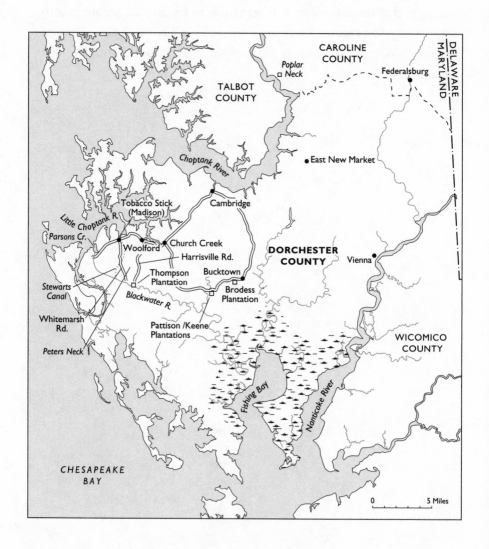

Dorchester County, circa 1800–1860.

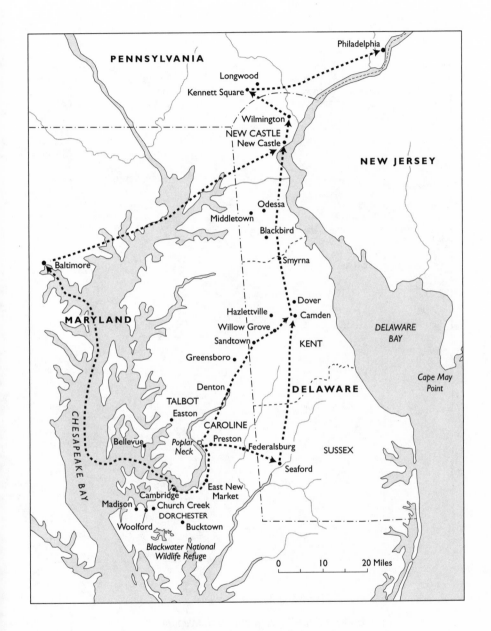

*Harriet Tubman's southern
Underground Railroad routes to Philadelphia.*

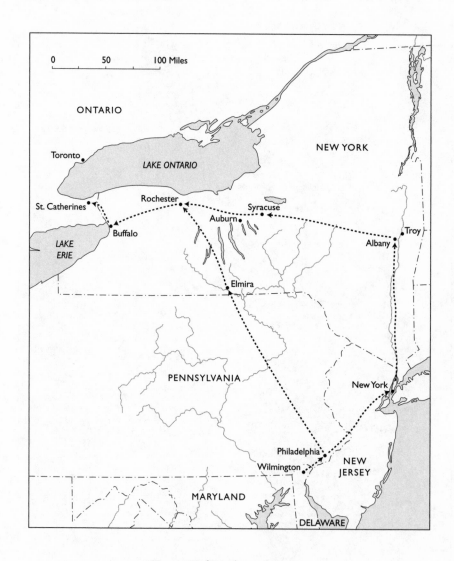

*Harriet Tubman's northern
Underground Railroad routes to freedom.*

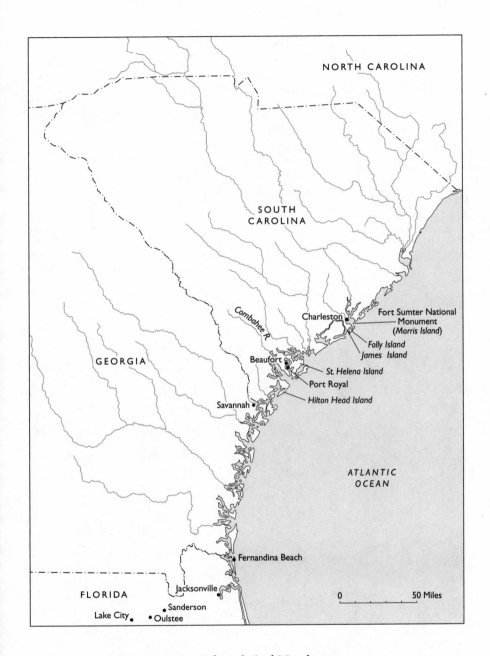

Harriet Tubman's Civil War theater.

BOUND *for the* PROMISED LAND

CHAPTER 1

LIFE ON THE CHESAPEAKE
IN BLACK AND WHITE

WHEN HARRIET TUBMAN FLED HER DEAD MASTER'S FAMILY IN 1849, she was not the only slave from the Eastern Shore of Maryland racing for liberty. In 1850 a total of 279 runaway slaves earned Maryland the dubious distinction of leading the slave states in successfully executed escapes.[1] The motivations for running away are no mystery; however, in many cases the methods of escape remain unknown even to this day. Despite stepped-up efforts in Maryland and other southern states to thwart escapes during the ten years before the Civil War, some slaves did marshal the strength and courage to take their liberty. But few returned to the land of their enslavers, risking capture and reenslavement, even lynching, to help others seek their own emancipation.

How did Tubman successfully escape bondage in Dorchester County, and how did she manage to return many times to lead out family and friends? Not merely the recipient of white abolitionist support, Tubman was the beneficiary of, and a participant in, an African American community that challenged the control of white Marylanders, from the time of the earliest Africans brought from Africa to the outbreak of the Civil War.

Tubman's story begins several decades before her birth with a complicated set of interrelationships, black and white, enslaved and free, of several generations of families living on the Eastern Shore of Maryland. As historian Mechal Sobel describes it, this was a "world they made together."[2]

DORCHESTER COUNTY LIES between two rivers, the Choptank to the north and the Nanticoke to the south and east, and extends from the Chesapeake Bay to the Delaware state line, encompassing almost 400,000 acres of dense forest full of oak, hickory, pine, walnut, and sweet gum; marshes and waterways; and extensive farmland. Numerous navigable rivers and creeks crisscross the county, offering access to trade and suitable sites for shipbuilding. The flat terrain provides abundant tillable lands for tobacco, wheat, corn, fruit, and other agricultural products, and before modern times, the vast supply of oyster shells helped keep soils fertile.

The Choptank River rises near the Delaware line, flowing south between Caroline and Talbot Counties and on to Dorchester County, finally emptying into the Chesapeake. In the nineteenth century, the river remained navigable for nearly forty miles upstream from the Chesapeake Bay.[3] Dorchester's southern border, the Nanticoke River, was navigable throughout its course from Seaford, Delaware, to the Chesapeake; the town of Vienna served as its port of entry and became a major trading center during the early nineteenth century, providing bay access to neighboring Somerset County and southwestern Delaware.[4]

It was to this landscape that Harriet Tubman's African ancestors were forcibly brought to labor in servitude to white masters. Enslavement of Africans in Maryland, and the laws and regulations that codified slavery's existence, evolved slowly over a hundred-year period. Until the early eighteenth century white indentured servitude was common, particularly on the Eastern Shore. Some planters had both slaves and indentured servants; by the 1730s and 1740s, however, shipments of black captives from Africa to the Americas had increased dramatically. Numerous laws were enacted relating to ownership of slaves, including ones specifying that any children born to an enslaved woman would carry the status of the mother, with ownership remaining with the slave woman's owner, even if the father was a free black or a white man.[5]

Thus Tubman's story begins with the history of some of the white families who claimed ownership of her and her family. The detailed records of the lives of the white families who enslaved Tubman, her family, and her friends, demonstrate the sharp contrast between the lives of whites and blacks, lives intimately entwined yet irreconcilably different. Following these white families' lives as closely as the remaining records allow reveals the lives of their enslaved people, bringing to life the web of community into which Tubman was born. The white Pattisons, the Thompsons, the Stewarts, and the Brodesses played key roles in the lives of Tubman's family. On the Eastern Shore of Maryland, most black people, slave and free alike, moved around according to the land ownership patterns, occupational choices, and living arrangements of the region's white families. Out of necessity, many black families maintained familial and community ties throughout a wide geographic area. Family separations were not always precipitated by sale; some whites owned (or rented) land and farms across great distances, requiring a shifting of their enslaved and hired black labor force at varying times throughout the year, or at various times over a period of decades when new land had been purchased and the cycle of clearing and establishing new farms began. This pattern of intraregional movement forced families and friends (both black and white) to create communication and travel networks in order to maintain ties with family and community. These complicated networks made it possible for Tubman to become one of the rare individuals capable of executing successful and daring rescues repeatedly.

A devastating fire at the Dorchester County courthouse, set by an unknown arsonist in May 1852, destroyed a great portion of Dorchester County's historical records.[6] Because few records survived from before 1852, piecing together the nature of black and white relationships in Dorchester County can be done in only a limited way. For instance, we do not know the names of all the slaves owned by Edward Brodess, Harriet Tubman's owner, nor all of those owned by Anthony Thompson, the owner of Tubman's father, Ben Ross, from the first half of the nineteenth century.

Several documents did survive the fire: the records of the Orphans Court from 1847 to 1852 were saved because the clerk of the court brought the logbook home to work on it over the weekend. This quirk of fate secured a five-year segment of history important to revealing details of Tubman's life and of those black and white families who were part of her community. Other records were saved, too: the books listing manumissions, freedom papers, and many chattel records (where slave sales were recorded) were preserved, providing important information about the black community and vital genealogical data for many families in the area. District court cases, heard at the appeals court located in neighboring Talbot County, were recorded at the state level, as were most land transactions, thereby preserving some information from the colonial era and the early republic. Fortunately, these court records contain some of the most dramatic documentation available detailing Harriet Tubman's life in slavery.

Reaching Beyond the Grave: The Legacy of a Patriarch

In 1791 Atthow Pattison, the patriarch of a long-established Eastern Shore family, sat down to contemplate his legacy to his children and grandchildren. A Revolutionary War veteran, a modest farmer, and an even more modest slaveholder, Pattison could proudly trace his roots in Dorchester County back at least a century. Intermarrying for generations, the Pattisons and other Eastern Shore families consolidated their control over vast tracts of dense timberland, rich marshlands, and productive farms.

Standing at his front door, Pattison could view much of his approximately 265-acre farm, situated on the east side of the Little Blackwater River, near its confluence with the larger Blackwater River.[7] From the wharf in front of his home Pattison probably shipped tobacco, timber, and grain, destined for England and other markets, and received goods originating from the West Indies or England as well as other trading points in New England and along the Chesapeake.[8]

After dividing tracts of land, including his home plantation, and arranging for payments to his grandchildren when they came of age, Atthow bequeathed his remaining slaves and livestock to his surviving daughter, Elizabeth, and her children, Gourney Crow, James, Elizabeth, Achsah, and Mary Pattison, and to his son-in-law, Ezekiel Keene, and his children, Samuel and Anna Keene. Elizabeth, in keeping with her father's implicit understanding that his children marry "in the family," had married her cousin William Pattison, and they lived on a nearby plantation.[9] Atthow's second daughter, Mary, had married her cousin Ezekiel Keene and moved to a farm south of Atthow's land, though she was dead by the time the will was written.

When Atthow Pattison died in January 1797 he gave to his granddaughter Mary Pattison one enslaved girl named "Rittia and her increase until she and they arrive to forty five years of age."[10] This phrase, limiting Rit's and her children's terms of service to forty-five years, provided for Rit's eventual manumission, or freedom, from slavery.[11] Maryland manumissions had taken place even in the earliest days of slavery. Never an informal procedure, manumissions were taken quite seriously and were often recorded in land records (as deeds) for each county. Some slaves were able to earn enough money to buy their own freedom, and on occasion slaves sued for their freedom, some eventually prevailing. In 1752 Maryland passed a law restricting manumission by will to slaves "sound in body and mind, capable of labor and not over fifty years of age," so as to prevent slaveholders or estates from avoiding responsibility for the care and maintenance of "disabled and superannuated slaves." Manumitting slaves was illegal if the grant of manumission was written in part "during the last fatal illness of the master," or if the freeing of slaves affected the ability of creditors to settle their claims against the estate of the deceased.[12] This legislation, it was hoped, would slow the increasing number of deathbed manumissions and hold slaveholders more accountable for the support and maintenance of indigent slaves.

Limiting Rit's term of service lowered her market value to Pattison's heirs if they were inclined to sell her after gaining possession of her. No doubt Pattison was aware of this, but he may have been influenced by the spirit of the times. On the Eastern Shore, as elsewhere in the new nation, a complex movement was emerging, both religious and secular, that spurred a marked increase in manumissions during the 1790s. While elite families still maintained much control, wealth could be achieved readily with the expanding production of wheat and other grains for export markets, providing viable roads to prosperity for entrepreneurial families in Dorchester and the surrounding counties. The rise of intensive grain agriculture and timber harvesting transformed work patterns on the Eastern Shore. Tobacco production required a year-round labor force, but grain agriculture did not. While timber harvesting could be carried on throughout the year, it also required continuous acquisition of land once one lot had been cut, and it demanded a predominantly male labor force. These factors, among others, altered the nature of black slavery and freedom on the Eastern Shore by 1800; on one hand, free black labor became, to some extent, a more attractive economic alternative to owning slaves, while on the other hand, some white slaveholders found it lucrative to sell off their excess slaves.[13]

The Debate over Slavery: Manumission and the Question of Freedom

An increasingly important religious awakening—founded upon Quakerism and Methodism—and an ideological legacy of freedom from the American Revolution sparked intense debate about the moral, political, and economic validity of slavery. While the rise in manumissions and petitions for freedom immediately following the American Revolution was in part a function of the Revolution's rhetoric of liberty, it was also a function of fluctuating economic conditions, less labor-intensive agricultural work, and a self-sustaining and economically viable free African American population, all of which made term limits and manumissions more palatable to slaveholders as an alternative to perpetual bondage.

An increasingly pronounced antislavery sentiment in England also sparked intense debate in America. In Maryland, citizens from the Eastern Shore, including those from Talbot, Dorchester, and Caroline Counties, petitioned the House of Delegates in 1785 for the abolition of slavery. Abolitionist voices throughout Maryland became quite influential, so much so that increasing numbers of slaves initiated successful lawsuits against their masters for their freedom. Outraged, slaveholders forced the Maryland state legislature to impose sanctions against the

Maryland Society for Promoting the Abolition of Slavery, effectively dismantling it by the mid-1790s.[14]

On the Eastern Shore, Quakers manumitted hundreds of slaves by deed and by will in the 1780s. Methodism evolved slowly in Maryland at first, but during the 1790s it spread rapidly throughout Dorchester and surrounding counties. Though the most elite families of the Eastern Shore initially remained loyal to the Anglican Church, Methodism played an important role in the increasing number of manumissions.

But elite slaveholder concerns about the impact of the growing free black population on their ability to control the economic, political, and social dynamics in their communities became a powerful counterpoint to antislavery sentiment on the Eastern Shore. While immediate emancipation remained a choice for some Methodist slaveholders (and some non-Methodist ones), it appears that the majority who considered manumission for their enslaved people followed a policy of delayed manumissions, executing deeds of manumission for some future date. In this way, the slaveholder ensured that he remained the beneficiary of a slave's most productive years. Others sold their slaves for a limited term of years, putting cash in their pockets while assuaging their consciences by providing for eventual manumission, which in all cases of delayed manumission "afforded the greatest amount of protection for the master's purse while still appeasing the troubled conscience."[15]

The Abolition Society argued in the 1780s that restrictions on the ability of a slaveholder to manumit his slaves (as defined in the 1752 law) was in direct conflict with the rights of free individuals to control their property, regardless of whether it was a slave or a piece of land. The question of limits on deeds of manumission was debated at yearly meetings of the Society of Friends, at the General Court, and finally before the House of Delegates in Maryland. After several defeats in the Maryland Senate, a revised bill was passed in 1790, allowing for "manumission freely by deed, properly executed, as before [per the 1752 law], or by will at any time, saving only the rights of creditors, and provided that the slave be not over fifty years and be able to work, at the time he was to be free." In 1796 the law was amended to restrict manumissions to those slaves under forty-five, which at the time was still a relatively advanced age.[16] Atthow Pattison's intention was to manumit those slaves specifically mentioned in his last will and testament of 1791 when they turned forty-five, five years sooner than the maximum allowed under the 1790 law.[17]

Limiting a slave's term of service was one method of ensuring loyalty from enslaved people, who could eventually join the growing freed and freeborn black population. Term limits also allowed slaveholders to ease their conscience within the context of the newly formed ideas of democracy and Christianity in the early republic.[18] This attitude was not incompatible with a belief that slavery could remain intact and be perpetuated.

Born sometime between 1785 and 1789, Tubman's mother, Rit, grew up in the Pattison household, probably with her mother, Modesty, and other close kin. According to Maryland's colonial census taken in 1776, Atthow Pattison owned five slaves.[19] Slave names were rarely recorded in the census, as slaves were considered chattel, much like sheep, cattle, and horses. By 1790 Pattison's household consisted of twelve individuals, five whites and seven slaves.[20] The higher number could reflect the birth of additional slave children to the enslaved women in Pattison's household. While Modesty is not mentioned in Atthow Pattison's will of 1791, she was at one time owned by Pattison and may have been one of the seven slaves listed in 1790.[21] Another slave, Minty, was bequeathed to Pattison's grandson Samuel Keene. Pattison bequeathed two enslaved women, Bess and Suke, to his daughter Elizabeth Pattison. All of them were to be freed when they turned forty-five.[22] These enslaved women were more than likely part of a family grouping of their own. As a child, Tubman had been given the name Araminta and was called Minty. Rit might have named her daughter after a favorite aunt, perhaps the sister of her mother. At the least, she named her child after a woman for whom she felt familial affection.[23] Later, Samuel Keene sold the elder Minty and a child called Ritty to his cousin, also named Samuel Keene.[24]

Atthow Pattison's granddaughter Mary Pattison married Joseph Brodess, a local farmer from Bucktown, in central Dorchester County, in 1800. Joseph and Mary settled into a home adjacent to her mother Elizabeth's plantation, south of the Little Blackwater Bridge, with five slaves.[25] Elizabeth, a widow in 1800, was the head of a rather large household of fifteen white and black people, including seven slaves. Brodess probably helped his mother-in-law manage her plantation. Indeed, given such a large household, including six minor white children and no adult white males, Elizabeth most likely needed her son-in-law's assistance. Joseph's own property, north and slightly east of his mother-in-law's, had not been developed yet, or his family was farming the land for him.[26] Brodess and his siblings, Edward and Elizabeth, had inherited several hundred acres in Bucktown from their father, Edward Brodess Sr., who died in 1796.

Mary Pattison Brodess gave birth to a son, Edward, on June 14, 1801. Sometime after June 1802 Joseph Brodess died, leaving Mary a young widow.[27] By 1803 Mary had married Anthony Thompson, a moderately successful landowner, with interests in several businesses on the Eastern Shore, and a descendant of early Dorchester County settlers. Mary's rapid remarriage represented the reality of life for women in the early republic. In need of support, possessing some limited wealth of her own, and the custodian of her infant son's inheritance, Mary sought to secure her future and that of her son by marrying within the community a man of equal or better social and financial standing. A woman's right to her own inheritance or to that of her dead husband was circumscribed by laws that limited her ability to control and own property outright. Though Mary entered the marriage with perhaps some yearly income from the residue of her grandfather's estate, she was more than likely not secure enough to maintain herself and her son independently.

Anthony Thompson was also a widower; Polly (Mary) King, his first wife, died sometime between 1800 and 1803. Thompson inherited his property in the 1780s; the majority of it sat near the Blackwater River in central Dorchester County. Over the years he added considerably to his land holdings in the area.[28] When Polly died, she left Anthony with three young sons, Edward, Anthony C., and Absalom Thompson, who were all under the age of fifteen. Thompson, who lived in Church Creek at the time, also owned about nine slaves.

It was to this household that Mary Pattison Brodess brought her young son, Edward, her personal slave, Rit (Harriet Tubman's mother), and four male slaves who had been owned by her deceased husband,

Joseph.[29] One of Thompson's slaves, Ben Ross, was a highly skilled and valued timber inspector and foreman, who managed the timbering operations on Thompson's heavily forested property. Through Mary and Anthony's marriage, Rit and Ben became members of the same household, and they eventually married and started their own family around 1808.[30]

The Trade in Black Bodies

Although it is unclear how Anthony Thompson came to own Ben Ross, Ben may have had extensive kin relationships with both free and enslaved blacks in the immediate area.[31] By 1810 Thompson had fifteen slaves; these additional slaves could be Rit, the four male slaves, and perhaps Rit's young daughter Linah, who was born around 1808.[32] Where Thompson and the Pattisons acquired their slaves in the first place is not known, but historical records reveal an active slave trade from Africa to the Chesapeake during the mid-eighteenth century, disembarking over eighteen thousand slaves onto Maryland soil.[33] According to Harriet Tubman's first biographer, Franklin Sanborn, Harriet was "the grand-daughter of a slave imported from Africa, and has not a drop of white blood in her veins."[34] In a later interview, another newspaper reporter wrote that "the old mammies to whom she told [her] dreams were wont to nod knowingly and say, 'I reckon youse one o' dem "Shantees," chile.' For they knew the tradition of the unconquerable Ashantee blood, which in a slave made him a thorn in the side of the planter or cane grower whose property he became, so that few of that race were in bondage."[35] It has been generally assumed that at least one, if not more, of Tubman's grandparents came directly from Africa. Another interviewer later reported that Tubman believed that Rit's mother, Modesty, had been "brought in a slave ship from Africa" and that Rit "was the daughter of a white man, an American." She also claimed that Ben was "a full blooded Negro."[36] Modesty is the only person noted in the historical record as being one of Tubman's grandparents.[37] Ben Ross's parentage remains unknown, though there is evidence of possible siblings and other relatives living in the county, both free and enslaved.[38]

Slave trade patterns in the Chesapeake during the eighteenth century offer some clues to Tubman's African heritage. Modesty, or any one of Tubman's other black grandparents, may have been taken as a child sometime during the mid-1700s while living on West Africa's Gold Coast, in the region now known as Ghana, populated by the Asante ethnic group, among others. Though "prone to revolt," the Asante were highly prized by slaveholders in Maryland and Virginia because of their strong physical ability and flexibility in performing different work tasks.[39] Most likely sold directly from the deck of a slave ship somewhere along the Chesapeake Bay or at the eighteenth-century slave market in Oxford, Maryland, these slaves eventually settled with the expanding planter families who were clearing and managing property in Dorchester County.

The Asante empire defended itself against colonial rule far longer than most African states, finally succumbing to the British in 1896. They did not succeed, however, in protecting themselves from capture and enslavement in the Americas. Years of conflict between the Asante and their neighbors in the eighteenth century offered a steady supply of Fante, Asante, and other Gold Coast captives who were sold as slaves to New World markets.[40] Most of these captives belonged to a variety of "Akan linguistic subgroups."[41]

Though gold was an enormously important trade commodity, the Asante economy was also based on agriculture. The Asante culture was highly spiritual, believing in the sacredness of land and water. Asante society was rooted in the power of great ancestresses and was noted for the roles its women played as advisors and leaders in the community. Asante ancestresses "came from either the sky or the earth to the forests," enabling the transition of the Asante people from hunter-gatherers living in the forests to farmers living in established villages and towns throughout the region. The Asante became adept at clearing densely forested land for small farms, establishing specific timetables for alternating fallow and production, and they were keenly aware of the need to protect the newly cleared land from the disastrous effects of soil erosion, particularly near rivers and streams. European observers noted the well-ordered and fenced farms of the Asante producing abundant crops of yams, corn, nuts, cassava, and plantains. It was perhaps these skills associated with forest clearing and agriculture that made the Asante and the related peoples of present-day Ghana so attractive as slave labor on the Eastern Shore.[42] The Asante developed social and cultural imperatives that placed a high value on "fruitfulness, increase, maximization, [and] abundance." New World planters very well may have detected this "principle of accumulation" among the Akan.[43]

Like other West African peoples, the Asante believed in a variety of deities linked to both the natural and spiritual worlds. The most powerful were associated with bodies of water, but the land was the link between the dead and the living, from which all Asante individual and communal values emanated. After death the ancestors continued to live in a parallel world and could be sought out in times of need. "Displacement was therefore a traumatic, personality-altering experience, especially as it terminated in a sugar cane or tobacco field on the other side of the world."[44]

The cultural traditions of West African peoples enslaved in the Chesapeake region and elsewhere may have persisted in the New World far longer than has previously been thought. Enslaved Africans from the Gold Coast "brought an acute understanding of the role and significance of land with them to the New World. They were among those who saw the need for a connection both tangible and spiritual."[45] Historians long believed that cultural retention was nearly impossible due to significant cultural mixing among Africans during the Middle Passage, leaving little opportunity for maintaining an ethnic or cultural identity once established on the plantation. Recent research suggests that slaves brought to the New World were not distributed randomly, creating opportunities for ethnically similar peoples to establish communities in the New World.[46] London traders brought the majority of African slaves to Maryland, and of those, the greatest number came from the Gold Coast and Upper Guinea.[47] This may have worked well for slaveholders in the long run. Planters may have wanted slaves with similar ethnic and cultural backgrounds to ensure more congenial work groups and ease the transition for frightened and angry new slaves.[48] Once a slaver arrived in the Chesapeake and began selling slaves on the Eastern Shore, several buyers from the same area would most likely purchase slaves at the same time, thus increasing the possibility that slaves could have culturally similar people nearby, if not on the same plantation.

As the planter class expanded on the Eastern Shore throughout the eighteenth century, slave ships plied their trade on both sides of the Chesapeake, in ports such as Cambridge, Oxford, and St. Michaels, in addition to selling slaves directly to plantation owners on their own docks along the rivers and bays. By the 1740s enslaved Africans had become the dominant labor resource for the expanding agricultural and timber economy of the Chesapeake. Slave imports rose steadily in Maryland between 1720 and 1770, culminating in over fifty-three hundred slaves disembarking during the decade prior to the Revolution.[49] After banning slave imports in 1783, Maryland relied more and more on intraregional trading, smuggling, and the natural growth of the slave community to increase its slave labor force. But African cultural practices surely persisted, as evidenced by such African names as Ibo, Mingo, Winnebar, Sinta, Suke, and Binah in the census records, and descriptions in manumission records that include such identifying characteristics as "has holes in his ears for bobs" and "pattern on jaws." As late as 1840 names such as Winnibar, Sinta, and Mingo persisted.[50] One Eastern Shore man recalled that his grandfather owned an African slave by the name of Suck and that his grandfather had purchased her from a "slave ship which had come up the Chesapeake Bay." When he was a young boy, Suck told him that she had been a member of an African tribe that "was defeated in battle with another tribe and numbers of her people were captured" and sold to slave traders plying the African coast.[51]

Meanwhile, the state's free black population grew from approximately 1,800 in 1755 to over 8,000 in 1790 and almost 34,000 by 1810.[52] In Dorchester County, there were 5,337 enslaved and 528 free blacks in 1790; by 1800 the free black population had increased dramatically to 2,365, while the enslaved population fell to 4,566.[53] Over the same period, Dorchester County's white population was largely stagnant, at around 10,000. Younger white Dorchester County residents migrated to North Carolina, Georgia, and farther west and south in search of better opportunities.[54]

The status of free blacks did not improve in relation to their growing numbers. In fact, as the free black population increased, whites became alarmed and quickly enacted new laws and codes to restrict free blacks' political rights as well as their economic and social options. By 1796 free blacks could no longer testify in court. Though some were given the right to vote if they had been free before 1783 and owned property, by 1802 all free blacks were stripped of voting rights, just as landless whites were gaining access to the vote. Methodism, the great hope for many slaves in the 1790s, became increasingly more conservative and restrictive while appeasing the needs and desires of the more recent converts, elite slaveholders. During the summer of 1800 a secret network of slaves living in and around Richmond, Virginia, made plans for an armed rebellion against their masters and the government. Their leader, Thomas Prosser's slave Gabriel, was betrayed the night before the raid. Though scores of African Americans were arrested and twenty-seven were eventually hanged, some southern whites became more fearful of their enslaved people. In 1805 a local Dorchester County slave was arrested and hung for planning an "insurrection to kill the white citizens of this county," permanently disabling any hopes for black liberty.[55] During the War of 1812 British forces established a base on Tangier Island in the mouth of the Chesapeake, where they made numerous successful attempts to entice slaves away from their owners to join the ranks of the British military, as the "Colonial Marines." Visions of armed former slaves renewed slaveholders' deep-seated fears of insurrection.[56]

Throughout the 1810s the Eastern Shore struggled with economic uncertainty. While demand for export products such as grain and timber reached all-time highs during the War of 1812, peace brought European products flooding back into American markets. Grain and timber prices dropped dramatically, severely affecting Eastern Shore farmers and manufacturers. Chesapeake traders faced increasing competition and barriers to freer trade, with escalating tariffs and taxes imposed on both sides of the Atlantic.[57] The fortunes of many of Dorchester's elite families waned; in fact, Anthony Thompson, one of the county's largest land- and slaveholders and a pillar of the community, was imprisoned for debt in 1817. Despite debt problems, Thompson remained in Dorchester County, expanding his landholdings and continuing to farm his plantation and harvest virgin timber on tracts of land for local and Baltimore mills and shipyards.

As the Eastern Shore turned from a predominantly tobacco-based economy to one of grain and timber export, many slave owners started reducing their slave holdings to accommodate the shift from year-round labor-intensive tobacco growing to cyclical crops. A slowing local economy and the rise of cotton in the lower South also dramatically altered the incentives for Maryland's slave owners. Rather than manumit their excess slaves, many planter families began to sell them to traders plying the Chesapeake communities, looking for fresh sources of labor for the rapidly expanding economies of Alabama, Mississippi, Louisiana, Florida, and Texas. For black families, the constant possibility of separation emerged in the nineteenth century as one of the greatest threats to their well-being.

SOMETIME BEFORE THE CENSUS was taken in 1810, Mary Pattison Brodess Thompson died, leaving her minor son and her slaves in the care of her second husband, Anthony Thompson.[58] Rit presumably worked for Thompson or was hired out by him for the benefit of young Edward Brodess's future inheritance, enabling her and Ben to maintain a stable family life. Their young family grew to five children; in addition to Linah, who was born in 1808, Mariah Ritty arrived around 1811, Soph in 1813, Robert in 1815, and Minty in early 1822.[59] For Ben and Rit, the crisis of separation loomed as Edward approached twenty-one in 1822, the age at which he could claim his inheritance and independence from his stepfather's control. Now the Ross family's hitherto stable life was about to be dramatically altered.

SWEET GUM AND PRICKLY BURRS:
THE CHANGING WORLD
OF THE EASTERN SHORE

O N MARCH 15, 1822, ANTHONY THOMPSON PAID A MIDWIFE $2 TO assist Harriet "Rit" Green in childbirth.[1] This could be a fortuitous record of Tubman's birth; Harriet, like most slaves, was unsure of her own birth date.[2] Frederick Douglass, the famous abolitionist and runaway slave and, like Harriet, a native of the Eastern Shore, lamented his ignorance of the date of his birth: "I have no accurate knowledge of my age, never having seen any authentic record containing it. By far the larger part of the slaves know as little of their ages as horses know of theirs, and it is the wish of most masters within my knowledge to keep their slaves thus ignorant. I do not remember to have ever met a slave who could tell of his birthday. They seldom come nearer to it than planting-time, harvest-time, cherry-time, spring-time, or fall-time."[3]

By the time Tubman was born, Rit had already been passed down through several generations of Atthow Pattison's family under a series of inheritance bequests, like a chest of drawers or a coveted piece of jewelry. Ultimately owned by Edward Brodess as a collateral member of the Pattison family, Rit and her children became Edward's personal property when he became an adult in 1822. Eventually Tubman and her

siblings were moved from Thompson's plantation, spending their childhood and early adulthood in and around Bucktown, where Edward
Brodess farmed his own small plantation.[4]

Since the death of his second wife, Mary Pattison Brodess Thompson, sometime around 1810, Anthony Thompson had continued his
role as legal guardian to Mary's son, Edward Brodess. As Thompson's
ward, Edward was dependent on the wise and prudent management of
his assets by his stepfather. These assets, which included over two hundred acres in Bucktown, slaves, cash and investments, and other real
and personal property, were to come into Edward's possession when he
turned twenty-one in June 1822. Thompson was legally bound by
Maryland law to use Edward's estate for the maintenance and education of his ward only, and to secure and preserve the estate's assets for
Edward's use once he reached the age of maturity.

In June 1820 the Orphans Court of Dorchester County authorized
Anthony Thompson to proceed with the construction of a house, "a
single story 32 by 20 [ft.] two rooms below with two plank floors and
brick chimney, and also a barn of good material" on the Brodess property under the supervision of Brodess's uncle Gourney Crow Pattison.
At a cost of $1,300, the improvements to Brodess's property exceeded
the value of his inheritance. Unable or unwilling to reimburse Thompson for funds expended for the construction, Brodess was facing the
prospect of having to sell part of his land or some of his slaves. In open
defiance of his stepfather, Brodess forced Thompson to take the matter
before the county court. Subpoenaed to appear in October 1823,
Brodess eluded attempts to bring him before the Dorchester County
Orphans Court in Cambridge for several months. Thomas H. Hicks, a
lawyer and local sheriff (and future governor of Maryland), was commanded to take Brodess into custody to ensure that he would "have his
[Brodess's] body before the Judges" to answer Thompson's suit for payment. Brodess was clearly in no hurry to appear before the court.[5]

Brodess finally stood before the justices in April 1824 with his attorney, Robert P. Martin. Thompson charged that Brodess owed him over
$1,800 "for diverse goods wares and merchandise."[6] This included ex-
penses for clothing, board, food, the care of slaves, and other similar
items, totaling approximately $570. During continued court action over

the next two years, Brodess promised time and time again to pay Thompson, but by April 1827 Thompson still had not been paid. Finally a jury decided in Thompson's favor, and Brodess was ordered to pay Thompson immediately.

Supported by his Pattison relatives, Brodess appealed the case to the District Court of Appeals in Easton, Talbot County. Arguing that the Orphans Court of Dorchester County did not have the legal authority in 1820 to authorize Thompson to build on Brodess's land, Brodess made a final attempt to avoid reimbursing his stepfather. The appeals court agreed, charging the Orphans Court had exceeded its legal authority and had, in effect, encumbered Brodess's estate beyond what was legally allowed.[7] Thompson had lost his case, leaving a bitter legacy between the two men.

Brodess moved into his new house in Bucktown sometime between early 1823 and early 1824, leaving behind the social and community network that surrounded Thompson's plantation in Peters Neck. Thompson had leased the Brodess property in Bucktown in 1821 and 1822, and probably for prior years as well.[8] While it is possible that Rit and her young children accompanied Brodess to his new home, they may have remained with Thompson for some time. Still the guardian to Edward Brodess in 1822, Thompson maintained accounts for the hire, care, and maintenance of Brodess's slaves and other property, both real and personal. When Tubman was born in early 1822, her mother, Rit, would have been under the control of, and probably working for, Thompson. According to testimony provided in his lawsuit against Brodess, Thompson also provided "board and clothing for two Negro children" from January to November 1822 at a cost of $2 per month.[9] These children are probably Robert and Soph, who were both under the age of ten at that time and may not have been hired out, but rather worked about the Thompson farm. Mariah Ritty, at ten or eleven years old, may have been hired out for food and clothing. Linah, who was thirteen or fourteen years old, was hired out at $12 per year during 1821 and 1822, and Samuel, Shadrach, and Frederick, three of the four male slaves Mary Pattison inherited from her first husband, Joseph Brodess, were also hired out for the benefit of Edward's inheritance.

Thompson credited his ward's account for the "hire of negro Rit for

1821," for the sum of $16. Rit was ill during the year, however, so Thompson debited the account for forty-three days' lost time and charged Brodess for "board and attendance" for Rit for those lost days.[10] This may have been for lost time associated with her pregnancy. There are similar debits for lost time for Sam and Frederick, suggesting that these slaves suffered from a local epidemic of some sort.[11] Rit was not hired out for money in 1822; she either remained in his household for the year or was hired out for merely clothing and food. This practice of hiring out pregnant women and women with small children for board and clothing was not uncommon.[12]

It is very likely that the midwife whom Thompson paid in March 1822 was there to assist Rit as she gave birth to Tubman. Tubman recalled,

[I]n the eastern shore of Maryland Dorchester County is where I was born. The first thing I remember, was lying in de cradle. You seen these trees that are hollow. Take a big tree, cut it down, put a bode in each end, make a cradle of it and call it a 'gum. I remember lying in that there, when the young ladies in the big house where my mother worked, come down, catch me up in the air before I could walk.[13]

Indeed, according to the 1820 U.S. Census for Dorchester County, Thompson had two white females between the ages of ten and twenty-six living in his house.[14] One was probably his niece, Barsheba, and the other his daughter-in-law, Anne Gurney, the wife of his son Absalom Thompson. Perhaps these were the young women in the "big house." Tubman herself states in an affidavit for her dead husband's Civil War pension that she was born in Cambridge, the county seat and the largest town in Dorchester.[15]

Edward Brodess married Eliza Ann Keene on March 2, 1824.[16] By the time Brodess and Eliza set up their household, Rit had given birth to a sixth child, Ben, and possibly a seventh, Rachel. It is unlikely that Edward would have insisted that Rit move to his home once he settled there. He was a bachelor at first, then a young husband with a new bride, so crowding his small house with a slave woman and all her children, three of them very young, does not seem likely. In fact, Brodess would more likely have required the services of Sam, Frederick, and Shadrach to help him run his farm. Though no records exist detailing the building of slave quarters on his property, Brodess could have built a separate shelter for his slaves. They may have lived in his barn, and Rit could have lived in the kitchen house, but by 1830 Brodess's growing family of small children in addition to nine slaves suggests that he probably had separate slave quarters.[17]

In 1825 Edward Brodess sold a sixteen-year-old slave by the name of Rhody to Dempsey P. Kane, a slave trader from Mississippi.[18] Rhody is most likely Mariah Ritty; the transcription in the chattel records could have erroneously used "Rhody" instead of "Ritty." Brodess sold a fifteen-year-old boy named James on the same day.[19] Eliza Ann Keene, Brodess's wife, may have brought some slaves with her into the household when she married Brodess, and James may have been one of these Keene slaves.[20]

Given the animosity the lawsuit created between Thompson and Brodess, it seems unlikely that Rit remained in Thompson's employ for very long. While Brodess was establishing himself on his own farm and starting a family in Bucktown, he also could have hired out Rit and the children to his new neighbors for ready cash until he could use their labor himself. By 1827 Edward and Eliza Anne Brodess had started a family of their own, and no doubt Eliza required the services of an experienced house servant, so it is likely that Rit and her children would have been settled on Brodess's farm by then.

Such hiring-out practices made life difficult for Rit and her children. Harriet later recalled that at the age of about five she was left with the responsibility of caring for several younger siblings, probably Ben, born around 1823 or 1824, and Rachel, born about 1826, but also perhaps Henry, born about 1829 or 1830.[21]

> When I was four or five years old, my mother cooked up to the big house and left me to take care of the baby an' my little brother. I use to be in a hurry for her to go, so's I could play the baby was a pig in a bag, and' hold him up by the bottom of his dress. I had a nice frolic with that baby, swinging him all around,

his feet in the dress and his little head and arms touching the floor, because I was too small to hold him higher. It was late nights before my mother got home, and when he'd get worrying I'd cut a fat chunk of pork and toast it on the coals and put it in his mouth. One night he went to sleep with that hanging out, and when my mother come home she thought I'd done kill him. I nursed that there baby till he was so big I couldn't tote him any mo'.[22]

While Tubman may have had fond memories of playing with her baby brother, the dangers inherent in leaving such young children alone to fend for themselves must have weighed heavily on Rit's mind, a painful reminder of the daily injustices and cruelties inflicted upon slave families.

White Entrepreneurs, Black Labor, and Cold Cash

Throughout the first three decades of the nineteenth century Anthony Thompson continued to expand his landholdings, buying vast tracts of virgin timber that his slaves, including Ben Ross, set about cutting, hauling, and shipping to the Baltimore shipyards. Ross was "a timber inspector, and superintended the cutting and hauling of great quantities of timber for the Baltimore shipyards."[23] Talbot County had long dominated the shipbuilding industry on the Eastern Shore, but by the turn of the nineteenth century that county had effectively been timbered over. Shipbuilders turned their attention to neighboring Dorchester County, with its thousands of acres of dense forests, and established shipbuilders in Dorchester eagerly expanded their own operations to meet demand. Thompson maintained long-standing familial and economic ties with many of these shipbuilding families, including the Richardsons, Stewarts, and Linthicums. His supply of timber was crucial to other shipbuilders along the shore, particularly at Church Creek, Tobacco Stick, Cambridge, and Baltimore. Dorchester County shipbuilders made their wealth building "West Indies traders, coastal schooners and brigs for tramp trading, and vessels for the growing number of packet services that called at ports from New England to New Orleans."[24] The demand for fast and sturdy schooners during the War of 1812 was great and provided a significant boost to the local economies of the Eastern Shore. At the end of the war demand dropped. But the swiftness of the Chesapeake schooners proved irresistible to illegal slave traders. Outlawed in 1793, the building of slave ships became a clandestine operation; it would take another twenty-five years before the penalties were serious enough to "drive most Americans out of direct participation in the trade."[25] Poor enforcement, however, tipped the risk-reward assessment in favor of building these ships. From about 1835 to 1855, risking capital punishment, Chesapeake shipbuilders, including those in Dorchester County, provided the fast schooners and brigs for the illegal trade. They also retrofitted existing ships to accommodate the particular cargo.[26]

For some enterprising Eastern Shore landowners and entrepreneurs, new economic opportunities in timber encouraged the building of canals and roads, sawmills, and small shipyards to ease access and accommodate shipments of timber to the Baltimore market. With its abundant creeks, rivers, and navigable marshes, Dorchester County became the ideal location for large-scale agriculture and timber harvesting, as well as shipping and trading. These same rivers, creeks, and bays offered ideally protected locations for shipyards. Growing demands for corn and other agricultural products, matched by the escalating demands for timber, sparked great hope for the county. Canals were needed to supplement the many small rivers and streams throughout the county to increase that access.[27] The Blackwater and Parsons Creek Canal Company was finally finished as Stewart's Canal during the 1830s. Taking twenty years to complete, the canal was originally carved out of marshland from Parsons Creek south to the head of the Blackwater River, eventually sweeping northeast, joining Tobacco Stick Bay.[28] Joseph Stewart, Anthony Thompson, and Robert Tubman were among the seven commissioners appointed to oversee its construction and operation.[29] Requiring a tremendous amount of manual labor, the canal was probably built by enslaved and free blacks. Now known as Coursey's Creek, the canal still exists, little changed from its original configuration in the 1830s.

The harvesting of timber cleared great swaths of land for agricultural production. Windmills dotted the low-lying landscape, pumping water from marshy lands and turning great grindstones for the milling of corn, wheat, and oats. This once less-than-desirable marshy land held great promise for the future, as access to the Chesapeake ensured access to trade and capital.

Anthony Thompson could not wait for the canal. He petitioned the Maryland assembly to open a road from the Baptist Meeting House in Woolford south to "Indian Landing on Black Water River," passing near and through his property.[30] Called Thompson's New Road, and then later Harrisville Road, it provided access to water on either end; Tobacco Stick Bay on the Little Choptank River to the north, and the Big Blackwater River and Fishing Bay to the south. Before the canals were built, teams of oxen and large timber gangs were necessary to haul the heavy white oak and other lumber from the forests. Marshy wetlands made hauling the timber incredibly difficult. Split logs created a marginally effective road surface upon which oxen and slaves gained footholds to pull their great loads. It was exhausting and backbreaking work, and only the youngest and strongest could endure it. Even with the addition of the canals, timber still had to be hauled great distances from the interior.

Not all landowners were as entrepreneurial or as ambitious as Thompson or the other leading citizens of the Eastern Shore. In the decade leading up to 1820, Eastern Shore planters were faced with a declining agricultural base, competition from expanding territories in the southwest, and an ever-increasing free black population that lived in stark contrast to the large numbers of enslaved Maryland blacks. Facing economic pressures, many Eastern Shore planters began selling their excess slave labor to slave traders plying the Chesapeake markets. With the importation of slaves to the United States becoming illegal in 1808, traders from the Deep South and southwest territories turned to internal markets to meet the voracious demand for fresh labor to clear and tame vast new territories in the southwest. Eastern Shore families also moved to these areas, eager for an opportunity to buy and develop large tracts of land, establish productive plantations, and become landed gentry in their own right. William and Thomas Hayward, for instance, moved their families and slaves to Florida; as early settlers, they became part of that territory's economic and political power structure. Returning years later to Dorchester County as successful entrepreneurs, they settled comfortably among the political, economic, and social elite of the Eastern Shore. Their slaves, however, were permanently separated from their extended families and friends, remaining behind on the Haywards' plantations in Tallahassee.[31]

By the mid-1810s manumissions were on the wane, with far more slaveholders opting to sell their slaves. Quaker complaints and other abolitionist arguments fell on deaf ears, although several unsuccessful attempts were made during the 1820s and 1830s to introduce legislation that would have provided for gradual emancipation. One movement did gain momentum, however: the American Colonization Society, founded in 1817 by prominent slaveholders, antislavery activists, and nonslaveholders alike, sought to establish a colony in Africa to resettle free blacks. Faced with one of the largest free black populations among the slave states, Maryland eventually established its own colonization society to expedite settlement to Cape Palmas in Liberia. Dorchester County slaveholders represented a significant number of the Maryland Colonization Society's leadership, and one of the colony's first settlers and leaders was a free black named James Benson from Cambridge. But the majority of freemen, many of them raised in Maryland, were reluctant to leave the homes they knew and move to Africa. Their enslaved families and friends represented ties most of them were unwilling to sever.[32]

The transformation of cash-crop agriculture on the Eastern Shore had dramatically affected the nature of slavery by the beginning of the nineteenth century. Soil depletion, expansion into the Deep South, production of corn, wheat, and other grains, and timber harvesting for the burgeoning shipbuilding industry in Baltimore drastically reduced the need for a large slave labor force in Maryland. Meanwhile, there was a growing demand for labor on the rapidly expanding cotton and sugar plantations of Georgia and South Carolina, and later Alabama, Mississippi, Louisiana, and Texas. Like Virginia, Maryland began to earn a reputation as a "breeder" state. While some slaveholders were determined to sell their enslaved people within the community to avoid breaking apart families, the economic incentives were often too tempting for cash-strapped masters, especially indebted landowners and owners of encumbered estates. Slave traders eager to sell to high-paying Deep South plantation owners paid much more than locals. Professional slave traders were becoming more common on the Eastern Shore, and the sight of slave coffles, groups of slaves chained together for their journey south, was a destabilizing force within the slave and free black community.

Sales of slaves to parties from outside the county and state sent shock waves throughout the black communities of the Eastern Shore, in part because of the intricate connections among black and white families that span several generations and the consequences of those ties for enslaved African Americans. Patriarchal, almost feudal attitudes toward inheritance from the seventeenth through the early nineteenth centuries encouraged intrafamily marriages that kept white family assets intact, including groups of slaves. This, in turn, ensured the stability of slave families within the region. Also, the importation of new slaves into the community became inconsequential during the early part of the nineteenth century, and a growing free black community supported by manumissions, natural increases, and localized trading kept the slave community relatively stable and many family units somewhat intact. Harriet Tubman's family was no exception.

The Pattison family, the Thompsons, and the Stewarts all practiced various forms of manumission, including immediate freedom, term slavery, and manumission upon the death of the master. On July 28, 1817, Levin Stewart strode into the Dorchester County courthouse and manumitted his slaves. Witnessed by James Pattison, who would manumit his slaves the following September, Levin recorded that "for diverse good causes and considerations . . . have and do release from slavery, liberate, manumit and set free . . . all my Negroes that I am at present possessed of, after serving, as is hereafter mentioned." Levin calculated the exact number of years each one of his enslaved people would serve him. Six-month-old Dick Bowley was to remain enslaved for thirty-one years, while his mother, Binah, age twenty-eight, was to receive her freedom in ten years.[33] Binah was more than likely African-born, like Modesty, Harriet's grandmother.[34] Perhaps married to a free black, Binah had five children, all enslaved by Levin Stewart. Her two other boys, Major and John Bowley, were included in the 1817 deed of manumission; two daughters, Harriet and Terry, were born shortly thereafter. Stewart manumitted them later, setting their terms of enslavement at twenty-six years. These Bowleys would become intimately involved with Tubman's family. Living and working in the same area of Dorchester County, they would become part of a well-established free black community centered around Harrisville Road south of Woolford, and the shipyards in Tobacco Stick (Madison), Woolford, Church Creek, and Cambridge.

In manumitting his slaves, eschewing top dollar for each healthy slave he could have sold to a Baltimore or New Orleans trader, Stewart was operating in contrast to the prevailing mood on the Eastern Shore. Moving to Georgetown to pursue shipbuilding and trading with his half brother Zachariah Skinner, Stewart no longer needed great numbers of slaves. He sold or gave many of them to his brother Joseph and to his son, John T. Stewart. Trained as shipwrights and carpenters, blacksmiths, and sail makers, Stewart's enslaved people were part of an elite group of highly skilled slaves. They were also highly mobile, which afforded them unusual freedom. After Levin died in 1825, his brother and son honored the manumission schedules he had set before his death.

As previously noted, Levin's friend James Pattison followed suit that September. The Rev. John Seward, a prominent local Methodist minister, may have influenced both Pattison and Stewart. Seward had acquired more than thirty slaves, probably through his three marriages. In January 1817 Seward manumitted all of his slaves based on staggered manumission dates, much like Stewart. Perhaps Seward had directly pleaded with his congregants to do as he did.[35] These three sets of manumissions from 1817 represent a significant portion of manumissions for that year; because of the staggered manumission schedules, these groups of slaves also represent a noteworthy number of the many Certificates of Freedom to be awarded during the next four decades.

Anthony Thompson's slave holdings increased dramatically during the three decades before his death, from fifteen slaves in 1810 to thirty-nine slaves in 1820, including fourteen female slaves under the age of fourteen.[36] Thirty-two slaves were recorded as living on his property at the end of Harrisville Road in the 1830 census. By the time he died in

1836, Thompson held in bondage over forty slaves. Though Thompson may have liberated several slaves prior to his death, his will provided for the eventual liberation of the majority of his slaves. Ross, who had earned a reputation for honesty and integrity, was manumitted by Thompson's will in 1840. Ben and fellow bondsman Jerry Manokey were clearly among Thompson's most highly favored slaves. When Thompson died, both men were given ten acres of land to live on for the remainder of their lives. Jerry was given his freedom immediately.[37] In his will, Thompson specified terms of enslavement for each of his forty-three enslaved people, from immediate emancipation to the forty-four-year terms of service required of infants.[38] Thompson viewed himself as the benevolent caretaker, providing the future promise of liberty in return for loyalty and good behavior. By liberating his slaves after a term of servitude, Thompson was guaranteeing that the benefits of their labor would accrue to his sons Anthony C. Thompson and Absalom Thompson, thereby perpetuating the economic benefit from the slaves' labor while ultimately providing for staggered manumission. Gradual emancipation reduced the slave owners' obligation to provide board and care for aged slaves, and the children born of enslaved women would provide slave labor into perpetuity.

By 1820 the Thompson slave population had grown to thirty-nine, an increase of twenty-four slaves in ten years. But the majority of this increase is to be found in the incredible number of young children: twenty-two of these slaves were under the age of fourteen.[39] The majority of Thompson's enslaved women were not married to his enslaved men. Some were married to free men; several were married to men enslaved by nearby slave owners in Church Creek, Tobacco Stick, and Cambridge, while still others appear to be married to slaves owned by masters living in Talbot County. Betsy, for instance, was married to Major Bowley, the son of Binah Bowley. Binah and Major were both eventually manumitted by Levin Stewart. Sarah Ann Reed was married to a slave of Dr. Robert Tubman. Both of these women lived near their husbands and therefore were able to maintain relatively stable family relationships. Hanner, on the other hand, was married to a man owned by a Mr. Haddaway of Talbot County. While it might appear that this particular relationship would have problems due to separation, in fact

Hanner was hired out to Absalom Thompson, one of Anthony Thompson's sons, who was living at Mary's Delight at Bayside in Talbot County, a few short miles by boat, or thirty miles by land from Dorchester County.[40] Hanner may have been living with Absalom, which could have precipitated her meeting and marrying her husband, or she could have met him beforehand and the Thompsons accommodated the relationship.[41] This practice was not unheard of, and from the point of view of the master, having "contented," family-oriented slaves kept them closer to the plantation and less likely to run away.

"1839, Jan. 1, Negroes of Anthony Thompson."
Ben Ross, Harriet Tubman's father, tops this list of Thompson slaves.

Thompson's male slaves likewise were married to women who did not belong to him. Bill Banks and Isaac Kiah were married to women enslaved by a Mrs. Stapleford, who lived on the west side of the Blackwater River near Thompson's property.[42] Ann Stapleford was also the enslaver of Harkless Jolley, Linah Ross's husband and the father of Kessiah Jolley Bowley, Harriet Tubman's niece. These relationships demonstrate the mobility of slaves, and indicate important social relationships cultivated through the social and economic interactions of slaveholding white families, in this case, the geographic and economic ties between Thompson and his neighbors. Absalom Thompson had few slaves of his own; as a doctor, he had less need for a large labor force. The few slaves he owned farmed his property at Bayside in Talbot County, and perhaps helped him maintain the rudimentary hospital he built on his property. No doubt the Thompsons shared their enslaved labor when the times required.[43]

For a small planter such as Brodess, however, slave children appeared to have been a burden, possibly seen as a distraction for their more useful and productive slave mother. By hiring out his excess slaves, Brodess was able to maintain his social status within the community and feed his own growing family of eight children without the added responsibility of providing for troublesome, and hungry, slave children.

Brodess did not always choose to hire out his excess slave labor, however. Throughout her youth Tubman heard the stories about older siblings who had been sold away before she was born, and she remembered the "agonized expression" of two other sisters as they were taken away, and the "hopeless grief" of her parents. Tubman claimed that for many years "she never closed her eyes that she did not imagine she saw the horsemen coming, and heard the screams of women and children, as they were being dragged away to a far worse slavery than that they were enduring there."[44] For Edward Brodess, the funds from sales of several of Tubman's siblings provided opportunities to expand his land holdings and sustain his growing family. Though Brodess was probably nursed and cared for by Rit as a child, it did not prevent him from taking her children away from her.

For slaves in the declining Eastern Shore and southern parts of the state, sale into the expanding plantation economies of the Deep South and the southwestern territories was increasingly common. The courthouse at Cambridge, Dorchester's county seat, was the center of the largest slave market on the Eastern Shore. The Woolfolk brothers, slave dealers from Baltimore, eventually opened a branch office in Cambridge, advertising in the Cambridge and Easton newspapers; they were met by such competitors as Thomas Overlay, who on one occasion advertised for "50 to 100 likely Negroes, from ten to twenty-five years of age, of both sexes, for which the highest market prices will be given in cash."[45] Other dealers included Hope Slatter of Baltimore; Henry Boyce of Louisiana, who was willing to "give the best price for those between the ages of 12 and 25 years";[46] and James Cox of Scott County, Kentucky, who on one occasion purchased thirty-eight slaves, including men, women, and children, six months to thirty-one years, from John W. Hanes for $6,610.[47] Austin Woolfolk, one of the largest, most successful, and most notorious of slave traders from Baltimore, assured his Eastern Shore slaveholders that he "still lives to give them cash and the highest prices for their NEGROES."[48] Most of Woolfolk's slaves ended up in the New Orleans market.

Local dealers often posed as representatives for larger slave traders from outside of Maryland. Charles LeCompte, a local slave dealer located in East New Market, sold over one hundred slaves during 1827 to traders from Mississippi and Kentucky; most of those he sold were teenagers and young adults, though he also sold infants and young children separately from their parents.[49] Slave traders often relied on these local dealers to provide the goods and to negotiate better deals. Peter Lowber, who would later become constable of East New Market, became quite active in the local trade. In November 1829 Lowber sold to James Baldock of Scott County, Kentucky, ten slaves, mostly under the age of ten, for $1,210.[50] Over the next few months, Lowber would sell more slaves to Bartholomew Manlove, Winder C. Dingle, and George Bates, all of Kentucky.[51]

Sales to traders were supplemented by sales to small individual planters who traveled the Eastern Shore to purchase slaves directly for their own use on plantations in the Deep South. These young entrepreneurs sought to buy directly, cutting out the middleman, and save themselves hundreds of dollars on each slave. A slave purchased for $400 in Cambridge could be sold for nearly $800 in Mississippi or Louisiana.[52]

Many slaveholders were reluctant, even in the face of greater economic gain, to sell beyond the county limits, let alone beyond state lines. Social customs reinforced the notion of guardianship and benevolence over one's slaves; also, slaves would be distraught over the loss of their loved ones to traders outside the state, and thus less productive. Too, the sight of large slave coffles trudging off to Baltimore overland or via boat from Cambridge was distasteful and uncomfortable to some Eastern Shore whites. Some felt such social pressure not to sell that they sold their slaves secretly elsewhere and then claimed they had run away. According to one local story, one slave dealer handled the "problem" quite successfully for years. "Joe Johnson was greatly feared and also very popular in his home neighborhood. Many times he sold slaves for Sussex and Dorchester neighbors who could not sell them publicly. In those abolitionist times citizens who did not wish the financial lose [sic] of freeing their slaves claimed them runaway and instead had Johnson sell them south. This had been illegal in DE since 1787 and in MD and VA since 1789." Johnson would later be tried for kidnapping free and enslaved blacks and selling them; after that, he was implicated with the notorious Patty Cannon of Dorchester County in several murders, with the bodies buried in the backyard of Cannon's house.[53]

For Harriet and her family, the sale of Mariah Ritty (Rhody) and James would mark the beginning of increased threats to their family stability. Already separated from their father, Ben Ross, Harriet and her siblings would at times find themselves traveling great distances to work for temporary masters. Other relatives and friends would find themselves on the auction block at the Cambridge courthouse or sold in private deals to traders or local slaveholders. The economic pressures on Brodess only intensified as his family grew and he saw his social and economic status fluctuate uncomfortably. Spoiled to a degree, and perhaps in competition with his economically and socially more successful stepbrothers, Anthony C. Thompson and Absalom Thompson, Brodess may have seen his excess slave labor as ready cash. Raised in comfortable circumstances, provided amply for by his stepfather, and living the life of a middle-class bachelor prior to his marriage, Brodess may have had little experience, and perhaps even little desire, to run a small plantation and care for numerous slaves. In fact, during the two years prior to his leaving Thompson's guardianship, Brodess's expenses did not include expenditures for farm equipment or clothing appropriate for the life of a yeoman planter; rather, he made purchases of cashmere and silk clothing, numerous pairs of shoes, pantaloons, vests, coats, handkerchiefs, gilt buttons, ribbons, and fine stockings.[54]

Sometime during the 1830s, or even as late as 1841, Brodess sold Harriet's sisters Linah and Soph. "She had already seen two older sisters taken away as part of a chain gang, and they had gone no one knew whither; she had seen the agonized expression on their faces as they turned to take a last look at their 'Old Cabin Home'; and had watched them from the top of the fence, as they went off weeping and lamenting, till they were hidden from her sight forever."[55] Linah and Soph "were sold out of State," thought Anthony C. Thompson.[56] Polish Mills, Brodess's neighbor and a local farmer who hired Rit and Linah in 1833, remembered that Brodess sold Linah for $400, turning "her proceeds into Land." Mills also claimed that Brodess sold Linah, and later her sister Soph, beyond state lines for top dollar, as "slaves for life . . . as a general rule . . . sell for one third more."[57]

Ben and Rit, of course, had little control over Brodess's actions. While slaves were sometimes given the chance to secure a local buyer, the Rosses probably had no such opportunity. No records exist for the sales of these two sisters. Curiously, most buyers would have required a bill of sale to secure their title; registering the sale at the local courthouse ensured legal ownership. Brodess may have avoided such a process by selling to a less-than-scrupulous buyer; by not registering the sale at the Dorchester County courthouse, he could avoid paying taxes on the transaction. Also, out-of-county traders, such as the Woolfolks or the Slatters, could have simply recorded the sales in Baltimore, though it appears that many of their transactions were recorded in the local chattel records.[58]

One of Harriet's sisters had

a young child, about two or three months old, & the master came after her to sell her to Georgia. Her husband had great confidence in a gentleman, who was a class-leader, & he takes my sister and carries her to him to keep her from her master. He told him—"Get your wife and bring her to me, and I will take care of her." So he did it. At the same time, the old master [Brodess] had got him to look out and get her, and after her husband carries her there, this man turns round and lets the master understand it, & he comes and gets her & sells her down to Georgia, and leaves that young child.[59]

Tricked by Brodess and unable to prevent or forestall the sale of her children, Rit no doubt remembered his betrayal. At an unknown later date Brodess attempted to sell Rit's youngest son, Moses. According to Tubman's brother Henry,

a Georgia man came and bought my brother; and after he had bought him, the master calls him to come to the house & catch the gentleman's horse, but instead of his coming to catch the horse, my mother, who was out in the field, and knew what the master was doing, comes in. She had a suspicion that they were going to sell the boy, and went to the backside of the house, and heard the master count the money; and after he had counted out the money, the master says, "I ought to have fifty dollars more yet," and . . . the mother comes, she says, "What do you want of the boy?" He wouldn't tell her, but says to her, "Go and bring a pitcher of water"; and after she brought the pitcher of water, she goes to work again. Then he makes another excuse, & hollers to the boy to come & put the horse in to the carriage. But the mother comes again. Then he says, "What did you come for? I hollered for the boy." And she up & swore, and said he wanted the boy for that (ripping out an oath) Georgia man. He called three times, but the boy did not come; and a third time, he came to look for the boy, but the mother had hid him, & kept him hid, I suppose for a month.[60]

Brodess held on to the money, thinking he would eventually get Moses from his hiding place and turn him over to the Georgia trader. As in most instances, nonlocal traders would stay for one or two months and purchase scores of slaves, holding them in slave pens or the county jail until enough purchases had been made to make the trip south worthwhile economically. But Brodess had not bargained on Rit or on the community network that would help conceal her son. Rit must have been confident that she had more to gain than lose by resisting Brodess's attempts to take her son away from her.

Brodess enlisted the aid of a loyal servant, perhaps one of the Keene slaves, who apparently felt pressured or compelled to find favor from his master. He revealed Moses's location in the woods. Isolated and remote, south-central Dorchester County was probably an ideal hiding place for recalcitrant and defiant slaves. Indeed, Greenbriar Swamp, just south of the Brodess property, is today still considered inhospitable and treacherous territory for humans.

Rit was wary when the servant suggested that he bring food to Moses in the woods. Not letting on that she was aware of his betrayal, she warned Moses ahead of time, and sent the man into the woods with food. "At noon" the servant went to the "bush, expecting the boy would be there . . . but the boy wasn't." Later that evening, he came to Rit with a white neighbor, John Scott. Standing at her cabin door, he asked to be let in,

> but she was suspicious and she says, "What do you want?" Says he, "Mr. Scott wants to come to light a segar." She ripped out an oath, and said; "You are after my son; but the first man that comes into my house, I will split his head open." That frightened them, and they would not come in. So she kept the boy hid until the Georgia man went away, and then she let him come out. Then the master came to the mother, and said he was exceedingly glad she hid the boy, so that he couldn't sell him. He told her, "when we wanted you to send the boy to the woods, we were there to catch him."[61]

Rit gambled and won. Her defiant attitude toward her master and another white slaveholder from her community reflects Rit's desperation as she faced the prospect of losing another child. She risked her own safety to protect her son, perhaps believing that Brodess would not confront her directly and take her son from her with her full knowledge. She may not have been able to prevent the sale of her daughters, but this time Rit played her hand and won.

With the constant threat of the sale of family members permanently affecting Harriet's family emotionally, they still had to endure the uncertainty of daily survival. Merely assets for Brodess's gain, they were hired out to temporary masters throughout the region, never confident in the stability of their home life, occupational status, or what the next day might bring. Rit could protect Harriet only when the child was with her. Hired away from the Brodesses at Bucktown, Harriet would endure beatings, whippings, and general neglect at the hands of temporary masters, marring her childhood and young adulthood and forever scarring her mind and body.

CHAPTER 3

"DEVILISH" MISTRESSES AND HARSH MASTERS: BLACK FAMILY LIFE UNDER THE LASH

HARRIET TUBMAN HAS PROVIDED US WITH FEW DETAILS ABOUT HER owner, Edward Brodess, or the various masters to whom she was hired out for the nearly thirty years she spent in slavery. She told Ednah Cheney that she seldom lived with Brodess and his wife, Eliza Ann.[1] He was "never unnecessarily cruel; but as was common among slaveholders, he often hired out his slaves to others, some of whom proved to be tyrannical and brutal to the utmost limit of their power."[2] Harriet's brothers Ben and Robert recalled harsher treatment at the hands of the Brodesses, however. Eliza Ann was "very devilish," Ben claimed, and he and his siblings were forced to "work hard and fare meagerly" to support the Brodesses in "idleness and luxury."[3] Robert felt Edward Brodess "was not fit to own a dog." Ben was more to the point: "Where I came from," he later recalled, "it would make your flesh creep, and your hair stand on end, to know what they do to the slaves."[4]

The practice of hiring out excess slave labor was very common on the Eastern Shore. It provided valuable income to slaveholders who could not profitably use all of their slaves, and it provided a ready labor force to nonslaveholders and other slaveholders who could not, or did not want, to own more slaves. For the slaves themselves, it often meant painful separations. For children it was particularly difficult, and like Tubman, they became terribly homesick and despondent.[5] While most rental contracts stipulated that the slaves be clothed, fed, and sheltered properly, this was not always the case.[6] William Still, the famous Philadelphia Underground Railroad operator, interviewed many runaway slaves who described mistreatment from temporary masters, particularly frequent beatings and a lack of food. Often their frustration was compounded by their owner's supposed disinterest.[7]

Slaveholders often viewed the hiring out of their slaves, even children, as an attractive alternative to selling them; the hiring out of a young male slave could command as much as $120 per year, much more than the interest that could be earned on the investment if the slave was sold for cash. Edward Brodess, with a small farm and few livestock, did not have enough work to fully employ all of his slaves, so he frequently hired them out to neighboring farmers and possibly relatives, preserving his investment in slaves until a later date when he could more profitably turn them into an investment in land.[8]

Tubman was first hired out to James Cook, a planter of limited means who lived on a nearby farm, to learn the trade of weaving.[9] Though only six or seven years old at the time, Tubman vividly remembered the man coming on horseback to get her. Young and obviously uninformed about what might lie ahead, Tubman "was anxious to go." She had no clothes, so Eliza made her a dress, and off she went with him, for the first of many separations from her family. Accustomed to spending most of her time with her family and other slaves, Tubman was at first reluctant to find herself in the house with her new master and his family. "When we got there," Tubman recalled, "they was at table eating supper. I never eat in the house where the white people was, and I was ashamed to stand up and eat before them."[10] Her new mistress offered her a drink of milk, which Tubman refused; she was so nervous standing in front of unfamiliar white people that even her hunger was not enough to overcome her fears. "I was as fond of milk as any young shoot. But all the time I was there I stuck to it, that I didn't drink sweet milk."[11] She may have stayed with the Cooks for as long as two years. Cook and his wife were cruel, and her time spent with them left her ill and physically scarred.

As one of her first tasks, Harriet was sent into the nearby marshes to check Cook's muskrat traps. The marshy wetlands of Dorchester County provided an ideal habitat for muskrats, with plenty of vegetation, soft peaty soil to build burrows, and ample, shallow fresh water suitable for a semiaquatic life. Catching them, of course, requires setting traps on the banks of streams where they burrow, or in the marshes, where they build domed houses. Trapping muskrats would be a difficult task for a young child, but in cold water during the winter trapping season, when muskrat pelts are at their finest, it would be even more so. At some point Tubman became sick with measles but was forced to continue working the traps in the cold water. She became gravely ill. Rit then convinced Brodess to bring little Harriet home.[12]

Rit nursed her weakened child back to health, only to have her hired out again and again. "I use to sleep on the floor in front of the fireplace an there I'd lie and cry and cry. I used to think all the time if I could only get home and get in my mother's bed, an the funny part of that was, she never had a bed in her life. Nothing but a board box nailed up against the wall and straw laid on it," Harriet recalled seventy years later.[13] She was sent back to the Cooks', but she hated them and would not learn to weave as she was expected to do.[14] Harriet became increasingly homesick, remembering later that she was "like the boy on the Swanee River, 'no place like my ole cabin home.' Whenever you saw a child was more homesick than I was, you see a bad one."[15]

Tubman also worked as a nursemaid and house servant to a young married woman, Miss Susan. Susan provided enough food and clothing for her enslaved people, but she had been taught that slaves would do no labor but under the "sting of the whip." Harriet, young and untrained, was ordered to sweep and dust the floors and furniture.[16] Ever mindful of the whip located on the fireplace mantel, Harriet struggled to complete her tasks quickly and well. She "swept with all her strength, raising a tremendous dust. The moment she had finished sweeping, she took her dusting cloth, and wiped everything 'so you could see your face in 'em, de shone so,' in haste to go and set the table for breakfast, and do her other work. The dust which she had set flying only settled down again on chairs, tables, and the piano."[17] Seeing only the settled dust, Susan suspected that Harriet had not done her work. Taking the whip from the mantle, Susan beat Harriet repeatedly on the "head and face and neck."

While enduring a fifth beating, little Harriet received a momentary reprieve. Susan's sister Emily appeared at the door. "Not being able to endure the screams of the child any longer," Emily scolded her sister for her cruelty and impatience. According to Bradford, Emily instructed Harriet on how to clean the room properly so as to prevent the dust from resettling on the furniture. Instructive and moralizing, this tale offered nineteenth-century readers two versions of the southern slave mistress, one wicked and cruel, the other saintly and patient, apparently with no slaves of her own to cloud the picture or corrupt her. Emily's kind instructions to the child Minty "saved Harriet her whippings for that day, as they probably did for many a day after."[18] This story of a kind southerner may have been Tubman's own view of the events as well, or perhaps Tubman and Bradford wanted to offer encouragement to a genteel northern public eager for some sort of hopeful reconciliation after the Civil War, even as early as 1868.[19]

Tubman later recalled that she was so young and small when she was called upon to care for Miss Susan's baby, that she had to sit on the floor in order to hold it. "An that baby was always in my lap except when it was asleep, or its mother was feedin' it."[20] Indeed, her workday was never over; "she was obliged to sit up all night to rock a cross, sick child. Her mistress laid upon her bed with a whip under her pillow, and slept; but if the tired nurse forgot herself for a moment, if her weary head dropped, and her hand ceased to rock the cradle, the child would cry out, and then down would come the whip upon the neck and face of the poor weary creature."[21] Samuel Hopkins Adams, grandnephew to Sarah Bradford, recalled Tubman reluctantly drawing "down her dress," in front of him and his cousins, to "exhibit the cruel weals on [her] neck and shoulders." She told them, with a "gleam in her button-bright eyes," that these cruel masters never made her "hollah," and that her revenge came when she returned to those plantations and helped relieve them of their bondsmen, women, and children.[22]

Apparently Susan's bad temper also often flared up against her husband. While watching a heated argument unfold in front of her one morning, Harriet took the opportunity to steal a small lump of sugar from a bowl on the table near her. But Susan had spied her; she grabbed for the whip, but Harriet ran out the door. "I just flew, and they didn't catch me. I run, and run, and I run, I passed many a house, but I didn't dare to stop, for they all knew my Missus and they would send me back."[23]

Harriet ran to a neighboring farm and hid in a pigpen. Exhausted from running away, and too small to climb in carefully, she tumbled into the pen and landed in the midst of "an ole sow, an' perhaps eight or ten little pigs . . . I was so beat out I couldn't stir." She stayed from Friday until the following Tuesday, fearful of the mother pig as she fought over scraps of food that came down the trough. "I was so starved I knowed I'd got to go back to my Missus, I hadn't got no where else to go, but I knowed what was coming." When she returned home, her master whipped her.[24]

Harkless Bowley, Harriet Tubman's greatnephew, recalled in 1939 that Tubman told him she was "shamefully beaten. She showed me a knott in her side by being struck by one cruel man with a rope with a knot in one end . . . for some trivial offence. The woman attempted to whip her," but Harriet would not submit to her. When the master came home, Harriet's mistress complained, but he decided not to "attack her at that time but sent her [Harriet] upstairs to roll some carpets. When she was thus engaged he crept up behind her and delt an awful blow."[25] The beating broke her ribs and may have lacerated her internal organs, and Harriet could no longer work. Half starved and unable to work, Harriet was returned to Brodess, carrying wounds that "pained her all of her life."[26]

These two early childhood stories of the Cooks and Miss Susan are often conflated in the retellings of Tubman narratives. James Cook and his wife do not appear to be related to Susan and Emily.[27] Nevertheless, cruel treatment, whippings, and beatings inflicted upon Tubman during this time period left scars "still plainly visible where the whip cut into the flesh," forty years later.[28]

During 1833 Brodess hired Rit and her daughter Linah out to a neighboring farmer, Polish Mills, separating Harriet and her siblings from their mother once again. Mills provided food and clothing only; Rit was nursing her youngest child, Moses, at the time, and another child, Henry, age two and a half or three, "could run about." Linah may have been ill, for according to Mills she was weakly and he thought her not to be very valuable as a slave.[29] Harriet, in the meantime, either was living with the Brodesses nearby or had already been hired out as a field hand to a neighboring farmer. She risked defying her master by sneaking out in the evening to visit her mother at Mills's plantation. In the years following the Nat Turner rebellion, restrictions on the movements of slaves and free blacks, particularly at night, had markedly increased. One of Harriet's brothers stood guard outside the slave cabin door, watching the road in the event slave patrols or her master appeared unexpectedly.

One evening as he was standing guard, Tubman's brother "called her to come out and see the stars. 'They were all shooting whichway.' "[30] During the evening of November 12 and into the early morning hours of the thirteenth in 1833, thousands of shooting stars illuminated the night sky as the annual Leonid meteor shower put on a particularly spectacular show. An Annapolis, Maryland, observer noted that the "light was so intense" and that the meteors "fell like snow." Another observer in Boston wrote that the sky had the "appearance of a thick shower of fire."[31] An Eastern Shore resident recalled the meteor shower resembled a "snow storm of fiery flakes—so thick and numerous were they."[32] The meteor shower was seen throughout the country, sparking fear and awe in millions of people. Tubman and her family "all thought the end of the world had come."[33] Other slaves in the area may have taken this natural phenomenon as a harbinger of some impending calamity. So much of their lives were shaped and dictated by outside forces, both human and natural over which they had little control, it is no wonder they imagined the end of the world was at hand.

It was probably not too long after this event, when Tubman was still an adolescent and hired out as a field hand on a neighboring plantation, that she received an almost fatal blow to the head from a stone or iron weight intended to fell another slave. This injury changed the course of her life, not only through the physical disability it caused, but also because it sparked physiological changes that redefined the way Tubman viewed the world.

Tubman had been hired out for her clothing and food to "de wust man in de neighborhood."[34] It was in the fall, a busy time on farms, and Tubman was assigned to break flax in the field. "My hair had never been combed and it stood out like a bushel basket," Tubman recalled, "an' when I'd get through eatin' I'd wipe the grease off my fingers on my hair and I expect that thar hair saved my life."[35] One night Tubman and the plantation's cook went to a nearby store to purchase a few items for the house. A dry goods store, located at the crossroads of Bucktown Road coming from the northeast, Bestpitch Ferry Road from the south, and Greenbrier Road from the west (toward the Brodess plantation), is the most likely scene of the tragic event.[36] A slave belonging to a local farmer named Barnett left his work without permission and was pursued by his overseer to the store.[37] When the overseer found the young slave, he ordered Harriet to help him tie the slave down. Tubman refused, and the slave broke free and ran away. The "overseer caught up a two-pound weight from the counter and threw it at the fugitive, but it fell short and struck Harriet a stunning blow on the head."[38]

Tubman later told Emma Telford that "I had a shoulder shawl of the mistress over my head and when I got to the store I was ashamed to go in." The last thing she remembered was the overseer "raising up his arm to throw an iron weight at one of the slaves and that was the last I knew." She remembered vividly how the weight "broke my skull and cut a piece of that shawl clean off and drove it into my head. They carried me to the house all bleeding and fainting. I had no bed, no place to lie down on at all, and they lay me on the seat of the loom, and I stayed there all that day and next." Receiving no medical attention, Tubman was returned to the field. "I went to work again and there I worked with the blood and sweat rolling down my face till I couldn't see."[39] "Disabled and sick, her flesh all wasted away," she was returned to Brodess. He attempted to sell her, but no buyer was interested in purchasing a wounded slave. "They said they wouldn't give a sixpence for me," Tubman later recalled.[40]

It was a very long time before Tubman recovered, with "a wound ever afterwards visible."[41] Thereafter Tubman was often subject to unexpected episodes of "lethargy . . . coming upon her in the midst of conversation, or whatever she may be doing, and throwing her into a deep slumber, from which she will presently rouse herself, and go on with her conversation or work."[42]

Tubman was unable to control the aftereffects of this injury. Sometimes it was "almost impossible to rouse her."[43] Her episodes of dropping off to sleep in the midst of conversation or while performing a task were frequent and unsettling. The *Freedmen's Record* reported in 1865 that the injury "still makes her very lethargic. She cannot remain quiet fifteen minutes without appearing to fall asleep. It is not a refreshing slumber; but a heavy, weary condition which exhausts her."[44] Wilbur Siebert interviewed Harriet Tubman in the mid-1890s and noted with surprise that her injury "caused her at frequent intervals (say of half an hour or so) to lose consciousness for three or four minutes. She explained that her head would drop and she would become silent, but I was not to become alarmed; she would arouse and continue her talk without losing the thread of her conversation."[45]

The head injury also coincided with an explosion of religious enthusiasm and vivid imagery in the young slave woman. Tubman broke out, often unexpectedly, into loud and excited religious praising. If this injury caused her great suffering, it also marked the beginning of a lifetime of potent dreams and visions that, she claimed, foretold the future. Some of her dreams eventually took on an important role in Tubman's life, influencing not only her own course of action but also the way other people viewed her.

Taken together, the range of symptoms and behaviors that followed Tubman's terrible head injury strongly point to the likelihood that she suffered from temporal lobe epilepsy (TLE). Her seizures, or sleeping spells, and visions are typical of TLE brought on by severe head injuries.[46] Furthermore, the bright lights, colorful auras, disembodied voices, states of tremendous anxiety and fear alternating with exceptional hyperactivity and fearlessness, and dreamlike trances while appearing to be conscious, followed by the episodes of overwhelming and crippling fatigue that Tubman experienced, are classic symptoms of temporal lobe epilepsy. TLE visions often have religious overtones, a phenomenon Tubman experienced throughout her life. Sounds of music, rushing water, screaming, and loud noises would overcome her without notice. Her dreams, visions, and hallucinations often intruded amid daily work and activities. "We'd been carting manure all day," Tubman once explained to an interviewer, "and t'other girl and I was gwine home on the sides of the cart, and another boy was driving, when suddenly I heard such music as filled all the air." Soon she began to experience a powerful religious vision, "which she described in language which sounded like the old prophets in its grand flow." Persistent shaking by her fellow slaves brought her back to reality, though she protested that she hadn't been asleep at all.[47]

Her frequent periods of semiconsciousness with an inability to speak, hyperreligiosity, paranormal experiences, and recurrent nightmares appear to have become integrated into the young woman's personality, a phenomenon not unknown in TLE. Unlike other forms of epilepsy, temporal lobe seizures do not include convulsions. In fact, the temporal lobes are associated with the sensory regions of the brain (which include smell, taste, vision, and hearing), memory, and emotions, and therefore the seizures most often affect those sensory activities. Tubman's religiosity was unquestionably rooted in powerful Methodist evangelical teachings and was also a mystical and deeply personal spiritual experience. But it may have been enhanced by the epiphany-like manifestations of TLE seizures. Some of her dreams reflect the out-of-body encounters reported by some TLE patients. Such experiences reinforced her notions of an all-powerful being that guided her throughout her life, protecting her and providing divine instruction. Tubman "used to dream of flying over fields and towns, and rivers and mountains, looking down upon them 'like a bird.' "[48] She claimed she had inherited this ability from her father, who "could always predict the weather, and that he foretold the Mexican war."[49] As Bradford put it, "when these turns of somnolency come upon Harriet, she imagines that her 'spirit' leaves her body, and visits other scenes and places, not only in this world, but in the world of spirits. And her ideas of these scenes show, to say the least of it, a vividness of imagination seldom equaled in the soarings of the most cultivated minds."[50]

The visions Tubman experienced were central to her inner spirituality and reinforced religious beliefs nurtured through strong African cultural traditions and powerful evangelical thought. Occasionally, Tubman was forced to attend services held by Dr. Anthony C. Thompson, Anthony Thompson's son, who had been licensed as a local Methodist minister in 1828. In mandating the attention of his slaves, Dr. Thompson fulfilled what he believed to be his role as the benevolent caretaker and provider for the spiritual well-being of his slaves. Ben and Rit Ross claimed Thompson was just "pretending to preach" and was nothing but "a wolf in sheep's clothing."[51] (Frederick Douglass once noted upon the religious conversion of his master, Thomas Auld, that "slaveholders may sometimes have confidence in the piety of their slaves, but slaves seldom have confidence in the piety of their masters."[52]) Though they attended Thompson's services, the Ross family may have also been influenced by Episcopal, Baptist, and Catholic teachings. Tubman and her family likely integrated a number of religious practices and ideas into their daily lives. The Pattisons, Thompsons, and Brodesses initially belonged to Anglican and Episcopal churches in Dorchester County before becoming Methodists; some of the white Keenes, Tubmans, and Rosses were originally Catholic.

Tubman was known to fast on Fridays, a practice then typical of Catholics, though some Methodists and Episcopalians also followed this habit; her parents abstained entirely from food on Fridays.[53] Tubman said her father did "it for *conscience*; we was taught to do so down South. He says if he denies himself for the sufferings of his Lord an' Master, Jesus will sustain him."[54]

The rise in evangelicalism and its concentration on spiritual freedom, particularly in the early to mid-nineteenth century, had potentially troubling consequences for slaveholders' interests. Slaves' access to religious instruction depended upon individual slaveholders, but it was generally allowed on the Eastern Shore of Maryland. To deny slaves the opportunity for religious experience was, for some masters, a violation of religious freedom and the much hoped-for spiritual conversion within the evangelical tradition.[55] During the early nineteenth century, free blacks began forming their own denominations within the Methodist tradition, establishing the African Methodist Episcopal and African Methodist Episcopal Zion churches in Philadelphia and Baltimore.

In the early years of the nineteenth century slaveholders became increasingly concerned about the possible subversive messages preached by black ministers, so many slaves were required, like Tubman's family, to attend the churches of their owners. In Bucktown, oral tradition suggests that Tubman, her family, and many of the area's free and enslaved blacks may have attended two other possible sites of worship. One was Bazzel's Methodist Episcopal Church, located on Bucktown Road, slightly southwest of the Bucktown crossroads, and only half a mile southeast of the Brodess property. Though the church was built in 1876, Tubman's family, it is reported, attended services at that location, perhaps in the woods directly behind the current church.

Scott's Chapel, slightly north on Bucktown Road, is another historically significant church for the local African American community and probably the most likely place of worship for the area's enslaved community.[56] Founded in 1812 as a Methodist church, the current building was constructed in 1891 on land donated to the church in 1858 by John Scott. The graveyard directly across the road contains headstones as early as 1792.

Whatever her place of worship, there can be no doubt Tubman's faith was deep and founded upon strong religious teachings, whether these were specifically Methodist, Catholic, Episcopal, Baptist, or of African origin. Thomas Garrett felt that he "never met with any person, of any color, who had more confidence in the voice of God, as spoken direct to her soul . . . and her faith in a Supreme Power truly was great."[57]

The role that evangelical Protestantism played in the lives of nineteenth-century slaves, particularly those in the region where Harriet lived in her formative years, is crucial to understanding the elements of Tubman's spiritual strength and endurance. Religion was a major support system within the African American community, for both the free and the enslaved, many of whom daily endured threats to their lives, their family stability, to the existence of their very community. The role of evangelicalism in nineteenth-century America is fundamental to any exploration of the cultural and human complexities of slave and free communities alike, and is crucial to understanding Tubman.

In this oppressive environment, then, Tubman and her family found ways to negotiate the cruelties of slavery and lack of control in their lives. Evangelical Protestant Methodism was one source of strength, blending smoothly with cultural and religious traditions that survived the Middle Passage. First-generation Africans, such as her grandmother Modesty, embodied a living African connection and memory for Tubman and her family. Tubman's religious fervor and trust in God to protect and guide her evolved from a fusion of these traditions.

In many ways, evangelical Protestantism represented a paradox in the antebellum South. On one hand, many white southerners who believed in slavery and accepted it as a cultural, economic, and institutional foundation of southern society were deeply committed to the preaching and spiritual guidance evangelical Protestantism provided. On the other hand, evangelicalism sustained and fortified generations of enslaved African Americans, even while white preachers instructed them to remain subordinate to their masters. For slaves, the spirit and meaning of biblical texts had a fluidity to them that allowed slaves to embrace a worldview shaped by African and American influences. African American spirituals, for instance, reflect a clear belief in alternative meanings for Holy Scripture.[58]

Black evangelicals rejected white versions of the Bible; they believed that God intended to set them free, delivering them in *"this* world."[59] Spirituals emphasized the Old Testament and the trials of God's chosen people, who hoped for deliverance in their own lifetimes.[60] While evangelical Protestantism did not protect slaves per se in the South, "it does not follow that the spiritual message of Protestantism failed as well . . . [for] [r]eligion is more than an institution."[61]

For Tubman, this fusion appeared seamless, though it could be bewildering to those who knew her. Sarah Bradford wrote, "I hardly know how to approach the subject of the spiritual experiences of my sable heroine. They seem to enter into the realm of the supernatural. . . . Had I not . . . seen such remarkable instances of what seemed to be her direct intercourse with heaven, I should not dare risk my own character for veracity by making these things public in this manner."[62]

The increased attention on the morality of slavery during the 1830s, 1840s, and 1850s coincided with an explosion of religious renewal that focused on spiritual freedom.[63] Setting this movement apart from the more traditional, white-controlled Methodist Church was the emergence of free black women preachers, including Jarena Lee, Maria Stewart, Sojourner Truth, and Zilpha Elaw. Viewing themselves as "agents with power of their own,"[64] Elaw, Lee, Truth, and Stewart believed that they were God's instruments, much like Tubman, who believed that "de Lord" had delivered her as she *expected . . . when she prayed . . . [and] Jes' so long as he wanted me, he would take keer of me, an' when he didn't want me no longer, I was ready to go."*[65]

Preaching at camp meetings throughout the Eastern Shore, Elaw and Lee operated quite successfully under the watchful eye of suspicious whites. Coming from black women, their words seemingly posed no threat to slaveholding elites. These women were able to preach messages of salvation and liberation with impunity, unlike their male brethren, who were often silenced through harassment or outright violence.[66] Their prayers were powerful tools, guiding Tubman and her family to insulate themselves from Thompson's messages to maintain patience and "obey your master."[67]

Maria Stewart, an early black female political and spiritual theorist, emerged as an important preacher in the Methodist Church during the early 1830s, eventually becoming the first woman preacher to speak before mixed audiences of men and women. Her messages of female strength and spiritual authority resonated with many free northern black women who were frustrated by their lack of control in their community and spiritual lives. Stewart suggested that God "makes use of feeble means sometimes to bring about his most exalted purposes."[68] In fact, Tubman believed that God used her for his own purposes, to free slaves and irritate slave owners with her uncanny ability to escape capture. The evangelicalism of the African Methodist Episcopal Church provided a very personal ideology for Tubman and sheds some light on the power of Tubman's religious fervor and trust in God to protect and guide her.

Women like Stewart challenged accepted notions about women's roles in society and in the Church, and about black women's rights to public discourse. They made female self-determination an important theme and demanded a radical reexamination of the accepted notions of the spirituality of blacks. Zilpha Elaw and Jarena Lee both spoke at camp meetings along the Eastern Shore of Maryland and in Baltimore throughout the three decades prior to 1850. It seems highly probable that Tubman, her family, and others from her community heard them speak. Perhaps this is how Tubman first became cognizant of the possibilities of a "spiritual birthright."[69]

Zilpha Elaw and Jarena Lee both risked arrest, sale into slavery, and even death to preach in the South, often at camp meetings, but also at a variety of Methodist, Presbyterian, and Baptist churches. Elaw, a free black Philadelphian, became convinced in 1819 that she had been called to preach. She claimed that "Christ sen[t] women to inform the disciples and Peter, that he had risen from the dead . . . that [therefore] the first preachers of the resurrection were women."[70] In 1828 Elaw left Philadelphia to preach in Maryland, Delaware, and Virginia.[71] Though she risked enslavement, many whites apparently did not consider her a threat. The slaveholders, she wrote, "thought it surpassingly strange that a person (and a female) belonging to the same family stock with their poor debased, uneducated, coloured slaves, should come into their territories and teach the enlightened proprietors the knowledge of God."[72] Elaw had no doubt "but God hath chosen the weak things of the world to confound the mighty."[73]

During the 1820s, 1830s, and 1840s Jarena Lee spoke at camp meetings in Cape May, New Jersey, southern Maryland, Philadelphia, Baltimore, and extensively throughout the Eastern Shore. In 1824 Lee spoke at camp meetings in Concord and Easton, then in Denton, Maryland, less than thirty miles from Bucktown. She continued past Bucktown to the southern part of the state, to Salisbury and Snow Hill, preaching to "slaves and the holders" in predominantly black churches, remarking that "they came seven miles' distance from only three or four hours' notice."[74] Writing of another camp meeting, Lee noted that many slaves walked twenty, thirty, or more miles to come to meetings, knowing they had to return the same number of miles to be ready to work the next day.[75] She repeatedly wrote of the comfort and power she found in the scriptures, feeling "so much of life and liberty in the word."[76] Lee was not without her problems, however. On at least one occasion, the authorities in Greenesboro, Caroline County, sought to have her thrown in jail. Assuming she had no freedom papers (a certificate issued to free blacks—sometimes required for travel in slaveholding regions), they eagerly waited for her to "say something to implicate myself"; the local magistrate, however, "was bound to protect her," and allowed her to continue preaching.[77] She prayed to God to "forward on the work of abolition until it fills the world," and "as we are all children of one parent, no one is justified in holding slaves."[78]

Camp meetings were frequent and well attended by both whites and blacks in Talbot, Dorchester, and Caroline Counties on the Eastern Shore. Ennals Springs, located three miles from East New Market and ten miles northeast of Bucktown, was a popular site for camp meetings, with fresh water, shade trees, and easy access by water and road. Notices appeared periodically in the local newspapers announcing the next camp meetings, some of which were sponsored by Methodist plantation owners on their own property. "A Camp Meeting will be commenced on the 12th of September next, in the woods of Mr. Levin Stephens, near Buck Town—where there is a sufficiency of water, and where ample provisions will be made for horses."[79] Given the close proximity to the Brodess plantation, Harriet's family could have attended camp meetings like this. William Cornish, a local slave who later fled to Canada, was allowed by his trustful owner to go as far away as Baltimore and "stay a week or two, or to go to a camp meeting."[80] Jacob Johnson was allowed by his Calvert County master to cross the Chesapeake in a canoe to attend a camp meeting at Taylor's Island in Dorchester County in August 1828. After Johnson failed to return, his master posted a runaway notice in the local Cambridge, Maryland, newspaper, where Jacob's free father was found to be living.[81] Many Maryland whites had been concerned about free and enslaved blacks, "roaming abroad or meeting in numbers on Sunday," and legislation was often proposed to impose restrictions, though little resulted from it.

Nat Turner's slave rebellion, in which nearly two hundred whites and blacks were killed in Southampton County, Virginia, in the summer of 1831, changed the nature of white-black relationships in the South. Southern slaveholders saw their worst nightmare made real: being murdered by their enslaved people while they slept.[82] For Dorchester County residents, however, Turner's attack only added to fears already festering in the community. In February 1831, a few short months earlier, a young slave woman by the name of Henny murdered her mistress, Betsy Thompson Insley. After having been refused sausage for her breakfast and then complaining about it, the Dorchester newspapers recounted, Henny received a "slight whipping" from her master. After Mr. Insley left the house in the morning, Henny threw lye in her mistress's face, butchered her with an ax, and hid the body in a closet. Tried and convicted, Henny was hanged to great fanfare in Cambridge the following June.[83]

No doubt many slaveholders began to look at their enslaved people with a different understanding, and perhaps their fears and anxieties prompted many to relieve themselves of the situation.[84] The Dorchester County manumission records record a remarkable rise in manumissions and requests for freedom papers, required by whites of free blacks to prove they were free, and an absolute necessity in this more restrictive environment.[85] For other slaveholders, however, more sales to southern slave traders relieved them of lingering fears.

Though gatherings by blacks were terribly circumscribed already, new legislation was passed forbidding blacks to "assemble or attend meetings for religious purposes which were not conducted by a white licensed clergyman or some respectable white of the neighborhood authorized by the clergy."[86] However, free and enslaved blacks found ways to absorb and negotiate the messages they received from itinerant or local white ministers. Also, the opportunity to gather at camp meetings allowed family and friends to meet and to renew their faith and hope for deliverance from their bondage. Those few black ministers who were allowed to preach on occasion, including Samuel Green (probably related to Tubman and her family), William and Joseph Cornish, and others, found ways to send messages of deliverance without the white authorities understanding it. Bill Cornish, a runaway slave from the Eastern Shore, became an approved minister after he was caught and returned from his hiding place in Calais, Maine. When he returned to the Eastern Shore, "Bill's arrival was hailed as a great triumph by the surrounding slave-owners, especially so when they were made acquainted with his sentiments of Northern negro freedom, and its horrors generally."[87] Bill recognized that his only chance to keep himself from being sold into the Deep South was to play the repentant slave. Always looking for the next opportunity to run away, Bill bided his time, and "while the masters were thus teaching over Bill's back the horrors of Northern freedom and the North generally, Bill, wide awake, and adroit in manner, was instructing far more effectively in quite the opposite direction."[88]

Whites on the Eastern Shore had long been wary of black ministers, and were often fearful that they could incite rebellion. In July 1830 local newspapers reported an "insurrection" of blacks, though the incident actually involved two black preachers who were believed to have incited rebellion, although nothing really happened. According to the *Cambridge Chronicle*, "supposed emissaries under the specious clock [cloak] of religion, and in the character of *Bethel Preachers*, have been amongst us sowing the seeds of sedition, and inciting the blacks to rebel, and those misguided, infamous wretches had but few disciples and have made still fewer proselytes."[89] A few local blacks were imprisoned, and the matter was dropped. The Reverend Noah C. W. Cannon, an AME minister from Baltimore, came under suspicion for the murder of "several women and children" in Cambridge. Though Cannon was dark-skinned and the suspected perpetrator a "bright mulatto," Caroline County officials attempted to arrest him. Suspicious of "movements they supposed were going on among the colored people," the authorities assumed the troublemaker was Cannon, an itinerant black preacher.[90]

While black ministers were prevented from preaching, black women found white audiences and local white authorities less suspicious of them. The preachings of women such as Lee, Elaw, and Stewart, however, suggest ways that Harriet Tubman experienced Christianity and shed light on the possible sources for her emotional and intellectual strength. Tubman did not necessarily have to hear Jarena Lee, Zilpha Elaw, or Maria Stewart to share their ideologies and religious sensibilities. What is most important is what these preachers represented for women as spiritual and intellectual beings. We cannot be sure where Tubman acquired her spiritual inspiration or how she came to know scripture by heart. We can assume that she experienced a spiritual awakening sometime in her adolescent years, perhaps as a natural progression of teachings heard at white Methodist services, camp meetings, at clandestine services in the woods, at Scott's Chapel in Bucktown, or in the slave quarters. Religious expression was a very personal experience for Tubman. When invited to join in prayers with a white master's family, "she preferred to stay on the landing, and pray for herself." Praying for strength to make her "able to fight," Tubman's pleadings became her own private rebellion.[91] Later Tubman would come to believe that her repeated attempts to retrieve enslaved blacks from the South were a holy crusade and that her God was the same God that so moved Elaw, Lee, and Stewart.

The influence of this fusion of African cultural and spiritual ideology and evangelical Protestantism, particularly its female voices, on Tubman's life has been lost in the retelling of her narrative. At the same time, it is also the nation's inflexible secularism that contributes to a devaluing and misinterpretation of the importance of religion and its defining influence in African American life. Harriet Tubman's courage and "utter disregard of consequences" elevated her to the status of Moses. William Still characterized Tubman as "wholly devoid of fear" and placed her within a long tradition of resistance, a tradition that may help explain at least part of her view of the world.[92] While her spirituality is a staple of her iconography, it is these intricate patterns of influence, from West African belief systems to the specific messages of evangelical women, that reveal the depth of Tubman's psychological and spiritual power.

Regardless of the exact nature of Tubman's religious instructions, daily survival remained her biggest challenge. Her profound faith and the care and nurturing by family and friends helped her survive her darkest hours. Disabled and weakened by her severe head injury and years of harsh treatment and neglect under temporary masters, often stricken with severe headaches that prevented her from working, Tubman's productivity declined significantly. Her worth to Brodess greatly diminished, and though he tried to sell her while she was recovering from her head injury, her ill health precluded any interested buyers. Indeed, Dr. Anthony C. Thompson remarked in his deposition in 1853 that Minty was not worth much, as she was "always sickly."[93] "I grew up like a neglected weed," Harriet once told an interviewer, "not happy or contented: every time I saw a white man I was afraid of being carried away."[94] Tubman would regain her strength, however, and mature into an accomplished worker, hiring her own time after paying Brodess a set wage for the year, and setting the stage for her own deliverance from slavery. "Slavery," she said, "is the next thing to hell."[95]

"SHADOW OF A VOICE IN THE TALKING LEAVES": THE HIDDEN WORLD OF BLACK COMMUNICATION

Hoot-owl calling in the ghosted air,
five times calling to the hants in the air.
Shadow of a face in the scary leaves,
shadow of a voice in the talking leaves.

—From "Runagate Runagate" by Robert Hayden

OVER THE MONTHS FOLLOWING HER HEAD INJURY, HARRIET STRUG-gled to regain her strength and resume a productive life. Under the care of her mother and other members of the community, including perhaps medical care from Dr. Anthony C. Thompson, who was then living in the Cambridge area, Harriet's head injury slowly healed.[1] Her ability to work fluctuated over time; headaches and seizures occasionally prevented her from performing assigned tasks, which gave her the reputation of being an unreliable slave. Brodess attempted to sell her on various occasions during this time period, but no buyer could be found.

After Harriet had sufficiently recovered, presumably sometime during 1835 or 1836, Brodess hired her out to a John T. Stewart, with whom she lived for five or six years.[2] This was probably John Trevalian

Stewart, the son of Joseph Stewart, a prominent shipbuilder, merchant, and slaveholder in the Tobacco Stick area of Dorchester County.[3] Joseph was the brother of Levin Stewart, who had owned and provided for the manumission of all of his slaves, including the Bowley family, before he moved to Georgetown in 1820.[4] When Levin Stewart died in 1826, Joseph Stewart purchased or assumed control of many of his brother's slaves, granting the manumissions that Levin executed for staggered dates beginning in the late 1810s.[5]

Tubman's work assignments may have varied considerably while working for Stewart. His father's 225-acre plantation sat upon the north side of Tobacco Stick Bay, west of Church Creek and Cambridge, extending along the shoreline "for a considerable extent down the creek." The plantation included tillable acreage used for wheat and corn, a shipyard, a store, windmill, a "work house," and two blacksmith shops, in addition to a main residence and assorted outbuildings, including, presumably, slave cabins.[6] The Stewarts' mercantile, farm, shipbuilding, and lumbering businesses required the labor of many people, including slaves and freemen, with varying levels of ability, from highly skilled blacksmiths to ship carpenters and sail makers, sawyers and timber inspectors, stevedores and drivers, and farm laborers. John T. Stewart probably operated the store and managed the lumbering operations connected with this property during the mid- to late 1830s for his father, and then later for himself during the early 1840s after his father had died. Tubman worked here first as a domestic slave, where, she later told a friend, she "would beat up the feather beds, make believe she was working hard, and when she had blown them up she would throw herself in the middle of them."[7] She may have also labored in Stewart's store, hauling goods to and from the wharves along the shore of Tobacco Stick Bay, or packing and hauling grain milled at the Stewarts' windmill. She lifted "huge barrels" loaded with goods bound for the market, and pulled heavily laden boats through the canal system "like an ox."[8]

She was eventually employed in the fields and woods, in the "rudest of labors,—drove oxen, carted, and plowed and did all the work of a man."[9] Working in the woods, Harriet cut sometimes half a cord a day.[10] She hauled logs, and reportedly was the marvel of her white master, who "would often exhibit her feats of strength to his friends."[11] It appears that Tubman was proud of her physical strength and prowess, particularly in work assignments that were traditionally, according to white northern abolitionists, assigned to men. Escaping the "petty tyranny" of the household may have been the source of Tubman's own motivations, especially in light of the horrible treatment she received as a child at the hands of intolerant and exacting mistresses.[12] Slave women themselves did not always view domestic work in a positive light.[13] The close scrutiny of mistresses and masters within the household, the tremendous variety of tasks required, and the sometimes dangerous sexual vulnerability to which household servants were exposed led many slave women to prefer outdoor work. On smaller farms and plantations, slave women were expected to both labor in the fields and contribute to household production and other domestic chores, while white women remained focused on household work. Regardless, most slaveholders were primarily concerned with economic success, and this often meant that most hands, both male and female, worked in the fields. White mistresses, unless they were elite women with large household staffs, also participated in household production, working with their enslaved women in contributing to the functioning of the household.[14]

In Edward and Eliza Brodess's household, the division of labor was less clearly defined. Rit may have worked for Eliza at times, but the fact that Rit and her daughter Linah were both hired out in 1833 raises the question of who was helping Eliza run her busy and growing household. Rit may have been primarily a cook and domestic servant, though she may have labored in the fields for Brodess or for temporary masters to whom she had been hired. With four young boys at home, including one infant, Eliza Brodess needed the help of an experienced house servant. Harriet's twenty-one-year-old sister, Soph, may have been assigned domestic duty within the household.[15] Edward's small farm did not necessarily need the field labor of his enslaved women; he had plenty of male slaves to work the fields. On the other hand, the money Brodess could earn by hiring out his male slaves, a fee nearly double what he could earn from his female slaves, may have been more attractive, on balance, than using all of them on his own farm.[16]

Working for John T. Stewart allowed Harriet to be closer to her father, Ben, who lived and labored just south of Woolford and Tobacco Stick in the Peters Neck area near the Big Blackwater River. She claimed to have loved "great physical activity,"[17] and noted that the "amount exacted of a woman for her time was fifty or sixty dollars,—of a man, one hundred to one hundred and fifty dollars," implying that she was worth what a man could earn for himself or his master. [18] By 1840 Ben Ross had been manumitted by a provision in Anthony Thompson's will and was now free to work for wages. Ben probably continued to labor for the Thompsons for a while, but then he hired himself to the Stewarts. Timber from the interior of Dorchester County was still being harvested and hauled to Tobacco Stick via Stewart's Canal, which was completed sometime in the 1830s. Joseph Stewart owned several tracts in this region, having purchased several parcels of property from Anthony Thompson's estate in 1837. Purchasing Thompson's land and acquiring the labor of Thompson's former slaves and those free blacks living and working in the area allowed for little interruption in harvesting and distribution of timber and agricultural products. For the black people in this community, it represented continuity in their lives, economically and socially. Hiring Ben was a logical and probably desirable thing to do; Ross was familiar with the territory and the work, and Joseph Stewart's own shipbuilding and merchant shipping business required the experience of a master timber cutter and foreman such as Ross. Stewart "was a builder, and for the work of Ross used to receive as much as five dollars a day sometimes, he being a superior workman."[19]

A dense community of slave and free black families, brought together by virtue of their work patterns and the social interactions of their white masters and employers, was home to Ben Ross. This community was ultimately the social world of Harriet Tubman and her family as well, even though their owner, Edward Brodess, lived several miles to the southeast, near Bucktown.[20] In fact, Anthony Thompson's home at the end of Harrisville Road near the Big Blackwater River was surrounded by many free black households, some of whom may have been former Thompson slaves; others, like Simon Ross, who was born free but who may have been a blood relative to Ben Ross, also lived here, constituting another part of this dynamic black community whose labor supported the commercial and agricultural aspirations of the area's white landowners.

Throughout the antebellum period Cambridge and Dorchester County continued to expand economically, adjusting to the changing markets in fisheries, timber, and agriculture. Many of the wealthiest white citizens owned property in several counties and moved about quite often between their various landholdings and the local towns and cities. But this patchwork of land ownership opened lines of communication for the black community as well; as slaveholders moved their slaves from one location to the other, depending upon the season and the nature of the operations on particular pieces of property, they fostered the establishment of widely dispersed communication networks. These lines fed in turn into larger trade networks connected to the water, as growth depended upon water traffic populated by a diverse group of maritime professionals, from ferrymen to experienced navigators, from single boatmen to crews manning large schooners, to stevedores and other dockworkers, ship carpenters, and caulkers. All contributed to a network of trade and commerce, which provided a consistent means of communication throughout the Chesapeake and beyond.[21] Even in remote parts of Dorchester County, new commercial links required a constant flow of ships and boats of all sizes, and seamen and watermen of different races, to provide and operate a dependable network to transport their cargo to markets, near and far.[22]

The towns and villages that were settled in this area were devoted to merchant shipping and shipbuilding, providing a market for timber, shingles, staves, boards, and wood pulp. Below the Little Choptank River, and traversed by the Big Blackwater River in the Peters Neck region, stood great swaths of thick virgin forest, so dense visitors imagined them to be towering black walls of great fortresses. During the eighteenth century, the timber brought out from this region was floated through a circuitous route south through the Blackwater River to Fishing Bay at the mouth of the Transquaking and Nanticoke Rivers. This route may have been less than ideal, although in the absence of a northerly route, it was the only option available. It did not provide for easy transport of timber from deeper in the interior. Those entrepreneurs who settled along the Little Choptank north of the Blackwater River quickly sought a more direct route for accessing and transporting the county's rich lumber, and then later its bountiful agricultural products. A canal, they thought, would provide that route.

Joseph Stewart, who purchased hundreds of acres of Anthony Thompson's former landholdings in the Harrisville and Peters Neck area in 1837, was one of the more successful businessmen in that area of Dorchester County.[23] He was instrumental in the building of what became known as Stewart's Canal throughout the late 1820s and early 1830s. The canal connected the Big Blackwater River to Parsons Creek to the northwest and Tobacco Stick Bay to the northeast, easing the transportation of timber from the interior of the Blackwater region to the shipyards and merchants on the water. Timber could be floated freely or by barge to local shipbuilders, or to waiting merchants contracted to ship logs, planks, shingles, and staves to Baltimore, Annapolis, Norfolk, and New England, where shipbuilders and other manufacturers prized the Eastern Shore's sturdy white oak, often used for keels, and abundant white and yellow pine.[24] Stewart trained and employed numerous slaves and free white and black labor in his own shipyard. Teams of oxen and scores of men dragged the huge cut trees along logging roads carved out of the dense forests. Icy and slippery in the winter and spring, stiflingly hot and humid in the summer and fall, the work required stamina and strength. With the canal, the difficult task of hauling the region's white oak, walnut, and pine was somewhat alleviated, creating increased supply for the area's shipbuilders and lumber merchants. Farmers also quickly took advantage of these canals to ship agricultural products from the area's rapidly expanding farms.

The construction of this canal required enormous numbers of laborers. Many enslaved workers, drawn from such areas as Slaughter Creek, Parsons Creek, Tobacco Stick, and Church Creek, dug this canal. It was incredibly difficult work; canal laborers toiled in water all day, digging, dredging, and tearing out hundreds of acres of marshland, forest, and swamp. Disease was rampant and the mortality rate extremely high. In contrast to the free, mostly immigrant laborers who built northern canals, the great majority of southern canal workers were enslaved. Free white and black workers rarely risked the high injury and death rates common among canal builders. Some slave owners, too, were reluctant to commit their enslaved labor when faced with the possibility of losing a slave to either death or permanent disability.[25]

A group of investors eager to clear parts of the Great Dismal Swamp in North Carolina, for instance, imported a cargo of slaves directly from the African coast to dig the canals that would drain it. In this isolated and remote area, suffocatingly ill-suited for human habitation, local slave or free labor was unattainable. Reasoning that unseasoned slaves fresh from Africa would be the best investment, the investors of the Lake Company noted unapologetically, "they are indispensable in this unhealthy and laborious country; for these long canals, that are all important in rendering our swamplands valuable, must be dug by them, or not at all."[26] Many slaves died from disease, injury, and the brutal treatment they endured from masters and overseers who worked them from dawn until dusk. Some committed suicide to escape the physical and psychological trauma.[27]

Stewart's Canal was modest by the standards of the Great Dismal Swamp; six or seven miles long, it was built in fits and starts over a twenty-year period. As the canal affected new areas of the Parsons Creek district, nearby landowners invested in its development. Slaves were probably also hired from local slave owners who were willing to risk the loss or injury of their enslaved labor.[28] A large free black population in Dorchester County offered an additional labor source. Despite the debilitating and risky work, some free blacks may have found no alternative if they were unwilling or unable to leave the county for better work options elsewhere.

The work was arduous and hazardous. Dorchester's vast marshes and swamps provided ample stagnant water for millions of mosquitoes and other irritating and dangerous insects. The digging was treacherous, exhausting, and backbreaking. For those slaves unable to swim, a slip or a tumble could mean death, particularly during the winter months when the water was icy and weakened limbs could not react quickly enough to save a life. Often living in tents and moving along the path of the canal under construction, poorly fed and clothed, the laborers fell prey to pneumonia and other infections. Heat during the summer added to their physical and emotional misery.

Many free black workers remained in this area once the canal was built. Finding work in the forests or in newly developed farmland, they labored next to their enslaved family and friends, establishing foundations of several predominantly black communities near the canal. Several of Stewart's former slaves settled in this area, establishing the nucleus of a closely knit community of skilled and unskilled black labor, particularly in the Peters Neck area, south of Tobacco Stick on White Marsh Road, and south of Church Creek and Woolford on Harrisville Road. Several of the Stewart slaves married free blacks living and working in this area, later becoming central figures in the establishment of Malone's Church and the area's black school.[29] The Bowley brothers, for instance, manumitted by Levin Stewart, were apprenticed as blacksmiths and ship carpenters while still young and under the control of Joseph Stewart.[30] (John Bowley eventually married Harriet's niece Kessiah Jolley.) While these young men lived and worked at the epicenter of a thriving maritime community, many of their familial and community relationships also included the plantations and work camps in the forests deeper in the interior of the county. These slaves, and other black workers like them, represented spokes in the wheels of inter- and intraregional communication.

From approximately 1836 on, Harriet worked and lived in and near this community. Though she lived for a time at the Stewart plantation in Tobacco Stick, she may have also lived with or near her father, and possibly her mother, at Peters Neck, bringing her closer to relatives and friends she had been separated from as a child.[31] It was in this blended community of free and enslaved people that Minty Ross married John Tubman, a local free black, around 1844. It was at this moment she took the name Harriet, possibly in honor of her mother, or it may have coincided with a spiritual conversion requiring the adoption of a new name.

It was a bittersweet moment for a free man such as John Tubman to marry Harriet. He must have loved her deeply, for he forfeited many rights incumbent upon the marriage of a free couple. By the laws of Maryland and other slaveholding states, all children born to John and Harriet would bear Harriet's slave status. Ownership of their children would fall to Edward Brodess as Harriet's master. John Tubman lacked any legal or parental rights to his own children. Nor could he share a life with Harriet without the consent of Brodess. Their decision to marry was no doubt made only after careful deliberation. Perhaps they both hoped, against great odds, that they could in time purchase Harriet's freedom from Brodess.

John Tubman has been treated quite unsympathetically in the various narratives of Harriet's life. Very little is actually known of his family and his life in Dorchester County. After Harriet ran away sometime in late 1849, John turned to another woman. By 1851 he had remarried, and this infidelity has become the defining moment for a seemingly flawed and weak man. Sarah Bradford claimed that John called Harriet "a fool, and said she was like old Cudjo, who when a joke went round, never laughed till half an hour after everybody else got through," stamping him indelibly as a loveless and emotionally unavailable husband.[32] In contrast, John's decision to marry Harriet came with a great cost. It appears the choice of a man deeply in love with or at least powerfully drawn to Harriet.[33]

John Tubman lived and worked in the Peters Neck area, near Harriet's father, Ben Ross. Slightly older than Harriet at about thirty-two years of age, John was a dark-skinned mulatto, born to free parents, possibly Thomas and Priscilla Tubman.[34] As a free man, John had far greater mobility than Harriet, and he may have moved about the area quite frequently, working for various farmers or other employers, as labor needs changed throughout the seasons.[35] The Eastern Shore suffered greatly during the 1830s as the nation went through a banking crisis followed by a severe economic downturn. As the economy slowly recovered, the demand for labor on the Eastern Shore increased, providing a variety of work options for free blacks such as John Tubman and even some slaves. In fact, the labor of free blacks and hired slaves was a vital part of the Eastern Shore's economy. The availability of this flexible workforce enabled many Eastern Shore farmers, manufacturers, timber harvesters, and other entrepreneurs the opportunity to hire labor when needed, without the heavy investment in slaves.[36]

Harriet hired out her time quite regularly during the 1840s, paying Brodess a yearly fee for the privilege of hiring herself out to temporary masters of her own choosing—similar to that of a free laborer such as

John Tubman. Given that Harriet was frequently disabled by her head injury, Brodess may have found this arrangement quite appealing, especially since Dr. Anthony C. Thompson, a major figure in the lives of Ben Ross and his family since the death of the elder Anthony Thompson, "stood for her," that is, he guaranteed the $50–$60 yearly payment extracted by Brodess for her labor.[37] Harriet, in turn, repaid Thompson and kept any additional monies she earned for herself. She was able to earn enough excess funds " 'to buy a pair of steers,' worth forty dollars."[38] Independent and savvy, Tubman then hired herself out, with her team of oxen. Plowing in the fields and hauling timber in the woods, Harriet maximized her earning potential throughout the year. It seems likely that John and Harriet hoped that they would be able to earn enough money to buy Harriet's freedom from Edward Brodess. Once married, John and Harriet presumably lived together, or at least near each other, in the Peters Neck area.[39]

Harriet was thus spared the fate of three of her sisters, Linah, Mariah Ritty, and Soph. Brodess continued to struggle at farming; his property at Bucktown was not highly productive. His large family required ever-increasing income, but his farm was too small to consistently increase its yield to produce higher yearly returns. Brodess probably remained a simple farmer, lacking the resources or perhaps the drive to expand his farm or entertain other economic opportunities. Instead, he turned his slaves into cash. As previously noted, in the 1830s or early 1840s Brodess sold Linah and Soph.[40] Both women were supposed to be freed at age forty-five, but Brodess sold them illegally, possibly to slave traders, and most definitely out of the state. Soph may have been sold with one child, though the record is not clear.[41] Linah was sold away from her two children, Kessiah and Harriet. Tubman's brother recalled years later, while he stood imprisoned for debts owned by Brodess, that his sister, most likely Linah, was "taken away from her children, handcuffed, and put into the jail where I was. Her irons were taken off; she was in great grief, crying all the time. 'Oh my children! My poor children!' til it appeared to me, she would kill herself for grief."[42] Apparently Brodess turned the $400 he received from illegally selling Linah as a "slave for life" into a land purchase, the record of which has yet to be found.[43]

On the cusp of adulthood, the disabled Tubman went to work on a timber gang, exhibiting great skills laboring in the logging camps and in the fields. There she was exposed to the secret communication networks that were the province of black watermen and other free and enslaved blacks. Like her father, Harriet drove oxen, cut and hauled wood, plowed, and did "all the work of a man." Living "much with her father and mother," Tubman's life revolved around the farms and small cabins in the black community while she labored for larger landholders and farmers, men such as Joseph and John Stewart, John D. Parker, and others.[44] As one of the few women working in the forests on a timber gang, if not the only one, Tubman became part of an exclusively male world. Here in the forests, beyond the watchful eye of white masters, the male slaves had access to the black watermen who worked along the Big Blackwater River, Parsons Creek, Tobacco Stick, Woolford, and Church Creek. They communicated with the black mariners whose ships carried the timber to the Baltimore shipyards. The free black men who toiled next to their enslaved friends were able to move about freely, from one community to another, from one family member to another. These black men were part of a larger world, a world beyond the plantation, beyond the woods, that reached out to towns and cities up and down the Chesapeake, ranging as far away as Delaware, Pennsylvania, and New Jersey. They knew the safe places, they knew the sympathetic whites, and, more important, they knew the danger. They created a veiled and secret world parallel to the white masters' world.

While working for John Stewart in Tobacco Stick, Tubman visited the wharves often, either procuring shipments for the Stewarts' store or readying goods to be transported by boat to distant markets.[45] Tubman's unique ability to make effective use of this complicated communications network, combined with well-practiced skills of disguise and deception, may have set her apart from other slave women and men in her community. In the predominantly illiterate community in which she lived, oral and physical communication was key. Furthermore, in a world of suspicious whites, a letter could elicit unwanted attention. Like the heavily coded spirituals Tubman would later use to guide fugitive slaves north, a look, a glance, a movement, a shift of the foot, or a wave of a hand could be invisible to the white master, yet speak louder than words to fellow blacks, passing messages in times of need, when the stakes were life or death.

Ben Ross, an experienced and trusted slave, probably knew many of the local watermen and seamen who worked the boats in the region. From the Big Blackwater River to the Choptank, to Baltimore, Washington, Norfolk, and on to New York, Massachusetts, and Maine, these black watermen provided a communication substitute for the newspapers and written words of the white community.[46] Anthony Thompson and later John Stewart may have even allowed Ben to accompany timber to Baltimore, ensuring safe passage to markets on Baltimore's bustling wharves. In any case, Ben was in a perfect position, even as a slave, to participate in the regional system of black watermen. Once free, Ross would have been more likely to move about freely, since he no longer required the permission of his master.[47]

Black mariners were the hubs of a great communication wheel, spreading news, gossip, and personal messages to blacks living throughout the Atlantic diaspora.[48] Spreading notions of liberty and freedom, relaying the details of revolution in Haiti, sharing news of abolition and colonization efforts and other political issues, and passing messages between members of families separated from one another, black watermen and seamen were vital to the survival of many free and enslaved black communities.[49] Local messages relayed by these networks may have been the main sources of information about freedom and liberty in the North and for learning the best routes to get there.

Indeed, a slave's social and economic network was often derived from the social and economic relationships fostered by his or her slave owner and the work assignments distributed to the owner's bondswomen and men. Of course, market days, camp meetings, horse races, and other forms of economic and social gatherings also gave slaves and free blacks important opportunities to meet and spend time with one another.[50] For Harriet Tubman and her family, the social and economic connections that linked the Pattisons, Stewarts, Thompsons, Brodesses, and others were at the heart of her extended-family experience.

While the Thompsons, and other slaveholders like them, may have been aware of the familial and social relationships among their slaves, and even accommodated them on occasion, they remained woefully ignorant of the black inter- and intraregional networks that often paralleled the white networks of trade, travel, and communication. Thomas Dail of Dorchester County, for instance, allowed his trusted slave William Cornish to travel to Baltimore and attend distant camp meetings, as previously noted. Sometimes gone for two weeks, Cornish always returned, reinforcing Dail's confidence that Cornish was a devoted and trustworthy slave, even though Cornish, in fact, was secretly determined to escape his bondage.[51] Anthony Thompson may have felt the same sort of trust in his relationship with Ben Ross, Jerry Manokey, and others. Many free blacks, of course, traveled about the county and region quite readily for economic, social, political, or spiritual reasons. Free blacks' mobility expanded the world even for slaves who were compelled to remain under the vigilant control of white masters.

The rapid exchange of information across geographic, social, and cultural boundaries was central to the survival of the African American community and crucial in providing Tubman and her family and friends with an effective and secure means of operating beyond the gaze of white masters.[52] But despite its power, the network could be easily disrupted by the vagaries of planters' lives.

In November 1836 the elder Anthony Thompson died at the age of seventy-four.[53] For Ben Ross and the other enslaved people owned by Thompson, this marked the beginning of a period of uncertainty, instability, and apprehension. The death of a slaveholder usually initiated an extremely fearful mood among the enslaved people of the deceased's estate; the division of the estate among heirs and the payment of outstanding debts often meant the sale of slaves to satisfy creditors, the breaking up of families, and the fracturing of community relationships. Thompson never sold any of his slaves, and although they were hired out or were required to work away from family and friends on the plantation, these slaves did experience a modicum of stability, allowing the creation and maintenance of long-term and intimate community and family relationships. Several of his slaves had been manumitted prior to his death, and in his will Thompson provided for the eventual manumission of all of his slaves at staggered manumission dates, ranging from immediate freedom to liberty for some of the children when they reached the ages of twenty-four, thirty, or forty-five.[54] It is possible that these unequal manumission schedules were purposely established to provide incentives to his enslaved people to work hard and remain compliant, thereby continuing to serve the planter's remaining family while earning further reductions in the slaves' terms of service.[55] In fact, Dr. Thompson followed his father's example over the next twenty or so years, reducing the terms of service as incentives or rewards for good service and extending terms of service for defiant and uncooperative slaves.[56]

Although Thompson apparently never sold any of his enslaved people, the advent of his death still brought anxiety and tension to those bonded to his estate. Though enslaved, the Thompson bondsmen and women had led fairly stable lives in the tricounty area. Most of them were married to local free or enslaved people and were able to raise their children to adulthood. Though they did not all live in two-parent households, an ideal practiced by most white families, they had come to be assured that they would not be separated forever by sale or removal to a distant territory.[57] Most, in fact, had been given some sort of future hope of freedom in the form of limited terms of service through delayed manumissions set up by the elder Thompson before his death. But they also all would have clearly understood that a master's promises were not always carried through, and the uncertainty inherent in estate settlements always created havoc and tremendous anxiety for the affected slave community.

At his death, Thompson had approximately forty-three slaves, including ten men, eight women, and twenty-five children. Thompson provided for the manumission of his slaves by the time they neared the maximum age for manumission, that is, forty-five years of age, though some were set to be freed at even earlier ages. It was common practice to extend slaves' terms of service illicitly. Manumitting a slave over forty-five years old was illegal in Maryland, but to extend the bonded service of a healthy and productive slave, slave owners often shamelessly changed the ages of their slaves; planters were rarely prosecuted for this crime, and the practice continued right up to the Civil War. For example, though Ben Ross had been born sometime during the 1780s, Anthony Thompson provided for Ben's manumission in 1841.[58] This would have made Ben older than the legal age limit for Maryland manumissions; Ben was in his fifties in 1840. Though freedom at any age may seem preferable to perpetual bondage, in fact the freeing of aged slaves was much frowned upon and discouraged. Communities did not want indigent, vagrant, old, and worn-out slaves loitering in their neighborhoods. And some Eastern Shore whites, both slaveholders and those without slaves, professed a moral and religious responsibility to provide for aged slaves, holding the slaveocracy accountable and responsible for maintaining elderly, disabled, and dependent slaves.

Bound to serve another five years, Ben Ross was provided with ten acres of land "for and during his lifetime . . . laid out to his house binding with the road" on the west side of Harrisville Road, with the "privilege of cutting timber" for his support.[59] This arrangement was unusual; while manumission by will was hardly uncommon, Thompson's provision for the material support of Ross through life tenancy and rights to timber on the property was extremely unusual. In some cases a slave master awarded a prized female slave, who may have also been his mistress, freedom, property, and money, but even this situation was extremely rare.[60]

Ben Ross was not the only beneficiary of such a bequest. In fact, Thompson provided that Jerry Manokey and his wife, Polly, were to be set free immediately upon Thompson's death, and their children, John, Aaron, Moses, Eliza, and Matilda, were to serve anywhere from eighteen to thirty-three more years. Their youngest children, Mary and Susan, were to serve forty-one and thirty-eight more years but were allowed to remain with Jerry and Polly until they were fifteen and eleven years old, respectively.[61] In the context of antebellum plantation life, these arrangements were most uncommon. So, too, was Thompson's provision giving Jerry and Polly the use of ten acres of land and the right to cut timber on the Thompson plantation for the remainder of their lives. Thompson also bequeathed one year's worth of bread to Jerry and required his son Anthony to continue to provide for Jerry "in time of need."[62]

Thompson's favoritism suggests an intimate connection (at least on the part of Thompson) with Ross and Manokey. Thompson had probably enslaved Ben and Jerry since they had been children. They played a major role in the physical and economic development of Thompson's properties: stripping his land of prized timber, hauling it to the Big Blackwater River or Tobacco Stick for shipment to markets, preparing and planting hundreds of acres of agricultural property, and digging the vital canal that would transform economic investment in the Blackwater region. Thompson's bequest suggests that Ben Ross and Jerry Manokey were particularly valued and prized slaves, and that he felt some sort of responsibility to provide for them and their families. No other Thompson slaves, male or female, were awarded material support and freedom through Thompson's last will and testament.[63]

After Thompson's death, Jerry and Polly Manokey remained within the Peters Neck community, where they had been enslaved for decades. Surrounded by family and friends, the Manokeys carried on with their lives, working and raising their young daughters who remained at home with them. Jerry, like Ben, may have continued working for the younger Anthony Thompson on the Thompson plantation, or he may have hired out to Joseph Stewart or John D. Parker, both of whom continued harvesting the timber and expanding their local land under cultivation. In April 1840 Ben Ross received his freedom, one year sooner than the will specified.[64] Finally free, Ross chose to remain in the area, continuing to work in his capacity as a timber inspector for Joseph Stewart and his sons, and other area farmers and shipbuilders in need of his skills.

Though Anthony Thompson seemingly had fostered intact families with his enslaved people, his economic interests set the parameters of family life in his slave quarters. Thompson, like other slaveholders, hired his slaves out. Thompson bequeathed nearly all of his enslaved people to his younger son, Anthony, with a portion of the income from their yearly hire reserved for Absalom.[65] Though all of Thompson's slaves were given to Dr. Anthony C. Thompson, Eliza and Matilda Manokey, among others, were ultimately "awarded" to Absalom Thompson, who then lived in nearby Talbot County. Eliza, who was about fifteen at the time of Thompson's death in 1836, and Matilda, about twelve, could have already been working at Absalom's plantation at Bayside in Talbot County at the time. Absalom and his brother, Anthony C., may have worked out an arrangement of sorts whereby Absalom took several of the slaves in exchange for a one-third interest in their earnings.

Ben's world revolved around the enslaved families owned by Thompson. Nearby free black families, living along Harrisville, Indian Landing, and White Marsh Roads, represented another part of Ben's complex community life.[66] Spending time with Rit, who lived sometimes on the Brodess property at Bucktown several miles away, or who was hired out to other area farmers, was not altogether convenient, particularly considering the work assignments they both must have endured. Though the living arrangements for many of Thompson's slaves are unknown, it appears that a set of fictive or virtual familial relationships evolved in this slave community. In 1843 Ben Ross purchased the freedom of two of Thompson's slaves: Maria Bailey and Aaron Manokey, "a cripple." For the small sum of ten dollars, Anthony C. Thompson agreed to the transaction.[67] Living in the same slave community for most of their lives, Ben may have even helped raise these two people. Maria was married to Isaac Bailey, who bore the same name as Frederick Douglass's grandfather.[68] Aaron, whose disability is unknown, may have been an unproductive slave even though he was a young man. Maria, on the other hand, was considered "delicate," a term that could have meant weak and unproductive, or she could have been pregnant at the time she was sold.[69]

Dr. Anthony C. Thompson was not interested in pursuing farming in the Blackwater and Peters Neck region, as his father had done.[70] Seeking more lucrative investment opportunities, Thompson began in 1847 to acquire large tracts of heavily forested land, totaling over two thousand acres, in Caroline County, thirty miles northeast of Peters Neck in an area called Poplar Neck. Formerly part of the Goldsborough plantation, Poplar Neck was situated on the Choptank River as it slowly winds its way from its headwaters near Greensborough, Caroline County, to the Chesapeake Bay. Gambling his own modest fortune and his entire inheritance, Thompson hoped to become a major timber supplier in the region. He enlisted the help of his sons, Anthony, Edward, and perhaps John, and eventually moved the majority of his enslaved men, and possibly later the women, to Caroline County. There they were set to work cutting and hauling great quantities of timber to be transported by black and white watermen to the shipbuilders in Dorchester and Caroline Counties, and probably beyond.[71] Leaving all of his ancestral lands in Dorchester County behind, Thompson hoped to make a name for himself and for his sons at Poplar Neck in Caroline. Keeping a residence in the town of Cambridge, where his wife and many of his enslaved women probably lived, Thompson initially traveled back and forth to oversee his new operations.[72]

For years, Dr. Thompson had been involved in a variety of businesses in addition to his medical practice. He opened a drugstore in Cambridge, selling his own medicinal elixirs and medications, confectionary, and other fine goods, purchased during frequent trips to Baltimore.[73] Throughout the 1840s and early 1850s, Thompson maintained his residence at Bellefield, his fourteen-and-a-half-acre property near Boundary Road in Cambridge. During this period, Dr. Thompson took on more public and active roles within the community. He was an early supporter of colonization movements, which sought to transport free blacks back to sponsored settlement sites in Liberia on the west coast of Africa. He was also a member of the local Sons of Temperance and was appointed school commissioner for Cambridge.[74]

Harriet, meanwhile, had been hiring herself out to various employers until 1847, when she was hired by Dr. Anthony C. Thompson and lived with him. Whether she moved to Caroline County and lived and worked for Thompson there or labored at his residence in Cambridge is not known.[75] Harriet became ill during the winter of 1848–49, working only when she could. Thompson's need for Ben's services at his Poplar Neck properties may have induced Thompson to be flexible with Ben's daughter's uncertain health. Brodess, however, was still struggling financially and was eager to sell her. The $50 to $60 she brought him on a yearly basis was not enough to meet his immediate cash needs. Thompson was in no position to purchase her, even as a favor to Ben; his own financial situation was precarious, and he was already overburdened with debt after purchasing his Caroline County land.[76] Tubman later recalled that "from Christmas till March I worked as I could, and I *prayed* through all the long nights—I groaned and prayed for ole master: 'Oh Lord, convert master! Oh Lord, change dat man's heart!' " Harriet's prayers would be answered, but not in the way she could have ever imagined.[77]

Harriet's prayers took on a more urgent tone as the winter of 1849 wore on and the first signs of spring began to appear on the Eastern Shore. Still recovering from poor health and overwork, and recurring relapses due to her epileptic seizures, Tubman prayed relentlessly, pleading with God to forgive her sins and deliver her from this heartless master. "Appears like I prayed all the time," she said, "about my work, everywhere, I prayed and I groaned to the Lord. When I went to the horse-trough to wash my face, I took up the water in my hand and I said, 'Oh Lord, wash me, make me clean!' Then I take up something to wipe my face, and I say, 'Oh Lord, wipe away all my sin!' When I took the broom and began to sweep, I groaned, 'Oh Lord, what so ever sin there be in my heart, sweep it out, Lord, clear and clean!' "[78] More fearful than ever, her prayers took on a more urgent tone with each passing day. By March 1849 she imagined with a keen sense of foreboding that she was about to be sold. "I prayed all night long for master, till the first of March; and all the time he was bringing people to look at me, and trying to sell me. Then we heard that some of us was going to be sold to go with the chain-gang down to the cotton and rice fields, and they said I was going, and my brothers, and sisters. Then I changed my prayer. First of March I began to pray, 'Oh Lord, if you ain't never going to change that man's heart, kill him, Lord, and take him out of the way.' "[79]

Little did Harriet know when she prayed for Brodess's death that he lay dying in Bucktown. On March 7, 1849, Edward Brodess died at the age of forty-seven. Harriet was stunned. Despite her relief, she still felt a sense of responsibility that her prayers had indeed been answered, though not entirely as she had expected. "Next thing I heard old master was dead, and he died just as he lived. Oh, then, it appeared like I'd give all the world full of gold, if I had it, to bring that poor soul back. But I couldn't pray for him no longer."[80] While his death would spark a decade or more of anxiety and upheaval in the lives of Brodess's wife and dependent children, no one was affected more than the slaves who were part of his estate. His death actually resulted in just what Harriet had feared. Within three months of Edward's death, his widow, Eliza, began petitioning Dorchester County's Orphans Court to order the sale of several of the estate's slaves to accommodate the Brodesses' many debts.[81]

A day or two before he died, Edward Brodess instructed his lawyer, Thomas J. H. Eccleston, to write out his will, leaving his estate to his wife, Eliza. But he excluded his slaves, giving his wife Eliza only "the use and hire" of his slaves while she lived, "for the purpose of raising his children, and after her death, all his estate was to go to his children."[82] Several of Harriet's family members believed that their master's will provided for their freedom upon his death.[83] Harriet's brother Henry later said that "he promised us, that if we would only be faithful, he would leave us all to be free, . . . but he left us all slaves."[84] Harriet herself knew better. Brodess had long proved himself to be dishonest and untrustworthy.

Sometime during the late 1840s, Tubman hired a lawyer to check the probate records of her mother's first owner, Atthow Pattison.[85] Paying for the lawyer with money she had earned by hiring herself out, she soon learned that her mother had been manumitted by Pattison's will, written in 1791 and probated after his death in 1797. Tubman was enraged to learn that Pattison had instructed that his female slaves and their children serve his heirs only until the slaves reached the age of forty-five.[86] Rit, who had been bequeathed to Atthow's granddaughter Mary Pattison, had been entitled to her freedom sometime in the early 1830s.[87] She was now over sixty years old. Edward Brodess, Atthow Pattison's great-grandson, had not abided by the terms of the will. It is not clear whether Brodess had been aware of the terms of his great-grandfather's will, but it is certain that he violated them during the prior twenty-five years when he sold several of Rit's children to out-of-state buyers, transactions that were illegal for term slaves. Only one of those sales was recorded, however, leaving open the possibility that the other sales were not recorded because he was aware that they were illegal transactions.[88]

Whether Tubman initially learned of the provisions of Pattison's will through her mother or another member of the black community or through the Pattison heirs is not clear. But by July 1849, four months after Edward Brodess died, Gourney Crow Pattison, Atthow Pattison's grandson and Edward Brodess's uncle, filed suit against Eliza Brodess and John Mills, administrators of Edward's estate, claiming ownership rights to Rit and any of her children then over the age of forty-five. According to the complaint filed in the Dorchester County Orphans Court, Gourney Crow Pattison argued that the terms of Atthow Pattison's will implied that Edward Brodess was entitled only to the labor of Rit and her children until they reached the age of forty-five. Because Atthow had neglected to specify what was to happen to the slaves upon reaching this age (though his intention must have been freedom, like many such manumissions by will at that time), Pattison argued that Rit and her offspring should revert to the Pattison estate.[89] Atthow Pattison had instructed that his daughter, Elizabeth Pattison, receive the residue of his estate, after all debts and bequests had been paid and assigned, and that when her children arrived at the age of twenty-one, they were to share equally in the residue of the estate as well.[90]

Based on this narrow reading of the will and the interpretation of probate law, Gourney Crow Pattison, his siblings, and their children claimed ownership of Rit through their rights to the residue of Atthow's estate. Rit, he argued, belonged to him because she was well over the age of forty-five, and all wages Brodess had collected from hiring out Rit after she turned forty-five must be turned over to Atthow Pattison's estate. The lawsuit also claimed that because Brodess had sold two of Rit's children, Linah and Soph, illegally as slaves for life beyond the state of Maryland, the Pattison heirs were entitled to compensation for the loss of their labor. They also sought to prevent the sale of any of Rit's other children until the matter could be resolved.

It appears that Tubman's inquiry into the status of her mother's enslavement may have either precipitated or initiated this legal action. Gourney Pattison pressed his claim in court; depositions were ordered and documentary evidence produced over a period of several weeks, culminating in the dismissal of the suit on August 6, 1849. Pattison and his attorney, James A. Stewart, appealed, sending the case back to court.[91]

In the meantime, Eliza Brodess was fretting about managing her large household and growing debts. With several minor children still living at home, Brodess faced pressing financial obligations that left little security for a new widow.[92] Within a month of Edward's death, the court ordered the sale of all of his personal property, "negroes excepted."[93] In most such cases, the family of the deceased bought all of the estate's personal property, if they had enough money to pay all of the debts owed by the deceased person. Eliza, it appears, did not. She turned to her neighbor, John Mills, who had been appointed co-administrator of Edward Brodess's estate with her, for a loan. Indebted to him for $1,000, and probably pressed by him for repayment, Eliza turned to one of the most liquid assets she had available, and the assets she was most willing to part with: her slaves.[94]

On June 27 Mills and Brodess posted an advertisement in the local newspaper to sell twenty-year-old Harriet (probably the daughter of Tubman's sister Linah and presumably named after her grandmother Rit) and her two-year-old child, Mary Jane.[95] The auction, set for July 16 at the Dorchester County Court House, never took place, however, and the reasons are unknown.[96] Possibly Harriet's husband (unknown) was trying to negotiate her purchase, or the Pattison lawsuit blocked the sale temporarily. On August 29, however, an advertisement appeared in the *Cambridge Democrat* featuring the upcoming "public sale to the high-est bidder, at the Court house door . . . a Negro woman named Kizziah," Harriet's twenty-five-year-old sister and Linah's other daughter.[97] Brodess advertised Kessiah as a slave for life, a clear violation of the Pat-tison will.[98] Scheduled for Monday, September 10, that sale did not pro-ceed as planned, either. The Pattisons continued to appeal the dismissal of their lawsuit against Brodess, possibly hampering Eliza's efforts to sell her slaves. Brodess and Mills returned to court on September 17, pe-titioning the court to allow them to sell "Keziah [Kessiah] and her chil-dren until they arrive at the age of 45 years."[99] The two young children cited in the court order were James Alfred, aged six, and Araminta, an infant.[100] As descendents of Rit, Kessiah and her children should have been accorded the limited-term status as specified and mandated in Atthow Pattison's will.

Terror gripped the family. The court first ordered Kessiah sold "at public sale to the highest best bidder."[101] Six weeks later, however, the court rescinded the order to sell her.[102] Perhaps her husband, John Bow-ley, was attempting to negotiate a private sale with Eliza Brodess; as a

NEGRO FOR SALE.

I WILL sell at public sale to the highest bidder for cash, at the Court house door in the town of Cambridge, on MONDAY the 10th day of September next, a negro woman named KIZZIAH, aged about 25 years. She will be sold for life, and a good title will be given. Attendance given by

JOHN MILLS,

Agent for Elizabeth Brodess.

August 29th 1849.   2w

Auction announcement for the sale of Harriet Tubman's niece,
Kessiah Jolley Bowley.

free man working in a shipyard in Cambridge, he may have been hopeful that he could buy his wife and young children. John and his brothers were entrepreneurial shipbuilders and blacksmiths in Cambridge, co-owners of a schooner that they built at the Steam Mill Wharf in Cambridge with John T. Stewart, James A. Stewart's brother.[103] Between his own labors and that of his brothers, John may well have been able to raise the funds to purchase his wife and children.

This reprieve for Kessiah, however, came at a high price. In reversing itself, the court granted a new order, dated October 24, authorizing the sale of Kessiah's sister, "Harriet and her child Mary Ann [Mary Jane]."[104] Whether an auction actually took place is not clear; on June 17, 1850, Eliza Brodess and John Mills sold Harriet and her child to a local merchant, Thomas Willis, for $375.[105] Five months later, Eliza Brodess sold another slave, Dawes Keene.[106]

These sales in 1849 marked a turning point for the transformation of Tubman from a slave to a liberator. The first step was her own hazardous journey of self-liberation. Spurred by rumors of her impending sale to satisfy creditors of Brodess's estate, and against the wishes of her free husband, John, Tubman took the initiative and set out.[107] On

September 17, 1849, the very same day that Eliza Brodess petitioned the court to allow her to sell Kessiah, Tubman and her two brothers Ben and Henry ran away.[108] An advertisement for a reward for their capture did not appear in the local paper for over two weeks, suggesting that Eliza Brodess had hired them out to other masters and therefore did not have constant supervision of them, or she had become accustomed to short-term desertion by them as a matter of daily life on her plantation. While Tubman was working for Thompson during this time period, it is possible that her brothers Ben and Henry were also hired out to Thompson, making their escape together more likely.[109]

Brodess offered a typical reward for their capture and return:

Ranaway from the subscriber on Monday the 17th ult., three negroes, named as follows: HARRY [Henry], aged about 19 years, has on one side of his neck a wen, just under the ear, he is of a dark chestnut color, about 5 feet 8 or nine inches hight [sic]; BEN, aged aged [sic] about 25 years, is very quick to speak when spoken to, he is of a chestnut color, about six feet high; MINTY, aged about 27 years, is of a chestnut color, fine looking, and about 5 feet high. One hundred dollars reward will be given for each of the above named negroes, if taken out of the State, and $50 each if taken in the State. They must be lodged in Baltimore, Easton or Cambridge Jail, in Maryland.

Eliza Ann Brodess
Near Bucktown, Dorchester county, Md.

Oct. 3d, 1849.

The Delaware Gazette will please copy the above three weeks, and charge this office.[110]

Tubman's brothers, in the meantime, "disagreed with her about directions," and succumbed to the fear of being captured.[111] They were "appalled by the dangers before and behind them, determined to go back, and in spite of her remonstrances dragged her with them."[112] Runaway slaves, if caught, faced almost certain sale into the Deep South, severe whipping, or worse. Ben was a young father, and perhaps

THREE HUNDRED DOLLARS REWARD.

RANAWAY from the subscriber on Monday the 17th ult., three negroes, named as follows: HARRY, aged about 19 years, has on one side of his neck a wen, just under the ear, he is of a dark chestnut color, about 5 feet 8 or 9 inches hight; BEN, aged aged about 25 years, is very quick to speak when spoken to, he is of a chestnut color, about six feet high; MINTY, aged about 27 years, is of a chestnut color, fine looking, and about 5 feet high. One hundred dollars reward will be given for each of the above named negroes, if taken out of the State, and $50 each if taken in the State. They must be lodged in Baltimore, Easton or Cambridge Jail, in Maryland.

ELIZA ANN BRODESS,
Near Bucktown, Dorchester county, Md.
Oct. 3d, 1849.

☞The Delaware Gazette will please copy the above three weeks, and charge this office.

Eliza Brodess's runaway advertisement for Minty [Harriet Tubman],
and her brothers, Ben and Harry [Henry].

the prospect of leaving a wife and children behind was ultimately too great a sacrifice for him to make at that moment.[113] The brothers may have hoped for a local sale rather than the more frightening possibility of sale to a slave trader from Mississippi or Georgia. Slave traders boarding at the hotel across the street from the Dorchester County courthouse were a constant reminder of this threat. Perched on the hotel's veranda, traders would haggle with private sellers or bid on slaves placed at auction on the courthouse steps. Vulnerable slaves often attempted to negotiate a favorable sale to a local planter, and for some Eastern Shore whites this was the preferable course of action as well. No doubt Ben and Henry had such hopes.

Sometime after October 3, when her brothers returned after their failed attempt to flee, Harriet Tubman stole away again, this time alone, from her cabin on Dr. Anthony C. Thompson's property, though which specific property remains unclear. Using "her strength and her craft, which was great," Tubman traveled by night, using the North Star and instructions from white and black helpers to find her way to freedom in Philadelphia.[114] "Harriet knew the North Star," Helen Tatlock later told Conrad, "that was one thing she insisted that she was *always* sure of."[115]

Harriet was helped first by a white woman who apparently knew her and willingly assisted Tubman on her way. Helen Tatlock, a friend of Tubman's later in her life, remembered Tubman telling her that she confided her plans to a white woman who lived in the area. Tatlock thought the woman was a Quaker, because "it was Quakers who then gave escaping" slaves the most aid.[116] Tubman gave this unidentified woman a coveted bed quilt; she could not give it to another slave, as that person would soon come under suspicion for knowing of Tubman's plans to run away. This white woman gave Tubman two names and directed her to the first person on the way, who would then help her on to the second.[117]

The exact route and the identities of those who helped her remains a matter of great speculation. Dr. Thompson's vast plantation at Poplar Neck in Caroline County was located on the Choptank River between Skeleton Creek to the north and the village of Choptank to the south, and was where Tubman's father, Ben Ross, was living while managing some of Dr. Thompson's timbering operations there. The property included a brick "big house," grain fields, a fruit orchard, and slave quarters.[118] The 1850 census for Caroline County lists Ben and Rit Ross as free blacks living on Thompson's property, close to Thompson's son

Edward, who was probably living in the brick house while he oversaw his father's timbering and farming operations.[119]

Poplar Neck, however, was also located on an invisible path to freedom in the North. A small Quaker settlement, the Marshy Creek Friends of the Northwest Fork Meeting, had been rooted there for more than 150 years, and several of the area's most active Quaker abolitionists lived within a mile of Thompson's new home. A small black settlement had also been established there, and in fact the local Quaker community deeded a parcel of its Mt. Pleasant Church property to the black community in 1849 for a church and cemetery of its own.[120]

Quakers were among the most important members of an increasingly organized network to freedom for runaway slaves. Though some Quakers denounced the owning of slaves from the earliest colonial times, many Quakers continued to own, buy, and sell slaves until the mid-1700s, when the Quaker John Woolman of New Jersey made a tour of Maryland, Virginia, and North Carolina for a firsthand view of American slavery. Based on his observations, Woolman's influential tracts denounced slavery as incompatible with Christianity. His continued attacks on slaveholding within the Society forced many Quakers to reexamine their positions. By 1770, many Quaker meetings were expelling members for purchasing slaves, and manumissions by deed and will were becoming commonplace. By 1790, Eastern Shore Quaker meetings were free of all slave owners.[121] This Quaker experience was repeated in other states as well, providing a groundswell of activism to end slavery throughout the young nation, in addition to establishing a loose network of like-minded individuals who could be tapped to help freedom seekers find their way north and provide support and shelter once they arrived. Not all Quakers, to be sure, were willing participants in this network; many were neither interested in slaves nor inclined to help them run away. Residents of sparsely populated Caroline County perhaps more readily tolerated the antislavery views of its Quaker inhabitants because there were few slaves in the county, and the Quakers' abolitionist views seemed to have little impact in the community.[122] Poplar Neck, then, seems to be the most likely way station for Tubman's escape north, if not the starting point.

Harriet may have left from Dr. Anthony C. Thompson's Bellefield residence in Cambridge. Consisting of fourteen and one-half acres, a main house, several outbuildings, and two slave cabins, Bellefield had been Thompson's main residence for several years while he practiced medicine and ran an apothecary and fine-goods store in Cambridge. Thompson, his wife, Susan, and daughters Mary and Sarah were all living at this residence in 1850 when the census taker arrived.[123]

There were also non-Quakers living on the Eastern Shore who had abolitionist and antislavery feelings, though very few were vocal.[124] Thus, regardless of where Tubman initially ran from, she could have quickly tapped an existing local network of abolitionists and others, including free blacks and other slaves, who were willing to help slaves make their way to freedom. The Underground Railroad, as this secret network of places and people was known, was functioning well on the Eastern Shore by the time Tubman took her liberty.

Tubman could tell no one of her plans to run, particularly her mother. Rit was already emotionally spent from the loss of her other daughters; "her cries and groans would have disclosed the secret."[125] But Tubman could not leave without giving her mother some sort of message about her plans. On the evening of her escape, Tubman offered to do her mother's chores, sending her to her cabin to retire for the evening. Rushing up to the "big house," where several of her relatives lived and worked, Tubman sought out Mary, another slave in whom she felt she could confide.[126] There, in the kitchen, she hoped to tell Mary of her plans to run away, but the room was crowded. She began to "frolic" with Mary, and they both ran outside to continue playing when Dr. Thompson rode up on horseback and surprised them. Mary ran back to the kitchen, but Harriet hesitated. Thompson "was regarded with special awe by his slaves," and few dared sing or talk when he was around. But Harriet was desperate to leave a message, so she stepped forward, meeting him at the gate, singing:

I'm sorry I'm going to leave you,
Farewell, oh farewell;
But I'll meet you in the morning,
Farewell, oh farewell.

I'll meet you in the morning,
I'm bound for the promised land,
On the other side of Jordan,
Bound for the promised land.[127]

Thompson passed Harriet as he rode through the gate, but she continued to sing. He looked around at her and watched her casually close the gate and slowly walk away, continuing her message in song. A few moments passed, and Tubman tried again to return to the house and tell Mary of her plans. But Thompson was still there, watching for her, so she sang louder, bowing to Thompson as she walked by.[128] He was probably a little suspicious of her, since she had already run away once with her brothers. Nevertheless, he did not question her, and he rode on to the house.[129]

Once he was out of sight, Tubman fled, probably working her way north as far as safely possible during the night. When Tubman reached the first safe house, the woman of the house asked her to sweep the yard—a deceptive tactic that helped mask Tubman's purpose while she waited for the woman's husband to return from the fields. When darkness fell, the man loaded his wagon, covering Tubman so that she could not be seen, and took her to the next sympathetic home.[130]

The Leverton family, Quakers of Caroline County, were known to be active abolitionists and Underground Railroad operatives.[131] Though Jacob Leverton had died by the time Tubman took her freedom in 1849, his widow, Hannah, still lived in the area with her son, Arthur W. Leverton, who was run out of Caroline County in the late 1850s for aiding slaves in their attempts to escape from their masters.[132] Dr. Thompson's son Anthony C. Thompson Jr. married Mary Elizabeth Leverton, Jacob and Hannah Leverton's daughter, in November 1849. The Levertons lived very close to the Thompson property at Poplar Neck; it is very likely that young Anthony met Mary Elizabeth while he was working with his brother Edward for their father in Caroline County.[133] Thompson's slaves and hired labor, including Ben and Rit Ross and some of their children, would have known the Levertons. It is highly possible that the Levertons played a role in Tubman's escape.

Traveling mostly at night, following the North Star and stopping at each new house she was directed to, Tubman finally crossed the border and into freedom in Pennsylvania. "When I found I had crossed that *line*," Tubman later recalled, "I looked at my hands to see if I was the same person. There was such a glory over everything; the sun came like gold through the trees, and over the fields, and I felt like I was in Heaven."[134]

"MEAN TO BE FREE":
THE FRAGILE LIGHT OF LIBERTY

Rises from their anguish and their power,

Harriet Tubman,

woman of earth, whipscarred,
a summoning, a shining

Mean to be free

—From "Runagate Runagate" by Robert Hayden

*H*ARRIET TUBMAN'S ESCAPE WAS NOT, IN FACT, UNUSUAL FOR THE Eastern Shore. Despite efforts by white Marylanders and other southerners to thwart escapes during the ten years before the Civil War, some slaves raced for freedom successfully, and many of them were from Maryland. With 259 recorded runaways in the 1850 census, Maryland held the lead of all the slaveholding states in the number of escapes. This number is misleadingly low, as many slave owners did not report their losses to the census taker.[1] A perusal of Eastern Shore newspapers for the period 1847–1849 indicates a steady flow of slaves running away from their masters, many of them in company with family and friends. Dr. Robert Tubman advertised in a January 1847 Cambridge newspaper for his slave Comfort and her two daughters,

Nice and Ann. This family took their liberty over the Christmas holidays, when slave owners traditionally allowed their slaves to visit family and friends on other plantations. Dr. Tubman suspected they had gone far; his advertisements also ran in the *Baltimore Sun* and the *Delaware Journal*.[2] Dorchester County residents Peter Harrington and Henry McGuire advertised for Vince and Anthony Cornish on the same day Zachariah Linthicum sought the return of Martin Green, while William Willoughby offered a reward for the capture and return of Stephen and Peter Dockings.[3] Throughout 1849, scores of slaves ran away from Talbot, Dorchester, and Caroline County slaveholders, and while some were unsuccessful in getting away permanently, that so many remained free demonstrates the strength of the underground network and underscores the slaves' persistent hope for freedom and independence. Frustrated slaveholders suspected a conspiracy of abolitionists within their midst tempting slaves to run away, not considering, or admitting, that slaves wanted to be free and to get away on their own. The *Easton Star* of Talbot County, for instance, reported in August 1849:

RUNAWAYS. On Saturday night week, three slaves belonging to H. L. Edmondson, Esq., made their escape, and last Saturday night, one of Jas. L. Martin's Esq., one of Jos. R. Price's Esq., and one belonging to Mr. George Hale, also absconded, and nothing has been heard of any of them since. Almost every week we hear of one or more slaves making their escape and if something is not speedily done to put a stop to it, that kind of property will hardly be worth owning. There seems to be some system about this business, and we strongly suspect they are assisted in their escape by an organized band of abolitionists. We think it advisable for the Slave Holders of the Eastern Shore to establish a line of Telegraph down the peninsula, and organize an efficient police force along the line, as the most effectual means of protecting their slave property, and recovering such as may attempt to make their escape. At present, all efforts to recover them after they once made their escape appears fruitless.[4]

The following October at least twenty-four slaves in Talbot County took flight from their owners, and local authorities were in swift pursuit of those who aided their escapes. Colonel Edward Lloyd, the largest slave owner on the Eastern Shore, offered a $1,000 reward for the capture and return of two of the runaways. Some were apprehended, though the rest were suspected of having successfully made their way "south east, across Caroline county to the Delaware Bay shore, and thence to New Jersey."[5] By the end of the month, however, Talbot County authorities arrested two men whom they believed "enticed" the slaves to run away; they were tried and convicted in December to much fanfare, although the *Baltimore Sun* mockingly reported that the "tax payers of Talbot have to foot the bill," in the amount of "one-thousand ninety-four dollars and ninety-seven cents."[6]

Though the name Underground Railroad first appeared in the early 1830s (with the advent of the new transportation system by rail), the secret networks to freedom had been in operation long before then. Slaves had been running away from their masters since Africans were forcibly brought to the colonies in the early 1600s. By the end of the eighteenth century, however, a more organized system had started to take shape, one that provided some measure of support to runaways finding their way to freedom. Runaways found assistance in Maroon and Native American communities, in a few states in the North that ended slavery within their borders in the years after the Revolution, and even among some groups in the South opposed to slavery. The Underground Railroad, as this organized system eventually came to be called, has long been shrouded in mysteries and myths, many of which date back to the time when the system was a reality.

As the antislavery movement expanded and became more organized, it attracted people from all walks of life and many religious organizations, including Methodists, Presbyterians, Unitarians, and Jews, among others. Eventually those few individuals within the broader abolitionist movement who helped runaway slaves find their way north to freedom became part of a loosely organized network. As the antislavery movement gained momentum, particularly after 1830, and far more communities, individuals, and small groups of like-minded people (especially in Pennsylvania, New York, Ohio, Indiana, New Jersey, and Massachusetts) committed themselves to help end the institution of slavery, an active mission to help runaways was firmly and permanently established. People who participated in this clandestine operation were known as "agents," "conductors," "engineers," and "stationmasters," terms that mirrored positions on actual railroads.[7]

Harriet Tubman made her way to Philadelphia, long a center of abolitionist activity. Here she blended into a large community of free blacks and freedom seekers from the South. But Tubman was not entirely safe. Efforts were made by many slaveholders to retrieve their "property" in Philadelphia and other northern cities and towns. It was important that slaveholders maintain control of their slave property. The system of slavery could work only if those enslaved believed the costs of escape would be too great and the chances of successfully getting away too remote. Professional slave catchers and bounty hunters roamed the countryside and cities and towns, hunting runaways for the substantial rewards offered by slave owners.[8] A second runaway notice has not been found for Tubman, suggesting that Eliza Brodess may have assumed she would return, as she had the first time with her brothers Ben and Henry. It seems unlikely that Brodess would have ignored Tubman's escape, though it may have been some time before she realized Tubman was actually gone. Tubman's practice of hiring herself out may have protected her for several days before anyone realized she was no longer in Dorchester or Caroline County.

Though Tubman was nominally free in Philadelphia, she soon learned that freedom did not ensure happiness. Liberation from slavery had its own reward, but Tubman noted that "there was no one to welcome me to the land of freedom. I was a stranger in a strange land; and my home, after all, was down in Maryland; because my father, my mother, my brothers, and sisters, and friends were there. But I was free, and *they* should be free."[9] What set Tubman apart from thousands of other runaways was her determination to act: she quickly set upon a plan to liberate her family. She easily found work as a domestic and a cook in various hotels and private homes in Philadelphia, and later, during the summer months, at Cape May, New Jersey.[10] She hoarded her money, planning carefully for the days ahead when she could return to the Eastern Shore to bring her family away to freedom. She kept in touch with events back home by communicating with the extensive network of sources among the free black, fugitive black, and liberal white communities of Philadelphia, Baltimore, Wilmington, Delaware, and Cape May who shared information about the slave community.

It would not be long before she would be forced to act to save a member of her family from the dreaded auction block. In December 1850 Tubman received word from relatives and friends in Baltimore that her niece Kessiah was once again going to be auctioned off at the courthouse in Cambridge. Tubman went immediately to Baltimore, lodging with friends and relatives then living along the city's busy and diverse waterfront. Harriet's brother-in-law Tom Tubman concealed her until the appointed time.[11] Tom was possibly working as a stevedore on Baltimore's docks; in fact, there were many former Dorchester County free blacks (and possibly some runaways and a few slaves who had been hired out to Baltimore, much as Frederick Douglass had been) living and working in Baltimore.[12] John and Tom Tubman's brother Evans, a seaman, also lived there, as did several Bowleys, Manokeys, and others from the Eastern Shore black community. The work assignments and living arrangements of many of these individuals made Baltimore's waterfront an ideal location from which Tubman could operate. These friends and family members were also perfectly positioned to receive news about any threats to Harriet's family.

With little time to prepare, Harriet and Kessiah's husband, John Bowley, devised a scheme to spirit Kessiah and her two children away. By way of underground messages, all aspects of the plan were put into motion. On the day of the auction, a small crowd of buyers assembled in front of the courthouse doors a little before lunchtime. In front of them stood Kessiah and her two young children, James Alfred and Araminta. The spirited bidding started; the price for a healthy young female slave with two children could have been $500 or $600 at that time. For agonizing moments the bidding continued, and a buyer was finally secured; John Brodess, acting for his mother, was satisfied by the sale. Kessiah was removed from the courthouse steps and set aside while the auctioneer went to dinner. But when the auctioneer returned and called for payment, no one came forward. "It was found after the sale that she was purchased by her husband, a Negro man, who when called failed to comply."[13] Recognizing a ruse, the auctioneer started the bidding again, only to discover that Kessiah and the children were nowhere to be found; unbeknownst to the crowd at the courthouse, she and the children had been taken and hidden in "a [lady's] house only a 5 minutes walk from the courthouse."[14] Later that evening John Bowley secretly took his wife and children on a "small boat," or log canoe, to Baltimore.[15] A skilled sailor with contacts throughout the Eastern Shore and Baltimore, Bowley knew his best chance for escape was by water. This perilous journey would have taken a full day of sailing up the Chesapeake to get to Baltimore, and given the time of year, it might have taken longer. With unpredictable weather, often cold and wet, the journey to Baltimore was incredibly hazardous; with two small children, the escape was even more so. If they were caught, John Bowley risked being sold into slavery. Perhaps seeking shelter in black waterfront communities, Bowley successfully reached Baltimore.[16] There they met one of John's brothers, possibly Major, and they all found safety with Tubman, who hid them among friends. After they had recuperated for a few days, Tubman safely brought them on to Philadelphia.[17]

Emboldened by her success and fearful for the safety of her family, Tubman returned to Baltimore a few months later, this time to bring her brother Moses and two other men to freedom.[18] Tubman was once again successful in executing a flight without returning to Dorchester County herself. In the fall of 1851, however, Tubman decided to return to the Eastern Shore, for the first time since she had run away, to bring out her husband, whom she had not seen for two years. She saved up her earnings, bought him a new suit of clothes, and ventured back to Dorchester County.[19] How she did this is unknown; she may have taken passage on a boat or traveled by foot, following the same path she took north to freedom two years earlier. When Tubman arrived there, though, she discovered that John had taken another wife, a free woman named Caroline.[20] Rather than create a scene, she hid with friends nearby and sent word to John that she was waiting for him. But he refused to join her; he had moved on and was content to continue with his life in Dorchester County. Devastated, Harriet determined to "go right in and make all the trouble she could," not caring if she was caught by her master.[21] Spurned by her lover, overwhelmed with anger and hurt, she could hardly bear the loss of her dreams for a free future with her husband. But she soon realized "how foolish it was just for temper to make mischief" and that if her husband "could do without her, she could do without him," so she "dropped [him] out of her heart."[22] She decided not to waste an opportunity, though, and instead gathered a group of slaves and brought them with her to Philadelphia.[23]

Always doubtful, the prospects for permanent freedom and safety for runaway slaves in the North diminished even more in 1850. Frustrated over the increasing numbers of runaway slaves from their plantations, farms, and homes, particularly in the border states, southern slaveholders and the elected officials who represented them perceived an imbalance of power in Congress that threatened the institution of slavery. Free-soil Democrats and northern Whigs had gained control of Congress when President Zachary Taylor took office in 1849. Promptly advocating the admission of California and New Mexico as free states, Taylor, together with northern Whigs and most northern Democrats, hoped to curb the expansion of slavery beyond the existing southern slave states. The admission of these two states would have tipped the balance of power in Congress from slaveholding southern interests to nonslaveholding northern interests, and southern representatives threatened disunion. After months of debate and argument, Congress sought to enact a compromise to stave off what many believed would be an irreparable sectional conflict and perhaps civil war. As part of the famous Compromise of 1850, Congress admitted California as a free state, which led to an imbalance of free and slave states. To offset this concession to antislavery sentiment, though, Congress also passed a new Fugitive Slave Act to placate southerners, in September 1850. The act required federal judges, marshals, and commissioners to convene special commissions, or courts, to assess the valid status of an accused runaway slave. Slave catchers searching in the North for their slaves were given the power to force cooperation from local authorities for the return of their slave property.[24]

Anyone obstructing the efforts of slave owners trying to retrieve their slaves, or who helped a slave escape, was subject to heavy fines and jail time. Under this law, northern police authorities were bound by federal law to capture and return to his or her owners any fugitive slave caught within their jurisdiction. This new law created an uproar in the northern states, where it was perceived as an infringement upon local control and state sovereignty, and as more and more runaway slaves were captured and forcibly returned to the control of their enslavers, northern abolitionists actively encouraged resistance to this new law. Several high-profile and widely publicized captures of runaway slaves marshaled the fury of northerners—not just abolitionists—who resented being forced to act as agents for seemingly powerful southern slave interests. Abolitionists were infuriated by the act's powerful clauses, and in the North several slaves who had been turned over to their owners were dramatically rescued. In some cases, participants were severely wounded in battles with authorities and slave catchers. In one instance a slave owner was killed by an angry group of whites and blacks who were attempting to prevent the reenslavement of a runaway then living in Pennsylvania.[25]

After passage of the Fugitive Slave Act, Tubman and her family and friends were no longer safe in Philadelphia or any other northern city. The stakes were now greater and the threat more palpable as southern slaveholders pursued their runaway slaves aggressively, with the force of the federal government behind them. In the fall and winter of 1851 many fugitives began a second journey from their homes in northern cities and towns to a more secure freedom in Canada.[26] John and Kessiah Bowley and their daughter Araminta moved from Philadelphia to Canada in late 1851, possibly with other runaways who had also decided their liberty was at risk in Philadelphia. Yet Tubman continued to plot and plan; members of her family remained enslaved, and she could not rest until she brought them away, too.

After Tubman's failed attempt to bring her husband north in the fall of 1851, she may have returned to Dorchester again, in December, and brought out a group of eleven slaves, supposedly another brother and his wife.[27] There are no details about this rescue; Tubman may have just conveyed to Canada eleven fugitives she had already brought away during 1850 and 1851.[28] Taking a route out of Philadelphia to New York City, then on to Albany and Rochester, New York, this large group

sought shelter with none other than Frederick Douglass. In his autobiography *Life and Times of Frederick Douglass*, written in 1881, Douglass
described what may have been this event:

> On one occasion I had eleven fugitives at the same time under
> my roof, and it was necessary for them to remain with me until I
> could collect sufficient money to get them on to Canada. It was
> the largest number I ever had at any one time, and I had some
> difficulty in providing so many with food and shelter, but, as may
> well be imagined, they were not very fastidious in either direc-
> tion, and were well content with very plain food, and a strip of
> carpet on the floor for a bed, or a place on the straw in the barn-
> loft.[29]

In his first autobiography, *Narrative of the Life of Frederick Douglass,
An American Slave*, published in 1845, Douglass explained to his readers
that he could not reveal the secret network of supporters who constituted the Underground Railroad.[30] Though he eventually revealed the
names of his fellow agents in the North in a later autobiography, he
maintained his silence about the southern operators for the rest of his
life.[31] There is no doubt, however, that Tubman had tapped into part of
the same network that helped Douglass run away in 1838 and stay secreted in the North, and it was this network, ever expanding throughout the 1840s and 1850s, that helped Tubman ferry her friends and
family north to freedom. By 1881, however, Douglass obviously felt
some ease in naming a number of the northern agents of the Underground Railroad. According to Douglass, the route through which he
operated a station "had its main stations in Baltimore, Wilmington,
Philadelphia, New York, Albany, Syracuse, Rochester, and St. Catharines
(Canada)." The stations were manned by the same abolitionists with
whom Tubman would also become so intimately involved: Thomas
Garrett, of Wilmington, Delaware; J. Miller McKim, William Still,
Robert Purvis, Edward M. Davis, Lucretia and James Mott, and many
others in Philadelphia; Oliver Johnson and Isaac T. Hopper, among others, in New York City; the Mott sisters, Stephen Myers, John H. Hooper,
and others in Albany; and the Reverends Samuel J. May and J. W.

Loguen of Syracuse. In Rochester were J. P. Morris, Douglass, Amy and Isaac Post, and others who greeted weary fugitives.[32]

Tubman later told Wilbur Siebert, whose early work on the Underground Railroad helped document the legions of known and unknown stationmasters and operators involved in this secret organization, that when she left Philadelphia with a party of runaways, she "proceeded by steam railroad to New York, and from there she took the train to Albany, where Stephen Myers looked after her and her charges."[33] From there she boarded a train bound for Rochester, "where the fugitive slave, Frederick Douglass, would see that she got on the train for the Suspension Bridge and St. Catharines in Canada."[34]

Little documentation exists that definitively points to any relationship between Douglass and Tubman prior to Tubman's own liberation. While they admired each other greatly, both publicly and privately, Douglass and Tubman never revealed the true extent of their interactions or relationship, if any, on the Eastern Shore or in the North.[35] Perhaps they were protecting vulnerable blacks and whites still living in Maryland. Nevertheless, Douglass and Tubman may have had extensive common ties on the Eastern Shore. Dr. Absalom Thompson, Dr. Anthony C. Thompson's brother, lived at Mary's Delight, at Bayside in Talbot County, which was situated next to the farm where Frederick Douglass, then known as Fred Bailey, lived for a period of time while hired out to Edward Covey, a local farmer. It was to Covey's farm that Douglass, as a defiant young slave in 1834, was sent to be "broken," as Douglass recalled, for Covey "had acquired a very high reputation for breaking young slaves."[36] After his year with Covey, Douglass was hired out to William Freeland, another local farmer, whose property was also near Thompson's plantation.[37] All of these farms were not far from the town of St. Michaels, where Douglass's master, Thomas Auld, lived; not surprisingly, the Thompsons and Auld traveled in the same social circles. In an effort to discredit Douglass's famous 1845 autobiography, Absalom C. C. Thompson, Dr. Absalom Thompson's son, publicly claimed in the *Delaware Republican*, the *Liberator* (William Lloyd Garrison's renowned antislavery newspaper), and later the *Albany Patriot* that he knew Frederick Bailey, the illiterate slave, quite well. Thompson also affirmed the veracity of the names and places Douglass described so faithfully in his first autobiography, the *Narrative of Frederick Douglass*.[38] "I was for many years a citizen of the section of the country where the scenes of the . . . narrative are laid; and am intimately acquainted with most of the gentlemen whose characters are so shamelessly traduced" by Frederick Douglass, Thompson wrote.[39] A series of letters between the two men was reprinted in various antislavery newspapers for the northern abolitionist community to read. Douglass taunted Thompson, offering him "thanks for his free and unsolicited testimony, in regard to my identity." Thompson had claimed Edward Covey was a "plain, honest farmer," that Thomas Auld, Douglass's owner, was a "respectable merchant . . . and an honorable and worthy member of the Methodist Episcopal Church," and that all the rest whom Douglass disparaged in his *Narrative* were "charming," "honest," "respectable," and "irreproachable." Douglass, however, remembered their ill tempers, the harshness of the hunger and humiliation he felt at their hands, and the searing pain of the lash. Other white citizens of Talbot County wrote letters of support for fellow slaveholders mentioned in the *Narrative*, and Dr. Anthony C. Thompson even entered his opinion on the matter, writing a short note in defense of Thomas Auld, but the damage was done.[40]

Did Douglass know Tubman and her family before he fled Maryland in 1838? Anthony Thompson owned several slaves with the surname Bailey, and it seems more than likely that Ben Ross knew Frederick Bailey and his extended family, including the members of Douglass's family who were sold away. Because the Thompson slaves, both Anthony's and Absalom's, traveled back and forth between Dorchester and Talbot Counties to labor on the plantations of both men, there is a strong likelihood that many of them knew Douglass. In 1842 Ben Ross purchased the freedom of Maria Bayley (Bailey) and Aaron Manokey from Dr. Anthony C. Thompson, who had inherited them from his father, for the incredibly small sum of $10. Maria was married to Isaac Bailey, who had the same name as Douglass's grandfather. Isaac and Maria later lived in Bucktown, raising their eight children there until Isaac was murdered in 1859. Ultimately, the communication network that functioned between Baltimore and the Eastern Shore, and between Talbot, Dorchester, and Caroline Counties, was dependent upon people

Douglass and Tubman both knew. It is thus highly probable that Douglass and Tubman shared strong familial and community relationships throughout the Chesapeake, ties that eventually encompassed runaways and free blacks living in cities and towns throughout the North.[41]

After ferrying the party of eleven fugitives through Douglass's house in Rochester, New York, then on to Canada, Tubman remained in St. Catharines for several months. Arriving in late December, the party had no food supplies, shelter, or appropriate clothing for the harsh winter months ahead. "The first winter was terribly severe for these poor runaways. They earned their bread by chopping wood in the snows of a Canadian forest,—they were frost-bitten, hungry and naked."[42] Harriet "kept house" for her brother and the rest, working and praying, and "carried them by the help of God through the hard winter."[43] They managed well enough, with the help of local aid associations and other friends and family in the area, so Harriet returned to Philadelphia the following spring, determined to earn enough funds to bring away the rest of her family from Maryland. That summer she worked in Cape May as a cook, and from there she returned in the fall of 1852 to the Eastern Shore, bringing away an unidentified group of nine slaves.[44]

Tensions were rising on the Eastern Shore, however, as national politics came to bear on Maryland's social, political, and economic foundations. Debates over the nature of slavery and its place in American society and its extension into the new territories dominated daily life, as representatives of the South and North fought over control of the legislative process. In Dorchester County free blacks were organizing themselves against efforts to pressure them to emigrate to Liberia as part of the Maryland Colonization Society's attempts to rid the state of free blacks. Instead, these free black women and men attempted to stake a claim to the political and economic decision-making processes in Maryland.[45] On the Eastern Shore, slave escapes continued unabated, frustrating local authorities, who were increasingly looking toward northern abolitionists as the root cause of their economic and political problems.

During the early morning hours of Sunday, May 9, 1852, an unknown arsonist set fire to Dorchester County's courthouse. Most of the county's Orphans Court records were destroyed, erasing two hundred years of probate, land, tax, and some criminal and civil court proceedings. The arsonist was never discovered, in spite of a $1,000 reward for information leading to an arrest.[46] Two crucial volumes of documents did survive the fire: the "rough & the recorded minutes" of the county court had been removed from the courthouse on Friday by the court clerk, who planned to work on them over the weekend.[47] Covering the years 1846 through 1852, these volumes provide, in many cases, the only view into the political, economic, social, and familial dramas occurring in the county. These books also contain some of the only surviving records available regarding the fate of Harriet Tubman's family and document the dangers they faced at the hands of their white owners and neighbors.

Stunned Dorchester County residents scrambled to recover from their loss. The court was removed to a local hotel, the Dorchester House, and the trial docket was resumed, while county clerks began the process of recovering and reconstructing the court's voluminous records. Thomas H. Hicks, registrar of wills, called upon all residents of the county to deposit copies of wills, guardianship papers, indentures, land and tax records, and any civil and criminal suit court documents to replace those lost in the great fire. As luck would have it, the Pattison family had another copy of Atthow Pattison's will, so James A. Stewart, the Pattisons' attorney, continued to appeal their claim against Eliza Brodess for ownership of Rit. In fact, the Pattisons' appeal was the first order of business to come before the court after the great fire, on Tuesday morning, May 12.

James A. Stewart, a Dorchester County lawyer, politician, and businessman, had known Tubman and her family for decades; his brother John had hired Tubman and possibly her father years before, and it is likely that her brothers may have been hired out to the Stewarts as well. By the time Tubman ran away, Stewart's involvement in the Pattisons' protracted legal battle against Eliza Brodess over ownership of Rit and her children seemed of little significance, although he was one of the most powerful attorneys on the Eastern Shore. Involved in politics for over twenty years, a leading member of the Eastern Shore's aristocracy, and elected as a Democratic representative to Congress from Maryland in 1855, Stewart was a powerful and controlling figure in Dorchester's political, social, and economic spheres. He owned over forty slaves, as well as buildings, ships, farms, and timber throughout the Eastern Shore and in Texas, and sat on boards of banks and businesses; by the mid-1850s, his political career was flourishing. Why did this powerful man take on this case and appeal it? Was it personal for Stewart, or was there more to this lawsuit than is recorded in the case record?

For some reason, the case was important to win, and Stewart pursued it with vigor. He quickly reentered the Pattisons' suit, claiming that the Pattisons were still entitled to "Rittia and such of her children as are now forty-five years of age," and restitution and damages for the loss of their hire.[48] Stewart also demanded that the remaining slaves under the age of forty-five be sold and the proceeds be apportioned according to the "respective rights" of the Pattisons involved. Eliza Brodess refused, and the case dragged on for three more years.[49]

Then, oddly, on July 28, 1852, Stewart purchased from Thomas Willis the young slave woman Harriet, Tubman's niece whom Willis had bought from Eliza Brodess two years earlier. One of Rit and Ben's granddaughters, Harriet had been sold in spite of the Pattisons' attempts to prevent the sale until the lawsuit could be appealed. But Stewart did not buy Harriet's daughter, Mary Jane (Mary Ann); the four-year-old remained in Thomas Willis's household with two-year-old Sarah Ann, possibly another child of Harriet's. Willis and Stewart lived several miles apart, taking Harriet far from her children.[50] The cruelty of this sale is only compounded by what may have been a political or personal agenda on the part of Stewart, for less than four months later Stewart purchased the "right, title, claim and demand" to Rit from his client, John R. Brown, a Pattison heir, for a total of $30. The following June (1853) Stewart purchased the same rights to Rit from another Pattison heir, Achsah Pattison, for $75 in spite of the unknown outcome of the pending lawsuit.[51] The other Pattison heirs did not sell their interest in Rit to Stewart. Perhaps Stewart was gambling that the lawsuit would ultimately find in his client's favor, and he stood to gain something from his share in the residual value of Rit and her children then over the age of forty-five, and the future income stream from the rest of her children as they, too, turned forty-five. But the case seemed ill-conceived from the beginning, and the ultimate value of a share in Rit, after divisions were made among all the heirs, appears to be quite small. Did Stewart have another reason for buying ownership in this family of slaves? Or did he do this to protect Rit and her children?

The latter seems quite unlikely, though not impossible. Stewart was a staunch defender of slavery, and his seemingly heartless decision to remove most of his slaves from Dorchester County to Texas in 1855, leaving behind broken families, does not fit the image of a benevolent white slaveholder. Perhaps there was personal animosity toward Brodess, though nothing in the records indicates this to be the case. Ultimately Stewart lost his gamble; the case dragged on for so long that by the time it was finally dismissed, both Eliza Brodess and John Mills were dead.

The Rosses may have been confused and frustrated by the continuing court action; Rit believed she was supposed to be free, and yet white people were still trying to keep her enslaved.[52] When Tubman returned to Dorchester County in the fall of 1852, she may have been unaware of the lawsuit then reemerging in the courthouse; however, it did not alter her ultimate goal of retrieving her family and bringing them away from their enslavers. Anxious to get away before they could be sold to the Deep South, Tubman's remaining three brothers, Robert, Benjamin, and Henry, also attempted to escape several more times after the last two's first failed attempt, with Harriet, in 1849. Though these escape attempts were also unsuccessful, the lawsuit worked in the brothers' favor; Brodess was prevented from selling them until the case could be resolved, giving them time to plan yet another attempt.

Tubman would not give up, either; facing increasing danger, she became more dedicated to her decade-long mission of liberation. What set Tubman apart from even those brave souls who swelled the routes of the Underground Railroad were her trips back home. For self-liberators such as Tubman, it was unusual to return to the land of their enslavers, risking capture, reenslavement, or even lynching to help others seek freedom. As tensions continued to rise throughout the country over the issue of slavery in the 1850s, Harriet Tubman intensified her efforts. Tapping into the powerful communication and relief networks of the black community as well as the white abolitionist community in the North, Tubman began to gain recognition among a small group of radical antislavery activists committed to ending slavery. Driven by her desire to liberate her family and friends, guided by an unquestioning belief in God's protection, and confident in the vast underground network she had come to know so well, Tubman returned several times to the Eastern Shore to guide groups of slaves to freedom.

Relying heavily on trustworthy free and enslaved African Americans, sympathetic whites (and even a few unfriendly whites who could be paid off), the number of slaves Tubman brought north was remarkably high.[53] In total, she made approximately thirteen trips, spiriting away roughly seventy to eighty slaves, in addition to perhaps fifty or sixty more to whom she gave detailed instructions, nearly all from Dorchester and Caroline Counties in Maryland.[54] Tubman "would never allow more to join her than she could properly care for though she often gave others directions by which they succeeded in escaping."[55]

Maryland's self-liberators had several advantages. First, they were close to a free state. Second, these runaways' odds were improved by the existence of heavily traveled north-south trade routes populated with free black families and by the water traffic throughout the region, which was itself dependent on free and enslaved black labor. Potential self-liberators could travel by road, boat, or train. As in other slave communities, some slaves and slave owners on the Eastern Shore had become accustomed to occasional or even habitual short-term desertion, which allowed some slaves the flexibility to visit with relatives, avoid work assignments, or trade, hunt, or fish illegally.[56] Though punishments could be severe, such absences became a fact of life on some plantations.

This practice certainly worked in Tubman's favor, giving her time to leave Dorchester County with her charges before their departures were noticed. Tubman carefully organized her escapes to leave on a Saturday evening, because newspapers were not printed on Sundays and no runaway slave advertisements could be taken out until Monday. Though she "was never seen on the plantation herself," she arranged for a particular meeting place at an appointed time, for her own safety as well as those who were to join her.[57] Choosing a rendezvous point, sometimes eight or ten miles away from the plantations or homes of the runaway slaves and their masters, protected Tubman from discovery should any of the freedom seekers get caught as they attempted to flee their neighborhoods. One former slave recalled that Tubman selected a cemetery as a rendezvous point, a clever choice.[58] A group of slaves gathering in a cemetery might not arouse the same attention as a group of black people gathering in a home, or even in the woods, which was specifically forbidden by law.

Tubman preferred the winter, when the nights were long, although she did lead parties out of Dorchester in the spring and fall as well. Like most runaways, she usually traveled at night, hiding and sleeping during the day. The geography of the Eastern Shore, with its wide tracts of timber, numerous estuaries, swamps, tidal marshes, creeks, and inlets, provided adequate cover for runaways. But Tubman herself was sometimes confident enough to move about during the day in pursuit of food and information, as she "had confidential friends all along the road" who could be trusted to help her while her companions stayed safely secreted in the woods.[59]

Tubman also guided her groups of fugitives by singing spirituals and other songs with coded messages. If danger lurked nearby, Tubman would sing an appropriate spiritual to warn her party of an impending threat to their safety. When the road was clear, she would change her words or the tempo of the song and guide them on to the next safe place. She paid free blacks to follow white masters and slave catchers as they posted reward notices for the runaways she was trying to help escape, and tear the notices down. Absolute commitment was required of all members of her parties; the weakness of one person could endanger the whole group. After first satisfying herself that "they had enough courage and firmness to run the risks," she would complete her plans for their escape.[60] Tubman carried a pistol, not only as protection from pursuers but as added encouragement to weary and frightened runaways who wanted to turn back. A dead fugitive could not inform on those who helped him or her. Whether Tubman would have actually used the pistol in such a case we cannot know. Elizabeth Brooks of New Bedford, Massachusetts, recalled that Henry Carrol, a runaway from Maryland who took flight with Tubman, wanted to stop for a rest, even though slave catchers were closing in quickly.[61] Harriet told him to "go on or die," and he quickly moved along.[62]

Disguising herself frequently as an elderly woman or man, Tubman's skills at deception thwarted catastrophe several times along the way to freedom. During one complicated rescue of a large group of slaves, Tubman found herself confronting a small group of Irish laborers on a bridge, probably in Delaware. Sensing imminent danger, and knowing that she and her charges could not run, Harriet strolled up to the group and engaged them in a conversation about Christmas. The white men were curious and pressed her for an explanation for her presence on the bridge. Her first trick having failed, she launched into another topic—finding herself a new husband. "She had one colored husband and she meant to marry a white gentleman next time," she told them. Tubman cleverly deflected suspicion away from her group of runaways, to "a subject of absorbing general interest, matrimony,"— especially matrimony between the races.[63] Tubman employed a strategy that exploited what she may have perceived were the prurient racial and sexual interests of these workingmen. The ruse was successful, and the group safely passed beyond the bridge, where "they all had a great laugh so they went thro' the town all together laughing and talking," decreasing the likelihood they would all be stopped again.[64]

Tubman said she could tell time "by the stars, and find her way by natural signs as well as any hunter."[65] She often traveled in the woods at night alone, where she felt what she called a "mysterious Unseen Presence." Her seizures continued throughout this time, and the religious visions accompanying them often comforted her, lifting "her up above all doubt and anxiety into serene trust and faith."[66] While the seizures were disquieting to those who accompanied her on her rescue missions, Tubman's accepting attitude about them bespoke her overall confidence in God's will and reassured those around her.

Despite Tubman's success, the enormous obstacles she surmounted in assisting runaways should not be diminished. There was the constant fear of relentless slave catchers, who were armed with guns, knives, and whips and who hunted with vicious dogs that were trained to attack human beings. Natural barriers were plentiful as well. Many slaves running for freedom along the land route through eastern Maryland into

Delaware and north into Pennsylvania or east and north into New Jersey lacked adequate clothing and shoes. Spiny sweet gum burrs, thorny thickets, the sharp needles of marsh grass, and icy paths in the winter all took their toll on the feet and limbs of struggling runaways. The Eastern Shore's numerous rivers, streams, and wetlands presented a serious hindrance, particularly to runaways who could not swim. Wet clothing could draw unwanted attention, and cold weather could seriously debilitate drenched and hungry escapees. Sometimes, in the most severe wet weather, the slaves' coarse clothing, made of flax or other rough material, chafed against their skin, causing it to bleed, filling every step toward freedom with pain.[67]

William Still and Thomas Garrett, friends of Tubman and active agents on the Underground Railroad in Philadelphia and Wilmington, Delaware, respectively, reported the weakened conditions of the many runaways who appeared on their doorsteps. They frequently had to provide clothing and shoes; typical slave garments had to be replaced as quickly as possible, as this was one of the most obvious means of detection. Medical care and food and water revived dangerously weak and ill runaways. Occasionally fugitive slaves died under the care of Underground Railroad operators in the North. In 1857 Romulus Hall, whose frostbitten feet turned gangrenous, died within a short time of reaching freedom in Philadelphia.[68] The Rochester Ladies' Anti-Slavery Society sought donations on several occasions to pay the funeral expenses for fugitives who died while in that city.[69]

Other runaways who secreted themselves aboard boats faced suffocating journeys deep in the holds of ships. Often hidden in airless compartments, they had to fend off wharf rats. Southern port authorities often "smoked" the holds of ships before they were allowed to leave for northern ports; the smoking forced out or suffocated both rats and stowaways.[70] Trains provided rapid transit out of slave territory, but a fugitive needed a certificate of freedom, seaman's protection papers like those used by Frederick Douglass in his escape from Baltimore, or some other means to deflect questions from railroad agents and suspicious white travelers. Secretly hitching a ride on a train was hazardous as well; trains heading out of slave states were often searched for runaways. Johnson H. Walker, a runaway from Maryland, lost his foot when the train he was attempting to board at Wilmington, Delaware, ran over him after he lost his balance and slipped beneath its wheels.[71]

Nevertheless, most runaways were healthy enough to continue moving north, eventually making their way to Canada or some northern U.S. city or town, where they found employment and freedom—tenuous as it was, with the Fugitive Slave Act still making life for them precarious.

In spite of the great danger, Tubman continued her campaign for liberation of her family. Though she had been successful in helping her youngest brother, Moses, to run away in 1850, she failed in two trips between 1852 and early 1854 to bring the rest of her family north. But she would have more successes as the decade wore on. In 1849 Tubman did not anticipate how her original lone act of survival would change the landscape of a community so completely for generations to come. While Tubman was not responsible for all the slaves who would run away from Dorchester and its surrounding counties in the 1850s, it would be her example that impelled many to do so.

—

CHAPTER 6

ALL FOR THE LOVE OF FAMILY

BETWEEN 1851 AND 1854, TUBMAN'S BROTHERS BEN, ROBERT, AND Henry Ross attempted several times to flee the Eastern Shore. It is a wonder that Eliza Brodess retained ownership of them throughout this period. "We started to come away," Tubman's brother Henry told an interviewer in 1863, "but got surrounded," so they turned back.[1] A white man who was a friend offered to buy them, but Eliza Brodess refused, telling him, "I'd rather see them sold to Georgia."[2] The unknown white buyer told the brothers to run away.[3] They tried to run away again, this time staying away for several months but were still unable to leave the Eastern Shore. Advertisements were posted for their capture, making it difficult for them to leave their hiding place. Ben Ross tried to help his sons; he sent them to a man "who said he could carry us away . . . but he disappointed us."[4] Once again they had to turn back, vowing they would try again. The brothers' attempts to flee and hide until they could safely complete their journey north must have frustrated and worried Brodess, who perhaps thought it was better to sell them than to risk losing everything if they were to be successful in taking their own liberty, but she may have been restrained by the

Pattison lawsuit from selling any more of Rit's children or grandchildren, buying valuable time for Robert, Ben, and Henry.

This gave Harriet additional opportunities to effect their escape; she tried at least once in the spring of 1854 but failed.[5] She did, however, successfully bring away twenty-seven-year-old Winnibar Johnson, the slave of Samuel Harrington of Tobacco Stick, in early June.[6] Johnson passed through William Still's office on June 29, where Still noted that Johnson had been "brought away by his sister Harriet two weeks ago."[7] It was too dangerous for Johnson to remain in Philadelphia, and he was passed on to New England.[8]

Before Tubman left the Eastern Shore with Johnson, she gave Sam Green Jr. detailed instructions to guide him on his secret journey to Philadelphia. Sam was the enslaved son of the Rev. Samuel Green, and possibly a relative of Tubman's mother, Rit. Trained as a blacksmith, Sam junior was held in bondage by Dr. James Muse, whom Green described as cruel and violent, "the worst man" in Maryland. Literate, possibly through his father's efforts, Green lived at Indian Creek in Dorchester County, not too far from his parents, Sam senior and Catherine, who were both free.[9] It took several months of waiting before he could effect his escape; on August 28, though, he arrived in William Still's office in Philadelphia. Still sent him on to the home of Charles Bustill, a member of one of the most important black Underground Railroad families in the region, who then passed him through to Canada.[10] A few months later Green wrote to his father, reassuring him that not only had he found a safe and easy passage to Canada but he had seen Harriet in Philadelphia.[11]

Tubman continued to live and work in Philadelphia throughout 1853 and 1854, saving her money and making friends and valuable connections within Philadelphia's active and multiracial antislavery community. Tubman had pressing responsibilities in Philadelphia and could not often return to Maryland to bring away the rest of her family.[12] Her young nephew James A. Bowley, the son of Kessiah and John, had remained in Philadelphia under Harriet's care after his parents moved on to Canada in 1851. Tubman was eager that James receive a good education; schools for black children in Canada were few, and because he was a child, he may have been less noticeable to roving slave catchers and bounty hunters on the watch for their next victim in Philadelphia's black community. Illiterate herself, Tubman knew the value of an education. James recalled that Tubman was "compelled to work at service for one dollar a week," giving half of that for his support, until he eventually moved on to Canada to be with his parents.[13]

Fortunately, Tubman was becoming known to a small group of powerful northern abolitionists.[14] Marveling at her devotion to freeing her family and friends, these abolitionists were at times overwhelmed by the force of her personality. Lucretia Coffin Mott, a Quaker then living in Philadelphia, was among the earliest of these white supporters to provide for Tubman's financial and physical needs.[15] A member of the radical Hicksite Quaker sect, Lucretia Mott was a prominent and persistent supporter of abolition and of full rights for women, including the right to vote and own property. Through Mott and William Still, Tubman gained access to other prominent white and black antislavery activists and Underground Railroad operators in the greater Philadelphia community, including Isaac and Dinah Mendenhall, Allen and Maria Agnew, and John and Hannah Cox from the Longwood and Kennet Square community in Chester County.[16] Lucretia, her sister Martha Coffin Wright of Auburn, New York, Elizabeth Cady Stanton, and Frederick Douglass were part of the small group of reformers who organized and conducted the first women's rights convention, held in Seneca Falls, New York, in 1848. Mott was also a close friend and ally of the abolitionist William Lloyd Garrison, of Boston. For Garrisonians, as they were then called, commitment to liberty and equality extended to rights for women. The experiences of the mid- to late 1830s had taught them "that free speech and slavery could not coexist for long in any society . . . and the spirit that would cut off free speech *was* the spirit of slavery."[17] Though committed to nonviolent forms of protest, they were often subjected to violent and dangerous confrontations with angry protesters who picketed and disrupted their public meetings.

Based on classical republican ideology, abolitionists envisioned a society rooted in an active citizenry that placed the common good ahead of private gain. Abolitionists argued that the family was man's best hope to fight the moral delinquency inherent in the world around them. Home and family represented goodness, a place where mothers and fathers imparted moral influences on their children. For abolitionists, slavery presented a particularly egregious moral, physical, and spiritual dilemma. Slavery violated the slave family through selling of family members away from one another; it also promoted physical assaults on female slaves by their white masters, thus corrupting the slave owner and his family as well. The potential depravity of the human mind and body led many women abolitionists, in particular, to argue that the unlimited power of one man over another was morally and spiritually unacceptable, that it led to sin, both physical and moral.[18]

Women's participation in antislavery work began early. But in the 1830s proslavery sentiment still ran strong even in northern nonslave states, and women's participation in political discourse challenged many citizens' understanding of nineteenth-century gender conventions. Women's attempts to join the political and very public discourse on slavery marked a turning point in abolitionist campaigning; their challenge to strict codes of gender behavior was the beginning of a new tactical program that would eventually transform the nation's political process.

Prominent white antislavery feminists such as Lydia Maria Child, Lucretia Mott, sisters Angelina and Sarah Grimké, and Abby Kelly helped focus the movement's attention on enslaved black women, using the image of the bound and chained slave woman as a metaphor for the status of all women in American society.[19] Some abolitionists, however, though supportive of women's expression of equality, shied away from including demands for women's rights on the antislavery platform.

Many black and white abolitionists did, however, recognize the gulf between rhetoric and reality and acknowledge that racial and sexual inequality were both symptoms of subordination to white men. While the image of the oppressed slave was used to define the nature of the oppression of women, the chained slave woman was in reality the victim of a double oppression: race and gender. Many free black women organized or joined antislavery societies, some of which had a mixed racial membership, but racism prevailed in these societies as well. Black women ultimately found it most practical to focus on the needs of their immediate community, such as providing for the growing numbers of runaway slaves seeking protection and aid. Indeed, the arguments of white women, which at times centered so much on gender oppression, were too narrowly focused for many black women, whose work on racial, economic, and educational improvement, in addition to aiding freed slaves, demanded their immediate attention.

Tubman became politicized very early on, attending antislavery meetings and then women's rights meetings and black rights conventions throughout the latter part of the 1850s. It was not long before Tubman found herself challenging women's and African Americans' subordinate political, economic, and social roles. This trustworthy network of active reformers proved worthy in Tubman's eyes; they often risked their own lives and livelihoods to defend and protect runaway slaves. Among them she found respect and the financial and personal support she needed to pursue her private war against slavery on the Eastern Shore of Maryland. The ideologies of racial and gender equality became central to her activism for the remainder of her life.

Many free black women combined antislavery work with racial uplift, while fewer white women felt the need to do so. African Americans fought and struggled for freedom as well as economic and educational advancement. Fund-raising, propaganda campaigns, boycotts, and other community and church-based programs dominated most black women's activities. It was often the responsibility of black women to provide for the material needs of recently freed slaves living in their communities, particularly before the Fugitive Slave Act of 1850. After that time, much of their fund-raising went to providing resources to move the freedmen and women to Canada and England. Lucretia Mott, on at least one occasion, spoke to the problem of stretched financial resources. She argued that aiding fugitive slaves was "not properly Anti-Slavery work" because the "primary goal of the society was to eliminate slavery" and to "destroy the system, root and branch, to lay the axe at the root of the corrupt tree."[20] Many others disagreed, and despaired of the movement's limited agenda when there was still so much work to be done once the slave was free. On the other hand, Mott was a devoted friend and supporter of Tubman, and her home was a stop on the Underground Railroad. She may have recognized that with limited resources, the movement's primary goal should be the total elimination of slavery immediately, so there would be no need to support a system to help slaves run away. Black women activists confronted the continuing realities of slavery directly. As arbiters of moral, educational, and spiritual well-being, they could not turn their backs on the destitute and poor, particularly recently freed bondsmen and women. It was within this bifurcated world that Tubman maneuvered. She was dependent upon white benefactors such as Mott to provide funding to support not only her trips south but also the security and settlement of fugitive slaves. But Tubman was also devoted to humanitarian work in the black community, through black churches and benevolent aid societies, which were often ignored by white activists.

In December 1854, Tubman made another attempt to retrieve her brothers after she learned that Eliza Brodess was planning to sell them over the Christmas holiday. Tubman enlisted the help of a literate friend in Philadelphia, who wrote a letter to Jacob Jackson, a free black then living in Dorchester County.[21] Jackson could read and write, which was not common for a black person in Dorchester County. Though his exact relationship to Tubman and her family is unknown, as a literate free black, Jackson may have been a hub of communication in the community, writing and reading letters for those who could not read and write for themselves.[22] Regardless of the relationship, Tubman was extremely cautious not to reveal anything in the letter that might pique the interest of a suspicious white postmaster. She first wrote of "indifferent matters," then asked him to "read my letter to the old folks, and give my love to them, and tell my brothers to be always *watching unto prayer*, and when the *good old ship of Zion comes along, to be ready to step aboard.*"[23] The letter was signed "William Henry Jackson," the name of Jacob's adopted son who had left Dorchester County for the north some years before. Tubman and Jacob must have established a specific code at some point during the years prior to 1854, and their caution proved wise; the postal authorities became suspicious because there had been several escapes in the area, and Jackson was suspected of providing a helping hand.

> Jacob was not allowed to have his letters till the self-elected inspectors had had the reading of them, and studied into their secret meaning. They, therefore, got together, wiped their glasses, and got them on, and proceeded to a careful perusal of this mys-

terious document. What it meant, they could not imagine; William Henry Jackson had no parents or brothers, and the letter was incomprehensible. White genius having exhausted itself, black genius was called in, and Jacob's letter was at last handed to him. Jacob saw at once what it meant, but tossed it down, saying, "Dat letter can't be meant for me, no how. I can't make head nor tail of it," and walked off and took immediate measures to let Harriet's brothers know secretly that she was coming, and they must be ready to start at a moment's notice for the North.[24]

Harriet made her way back down to the Eastern Shore, probably by train to Baltimore and then by boat to Cambridge or some other convenient landing along the Choptank. She arrived on Christmas Eve, a Saturday, the perfect timing for an escape. Slaveholders usually allowed some of their slaves, especially field slaves, to take time to visit with relatives and friends on other plantations during the holidays. Ben, Robert, and Henry were expected to visit their parents for Christmas dinner at Poplar Neck. Upon Harriet's arrival, however, she discovered advertisements had been posted for a public auction to be held on Monday, the day after Christmas, when her three brothers would be sold to the highest bidder. With no time to waste, Robert, Ben, and Henry were alerted to her presence; they were to meet after dark and start immediately for "their father's cabin, forty miles away."[25] Unbeknownst to Tubman, though, Robert's wife, Mary, was in labor, about to give birth to their third child.

The baby was coming, and Mary needed a midwife. Torn between freedom in the North and his devotion to his wife and his unborn child, Robert hesitated, raising Mary's suspicions. She was not aware of his plans, though she lived with the possibility that he would try to flee to freedom again after his past attempts ended in failure. Within a couple of hours, Mary gave birth to a little girl, and they named her Harriet.[26] Robert then turned his thoughts to joining his sister and brothers again. It was so late, and he knew he must go, but Mary kept calling for him, sensing there was something wrong. Robert agonized over the deceit he was about to commit; he was leaving his wife, his two little boys, John and Moses, and now his infant daughter. He could not be sure of their fate, but he knew that staying behind meant certain sale for him to the Deep South. So he lied to Mary, claiming he was going to hire himself out for Christmas Day. Mary did not believe the rumors that he was to be sold, and he hoped that this lie would calm her worries. But she soon realized his true intentions, and finally, after pleading with him to stay, she relented and let him go, comforted, perhaps, by the hope of following him later. With what must have been great distress, Robert left his family behind and set out to meet his sister and brothers.[27]

Tubman had not waited for Robert, however; she had specified a time and place, and according to her rules, she "never waited for no one."[28] She gathered those who had arrived on time and set out for Poplar Neck. Ben had arranged for his fiancée, Jane Kane, to join them; she was enslaved by Horatio Jones, "the worst man in the country."[29] Jones, Kane told an interviewer, was a cruel man who beat, tortured, and flogged his slaves.[30] He starved them and took away their clothes to keep them from leaving the farm where they labored. He whipped Jane's brother "until his back was as raw as a piece of beef"; he beat her "until the blood ran from my mouth and my nose," then locked her in a cupboard, where she almost suffocated.[31] Jones would not allow Jane to marry Ben, so they planned to run away together when the time was right. On the night of the escape, Jane put on a suit of men's clothing that Ben had secreted for her in one of Jones's gardens. When she was discovered missing, the other slaves on the farm did not imagine that the young man walking up from the garden, "as if from the river," was actually Jane. The disguise had worked well, and Jane was soon on her way to Poplar Neck with Ben.[32]

Robert, in the meantime, raced directly for Poplar Neck himself, hoping to catch up with the group there and travel on to freedom with them. On Christmas morning he reached Dr. Thompson's property. There, in the corn crib not far from his parents' cabin, Robert found his sister, his brothers Ben and Henry, Jane, and two others: twenty-year-old John Chase, the slave of John Campbell Henry from Cambridge, and Peter Jackson, the slave of George Winthrop, also a farmer from the Cambridge area.[33] It was raining heavily that day, so they remained hidden together in the fodder house to wait for the cover of darkness to run north.[34]

Rit, meanwhile, was waiting impatiently for her sons to arrive for Christmas dinner. From the "chinks" in the fodder house walls, Harriet and her brothers watched their mother step out of her cabin, "shading her eyes with her hand, take a long look down the road to see if her children were coming, and then they could almost hear her sigh as she turned into the house, disappointed."[35] Harriet had not seen her mother for over five years, but she could not risk letting Rit know that her children were hiding but a few yards from her cabin door, lest she cause such an "uproar in her efforts to detain them with her, that the whole plantation would have been alarmed."[36] The night before, after arriving at the fodder house, Harriet sent John Chase and Peter Jackson to her father's cabin door to rouse him without letting Rit know what was happening. Ben gathered some food for the hungry and weary runaways and brought it to the fodder house. Using every caution, he passed food to them, "taking care not to *see* his children."[37] Ben knew that he would be asked if he had seen them when the slave catchers came looking, and he cleverly decided he could tell them that he truly had not "seen" them. It was very hard for Ben, though; he had not seen his daughter Harriet since she had run away, and now she was there with her brothers, ready to run north, leaving him and Rit behind. He checked on the group several times on Christmas day, and by nightfall they were rested, well fed, and ready to start their journey. Harriet and her brothers took a moment to peer through the cabin window; there Rit sat "by her fire with a pipe in her mouth, her head on her hand, rocking back and forth as she did when she was in trouble, and wondering what new evil had come to her children."[38] Sadly they turned their faces north, not knowing if they would ever see their dear mother again. Ben tied a "handkerchief tight over his eyes, and two of his sons taking him by each arm, he accompanied them some miles upon their journey. They then bade him farewell, and left him standing blind-fold in the middle of the road. When he could no longer hear their footsteps, he took off the handkerchief, and turned back."[39]

Tubman most likely took one of two routes north. She could have gone east through Federalsburg, then over to the Bridgeville area in Delaware, then north to Camden, Dover, New Castle, and Wilmington, stopping at various safe houses along the way in Blackbird, Smyrna, and other places. Tubman could also have headed northeast along the Choptank River, through Denton and Greensboro, and into Delaware through Sandtown and Willow Grove, then on to Dover and Wilmington. Once in Wilmington, Tubman and her group stopped at Thomas Garrett's home, where he provided them with food and clothing. Harriet and one of the men "had worn their shoes off their feet," so Garrett gave them $2 to buy new shoes. Garrett, a hardware and iron merchant, used his own income to provide refuge and necessities for the estimated twenty-five hundred runaways who came through his home over a thirty- to forty-year period.[40]

Garrett secured a carriage for Tubman and her party, directing them on to Allen Agnew's house in Kennett, Chester County, Pennsylvania, where Agnew would forward them to William Still's Anti-Slavery Office in Philadelphia.[41] At Still's, the party felt relieved to have "eluded pursuit."[42] It was December 29, and they had spent four days traveling over one hundred miles to freedom. William Still had already welcomed six freedom seekers that month into his home or office. By the time Tubman arrived, her group had grown to nine, including two additional men who had joined Tubman and her charges earlier in their journey. George Ross and William Thompson were both enslaved by Lewis N. Wright, a Delaware farmer from Seaford. Wright's family had extensive landholdings and business relationships to the west in Dorchester County, where the Wrights and families like them traveled back and forth between the two states and counties several times throughout the year. Seaford, just south of Bridgeville, was a major trade terminus at the headwaters of the Nanticoke River and had been settled by many people with familial and economic relationships in Dorchester County.[43] The Wrights transported their slave labor back and forth across state lines, depending upon the seasonal labor requirements of their various farming and fishing enterprises.[44] George Ross and William Thompson may have been laboring for Wright in Dorchester County when they ran away.[45]

William Still was responsible for securing passage from Philadelphia to a variety of other stations along the Underground Railroad route north. He depended upon a large network of white and black abolitionists throughout the area, predominantly in Philadelphia and neighboring Chester and Lancaster Counties and across the Delaware River in New Jersey. He forwarded many of his charges directly on to New York City, New Bedford, Boston, and beyond, as well as to central New York cities and towns such as Troy, Albany, Syracuse, and Rochester, where fugitives were then directed to Buffalo or some other convenient place for safe passage across Lake Ontario, Lake Erie, or Niagara Falls. Some went to Elmira, New York, where John W. Jones, a longtime black Underground Railroad operator, funneled hundreds of fugitives making their way though eastern and central Pennsylvania, then on to Syracuse, Rochester, and Buffalo for transfer to the suspension bridge over Niagara Falls.[46]

William Still kept a record of most of the freedom seekers who sought shelter and aid through his office at the Anti-Slavery Society in Philadelphia. Still noted each person's name, age, height, and skin color, the name of their enslaver, where they had lived, and sometimes the runaway's personal family information, such as number of brothers and sisters and names of parents, spouses, and children. He recorded any aliases the runaways chose, ensuring that they could be found by friends and family in the future. On occasion he took testimony from the former slaves, recording their experiences under slavery, their reasons for taking flight, and their opinions of their masters. Still also maintained detailed accounts of funds spent on each freedom seeker who came through the society's office.[47]

On December 29 Still interviewed Tubman and her brothers. He recorded the names Harriet's brothers would take, and keep, for the rest of their lives. Shedding their Ross surname, they chose Stewart, the name of one of Dorchester County's more prominent white families. While many runaway slaves apparently chose aliases to protect their identities from slave catchers in the North, some probably adopted the names that they themselves recognized as their rightful names even under slavery. Some rejected outright the names their white masters had assigned them, assignments that may have often disregarded blood and familial ties. Whether this was the case for the Rosses is uncertain. Ben took the name James Stewart; Robert chose John Stewart; and Henry first chose Levin Stewart, but then changed it to William Henry Stewart.[48] James A. Stewart, the Pattisons' lawyer and one of the most powerful white men on the Eastern Shore, may have represented power and control. But James A. Stewart was also a major slaveholder and quite unsympathetic. John T. Stewart, son of Joseph, and James A. Stewart's brother, was a local shipbuilder and merchant, had a modest number of slaves, and was not nearly as powerful as his brother. John T. Stewart did, however, work with and own a boat with the Bowley brothers. The other white John T. Stewart was the son of Levin Stewart (Joseph Stewart's brother), who had manumitted all of his slaves, including the Bowleys, decades before. This John T. did not own slaves, was a Union sympathizer, and was in partnership with a free black man named Denwood Clash during the Civil War.[49]

Robert, Ben, and Henry Ross's choice of the Stewart name may have had different meanings for all of them; it remains a curiosity, however, that they took the name of this complicated and powerful white family. Living and working in the same community as the white Stewarts, the brothers may have been claiming a familial connection not apparent in the existing records. Two men who fled with Tubman and her brothers, John Chase and Peter Jackson, also chose aliases that were the names of powerful white Eastern Shore men. John Chase became Daniel Lloyd, and Peter Jackson became Tench Tilghman. The white Daniel Lloyd had been Frederick Douglass's playmate when they were children; he was the son of Edward Lloyd, the largest slaveholder and probably the richest man on the Eastern Shore. Daniel Lloyd was married to Kate Henry, the daughter of Chase's enslaver, John Campbell Henry. Tench Tilghman was also a very wealthy man, owning vast tracts of land in Talbot County, and was descended from a famed Revolutionary War hero.[50] Perhaps these newly liberated men felt powerful and wealthy in spirit as they embraced freedom, much like their white counterparts.

Ben, William Still wrote in his Journal C, was twenty-eight, of medium height and "chestnut color," and intelligent, and had been owned by "Eliza Ann Brodins" (Brodess), who lived near "Bucktown, Cambridge," Maryland. Ben described Eliza as being "very Devilish." He told Still that it was "difficult for 3 slaves to support a family of 8 whites," and that they had fled out of fear of being sold. Ben also told Still that he had left behind a sister, Mary Ann Williams, who wanted to run away as well. Jane Kane was twenty-two, and she told Still that she had been used "very hardly" by her master, "Rash [Horatio] Jones," and that her new name would be Catherine Kane. Still described Henry as "smart," twenty-two years old, of chestnut color, who left behind a wife, Harriet Ann, and two little sons. Harriet's oldest brother, Robert, was thirty-five years old, Still recorded, of chestnut color, and he too had left behind two children.[51] Still provided them with funds to get to the next station, probably New York City, where Jacob Gibbs most probably helped them along to Albany, New York.[52]

In Albany and Troy, Tubman sought aid from Stephen Myers, a black abolitionist, a member of the local Vigilance Committee, and publisher of the area's black newspaper. Tubman had several friends and relatives in Troy and Albany; some were Maryland runaways, including John and Mary Hooper, Anthony and Lucy Hooper, William and Margaret Jones, and William J. Bowley.[53] John Hooper was a fugitive himself, having fled from the Eastern Shore possibly in the early 1840s. He had "lived near Frederick Douglass in his boyhood" and was "an acquaintance then of Fred Douglas [sic]."[54] The Hoopers were well-known Underground Railroad operators in the area.[55] Tubman and her brothers may have stopped at their home for a few days' rest, or they may have headed straight to Syracuse or Rochester and then St. Catharines, Ontario, Canada, where family and friends awaited them.[56]

In Canada, the three brothers and Jane (now named Catherine) settled into a home with other runaways then living in St. Catharines. The Bowleys had moved to Chatham, 140 miles west of St. Catharines, where they found a place in a rapidly growing community of fugitive slaves, most of whom had made their way to Canada from the Midwest through Detroit and the western shores of Lake Erie.[57] Ben (now James Stewart) and his bride, Catherine, moved on to Chatham to live with John and Kessiah Bowley and their family sometime between the summer of 1855 and the spring of 1856. John and Kessiah had settled in Chatham probably not long after they had arrived in Canada in 1851, where John may have tried farming, blacksmithing, or other types of manual labor.[58] The following year Catherine gave birth to a son, Elijah Ross Stewart, who was soon followed by the arrival of John and Kessiah's son, Harkless.[59] Chatham and nearby communities had larger and more well-established black fugitive communities; aid, in the form of housing, schooling, and economic advancement, held greater promise there than in St. Catharines.

William Henry [Ross] Stewart, one of Harriet Tubman's
brothers who ran away with her during Christmas 1854.
Photo probably taken in Canada circa 1860.

Tubman's other brothers, Robert (now John Stewart) and Henry (now William Henry Stewart), settled in St. Catharines. Both were common laborers for a time, but eventually John became a coachman for two local white doctors, and William Henry tried his hand at farming.[60] William Henry later told an interviewer that "at first, I made pretty good headway," but he then lost a $200 investment in a rented farm when he and one of his brothers "got into some trouble."[61] In 1861 William Henry bought six acres of land in Grantham, Lincoln County, Ontario, on the outskirts of St. Catharines, where he settled down with his wife, Harriet Ann, and his four children, William, John, Caroline, and Mary.[62] Harriet Ann had arrived from Dorchester County shortly after William Henry, making her way north with at least one of their children, then called William Henry Stewart Jr., and possibly a second, John Isaac.[63] The whereabouts of Tubman's youngest brother, Moses, however, remains unknown. No record of him after his escape from slavery has been located.[64]

Back on the Eastern Shore, it was not long before the three brothers, Jane, and the other two men were discovered missing. Slave catchers arrived at Dr. Thompson's plantation, looking for information as to the whereabouts of the brothers—for at first they may not have suspected that the other runaways were involved. Dr. Thompson told them that he thought they were supposed to have visited Ben and Rit for Christmas but that he had not seen them himself. Thompson was to have been asked,

'Have you been down to Old Ben's?' . . . 'Yes.' 'What does Old Rit say?' 'Old Rit says not one of 'em came this Christmas. She was looking for 'em most all day, and most broke her heart about it.' 'What does Old Ben say?' 'Old Ben says that he hasn't seen one of his children this Christmas.' 'Well, if Old Ben says that, they haven't been round.' And so the man-hunters went off disappointed.[65]

Ben's clever play on words helped him avoid telling the truth, but it would not be so easy as time went on. As more and more slaves took flight from the region, suspicion started to settle on a few free blacks then living in Dorchester and Caroline Counties. Because most of their children had successfully run away at this point, Ben and Rit were increasingly at risk. Ben's reputation as a trusted and reliable former slave protected him for a time. Being an important asset to Dr. Thompson also gave Ben some protection, but not for long. Eastern Shore slaveholders were becoming restless, and even a man like Thompson could not protect a suspected Underground Railroad agent indefinitely.

Ben must have been getting nervous; on June 11, 1855, a bill of sale was filed at the Dorchester County courthouse, recording Ben's prior purchase of his wife, Rit, from Eliza Brodess for $20. The transaction, however, demonstrates Eliza's deviousness and underhanded treatment of Rit.[66] Though Rit was close to seventy years old and the lawsuit had made it apparent that Rit should have been freed at age forty-five, Eliza still managed to sell her for cash. The bill of sale, "having been neglected to be filed" by Eliza Brodess, was finally recorded when she appeared before the court on June 11, 1855, to acknowledge the prior transaction. When Ben may have actually purchased Rit is not known. He may have felt he had no choice; to secure his wife's freedom meant he had to have ownership of her. Her slave status remained ambiguous, though, and Ben could not manumit her, as he did Maria Bailey and Aaron Manokey in 1843, because Rit was then over forty-five years of age, the maximum age for legal manumission. Worried over increased attention to his activities after his sons had run away, Ben may have gone to Brodess and insisted that she file a record of the transaction, anticipating that he might need to flee and take Rit with him. Ben would need proof of his ownership of Rit to travel out of the state with her.

Eliza Brodess, in the meantime, must have been increasingly frustrated with the turn of events. Though the Pattison lawsuit had been permanently dismissed by the court in September 1854, making it possible, finally, for Eliza to sell any or all of Rit's children or grandchildren, her financial situation remained unsettled. When the three brothers ran away that Christmas, Eliza lost over one-third of her assets.[67] She began to suspect that John Mills was not acting in her best interest as co-administrator of Edward Brodess's estate. On December 20, 1855, Eliza filed a bill of complaint against Mills, charging him with fraud in the administration of her husband's estate. Eliza wanted the court to force Mills to deliver up the balance of the estate, because, she claimed, he was indebted to her for "a large sum of money, which he has hitherto refused to pay."[68] She may have suspected that Mills had actually sold Robert, Ben, and Henry illegally and then claimed they had run away. She asked the court to force Mills to produce a list of the "sales of Negroes, stating in particular what Negroes were sold by him, to whom they were sold, by what authorization and for what price?"[69]

All of this gave Harriet Tubman reason to worry about the rest of her family remaining on the Eastern Shore. Her sister Rachel, still owned by Brodess, was at higher risk of being sold now that her brothers had escaped. At the same time, other factors made it increasingly difficult to bring away slaves. The New Year had brought more tension to the area, and frustrated Eastern Shore slaveholders were increasingly angered by the growing numbers of runaway slaves, who were urged on, they imagined, by unknown abolitionist forces that lurked in free blacks' homes, sowing notions of freedom and liberty among the slave community. By Easter 1855 rumors stoked fears of an impending insurrection by unidentified free and enslaved blacks in Dorchester and Talbot Counties. Meetings of concerned white citizens were held to formulate plans to suppress gatherings of local blacks, particularly illegal black schools, unless they were held under the supervision of a white person.[70] Searches were made of black homes, where guns and other weapons were supposedly seized. Slaveholders, the newspapers announced, were to keep their slaves home during the Easter holiday. The editor of the *Cambridge Chronicle* discounted the possibility that white abolitionists were in their midst, readying the black community to strike out against whites. He was in the minority, apparently. Swift condemnation of his call for reason followed from fellow citizens of Dorchester County, and shortly thereafter the newspaper folded. One irate resident called for the expulsion of all free blacks from the state of Maryland. Many others agreed.[71]

Tubman remained in Canada for some months with her family members during the winter of 1855. That spring or early summer, Tubman, her brothers John and James Stewart, and James's wife, Catherine Kane Stewart, were interviewed by Benjamin Drew, a Boston abolitionist, school principal, and journalist, who had traveled to Canada to meet former slaves who had fled farther north to escape the Fugitive Slave Act. Drew wanted to record stories of life under slavery from the fugitive slaves themselves and to document the living conditions of the freedmen in Canada. His efforts were in direct response to events that had dealt a heavy blow to the antislavery movement. The Kansas-Nebraska Bill of 1854 provided for two new territories to be carved out of the remains of the former Louisiana Purchase, the northernmost part called Nebraska and the southern portion Kansas. The settlers of each new territory then had the right to decide for themselves whether to allow slavery. Northern opponents of the extension of slavery into the new territories balked at this repeal of the Missouri Compromise agreement to keep slavery out of the area. This strengthening of southern slave power repudiated abolitionists' efforts to end slavery in all states.

Two books were published during this period that defended the institution of slavery as a benevolent and caring institution that provided for the protection of black people. George Fitzhugh's *Sociology for the South; or, the Failure of Free Society* and Reverend Nehemiah Adams's *A Southside View of Slavery* both argued the view that slavery was far more beneficial and less oppressive than abolitionists had led the public to believe and that the northern wage labor system was in fact worse. They both claimed that slaves were actually happy in the South. Directly challenging Harriet Beecher Stowe's description of slavery in her runaway best-seller *Uncle Tom's Cabin* (1852), Fitzhugh and Adams claimed authority through firsthand observations of the slave system at work, challenging northern abolitionists' claims about the injustices and horrors of slavery as purely emotional and without merit.

Benjamin Drew sought to counter such claims by publishing his interviews with the Canadian fugitives in *The Refugee: or the North-side View of Slavery*. Drew's interview with Tubman was the first of its kind to be published; unfortunately brief, it does draw attention to the fact that she chose to be known by her real name, Harriet Tubman. Her brothers John and James preferred the surname Seward, a variation on the name Stewart.[72] Fresh from slavery, they minced no words about its horrors. John told Drew he had been waiting twenty years to come away. He had been suspicious of abolitionists at first; he was "afraid of a trick."[73] James lamented the sale of his niece before they could get away.[74] Catherine told Drew that her owner had inflicted brutal treatment upon her and her family.[75] Tubman told him that they longed to return to Maryland to be with family and friends but "wished they could be as free there as we are here."[76]

With her family safely in Canada, Tubman returned to Philadelphia to earn more money to continue her personal campaign of liberation. In October 1855 she probably attended the National Colored Convention, held at Franklin Hall in Philadelphia. Frederick Douglass, Jacob Gibbs, and Stephen Myers, of New York; William Cooper Nell, Charles Lenox Remond, and John S. Rock, from Massachusetts; and William Still, Robert Purvis, and many others from Philadelphia were in attendance, along with sixty other delegates from northern states. Tubman's friends from Dorchester County, the Rev. Samuel Green and his wife, Catherine "Kitty" Green, may have been among the forty delegates from the "cotton states."[77] The convention gave Tubman the opportunity to meet with powerful black abolitionists in other cities and towns in the Northeast. It also provided an outlet for her expanding notions of liberty and freedom beyond the confines of the Underground Railroad. Intimate with Philadelphia's community of women's rights activists, black mutual aid societies, and black suffrage organizations, Tubman was eager to participate in an organized national black rights movement. Men dominated the convention. Mary Ann Shadd, publisher of the *Provincial Freeman*, an influential black Canadian newspaper, was the only woman allowed to attend as a delegate. Nevertheless, Tubman and other women like her were a visible presence.

Many attendees took time to visit Passmore Williamson in Philadelphia's Moyamensing Prison, where he was being held in contempt for refusing to produce a fugitive slave woman named Jane Johnson and her two young sons in court. Williamson, among others, had been successful in helping Jane and her children escape from her owner, who was then in Philadelphia transacting some business. Williamson, a white man, was a member of the Pennsylvania Anti-Slavery Society and was closely associated with William Still and Philadelphia's Underground Railroad networks. Tubman probably knew Williamson before his incarceration; in any case, on October 20, two days after the closing of the convention, Tubman and her friend, Catherine Green, visited him in his cell.[78] Williamson was one of many influential white abolitionists Tubman was drawn to; standing firm on principle, they risked their freedom and livelihoods to protect fugitive slaves and fight to end slavery. Williamson and many like him came to admire, some with great awe, Tubman's tenacity and commitment, recognizing that her efforts far exceeded even their most impassioned and dangerous work on behalf of the slave.

Among her many admirers was Thomas Garrett, who in mid-December 1855 wrote to Eliza Wigham, secretary of the Ladies' Emancipation Society of Edinburgh, Scotland, about Tubman, and described her as "a noble woman . . . in whose veins flow not one drop of Caucasian blood." Garrett went on to describe the missions she was undertaking to liberate her family and friends. Wigham and her sister Mary Edmundson were both staunch abolitionists and Quakers who raised funds not only for Garrett's efforts to help liberate slaves but also for Frederick Douglass, William Lloyd Garrison, and Wendell Phillips and their campaigns against slavery in the United States. Garrett wrote to the sisters, keeping them informed of the latest struggles in Wilmington, Delaware, and to relay some of the more compelling and dramatic slave stories and rescues with which he was familiar. Such communication was vital to raising funds from sources both in the United States and abroad, for these tales fed abolitionists' constant thirst for authentic slave experiences to validate and support the cause of the slave.[79] Though Garrett did not mention Tubman by name, he told Wigham that Tubman had made four trips to her "neighborhood," bringing away seventeen of her family and friends, in the process spending "every dollar she could earn." Garrett told Wigham he was proud of his acquaintance with Tubman and that he marveled at her devotion to her family and friends at the risk of her own health and liberty.[80]

Though Tubman successfully brought north William Henry's wife, Harriet Ann, and their son William Henry Stewart Jr. and possibly a second, John Isaac, sometime between 1855 and 1856, the diligence of the slaveholders and slave catchers on the Eastern Shore made rescues increasingly difficult. To avoid endangering her parents, she tried to vary her hiding places. She stayed at times with the Rev. Samuel Green and his wife, Kitty, in East New Market, but she may have also stayed with other black families in the area, or secreted herself in swamps and other hideouts.[81] During one attempted rescue mission she spent three months in Dorchester County waiting for the opportunity to bring away family members, possibly her sister Rachel and Rachel's children, Angerine and Benjamin, and possibly Mary Manokey Ross and her children.[82] It is remarkable that Tubman was not betrayed, as so many other southern agents and runaways had been.

Tubman faced great risks while waiting; there was always the opportunity for unexpected exposure. On one occasion Tubman ran into her master, probably Dr. Thompson, "in the fields," but Garrett wrote her "color had changed so much that he did not recognize her," nor did her brother and sister. Garrett imagined that, because Tubman no longer toiled under the sun, her skin color had changed enough to make such a difference. It may have been her clothing, too. On occasion, Tubman purposely wore fine clothing, including a silk dress, to add to the illusion that she belonged in the world of middle-class free blacks, not that of the poorly clad field hands.[83]

On another occasion, Tubman "went even to the very village where she would be most likely to meet one of the masters to whom she had been hired; and having stopped at the Market and bought a pair of live fowls, she went along the street with her sun-bonnet well over her face," acting the part of an aged and "decrepit" woman. Upon seeing her "master . . . she pulled the string which tied the legs of the chickens; they began to flutter and scream." While Tubman lowered her bonnet over her eyes and stooped down to attend to the squawking birds, "her master . . . went on his way, little thinking that he was brushing the very garments of the woman who had dared to steal herself, and others of his belongings."[84] Later Tubman recognized one of her former masters seated near her on a train. She quickly grabbed a newspaper that had been left on her seat and pretended to read it. Tubman was not sure if it was "bottom side up or not," but her master, knowing she could not read, did not bother with her. "The Lord," Tubman later said, "save me that time too."[85]

In early December 1855 Tubman brought away one man, probably Henry Hooper, who arrived in William Still's office on the sixth; she immediately returned to Dorchester County, determined to bring away her sister—probably Rachel—"now the last one left in slavery," Rachel's children, her sister-in-law Mary Manokey with her three children, and "one male friend."[86] She did not succeed, but she was probably responsible for directing Joseph Cornish, a local Dorchester County freedom seeker, to William Still's home in Philadelphia on Christmas Day. Cornish, forty, had been a preacher in the African Methodist Church for about seven years, but his owner, Captain Samuel W. LeCompte, had decided recently to sell him, so Cornish set his sights on freedom instead. Leaving behind a free wife and children, Cornish was forwarded to Canada after a couple of meals and a good night's sleep.[87] On the following day, Garrett forwarded George Wilmer, a slave from Kent

County, Maryland, who was himself an agent on the Underground Railroad.[88] Whether Wilmer was being pursued or not is unclear; curiously, he passed through Still's office again the following fall with William Cornish of Dorchester County, possibly a clue to one of the many paths to freedom Tubman and her friends had come to rely on—this one through the Sassafras River region of Kent County. Somehow Wilmer juggled a variety of roles as both a slave and an Underground Railroad operator living a very precarious dual life on Maryland's upper Eastern Shore.[89]

Tubman could not rest; her sister Rachel was still trapped on Brodess's plantation. During Tubman's trip at Christmastime in 1855, Rachel could not get away; her children had been separated from her, and she would not leave them behind. Eliza Brodess and her son John, who had taken over the administration of his father's estate, probably would not let Rachel visit her parents at Poplar Neck that Christmas, as they had allowed Ben, Henry, and Robert to do the year before. Whether they suspected Ben and Rit of aiding the brother's escape or not, they were not about to take any more chances with the last of their slaves by allowing Rachel traditional freedoms over the holiday. Where Rachel's children, Ben and Angerine, were at this time is not known. Tubman returned to Philadelphia gravely disappointed but still determined to return to bring her whole family together in the North.

It would take another five months before Tubman could earn and collect enough money to make another trip. On May 11, 1856, Thomas Garrett wrote J. Miller McKim and William Still that he had forwarded four young men to Longwood on the ninth, with Tubman following on the tenth.[90] The next day Still noted that Harriet Tubman had arrived with the four unidentified men after having made a stop at the home of a Mrs. Buchannon. With the help of Nathaniel Depee, a member of the Vigilance Committee who boarded the men for two days, the party was forwarded to Canada. Harriet had been lucky again.

Just two weeks earlier, two men had been hauled into Dorchester County court for aiding and abetting a slave to run away.[91] Five days after Tubman had stopped at Still's office with the four runaways, another freedom seeker, Jesse Slacum of Dorchester County, made his way to Still's office.[92] Possibly a slave of Dr. Thompson or related to a

slave owned by him, Slacum was just one of several running away during that spring and summer. Though slaveholders on the Eastern Shore
were increasingly frustrated and sought to penalize their slaves and
members of the free black community, Dr. Thompson apparently responded to this rash of runaways by decreasing the terms of servitude
of twenty-seven men, women, and children. Among them was twenty-
four-year-old Mary Manokey Ross, the wife of Robert, now John Stewart, who had fled a year and a half earlier. Thompson, "for divers good
causes and considerations," manumitted Mary and her children, John
Henry, age six, Moses, age four, and Ritty, age two years, when they
reached the age of thirty.[93] Mary, then, would be free in 1862, while her
children would remain enslaved until the late 1870s and 1880s. This
manumission record also provided for the same term limits, that is, until the age of thirty, for twenty-three other slaves, including members of
the Sprig, Slacum, Kiah, Young, and Manokey families, some as young
as two months old.[94] Thompson probably hoped that such reductions
in the terms of service might induce these young slaves to reconsider
any thoughts of running away.[95]

But Thompson was inconsistent in his treatment of his enslaved
people. In fact, he was having many problems of his own, only some of
which were connected to notions of liberty surfacing in his slave quarters. He had overextended his credit when he bought thousands of
acres in Caroline County and could not meet the terms of the notes.
During the 1840s and early 1850s Thompson sold several of the slaves
from his father's estate. All of the slaves had limited terms of service, so
they could not be sold out of the state. To the complete shock and dis-
belief of Ben Ross and most of Thompson's slaves, Thompson sold
young Susan Manokey, Mary Manokey's sister and Jerry and Polly
Manokey's daughter, in 1847 to an East New Market man, who then
sold her to the wife of a slave trader, Miles Tindle. Tindle immediately
sold Susan, then eighteen years old, illegally beyond the limits of the
state. He was brought before the county court, but the damage was
done. Jerry and Polly had lost a daughter; Mary and her siblings had lost
their sister. It was a betrayal that would not be forgotten by Thompson's slave community.[96]

By the mid-1850s, Thompson was experiencing severe financial difficulties. Facing bankruptcy, he began in 1854 to consolidate some of his landholdings still left in Dorchester County, hoping to keep his creditors at bay. Though he had been bound by the terms of his father's last will and testament to manumit his father's slaves at specific dates, Thompson started to sell some of them instead. Over the next few years Thompson continued to sell slaves, creating lasting bitterness and increasing tension in the slave quarters.[97] No slave seemed exempt; slaves with very limited terms of a year or two and young children with twenty or more years of service were sold, providing the easy cash he desperately needed.[98] Dr. Thompson's actions were an unforgivable betrayal, and his enslaved people knew well that his poor business judgment had caused his financial predicament.[99]

If Thompson did not know definitively, surely he must have suspected that Mary Manokey was hoping to get away as her husband, Robert Ross, had done. Selling Mary and her children was not an attractive option; Thompson's earlier efforts to sell some of his own and his father's slaves had created such havoc in the slave quarters that he may have felt it was too risky. It was probably during this time that he sent Mary and her children to live with his daughter, Sarah Catherine Haddaway, in Talbot County, removing her from what he may have perceived as a persistent threat of escape.[100]

Tubman was determined to bring Mary Manokey, along with Tubman's sister Rachel and both women's children, north. But after escorting the unidentified men to Canada in May, she became quite ill. A respiratory ailment, possibly pneumonia brought on by exposure to the elements during her last raid, weakened her considerably, so much so she could not make another trip south until the following September. By that time she was "quite feeble, her voice much impaired from a cold taken last winter."[101] Garrett was deeply worried that her health had been permanently affected.

It was possibly during this trip in May, when Tubman was escorting the four men north, that she became uneasy, sensing that something was wrong and that they were in danger. She told Sanborn that she always seemed to know when danger was near; her heart would "go flutter, flutter."[102] Some thirty miles from Wilmington, probably in the vicinity of Blackbird, her intuition led her to immediately change her planned route. "God told her to stop," which she did, "but then he told her to leave the road, and turn to the left." As they approached a "small stream of tide water," they looked for a boat or a bridge to cross over but found none. Their only option was to wade across, but it was cold and the depth of the stream was unknown to them, so the men refused to go into the water. Tubman, convinced they had no choice and that the risk of capture was too great, plunged in and waded across without them. The water nearly reached her shoulders, but no higher, and she safely reached the other side. Seeing that she had not drowned, the men reluctantly followed. They came upon a second stream, and after crossing that they made their way to the house of a black family who took them in, dried them off, fed them, and hid them until the next evening, when they could proceed to Wilmington. Having run out of money, Tubman gave the woman of the family her undergarments to "pay for their kindness." Garrett recalled that when Tubman finally made it to his office, "she was so hoarse she could hardly speak." She also had a "violent toothache," which she remedied by knocking out the offending tooth with a rock.[103]

Tubman confronted many unforeseen barriers on her paths to freedom. But she would not rest until her family was all in Canada. Risking her own health and safety, she would return several more times to the Eastern Shore, escalating the chances that she would be discovered and reenslaved.

CHAPTER 7

STAMPEDE OF SLAVES

AS THE 1850S WORE ON, SLAVEHOLDERS ON THE EASTERN SHORE OF Maryland faced a complicated political, economic, and moral battle that was threatening the very foundations of the institution of slavery. Rising racial tensions and northern abolitionist threats to the institution of slavery contributed to a reactionary response in Dorchester County that resulted in an ever-more-oppressive environment for black people, both free and enslaved. This compelled more slaves to strike out for freedom, wreaking havoc on the stability and security of the white community. Though Tubman's identity remained veiled from Eastern Shore whites, who were probably not even aware of her role, each new mission placed her at greater risk of being discovered.

Tubman often faced severe restrictions on her ability to travel freely, save money, and coordinate her missions to coincide with an opportune time to effect an escape. When she was finally able to return to Philadelphia from Canada in September 1856, for instance, she discovered that her landlord had died during the summer. His widow had sold the house and left Philadelphia for Harrisburg, Pennsylvania, taking Harriet's clothes and money with her. Thomas Garrett wrote to his friend and benefactor, Eliza Wigham, that Tubman had asked that Wigham kindly send "five pound sterling" to help her with her efforts, and to direct the funds to William Still's office in Philadelphia, where Tubman would be stopping, now that she had lost her rented room, whenever she was in Philadelphia.[1]

On September 12 an undeterred Tubman left Garrett's office for Baltimore to bring away two children. She told Garrett that once she returned she would make her way back to the Eastern Shore to make still another attempt to retrieve Rachel and Rachel's children from Dorchester County.[2] Later that month, Garrett notified Still to be on the lookout for five runaways from the Eastern Shore who had been sent along from his home earlier. Francis Molock, Cyrus Mitchell, Joshua Handy, Charles Dutton, and Ephraim Hudson had probably either left with Tubman or used instructions provided by her.[3] Tubman's illness throughout the summer had delayed their escape; in fact, Garrett had been waiting for Tubman to bring them on since May.[4] She may have organized their efforts, or she could have accompanied them just part of the way, preferring to remain close to the Eastern Shore or in Baltimore to embark on another mission of her own.

One month later Tubman arrived in Wilmington with Tilly, a young woman whose lover had pleaded with Tubman to bring his fiancée away from Baltimore to Canada.[5] Perhaps while in Baltimore to retrieve the two unnamed children, Tubman sought out Tilly and pulled off one of her most complicated and clever escape attempts. The story of Tilly's rescue so intrigued Garrett that he immediately sat down and wrote to Eliza Wigham, who had just sent a five-pound note specifically for Harriet's use. In writing to Wigham again, Garrett's motives were no doubt financially driven, knowing that Wigham and her friends would send more money to support his and Tubman's efforts to help runaways.[6] Tubman's latest adventure was, Garrett knew, just right to pique the interest of his English friends, while it also gave him the opportunity to promote and celebrate the attempts of "that noble woman, Harriet Tubman," whom he admired so greatly.[7]

Garrett told Wigham that "the history of this trip was remarkable, and manifested great shrewdness."[8] A refugee living in Canada had left his fiancée in Baltimore some seven years before, when he had to run away to avoid being sold south. He gave Harriet money, and Tubman made her way to Philadelphia, where a steamboat captain gave her a certificate stating she was a resident of Philadelphia and a free woman. Traveling through the Chesapeake and Delaware Canal on this vessel, Tubman reached Baltimore and in time found Tilly. Tubman was well aware that she could not bring a black woman from Baltimore to Philadelphia without paying a bond of $500 or producing a certificate of freedom of some sort, neither of which Tubman had. Tubman, not to be deterred, purchased fares for passage on a steamboat bound south through the Chesapeake Bay to Seaford, Delaware, far up the Nanticoke River from Dorchester County. Eventually Tubman convinced the captain of the steamboat, who knew the captain from the Philadelphia steamer, to provide a travel pass or some other certificate to Tilly. Two black women traveling south did not raise much suspicion, and providing Tilly with a pass probably seemed harmless, or perhaps the steamboat captain was an antislavery man.

Tubman and Tilly soon found themselves far south of Baltimore and even farther from free soil. Upon their arrival in Seaford, Tubman "boldly went to the Hotel & called for supper and lodging."[9] How restful their sleep was, Garrett did not report, though Tubman probably prayed through the night, seeking their safe deliverance north. In the morning they were confronted by a suspicious slave dealer who tried to arrest them. Tilly was on the verge of hysteria—she was convinced they had been discovered—"but on showing the captain's certificates," they were allowed to pass. Tubman later said that she prayed, "Oh, Lord! You've been with me in six troubles, *don't* desert me in the seventh!"— meaning, presumably, this was her seventh trip.[10]

They purchased tickets for the train through to Camden, Delaware, where William Brinkley, a local free black who had been befriended by Tubman some time before, and other Underground Railroad operators brought them by carriage the fifty miles to Wilmington. Garrett gave Tubman the $25 that Eliza Wigham had sent for her. Tubman and Tilly both needed new shoes, but more important, Tubman needed at least $20 to "go for her sister and children," still waiting on the Eastern Shore.[11] Tilly was sent along to Canada, while Tubman immediately returned to Dorchester County. Garrett told Wigham that he was amazed that Tubman "does not know, or appears to not know that she has done anything worth notice."[12] Tubman cared more about success than celebrity. She assured Garrett that she had great confidence that God would protect her "in all her perilous journeys," for she never went "on a mission of mercy without his consent."[13]

Tubman had made arrangements to meet her sister, and had "one or more interviews with her," but after waiting for ten days, her sister could not leave without her children, who were then living away from her.[14] They planned then that Tubman would return over the Christmas holidays. Her sister was hopeful that she and her children would be allowed to be together over the holiday, and they would make their bid for freedom then. Harriet gathered another group of eager freedom seekers and headed north.

Tubman knew her latest charges, and probably fairly well. Josiah (Joe) Bailey and his brother Bill, Peter Pennington, and Eliza Manokey struck out with Tubman in mid-November. Laboring together in William Hughlett's timbering operations, Joe and Bill had both been eager to escape.[15] A prominent planter who owned thousands of acres of farmland and timber along the Choptank River, and the owner of some forty slaves, Hughlett "was in the habit of flogging" his enslaved people, and when he whipped the Bailey brothers, they decided to run away.[16] As a timber foreman who managed the harvesting and hauling of ship timber from Hughlett's land along the Choptank River, Joe Bailey was well connected to the black maritime and shipbuilding networks in that region. Bailey knew Ben Ross and knew of Harriet's forays into the neighborhood to help lead away her family and friends. Setting out from Jamaica Point in Talbot County on the Choptank River one evening, Joe "took a boat and went a long distance to the cabin of Harriet's father," at Poplar Neck in Caroline County. There he told Ben to let Tubman know he and his brother wanted to leave with her the next time she came through. Within a week or two Tubman had arrived, and because of her sister's inability to leave, she was ready to take another party of fugitives north.[17] Joe and Bill Bailey probably contacted Peter Pennington, who labored for Turpin Wright at Wright's farm at Secretary Creek, across the Choptank River from Hughlett. How Eliza Manokey came to join the party remains a mystery.[18]

Whatever the ease in coming together as a group, they faced serious obstacles in their escape north. They were hotly pursued. It took them nearly two weeks to reach Wilmington, a trip that had in the past taken Tubman only three or four days. The slave catchers' persistent tracking of the group forced them to proceed slowly and remain hidden for a longer period than Tubman was used to. They hid in potato holes while the slave catchers passed within feet of them. They sought shelter with Sam Green in East New Market and were "passed along by friends in various disguises," where they were "scattered and separated" and led "roundabout" to a variety of safe places while their pursuers relentlessly searched for them.[19]

William Hughlett, who had only recently purchased Joe Bailey, posted runaway advertisements throughout the Eastern Shore of Maryland, offering an extraordinary reward of $1,500 for the twenty-eight-year-old. Joe was a valuable slave, obviously a skilled timber man whose services were vitally important to Hughlett's operations. Hughlett had paid close to $2,000 for Joe, and to have him run away so quickly after buying him must have infuriated him. Still, a $1,500 reward seems excessive; Hughlett may have taken Bailey's escape as a personal affront and determined to get him back at all costs. Perhaps Hughlett wanted to send a message to the slave quarters. John Campbell Henry, who owned Joe's older brother, Bill Bailey, offered a more typical reward of $300 for his return, while Turpin Wright offered another high reward, $800, for the capture and return of thirty-year-old Peter Pennington.[20] Such high rewards increased substantially the danger of capture for the runaways.

Weaving their way northeast through Caroline County, perhaps following the Choptank River into Sand Town and Willow Grove in Delaware, the party of freedom seekers relied heavily on the secret network of safe houses belonging to blacks and whites. Near Camden, they probably sought shelter with Tubman's friends William Brinkley and his brother Nat, or Abraham Gibbs, where Tubman felt "safe and comfortable."[21] Gibbs and the Brinkleys, active black Underground Railroad operators in this region of Delaware, probably brought Tubman and the group farther north past Dover and Smyrna to Blackbird, where other Underground Railroad operators took charge of them and sent them over or around the Chesapeake and Delaware Canal to New Castle and other towns outside of Wilmington.[22]

When they finally reached the outskirts of Wilmington, they discovered that Hughlett, Wright, and Henry had arrived three days before, posting reward notices and hoping for news that the fugitives were near. Though the members of the black community followed these men around town and tore the reward notices down, the high reward offers had become common knowledge.[23] Police were patrolling all routes into the city, and there was no safe route to Thomas Garrett's house or store. So they were separated again, sent to wait at the homes of various black friends who sent word to Garrett that Harriet and the fugitives were seeking help to get across the Christiana River, probably by way of the Market Street Bridge. Garrett engaged the services of a couple of black bricklayers, who loaded their wagon with bricks and journeyed across the bridge in the morning, "singing and shouting," greeting the police and others watching the traffic. The bricklayers located Harriet, Joe, Bill, Peter, and Eliza, and loaded them into the wagon, concealing them in a compartment built into the wagon beneath a strategically placed mound of bricks. Back they proceeded, still "singing and shouting," passing undetected by the police and slave catchers waiting about the bridge.[24]

One day later, on November 26, the party arrived in Philadelphia at Still's office.[25] They were not safe, however, and it was imperative that they get to Canada as quickly as possible. On the twenty-seventh they traveled by train to Oliver Johnson's office in New York City, who then forwarded them by train to Albany and then Syracuse.[26] The Fugitive Aid Society in Syracuse, however, had run out of money, and was able to forward the group only as far as Rochester, not directly to the suspension bridge at Niagara Falls, as it customarily did. The treasurer of the Syracuse society, W. E. Abbott, sent them to various safe houses along the way instead.[27] Abbott wrote to Maria G. Porter, treasurer of the Rochester Ladies' Anti-Slavery Society, that this was Tubman's second trip through their office, indicating that she had managed to circumvent Syracuse's main Underground Railroad station for most of her earlier trips to Canada.[28]

Joe had been terrified for much of the trip. When he learned that runaway notices had been posted for their capture in New York, Joe "was ready to give up."[29] He grew silent, gripped with anxiety over the possibility of getting caught. As they approached the suspension bridge, which spanned the Niagara River separating New York and Ontario, Canada, Tubman called out to her friends to look at the great falls. But Joe was inconsolable and would not look. When they reached the Canadian side of the bridge, Tubman shouted out, "Joe, you're free!" Overcome with relief, Joe's shouts of joy and singing drew a crowd. Praising God for his good fortune, Joe told Tubman that the next trip he planned on taking would be to heaven. "You might have looked at the Falls first," Tubman replied, "and then gone to Heaven afterwards."[30]

The fugitives settled in Ontario; Joe and his brother stayed in the St. Catharines area, while Peter Pennington eventually made his way to Sarnia, in Lambton County on the west side of the province, near the Canadian border with Michigan.[31] What became of Eliza Manokey is not known. Joe became something of a celebrity; the fact that he was so highly valued a slave, that the reward was far greater than most, provided abolitionists on both sides of the border with more dramatic stories for the lecture circuit and the antislavery press. The Rev. Hiram Wilson, who was then operating a relief operation in St. Catharines to aid fugitive slaves, noted in his semiannual report to the Rev. Dr. Lathrop, secretary of the Society for the Propagation of the Gospel, that these men were brought north by "a remarkable colored heroine" in one "of the many instances of her deeds of daring." The men, he wrote, were "of fine appearance and noble bearing," and the woman was "unusually intelligent and fine appearing . . . They manifested great joy & appeared truly grateful when relieved and furnished from our stores."[32]

Tubman's reputation as Moses was taking shape. Her trips back and forth into slave territory inspired tremendous respect and awe from many people, white and black. To some people, that she was a woman made her raids even more remarkable. Small in stature, neatly but often poorly dressed, with an understated modesty about her accomplishments, she seemed no different from anyone else. But she was different. Her head injury continued to plague her; headaches and lethargy often came upon her with no notice, and during her rescues she would occasionally drop off to sleep, jeopardizing the safety of her parties of runaways. But she never "lost a passenger," and her friends and family marveled at her ability to run the "gauntlet of the most difficult parts of the Southern country."[33] William Wells Brown, a prominent black author and former runaway slave himself, went to Canada in 1860 and interviewed some of Tubman's friends and family members who had fled north with her during the 1850s. They told him that Tubman had the "charm." The "whites can't catch Moses," they told Brown, "cause you see she's born with the charm. The Lord has given Moses the power."[34] Tubman also believed she had the "charm"—her devout faith in God's design and power through her gave her the strength and courage to carry on when all seemed lost.

After securing food and lodging for the Bailey brothers, Pennington, and Manokey, Tubman was supposed to return immediately to the Eastern Shore to try to bring away Rachel and her children, Ben and Angerine, over the Christmas holiday. Apparently Tubman did not make it back, for in March 1857 Thomas Garrett wrote to William Still that he had not seen her since the previous fall, when she had come through his office with Joe Bailey. "It would be a sorrowful act," he wrote, "if such a hero as she, should be lost from the Underground Railroad."[35] He expressed his concern again in a letter two days later to Mary Edmondson, Eliza Wigham's sister, telling her, "I fear something has happened to her."[36]

Tubman's need for money to complete her missions remained a constant problem throughout the 1850s, and the continual lack of funds probably prevented her from returning to the Eastern Shore as she had hoped to on several occasions. She was also frustrated with abolitionists who could not or would not provide her with funds as she needed them. The Rev. Jermain Loguen, a leading abolitionist and Underground Railroad operator in Syracuse, refused to provide Tubman with money when she desperately needed it to retrieve a group of slaves, possibly her sister and children. She was thus forced to travel about the city, searching for odd jobs to raise the necessary funds.[37] On another occasion she planted herself in the offices of the New York City Anti-Slavery Office, refusing to leave until she had been given enough money to return to the Eastern Shore to bring her aged parents away. When Oliver Johnson could not give her the $20 she demanded, she promptly sat down and waited. Dozing off and on all day, Tubman was surprised and pleased to find she had collected $60 for her rescue mission from visitors to the office while she slept.[38] With money in her pocket, Tubman made her way to Still's office in Philadelphia. Still immediately wrote to Garrett, informing him that Tubman had just arrived and that she was preparing for another trip south "this week."[39]

Garrett was worried about Tubman's safety, more so than he had been in the past. Earlier in the month, on March 8, eight slaves from Dorchester County had escaped, but they were trapped in Dover, Delaware. Henry Predeaux, Thomas Elliott, Denard Hughes, James and Lavinia Woolfley, Bill and Emily Kiah, and an unidentified eighth man had followed a route given them by Tubman.[40] She advised them to contact a black man, Thomas Otwell, then living outside of Dover, Delaware, who could guide them to the next stops on the Underground Railroad north to Wilmington.[41] Otwell, who knew the Underground Railroad network in the Camden and Dover region, was also familiar with William Brinkley and his brother Nathaniel, who were active agents in the area. Otwell was a highly trusted agent; William Brinkley told Still that Otwell had "come with Harriet, a woman that stops at my house when she passes to and through you."[42]

Otwell, however, "decoyed and betrayed" this group of eight runaways into the Dover jail. Revealing his role as an Underground Railroad operator to a local white man, James Hollis, Otwell conspired to trap the group coming through and claim the reward money, estimated at nearly $3,000.[43] Otwell and Hollis approached Dover's Sheriff Green and informed him of the plan to lead the unsuspecting runaways to the jail, where they were to be held, ostensibly, for protection for the night. On the evening of March 9 or 10, Elliott, Predeaux, Hughes, and their fellow fugitives, armed with knives and pistols, met up with Otwell, who for the sum of $8 was to guide them from Milford, Delaware, north to past Dover, a total of thirty miles. By four o'clock in the morning they were near Dover, and Otwell took them to the jail and introduced them to Hollis, who, they were assured, was a "great friend of the slaves."[44] Hollis brought the cold and tired fugitives to the second-floor jail cells, where, he assured them, they "would soon have a good warming."[45] The moonlight shone through the barred windows, and Henry Predeaux became suspicious, commenting that he "did not like the looks of the place."[46] Sheriff Green followed them to the second floor with the intention of locking the runaways into the jail cells. Unsettled by Predeaux's suspicions, however, the group refused to leave the hallway, so Green ran downstairs for his pistols. Startled by Green's hasty departure, the runaways followed him to his private quarters, waking Green's wife and children. As the sheriff reached for his pistols, Predeaux grabbed "a shovel full" of embers from the fireplace, scattering burning coals throughout the room and onto the beds.[47] With a red-hot poker he smashed the window and kept the sheriff back while the rest jumped out the window, dropping "twelve feet to the soft mud" below.[48] They scaled the wall surrounding the jail and disappeared into the night. Predeaux, the last to make it out of the jail, "lost sight of his comrades," and, as fortune would have it, was spared when the sheriff's pistol jammed as he tried to shoot him.[49]

The group scattered. Predeaux made his way to Garrett's house, while six of the others backtracked, "not knowing which way to run."[50] They made their way back to Camden and within a short time overtook Otwell. Pleading for his life, Otwell promised he would take them to the next Underground Railroad station at William Brinkley's, where he was originally supposed to have taken them. Once there, Otwell disappeared, and Brinkley took charge of them. The sheriff and a posse of slave catchers were on the lookout for the party but could not obtain a warrant to enter the home where the fugitives were suspected of hiding. Somehow the six were taken on to "Willow Grove, whence they were forwarded by the forest roads."[51] Brinkley traveled as quickly as possible through Dover and Smyrna, "the two worst places this side of the Maryland line," taking the runaways nineteen miles to the next station, a round-trip of thirty-eight miles. It was "too much for our little horses," he wrote Still.[52]

Thomas Garrett was waiting in Wilmington, worrying that they would all be captured. The owners of three of the men were in town, looking and waiting for their arrival. Garrett sent word to the fugitives that they must keep from "crossing the bridges."[53] Thomas Elliott and Denard Hughes may have been trying to get to the residence of Moses

Pinket, Elliott's uncle who lived in Wilmington.[54] Garrett watched the roads himself for several nights, eventually finding them near Wilmington and bringing them safely to his home.[55] Four more were met outside of the city by two men commissioned by Garrett, who were directed to take them across the Christiana River to another stop on the Underground Railroad, ten miles from Wilmington.[56] Eventually five of the eight made it to William Still's office, including James Woolfley, who became separated from his wife, Lavinia, and they were directed on to Canada and freedom. William and Emily Kiah, however, remained either in Delaware, Maryland, or Pennsylvania. They may have been waiting to bring away their daughter Mary, whom they apparently had had to leave behind.[57] Though separated from the group, Lavinia Woolfley did elude capture. Hiding out for several months, she successfully made it to Philadelphia, where she learned from William Still that her husband was waiting for her in Canada.[58] The identity of the eighth runaway remains unknown, though he or she apparently found a way to Canada with the rest. What became of Otwell is not known. He apparently did not divulge the names of some of his contacts on the Underground Railroad in the Dover area.

Garrett noted in his letter to Mary Edmondson in late March that this group of self-liberators, who came to be known as the Dover Eight, had come "from the immediate neighborhood" of Harriet's "old Master."[59] Pritchett Meredith, a wealthy and prominent farmer in Bucktown, enslaved Thomas Elliott and Denard Hughes.[60] Meredith, Hughes later told Still, was "the hardest man around," and his mistress, at eighty-three years of age, "drank hard" and was "very stormy."[61] Elliott and Hughes knew Harriet and her family, and William and Emily Kiah probably did, too. Benjamin G. Tubman owned William Kiah, and Emily belonged to Ann Craig's family of Vienna.[62] Ara Spence, a prominent jurist who sat on Dorchester County's district court, owned Henry Predeaux, who was twenty-seven years old and a "giant." Predeaux may have been hired out to the Bucktown area, possibly to Pritchett Meredith, though Predeaux believed that Spence was considering selling him "south."[63]

The news of the successful escape from the Dover jail spread

through newspapers from Wilmington to Chatham, Ontario. Abolitionists and Underground Railroad agents made the group's dash to
freedom a rallying cry. This infuriated Eastern Shore slaveholders. On
April 14, 1857, a group of prominent Dorchester County slaveowners
convened a hasty meeting to "devise means for a better protection of
the [sic] slave property." While the slaveholders were publicly decrying
the loss of their slaves, police and white vigilante groups were determined to find the people who were responsible for "exciting slaves to
escape."[64] The weather was exceedingly cold that April, destroying
thousands of bushels of fruit, with major storms pelting freezing rain
and hail, wreaking havoc on all the major crops on the Eastern Shore.[65]
Farmers watched helplessly as nature destroyed their livelihood, and
their frustration was compounded by the insecurity of the human capital in which they were so invested. They could not control the weather,
but they believed they had to find a way to control black people.

By mid-March rumors were circulating that the Rev. Samuel Green,
Tubman's confidant, friend, and possible relative, had played a role in
the escape of the Dover Eight and presumably many other escapes. He
had apparently been suspected before this, but he was so highly regarded in both the black and white communities that he was able to deflect suspicions for some time. When it was discovered, however, that
the Dover Eight "had passed in their flight immediately by his house,
which stands near the road leading from Cambridge to the State of
Delaware," suspicions were aroused once again. On April 4, Sheriff
Robert Bell arrived at Green's house with a search warrant.[66] Green was
promptly arrested when they found a Canadian map, letters from other
Dorchester County runaways living in Ontario, "six or eight schedules
of a rail-road route through New Jersey," a letter from Green's son,
Samuel Green Jr., who had fled from his owner, Dr. James Muse, some
three years before, and a copy of Harriet Beecher Stowe's *Uncle Tom's
Cabin.*[67]

Once settled in Ontario, Sam junior wrote to his parents, telling
them news of his successful journey to freedom, which included
"plenty of friends, plenty to eat, and to drink." He told his father to tell
Peter Jackson and Joe Bailey to "come on[e], come more."[68] The letter,

written September 10, 1854, preceded the escape of Peter Jackson, who fled north with Harriet Tubman and her brothers over the Christmas holiday in 1854, a few short months after Sam himself had fled. Joe Bailey ran away two years later, in late November 1856. Adding to local whites' suspicions, Green had recently returned from a trip to Canada to visit his refugee son. The slaveholders felt sure, then, that Green had been involved in these and other escapes as well. Green was charged with illegal possession of material that could rouse feelings of "discontent" and dissatisfaction among the slaves. He was in violation of the Act of 1841, Chapter 272, which stated that if any free black "knowingly receive or have in his possession any abolition handbill, pamphlet, newspaper, pictorial representation or other paper of an inflammatory character," which could "create discontent amongst or to stir up to insurrection the people of color of this State, he or she shall be deemed guilt of felony," subject to a prison term of ten to twenty years.[69]

Prosecutors tried to claim that the maps, railroad schedules, and letters from Green's son describing life in Canada were designed to create discontent among the slaves. The court acquitted Green, though, ruling that those materials in and of themselves were not incendiary publications. New charges were lodged against him, citing his possession of Uncle Tom's Cabin, and this time he was convicted.[70] Though local newspapers acknowledged that Green never would have been charged with this "crime" if he had not been under suspicion for aiding slaves to run away, they congratulated themselves for "testing the applicability of the Act" to Uncle Tom's Cabin.[71]

> The result is a practical commentary upon the insane efforts of abolition writers. Where can an instance be found of real benefit having accrued to any slave by reason of the production of Mrs. Stowe's book! Until he was wrought upon by such publications, and by the more direct appeals of abolition emissaries, Green had lived quietly and contentedly in the community in which he was born and had the respect and confidence of all who knew him . . . There is no doubt of the fact that Green was instrumental, and had been for a long time, in the escape of slaves from this county.[72]

Fifty-five years old, the Rev. Sam Green represented what some slaveholders suspected and feared the most: a literate, well-respected free black who could move about and freely converse with whom he pleased and whose conversations may well have encouraged resistance to the slave system. Green was sentenced to ten years in the Maryland State Penitentiary, officially for "having in his possession a certain abolition pamphlet called Uncle Tom's Cabin."[73]

As Tubman started to make her way south from Philadelphia the first week of April 1857, she was probably aware of the tensions rising on the Eastern Shore and may have been well aware of the rumors and ultimate arrest of the Rev. Sam Green. In Caroline County, Ben Ross had come under suspicion of aiding slaves in their attempts to escape, and he was suspected of being involved in the flight of the Dover Eight. Indeed, Ben had sheltered "in his hut" the eight runaways from Dorchester County at the beginning of March.[74] Garrett thought that the original party of slaves was in fact nine but that they had been "betrayed by one who started with the rest," who had turned back and informed on the person who piloted them to Ben's house the first day of their escape.[75]

Ben and Rit were more than likely aware of their precarious situation. The authorities were preparing to arrest Ben "when his master secretly advised them to leave."[76] Dr. Anthony C. Thompson, whom Ben would later criticize for his emotional cruelty, may have suggested to Ben that he leave the state immediately. However, it took Tubman some time to safely make her way down to the Eastern Shore; the increased vigilance of slave patrols, the loss of key Underground Railroad operatives she was dependent upon, and the unseasonably cold and stormy weather slowed her progress, making the journey more hazardous than ever. By the end of May, with the weather more predictable and warm, Harriet was ready to take her parents north.

Ben and Rit were both in their seventies, and the prospect of journeying to Canada must have seemed daunting to them. Rit was not eager to go without her meager belongings, particularly her "featherbed-tick," and Ben wanted to bring along his prized broad-axe.[77] Tubman took an "old horse, fitted out in primitive style with a straw collar, a pair of old chaise wheels, with a board on the axle to sit on, another board swung with ropes, fastened to the axle, to rest their feet on."[78] Fleeing in the face of great danger, Tubman led her parents north to Wilmington. On June 4 Tubman arrived at Garrett's house, where he provided them with $30 and sent them along to William Still's in Philadelphia. Though Ben and Rit were essentially free people, Still treated them as newly liberated slaves. There, finally on free soil, Ben and Rit told Still of their deep sorrow over having a "portion of their children . . . sold to Georgia." Dr. Thompson, Ben reported, was a "rough man towards his slaves," and they had been "stinted for food and clothing." He also complained that Thompson "had not given him a dollar since the death of his [Dr. Thompson's] father, which had been at least twenty years prior to Benjamin's escape."[79] Oddly, Still neglected to note that Ben and Rit were Tubman's parents.

Ben, Rit, and Tubman most likely went on to New York City, where Oliver Johnson and Jacob Gibbs would have tended to their needs. When they reached Rochester, Ben and Rit stayed with Maria G. Porter, the secretary of the Rochester Ladies' Anti-Slavery Society and a close associate of Frederick Douglass's, for two weeks before moving on to St. Catharines, where Ben and Rit's sons, William Henry and John Stewart, and several grandchildren and great-grandchildren were living.[80]

Tubman did not stay with her parents in Canada; in fact, she may have left them with the Porters, knowing they would be safe and well cared for until one of her brothers could come for them from St. Catharines. Instead, Tubman returned to the Eastern Shore that summer to try again to retrieve her sister Rachel and her children. Rachel, who was separated from her children by some twelve miles, was probably hired out to another master somewhere in Dorchester County. By this time Angerine was ten years old and Ben was eight, both old enough to be helpful and productive around the Brodess farm. But Tubman was again unsuccessful, and it appears that while she remained on the Eastern Shore for some time during that summer and fall, she did not bring away another party of slaves.

She did, however, help a large group of thirty-nine slaves make their own plans to run away together that fall.[81] During a three-week period in October 1857, more than forty slaves ran away from masters in Dorchester County. Though a few runaways had taken flight during September, it was not until the early part of October that a wave of escapes threatened the stability white slave owners imagined they had created after the high-profile imprisonment of Green and other Underground Railroad operatives in the area. Caroline Stanley, her husband, Daniel, and their six children fled Dorchester County in early October with Nat and Lizzie Amby and several other adults in a group of about fifteen runaways. They passed through Norristown, Pennsylvania, on the eighteenth and were forwarded to Still in Philadelphia by John Augusta.[82] With masters and slave catchers already on the lookout, another group, nearly twice as large, fled from their enslavers, heightening anxiety in an already tense community.[83]

On the evening of Saturday, October 24, twenty-eight men, women, and children sneaked away from the homes and slave quarters of their enslavers, Samuel Pattison, Jane Cator, Richard Keene, Willis Brannock, Reuben E. Phillips, and the Rev. Levi D. Travers.[84] Pattison, in fact, started his day with the shocking discovery that nearly all his slaves, fifteen in number, had "absconded" the night before, leaving him with no labor to operate his farm or, indeed, to cook his morning breakfast.

How such a large number of runaways successfully eluded capture remains a mystery. For two substantial groups of slaves to successfully escape from the same county in less than two weeks was an extraordinary achievement in itself. But that these two large groups of self-liberators also brought away twenty children, several of whom were infants, makes their escapes all the more remarkable. Aaron Cornish and his wife, Daffney, brought away six of their eight surviving children, including a two-week-old infant. The Rev. Levi D. Travers owned Aaron, but Daffney and six of her children were owned by Jane Cator and her stepfather, Reuben Elliot Phillips. Two more of the Cornishes' children had to be left behind; as young teenagers, they had been hired out to another master, making it difficult for Aaron or Daffney to retrieve them the night the rest of the family ran away.[85]

Among the fifteen who absconded from Samuel Pattison that rainy night were two complete families. Susan Viney and her husband, Joe (who was owned by a Virginia planter but hired out in Dorchester County), effectively brought away their four young children, Lloyd, Frank, Albert(a), and nine-month-old J.W., in addition to Joe's three older sons, Henry, Joe, and Tom. Kit and Leah Anthony brought with them their three small children, Adam, Mary, and one-year-old Murray. Another slave, Joseph Hill, also owned by Pattison, was able to get away, bringing his free wife and son, Alice and Henry. The fifteenth slave Pattison lost that evening was Joseph Hill's sister, twenty-five-year-old Sarah Jane, who may have been hired off the Pattison plantation at the time she ran away with the rest; it was not until a few days after the escape that Pattison realized that she, too, was gone.[86]

It rained heavily over the three days these self-liberators traveled the route to northern Delaware and then to Pennsylvania. Several adult male slaves joined the group: Solomon and George Light, Marshall Dutton, and Silas Long increased the number of freedom seekers to an astonishing twenty-eight runaways (excluding free Alice and son Henry).[87] They were heavily armed, carrying pistols, revolvers, knives, and one paw, a three-pronged weapon for "close combat."[88] The weapons indicated they were not going to be captured without a fight. The escaping slaves found their way to Tubman's friend William Brinkley, who, with his associates, brought the group from the Camden area to the outskirts of Wilmington. But they had been warned ahead of time to stay clear of the city. The news of the great escape had reached Wilmington, and Samuel Pattison, having learned that the fugitives were expected in the city, was following them and closing in quickly. In an all-out effort to outrun Pattison and other slave catchers, Brinkley's carriage, "owing to fast driving with such a heavy load," broke down and his horse was severely injured.[89] The fugitives were sick and hungry. Traveling in the cold rain for days, some of them barefoot, took a great toll on the children in particular. They were not able to rest or recuperate for long, however.

On the thirty-first Thomas Garrett wrote Still, informing him that he had received word that twenty-seven of the runaways were outside the city, in Centreville, near the border on the road to Kennett Square, Pennsylvania. Part of the group, eighteen men, women, and children under the care of a black conductor named Jackson from Wilmington, had an altercation with "several Irishmen" who attacked the runaways with clubs. Garrett was not sure whether the Irishmen were "on the lookout" for the fugitives or whether they were just "rowdies out on a

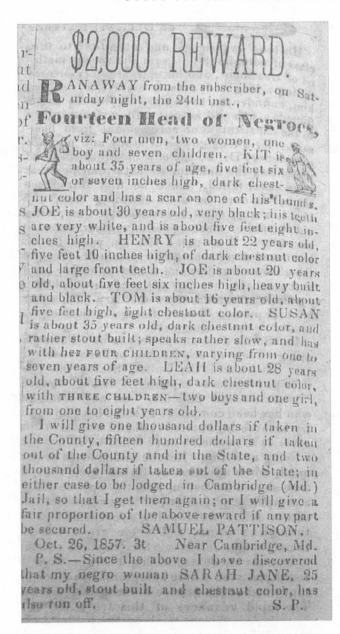

*Samuel Pattison's advertisement for the return of the fifteen
enslaved people who ran from his plantation in October 1857.*

Hallow-eve frolic."[90] One of the runaways had used his revolver, shooting one of the Irishmen in the forehead. The man survived, but
the shooting increased the tension in an already stressful situation. A

fourteen-year-old boy, probably one of the Cornish children, had been separated from the rest. He was barefoot, and there was great anxiety that he would be caught and perhaps inform on the rest.[91] The runaways had to be sent along as quickly as possible.

The fugitives were separated and sent to different Underground Railroad operators outside Philadelphia, as the city itself was not safe for them. Some of the eighteen were secreted at John and Hannah Cox's home at Longwood in Chester County, Pennsylvania.[92] Joe and Susan Viney and their children were sent to Georgiana Lewis and Elijah Pennypacker outside of Philadelphia; Joe's older sons were sent on ahead while Susan, Joe, and the younger children followed later.[93] Traveling through a blinding snowstorm in late November, the weary and frightened runaways were greeted by some of the worst weather to hit the northeast and central New York in years.[94] The Vineys, the Stanleys, the Cornishes, and many of the others eventually made it to St. Catharines, Ontario, where they joined a growing number of their friends and neighbors from the Eastern Shore of Maryland.

On the Eastern Shore, in the meantime, a torrent of accusations and counteraccusations were unleashed. Slaveholders and nonslaveholders were struggling to make sense of a world crumbling around them. On November 2, leading citizens and prominent slaveholders convened another slaveholders' meeting in Cambridge to "take into consideration the better protection of the interests of the slave owners."[95] Imagining a northern conspiracy infiltrating their community with "abolition emissaries," James A. Stewart and his fellow slaveholders passed resolutions calling for tighter restrictions on black people, but they struggled in vain to stifle the national media frenzy.[96] Their anger focused on the free black community, by whom they felt "greatly annoyed and injured" and who, they believed, were "agents of the 'negro worshipers' of the North."[97]

One of the more prominent slaveholders calling for immediate action was James A. Stewart. Stewart had been elected as a Democratic representative from Maryland in 1855. His fiery proslavery speeches on the floor of Congress marked him as a man with greater, and promising, national ambitions. The "negroe," he argued, "is in his happy element on a sugar or cotton plantation, and in this condition will laugh to scorn the mistaken views of the Abolitionists to benefit him by placing him on a different theater." Stewart scoffed at the vociferous criticism hurled at him from antislavery and moderate members of Congress.[98] He was comfortable in his role as representative of a strong coalition of powerful and conservative southern states-rights Democrats. And he appeared to be gaining the upper hand over his opponents, at least rhetorically, while briefly enjoying a national reputation. Stewart had "measured lances with, and vanquished, the most powerful champions of abolition" in Congress, the editor of the *Easton Star* boasted in the fall of 1857. The newspaperman assured his readers that Stewart's "sound national views" on slavery kept the "institutions of the South secure."[99]

Little did Stewart and the rest realize, however, that Harriet Tubman, the disabled slave they had known a few years before, had become part of the vehicle that set in motion a sequence of events culminating in their national humiliation. Despite a harsh crackdown on the personal liberties of free and enslaved blacks, and even nonslaveholding whites, slaves in Dorchester County continued to run away in unprecedented numbers. Soon national newspapers were running articles mocking Eastern Shore slave owners, reporting that the "stampedes of slaves" from the area certainly did not support Stewart's view of their happiness.[100]

The growing national attention served to mobilize increased vigilance on the part of slaveholders on the Eastern Shore, making it impossible for Tubman to get her sister and her sister's children. She eventually gave up and returned to Canada. Staying on the Eastern Shore was far too precarious now; the increased activity of slave patrols and the diligence of slaveholders created a climate of oppression and fear. Tubman could not be sheltered safely anymore.

Without Tubman's help, and in spite of active patrolling by whites, slaves continued to run away throughout December 1857 from many parts of the Eastern Shore and southern Delaware. Unfortunately, a group of seven runaways from Cambridge were caught in Caroline County as they were trying to make their escape in early January 1858.[101] Hannah Leverton's son, Arthur Leverton, and his free black neighbor, Daniel Hubbard, were immediately suspected. With tempers already at the breaking point, a white mob formed to forcibly carry the men to Cambridge with the intention of lynching them, but Arthur and Daniel received word of the mob's plans beforehand and made a run for Philadelphia.[102]

Up and down the Eastern Shore, vigilante groups were meting out their own form of justice on those who they believed harbored and aided runaway slaves. In June 1858 James Bowers was dragged by a "party of ruffians" (in fact local farmers and prominent members of the community) from his home outside of Chestertown in Kent County, Maryland, where he was beaten, stripped, tarred and feathered, and threatened with hanging if he did not leave the county immediately. The noose around his neck and the preponderance of guns and knives held by his abductors convinced him to flee for Philadelphia, leaving his nine-month-pregnant wife behind.[103] That same evening the mob committed the same "outrage" on a free black woman named Harriet Tillison, who was described as "dwarfish in appearance, scarcely weighing fifty pounds," and whose visits to the area supposedly preceded the escape of a number of slaves.[104] Tillison was not as lucky as Bowers; after being tarred and feathered she was arrested and thrown in jail on charges of "preaching and circulating pamphlets of an incendiary character."[105]

In August 1858 another group of runaways from Dorchester County made an effort to break for freedom, but they were apparently betrayed by a free black, Jesse Perry, who in collusion with a group of white men set an ambush for them seven miles north of Greensborough in Caroline County.[106] Their white conductor, Hugh Hazlett, was arrested and thrown into jail. When the steamer was transferring the eight fugitives, including Hazlett, to Cambridge, a large crowd gathered at the wharf. The sheriff, fearful of a lynching, directed the steamer to disembark the fugitives at another location, thereby avoiding the angry and potentially murderous mob.[107]

More slaveholders' conventions were convened and planned in various communities throughout the Eastern Shore. Though the *Easton Star* condemned lynching, the editor argued that, given the diversity of opinion on the methods that might be used to stop the flood of runaways, a public slaveholders' convention was not in the best interests of the Eastern Shore. He recommended that each slaveholder and each community "keep strict watch over their respective neighborhoods" and avoid "constant discussion through the public journals," which proved to be "injurious to the institution of Slavery on this Shore." Furthermore, he emphasized the importance of saying "nothing more about it through [the press] and let an entirely private means be adopted to detect these aiders and abetters." The newspaper decided to put the best face forward for the national media. Its editor continued to argue that slaves absconding from their masters was a "thing of rare occurrence," as slaves on the Eastern Shore "met with more humane treatment" there than anywhere else, and that there "existed between master and slave that feeling of mutual confidence." This had lasted until northern abolitionists and their "emissaries" had challenged the peace and serenity of their community.[108]

The timing could not have been worse for Sam Green. One hundred and fourteen ministers of the Black River Conference of the Methodist Church forwarded a petition to Governor Thomas H. Hicks, formerly of Dorchester County, asking for the release of the Rev. Sam Green.[109] If Hicks had been inclined to pardon Green, and there is no indication he was, the growing firestorm whipping up on the Eastern Shore made such a move politically impossible for him. With slaveholders looking around every corner for "northern fanatics" spreading "the evil influence of abolitionism," Hicks could not have released Green without a tremendous outcry from his own community and constituents.[110] For Eastern Shore whites, the drama of a "stampede of slaves" out of Dorchester County, as local and national newspapers were wont to describe it during the 1850s, was surpassed only by the Civil War itself.[111]

During the uproar in Maryland, Tubman became more involved in the relief activities in St. Catharines, aiding newly arrived fugitives and helping them settle into free lives there.[112] She was now well known as Moses among the refugee community. She was often asked to help bring away family and friends of other runaways, but she could no longer make plans for such missions. She channeled her energies into building and strengthening her network of black and white friends and supporters throughout central New York and New England. Living on North Street in a home once occupied by her brother William Henry and his family, and across the street from the newly built British Methodist Episcopal Church, Salem Chapel, in St. Catharines, Tubman became more active in the social, spiritual, and benevolent life of the community.[113]

Though Ben and Rit were reunited with their sons, friends, and other family members, the journey north took a great toll on them. They suffered terribly that first winter (1857–58), and Rit complained to Harriet so much that Tubman's patience was "a lesson of trust in Providence better than many sermons."[114] The cold winter weather, the loss of longtime friends and family, and the unfamiliar landscape weighed heavily upon Rit.

Discouraged by her inability to return safely to the Eastern Shore, and financially and physically burdened with supporting her aged parents, Tubman channeled her frustrations into a more public and activist role in northern abolitionist circles. Already the subject of great admiration from those who knew her, and the object of even greater speculation and awe on the part of those who did not, Tubman's courageous exploits garnered close attention from one of the most serious, and ultimately one of the most hated and celebrated abolitionists of all time: John Brown.

MOSES MEETS JOHN BROWN

OR THE THOUSANDS OF REFUGEES WHO FLED NORTH FOR A CHANCE at a free life, daily struggle did not end when they left the South. Liberty did not guarantee food, clothing, and housing. The daily work of survival continued and often required the communal efforts of family, friends, and supporters. The arrival in St. Catharines of over forty runaways from Dorchester County in the late fall of 1857, for example, required a tremendous relief effort on the part of the refugee community. Scrambling to provide shelter, clothing, fuel, and food to the weary and weak families taxed an already poor community. Southern blacks often came ill-prepared for the long, cold winters. Many suffered from respiratory illnesses when they first arrived; inadequate food, clothing, and housing exacerbated the problems. William Cornish, for example, who arrived in the fall of 1856, fell ill for several months. After his wife, Delia, followed him to Canada in December 1856, she also became very sick; William, already weak himself, spent "three weeks . . . just [turning] her over in bed." By 1863, three of their six children were dead.[1]

Depending upon the season and the connections fugitive slaves could make upon arrival, work options varied dramatically. Agricultural

work throughout Canada West attracted thousands of former plantation slaves. But the shorter growing season made for difficult times
through the long winters. High rents, low agricultural prices, and the
tactics of some unscrupulous Canadians made independence difficult
for some runaways to achieve. Several planned and segregated communities were founded throughout Canada West, supported by organizations such as the American Missionary Association, to help former
slaves rebuild their lives and develop economic and agricultural resources. In these all-black cooperative settlements, land was sold to
former slaves, who timbered and then cultivated it, creating small functioning communities. Though some of these communities and land co-
operatives remained dependent upon charitable contributions, their
efforts did help some refugees build new lives in freedom.[2]

To carry out her own charitable relief activities, Tubman turned to
the Rochester Ladies' Anti-Slavery Society, among other organizations,
for support. In their 1857–58 annual report, the Rochester society highlighted Tubman's past history of rescuing "about fifty persons," providing a fresh new face of slavery for the thirsty antislavery readers and
donors anxious for personal stories to justify their monetary support.[3]
The society conducted antislavery fairs and collected clothing and food
to pass along to Canada, helping to ease Tubman's and the other fugitives' burdens.

Newly arrived former slaves also struggled with discrimination, prejudice, and racism. Many cities and towns refused to educate young black
children, for instance, in integrated classrooms, forcing black communities to establish, staff, and fund private segregated schools. In some
ways, the situation in Canada was little different from that in the
northern states. In Canada, however, blacks enjoyed political liberties
not often shared by African Americans in the northern United States.
Under Canadian law, blacks were guaranteed the same rights as whites;
they could vote, serve as jurors, testify in court, own property, and run
for political office. Racism and discrimination tempered the enjoyment
of those rights, but for many former slaves who had fled from the
South, a life of freedom and relative independence in Canada far outweighed the myriad of prejudices and indignities they faced in the
North.[4]

On the whole, many freedom seekers eventually found work and stability once they arrived in Canada. In St. Catharines, runaways from Dorchester County found ready employment as day laborers, servants, coachmen, farmers, cooks, waiters, blacksmiths, painters, and barbers, and at least one, Joseph Cornish, became a full-time minister. There they re-created the familial and social relationships and networks they had established in Dorchester County. St. Catharines assessment records, rent rolls, and census records reveal a tightly knit community of Eastern Shore runaways living within a several-block radius of North Street, where Tubman's brothers John and William Henry Stewart and her parents settled for a time during the mid- to late 1850s. Several refugee families also wound up in Grantham, on the outskirts of St. Catharines; William Henry Stewart and his family settled on six acres of land there in 1861, near the Stanleys, the Anthonys, Thomas Elliott, and his brother Abraham, among others.[5]

Some of the Eastern Shore's runaways also settled in Auburn, New York, and probably other central New York communities as well. Nat Amby and his wife, Lizzie, settled in Auburn after they had successfully eluded pursuit with the other twenty-six runaways who had fled Dorchester County in October 1857. Nat Amby, writing from Auburn in August 1858, told William Still that he and Lizzy were doing well but that he was eager to communicate with family left behind in Maryland. Living in a small black settlement known as New Guinea, on the east side of Auburn running along the Owasco River, Nat and Lizzie found support and shelter with P. R. Freeman, a descendant of one of the very first black families to settle in Auburn.[6] Some of the runaways who fled the Eastern Shore during the late fall of 1857 had apparently been directed through Auburn on their way to Rochester and Canada by way of Albany and Syracuse. These Dorchester County fugitives may have settled in Auburn because of Tubman's relationships with Auburn abolitionists Martha Coffin Wright and her husband David's law partner William H. Seward. Tubman more than likely became close to Martha Coffin Wright through Wright's sister, Lucretia Coffin Mott, of Philadelphia, a longtime Tubman friend and supporter. Tubman's knowledge of and use of central New York's Underground Railroad network also would have led her to Auburn and the black and white families who sheltered and aided freedom seekers running through the Finger Lakes region. Though this was not a main branch of the Underground, an estimated five hundred fugitives passed through the area during the thirty years prior to the Civil War.[7]

Tubman's network of black and white abolitionists brought her into contact with the legendary John Brown, a zealous and militant freedom fighter and antislavery activist destined to martyrdom in a failed attack on Harpers Ferry, Virginia, in 1859. In early January 1858 Tubman spent a few days with Frederick Douglass and his wife, Anna Murray, at their home in Rochester. Tubman had "been spending a short time with us since the holidays," Douglass wrote the Irish Ladies' Anti-Slavery Association. Hoping to solicit more funds to help with the Underground Railroad operations in Rochester, Douglass told them Tubman "escaped from Slavery some eight years ago, has made several returns at great risk, and has brought out, since obtaining her freedom, fifty others from the house of bondage."[8]

Douglass may have been the initial connection between Tubman and John Brown. Perhaps he suggested Tubman as a possible recruiter and practical guide who could help Brown in his scheme to lead an insurrection in the South and establish a new free state for liberated slaves in the mountains of Virginia and western Maryland. Perhaps the one white person Tubman most admired was John Brown. During the winter and spring of 1858 Brown was advised by the prominent abolitionists and Underground Railroad operators Frederick Douglass, Gerrit Smith, and Jermain W. Loguen to travel to St. Catharines, where Tubman was then living with other fugitive slaves. Brown had heard a great deal about the extraordinary woman who had made several successful rescue missions to the Eastern Shore. He hoped that her expert knowledge of the communication and transport lines on the Underground Railroad might be used to his advantage during his planned assault on Harpers Ferry to liberate slaves and strike a fatal blow to slavery.

Brown visited with Douglass at the end of January, after Tubman had left, spending a week discussing his plans and then writing a draft constitution for a provisional government for his visionary state for newly freed slaves. From Rochester, Brown moved on to Gerrit Smith's house in Peterboro, where he stayed a few days to try to convince Smith of the viability of his plan for an armed attack in Virginia. Smith was one of Brown's Secret Six, a group of supporters (mostly from the Boston area) who knew of Brown's secret plans for an armed raid and who provided funds and connections for Brown. Though Frederick Douglass was not one of the Secret Six, he was intimately involved in the plot; Brown had hoped to get Douglass's full support for his scheme, but Douglass ultimately believed that Brown's plans were doomed to fail.[9]

After staying with Smith for a short period in February, Brown headed to Boston with Franklin Sanborn, a writer, schoolmaster, and active abolitionist. Sanborn had come from his own home in Massachusetts to confer with Brown about his plans and to ready him for meetings with other prominent, well-connected, and wealthy abolitionists in the Boston area. Brown desperately needed funds for himself, his family, and his campaign. Staying at Sanborn's residence in Concord, Brown made the rounds of selected abolitionist homes, soliciting money and raising interest in his scheme to incite rebellion among the slaves in a border state. It was here in Boston that the decision to launch the attack on Harpers Ferry was finally made with the approval of Brown's secret support committee, though the timing and exact location remained secret, even from many of Brown's supporters.[10]

Through introductions made by Douglass, Smith, and the Rev. Jermain W. Loguen, Brown met with Tubman in early April 1858 to discuss recruiting former slaves, then living in Canada, to join the small band he would lead on his raid.[11] He believed her crucial knowledge of terrain in Maryland and Pennsylvania would be critical to conducting a successful attack.[12] Though Harpers Ferry was in unfamiliar territory for Tubman, her expertise in traversing the border, her uncanny ability to move about undetected, and her familiarity with clandestine black communication networks would be valuable to any operation Brown was planning.

"I am succeeding in all appearance, beyond my expectations," Brown wrote his son enthusiastically on the eighth.[13] He had met Tubman the day before in St. Catharines; referring to her as "General," Brown quickly recognized her great intelligence.[14] "*He* is the most of a *man*," Brown wrote, "that I ever met with."[15] Blurring the gender conventions of the time, Brown acknowledged Tubman's leadership abilities—a quality he would have considered masculine—from the beginning. The respect and admiration Tubman commanded in St. Catharines' fugitive community, her seemingly tireless and persistent battle to free her friends and family from enslavement on the Eastern Shore, her deep religious faith, and her obvious enthusiasm for Brown's scheme defined the type of "man" Brown was looking for to accompany him on his attack. To Brown, Tubman was a doer; acting on her convictions and risking her life like few others, she stood apart from most men Brown knew.

Tubman claimed that she had had a vision of Brown before she met him. "She laid great stress on a dream which she had just before she met Captain Brown in Canada":

> She thought she was in "a wilderness sort of place, all full of rocks and bushes," when she saw a serpent raise its head among the rocks, and as it did so, it became the head of an old man with a long white beard, gazing at her "wishful like, jes as ef he war gwine to speak to me," and then two other heads rose up beside him, younger than he,—and as she stood looking at them, and wondering what they could want with her, a great crowd of men rushed in and struck down the younger heads, and then the head of the old man, still looking at her so "wishful." This dream she had again and again, and could not interpret it; but, when she met Captain Brown, shortly after, behold, he was the very image of the head she had seen. But still she could not make out what her dream signified.[16]

Tubman's respect and admiration for Brown overshadowed any doubts harbored by her subconscious. He was unlike any white man she had met before, and their mutual admiration and respect both elevated Brown's stature among the fugitive community and likewise raised Tubman's own stature in white antislavery circles. Brown entrusted her with organizing a band of fugitive slaves willing to fight along with him, hoping that she, too, would be at his side when the attack came. Loguen had accompanied Brown to St. Catharines, and it was he who set up the meeting between the two on April 7. Brown was cautious; he did not want to arouse suspicions as to his reasons for being in St. Catharines. When Loguen requested that Tubman meet Brown at his hotel, she told Loguen "that the old man might visit her home, for nobody would hurt him there."[17] A small group of fugitives from Dorchester County assembled at Tubman's request at her house on North Street.[18] She told them of Brown's scheme to liberate slaves through armed revolution, striking a first, and unexpected, blow to southern slavery. Brown, with fiery blue eyes, wild gray hair, and a flowing beard, spoke to the small gathering, perhaps reading the draft constitution for the provisional government he envisioned for the hoped-for state for freed slaves. (That document had been drafted at Douglass's house a few short months before.) He spoke Tubman's language; with his claim that he had heard God's voice directing him to this revolutionary cause, Brown's evangelical fervor was not out of step with the worldview of many fugitive slaves. His vision, resounding in apocalyptic and judgment day metaphors, seemed to answer the prayers with which so many slaves had comforted themselves while enslaved. Brown told his audiences that it was time for "God's wrath to descend" and that he, and they, were God's instruments through which "swift justice" would be served to "unrepentant slaveholders."[19] Slavery was murder, he probably told them, and God had chosen him to lead an army into slave territory and incite rebellion among the slaves.[20] Coming from a white man, this must have seemed incredible to those former slaves gathered to listen to his plan; many had just arrived from bondage and were very suspicious of whites, "afraid of some trick" or lie.[21]

Brown's passionate plea had its intended effect. "Harriet Tubman hooked on *his* whole team at once," Brown wrote gleefully to his son, "there is the most abundant material, and of the right quality, in this quarter, beyond all doubt."[22] Thomas Elliott and Denard Hughes of the famous Dover Eight joined up, as did Peter Pennington, Joe Bailey, and his brother William, who had all come away with Tubman in November 1856. Charles Hall and John Thompson, friends of Tubman's in Canada, rounded out the group.[23] It is possible that Tubman's parents and her brothers John and William Henry were also there. William lived a few doors away on the corner of North and Geneva Streets, and John lived a few short blocks away. When Brown left Tubman that day he shook her hands and called her "General Tubman" three times, determining then that she "was a better officer than most" men he had known. He had no doubt she "could command an army as successfully as she had led her small parties of fugitives."[24]

Over the next few days Tubman continued to solicit support for Brown; on the twelfth Brown gave her $15 toward her rent and other expenses.[25] By the fifteenth, however, Brown was troubled by her conspicuous absence from St. Catharines; they had planned to meet at the train station, but she failed to arrive. Concerned that she might have fallen ill, Brown wrote to black publisher William H. Day inquiring as to her whereabouts.[26] "May I trouble you to see her at once," he wrote anxiously to Day, and "if she is well; by all means have her come on immediately." Brown knew she was in dire financial straits, but he also apparently knew that she was prone to ill health. "If she is unwell get her to send on Thomas Eliot," he told Day. Thomas Elliott had emerged as Tubman's right-hand man, and he was probably working to drum up interest among the St. Catharines fugitive community in Brown's insurrection plans. Waiting for her at the Daly House in Ingersol, where Brown was conducting another recruitment and planning meeting, he told Day, "I would not *on any account fail* of having her come if she is able to do so . . . but I am very anxious to have her come."[27] Tubman, it seems, had become a major player in Brown's plans.

Unbeknownst to Brown, however, Tubman had already left for Toronto on her way to Ingersol, perhaps in an apparent mix-up of plans or communication.[28] Day informed Brown that Denard Hughes, Peter Pennington, the Bailey brothers, Hall, and Thompson were all waiting for him at Thompson's rooming house, "Bachelor's Hall" at Ingersol.[29] Within a few days Brown left Canada and traveled to Iowa and Chicago, rounding up a small band of recruits he had left behind while he traveled throughout New England and Canada soliciting more money and aid. He returned with them to Canada, and by the first of May he was arranging a meeting of interested recruits at Chatham's Masonic Lodge. Brown was still looking for Tubman, but she was nowhere to be found. On May 6 Loguen wrote anxiously to Brown inquiring if Tubman was with him.[30]

On May 8 Brown convened his Chatham Convention, without Tubman or Frederick Douglass, or any member of his Secret Six supporters. He explained his vision for a slave insurrection and invasion at Harpers Ferry, Virginia, and laid out his plan to wage war against southern slaveholders. He believed that once the attack began, blacks throughout the North, Canada, and the South (both slave and free) would come rallying to the cause. He presented his newly printed Provisional Constitution for the new free state, and the convention delegates voted unanimously to approve the constitution.[31] None of Tubman's friends were among the constitution signers. Perhaps the constant shortage of money prevented them from attending the meeting. The Rev. Jermain Loguen had already expressed concern to Brown that some of the men lacked funds to travel to Chatham.[32]

Ultimately, Elliott, Hughes, the Bailey brothers, Pennington, Hall, and Thompson decided not to join Brown. They had already come to Canada at great sacrifice and risk; perhaps they felt they had battled slavery enough. Their new lives in freedom were precious now and outweighed any visionary dream of Brown's. They may have also sensed the folly in Brown's plans. But Tubman continued to support Brown by recruiting more fugitives for his cause, maintaining interest among her friends, and directly assisting in the military planning for the assault. Indeed, she remained a fixture in his plans until nearly the end.

While Brown was galvanizing his small army in Chatham, a disgruntled Brown associate, Hugh Forbes, leaked the plans to a few members of Congress. Desperately afraid of exposure, the Secret Six met in Boston at the end of May to discuss delaying the planned attack (except for Higginson, who disapproved of postponement). Under severe financial pressure, Brown agreed to delay his scheme, and with $500 in his pocket and with more promised to him by his supporters, he set out for Kansas until things quieted down.[33]

With the raid on hold indefinitely, Tubman turned her attention to her household and the pressing needs of her aging and fragile parents.[34] During the summer or fall of 1858 Tubman visited Boston, hoping to raise funds for herself and the St. Catharines fugitive community. It was then that she finally met Franklin B. Sanborn. Sanborn was not only a supporter and confidant of Brown and a member of Brown's Secret Six, but also a friend and admirer of some of New England's more famous, and controversial, Transcendentalists and literary giants.[35] He was also actively engaged with New England's abolitionist vanguard; he knew William Lloyd Garrison, Wendell Phillips, Samuel May, Lewis Hayden, William Wells Brown, William Cooper Nell, John S. Rock, and Brown's Secret Six, Sanborn, Higginson, Howe, Parker, Stearns, and Gerrit Smith of New York. Sanborn thought Tubman to be "the heroine of the day."[36] He took an instant liking to her and would eventually become one of her most staunch and reliable supporters, writing the first, and perhaps the most accurate, biography of Tubman's early life.

As one of Brown's confidants, Sanborn overcame Tubman's cautious and suspicious nature, and they quickly developed a close bond. Over the next year Tubman visited Boston on several occasions, seeking to raise interest in and funds for the growing fugitive community on Canada, as well as to raise money for her own stalled effort to return to Dorchester County. Boarding in a house on the north side of Beacon Hill, Boston's pre–Civil War African American neighborhood, Tubman received visitors who had heard of her through a tightly connected abolitionist network. With letters of introduction from her friends in New York, probably Gerrit Smith, Martha Coffin Wright, William H. Seward, and Frederick Douglass, Tubman hosted a succession of meetings and visits to her little room. Probably through her acquaintance with William Lloyd Garrison, which helped provide comfortable access to the highest echelons of abolitionist society in Boston, Tubman also found an open door to the inner circles of Boston's powerful woman suffrage community. The Garrisons, through their relationship with Thomas Garrett in Wilmington, and Lucretia Mott, William Still, and others in Philadelphia, had known Tubman for some years.[37]

Tubman took considerable risks on such visits. Unable to read or write, she was vulnerable to betrayal, especially were she to be exposed by an unscrupulous proslavery Bostonian or mercenary slave catcher. Sanborn recalled that Tubman used extreme caution before agreeing to meet a stranger at her boardinghouse. "One of her means of security," Sanborn wrote, "was to carry with her the daguerreotypes of her friends, and show them to each new person. If they recognized the likeness, then all was right."[38] Tubman charmed many of her visitors, endearing herself to them and establishing the foundations for friendships that would span the rest of their lifetimes. Edna Dow Cheney, reformer, suffragist, and another early biographer of Tubman, wrote that Tubman had "a very affectionate nature, and forms the strongest personal attachments."[39]

Her loyalty and love for her family dominated Tubman's life, and she worried constantly over their well-being, particularly that of her aging parents. Another winter in Canada proved too difficult for Ben and Rit. Tubman wanted desperately to secure a home for them, and she shrewdly recognized that their survival depended upon returning to the United States, where they might be sheltered and protected by the growing circle of black and white friends then living in New York and Boston. Sometime during the late winter or early spring of 1859 William H. Seward offered Tubman a small parcel of property on the outskirts of Auburn, New York. Seward had inherited a seven-acre farm from his father-in-law, Elijah Miller, on South Street, near the tollgate on the Auburn and Fleming town lines. For a total of $1,200, Seward sold the property to Tubman. Originally known as the Burton Farm, the lot consisted of a house, a barn, several outbuildings, and tillable land, providing ample room for Tubman, her parents, and any other family members or friends who were in need of a home.[40]

Seward himself spent little time in Auburn during that year. Then a powerful and high-profile member of the U.S. Senate who was nurturing presidential aspirations, Seward shouldered numerous responsibilities that kept him in Washington a significant amount of time.[41] Seward's wife, Frances, may have been instrumental in the transfer of the property. Their son, William H. Seward Jr., may have negotiated the deal with Tubman, handling the financial and legal terms in his father's absence. According to Sanborn, "to the credit of the Secretary of State [Seward] it should be said, that he sold her the property on very favorable terms, and gave her some time for payment."[42] This was not the first time Seward had sold property on "favorable terms" to individuals in need. Seward, and later his son, built small frame dwellings in and around Auburn on property they owned, selling them for sums ranging

Harriet Tubman's home in Fleming, New York, on the outskirts of Auburn.
Her original wood-frame dwelling was replaced sometime before 1885
with this brick residence.

from $300 to $500 to immigrant and black families.[43] Seward had long been a supporter of immigration and sought to protect the rights of immigrant families, and his commitment to the abolition of slavery and the attainment of equal rights for African Americans was well documented by this time.[44] Though this property was larger and more valuable that the other properties Seward sold to needy families, Seward's decision to assist Tubman was consistent with his other philanthropic and community commitments.

In lieu of a $1200 payment, Seward accepted a mortgage on "easy terms," that is, Tubman put $25 down on the home, and contracted to make quarterly payments of $10 with interest.[45] This offer is remarkable for several reasons. First, Seward was selling the property to a woman, a black woman at that, with no obvious or steady means of income. Property ownership by women was uncommon in this period, and Seward could have required that the property be sold to Tubman's father, who was legally free. But Tubman must have made a strong argument for selling the property to her and her alone. There were legal considerations, however: What if her husband, John Tubman, appeared and demanded his rights to the property? Did her suffragist friends advise her as to the best legal course of action to protect herself, her property, and her family? As a New York resident, Tubman would have had limited citizenship rights. But her status as a fugitive slave added legal complexity to an already unusual legal transaction. Tubman was not a citizen; she held no rights either as a free black or as a slave. The Dred Scott decision, handed down by the Supreme Court in 1857, had denied that blacks, free or enslaved, could be citizens. The Fugitive Slave Act of 1850 also placed Seward in a precarious position. Seward was probably committing an illegal act by selling the property to a known fugitive slave. Conceivably he could have been arrested for aiding Harriet Tubman.

But providing a home for a known runaway and her family of fugitives would not have damaged Seward's reputation—in fact, it probably enhanced it. A staunch abolitionist, Seward was increasingly frustrated by the powerful slave interests in Congress, who were supported by President Buchanan. Seward was eager to rally free-soil Republicans and northern Democrats to retake the halls of Congress and the presidency from proslavery forces. Perhaps Seward was positioning himself for his own presidential nomination, though Seward and Tubman must have considered the possibility that she and her family would be at risk of capture if they moved to Auburn.

In addition, Seward probably was aware that Tubman had known James A. Stewart, the congressman from Cambridge, Maryland. Stewart, who was a staunch defender and supporter of President Buchanan, had been raising quite a ruckus on the Eastern Shore. He had conducted slaveholders' conventions and demanded state and federal protection of their slave assets, which were continuing to run away in great numbers. Tubman also knew Samuel D. LeCompte, formerly of Dorchester County, who had been appointed as a jurist for the territory of Kansas and who was the architect of the highly controversial constitution that would have made Kansas a new slave state, in defiance of the majority of antislavery forces in Kansas. As someone who was intimately familiar with Stewart, LeCompte, and their slaves, Tubman could provide

Seward with ample ammunition if he needed it. Could Seward have viewed her as an insurance policy of sorts?

Whatever the motivations, Seward and Tubman reached an agreement that benefited both of them. Though Tubman knew full well the risks involved in moving to Auburn, she was also assured of as much protection as the black and white community could provide in the event that slave catchers might threaten her. Martha Coffin Wright and her small circle of antislavery and suffragist friends could be counted on to help provide comfort and security for Ben and Rit. Living in New York also provided Tubman with closer contact with other New York abolitionists such as Gerrit Smith, Samuel May, and her close allies in Albany, including her cousin John Hooper.

The need for money became paramount for Tubman after she purchased her home. Tubman started right away soliciting funds.[46] With her parents and her brother John safely ensconced in her house in Auburn, Tubman headed to Boston. Arriving in late May, she began her rounds of visiting the homes of antislavery activists, giving lectures and speeches on her life in slavery and recounting some incidents of her many slave rescues. John Brown was in town that spring as well, raising more funds for his planned assault on Harpers Ferry. Tubman and Brown met on several occasions, planning and scheming. Harriet had suggested the Fourth of July as the best time to "raise the mill."[47] Tubman had two missions at hand; helping Brown raise money and also raising money for herself. Wendell Phillips recalled that the last time he "ever saw John Brown was under my own roof, as he brought Harriet Tubman to me, saying: 'Mr. Phillips, I bring you one of the best and bravest persons on this continent—*General* Tubman, as we call her.' "[48] This was probably the last time Tubman saw Brown, too.

Brown had successfully raised $2,000 after spending three weeks in May in Boston; Tubman no doubt hoped to tap into the same wellspring of supporters eager to help Brown put an end to slavery. On May 30, Sanborn wrote to Thomas W. Higginson, suggesting that he see Tubman, "the woman who brought away 50 slaves in 8 journeys made to Maryland."[49] He told Higginson that she was staying at "168 Cambridge St." and that she would be holding an audience the following Wednesday at "Mrs. Bartol's on Chestnut St.—can you not attend?

Even you would be amazed at some of her stories."[50] Tubman's reception was a success, apparently. Lucy Osgood reported, secondhand, to Lydia Maria Child, on the "unique entertainment."[51]

> Where Mrs. Cheney found her I do not know, but her name is Harriet. She is coal black & was a slave only three years ago, but within that time she has taken leg bail herself, & assisted no fewer than fifty others to do the same. Two or three times she has returned to the very plantation where she had served, & brought away with her companies of her relatives & friends. Her old father & mother she had helped out of bondage, & the object of this gathering was to assist her to buy a little place for them in Auburn. Her course had not been always smooth.[52]

Tubman told them how she journeyed at night and slept by day. She also sent them into fits of laughter when she told them of her attempt to bring away her husband in 1851. Tubman "went for her husband," Osgood wrote, and "she had carefully provided herself with clothing to make him, she said, fit to be seen among folks—Lo! However, the recreant had taken to himself another helpmeet & strongly advised her to give up the nonsense of freedom, & 'I had his clothes' said she, 'but no husband.'—Mrs. Follen & Mrs. Putnam shouted at her comic pathos—They dubbed her Moses the deliverer, instead of Harriet."[53]

The story of Tubman's husband's rejection, and her humorous delivery of the event, resonated with these women. While they were deeply interested in her tales of the horrors of slavery and her own courageous efforts to bring away her family and friends, Tubman's "comic pathos" provided an alternative antislavery story that was unmatched by the legions of male ex-slave lecturers and performers.[54] For white women, Tubman's portrayal of her husband's philandering would have, perhaps, resonated on a personal level; it evoked the fear of male power and the unacknowledged sacrifices they had often made for the men in their lives. Tubman's tale would have also fit a cultural stereotype that white women had come to accept of many black men: that of the unfaithful black husband all too willing to abandon his wife for another.

Tubman's retelling of her heroic feats on the Underground Railroad also challenged white male authority, a topic close to the hearts of reform-minded women in Boston's antislavery circles. Capturing her audiences' imagination, Tubman's legendary exploits portrayed a very personal and yet collective experience of resistance and liberation that resonated for both white and African American women. Whether Tubman recognized this subliminal appeal is not known; no doubt she quickly realized how eager and receptive abolitionists were to hear her stories and to give her money. Tubman's political savvy helped establish her as more than a mere storyteller.

A great storyteller she was, however. She moved her audiences deeply. Plainly dressed, very short and petite, quite black-skinned, and missing front teeth, Tubman physically made a stark contrast to Sojourner Truth, one of the most famous former slave women then speaking on the antislavery lecture circuit, who was nearly six feet tall. Both women had their femininity challenged, though in entirely different ways. In 1858 Truth bared her breasts during a public suffrage meeting when proslavery hecklers doubted she was a woman. Tubman, on the other hand, was considered the "most of a man" by none other than John Brown. Unlike Truth, who used the incident in the meeting to defend her womanhood and denigrate the manhood of her critics, Tubman embraced an identity that crossed gender lines. She basked in the apparent compliment to her great military genius and leadership qualities, virtues most certainly reserved in the nineteenth century for white men.[55] Of course, her femaleness was not questioned despite her obvious physical strength: Tubman's petite frame and beautiful singing voice gave the lie to any taunts of masculinity. Like Truth, however, Tubman shocked her audiences with stories of slavery and the injustices of life as a black woman. Black men dominated the antislavery lecture circuit. Tubman and Truth stood for millions of slave women whose lives were marred by emotional and physical abuse at the hands of white men.

Both women also laid claim to a deep spiritual connection to God. As Nell Painter has argued, Truth relied "on the gifts of the Holy Spirit and a remarkable network of abolitionist, feminist, and spiritualist supporters," through which "she healed the fear and insecurity embedded in her wretched childhood."[56] The same could be said of Tubman, who also believed that she was God's instrument. Thomas Garrett later wrote that Tubman "had more confidence in the voice of God, as spoken direct to her soul . . . that she talked with God, and he talked with her every day of her life, and she has declared to me that she felt no more fear of being arrested by her former master, or any other person, when in his immediate neighborhood, than she did in the State of New York, or Canada, for she said she never ventured only where God sent her, and her faith in a Supreme Power truly was great."[57] For both Truth and Tubman, profound religious devotion allowed them to claim respectability and authority with white audiences.

Harriet, however, was also charming and witty, and her audiences were deeply intrigued by her. "She has great dramatic power," Ednah Cheney wrote, "the scene rises before you as she saw it, and her voice and language change with her different actors."[58] Higginson was more blunt: "She is jet black and cannot read or write, only talk, besides acting."[59] Unlike Sojourner Truth, however, Tubman rarely spoke in public. Prior to the summer of 1858, most of Tubman's lectures, or what Jean Humez calls "performances," remained within the sheltered and intimate parlors of abolition's elite, or the homes of her fellow fugitives in Canada and elsewhere.[60] Her identity remained obscure for obvious reasons: She needed protection from people who would have been more than happy to claim her as their prize. She was constantly moving, too, in and out of the South ferrying fugitive slaves, meeting privately with prominent antislavery activists in search of funds, or working odd jobs to support herself. She did not have time for a more public life. Therefore, though she frequented antislavery rallies and lectures throughout the 1850s, she mostly remained a spectator.

But the new urgency of her needs in the spring and summer of 1859 changed all that. By June, having had a successful event on Chestnut Street and probably in other places, she began to see the financial rewards for telling her stories. John Brown, however, was anxious for her to return to Canada and gather her recruits for him, as he intended to conduct his raid the following month. In early June 1859 Tubman told Sanborn that she could not or would not go, so Sanborn hurriedly wrote Higginson (who was then living and preaching at a church in

Worcester), asking him to make the trip to Canada instead. "You have already some acquaintance with the Canada people—and you would be able to go instantly to the right places and get the right men," he told Higginson. As further enticement, Sanborn told Higginson that Tubman was concerned about "a society in aid of destitute fugitives at St. Catharines—which has some reason to complain of Mr. Wilson the missionary among fugitives in that town—whom you probably know— It is said that the contributions of the friends do not reach the fugitives at all and they are desirous to have the matter looked into."[61] Tubman was still trying to fulfill two missions: that of providing for herself and her parents, and that of looking after the welfare of desperately needy fugitives in Canada. Hiram Wilson had been under suspicion for some time for mismanaging funds intended for refugees in Canada. Tubman may have had firsthand knowledge of this, or perhaps she was merely passing along communication sent to her from her family and friends still in Canada.

In either case, Tubman spent several days in Concord, visiting with Sanborn and his circle of friends, the Whitings, the Alcotts, Mrs. Horace Mann, and the Brookses, retelling her stories of aiding the escapes of "fifty slaves."[62] Ann Whiting attempted to teach Harriet to read, to no avail.[63] It was also during the month of June that Tubman was evidently contemplating a visit to New Bedford, "where many of her protégés are in hiding," including Winnibar Johnson and Henry Carrol.[64] Maria Weston Chapman provided Tubman with a letter of introduction to a Mrs. Arnold of New Bedford, where, Chapman told Arnold, Tubman was hoping to raise funds to pay for her home in Auburn.[65] Chapman suggested that Tubman was "the suitable person to undertake to bring off the children of Charles, about whom I had so fruitless a correspondence with the Philadelphia Vigilance Committee & others."[66] Who Charles was, or where his family was being held in slavery, remains a mystery. Tubman's identity as "Moses the deliverer," though, now expanded well beyond the black community.[67]

Whether Tubman went to New Bedford or not is not known. In mid-June she spoke at Thomas Higginson's church in Worcester, regaling the audience with "tales of adventure" that were "beyond anything in fiction."[68] Higginson now thought she was the "greatest heroine of the age," and he found her "ingenuity and generalship . . . extraordinary."[69] Higginson wrote his mother that Tubman had "been back eight times secretly and brought out in all sixty slaves with her, including all her own family, besides aiding many more in other ways to escape." There was a "reward of twelve thousand dollars offered for her in Maryland," he wrote, making this the first mention of a specific monetary reward for her capture.[70] Already Tubman was creating a larger-than-life persona, one that would endure for the rest of her life. Her risk-taking and courage were the marvel of the antislavery circuit, and so genuinely authentic that even seasoned abolitionists such as Higginson were deeply impressed.

Tubman did not go to the Eastern Shore again for quite some time. She was raising good money and extended her stay in New England throughout the summer. It was a busy antislavery season in New England: Tubman evidently became quite popular on lecture platforms throughout the greater Boston area, sharing the stage with numerous more professional and salaried black and white antislavery activists. Some of abolition's most prominent black activists, including William Wells Brown, William Still, the Rev. Jermain Loguen, Frederick Douglass, William Cooper Nell, and many others, headlined numerous fairs, conventions, meetings, and lectures. Though Tubman stayed with white families in Concord for a few nights, she mostly depended upon the hospitality of blacks living in Boston, including Lewis Hayden, John S. Rock, and probably other friends and relatives living in Boston's historic black neighborhood.[71]

On July 4, 1859, Tubman addressed the Massachusetts Anti-Slavery Society meeting at Framingham. Higginson welcomed her to the platform, telling the audience he wished to introduce them to "a conductor on the Underground Railroad." For dramatic effect, he did not tell them her real name, but rather declared that he found it difficult to introduce her—raising the excitement as to who this little woman standing on the stage with him could be. "She came here from a place in the slave States; she came by land, and had been here in a reasonable time. (Laughter) At the South, she was called 'Moses'—after an ancient leader, who took men and women into the Promised Land. (Applause)."[72]

Many people in the audience had probably already heard rumors of this "deliverer" who returned to her old home in Maryland to bring away family and friends. Tubman stepped forward and greeted the cheering audience. After the applause subsided and a hushed silence fell over the crowd, Tubman began to speak. First she told of her "sufferings as a slave, her escape, and her achievements on the Underground Railroad, in a style of quaint simplicity, which excited the most profound interest in her hearers," a reporter from the *Liberator* wrote. When she was finished, Higginson informed the crowd that

> this brave woman had never asked for a cent from the Abolitionists, but that all her operations had been conducted at her own cost, with money earned by herself. Now, however, having brought her father and mother out of slavery, she found that the labor required for their support rendered her incapable of doing anything in the way of business, and she therefore desired to raise a few hundred dollars to enable her to buy a little place where her father and mother could support themselves, and enable her to resume the practice of her profession![73]

The audience roared, applauding enthusiastically, and a collection was started, yielding the modest sum of $37. With this and additional monies she was able to raise, she paid Seward $200 toward her debt, offering more than the terms of their agreement required.[74]

Such successful public performances kept Tubman actively involved in New England's antislavery circuit that summer. On August 1 "jubilees" were held throughout New England, celebrating the twenty-first anniversary of full emancipation and freedom for West Indian slaves held in bondage by the British government.[75] In Boston, the celebration coincided with a meeting of the New England Colored Citizens' Convention, held at Tremont Temple. The delegates to the convention adopted resolutions condemning the Fugitive Slave Act, proslavery religious organizations, the Dred Scott decision, segregated schools, and the American colonization movement, and in particular the African Civilization Society, which sought to repatriate African Americans, slave and free alike, to Africa. On the evening of the first, Tubman once again took center stage. This time she was afforded an opportunity to express her own political views. Introduced to the audience as "Harriet Garrison," in an obvious attempt to obscure her identity, Tubman "denounced the colonization movement" and

> told the story of a man who sowed onions and garlic on his land
> to increase his dairy productions; but he soon found the butter
> was strong and would not sell, and so he concluded to sow clover
> instead. But he soon found the wind had blown the onions and
> garlic all over his field. Just so, she said, the white people had got
> the "nigger" here to do their drudgery, and now they were trying
> to root 'em out and send 'em to Africa. "But," she said, "they
> can't do it; we're rooted here, and they can't pull us up."[76]

As the crowd was applauding her, though, the Rev. John B. Smith from New Bedford, a member of the African Civilization Society, stepped onto the stage, signifying a challenge to Tubman's speech. Smith insisted that the repatriation of African Americans was "for evangelizing and civilizing Africa."[77] The crowd was not sympathetic, and ultimately it was Tubman's simple parable that carried the day.

In early to mid-August Tubman mingled with many of the antislavery movement's black leaders, who had remained in the Boston area after the convention to attend and participate in lectures.[78] William Still came from Philadelphia to speak at the Twelfth Street Baptist Church on the Underground Railroad; Loguen also spoke there on his Underground Railroad efforts in Syracuse, claiming, oddly, that he "very seldom . . . sends fugitives to Canada, unless they are of the timid class, who dare not run the risk of remaining in the States."[79] One wonders how this would have sounded to Tubman, who understood the dangers that existed for any fugitive slave living in the North.

John Brown's son expected to meet with Tubman in Boston in the middle of August, but there is no record of such a meeting. On August 27 Sanborn wrote to John Brown, who had apparently inquired about her whereabouts, that she was "probably in New Bedford, sick. She has staid in N.E. a long time, and been a kind of missionary."[80] By the middle of September Brown was already ensconced at his base of operations in Chambersburg, Pennsylvania, just across the state border from

Harpers Ferry, Virginia, where he was finalizing his attack plans and waiting for Tubman to join him. Brown was impatient and anxious—he had sent inquiries to Sanborn and others in search of her. Lewis Hayden wrote to Brown on September 16 that he had just written Tubman, telling her to hurry back to Boston.[81] By the end of September, though, Tubman had still not been heard from.[82]

It has long been assumed that Tubman was incapacitated by illness in New Bedford, Massachusetts, in the fall of 1859 and that this was why she could not join Brown in his attack at Harpers Ferry. There is a possibility, however, that she actually may have been in Maryland. According to Talbot County, Maryland, historian Dickson Preston, local Talbot County newspapers reported in October 1859 that "Brown had wandered through southern Talbot County dressed as a woman, seeking recruits for the insurrection he planned. Among other places, he was supposed to have appeared at such places as Trappe District estates at Boston, Crosiadore, Howell's Point, and Compton. According to the papers there was little doubt that someone had been traveling through the county in disguise, but no proof that it had been Brown."[83] It may have been Tubman, traveling among the slaves and free blacks on the Eastern Shore, trying to recruit followers to join in Brown's attack. Given her propensity for disguise and trickery, she could have left the impression that she was a man dressed as a woman. Another possibility concerns two of her nephews and a niece, John and Moses Ross and their sister Harriet, the children of her brother John Stewart. Dr. Anthony C. Thompson had sold them to his daughter, Sarah Thompson Haddaway, who was then living in Trappe in Talbot County. Could Tubman have been hoping to bring away the children, too? Was she hoping to bring her sister Rachel away then as well? There is no proof that Tubman was in Maryland at this time. It remains, though, an intriguing possibility. Another possibility, of course, is that Tubman herself got cold feet. She may have decided that Brown's attack was doomed to failure; she probably knew he had few followers, leaving him incredibly vulnerable. Douglass had rejected Brown's scheme as unworkable, and perhaps Tubman, too, came to the same conclusion, and that it was better to feign illness than to endure Brown's disapproval. Her strong survival instinct may have protected her in the end.

Nevertheless, her silence on this issue, even years later, may indicate a careful decision not to reveal the full extent of her participation in Brown's raid.

Brown commenced his attack on the federal arsenal at Harpers Ferry on Sunday night, October 16, 1859. By Tuesday, Brown and his small group of twenty-one men were holed up inside an engine house, where Robert E. Lee and a party of U.S. Marines had forced them to retreat. The insurgents were captured and the raid was squelched. Both of Brown's sons, Watson and Oliver, were killed, as were eight others. Only five rebels were able to escape, including one of the original group of five African Americans, Osborne P. Anderson, who had joined Brown in Chatham. Seven, including Brown, were arrested and thrown in jail, where they awaited trial on charges of treason and inciting a slave insurrection.[84]

John Brown's attack on Harpers Ferry sent shock waves throughout the country. To many southerners, this was confirmation that northern aggression and hostility were incontrovertible. The insurrection thus only served to strengthen their resolve to resist any attempt to restrict or abolish slavery. Southern secessionists pressed harder, and the Democratic Party, already splintering over the slavery issue, divided further. In Boston, Brown's Secret Six panicked. A search of Brown's temporary residence in Chambersburg had produced incriminating letters and documents, implicating members of the secret committee as well as many others who had supported Brown (though many remained uninformed of the extent of Brown's true plans). Sanborn fled to Canada, as did Douglass and others who were fearful of being arrested and carried off to Virginia for trial.

Tubman was in New York City when the raid failed. "She felt her usual warning that something was wrong—she could not tell what. Finally she told her hostess that it must be Captain Brown who was in trouble, and that they should soon hear bad news from him. The next day's newspaper brought tidings of what had happened."[85] Her dream finally made sense to her. Of the three-headed serpent, the two younger heads, which had been struck down, represented Brown's sons, who had been killed by Lee's men during the raid. The third head, the "old man, still looking so wishful," was Brown, soon to be found guilty of treason and hanged at the gallows in Virginia.[86] Over the next six weeks confusion reigned, as co-conspirators and supporters watched while Brown and his accomplices were tried and convicted.

In the midst of all the excitement, Tubman's family had been settling into their new home in Auburn. Her brother John had been caring for their aged parents, but the responsibility was weighing heavily on him. On November 1, in the only known surviving letter from one of Tubman's family members, John Stewart wrote to her, seeking help and advice on the best way to handle their sometimes difficult parents.[87]

Sister Harriet Tubman,

I am well and hope you are the same. Father's health is very good for him. I received your welcome latter yesterday which relieved my uneasiness. we thought quite hard of you for not writing before. we would like to see you much, but if you can do better where you are you had perhaps better stay. Father wanted to go to Canada after his things on foot but I would not consent as I thought it would be too much for him and he consents to stay until he gets your advice on the subject as he has no means for going. please write as soon as possible and not delay. We three are alone, I have a good deal of trouble with them as they are getting old and feeble. There was a man by the name of Young that promised father a stove and some things to go to keeping house but has refused to do anything for them. Brother John has been with father ever since he left Troy and is doing the best he can. Catherine Stewart has not come yet but wants to very bad. send what things you want father to bring if you think best for him to go. I am going to send a letter to Wm Henry. if you wish me to say anything for you to him let me know when you write. Seward has received nothing as Payment since the 4th of July that I knows of. Write me particularly what you want me to do as I want to hear from you very much. I would like to know what luck you have had since you have been gone. have heard that you are doing well. hope to find it so. Direct my letter to me Box 750, Auburn.

Truly Yours, John Stewart.[88]

Harriet probably traveled back to Auburn to help her brother with their parents, set up housekeeping, retrieve her father's belongings in Canada, and perhaps discuss her debt obligations to Seward.[89] But by the beginning of December she was back in Boston. Brown's execution was set for December 2, 1859, in Charlestown, Virginia, and Harriet may have wanted to be near other Brown friends on that day. At the time of Brown's death, Tubman went to Ednah Cheney's home to find comfort, but could not be consoled. "Her heart was too full, she must talk," Cheney later wrote.

> "I've been studying and studying upon it," [Tubman said], "and its clar to me, it wasn't John Brown that died on that gallows. When I think how he gave up his life for our people, and how he never flinched, but was so brave to the end; its clar to me it wasn't mortal man, it was God in him. When I think of all the groans and tears and prayers I've heard on the plantations, and remember that God is a prayer-hearing God, I feel that his time is drawing near."[90]

Tubman had perhaps a clearer understanding of the implications of Brown's fateful raid than did Cheney. "God," Tubman told her, "was always near. . . . He gave me my strength, and he set the North Star in the heavens; he meant for me to be free."[91] And so did John Brown. Later, while visiting Sanborn in Concord, Tubman spied a bust of Brown in Sanborn's library. "The first time she came to my house, in Concord, after that tragedy, she was shown into a room in the evening, where Brackett's bust of John Brown was standing. The sight of it, which was new to her, threw her into a sort of ecstasy of sorrow and admiration."[92] Tubman admired Brown more than any other acquaintance she had made through her long involvement with the antislavery movement. To her great satisfaction, his attack and death would immortalize him in the minds of many free and enslaved blacks throughout the country, who would rally around invocations of his memory and set their sights on overthrowing slavery.[93] In fact, she later told a close ally, "he done more in dying, than 100 men would in living."[94]

In the middle of December the U.S. Senate convened a commission to investigate the Brown affair. Headed by James A. Mason of Virginia and Jefferson Davis of Mississippi, the Mason Commission, as it would be called, began a broad inquiry into Brown's "crime," a development that quickly renewed in Sanborn, Howe, Smith, and others the fear that they would be arrested.[95] On the twentieth of December Sanborn wrote to a friend that Howe and the others were expected to leave soon for Canada, and that Tubman would also return there.[96] Given her vulnerability as a Brown co-conspirator (Virginia authorities had located several letters among Brown's papers that mentioned her role in his plans), Tubman probably packed up her family and moved back to the relative safety of St. Catharines.[97] In fact, on January 17, a U.S. marshal from Harpers Ferry was in Auburn, possibly "engaged in summoning witnesses for the Senate Investigating Committee," including, conceivably, Tubman, when the marshal, by design or by sheer luck, ran into John Brown's co-conspirator, Osborne P. Anderson, who had escaped from Harpers Ferry back in October. What Anderson was doing in Auburn is not known; it had been nearly two months since his escape from Harpers Ferry. Why he was not in Canada is a mystery. The U.S. marshal attempted to arrest him, but "friends" sent Anderson to Canada, "or parts unknown."[98]

The New Year brought enormous tensions in the United States as the drumbeat of secession grew louder in the wake of the Brown affair. War was coming, but Tubman was already prepared for battle.

FRACTURED FAMILY

TUBMAN DID NOT GIVE UP HOPE OF REUNITING HER FAMILY. WITH HER parents safely ensconced once again in St. Catharines, Tubman turned her thoughts to earning more money. During the late winter and early spring of 1860 she traveled throughout central New York, giving lectures and attending receptions in her honor, where she collected funds for her Canadian relief work and for her personal support.[1] At the end of April Tubman found herself in the center of one of the most dramatic slave rescues to occur in central New York since the "Jerry Rescue" of Syracuse in 1851.[2] On April 27, 1860, Tubman was visiting with her cousin, John Hooper, in Troy, New York, as she passed through on her way to an antislavery meeting in Boston.[3] On the morning of the twenty-seventh a young fugitive named Charles Nalle was arrested as he was walking to a local bakery to procure bread for the family of his employer, Uri Gilbert. Gilbert, a wealthy industrialist and antislavery activist in Troy, had recently hired Nalle to be his coachman, knowing full well Nalle's status as a runaway slave.[4]

Nalle had taken flight from his slave master, Blucher Hansbrough of Culpepper County, Virginia, in October 1858. Married to a free woman and the father of six children, Nalle fled with his family to Columbia, Pennsylvania, where they thought they might be safe. Feeling threats to his freedom there, Nalle decided to head farther north, while his pregnant wife stayed behind until he could settle someplace and send money to have them follow him. Finding safety in Troy, Nalle worked at various jobs trying to save enough money to bring his family north. His wife, in the meantime, was arrested and then jailed in Washington, D.C., on suspicion of aiding Nalle's escape.

Illiterate and dependent upon others to write and read for him, Nalle paid Horace Avril, a "shyster lawyer" from Troy, to write letters for him to his wife and friends in the hope of securing his wife's freedom and his children's safe passage north. Avril betrayed Nalle, however, to Hansbrough, who, under the Fugitive Slave Act, procured a warrant for Nalle's arrest and return to Virginia.[5] Nalle had been boarding with a prominent local black antislavery activist named William Henry, who ran a grocery store on Division Street in Troy.[6] When Henry discovered Nalle had been arrested, he immediately alerted the black community and his white antislavery associates that Nalle was being held at the U.S. commissioner's office. Time was of the essence; Nalle was going to be turned over to Hansbrough's agent, Henry Wall, without the benefit of a trial or hearing. While Martin I. Townsend, a prominent local attorney, set out to obtain a writ of habeas corpus, a crowd gathered outside the U.S. commissioner's office, then located on State Street in Troy at the Mutual Bank building.

Tubman was only a short distance away when she heard the alarm and joined the crowd at the commissioner's office. William Henry, Tubman, and others started to whip the growing crowd into a frenzy. They then settled on a plan to rescue Nalle from the agent. Acting the part of an old woman, Tubman stole inside the building to keep watch on the activities in the commissioner's office, where the police took no notice of her presence. "On the opposite side of the street stood the colored people, watching the window where they could see Harriet's sun-bonnet, and feeling assured that so long as she stood there, the fugitive was still in the office."[7] The local newspaper noted a "somewhat antiquated colored woman," standing near the window, who was "provided with a signal to prepare those on the outside for an attack, when the prisoner should be brought forth."[8] But the police were wary of bringing Nalle out into the crowd. Someone shouted "fire," in hopes of forcing them to come out of the building, but it only served to create more confusion on the street.[9]

Finally, after hearing word that Townsend had obtained the writ of habeas corpus, the authorities decided to move Nalle to Judge Gould's office on Congress Street, a few blocks away, where Townsend could argue his case for Nalle's release. Tubman gave the signal to the crowd below, then rushed down the stairs and made an attempt to wrestle Nalle from the grasp of the sheriff and his deputies as they were exiting the building. Hanging on to the neck of one officer, Tubman began choking him, but she was beaten back.[10] Again she struck, fighting to keep hold of Nalle as the sheriff and other officers dragged him out of the building and into the angry crowd. Bradford has suggested that the sight of Nalle further enraged the crowd. He was apparently a very light-skinned mulatto, "a tall, handsome, intelligent *white* man, with his wrists manacled together," who looked, according to Bradford, remarkably like his master.[11] Bradford's description of the reaction of the crowd, if accurate, reveals contemporary notions of color that equated slavery with black skin, not white skin.[12]

A fight ensued; Nalle and Tubman were dragged and beaten as the crowd tried to pry Nalle loose from the grip of the officers.[13] A few voices in the crowd called out for calm, urging the people to trust in the law to gain Nalle's freedom. But Tubman, among others, disagreed. Tubman was well known in the Troy community; word probably traveled quickly that it was she who was leading the charge, and many were eager and ready to follow her command. The Troy *Daily Times* reported that "the most conspicuous person opposed to the legal course was the venerable old colored woman, who exclaimed, 'Give us liberty or give us death!' "[14]

Pistols were drawn, and one officer threatened to kill a rescuer he had grabbed from the crowd; instantly a knife was drawn under the throat of the policeman, and the pistol was dropped. "Twenty times the prisoner was taken from the officers, and twenty times they recovered him," the Troy *Daily Times* reported.[15] "Colored women rushed into the thickest of the fray; the venerable Moll Pitcher of the occasion fighting like a demon, and losing all her gearing save a dilapidated out-shirt."[16] Tubman cried out, "Drag us out! Drag him to the river! Drown him! but don't let them have him!"[17] One man offered $200 for Nalle's rescue, "but not one cent to his master!"[18] The crowd carried both Tub-man and Nalle, who by then was wearing Tubman's bonnet, down Congress Street toward the riverfront. Two men had gone ahead to se-cure a boat at the docks, near the foot of Washington Street, to carry Nalle across the Hudson River to West Troy. Tubman let go of him when they reached the docks, and he was placed on the boat, still shack-led, and taken to the other side.[19]

The officers, who had been held back by the crowd, soon found their way to the waterfront and boarded a ferry with about "300 of the rescuers."[20] Police officials in West Troy had been notified by telegraph of Nalle's escape and were prepared to capture him when he landed. Bleeding profusely from his head, arms, and hands, where the hand-cuffs remained locked around his wrists, Nalle tried to run from the waiting officers but was seized and taken to Judge Stewart's chambers near the ferry terminal on West Troy's waterfront. Tubman, the other rescuers, and Troy's sheriff and deputies landed soon after. Racing for the judge's office nearby, the crowd was joined by sympathizers from West Troy. Officers guarding the judge's chambers fired upon the first rescuers storming the building; several were shot, driving the crowd out of the building and back onto the street. The sight of wounded men infuriated some in the crowd, and another attempt was made to storm the building. "More stones and more pistol-shots ensued," and fi-nally the door to the judge's chambers was forced open by an "im-mense negro" named Martin, who was immediately "felled by a hatchet in the hands of Deputy Sheriff Morrison."[21] Stunned but not fa-tally injured, Martin lay unconscious in the doorway, blocking attempts by the sheriff and others to close the door. "Harriet and a number of other colored women rushed" over Martin and the bodies of the other wounded rescuers to reach Nalle.[22]

Tubman later told young audiences that she threw Nalle "acrossed my shoulder like a bag o' meal and took him away out of there."[23] Down the stairs the women ran, "bullets whistling past" them as they emerged onto the street. A farmer passing close by was "compelled" to give up his horse and wagon for Nalle's escape; the wagon broke apart, however, a few blocks away, necessitating a transfer to another horse and wagon.[24] Nalle successfully made his escape from the authorities; while the newspapers reported that he was safe in Canada, he was, in fact, hiding in the countryside.[25] Through the effort of the local antislavery community in Troy and Albany, Nalle's freedom was purchased from Hansbrough, and he was able to return to Troy.[26]

Tubman slipped back into the crowd once Nalle was out of sight. She had been badly beaten; she was bruised and bloody, and her clothes were torn and tattered. National newspapers picked up the story. Antislavery societies celebrated the successful rescue, crediting not only "many of our most respectable citizens,—lawyers, editors, public men, and private individuals," but "the rank and file, [who] were black . . . African fury is entitled to claim the greatest share in the rescue."[27] Ednah Cheney later wrote of the Troy event, remarking that Tubman loved "fighting in a good cause."[28]

Throughout the summer of 1860, Tubman continued to visit and speak at small antislavery meetings, intimate parlor gatherings, and larger, more public venues. Visiting with Sanborn in Concord in June, she probably delighted him with tales of the Nalle rescue. She was "an extraordinary person," he wrote his friend Benjamin Lyman.[29] On July 4 she spoke at a woman suffrage meeting held at the Melodeon Hall in Boston. "A colored woman of the name of Moses," the *Liberator* reported the next day, "who, herself a fugitive, has eight times returned to the slave States for the purpose of rescuing others from bondage, and who has met with extraordinary success in her efforts," told the audience of "her adventures in a modest but quaint and amusing style, which won much applause."[30] Joining Tubman were some of Boston's and New England's women's rights vanguard: Caroline Dall, Caroline Severance, Helen Garrison, Samuel May, James Freeman Clark, and Wendell Phillips, among others.[31]

Southerners were taking notice, however. How long Tubman's activities were known to Eastern Shore slaveholders has not been recorded. John Bell Robinson, a proslavery writer in Philadelphia, noted in 1860 that Harriet Tubman had been featured as "A Female Conductor on the Underground Railroad" at the meeting at the Melodeon in

July. He was horrified, he told his readers, that she was applauded for bringing her parents "away from ease and comfortable homes" where they had been "caressed and better taken care of . . . around the plentiful board of their master."[32] He argued further that Tubman's "cruelty" to her parents was "a thousand times worse than to sell young ones away!"[33] No doubt Ben and Rit, and many other slaves, would have disagreed on that point.

Despite her growing notoriety and the risks it brought to her, Tubman continued to appear in public, telling her audiences of her life in slavery, her escape and rescue missions, earning as much money as she could to support herself, her family, and relief efforts in St. Catharines. Tubman may have been having a difficult time earning enough money to meet all of her obligations. By August 1860 Tubman had not made a single payment to Seward since the prior January. Interest was accruing monthly, and property taxes and insurance payments added to her debt obligation; Seward, however, made sure the taxes and insurance were paid on the property. Perhaps Seward was distracted by his own battles. He was, that summer, fighting a political battle at the Republican National Convention in Chicago, hoping to secure his party's nomination for the presidency. Abraham Lincoln, a more moderate candidate, won the ballot instead, and Seward committed himself to support Lincoln's campaign for election in November.[34]

There is no indication Seward pressured Tubman to make payments at that time.[35] She therefore could focus on earning the $100 she needed to fund another trip back to the Eastern Shore to retrieve her sister Rachel and Rachel's two children, Angerine and Ben. In early August Tubman sent a letter to Wendell Phillips requesting money from him, money that he had apparently promised her sometime before then. "I am about to start on my mission," she told Phillips, "you promised if I would let you know in case I did not make off my $100 . . . I lack after paying my board 19 or $20 of that amount."[36] She asked him to send the money to "Mr. Walcott," who was probably Robert F. Walcutt, manager and business agent for *The Liberator*, who was to forward the money to Tubman once she reached Philadelphia.[37] As a reminder of her sometimes unpredictable health, she added a closing line: "I am as well as usual for me to be and in good spirits."[38]

On December 1 Thomas Garrett wrote to William Still that Harriet had arrived, alone, at his home the evening before. She had left two men, Stephen Ennals and another named John, near New Castle; the roads were dangerous, and she felt it unsafe to bring them to Wilmington.[39] Garrett paid someone to find them and take them to Chester County in Pennsylvania, and he gave Harriet $30 to travel back thirty miles to the place where she had secreted Maria Ennals, Stephen's wife, and their three children, Harriet, Amanda, and a three-month-old infant.[40] There she hired someone to take them safely by carriage to Chester County.[41]

Bringing away the Ennals family was probably a last-minute decision for Harriet. Her every intention had been the retrieval of her sister Rachel and Rachel's two children, the very last of the Brodesses' slaves. Sadly, Rachel had "died a little before Harriet reached her neighborhood," news that Tubman had not received before she returned to the Eastern Shore.[42] Ednah Cheney later wrote that Tubman "had to leave her sister's two orphaned children in slavery the last time, for the want of thirty dollars."[43] It is possible that she may have needed more money to bribe or pay someone else to bring the children to her.[44] The sequence of events is unclear, however. Bradford later wrote that on Tubman's last trip, the runaways "were to meet her in a wood, that she might conduct them North. For some unexplained reason they did not come." Tubman spent a final night waiting hopefully in a "blinding snow storm and a raging wind. She protected herself behind a tree as well as she could," leaving herself "exposed to the fury of the storm."[45] Restrictions on liberties were still being strictly enforced on the Eastern Shore; slave patrols and slave catchers continued to monitor and watch movements in the countryside.[46] Whatever happened during the attempted rescue of the children, Angerine and Ben remained enslaved in Dorchester County.

Tubman could not wait for the right moment to get the children; she knew from years of experience that such a chance might not come. The Ennals family was ready to go, however, so Tubman started toward Wilmington with them, intending perhaps to turn around and try again later for her niece and nephew.[47] According to William Still, Stephen was enslaved by either James Craig, from Madison, or John E. Cator, from the Parsons Creek District.[48] Maria and her children were enslaved by Algernon Percy, of Vienna.[49] Maria "hired her time" but still lived eight miles from her husband, who was not allowed by his master to live with her.

Somewhere along her escape route, Tubman brought her party of runaways to the home of a black man she knew to be an Underground Railroad stationmaster. Arriving in the rain during the early morning hours, "Harriet went to the door, and gave the peculiar rap which was her customary signal to her friends."[50] After knocking on the door several times with no response, Tubman became alarmed. A white man appeared at the window "with the gruff question, 'Who are you?' and 'What do you want?' " Tubman soon learned that her black friend had been "obliged to leave for harboring" fugitive slaves.[51]

The underground network had disintegrated considerably on the Eastern Shore due to increased vigilance on the part of the slaveholders and local authorities since the great number of escapes in the fall of 1857. Several known and unknown agents had been caught and jailed, chased out of the area, or possibly even killed. Though Tubman may have been aware of some of these arrests, she may not have known the fate of some of her particular allies. Finding herself caught off guard by the white man living in a former black-occupied Underground Railroad safe house put Tubman and her party of runaways at greater risk of exposure. She hurried them to the outskirts of the town, where she found a small island in the middle of a swamp. The tall grass growing there was the ideal camouflage until they could move on. They waded through the water to the island, carrying the baby in a basket, and the group lay quietly in the damp grass, where they prayed "and waited for deliverance."[52] They were hotly pursued; patrols passed by, searching nearby homes and fields for the runaways, making it difficult for Tubman and her charges to get to the next Underground Railroad station. They were hungry and cold; the baby had to be drugged with paregoric to keep it quiet.

Eventually a Quaker man appeared, "slowly walking along the solid pathway on the edge of the swamp."[53] Tubman and the others, thinking he was "talking to himself," finally realized he was giving them instructions to get to his nearby barn, where a horse and a wagon filled with provisions awaited them. A seemingly miraculous answer to Tubman's prayer, Bradford later wrote, "never seemed to strike her as at all strange or mysterious; her prayer was the prayer of faith, and she *expected* an answer."[54]

Tubman guided them to the next town, to the safety of another Quaker she knew, who sheltered them and sent them along to the next station.[55] The trip was long and cold, though, with only an "old comfort [and] blanket" and "a basket with a little kindling, a little bread for the baby with some laudanum, to keep it from crying during the day," Martha Coffin Wright wrote to her daughter Ellen Wright Garrison. Tubman and the group "walked all night, carrying the little ones, and spread the comfort on the frozen ground, in some dense thicket, where they all hid."[56]

The journey took some time to complete because of the intense scrutiny and the vigorous searches being conducted in the pursuit of these runaways. They had to hide in the woods longer than Tubman anticipated; they were starving, so Tubman attempted to find food.[57] While the refugees were secreted in the woods, Tubman "went out foraging, and sometimes could not get back till dark, fearing she would be followed. Then if they had crept further in, and she couldn't find them, she would whistle, or sing certain hymns and they would answer."[58]

Bradford recorded these songs, "as I have so often heard them sung by herself [Tubman]":

Hail, oh hail, ye happy spirits,
Death no more shall make you fear,
Grief nor sorrow, pain nor anguish,
Shall no more distress you dere.
Around Him are ten thousand angels,
Always ready to obey command;
Dey are always hovering round you,
Till you reach de heavenly land.
Jesus, Jesus will go wid you,
He will lead you to his throne;
He who died, has gone before you,
Trod de wine-press all alone.

He whose thunders shake creation,
He who bids de planets roll;
He who rides upon the tempest,
And whose scepter sways de whole.
Dark; and thorny is de pathway,
Where de pilgrim makes his ways;
But beyond dis vale of sorrow,
Lie de fields of endless days.[59]

Tubman instructed her party not to come out of their hiding places until she had sung the song twice. If it was too dangerous for them to come out, she would sing:

Moses go down in Egypt,
Till ole Pharo' let me go;
Hadn't been for Adam's fall,
Shouldn't hab to died at all.[60]

But once danger had passed then she would change the song to a joyous refrain, which, Bradford wrote, was "forbidden to her people at the South."

Oh go down, Moses,
Way down into Egypt's land,
Tell old Pharaoh,
Let my people go.
Oh Pharaoh said he would go cross,
Let my people go,
And don't get lost in de wilderness,
Let my people go.
Oh go down, Moses,
Way down into Egypt's land,
Tell old Pharaoh,
Let my people go.
You may hinder me here, but you can't up dere,
Let my people go,

He sits in de Hebben and answers prayer,

Let my people go!

Oh go down, Moses,

Way down into Egypt's land,

Tell old Pharaoh,

Let my people go.[61]

Eventually they made it to Wilmington and then safely to Philadelphia, where Still reported that the group was given food, clothing, and money.[62] Marveling at Tubman's continued success, Garrett wrote Still that Harriet "seems to have had a special angel to guard her on her journey of mercy."[63]

It took some time for Tubman and the rest to reach Canada. On December 30 Martha Coffin Wright in Auburn reported to her daughter Ellen in Boston that she and other Auburnians had "been expending our sympathies, as well as congratulations, on seven newly arrived slaves that Harriet Tubman has just pioneered safely from the Southern part of Maryland."[64] News traveled quickly that Tubman had made another successful trip. The news of her sister's death was also widely reported, indicating how much many of the white abolitionists knew about Tubman's family and her plans. There was probably great grief and disappointment in her own household; Ben and Rit had lost another daughter, and their grandchildren remained enslaved while others made their way to freedom.

Many were deeply concerned for Tubman's continued safety, though, and that of her family.[65] Gerrit Smith wrote to Fanklin Sanborn on January 29 that Tubman "sits by my side . . . she returned Christmas from another of her southern expeditions, bringing with her 7 slaves."[66] Tubman had been staying with his family for five days, and he expected her to stay several more; she had "badly frosted" her feet while on her last mission. Tubman wanted Sanborn to know, Smith wrote, that "her father has a lame hand," possibly a message that they were in need of help.[67] In spite of the continuing threats to her safety while on U.S. soil, Tubman seemed relaxed and at ease at the Smiths' residence—"the Big House," as Tubman called it.[68] She found great comfort and a warm welcome from Gerrit Smith and his family. It was probably this respite at the Smiths' that Tubman later recalled fondly to an interviewer; Green, Smith's son, invited Tubman to go hunting with him, but her shoes had been ruined and she could not go. "I remember," Tubman recalled, "once after I had brought some colored people from the South . . . Gerrit Smith's son, Green, was going hunting with his tutor and some other boys. I had no shoes. It was a Saturday afternoon and—would you believe it?—those boys went right off to the village and got me a pair of shoes so I could go with them."[69] They considered Harriet to be "equally skilled with a gun or a hoe, in the laundry or the kitchen."[70]

In early February, however, the issue of Tubman's safety reached a crisis point. David Wright had received a letter from a fellow abolitionist, Charles Mills in Syracuse, who informed him that "a slaveholder was there the day before enquiring as to the possibility of retaking slaves here [Auburn]."[71] There had already been several narrow escapes in the Auburn area.[72] This new warning, however, heightened the sense of danger for Harriet, her family, and her friends. Wright (who had been traveling in New York or Washington at the time) wrote to Martha that he had "immediately called on several whom I knew could be trusted, on—men amongst others, who promised to warn Harriet and her *children*."[73] Wright sent Mills's letter to Mr. Hosmer, the editor of the local newspaper in Auburn, who in turn rode out to Tubman's house on South Street and read it to Tubman's parents.[74] Martha Wright suspected that Tubman had already gone on to Canada with Gerrit Smith, and she was right.[75]

There were other reasons to be concerned for Tubman's safety. In November 1860 Lincoln had been elected president. While Lincoln prepared to take office in March 1861, Seward was working on a compromise to avoid secession. Seward was in line to be appointed Lincoln's secretary of state, and in that position, Seward hoped, he would have a powerful influence on the administration's policies toward the South. Though a devoted antislavery man, Seward was also a strict unionist, and he was determined to maintain the Union without resorting to war, a position that he stood firm on, even if that meant making concessions to southern states. To his longtime abolitionist friends, Seward suddenly appeared all too willing to accept compromises that many antislavery activists were loath to support. They turned away from Seward, thinking he was a traitor to the cause.

Adding to the sense of urgency was the decision by seven southern states, South Carolina, Mississippi, Louisiana, Georgia, Alabama, Florida, and Texas, by February 1861 to pass resolutions to secede from the Union.[76] Tubman's friends and allies became increasingly concerned that Seward himself, hoping to compromise and bargain his way back to reunification, might betray her. Sanborn later wrote:

> Seward knew the history of this poor woman, he had given his enemies a handle against him by dealing with her, it was thought that he would not scruple to betray her. The suspicion was an unworthy one, for though the Secretary could betray a cause, he could not surely have put her enemies on the track of a woman who was thus in his power, after such a career as hers had been. But so little confidence was then felt in Mr. Seward, by men who had voted for him and with him, that they hurried Harriet off to Canada, sorely against her will.[77]

Indeed, on February 3, 1861, Gerrit Smith left Peterboro for Canada, taking Tubman with him. A recent slave case in Ohio, where a fugitive named Lucy had been returned to her master under the Fugitive Slave Act, had shaken Smith's confidence in the justice system, and that, combined with anger and suspicion toward Seward, made him "alarmed" for Tubman's safety.[78] Tubman's notoriety as a conductor on the Underground Railroad, especially since she had been lecturing in public in New England for nearly two years, probably made her a choice target. Though a reward notice for Tubman's capture has yet to be found, it is likely that there was one; whether it was $1,200 or $12,000, Tubman would have been a significant catch for southern bounty hunters. While she fled back to Canada, her family remained in Auburn. Chas. Mills informed Martha Wright of Tubman's whereabouts, asking her "see that the family did not suffer, [and] a message came from her, thro' her favorite slave, desiring that we send them a bbl of flour [and] she [would] pay us on her return."[79]

Harriet probably did not stay long in St. Catharines.[80] With part of her family in Auburn and the rest in Canada, Tubman most likely spent time in both places in the spring of 1861. Smith, Sanborn, and other allies continued to raise money for her, sending it to her in small installments of $10 and $20 at a time.[81] They had become concerned over her ability to manage the money in a way they deemed best. Sarah Bradford later wrote that Tubman's "heart is so large, and her feelings are so easily wrought upon, that it was never wise to give her more than enough for present needs."[82] What Tubman may have thought was an appropriate use of the money may have differed from what white benefactors envisioned as worthy. Lacking any documentation from Tubman herself, we are left to speculate that perhaps Tubman's supporters were influenced in part by paternalistic attitudes toward her.

Tubman's burdens remained great, however. In April Catherine Stewart, the wife of James Stewart, Tubman's brother, and their son, Elijah moved from St. Catharines to Tubman's home in Auburn, crowding the small home even more.[83] Bradford wrote that Tubman's mother "was querulous and exacting, and most unreasonable in her temper, often reproaching this faithful daughter as the Israelites did of Moses of old, for 'bringing them up into the wilderness to die there of hunger.' "[84] John Stewart procured work as a laborer, and possibly as a coachman or a teamster, but the whereabouts of Catherine's husband, James, remains unknown.[85]

Nearly seventy-five years old, Ben was probably unable to work much; that left Catherine and thirty-nine-year-old Harriet as the only other wage earners in the household. Harriet's mother, Rit, spent some time with the Smiths in Peterboro; Tubman may have asked her friends to care for her aging parents, away from the crowded household in Auburn.[86] Funds from supportive antislavery friends helped the family survive through the winter, spring, and summer, when they could plant some crops in hopes of a good fall harvest to see them through the next winter.

Traveling throughout New England raising money, checking in on her family in Auburn, and visiting refugees in St. Catharines, Tubman had a particularly active spring and summer. Sometime during that period she formally established her own relief organization in St. Catharines to aid needy refugees living there.[87] Continued frustration with Hiram Wilson and questions over the management of funds given to him for refugee relief forced Tubman to establish the Fugitive Aid Society of St. Catharines. She staffed the organization with people she knew and trusted; many had fled slavery in Maryland and Delaware. Charles H. Hall, the president, had run away from Maryland twenty-five years before; Benjamin Fletcher, the vice president, had only arrived in 1859; Christopher "Kit" Anthony, the secretary, was one of the twenty-eight fugitives who had run away from Dorchester County in October 1857; H. W. Wilkins (Wilkinson), the assistant secretary, had left Dorchester in February 1858 with a party of five other men, all of whom settled in the St. Catharines area.[88] A fifth man, William Hutchinson, served as treasurer for the newly formed society. Tubman, her brother William Henry Stewart, John Jones, and Hutchinson's wife, Mary, served as the society's committee. The Fugitive Aid Society assured its potential donors that the association "may be relied on as worthy of confidence by those who wish to help the fugitives in Canada."[89]

Ironically, when Horatio Wilkins (Wilkinson) passed through William Still's office in February 1858, he told Still that his master, Thomas Hodges (Hodson), had visited Canada and upon returning told his slaves that Canada was "the meanest part of the globe" he had ever seen. Hodson told them that he had not seen one black person; a "custom-house" official informed him that all the runaway slaves had been sent "round Cape Horn" and sold. Just in case his slaves still doubted him, Hodson told them "the suffering from deep snows and starvation was fearful."[90] Though Horatio told Still he was aware it was all a lie, little did he know that he and other runaways would indeed face some harsh conditions in Canada.

Tubman felt, like many people, that the country was headed for a profound and lengthy war.[91] She had a vision that the slaves would be emancipated.[92] During a visit with Henry Highland Garnet, a prominent New York black abolitionist, she told him of her vision. He did not believe that they would see emancipation in their lifetimes, nor during the lives of his grandchildren. No, she told him, "you'll see it, and you'll see it soon. My people are free! My people are free."[93] It was not long after, in April 1861, that shots were exchanged for the first time at Fort Sumter, the federal garrison located in the harbor of Charleston, South

Carolina. After two days of heavy bombardment of the garrison, the federal commander, Major Anderson, surrendered the fort to the Confederate commander in Charleston, General Beauregard. The Civil War had begun.[94]

Maryland, however, had not seceded from the Union, and Lincoln was determined to prevent it from doing so. In the middle of April a Massachusetts regiment marching through Baltimore was attacked by an angry secessionist mob. Additional Union troops were sent in to protect rail lines and major thoroughfares; the pressure resulted in Maryland's legislature voting in May to remain within the Union. Though southern sympathies ran strong in Maryland, particularly on the Eastern Shore, pro-Union factions soon dominated.[95]

Reaction to the sectional crisis on the Eastern Shore was divided. Fears of slave insurrection dominated correspondence between Governor Thomas H. Hicks and Union general Benjamin Franklin Butler in April.[96] Maryland had a much smaller slave population and smaller slaveholding class, and a much larger free black population, than its recently seceded Confederate neighbors. Maryland slaves, perhaps sensing a moment of opportunity in the confusion, started to run away again in higher numbers than before.[97] In the late fall Sanborn reported to Benjamin Lyman in Philadelphia that Harriet had told him that the number of slaves escaping from Maryland and Virginia was "unusually great."[98]

Though Union regiments were quickly formed on the Eastern Shore, Governor Hicks was particularly concerned about the strong support for the Confederacy manifesting itself there. He asked the federal government for more assistance in the form of arms and supplies to raise more regiments and to root out the "secessionists that are now passing in great numbers through [there] to the Eastern Shore of Virginia," where they were joining Confederate regiments.[99] Perhaps because of this uncertainty in Maryland, Tubman never made the trip to rescue her niece and nephew.

On November 7, 1861, the Union navy captured two forts at the mouth of Port Royal Bay, on the southeastern coast of South Carolina. Confederate forces and many civilians fled from the area, leaving behind plantations, storehouses, and slaves.[100] Encompassing the Sea Islands and the whole Port Royal district, including Hilton Head Island, St. Helena's Island, and Beaufort, Union forces claimed a vital position from which to launch offensive raids throughout the region. A military zone was established, called the Department of the South, which encompassed South Carolina, Georgia, and Florida.

Within a very short period of time Tubman found herself swept up into war-related activities, forcing her to put aside her own plans and focus on helping the Union cause in the South. Many of the thousands of slaves who were left behind or who ran away in the confusion when their owners abandoned their farms and plantations in the Port Royal district sought shelter behind Union lines. Early in the war, in places where Union troops were encamped (Washington, D.C., North Carolina, and Virginia, for example), slaves from surrounding communities often attempted to flee to the protection of Union lines, only to be turned away or forced back to their owners.[101] Lincoln and his administration were not ready to make the war about emancipation; they wanted the southern states to return to the Union and the issue of the abolishment of slavery to be addressed at a later time.[102] But by the summer of 1861 General Butler, then at Fortress Monroe in Virginia, decided that slaves, who were considered property by their Confederate owners, could be taken into Union camps under his control, ostensibly under war resolutions allowing for the confiscation of rebel property. He called these fugitive slaves flooding to Union lines "contrabands of war."[103] It did not become an official Union policy until March 1862, when a new guideline was passed specifying that no Union officer could return a fugitive slave to its owner.[104] Major General David Hunter, a staunch abolitionist who had been assigned command of the department in South Carolina, went one step further and in mid-April declared all slaves within his jurisdiction free.[105] President Lincoln, however, revoked Hunter's order, infuriating abolitionists throughout the North. Though Hunter effectively ignored the revocation in practice, Lincoln's policy remained in effect until the Emancipation Proclamation was issued on January 1, 1863.[106]

The issue of what to do with all the "contrabands" flooding Union encampments became an immediate concern after the Port Royal district was secured. General Thomas W. Sherman ordered that former slaves in the area be hired to work in the camps in whatever capacity was needed.[107] He later wrote the War Department, requesting teachers be sent from the North to help educate and train the many former slaves seeking help from the Union army. He also requested that agents be sent "to take charge of the plantations and superintend the work of the blacks until they [can] provide for themselves."[108] Further appeals went out to northern churches and antislavery and relief societies for clothing, books, money, other supplies, and volunteers.[109]

Boston abolitionists were among the first to respond. They immediately established organizations and societies to provide for the needs of newly freed slaves. Boston, New York, and Philadelphia set up educational and relief associations within weeks of each other in the early months of 1862.[110] Meetings were held in Boston, privately and publicly, calling for volunteers, money, and supplies to be sent to the various Union encampments in the South. Tubman, who appears to have been in New England throughout that fall, "conceived of the idea of going there and working among her people."[111] She was irritated by Lincoln's position regarding contrabands and his refusal to abolish slavery.[112]

Through her contacts with William Lloyd Garrison, George L. Stearns, Elbridge B. Dudley, and others, Tubman was introduced to Massachusetts governor John Andrew, who quickly made arrangements for her to sail to Beaufort, South Carolina, headquarters for the Department of the South at Port Royal, to begin her work there.[113] Tubman probably returned to Auburn to make arrangements for the care of her elderly parents and others living in her house there; indeed, Ednah Cheney reported that the "only condition she made was that her old parents should be kept from want . . . with what shrewd economy she . . . planned all their household arrangements. She concluded that thirty dollars would keep them comfortable through the winter."[114]

The care and support of her parents was not Tubman's only worry. Sometime before May, and before she left for Port Royal, Tubman brought a little girl named Margaret Stewart to live with Lazette Worden, the sister of William H. Seward's wife, Frances. As Martha Coffin Wright reported, "Mrs. Worden . . . has taken a contraband 10 yrs. old, to live with her, a niece of Harriet Tubman."[115] Though Lazette Wor-

Frederick Douglass. Born Frederick Bailey on the Eastern Shore of Maryland, Douglass fled enslavement in 1838, and within a few years he became a fixture on the northern antislavery lecture circuit.

William Still, a member of Philadelphia's Vigilance Committee and the Pennsylvania Anti-Slavery Society, and one of the most famous black Underground Railroad agents of his time.

Thomas Garrett, notorious Underground Railroad agent operating in Wilmington, Delaware, where he reportedly helped more than twenty-five hundred runaway slaves over a forty-year period.

Lucretia Coffin Mott, abolitionist and suffragist, and a close friend and supporter of Tubman's in Philadelphia.

Gerrit Smith, Underground Railroad operator, abolitionist, John Brown co-conspirator, and early Tubman supporter.

John Brown, abolitionist and freedom fighter. Tubman considered him to be the greatest man she ever met.

Martha Coffin Wright, abolitionist, suffragist, and a close friend and supporter of Tubman's in Auburn, New York.

Colonel James Montgomery, commander of the South Carolina 2nd Regiment, Colored Volunteers, worked closely with Tubman during the war.

Franklin B. Sanborn, abolitionist, author, teacher, John Brown co-conspirator, and a very close friend of Tubman's.

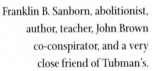

Sarah Hopkins Bradford, a Tubman friend and supporter, wrote *Scenes in the Life of Harriet Tubman* before sailing for Europe in the fall of 1868.

Taken in 1887 or 1888 at Tubman's residence. *Left to right:* Harriet Tubman, adopted daughter Gertie Davis, Nelson Davis, Lee Cheney, "Pop" Alexander, Walter Green, Blind Aunty (Sarah) Parker, and great-niece Dora Stewart.

Harriet Tubman,
date unknown.

Harriet Tubman, circa 1896–1898.

Margaret Stewart
Lucas and daughter
Alice Lucas Brickler,
circa 1900.

The Harriet Tubman Home for the Aged, circa 1908.

John Brown Hall, circa 1912. Tubman is seated in a wheelchair in the center, surrounded by friends, including nurses and matrons from the infirmary.

Harriet Tubman, circa 1908. Photographer:
Ernsberger, Auburn, New York.

Harriet Tubman in her last year, circa 1912.

den had her own home in Auburn, she often stayed for extended periods at the Seward residence, especially when William was away in Washington, D.C., and Frances was left behind at home.[116] Frances Seward, a devout abolitionist who had sheltered slaves in her home during the 1850s, was part of the close circle of white supporters who helped and admired Tubman.[117] It appears that it was to the Seward home that Lazette Worden brought Margaret to live.

The identity and exact relationship of this little girl, Margaret, to Tubman is mysterious and seemingly complicated. Margaret's daughter, Alice Lucas Brickler, recalled many years later that her mother was "Aunt Harriet's favorite niece," a description that was confirmed by another close friend of Tubman's, Florence Carter.[118] "My Mother's life," Brickler wrote, "really began with Aunt Harriet kidnapping her from her home on the Eastern Shore of Maryland when she was a little girl about eight or nine years old."[119] According to Brickler, Margaret had never been a slave. Her mother and her brothers were free as well, and her father was one of Harriet's brothers, "an ex-slave." Margaret's memories of her Maryland home were vague, however, but she told her daughter Alice that she remembered that the family owned "a slick pair of chestnut horses and a shiny carriage in which they rode to church. That was all she remembered of her home."

> Her next memory was of Aunt Harriet's visit to the home. She fell in love with the little girl who was my mother. Maybe it was because in Mother she saw the child she herself might [have] been if slavery had been less cruel. Maybe it was because she knew the joys of motherhood would never be hers and she longed for some little creature who would love her for her own self's sake. Certainly whatever the emotion, it was stronger than her better judgment for when her visit was ended; she, secretly and without so much as a by-your-leave, took the little girl with her to her northern home.[120]

They took a water route north, sailing on a steamer that impressed Margaret "so greatly that she forgot to weep over her separation from her twin brother, her mother & the shiny carriage she liked so much."[121] Brickler found this "kidnapping" as confusing as her mother apparently did. She speculated that Tubman "must have regretted her act for she knew she had taken the child from a sheltered good home to a place where there was nobody to care for her." Taking Margaret from her home on the Eastern Shore to live with her in the North did not "calm [Tubman's] restless soul and turn her into a domestic." Tubman had, in Brickler's view, "violated her brother's home & sorrow & anger were there."[122] Tubman, Brickler believed (and rightfully so), was too busy to care for Margaret, so she "gave the little girl, my mother to Mrs. William H. Seward, the governor's wife . . . [who] brought up mother—not as a servant but as a guest within her home."[123] Though Tubman left Margaret with Lazette Worden, she was raised in the Seward home and taught to "speak properly, to read, write, sew, do housework and act as a lady."[124]

Margaret's parentage remains a mystery, though there are some clues. Tubman did not have a free brother; Edward Brodess had enslaved all of them. One of her brothers, probably Ben (later named James Stewart), left behind two boys, Benjamin and David, when he fled enslavement in Dorchester County in 1854. The boys were free; they were indentured to John D. Parker in May 1857, which indicated that their unidentified mother was free.[125] Benjamin was eight years old in 1857, placing his birth somewhere around 1849.[126] He could be the twin that Margaret left behind. Tubman's brother Ben, however, ran away in December 1854, leaving behind his children, which then raises the question of who was taking care of them—particularly in a home that was financially secure enough to possess what Margaret recalled were "slick chestnut horses and a shiny carriage."[127] As a slave, Ben was not necessarily free to live with them.[128] Who, then, are Margaret's parents? Why, given all the family members then living in Tubman's home in Fleming, including her brother John, her sister-in-law Catherine and her children, possibly her brother James, and her parents, did she take this particular child and leave her with one of the most powerful and richest white families in Auburn? What made this particular child so much more important than the others?

There is one possibility that must be considered, regardless of how remote it may seem: that Margaret Stewart is in fact Harriet Tubman's own daughter. Such a scenario provides one of the few logical explanations, if not the only one, for Tubman's "kidnapping" Margaret from her home. Tubman understood the particular pain of separation of family; she never forgot the "hopeless grief" of her parents when her sisters were sold away.[129] Does it make sense that she would have stolen a child from its mother? Tubman's primary goal during the 1850s was family reunification; it was for family that she risked her life over and over again to return to the Eastern Shore to bring them north. Was she also returning time and time again to see the young child she had given birth to?

It is possible that Tubman gave birth before she left the Eastern Shore. Knowing that her child would be enslaved, Tubman could have given the child to another woman, a free woman, to raise for her—a woman who may have given birth at the same time, who could, in fact, claim she had twins. Tubman could have concealed her pregnancy, or she could have claimed the child had died. Though Margaret's daughter Alice had been told her mother was born on the Eastern Shore, her death certificate states she was born in Baltimore. After running away, Tubman could have given birth there, leaving the child with a free black family while she pursued her efforts to liberate her family.[130] In fact, Tubman was in Baltimore in December 1850, when she helped her niece Kessiah Bowley escape from the Eastern Shore with her husband, John Bowley, and children Araminta and James. Baltimore's waterfront was home to several of Tubman's extended-family members and friends. Irrespective of where Margaret may have been born, the large number of free black families in Maryland made such a plan a possibility.

While this scenario is highly speculative, it would help to answer several lingering questions about Margaret and her strong bond with Tubman, a bond that was obvious to those who knew them. Alice Brickler made another important comment. "Strange to say," Brickler wrote Earl Conrad, "mother looked very much like Aunt Harriet, and there was a hardness about her character in the face of adversity that must have been hereditary."[131] Conrad inquired of Florence Carter if this was true, and Carter confirmed it.[132] When Margaret died in 1930, the newspaper described her as Tubman's "foster daughter."[133]

Why, once safely in the North, would Tubman conceal the identity of her own child? There are several plausible reasons. The child may not have been John Tubman's, or once she ran away from slavery (and him) he may have shown no interest in the child, if he had been aware of its existence in the first place. John abandoned his marriage to Tubman as early as 1851, and she may have felt that leaving Margaret with an intact free family was better than trying to care for the child herself in Philadelphia, particularly if she remained at risk of recapture. In 1862 Tubman may have doubted that her middle-class white supporters would view her so favorably if she revealed the presence of an unknown daughter. Complex notions of slave women's sexuality throughout the antebellum period (and after) remained a titillating yet uncomfortable topic of fascination for whites. Antislavery texts, whether in newspapers, tracts, novels, or slave narratives, spoke to the particular problems black women faced in slavery. Sexual exploitation by white masters denigrated black women and men and contributed to a view that black sexual activity was aberrant, immoral, and uncontrollable. Children born out of wedlock and unfaithful husbands all fed into the racist stereotype of low moral character in black women and men. Tubman spent enough time with white northerners to know that many of them shared these stereotypical views. Therefore, she may not have wanted to confront this issue, nor burden herself or her daughter with such disapproval. Once the lie had been told, it may have been easier to maintain it. When Tubman settled Margaret with Lazette Worden in the Seward household in 1862, she had chosen not to care for Margaret herself; her commitment to going to South Carolina to help with the war effort superseded any thoughts of staying in Auburn with her family. Why risk being judged for abandoning her child again?

Brickler could not reconcile her mother's position within the various kin relationships in Tubman's household. She was confused, and rightly so, as it seems that no one made mention of who Margaret's parents were, nor is there any mention of whether Margaret returned to the Eastern Shore at any time after the Civil War to see the family she was allegedly taken from.[134] It appears, as well, that Margaret's favored position in Tubman's household provoked serious jealousy and resentment from others. Margaret was "very proud to the point of being snobbish . . . she was short and plump, light brown with long thick Negroid hair," Brickler told Conrad. Margaret had been favored with a good education, a lovely and wealthy home environment, and all the accouterments that came with being part of the Seward and Worden households. A Tubman relative, Brickler recalled, "disliked Mother very much [and] whenever Aunt Harriet was out of hearing she used to call Mother a 'pumpkin-colored hussey.' "[135] Much to the chagrin of some extended Tubman family members, Alice Lucas (Brickler) was chosen to unveil a bronze memorial tablet placed on the county courthouse in Auburn in Tubman's honor in 1914.[136]

Animosity toward Margaret spanned generations. In 1940 Eva Stewart Northrup, a great-niece who had been raised since birth in the early 1890s by Tubman, wrote to Earl Conrad to inform him "Mrs. Brickler is of no relation, neither by blood or through marriage, whatsoever, to my Aunt. I have already put her down in history as an imposture. She has no rightful claim to give out information or to claim credit for an[y] information that she might give."[137] Northrup asked Conrad to share the information Brickler had given him, in addition to all the other material he had collected while researching his book. "There are only a few sources that are authentic. But there are plenty of the other type. . . . I would also like to know what arrangements you intend to make [w]ith me for the information I could give you for the book? Also, what percentage of the royalty [sic] from the sale of your book?"[138]

Conrad confronted Brickler about Northrup's accusations: "Mrs. Northrup of Philadelphia has written to say that you are not in any way related to Harriet."[139] At first Brickler claimed she did not know who Northrup was.[140] Brickler attempted to defend herself; she told Conrad "there is a part of the family history that is better never told"; with such a large family as Tubman's there were naturally many different perspectives and stories to tell, prompting some relatives to "think of themselves as the sole heirs."[141] In a later letter, Brickler realized that she did in fact know Northrup. "I remember Katy Stewart Northrup. I did not know she is living in Philadelphia. This may sound catty—but—I'm not surprised at anything she says or writes."[142] Brickler summed up the situation quite effectively: "Being a member of the Harriet Tubman family is an empty honor at most but I do have this to say. Mother was always said by the older heads to be Aunt Harriet's niece."[143] Whether Margaret was Tubman's daughter, the daughter of an unknown brother, or someone else's child, her presence and importance to Tubman remain a mystery. Irrespective of the kin relationship, the story of Margaret's "kidnapping" remains one of the most puzzling, and troubling, stories of Tubman's life.

IT WAS RAINING BLOOD:
HARRIET TUBMAN'S CIVIL WAR

ARRIET TUBMAN'S CIVIL WAR STARTED YEARS BEFORE THE FIRST shots were fired on Fort Sumter in South Carolina in April 1861. Some might argue that it began with her first defiant act as a slave: running away at the age of six to avoid a whipping when she was caught taking a lump of sugar. But it was Tubman's battles to claim liberty for scores of friends and relatives that marked the beginning of a strategic, political, and even military consciousness that eventually prepared her for a role on the battlefields. Her leadership skills, honed on the escape missions she successfully conducted from the Eastern Shore, and the support systems and close community relationships she forged in the northern United States and Canada earned her the title "Moses of her people."

These leadership skills, combined with a passion and commitment to fight for freedom, brought Tubman to the attention of Massachusetts governor John Andrew. In January 1862 Andrew made arrangements for Tubman to travel to South Carolina, where he believed she would be useful in the Union war effort. He probably assumed that, as a natural leader of fleeing slaves, she would be helpful in dealing with the hundreds of "contrabands" flooding Union camps at Port Royal.

And given her ability to move in and out of hostile territory unde-tected, Andrew and Tubman believed that "she would be a valuable person to operate within the enemies lines in procuring information & scouts."[1]

Harriet later recalled that someone "changed the program" before she started for Beaufort, and instead redirected her to participate in the distribution of clothing and supplies being sent by the various charita-ble organizations forming in the North, as the numbers of slaves com-ing to Union lines continued unabated.[2] She was sent to New York, and from there, Colonel Francis Howe sent her along to Beaufort on the "Government transport Atlantic," although years later she offered a slightly different sequence of events that brought her to Beaufort.[3] "They wouldn't let no colored people go down South then," she told Emma Telford,

> unless they went with some of the officers as a servant; so they got a gentleman from New York to take me as a servant. He was stopping at a big hotel on Broadway and I went to the parlor and they sent for him and he came down: but I didn't like that man no how. He looked at me and said, "well, I guess you're young enough. You go to the quarter master and tell him I sent you." But I made up my mind that I wasn't going with that man. He looked brave and noble enough to be a gentleman if looks made one, a struttin' about; but I went out and I ain't seen the quarter master yet, nor him neither. So I just went on alone to Balti-more, and General Hunter sent for me to go to Beaufort, an the vessel that was going there didn't sail for two days, a waitin' for me till the General's orders were fulfilled.[4]

The needs were so great at the time of her arrival (sometime in the spring) that she immediately set about doing anything and everything she could.[5] Much of the early Union military, government, and philan-thropic efforts in Port Royal targeted the dismantling of the plantation slave labor system by replacing it with a wage-based system, a difficult task given the hundreds of years of forced labor that had denied educa-tion and economic opportunity to thousands of Sea Island slaves. This early effort was called the "Port Royal Experiment," a "proving ground for the freedmen," which would, they hoped, demonstrate how well former slaves could cope and function in a free, capitalist economy, given the right guidance and education by Northern abolitionists.[6]

Tubman was one of the very first northern blacks who traveled to South Carolina to participate in this grand effort. "I first took charge of the Christian Commission house at Beaufort," she explained, which had been set up by the YMCA to distribute supplies of clothing, food, books, and other items to Union soldiers.[7] Tubman established a "wash house" with $200 she received from the government; here she taught newly freed women to do washing, sewing, and baking for the Union soldiers, so that they could support themselves with wages instead of depending upon government support.[8] At first Tubman had been allowed to draw rations like other soldiers, but she later gave up that privilege because of the tension it created among the freedmen, who perceived her as receiving preferential treatment.[9] She purchased supplies in Beaufort and at Hilton Head, which she either resold or used to bake pies and make root beer that she then sold to the soldiers, who were eager to supplement their meager rations. In this way she supported herself and put away a little money to send to her parents.[10]

At some point during the spring or summer Tubman was introduced to General David Hunter.[11] She was attracted to Hunter's strong abolitionist and reform ideology; within weeks of his appointment to the Department of the South he declared that all "contrabands" in the Port Royal district were free. Shortly thereafter he declared all slaves within the jurisdiction of the Department of the South, which included South Carolina, Georgia, and Florida, free people.[12]

Hunter was intent on building a regiment of black soldiers, the First South Carolina Volunteers, made up of newly liberated slaves in the Port Royal district, and he set about recruiting at the various plantations in and around Hilton Head and the other Sea Islands.[13] Northern abolitionists loudly praised Hunter's independent actions, but, as previously noted, Lincoln was not ready for emancipation, nor was he ready to outfit a regiment of black troops. On May 17, Lincoln invalidated Hunter's orders.[14] Hunter initially ignored Lincoln's reprimand, continuing to recruit and drill his small band of soldiers.

Tubman believed Lincoln was shortsighted and that he was blinded by his inability to see that the war could not be won without the direct participation of black people. In the early days of the war Lincoln had not yet decided the fates of millions of slaves still held in bondage in the Confederacy. For Tubman and many antislavery activists, there was but one decision to make: emancipation. Tubman noted:

They may send the flower of their young men down South, to die of the fever in the summer, and the ague in the winter.[15] (For it is cold down there, though it *is* down South.) They may send them one year, two years, three years, till they are *tired* of sending, or till they use up all the young men. All no use! God's ahead of master Lincoln. God won't let master Lincoln beat the South till he does *the right thing.* Master Lincoln, he's a great man, and I am a poor negro; but the negro can tell master Lincoln how to save the money and the young men. He can do it by setting the negroes free. Suppose that was an awful big snake down there, on the floor. He bite you. Folks all scared, because you die. You send for a doctor to cut the bite; but the snake, he rolled up there, and while the doctor doing it, he bite you *again.* The doctor dug out *that* bite; but while the doctor doing it, the snake, he spring up and bite you again; so he *keep* doing it, till you kill *him.* That's what master Lincoln ought to know.[16]

Tubman played an important role in advancing her cause by helping Union recruitment of black soldiers. Many of these former slaves were suspicious of whites, regardless of who they were, and were unwilling to leave their families and their newfound liberty on the plantations and in the countryside where they were living. Hunter needed help to persuade them; he may have called on Tubman to reassure the suspicious blacks, who "were as much afraid of 'de Yankee Buckra' as of their own masters. It was almost impossible to win their confidence, or to get information from them."[17] When Hunter, frustrated by the slow enlistment of local blacks, started forcibly drafting local African American men into his regiment, he created even more fear and anger among the men and their families. Some were eager and willing to join, while others panicked.[18]

Hunter's actions contributed to the already anxious debate among abolitionists and some members of Lincoln's administration who were eager to keep the discussion of emancipation alive, albeit behind closed doors, at the highest levels of government. At the end of July 1862 Lincoln handed his cabinet a draft resolution to emancipate slaves. By September the Emancipation Proclamation had been announced to the world; effective January 1, 1863, slaves in those states still in rebellion against the United States were to be freed.[19] While the proclamation did not provide freedom for slaves living in border states such as Maryland, still loyal to the Union, it marked a dramatic change in the policies of the Lincoln administration.[20] The proclamation authorized the call into service of any able-bodied African American who could be of assistance to the Union forces in the South, opening the window for the official establishment of African American regiments.[21]

Even before the preliminary Emancipation Proclamation was issued, General Rufus Saxton, military governor of the Department of the South, was formally authorized in late August 1862 by the secretary of war, Edwin Stanton, to raise five regiments of black troops. He began with Hunter's disbanded First South Carolina Volunteers; avoiding Hunter's tactics of conscription, he successfully filled the first regiment by November. He called upon Tubman's old Massachusetts friend Thomas Wentworth Higginson to lead the troops, and Higginson enthusiastically agreed. On November 24, 1862, Higginson arrived at Beaufort to take command; within a couple of weeks of his arrival he was greeted by Tubman, who had driven the three miles from Beaufort to Camp Saxton, the former Smith plantation where the First South Carolina was quartered, to see him. Higginson wrote to his wife, Mary, that Tubman was living in Beaufort "as a sort of nurse & general caretaker."[22]

As a nurse, she faced daily arrivals of sick and dying soldiers and civilians, who were ill not from battle wounds (as little combat was occurring in the region during 1862) but from contaminated water and food, poor sanitation and hygiene, and the particular natural environment found in the Port Royal area. Disease was rampant in the camps;

many northerners, whether soldiers or volunteers there to help with relief work, fell victim to the uncontrolled outbreaks of smallpox, dysentery, measles, malaria, scarlet fever, typhoid, pneumonia, and other
infections that weakened and killed thousands.[23] The Port Royal district, home to innumerable swamps, marshes, creeks, and irrigation
and drainage ditches, was an ideal breeding ground for mosquitoes,
which spread malaria and, at times, yellow fever during the warmer
months.[24] Ticks and fleas thrived in the close living quarters of army
camps, spreading typhoid and other infections. On August 28 Henry K.
Durant, assistant surgeon, told Captain Warfield to "let 'Moses' have a
little Bourbon whiskey for medicinal purposes."[25] She probably used
this in combination with quinine and other drugs and herbs to relieve
the symptoms of malaria and to ease discomfort associated with fevers
and other illnesses.[26]

Tubman was not paid for her nursing duties and relied on her cooking, sewing, and washing skills to make an income. Tubman ran an
"eating house" in Beaufort, which may have been for freedmen who
had been hired to work in the area, or perhaps for the better-paid officers and their families, who could afford to pay for the meals.[27] Tubman
would make "about fifty pies, a great quantity of ginger-bread, and two
casks of root beer," then hire "some contraband to sell for her through
the camps, and thus she would provide her support for another day."[28]
She lived, at least part of the time, at the Savan House, across from the
arsenal and not too far from General Saxton's headquarters and the local "contraband" and military hospitals.[29]

Charlotte Forten, a young black woman from Salem, Massachusetts,
who had come to Port Royal as a teacher with the Pennsylvania Freedmen's Relief Association in October 1862, recorded spending a day with
"Moses" at Beaufort in late January 1863.[30] Tubman entertained Forten
with stories of Underground Railroad rescues, including the flight of
Joe Bailey, sang songs, and recalled how a reward of $10,000 was offered
for her capture.[31] Forten noted that Tubman was eager to return to the
North. No doubt Harriet wanted to see her family and make sure they
were doing all right.[32]

General Saxton made a great effort to celebrate the Emancipation
Proclamation on the day it became official, January 1, 1863. Word

spread, not only through the black regimental camps but also throughout the countryside and outlying islands composing the Port Royal district, that Saxton was planning a daylong festival, to include a formal reading of the Proclamation. It was bright, clear, and warm for the New Year's Day festivities. Steamers ferried black men, women, and children from the various islands to Camp Saxton, and "carriages heavily laden" rolled alongside hundreds of "foot passengers" and people riding various kinds of pack animals to the "great celebration."[33] An estimated four thousand African Americans, now free, crowded the festivities. Dressed in their finest clothing, the freedmen continued to stream into "a beautiful grove of live oaks, whose fresh glittering leaves, and gray hanging moss" welcomed them all under its shade.[34] The women, "picturesque" in "bright colored turbans," gave the event an air of gaiety.[35] Mingling with the crowd, the soldiers of the First South Carolina stood out, their swords gleaming against their blue coats and dark red pants.[36]

Dr. William Brisbane, a former Sea Island planter who had freed his slaves some twenty-five years before, read the Proclamation to the crowd; Higginson was then presented with a flag for his black regiment, at which point a "spontaneous" performance of "My Country, 'Tis of Thee" erupted from the freedmen.[37] Two members of the First South Carolina, Sergeant Prince Rivers and Corporal Robert Sutton, addressed the crowd, urging freedmen to join and fight for the liberation of others still held in bondage. The three-hour ceremony ended with a rousing rendition of "John Brown's Body."[38]

In Tubman's eyes, the Emancipation Proclamation was only a half step. She recognized the political advantages and disadvantages of the proclamation, but she wanted more. The war would not be won with the freeing of *some* enslaved people in the South—they should all be free. While everyone was celebrating the proclamation, she was asked "why do you not join with the rest in their rejoicing!" Recalling her dream three years earlier while staying at the home of Henry Highland Garnet in New York, where she envisioned the emancipation of all slaves, Tubman replied, "I had *my* jubilee three years ago. I rejoiced all I could then; I can't rejoice no more."[39]

She set her sights instead on participating more directly in armed conflict, bringing herself into closer contact with generals and other officers. Tubman's reputation as "Moses" was obviously known in the camps; stories of her raids on the Eastern Shore inspired admiration and respect from some soldiers, and her relationship with white people in positions of power, such as Higginson, must have also played a role in making her a leader in the camps among the freedmen. Tubman effectively ferreted out information on rebel locations and movements from the local black population, and passed it along to Generals Stevens, Sherman, and Hunter.[40] Before long, Tubman was scouting into the interior regions, beyond the occupied areas of Port Royal district, up the rivers and streams to assess rebel troop activities, offering "much and very valuable service acting as a spy within the enemy lines."[41] She gained the confidence of several local men: Isaac Hayward, Mott Blake, Gabriel Cahern, Sandy Sellers, George Chisholm, Solomon Gregory, Peter Burns, Charles Simmons, Samuel Hayward, and Walter D. Plowden, who, through her influence, became "the most valued scouts and pilots in the Gov't employ in that Department."[42] On January 7, 1863, Tubman was given a requisition for $100 "secret service money."[43] With these funds, she and her band of scouts supported themselves and bribed nervous informants, such as slaves still living in Confederate-controlled territory nearby, for crucial information.

Tubman moved easily about the physical landscape, as the geography of Port Royal district was very similar to the landscape of Dorchester County and the Eastern Shore of Maryland. Numerous bays, rivers, streams, creeks, marshes, and swamps divided the land and defined daily life much in the same way water defined life in Dorchester County. The water was both a barrier between various places in the district and a means of access to them. Tubman was quite comfortable navigating both on land and by water. Although the fields sprouted rice and cotton rather than the grains of the Eastern Shore, the sameness of the physical landscape worked to Tubman's advantage.

At first the efforts of Tubman and others to recruit for the Second South Carolina Volunteers had been slow, but when the Emancipation Proclamation was formally enacted and announced on January 1, 1863, many more former slaves decided to join. On February 24 Colonel James Montgomery arrived at Port Royal to take command of the Second South Carolina.[44] Montgomery had been a comrade of John Brown's, "a veteran guerilla of the Kansas wars," during the late 1850s, fighting proslavery forces long before the start of the Civil War with the South.[45]

Tubman soon met Montgomery and developed a close working relationship with the Kansas freedom fighter. Though Tubman had known Higginson prior to the war, she and Montgomery had far more in common. Montgomery had been "acquainted with [Tubman's] character and actions for several years." It is likely that he had heard of her association with Brown from Brown himself, and therefore knew of the respect Brown felt for her.[46] While Higginson, Tubman, and Montgomery shared an adoration of John Brown, Montgomery had fought beside Brown, had risked his life to defend free soil, and in him Tubman saw a similarity to Brown, including the willingness to resort to extreme measures to secure the demise of slavery.[47] Her partnership with Montgomery would draw Tubman into direct armed conflict and position her to witness some of the most horrific fighting in the Department of the South.

Within two weeks of his arrival at Port Royal, in early March 1863, Montgomery led his regiment, along with Higginson's First South Carolina, to capture and occupy Jacksonville, Florida. They met little resistance, though there were small skirmishes and pockets of fighting, giving some of the black troops their first taste of battle. Both Higginson and Montgomery hoped to recruit more former slaves into their regiments, but to their great disappointment, local slave owners had fled with all their "able-bodied" slaves to the interior.[48] Montgomery was able to secure a few thousand dollars' worth of confiscated cotton and other supplies, but only thirty new recruits. Whether Tubman joined them on this expedition is not known, although the regiments were accompanied by the usual assortment of laundresses, cooks, nurses, surgeons, and other medical personnel, as well as scouts and spies. Like Susie King Taylor, a former slave from Savannah, Georgia, who served as a teacher, nurse, and laundress during the Civil War in the Department of the South, Tubman often followed troops into battle, if not as a scout and spy, then as a nurse, cook, or laundress.[49]

Tubman's importance and value to Hunter's operations are evidenced in a military pass issued in February 1863: "Pass the bearer, Harriet

Tubman, to Beaufort and back to this place, and wherever she wishes to go; and give her free passage at all times, on all Government transports. Harriet was sent to me from Boston by Governor Andrew, of Massachusetts, and is a valuable woman. She has permission, as a servant of the Government, to purchase such provisions from the Commissary as she may need."[50] These provisions, including flour, sugar, molasses, whiskey, and assorted other items, were used in cooking and administering nursing services to the sick and wounded.[51] That such broad powers and freedom of movement were granted to a black woman seems extraordinary; the language of the pass indicates not only familiarity with Tubman's past accomplishments but also an acknowledgment of her perceived importance to Hunter and other officers. She had already engaged in several espionage trips into the interior; as a sort of free agent, Tubman would not be hindered by the necessity of obtaining individual passes from various officers in command at different locations throughout the district. A cook and a laundress one day, a spy the next, Tubman continuously reinvented herself, adapting to and accommodating the immediate requirements of wartime crises with stunning success.

On June 1, 1863, Tubman became the first woman to plan and execute an armed expedition during the Civil War. Acting as an advisor to Montgomery, Tubman led a raid from Port Royal to the interior, some twenty-five miles up the nearby Combahee River. Using communication networks that were the province of black mariners, Tubman's successful spy mission provided crucial details about rebel enforcements and heavily mined waters. Leaving under the cover of darkness, the steam-driven gunboats *John Adams, Harriet A. Weed,* and *Sentinel* moved slowly along the river with three hundred men from the Second South Carolina and a smaller contingent from the Third Rhode Island Battery.[52] The *Adams* and the *Harriet Weed* were about a quarter of a mile apart; Harriet stood with Montgomery and another officer in the lead boat, the *Adams,* with Walter Plowden, the local scout who helped direct the ships around the mines.[53] After locating many "torpedoes," the pilots of the *Adams,* the *Harriet Weed,* and the *Sentinel* were able to navigate through the channels of the river without incident.[54] Under Tubman's leadership, Montgomery and his small force made their way to

the plantations where Tubman and her scouts had identified Confederate warehouses and stockpiles of rice and cotton.[55]

At about dawn on June 2, with fog rolling slowly off the rice fields,
Montgomery landed some of his black troops, sending them into the
fields and woods to rustle out any Confederates hiding in wait, and to
warn the slaves, telling them to come to the river and join the Union.[56]
The troops effectively dispersed Confederate gunners located at various
points along the river and met with little resistance. They set fire to several of the plantations, destroying homes, barns, rice mills, and steam
engines, and they confiscated thousands of dollars' worth of rice, corn,
cotton, horses, and other farm animals. What they could not take with
them they destroyed. "We broke the sluice gates," the regiment's surgeon reported to *Harper's Weekly*, "and flooded the fields so that the
present crop, which was growing beautifully, will be a total loss."[57] The
slaves fled to the Union boats.[58] Montgomery made his way to Combahee Ferry, where he ordered the destruction of the pontoon bridge.[59]

Montgomery ordered the whistles blown on the steamers, signaling
to the area's enslaved people to abandon the plantations and fields and
come aboard the ships.[60] Tubman recalled that some of the slaves were
reluctant to join them, though most quickly realized that "Lincoln's
gun-boats [had] come to set them free."[61] Overseers, plantation owners,
and managers tried in vain to keep the slaves from running away;
though they brandished whips, guns, and pistols, their threats of punishment and even death were almost useless against the mass desertion.[62] Several slaves were killed or wounded, however, by rebel soldiers
and others "as they swarmed to the protection of the old flag."[63]

Tubman later recalled that she had never witnessed anything like
the scene that unfolded.[64] Women and men, arms laden with children,
food, clothing, and other personal possessions, streamed from the fields
to the riverbanks. "Some had white blankets on their heads with their
things done up in them. . . . Some had bags on their backs with pigs in
them; some had chickens tied by the legs," Tubman recalled.[65] One
woman had "a pail on her head, rice a smokin' in it just as she'd taken it
from the fire, a young one hangin' on behind, one hand around her
forehead to hold on . . . [and a] hold of her dress two or three more
[children]."[66] With squealing pigs, squawking chickens, and crying

children, the cacophony alone was extraordinary. It reminded Tubman of "the children of Israel, coming out of Egypt."[67]

Montgomery sent small boats to the riverbanks to retrieve the liberated slaves, but their arrival produced a tremendous amount of confusion and panic. Many of the boats became dangerously overcrowded as men, women, and children scrambled to get aboard. Fearful of being left behind, some of the people held on so that the boats could not leave without them. The "oarsmen [had to] beat them on their hands, but they would not let go; they were afraid the gun-boats would go off and leave them."[68] It was turning into an alarming situation. Montgomery, eager to get away from the banks of the river and avoid a rebel attack, urged Tubman to encourage the people to stay calm and assure them that all would be taken onto the boats and away to freedom: "Moses Garrison . . . come here and speak a word of consolation to your people."[69] But Harriet did not consider them "her people." She later told Emma Telford that they "wasn't my people any more than they was his—only we was all Negroes—'cause I didn't know any more about them than he did. So I went when he called me on the gunboat, and they on the shore. They didn't know anything about me and I didn't know what to say. I looked at them about two minutes, and then I sung to them."[70] Tubman's singing was contagious; the people on the banks starting singing and clapping their hands, shouting "Glory!" to her melody. They let go of the boats, and the evacuation continued safely until Montgomery had brought away somewhere in the neighborhood of 730 "contrabands."[71]

They all spent the night of June 2 crowded together on board the three steamboats, making their way back to Beaufort; a violent storm during the night probably made the passage uncomfortable, but by morning the sun was shining brightly.[72] The refugees were led from the boats to a church in Beaufort, where they were housed temporarily while arrangements could be made for their settlement elsewhere. Montgomery delivered an address to them, which was followed by a speech from Tubman, "the black woman who led the raid," a reporter from the *Wisconsin State Journal*, who witnessed the victorious return, wrote, "and under whose supervision it was originated and conducted. For sound sense and real native eloquence, her address would do honor to

*"Raid of Second South Carolina Volunteers (Col. Montgomery)
Among the Rice Plantations on the Combahee, S.C."*

any man, and it created quite a sensation."[73] Headlining the triumphant
story to his readers, the reporter powerfully acknowledged Tubman's
role as "A Black She 'Moses'—Her Wonderful Daring and Sagacity."

> Col. Montgomery and his gallant band of 300 hundred black sol-
> diers, under the guidance of a black woman, dashed into the en-
> emies' country, struck a bold and effective blow, destroying
> millions of dollars worth of commissary stores, cotton, and
> lordly dwellings, and striking terror to the heart of rebellion,
> brought off near 800 slaves and thousands of dollars worth of
> property, without losing a man or receiving a scratch! It was a
> glorious consummation.[74]

The reporter, quite taken with Tubman's accomplishments, devoted
considerable column space on the role of "this black heroine." Since

the war, he wrote, she had many times "penetrated the enemy's lines and discovered their situation and condition, and escaped without extreme hazard . . . In patriotism, sagacity, energy, ability, and all that elevates human character, she is head and shoulders above the many who vaunt their patriotism and boast their philanthropy, swaggering of their superiority because of the cuticle in which their Creator condescended to envelop them."[75] His recognition of her accomplishment underscores the ways in which the legend of Harriet Tubman as a heroic figure was constructed and established even during her own lifetime. She was the heroine of the day.

Back in Boston, the *Commonwealth* picked up the story of the "black she 'Moses'," publishing part of it, and pointing out to its readers that the woman heralded in the article was none other than Harriet Tubman. Tubman, in fact, had dictated a letter to Sanborn informing him of the raid herself. She was extremely proud of the successful mission and asked Sanborn if he didn't think "we colored people are entitled to some credit for that exploit, under the lead of the brave Colonel Montgomery? We weakened the rebels somewhat on the Combahee River, by taking and bringing away *seven hundred and fifty-six* head of their most valuable live stock, known up in your region as 'contrabands,' and this, too, without the loss of a single life on our part, though we had good reason to believe that a number of rebels bit the dust. Of these seven hundred and fifty-six contrabands nearly or quite all the able-bodied men have joined the colored regiments here."[76]

From a military standpoint, it was a productive raid for Montgomery, too. He gained another 100 to 180 new recruits for his regiment.[77] Tubman claimed she brought nearly one hundred of the contrabands to the recruiting officer's headquarters herself and that she should have been paid for it but never was.[78] The confiscation of supplies of rice, cotton, and livestock was a great coup for Montgomery, but many officers disagreed with his guerilla tactics. Higginson "utterly" detested Montgomery's "burning and pillaging."[79] Robert Gould Shaw, the commander of the famous northern black regiment, the Fifty-fourth Massachusetts Colored Infantry, also disliked Montgomery's tactics, though he admired him greatly for his devotion to the cause. Montgomery was "enormously energetic" but a "bush-whacker,"

Shaw wrote, "[and] considers that praying, shooting, burning [and] hanging are the true means to put down the rebellion."[80]

Tubman and Montgomery apparently agreed on this point, but Higginson could not abide by it. He complained often in his letters and diary about Montgomery, and he was pleased when General Hunter was relieved of his command and replaced by General Quincy Gillmore, someone whom Higginson thought would exercise more control over the Department and Montgomery.[81] Sanborn later wrote that, under Montgomery's command, Tubman performed some of "her best service in S. Carolina; but her direct way of interpreting orders, and Montgomery's soldierly way of acting under general orders, offended the more fastidious Col. Higginson, and led to censures by him of both Montgomery and Harriet."[82]

Immediately after this successful raid, Tubman was called to testify at the court-martial of Private John E. Webster. Private Webster had been assigned to the superintendent position at Beaufort, allocating work to freedmen, including stevedore positions on the wharves and docks, carpentry, cutting and hauling wood, and other tasks required for the functioning of military and civilian life in and around Beaufort. He was also responsible for doling out rations of food and other supplies from the commissary.[83] He was charged with "embezzling and misapplying Military stores," including two counts for selling Tubman brown sugar on two different occasions, and another count for selling sugar to Walter D. Plowden, Tubman's fellow scout and spy.[84]

The unprecedented testimony of blacks against a white defendant marks an important moment in the Port Royal experiment. Though the civil status of the former slaves was still a contested issue even in the North, a new opportunity presented itself in this wartime environment, one that required an adjustment to accepted norms of political and civil rights. Though tentative at first, the Emancipation Proclamation, Benjamin Giterman writes, made the freedmen "irrevocably free" and thus required that they "be guaranteed certain basic legal powers," including testifying under oath. In Port Royal these freedmen were experiencing legal, social, and civil rights not enjoyed by African Americans elsewhere.[85]

It was this transition in black rights that allowed Tubman, Plowden, and four other black witnesses to testify before the court on June 5.[86] Webster, Tubman testified, had sold her brown sugar twice; unbeknownst to her, the sugar was part of the inventory of military stores and therefore not available for sale. Webster was supposed to provide these supplies in the form of rations to the freedmen working for the government and to the regiments in his jurisdiction.[87]

Tubman had purchased approximately fifty or sixty pounds of sugar from Webster on two separate occasions; the exact price and amount she could not recall. Plowden had done the same (150 pounds at 14 cents a pound) and later purchased coffee and other items.[88] Tubman and Plowden then tried to sell these items in and around Beaufort, raising the suspicions of another local shopkeeper, John Lilly, who suspected they had stolen the items. When Lilly confronted Tubman in Webster's presence, Webster admitted that he had indeed sold her the sugar. Webster later asked Lilly to keep the information to himself, but it was too late; Tubman had immediately gone to General Saxton and told him of her own suspicions.[89] Based on the testimony of all the witnesses, both black and white, Webster was convicted of illegally selling army supply rations and sentenced to six months in a labor detail without pay.[90] As the testimony indicates, Tubman's stature with General Saxton and other officers in the district was well known and had protected her, revealing her easy access to those at the highest levels of command.

On June 5 Montgomery led his regiment down the coast to capture Darien, Georgia.[91] Tubman stayed behind to help the newly arrived freedmen from the Combahee raid. "Most of those coming from the mainland are very destitute, almost naked," she wrote Sanborn in a dictated letter. "I am trying to find places for those able to work, and provide for them as best I can, so as to lighten the burden on the Government as much as possible, while at the same time they learn to respect themselves by earning their own living."[92] She was still struggling to earn money to support herself, though, while also trying to save enough money to send home to her family. Her parents needed her, and she experienced anxiety about their welfare in her absence.[93] She hoped that Sanborn would see to it that they were taken care of and that they would not be allowed "to suffer." She privately reminded Sanborn that he had told her "some time ago that you would furnish me with a small sum of money every year to help me carry on my work."[94]

Sanborn published her letter in the *Boston Commonwealth* on July 17, at the conclusion of a biographical sketch of her life. Using notes he had taken from interviews with Tubman in the late 1850s and early 1860s, Sanborn drew a brief but detailed sketch of Tubman's life in slavery and her rescue missions to bring away family and friends during the 1850s. His essay constituted the first biography of Tubman ever to be published.[95] Sanborn offered the portrait in the hope that his readers would send Tubman money she obviously needed to continue her work in South Carolina and to help support her needy parents in Auburn, "for none is better deserved."[96] Within three days, a $100 payment was made on Tubman's mortgage debt to William Seward.[97]

She also asked Sanborn to let it be "known to the ladies" that she needed "a *bloomer* dress, made of some coarse, strong material, to wear on *expeditions.*" Made popular by Amelia Bloomer, a suffragist and reformer, the dress was actually a modified pantaloon that combined the ease and comfort of pants with the more feminine look of a dress. The source of much ridicule and the subject of many jokes at the expense of suffragists, who were perceived as literally wanting to "wear the pants" or take over men's roles in society, the bloomer dress never really attained much public acceptance. But for a woman such as Tubman, it had immense practical application. She had lost all of her clothes during the fall of 1862, when Beaufort had to be evacuated temporarily. She explained to Sanborn that

all my clothes were packed and sent with others to Hilton Head, and lost; and I have never been able to get any trace of them since. . . . In our late expedition up the Combahee River, in coming on board the boat, I was carrying *two pigs* for a poor sick woman, who had a child to carry, and the order "double quick" was given, and I started to run, stepped on my dress, it being rather long, and fell and tore it almost off, so that when I got on board the boat, there was hardly anything left of it but shreds. I made up my mind then I would never wear a long dress on another expedition of the kind, but would have a *bloomer* as soon as

I could get it . . . for I expect to have use for it very soon, probably before they can get it to me.[98]

By the first of July plans were in the making for an assault on
Charleston, under the leadership of General Gillmore, and the regiments in the Port Royal district were mobilized for action. It would be
an immense undertaking and a difficult fight. After days of bombardment and combat, Gillmore was certain that the Confederate defenses
on Morris Island at Fort Wagner had been debilitated enough for a
frontal assault. Others, however, thought the defenses had not been sufficiently damaged and that the Union assault forces would be exposed
"like a flock of sheep."[99] On the morning of July 17 the Massachusetts
Fifty-fourth, under the command of Colonel Robert Gould Shaw, was
called into action and readied for the assault.[100] On the evening of the
eighteenth they moved into position on the beachhead on Morris Island, opposite Fort Wagner, in preparation for their attack the following
morning.

Tubman had followed the regiments up the coast to their positions
outside Charleston Harbor. Probably there as a nurse and cook, but
perhaps even as a scout, Tubman witnessed the carnage inflicted upon
the Fifty-fourth Massachusetts on July 19 at Fort Wagner.[101] She later
told an interviewer that she served Colonel Shaw his last meal.[102] She
had probably become quite familiar with Shaw and his regiment since
they had arrived in Beaufort six weeks before. Frederick Douglass's two
sons, Lewis and Charles, were members of the Fifty-fourth, and Tubman no doubt knew both young men.[103]

Tubman's description of that fateful day, as stunning in its poetic
form as it was haunting, would long be remembered: "And then we saw
the lightning, and that was the guns; and then we heard the thunder,
and that was the big guns; and then we heard the rain falling, and that
was the drops of blood falling; and when we came to get in the crops,
it was the dead that we reaped."[104] Union losses were horrific: 1,515
dead, wounded, missing or captured, compared to only 174 Confederate casualties. The Massachusetts Fifty-fourth was particularly hard hit,
with 256 casualties, many of them missing and presumed dead.[105]

The wounded were transported to Beaufort, where Tubman tended to them. Charles A. Smith, a member of the Fifty-fourth Massachusetts, recalled meeting Tubman at the hospital when she was assigned by Montgomery to provide nursing and comfort to the wounded and dying soldiers felled during the Wagner assault.[106] Tubman later recounted the dreadful conditions and the difficult environment in which they had to care for the wounded and ill soldiers:

> I'd go to the hospital, I would, early every morning. I'd get a big chunk of ice, I would, and put it in a basin, and fill it with water; then I'd take a sponge and begin. First man I'd come to, I'd thrash away the flies, and they'd rise, they would, like bees round a hive. Then I'd begin to bathe their wounds, and by the time I'd bathed off three or four, the fire and heat would have melted the ice and made the water warm, and it would be as red as clear blood. Then I'd go and get more ice, I would, and by the time I got to the next ones, the flies would be round de first ones, black and thick as ever.[107]

The fighting in Charleston Harbor continued through to the first week of September. Wounded and ill soldiers continued to overwhelm the hospitals at Beaufort. Tubman probably worked day and night caring for the sick and wounded men while also trying to support herself by baking and cooking in between shifts at the hospital.[108] Women all over the islands were asked to serve in the hospitals: wives of officers, teachers in the freedmen's schools, such as Charlotte Forten, and others offered their services.[109] Tubman must have been exhausted. Given her own fragile health, it is a wonder that she managed to maintain herself and survive through the summer and part of the fall, unlike many other volunteers who fell victim to the heat, disease, and exhaustion.[110]

Tubman eventually took a leave sometime in the late fall of 1863. She had not seen her family in over eighteen months. Her sister-in-law Catherine, who had buried her little boy, seventeen-month-old Adam Stewart, the previous February, had just given birth to another child, a daughter, Hester.[111] In addition, Tubman found her family and friends in Auburn working hard, trying to make ends meet; many of them were employed as coachmen and servants for the wealthier white families, some of them close friends of Tubman's, while others were day laborers or worked in the local factories.[112] Thomas Elliott, for instance, moved to Auburn and was living on South Street in a house owned by William H. Seward.[113]

In early November Tubman traveled to Canada, visiting with her brother William Henry and his family in Grantham on the outskirts of St. Catharines.[114] She may, in fact, have accompanied Samuel Gridley Howe on his fact-finding trip to Canada for the American Freedmen's Inquiry Commission to investigate the conditions of fugitives. Given her connections in the St. Catharines community, she would have been a likely choice to provide introductions to local former slaves still living there. She may have also been trying to recruit men to serve in black regiments in the South. Tubman left by mid-November and returned to service in South Carolina, where General Gillmore immediately ordered her to Folly Island, just south of Morris Island.[115]

In February 1864, George Garrison, the son of William Lloyd Garrison, who was stationed at Folly Island, South Carolina, ran into Tubman while on a day excursion with friends from Boston. Writing to his brother William Lloyd Garrison II, George described Tubman's surprise upon seeing him: "When we entered where she was at work ironing some clothes, Mrs. Severance went to introduce me by saying here is George Garrison, she no sooner saw me than she recognized me at once, and instantly threw her arms around me, and gave me quite an affectionate embrace, much to the amusement of those with me." She was "cooking and washing clothes at Gen'l Terry's quarters, who is now in command of Morris and Folly Islands," Garrison told his brother. Tubman wanted to go home, but General Gillmore would not allow her to. "He thinks her services are too valuable to loose [sic]. She has made it a business to see all contrabands escaping from the rebels, and is enable to get more intelligence from them than anybody else."[116]

They talked for a while; Tubman told Garrison and his friends that she was trying to save some money to send home to her parents, but that she had recently been robbed of $50. Caroline Severance offered to take the money Tubman had left and see to it that it reached her parents. Tubman seemed never to let an opportunity go by that could help her raise money. Though Garrison was, indeed, concerned for her financial welfare, he also noted that Tubman had "a chance of making a good deal of money here, and can easily get fifty times more work than she can do," stressing Tubman's value as not only a scout and spy, but also a nurse, laundress, and cook.[117]

HARRIET TUBMAN.

Woodcut of Harriet Tubman in her Civil War garb.

In the meantime, Montgomery had been sent back to Florida with his black troops. He was joined by a steady stream of white and black regiments under the command of General Seymour, including Garrison's Fifty-fifth Massachusetts Infantry and the Eighth United States Colored Troops (USCT) from Pennsylvania under the command of Colonel Charles Fribley.[118] Tubman probably accompanied these regiments from Folly Island to Jacksonville, Florida, providing cooking and laundry services, and serving as a nurse as the need arose.[119] Seymour, whose unauthorized strategy was to destroy the Atlantic and Gulf Railroad, ordered the troops under his command to advance toward Lake City; General Gillmore ordered him to halt, but the communiqué reached Seymour too late to stop the advance.[120]

On February 20 the Union regiments were met by unexpectedly heavy fire from Confederate forces at Olustee. The Eighth USCT was newly trained and had never been tested in battle before. Surprise fire from rebel regiments left the soldiers of the Eighth in disarray and confusion, which was exacerbated by Seymour's conflicting orders. Nevertheless, they fought hard and bravely, earning the regiment a place on the rolls of Civil War heroes. In less than two hours, over half the regiment's men were left dead, wounded, or missing in action, including the regiment's commander, Colonel Fribley, and several other officers.[121] Montgomery's brigade, along with the Fifty-fourth Massachusetts, and other regiments soon arrived, giving the Eighth the chance to withdraw and regroup. But the fire was so heavy, Seymour ordered the retreat of all Union forces on that field, leaving behind hundreds of dead and wounded. Most of the regiments suffered high losses, but the black regiments suffered the most. The advancing Confederates killed many wounded black soldiers who could not retreat with their regiments, compounding an already devastating situation.[122] It was a humiliating failure, and it cost the Union its hoped-for control of Florida.

Whether Tubman witnessed the Battle of Olustee or not, she most likely was called to Sanderson, where wounded and dying men crowded the railroad station, or to Jacksonville to tend to the hundreds of wounded and exhausted soldiers brought there.[123] Tubman's skill at curing soldiers stricken by a variety of diseases was well known.[124] At one point during the war, Tubman was called to Fernandina, Florida, by the Union surgeon in charge, to help cure the men of debilitating and often deadly dysentery. When she arrived, "they was dying off like sheep." She prepared a medicinal tea "from roots which grew near the water which gave the disease."[125] She went into the swamps and "dug some roots and herbs and made a tea for the doctor [who had been afflicted with the disease] and the disease stopped on him," she told Emma Telford. "And then he said, 'give it to de soldiers.' So I boiled up a great boiler of roots and herbs, and the General told a man to take two cans and go round and give it to all in the camp that needed it, and it cured them.' "[126]

It was during one of her assignments in Florida that the "wash house," which Tubman had had built in Beaufort and where she taught locals to do the washing for the soldiers, was destroyed. The location had been "appropriated by a Reg't of troops fresh from the North" to make camp for themselves.[127] The government money she had used to build the laundry was now gone to waste, and the place where she had been earning her own money had been taken away as well. Once again Tubman had to adjust quickly to a rapidly, and often unexpectedly, changing environment.

Throughout the spring of 1864, Tubman continued to labor for the Department of the South. In early May, acting assistant surgeon Henry K. Durant issued a testimonial to Tubman's character and the "esteem in which she is generally held." He noted that he had "frequent and ample opportunities to observe her deportment; particularly her kindness and attention to the sick and suffering of her own race." General Rufus Saxton added, "I concur with the above."[128] The purpose of the testimonial is unclear; Tubman may have been seeking a furlough to go home to Auburn, or she may have needed an introduction to other officers in charge or hospital directors in another area of the Department of the South. She may also have been trying to get some pay for her services to the government. Tubman had been paid little over the two years she had been employed by the Department of the South, and much of what she did receive she probably used to pay other scouts and spies for information.

Military pay for black soldiers had been an issue since the very first black regiments had been formed. Black soldiers were paid $10 per month, less $3 for clothing. White troops, on the other hand, were paid $13 per month with an additional allowance for clothing. Many black troops, including the Fifty-fourth Massachusetts, refused to accept the lesser pay; they waited until September 1864 before they would see equal pay.[129] Getting paid may have been even more problematic for Harriet. She was not a soldier, officially, and her on-again, off-again role as a scout and a spy made consistent payment for her services unlikely. Payments of $100 or $200 may have been deemed sufficient, even

though she used the money to pay for other scouts' services and information. She was never paid as a Union nurse, which may have been an
additional source of irritation for Tubman. Like the black troops, Tubman was performing her jobs as well as her white counterparts, but still
was not treated equally.

Nevertheless, Tubman was granted a furlough to go home to see
her family sometime in June 1864. She traveled to New York City,
where Wendell Garrison, another of William Lloyd Garrison's sons,
wrote to his brother William that Tubman had just arrived from Port
Royal. "Moses Garrison," he wrote, "alias Harriet alias General Tubman has just arrived. . . . What times."[130] She spent part of the summer
in Auburn with her family; by early August she was in Boston, making
rounds of visits with abolitionist friends.[131] Frank Sanborn printed a
short notice in the *Commonwealth* that she was in town, staying with Dr.
John S. Rock on Beacon Hill. He noted that Harriet had some reason to
complain, for "her services to her people and to the army seem to have
been very inadequately recompensed by the military authorities."[132] He
again asked for contributions of money or clothing for her support and
for distribution to freedmen in the South.[133]

Sojourner Truth was in Boston then, too, and the two women
met.[134] Truth had long been a very public antislavery lecturer and
women's and African American civil rights activist. Born a slave and
deeply religious, she and Tubman had much in common. They differed,
however, in their assessment of Lincoln. Truth had campaigned for Lincoln and believed he had done much for the betterment of African
Americans.[135] But Tubman still did not care for Lincoln.[136] Identifying
herself with the thousands of black troops during the Civil War who
were paid less than half of what white soldiers received for the same
service, Tubman remembered that "we colored people didn't understand then he was our friend. All we knew was that the first colored
troops sent south from Massachusetts only got seven dollars a month,
while the white regiments got fifteen. We didn't like that."[137] The
women discussed Lincoln and his policies, but Tubman could not be
swayed. Later, after Truth had gone to Washington and met with Lincoln, Tubman felt she had been too harsh in her assessment of him. She
had heard that Lincoln had been kind to Truth, telling her that he "had

done nothing himself; he was only a servant of the country."[138] This deeply impressed Tubman; she understood the meaning of service to the nation. "I'se sorry now I didn't see Master Lincoln and thank him," Tubman recalled thirty years later.[139]

She remained in the North at least through late November, when she met with Gerrit Smith in Peterboro, New York.[140] He provided her with a testimonial, which indicates that Tubman was still fighting a battle for recognition. "The cause of freedom owes her much," he wrote, "the country owes her much."[141] Exactly when Tubman returned to South Carolina is unclear. Later Charles P. Wood of Auburn wrote in Tubman's application for a pension and retroactive pay from the government that she became ill at this time and remained in New York longer than her furlough allowed. When she was finally able to travel, she was "refused return transportation." It would take her a month to obtain another pass from the War Department to take a government transport to Hilton Head, South Carolina.[142]

The New England Freedmen's Aid Society, in the meantime, made arrangements for her to be hired as a "practical teacher" in the Hilton Head district.[143] The government's refusal to pay Tubman may have prompted Tubman's Boston friends to devise a means of sending her money to keep her actively involved in the relief efforts in the South. Toward this end, an account of Tubman's life was published in the *Freedmen's Record*, the journal of the New England Freedmen's Aid Society, in March 1865. Ednah Dow Cheney, a writer, abolitionist, and friend of Tubman's, penned the article, drawing heavily upon Sanborn's sketch in the July 17, 1863, *Commonwealth* and her own conversations with Tubman.[144] This was the second published biographical account of Tubman's life. At its conclusion, Cheney informed her readers that Tubman was still in need of financial assistance. "This society," Cheney wrote, "considers her labors too valuable to the freedmen to be turned elsewhere, and therefore have taken her into their service, paying her a small salary of ten dollars per month that she asks for."[145]

In early April, before heading back to South Carolina, Tubman appeared at Camp William Penn, outside Philadelphia, where USCT regiments were being organized and trained. She spoke to the newly formed Twenty-fourth USCT regiment, giving them a "thrilling account of her trials in the South, during the past three years, among the contrabands and the soldiers."[146] A journalist from the *Christian Reporter* noted that she seemed to be "very well known by the community at large, as the great Underground Railroad woman." She "elicited considerable applause" from the crowd, who then offered her a "liberal collection."[147]

As she was about to make her way to New York City to take passage from there to South Carolina, she was stopped in Philadelphia by nurses of the United States Sanitary Commission, who convinced her to go with them to work in some of the Union hospitals along the James River in Virginia.[148] Tubman was persuaded that the need for her services was great, so she changed her plans, traveling instead to Fortress Monroe at Hampton, Virginia, to care for sick and wounded black soldiers.[149]

On April 9 Confederate general Robert E. Lee surrendered at Appomattox Court House. Five days later President Lincoln was dead and Tubman's dear friend, William H. Seward, lay gravely wounded from an attack by a would-be assassin made on the night of Lincoln's assassination. The Civil War was over, the slaves would be free, but many more hurdles lay ahead before the nation would recover from its wounds and accept African Americans as free and full citizens. For Tubman, these hurdles would define the remainder of her life.

A HERO IS REMEMBERED

ITH THE CIVIL WAR OVER, HARRIET TUBMAN'S INTELLIGENCE-gathering skills were no longer needed in the Department of the South. A devoted nurse, Tubman remained at Fortress Monroe in Virginia for several months, caring for wounded and dying black soldiers. Disturbed by "some dreadful abuses" taking place in the hospital, and frustrated by her inability to facilitate positive changes there, Tubman returned to Washington, D.C.[1] She spoke with Seward, who directed her to Dr. Joseph K. Barnes, the surgeon general, and informed him of the atrocious fatality rate for African American soldiers being treated at the hospital, two and half times greater than for whites.[2] Barnes, appointed in August 1864, was instrumental in enforcing reforms in the recruitment of doctors for the army hospitals, and he mandated guidelines for the adequate care of soldiers during the Civil War.[3] Barnes officially appointed Tubman "Nurse or Matron at the colored hospital" at Fort Monroe.[4] Tubman received a pass on July 22, 1865, from Louis H. Pelonge, assistant adjutant general to the secretary of war, Edwin Stanton, to return to Monroe by way of government transport.[5]

Before leaving Washington, however, Tubman solicited the help of

Seward in applying to the government for back pay. Though still recovering from the nearly fatal wounds he received the night of Lincoln's assassination, and still in mourning over the unexpected death of his wife, Frances, in June, Seward wrote to Major General David Hunter requesting that Hunter look into Tubman's claims against the government. "She believes she has claims for faithful services to the command in South Carolina, with which you are connected, and she thinks that you would be disposed to see her claim justly settled."[6] Seward loaned her $12, to be applied to her already mounting debt.[7] Less than two weeks later, the New England Freedman's Aid Society paid $20, two months of Tubman's salary, to Seward to apply toward that liability.[8]

Tubman did not stay at Fort Monroe for long; she was not given the promised appointment and soon returned to Washington.[9] Her frustration over the lack of payment for her services during the war and possibly as a nurse in the hospital at Fort Monroe must have forced her to make a difficult decision: return home and begin earning money to continue to support her parents and pay her debt to Seward, or remain where she was and continue providing valuable, though unpaid, services to wounded black soldiers. But her aged parents and struggling family back in Auburn and Canada required her attention as well, and the time was approaching when she would need to return there and begin rebuilding a life with them. No doubt her parents and her crowded household in Auburn were anxious for her return.[10]

On the first of October Tubman headed back to Auburn. She stopped by Lucretia Mott's home, Roadside, outside of Philadelphia, for a short visit and to pay her respects; Lucretia's daughter Elizabeth Mott Cavender had died one month earlier, and the household was still in mourning. Lucretia "was very glad" Tubman stopped by; they talked politics, specifically the "Freedmen & their right to vote."[11]

Suffrage and basic civil rights for African Americans dominated political conversations of the day. In January 1865 Congress had passed the Thirteenth Amendment to the Constitution, abolishing slavery forever. Section One of Amendment Thirteen states: "Neither slavery nor involuntary servitude, except as a punishment for a crime whereof the party shall have been duly convicted, shall exist within the United States, or any place subject to their jurisdiction."[12] But this amendment did not guarantee equality, citizenship, or the right to vote to African Americans; the Dred Scott decision in 1857 had virtually stripped free blacks of their citizenship rights, and a new amendment was needed to guarantee the full protection of citizenship. Discrimination against African Americans, particularly in the South, was rampant, and African Americans could not depend upon equal protection under the existing provisions of the Constitution. In fact, in the South many states began enacting "Black Codes," laws specifically targeting blacks such as denying them the right to vote, and in many cases restricting rights to own guns or land, to move freely, or to work for themselves. They also included harsh penalties for any breach of these codes, including enforced labor and apprenticeships, prison terms, and punitive levies and taxes.[13]

Liberal and moderate Republicans in Congress, therefore, sought to guarantee the citizenship rights of freedmen by passing a civil rights bill in March 1866. The bill was vetoed by President Andrew Johnson, but its key provisions were incorporated into the first clause of the Fourteenth Amendment, which guaranteed citizenship for anyone born in the United States and forbade states to "deprive any person of life, liberty, or property, without due process of law," "nor deny to any person within its jurisdiction the equal protection of the laws."[14] This amendment would become the cornerstone of the plans the Republican majority in Congress established to rebuild the South after the Civil War. While another amendment would be needed to guarantee the vote for African Americans, the Fourteenth Amendment represented the hope and goals of radicals and moderates in Congress for the rebuilding of a new political, economic, and social order in the South.[15]

For African Americans both in the North and in the South, bigotry and injustice lingered. In Washington, D.C., Philadelphia, and New York, for instance, African Americans faced daily indignities and resistance to their claims to equality in transportation, education, entertainment, and employment. Frederick Douglass and Sojourner Truth, for instance, were among many African Americans forcibly removed from trains and streetcars because of the color of their skin, and so was Harriet Tubman.[16] After the war, many such incidents occurred throughout the North; though slavery had ended, rampant discrimination against African Americans persisted.

In mid-October, with a "half-fare ticket" in her hand, Tubman took passage from Philadelphia to New York on a late-night Camden & South Amboy train. When the conductor ordered her to the smoking car, she refused. She explained that she was working for the government and was entitled to ride wherever she liked. "Come, hustle out of here! We don't carry niggers for half-fare," the conductor yelled at her.[17] He physically struggled with her, but Tubman's legendary strength apparently outmatched him. Clinging tenaciously to some part of the interior of the compartment, she resisted his efforts to forcibly remove her from the train car. He called upon two other men to help; they pried her fingers loose from the car, then wrenched her arm and broke it. She was then thrown violently into the smoking car, further injuring her shoulder and possibly breaking several of her ribs.[18] No one on the train came to her aid; in fact, several passengers shouted epithets and encouraged the conductor to toss her off the train.[19] She told the conductor "he was a copperhead scoundrel, for which he choked her ... She told him she didn't thank anybody to call her colored person—She would be called black or Negro—she was as proud of being a black woman as he was of being white."[20]

A young white man approached her when she left the train and suggested she sue the train company. He gave her his card and told her to contact him if she needed a witness, and then he disappeared.[21] After recuperating briefly in New York City, Tubman made her way to Auburn, arriving at her home physically and emotionally beaten.[22] Tubman was slowly nursed back to health by a network of supportive family and friends. Martha Coffin Wright was deeply concerned about Tubman's welfare, physically as well as financially. Wright encouraged her husband, David, to look into the train incident, and they enlisted the aid and support of Wendell Phillips's son-in-law, then working in the American Anti-Slavery Office in New York City, to see if any restitution could be had from the Camden & South Amboy railroad line. David encouraged Tubman to sue; advertisements for the witness who had given his card to Tubman were placed, calling for him to come forward, and Wright wrote to George Smalley of the New York Tribune, possibly to suggest some sort of story when the time was right.[23] The witness never appeared, and though letters from the doctor who treated her in Auburn and Tubman's own testimony may have been sufficient to pursue a lawsuit, it appears that, at least through the winter, nothing came of their efforts to pursue a claim against the railroad.

In the fall of 1865 Tubman's household was very crowded. Ben and Rit were living in the small wood-frame dwelling with Catherine Stewart and her two children, Elijah and Hester; Thomas and Ann Stewart Elliott, who had married in July 1864; Margaret Stewart; and Thornton Newton, a boarder.[24] The whereabouts of James, Tubman's brother and Catherine's husband, remain a mystery, though he probably was dead.[25] John Stewart had moved out of the house with his new wife, Millie, before 1865 and was living on the corner of South and Swift Streets, just a short walk up South Street from Tubman's home.[26]

By 1865 several former Maryland runaway slaves had settled in Auburn, some of whom had run north with Tubman or had known her in Maryland and St. Catharines. Bill and Emily Kiah, for instance, who had been part of the famous Dover Eight escape with Thomas Elliott, Denard Hughes, and Henry Predeaux in 1857, settled in Auburn under their new names, William and Emily Williams. Their daughter Mary, whom they had had to leave behind when they took flight in 1857, probably finally escaped in 1860, when William Still recorded her parents going through his office for a second time.[27]

Tubman could not work throughout the winter, increasing the financial and physical burdens already weighing heavily upon her and her family. She later told William Lloyd Garrison II when he visited the following April that "they would have suffered for food, the past winter, as she was disabled, if it had not been for the work of a woman in the house—They had to burn their fences for firewood."[28] Catherine was probably this woman. At one point, "everything eatable was exhausted, and the prospect was dark, indeed."[29]

Tubman's mother and father were totally dependent upon her, and she bore the brunt of their "reproaches," which fell "thick and fast."[30] There was no money for food, and Tubman's mother had to go without her tobacco and tea, which "were more essential to her than food or clothing." One desperate day, when the scoldings and the complaints were particularly harsh, Tubman "went into her closet and shut the door." She soon emerged, calling to Catherine to "take off that small pot an' put on a large one."[31] Catherine pointed out that they had no food for the pot. "Put on the large pot, Catherine; we're going to have soup to-day," Tubman told her, and off she went to the market. It was near the end of the day, and Tubman walked from stall to stall; with no money she could buy nothing. Noticing her empty basket, a "kind-hearted butcher" offered her a soup bone and told her she could pay him when she had the money. Other vendors followed suit until "the basket was full." She traded with other vendors until her basket contained all she needed; meat, potatoes, and vegetables. Tubman's rather wry memory of that day was that she "had not 'gone into her closet and shut the door' for nothing."[32]

Poverty would mar much of these early years of freedom for Tubman; her household was always full of boarders and people passing through, in addition to assorted friends and relatives seeking temporary or more permanent shelter. Her injuries from the train incident, together with her ongoing struggle with TLE seizures, limited her ability to earn money, forcing her to remain, to some degree, dependent upon white benefactors such as the Wrights, the Smiths, the Garrisons, and the Sewards. Back pay and a pension for her war service would have gone a long way toward alleviating those financial burdens. Compensation from the railroad company would also have alleviated some of her financial woes.

Wendell Phillips sent her $60, which "kept them warm for the winter."[33] After William L. Garrison II's visit in April, he sent $10 to Martha Wright for Harriet, telling Wright "his father [William Lloyd Garrison] had a fund of 2 or 300 given him to meet such cases as hers."[34] Later Tubman told Wright that the money could not "have come in a better time, for she wanted to get some potatoes to plant, but she was afraid Mr. Garrison misunderstood her, & tho't they were suffering for food, [which] she [said would] not be, while they had so many kind friends here—she has a good deal of that honest pride [which] makes her unwilling to beg." In spite of her struggles, Wright noted that Tubman "seems happy & exultant, except for 'the misery' in her shoulder & chest where that Camden & Amboy wretch hurt her."[35]

The Wrights and their friends continued to pursue action against the railroad company through the spring. In April David Wright followed up on the matter in New York with friends at the Anti-Slavery Office, and Martha tried to get more details from Tubman about which train she had taken and on what day, but to no avail.[36] Word was spreading about the incident, however. At the Eleventh National Women's Rights Convention in New York City on May 16, 1866, Frances Ellen Watkins Harper, a prominent African American writer, lecturer, and suffragist, told the audience that she had recently been mistreated on a railroad car coming from Washington to Baltimore, by being forced to sit in the smoking car. She was not the only one, she told them

> We have a woman in our country who has received the name of "Moses," not by lying about it, but by acting it out (applause)—a woman who has gone down into the Egypt of slavery and brought out hundreds of our people into liberty. The last time I saw that woman, her hands were swollen. That woman who had led one of Montgomery's most successful expeditions, who was brave enough and secretive enough to act as a scout for the American army, had her hands all swollen from a conflict with a brutal conductor, who undertook to eject her from her place. That woman, whose courage and bravery won a recognition from our army and from every black man in the land, is excluded from every thoroughfare of travel.[37]

Tubman's treatment by the railroad conductor was representative of another battle facing African Americans in general, and black women specifically. The injustices and indignities they were forced to endure provided ample fertile ground for arguments calling for protecting the civil rights of African Americans and ensuring equal protection under the law. Black women were not given the same courtesies and respect white women expected and were accorded in public (and some private) spaces, posing a special and particular burden for them. Harper noted that black women's interests differed from white women's, and that winning the vote would not eliminate the discrimination and prejudice confronting the black community. Would white women with the vote,

Harper asked, help protect the civil rights of black women?[38] In closing, Harper challenged the white women in the audience to stand by their black sisters, to look beyond their own white privilege. "You white women speak here of rights. I speak of wrongs," she reminded them. "Talk of giving women the ballot-box? . . . While there exists this brutal element in society which tramples upon the feeble and treads down the weak, I tell you that if there is any class of people who need to be lifted out of their airy nothings and selfishness, it is the white women of America."[39] For black women, however, the struggle for equal rights and the vote would continue to be an uphill battle well into the twentieth century.

The daily struggle of supporting a large household of dependents, and participating in community life, dominated Tubman's immediate postwar life. The needs of Tubman's household were great. In late October Gerrit Smith's wife, Ann Fitzhugh Smith, sent Harriet a box of clothing, including "some white things" for Rit, "when the time came for her to 'set out for the shining shore'—Harriet said she was brought up near the Fitz Hughs, and in their part of the country it was customary to prepare the grave clothes & have them ready—Mrs. Smith reminded her in her note of this custom."[40] Rit was about eighty years old and was probably in considerably poor health, prompting Ann Smith to send along the grave clothes without seeming inconsiderate or impertinent. Martha Wright saw to it that Harriet's household did not do without for Christmas; her sister, Lucretia Mott, noted that the Motts were doing without presents for each other for Christmas, "after putting up parcels for all the *Tubmans* around us—some 10 or 12 bundles of very homely yet useful articles, I really have had nothing left for anybody—so we old folks concluded not to try to make presents."[41]

It was during this year that John and Kessiah Bowley, who had been living in Chatham, Canada, probably came to live with Tubman for a year before returning to the Eastern Shore of Maryland. Harkless Bowley, John and Kessiah's son, later recalled that he and his family stayed with "Aunt Harriet a year or two before going to Maryland,"[42] placing the Bowley family there sometime between late 1865 and 1867.[43] The Bowley family by then had expanded to seven children, including James Alfred, Araminta, Linah, Anna, Harkless, Josiah, and Pleasant Ann.[44]

James Alfred, who had stayed in Philadelphia with Tubman when his parents moved to Canada around 1851, had rejoined his family in Canada by 1861. Well-educated, James sought employment as a teacher with the Freedmen's Bureau in Georgetown, South Carolina, after the war.[45] Having extra hands around the house probably eased Tubman's burden considerably. Tubman's brother John Stewart "had a fine team of horses" but was crippled with "rheumatism" and often could not work.[46] John and Kessiah remained at least a year, returning to Dorchester County sometime during late 1867 or early 1868, where they probably moved in with Kessiah's father, Harkless Jolley.[47] They left their son Harkless behind with Tubman, where he remained for "quite a while,"[48] perhaps because education, a priority in the family, would have been more accessible for a young black child in Auburn than in Dorchester County, or perhaps because the situation on the Eastern Shore since emancipation was still quite unstable for black families.[49]

Maryland had emancipated all of its slaves on November 1, 1864, nearly two years after Lincoln had issued his Emancipation Proclamation freeing all slaves in the Confederate states. Because Maryland had remained loyal to the Union, it was not required by the president to free all of its slaves according to the provisions of the Proclamation. Under intense internal and external forces, Maryland finally acquiesced and wrote a new constitution in November 1864, banning slavery.[50] Many former slaveholders, reluctant to adjust to a totally free labor system, indentured the children of their former adult slaves, virtually perpetuating the slave system under the guise of indenture and apprenticeship.[51] Court records throughout the state, and particularly on the Eastern Shore, show a sharp rise in the incidents of indenture, beginning in the few months before emancipation with free black children, and then newly freed children beginning just hours before November 1, 1864.[52]

The indenturing of Maryland's black children also ensured that the parents would remain tied to the former master, or at the very least in the area, keeping their labor available to the whites. John and Kessiah may have been leery of putting their son at risk of indenture. In fact, John Stewart's sons John Henry and Moses Ross, whom Tubman had never been able to bring north, were indentured on November 15, 1864, by their former master, Dr. Anthony C. Thompson's son-in-law Thomas Haddaway.[53] Haddaway had purchased Mary Manokey Ross, John Stewart's wife, and their children from Dr. Thompson in March 1857; at the time, John Henry, his brother Moses, and their sister Harriet were still young children.[54] By 1864 John and Moses were fourteen and twelve years old, respectively, and their labor was then becoming productive and valuable. For Haddaway, indenturing them was the quickest and easiest means to maintain the status quo on his farm.

John Stewart was "anxious" to have his boys with him in the North.[55] Though both John and Mary had hoped to be reunited as a family in the North after he had run away at Christmastime in 1854, Tubman had not been successful in effecting Mary and the children's escape. Dr. Thompson, probably fearful that Mary and her children would also take their own freedom like John, sent the family to his daughter's home in Trappe, in Talbot County on the north side of the Choptank River across from Cambridge.[56] As time went on, Mary fell in love with a freeman named Wilson Wells, who was then living in the Trappe area.[57] Though John eventually remarried in the North, he still wanted his children with him. Once John Henry and Moses were free, however, their indenture to Thomas Haddaway seems to have been the most significant barrier to their traveling north.[58]

John Stewart asked John Bowley to find his sons for him once Bowley resettled in Dorchester County. Sometime during 1867 or 1868, after the Bowleys had returned to the Eastern Shore, John Bowley "went across the [Choptank] river at night [and] brought away the oldest boy," secreting him in their home in Dorchester County until John Henry could safely be sent to Auburn.[59] After "things quieted down," John Bowley returned to the Haddaway plantation, retrieved Moses, and sent him along to Auburn, too.[60]

John Stewart had not seen his children in thirteen or fourteen years—John Henry and Moses probably had few, if any, memories of their father. While the change must have been difficult, they seemingly adjusted to their new family and community circle. John Henry hired himself out as a laborer, possibly working in the local factories or brickyard. Moses took over the management and driving of his father's team of horses when John Stewart was laid up because of crippling arthritis. Harkless Bowley recalled helping Moses load his wagon on occasion.[61]

The winter of 1867–68 was a harsh one, and the family continued to struggle. At one point Harriet found it necessary to ask for money to buy some food for her family. It had snowed heavily that winter, making it difficult to get into Auburn from her farm on the outskirts of the city; with no money, the situation was desperate. Tubman had no other choice and was "compelled to plunge through the drifts to the city" to seek some help. Arriving at the home of a white benefactor, Miss Annie, Tubman struggled with the words to convey her problem. Exasperated, Miss Annie finally asked, "Well, what *is* it, Harriet?" With her eyes "filled with tears," Tubman asked for a quarter. Tubman's supporters were immediately notified, and they soon "supplied all the wants of the family."[62] On the following Monday, Bradford assured her doubting white readers, Tubman "appeared with the quarter she had borrowed," bringing closure to the story with a moral lesson and a clear message about Tubman's integrity.[63]

Tubman also took in boarders. One of these boarders was a young Civil War veteran, Nelson Davis. Davis, a member of Company G, Eighth USCT that fought so valiantly at the Battle of Olustee, Florida, had been honorably discharged on November 10, 1865, at Brownsville, Texas. Originally a slave from Elizabeth City, North Carolina, Davis had fled north sometime during or before 1861. Settling in Oneida County, New York, for a couple of years, Davis went to Pennsylvania and enlisted in the Eighth USCT on September 10, 1863, at Camp William Penn outside of Philadelphia.[64] Nelson Charles, as he was known then, was only twenty-one years old when he was discharged from the army. He followed a fellow soldier, Albert Thompson, from Company G to Auburn, where he found a room at Tubman's home and a job nearby, probably at a local brickyard abutting Harriet's property.[65]

Not too long after Davis had settled into Tubman's home, she received word that her husband, John Tubman, had been murdered in Dorchester County. On September 30, 1867, John Tubman and a white man named Robert Vincent, a neighbor of Tubman's, had some sort of disagreement, and Vincent shot Tubman dead. The first news reports indicated that Vincent had threatened to kill John Tubman on the morning of September 30 after a disagreement over "the removal of some ashes from a tenant-house on Vincent's farm." Vincent chased Tubman down the road with an ax, though Tubman apparently escaped Vincent's wrath at that moment. Later in the day, around 5 P.M., Vincent and Tubman met again on the road and quarreled, and Vincent shot Tubman in the forehead and killed him.[66]

Violence against freedmen continued unabated in the South for years after the war, as whites struggled with a new social order.[67] For some in the white community, in Maryland as elsewhere, black displays of independence in addition to perceived insolence or disrespect warranted swift and sometimes violent reprisal.[68] Maryland was no different from other parts of the South, and its white residents struggled to adjust to emancipation and directives imposed by Reconstruction, which tried to control white efforts to reenslave the freedmen through a variety of legal and extralegal tactics.[69] Dorchester County, then, was experiencing the same transformative changes as the rest of the South.

The exact details of what actually happened between the two men on the day Tubman was killed, and perhaps in the days, months, and years leading up to it, will probably never be known. As a Baltimore newspaper reported, Vincent never "stopped to see if his shot proved fatal, but continued on his way home."[70] Vincent was arrested and tried for murder. At the trial, Vincent claimed that John Tubman had threatened him earlier in the day, and, when he started home later in the day along the same road, Tubman "rushed out of the woods with a club and made at him, whereupon he seized his gun and fired," fatally wounding his alleged attacker.[71] The state's case against Vincent hinged on the testimony of two African Americans, Rachel Camper, a neighbor, and Tubman's son, Thomas, then thirteen years old. Thomas, who had apparently been with his father at the time of the shooting, was actually the only one to have witnessed the killing. Baltimore's liberal newspaper, the *Baltimore American*, noted that "it was universally conceded that he would be acquitted" because only "a colored boy" had witnessed the deed, and that the jury "was composed exclusively of Democrats," meaning former southern sympathizers who were still reluctant to accept African Americans as their equals. Democrats, the paper charged, were still a long way from "convicting a fellow Democrat for killing a Negro. But even that will follow when the Negro is armed with the ballot."[72] The jury deliberated for ten minutes, whereupon they returned a verdict of not guilty.[73]

That fall Harriet continued to pursue her claim against the government for back pay as a scout and nurse for the Union army. In early November she visited Gerrit Smith to solicit support for her efforts; Sallie Holley, a writer, former abolitionist, and suffragist, was there, and Tubman showed her the documents she had been collecting for two years to support her claim. Holley immediately posted a letter to the *National Anti-Slavery Standard*, highlighting Tubman's struggles with the government and her injuries from the train incident two years earlier.[74] Expecting her readers to know Tubman's history, Holley asked, "[A]mong American women, who has shown a courage and self-devotion to the welfare of others equal to Harriet? Hear her story of going down to rescue her suffering people, bringing them off through perils and dangers enough to appall the stoutest heart, till she is known among men as 'Moses.' " Then, for unexplained reasons, she added, "[F]orty thousand dollars was not too great a reward for the Maryland slaveholders to offer for her," thus setting in print an exaggerated myth that still persists today.[75] Holley may have been trying to make the point that if the Maryland slaveholders found her so valuable, why couldn't the federal government find value in her services to the Union during the war? Nevertheless, Tubman could always depend on a small circle of friends, including the Smiths, Wrights, and Osbornes, to see her through the hardest of times. The Garrisons continued to send her funds; William Lloyd Garrison II had married Martha Coffin Wright's daughter Ellen, bringing the Garrison family in Boston into closer contact with the daily needs and wants of Tubman and her family.[76]

The struggles of the freedmen in the South for economic, educational, and political advancement occupied Tubman's thoughts as well. Tubman's nephew James A. Bowley had been working with the Freedmen's Bureau in South Carolina, and perhaps that, along with her connections to the bureau itself, provided Tubman the impetus to raise funds for the freedmen's relief effort. During 1867 and 1868 Tubman organized small fairs to raise money; they were modeled on the successful antislavery fairs from before the war, and local donations of clothing and household and personal items, as well as home-baked goods, were sold, all for the benefit of the southern freedmen.[77] Tubman solicited the help of a significant number of the Wrights' friends and fellow liberal activists, including the daughters of Auburn's social and liberal elite.[78] Articles appeared in the *Auburn Daily* newspaper featuring Tubman's activities on the Underground Railroad "hiding in the woods days, & traveling nights," and also her service "as a scout, during the War, & as a nurse," using the opportunity to draw attention to her humanitarian work.[79] Held at the Central Presbyterian Church, where Tubman and her family had been attending services since 1862, the fairs were a success, raising several hundred dollars for freedmen's relief.[80]

During the spring of 1868, Sarah H. Bradford, the sister of one of Central Presbyterian's founding pastors, Samuel M. Hopkins Jr., was persuaded to write a biography of Tubman. Bradford had earned a small degree of success as a writer of sentimental novels and short stories. Most featured such moralistic topics as overindulgent parents and naughty children who "owe their origin to the criminal neglect of proper parental discipline," dead mothers and orphaned children, impoverished widows and at least one story of a fugitive slave, "Nina."[81] Writing under the pseudonym "Cousin Cicely," Bradford published seven volumes of short stories, including several for young readers, one novel, two biographies, and a fictionalized history of the Linton family before starting her book on Tubman.[82] Though Bradford was probably antislavery in her sentiments, she was not known as an active abolitionist, and she seemingly was not well known to the Wrights and Osbornes, Tubman's closest white friends in Auburn.[83] But Bradford's father, Samuel Miles Hopkins, was a successful lawyer, judge, and former New York congressman who had been friends with William H. Seward. Sarah married John M. Bradford, a local lawyer and businessman, and they raised their six children in Geneva, several miles to the west of Auburn.[84]

During the late spring and into the summer of 1868 Bradford contacted several of Tubman's associates, many of whom she did not know, asking them to provide testimonials and reminiscences of Tubman and her activities.[85] Lucretia Mott, Franklin Sanborn, Gerrit Smith,

Thomas Garrett, Wendell Phillips, Frederick Douglass, the Rev. Henry Fowler, and Tubman's nephew James A. Bowley were among the notables who provided information and letters of support.[86] Bradford printed many of these letters in her biography, *Scenes in the Life of Harriet Tubman*. Frederick Douglass's letter, perhaps the most poetic in form, celebrated Tubman's great achievements:

> You ask for what you do not need when you call upon me for a word of commendation. I need such words from you far more than you can need them from me, especially where your superior labors and devotion to the cause of the lately enslaved of our land are known as I know them. . . . Much that you have done would seem improbable to those who do not know you as I know you. It is to me a great pleasure and a great privilege to bear testimony to your character and your works, and to say to those to whom you may come, that I regard you in every way truthful and trustworthy.[87]

Bradford was a poor choice for writing Tubman's biography.[88] Complicating matters, she was planning to sail for Europe on September 2, 1868, leaving just three or four months to write the biography.[89] Bradford's brother, Samuel Hopkins, wrote in the introduction to the book that Bradford made "no claim whatever to literary merit. Her hope was merely that the considerably numerous public already in part acquainted with Harriet's story, would furnish purchasers enough to secure a little fund for the relief of this remarkable woman." It seems surprising that Bradford had no hopes for a wide circulation of the biography, especially given the success of many former slave narratives, which were still popular in the early postbellum period. At any rate, Bradford felt that "outside that circle [those familiar with Tubman's story] she did not suppose the memoir was likely to meet with much if any sale."[90]

Writing in haste, Bradford hoped "the bare, unadorned facts are enough to stir the hearts of the friends of humanity, the friends of liberty, the lovers of their country" to purchase the book.[91] Bradford explained that she printed only stories told to her by Tubman if they could be independently verified by another source.[92] Tubman spent some time living with Bradford, giving her the opportunity to record many stories. "Much has been left out which would have been highly interesting," Bradford wrote in her preface to the book, "because of the impossibility of substantiating by the testimony of others the truth of Harriet's statements. But whenever it has been possible to find those who were cognizant with the facts stated, they have been corroborated in every particular."[93] Unfortunately, if Bradford had accepted more of Tubman's stories on their own merit, we might have a richer account of her life.

In the end, Bradford's volume was an imperfect memoir. As historian Jean Humez has argued, Bradford was not a "competent transcriber" of Tubman's oral stories, "apparently because of unfamiliarity with her cultural norms."[94] Bradford was more suited to sentimental dramatization than to recording and conveying the intricacies of the life of a black woman whose existence under slavery and in a highly racialized society was beyond her understanding. Tubman's version of her life was probably highly modified and censored; the rest is Tubman's life according to Sarah Bradford.[95] Bradford's claims of accuracy and the pursuit of truth only serve to reveal her as an interloper in Tubman's story, an omnipresent and all-knowing narrator whose white prejudices mistakenly informed her judgment. Bradford may have been more concerned with her own reputation than with writing Tubman's memoir. Harriet's life had all the elements of a dramatic novel, and Bradford needed only to record her story more deliberately, rather than dramatizing elements of her story for the sake of sentimentality.

Of the 132 pages in the biography, fewer than half were written by Bradford. The rest includes about twenty pages of letters of support and testimonials from friends and acquaintances, including several from Union Army officers familiar with Tubman's war service; a copy of Sanborn's 1863 *Boston Commonwealth* article; newspaper articles and a letter relating to Charles Nalle's rescue by Tubman in Troy, New York, in 1860; an introduction by Samuel Hopkins; a sixteen-page "Essay on Woman-Whipping" (whose authorship is under question); and a list of subscribers who donated funds to pay for the printing of the book.[96]

Bradford's interviews with Tubman and the resulting narrative through Bradford's hand are still perhaps the most important link to Tubman's history, in spite of Bradford's inaccuracies. While Franklin Sanborn's *Boston Commonwealth* article remains a vitally important biographical sketch of Tubman, and its placement in Bradford's book is a critical chapter, Bradford disclosed more important details of Tubman's youth, revealing essential names and places and providing additional clues to Tubman's past. Bradford offered several new stories, too, including the escape of Joe and Bill Bailey, Peter Pennington, and Eliza Manokey; the rescue of Tubman's aged parents in 1857; the dramatic mission to bring her brothers away; her Civil War activities; and more detail on Tubman's own escape and other escapes in which she was involved. These details added a new dimension to Tubman the hero, establishing a compelling narrative that has survived for over 140 years.

As a historical document rather than just a literary production, Bradford's biography performs a great service; compelled by the white community's expectations of veracity, Bradford eagerly provided it. The testimonials, letters of reference, and commendations offered proof to the reader of Tubman's (and Bradford's own) respectability and truthfulness. It also affirmed Tubman's right to reveal her narrative to the public. Tubman offered her life as representative of the horrors of slavery, and also staked a claim, based on an African American intellectual and spiritual tradition, to full participation in the public discourse about the still-uncertain fate of millions of ex-slaves.

Tubman's narrative in *Scenes* challenged conventional stereotypes of black womanhood. To be sure, in its twin themes of resistance and liberation, it followed conventions that a predominantly white audience had come to expect and understand from black memoirs. Yet more than this, *Scenes* recounts an experience that is simultaneously very personal and collective. Tubman's intense spirituality and humor drove a compelling drama for a public still eager to read lurid details of slavery and its injustices. Tubman told a tale of a physical and spiritual struggle against violence and oppression that sapped the very lifeblood from her community and family, but it also conveyed a message of ultimate justice, a message that resonated with a northern liberal public still celebrating its victory over the South and slavery.

Nevertheless, *Scenes* is still a mediated text, and we may never know the true extent of Bradford's intrusion into the narrative, nor will we ever know some of the stories Tubman may have told Bradford that did not find their way into print. There were errors, and several people were concerned that they be corrected. William G. Wise, for example, wrote to William J. Moses, the local Auburn publisher, that he expected future corrections. "I have not been able to examine the book," Wise wrote, "but as you wish the bill paid to-day, I send a check, relying on you to correct afterwards any errors there may be."[97] Ellen Wright Garrison wrote to her mother, Martha Wright, that the imperfections irritated her. "I don't think much of Mrs. Thingumbob's [Bradford's] effort," Garrison wrote, "she is continually apologizing for haste, & going off to Europe. If she hadn't time to do the subject justice, why undertake it? . . . Still it is an interesting account of marvelous things, & I only wish it could have been better worked up."[98]

Many of the mistakes found throughout the book were not corrected. Clearly Bradford did not understand who exactly owned Tubman and her family in slavery. For instance, she conflated the identities of Anthony Thompson, Dr. Anthony C. Thompson, and Edward Brodess (whom she never identifies) and their roles as guardian, master, and owner, three distinct and important relationships in Tubman's life. Bradford mistakenly believed that Dr. Thompson owned Harriet's family, and also erroneously believed that Edward Brodess was a child when he died, leaving his guardian (Dr. Thompson, in error again) in charge of Harriet and her family. However, even Tubman's closest friends recognized the difficult task assigned to Bradford, "A Mrs. Bradford of Geneva," Martha Coffin Wright wrote to her sisters in July 1868, "is writing a memoir of her—as well as she can, with Harriet's disjointed materials."[99] Martha Wright believed that Lydia Maria Child would have made the narrative more interesting, but she felt Bradford deserved "credit for having done so well, almost impossible as it is to understand Harriet's desultory talk."[100]

As an afterthought to the core narrative, Bradford or her publisher included the "Essay on Woman-Whipping," a daring and harsh indictment of the legacy of slavery on white southerners, its corrupting influence on male-female relationships, and its legacy of simmering racial animosities. It describes whipping as a "dish of torture . . . to be pep-

pered very high to please the palates of those epicures in brutality."
How, the author asked, could "the 'chivalric' mind endure the loss of
such gratifications?" "But," she continued, "the bloody morsel has been
snatched from the mouths of the 'chivalry' at one clutch. No wonder
their mortification vents itself in weeping and wailing, and knashing of
teeth, and in such miscellaneous atrocities as their 'Ku-Klux-Klan' can
venture to inflict on helpless freedmen and radicals."[101] The author re-
serves some of her harshest criticism for Southern women.

> The Southern mistress was a domestic devil with horns and
> claws; selfish, insolent, accustomed to be waited on for every-
> thing. She grew up with the instinct of tyranny—to punish vio-
> lently the least neglect or disobedience in her servants. The
> variable temper of girlhood, not ugly unless thwarted, became
> in the "Southern matron" a chronic fury. . . . It is the vindictive
> woman's nature in the South that protracted and gave added fe-
> rocity to the rebellion. These woman-whipping wives and moth-
> ers it was who hounded on the masculine chivalry to the work of
> exterminating the "accused Yankees," and thus made their own
> punishment so much sorer than it need have been.[102]

The author felt hopeful, however, that white southerners would
learn to assert "gentler virtues" under the influence of morally superior
northerners. This essay, even though it seems to have little to do with
Tubman's narrative per se (although Tubman bore the scars of being
whipped), reflects the mood of some former antislavery activists, who
were still willing and able to heap harsh criticism on the social and cultural norms that the radical Reconstructionists identified with the South
and were trying so hard to change. In 1868 rampant injustices and daily
acts of violence against blacks continued in the South, and this essay
was a reminder that some northerners were determined to revolution-
ize a repressive southern culture that denied African Americans social,
political, and economic opportunities.

We do not know how Tubman herself felt about the book. Whatever reservations she may have harbored, she knew sales would gener-
ate money for herself and her family, releasing herself from a large debt

that could not have been paid any other way. She must have felt some pride that she would join the ranks of other former slaves who had published their memoirs, with or without the help of an amanuensis. Though written and edited by a white woman, Bradford's *Scenes* contributed to a growing body of African American literature that was struggling to maintain the memory of slavery and the war and to reveal a history of African American family, community, and spiritual life that was becoming lost in the oppressive waves of discrimination that consumed the nation in the postwar years. Despite the book's limitations, Harriet's narrative emerged as a vivid view of the struggles of African Americans to create a historical memory. In doing so, it shared in the collective production of African American literature that emerged through the abolition and antislavery movements of the nineteenth century and served to promote political as well as personal agendas. This narrative, though mediated through a white lens, reveals that Tubman embraced the written word as a means to further her goals of liberty and economic independence, not only for herself but for other freedmen. She was able to establish a permanent record of her history, though she may never have imagined just how permanent her legacy would be and how important her historical memory would become.

The publication of Tubman's narrative allowed her to repay many of her debts. She still owed William H. Seward over $1,200 for her home, including taxes, insurance, and improvements. To ensure that Tubman received the greatest benefit from the sales of the book, Bradford agreed to forgo any royalties, and donors were sought to underwrite the cost of publishing the book with William J. Moses of Auburn. Sometime during the summer or fall of 1868, William G. Wise, a local Auburn businessman, organized a subscription drive "for the benefit of Harriet Tubman," raising over $430 to cover the costs of printing twelve hundred copies.[103]

WITH THE BOOK taken care of, Tubman turned her attention to organizing another fair for the relief of the freedmen in South Carolina. James A. Bowley arrived in early September for a visit, spending time with Harriet, his younger brother Harkless, and other family and friends, where he met some of Tubman's old antislavery associates. "Harriet Tubman just came with her mother's great-grandson," Martha Wright wrote to her nieces Anna and Patty, "he lived in Canada till the War, & now teaches the freemen in S. Carolina—He was one of the first that Harriet rescued from Slavery."[104] Wright, though, seemed to be tiring of the endless rounds of fund-raising and relief efforts for the freedmen, noting that she had "to look around & find a bundle of blamed things for the nephew to take to the Freedmen—& get it to Eliza's."[105] Bradford noted that "even now, while friends are trying to raise the means to publish this little book for her, she is going around with the greatest zeal and interest to raise a subscription for her Freedmen's Fair."[106] Seward, obviously frustrated with Tubman's perpetual need for money, told Tubman, "[y]ou have worked for others long enough. It is time you should think of yourself. If you ask for a donation for *yourself*, I will give it to you; but I will not help you to rob yourself for others."[107]

Within the month, however, Martha Wright was writing in a more positive tone to her sisters about the current activities in support of the freedmen and Tubman's upcoming fair. Martha was busy sewing aprons, some of which were to be sold at Tubman's fair in December. Harriet had collected a full box of clothing and was looking for more for the freedmen. "I couldn't think for a moment, what there was left, but I told her she needn't come all the way here for the bundle, I [would] send it to Mrs. Osborne's."[108] The Osbornes' home was on South Street, much closer to Tubman's home than the Wrights' residence on Genesee Street, making it more convenient for Tubman to pick up items from there. Tubman, however, must have told other people to send their donations to the Osbornes, and before they knew it, an advertisement appeared in the *Auburn Daily Advertiser* announcing that all items for the freedmen could be left at the Osborne home. "Bundles began to pile in," crowding Eliza Wright Osborne's "little sewing room."[109]

The Wrights, the Motts, the Osbornes, the Wises, the Dennises, and many other friends spent October and November making items to sell at the fair.[110] Henry Wise persuaded William J. Moses to print *Scenes* in time to sell copies at the mid-December fair—which may account for some of the typographical errors.[111] Sixty or seventy copies were sold at

$1 each, and Martha Wright noted that in all the excitement of the fair, "Harriet was quite the heroine . . . her talk . . . was as good as a play."[112] The fair successfully raised over $500 for Tubman's relief effort.[113]

Over the next few months the same circle of supporters ordered copies of the book to give or sell to friends, or to sell at antislavery meetings and other gatherings of former abolitionists and activists.[114] An unidentified buyer in Chicago purchased one hundred copies.[115] Franklin Sanborn wrote a lengthy review of the book for the *Springfield Republican*, encouraging people to buy it for the benefit of Tubman and "her protégés."[116] Harriet was "poor and partially disabled from her injuries," Sanborn told his readers, "yet she supports cheerfully and uncomplainingly herself and her aged parents, and always has several poor children in her house, who are entirely dependent upon her exertions." Three of these children, Sanborn noted, were then living with Tubman, "while their parents are working to pay back money borrowed to bring them on."[117] As if this was not enough, Sanborn informed his readers that she "maintains, by her exertions . . . two schools of freedmen in the South, providing them teachers and sending them clothes and books. She never asks for anything herself, but she does ask the charity of the public for 'her people.' "[118] By the end of January 1869, 594 copies of *Scenes* had been sold, with another 607 copies sold over the following three months.[119]

It would seem then, that Tubman's financial worries were at least temporarily over. Though the debt on her home was not paid off until 1873, the funds raised from the sale of the book brought some immediate relief to Tubman and her family.[120] She was still receiving small amounts of money from white supporters, and also became the beneficiary of a small inheritance from Laura Birney in the form of a $50 annuity.[121] Tubman's persistent efforts to alleviate the sufferings of her family and the struggling freedmen in the South represented a continuum of humanitarian work that would define the remainder of her life. Her fight for justice and equality would remain a singular focus for the next four decades.

MYTH AND MEMORY

ROM THE END OF THE CIVIL WAR TO HER DEATH IN 1913, TUBMAN'S
fame and notoriety fluctuated dramatically. Her public image as a heroine and a "Black Joan of Arc" was secured by the appearance of *Scenes
in the Life of Harriet Tubman* in 1869.[1] Its publication marked a new
phase in Tubman's life; bringing some financial relief and increased
public attention, it provided Tubman with more opportunities to raise
awareness of the plight of freedmen and women. But from this point
forward, Bradford's narrative also defined Tubman's public identity; the
account ends with her Civil War activities, arresting Tubman's life story
almost fifty years before her death, immortalizing her forever as an Underground Railroad agent and Civil War spy.

In a letter written for inclusion in her biography, Frederick Douglass
wrote that only "the midnight sky and the silent stars have been the witnesses of your devotion to freedom and of your heroism," drawing attention to the fact that Tubman's heroic deeds were not accomplished
in full view of the public.[2] With the publication of *Scenes*, Tubman
emerged as more than a Moses; she was also a David figure, striking a
fatal blow to an almighty Goliath. She had challenged white and male

authority, emerging the victor in an unequal battle of race and gender. But such imagery could work well only in the period immediately after emancipation, when the goals of racial and gender equality seemed ever closer. Later, such heroic images became obscured and forgotten in the oppressive decades of Jim Crow racism and constitutional segregation, when those dreams of equality were derailed.

The publication of *Scenes* did not help her win her claim for back pay from the U.S. government. Charles P. Wood, a local Auburn banker, took up Tubman's cause. He interviewed her and wrote an account of her war service, including testimonials from various Union officers, certifying Tubman's war activity.[3] Tubman claimed the government owed her $966 for "Services as a Scout," from May 25, 1862, to January 31, 1865, a total of thirty-two and a half months at $30 per month. She deducted $200 from the total to account for money she was paid while on duty in the Department of the South, leaving $766 unpaid.[4]

While regular army soldiers were paid $15 per month, the Union paid scouts, spies, and detectives approximately $2 to $2.50 per day for their services.[5] Tubman, then, was asking for less pay per diem than what other commissioned scouts would have been paid, but clearly she did not act as a scout or spy every day of her service during the war. Congressman McDougall of New York introduced a bill to Congress in 1874 asking for relief for Tubman, but to no avail.[6] Tubman's accomplishments and contributions to the Union cause went largely unrecognized by the government until the turn of the century.

Community, work, and family consumed much of Tubman's efforts during the latter part of her life. Finally in a position to think of her own personal needs after so many years of acting on the behalf of others, Tubman fell in love with Nelson Davis, her boarder of three years and more than twenty years her junior. On Thursday, March 18, 1869, in a ceremony officiated by the Rev. Henry Fowler at the Central Presbyterian Church in Auburn, Harriet and Nelson were married in the presence of "friends . . . and a large number of the first families in the city."[7]

Though Tubman maintained ownership of her home—the 1870 census records her as the owner of the property, valued at $600—she and Nelson ran a brickmaking operation at the rear of their property.[8]

Harkless Bowley recalled working in the brickyard when he lived with Tubman for two or more years before rejoining his family.⁹ The presence of a brickyard on and near such a small piece of property proved to be hazardous to Tubman's crops; in October 1869 Martha Wright reported that Tubman and her family were once again in need of assistance, as her "garden had failed, by the wet *season* & the masons turning water on it."¹⁰

Nelson Davis was a sick man for most of the time he lived in Auburn. Suffering with tuberculosis, he probably could not work consistently, so support of the household often fell on Tubman's shoulders. Some people believed Tubman married Davis in order to take care of him.¹¹ He was "a magnificent specimen in appearance," Helen Tatlock recalled, "big, black, a true African."¹² Alice Brickler, however, thought Davis was a "colorless creature," and to be "handsome and tubercular is not even romantic."¹³ Another friend of Tubman's recalled the marriage was not "very workable . . . Harriet was such a busy woman devoted to her social interests that perhaps a domestic life was never the foremost thing to her."¹⁴ Nevertheless, Davis worked in the brickyard, helped farm Tubman's property, and was also an active member of the community, joining the Board of Trustees of St. Mark's AME Church at its founding in March 1870 along with several former Marylanders.¹⁵

Harriet not only worked on her farm and in the brickyard, but also hired herself out as a domestic to Auburn's wealthier families. Lazette Worden and Martha Coffin Wright both hired Harriet for spring cleaning; Theodore Pomeroy, whose children "she had rocked and tended in infancy," also hired Harriet for domestic services.¹⁶ She bartered and sold items when she could, and with additional income from occasional boarders she and Nelson managed to support her increasingly frail parents and those who happened to make their way to her doorstep in search of food and a place to stay.¹⁷

Many of Tubman's family and friends had settled more permanently into residences of their own within a growing black settlement in Auburn, less than a mile or so from Tubman's own home. Auburn's wealthier families employed them, too, usually as coachmen, domestics, and day laborers, while some took employment in the city's various manufacturing businesses. Many earned enough money to buy homes, and some could afford to let mothers and wives stay at home "keeping house," a middle-class ideal that must have seemed far removed from their days in slavery.[18]

While Tubman's fame was still fresh from the publication of *Scenes*, William Still published his eight-hundred-page documentary volume, *The Underground Railroad*. Based on records he had kept while secretary of the Vigilance Committee of the Pennsylvania Anti-Slavery Society, Still's book highlighted the role slaves themselves played in their own liberation.[19] He gave special acknowledgment to Tubman's "adventurous spirit and utter disregard of consequences." "In point of courage," Still wrote, "shrewdness and disinterested exertions to rescue her fellowmen . . . she was without her equal."[20] Though he claimed Tubman was "utterly devoid of personal fear," he acknowledged that she was extremely cautious and intolerant of the "weak-kneed and faint-hearted,"[21] requiring total adherence to a "very short and pointed rule or law of her own, which implied death to any who talked of giving out or going back."[22]

Oddly, however, given the fact that Tubman brought away scores of slaves, many through Still's office, he devotes little more than these brief mentions to describing her career as an Underground Railroad agent. While he may have felt that Tubman's biography spoke for itself and there was no need to highlight her accomplishments further, the brevity (one page or so) with which he discusses Tubman's contributions to the Underground Railroad stands in direct contrast to the extensive sketch he devotes to praising the antislavery and postemancipation work of Frances Ellen Watkins Harper. A well-educated, freeborn African American woman, an accomplished poet and writer, Harper emerged from the antislavery lecture circuit to become an advocate for women's rights and temperance.[23] Still's descriptions of the two women are striking in their differences. "Harriet," he wrote, "was a woman of no pretensions, indeed, a more ordinary specimen of humanity could hardly be found among the most unfortunate-looking farm hands of the South."[24] Harper, by contrast to the illiterate former slave, represented an ideal of middle-class black womanhood. Harper was a "laborer, battling for freedom under slavery and the war . . . [and] for Equality before the law—education, and a higher manhood, especially in the south, among the Freedmen."[25] While Harper's accomplishments as an antislavery lecturer, sometime Underground Railroad helper and supporter, and prolific writer are without doubt laudable, Still's claim that "want of space forbids more than a brief reference" to her life seems specious given the thirty pages he devotes to her biographical sketch.[26] Apparently Tubman, whose many accomplishments are condensed into one page, no longer fit the model of the future of black womanhood, at least in the eyes of William Still and his perceived audience. But it may not have mattered to Harriet; her reputation as Moses was well entrenched in the African American and liberal white community.[27]

Harriet's father, Ben Ross, died sometime during 1871; in his mid-eighties, Ben had suffered much with rheumatism and probably had been quite incapacitated during his last years in Auburn. Harriet's mother survived for several more years.[28] While the proceeds from *Scenes* was supposed to have gone toward Tubman's mortgage with Seward, it appears that no payments were made for the three years following the publication of the book. On October 10, 1872, William Henry Seward died, and his son, Frederick, inherited the note on the property, which had grown to over $1,500.[29] There is no record of what Tubman did with the money from the sales of her book, and in fact there is no record that she received any of the funds directly. Seward may have agreed not to take payment until Tubman was more financially secure herself. Some of the funds may have been doled out to her in times of greatest need. Alternatively, Tubman may have used some of the money to support herself and her family, purchase equipment to run the brickmaking business, or sent funds to educational and relief efforts in South Carolina. On May 29, 1873, Frederick Seward signed over the seven-acre property to Tubman in exchange for a lump-sum payment of $1,200, the original mortgage of the home. The rest of her debt to the Seward estate was forgiven.[30]

Within months of this transaction, however, Tubman found herself and her brother John implicated in the theft of $2,000. In the middle of September a man named Stevenson, "a Yellow fellow," appeared in Seneca Falls, New York, attempting to persuade individuals there that he had access to "a large quantity" of gold hidden in neighboring

Cayuga County, which he was willing to trade for $2,000 in cash.[31] Various individuals in the black community were consulted, but the money could not be raised to complete the deal, so Stevenson moved on to Auburn to try his luck there. Zadoc Bell was the first man he approached, but Bell, suspicious, sent Stevenson away. Bell later told the *Auburn Daily Bulletin* that he remembered a similar incident occurring in St. Catharines a couple of years earlier, where several of his friends had lost $500 in a scam involving Confederate gold. Having been turned away by Bell, Stevenson and an accomplice, John Thomas, sought the help of John Stewart, Tubman's brother. Stevenson and Thomas told Stewart that they had a friend, a "contraband" from South Carolina, who had "a large sum of gold . . . which he had kept since the war—being afraid to use any of it, or to let any white man know about it."[32] The men convinced Stewart that they had approximately $5,000 in gold pieces but would take $2,000 in "greenbacks," or cash, "which would be worth more . . . in South Carolina than the entire sum of gold."[33]

John Stewart told them that he could not raise the money but that "his sister might be able to effect the transaction with some of her white friends."[34] After being rejected by a local banker, who told him he needed to see the gold first before he would get involved in the transaction, Stewart brought Stevenson and Thomas to see Harriet. She took them into her home, where they lodged for several nights. Stevenson convinced Tubman that he and Harris, the "contraband" from South Carolina, knew her nephew, "Alfred Bowley," and that he had told them about her, thereby deflecting doubts she might have initially harbored regarding their characters.[35] Tubman later told the local newspaper that she recalled seeing a "trunk full of gold and silver buried in Beaufort, South Carolina," during the war, so this claim did not seem impossible to her. Thus convinced of their honesty and sincerity, Tubman visited several white friends in Auburn and Fleming and asked for money to exchange for the gold. She was cautioned more than once, however, that she was probably dealing with "robbers [who] might eventually take her life."[36] Harriet approached John Osborne, who in turn inquired of David Wright, but Wright cautioned Osborne to "have nothing to do with it."[37] Charles P. Wood was approached, and he, too, declined involvement.

Tubman was persistent, so David Wright suggested that she "better leave such dealings to Shimer."[38] Anthony Shimer was a successful local merchant and real estate investor, like many of Auburn's elite businessmen a risk taker and entrepreneur. He was a member of Central Presbyterian Church, where Tubman and many of Auburn's liberal elite families met for religious services. He was also apparently a bigger gambler than most other Auburnians, which may account for his vast wealth at the time of his death in 1896.[39] It may also explain why Wright suggested Tubman discuss the suspicious deal with Shimer; as a known risk taker, Shimer's reputation for pursuing unlikely opportunities may have offered Wright a way out of shutting the door to Tubman's request for money.[40]

Stewart and Tubman eventually persuaded Anthony Shimer to provide the $2,000 to complete the transactions. In spite of protestations from his bankers, Shimer withdrew the cash from his accounts and gave the money to Tubman.[41] Shimer trusted Tubman, and he believed this opportunity was too good to pass up; the interest he could earn on the gold was far greater than what could be earned on cash. He was cautious, however; he requested that his banker, Charles O'Brien, accompany them to the rendezvous point at Fleming Hill. But Harris was not there when they arrived at the appointed time. Stevenson convinced Tubman, Stewart, Shimer, and O'Brien that Harris was leery of white men and would not come forward. After much discussion, it was decided that Tubman would go on alone with Stevenson to meet Harris and give him the money personally, while the rest waited at a nearby tavern for her return.[42]

Stevenson brought Tubman to where Harris was hiding; there she noted that Harris appeared "scared and troubled."[43] Leading her across a field and into some woods near Poplar Ridge, the two men showed her a trunk partially buried in the ground. Harris insisted he receive the money before opening the chest, but Tubman refused. Suddenly Harris remembered that he had "forgotten" the key to the box; Stevenson and Harris started back to the place where Harris had been hiding, while Harriet waited by the box, still holding the money.[44]

It was getting dark, and Tubman became suspicious and worried. She looked more closely at the box and realized there was no keyhole.

She later told investigators that she became frightened, "thinking of stories about ghosts haunting buried treasures."[45] She tried to walk out of the woods but was alarmed by "something white," which she feared was a ghost. As she moved closer to it, she realized it was a cow, which became frightened by her movements in the dark. The cow "started off in a mad run, which startled up numerous other cows, all joining in a wild prance about the woods."[46] She returned to the box and attempted to break it open, but she became somewhat disoriented, later recalling, that "all the woods seemed filled with the wild cattle, and specters." Then, suddenly, the "two men were at her side. She sank down grasping for the box, and lost all consciousness."[47]

Tubman awoke later to find herself bound and gagged. She stumbled and struggled over two fences "by resting her chin on the top rail, to steady herself while she climbed up, and then dropped to the ground."[48] In the meantime, her brother John, Shimer, and O'Brien were also becoming alarmed; Harriet had not returned at the expected time, so they set out to look for her. They found her trying to make her way to them; she was "cut and bruised, her clothing torn," and the money was gone. Tubman, Martha Wright wrote to her daughter Ellen in Boston the next day, was taken to "the tavern but she became insensible & all remains a mystery."[49] The box was later discovered to contain only rocks.[50] Shimer was furious; he demanded the return of his money, claiming he had only loaned Tubman the money for the deal, with her home as security.[51] Shimer's claims did not sway anyone, so he lost the $2,000—he was a prominent businessman who had taken a great risk and lost, and few people apparently felt sympathy for him. Years later, at his death, the local newspaper would claim that "in 1873, Shimer lost more money than he ever lost before or since through reposing too much confidence in fellow beings." Afterward, the newspaper declared, "a change was noticeable in the old man."[52]

Though Tubman and her brother may have found themselves under a cloud of suspicion, the newspaper reports seem to sympathize with Tubman, noting that her "sanguine imagination" over smuggled Confederate gold had outweighed her better judgment. Tubman's reputation as a heroine and a "celebrated colored philanthropist" carried public opinion in her favor, effectively deflecting any suspicion cast upon herself and her brother.[53] The newspaper was quick to point out that John Stewart was an "honest and industrious man," and Zadoc Bell, the first black Auburnian to have been approached by the con men, was a "reliable, straight-forward man, industrious and steady," in direct contrast to the "confidence" man, Stevenson.[54] The *Daily* insisted that though the scheme looked "very 'thin' . . . especially so to those who bit at the bait and were 'caught,' " it was, the *Daily Advertiser* implied, Shimer's own fault for going along with the scheme in the first place.[55]

Beaten badly enough to need some care, or perhaps needing to be out of the spotlight for a few days, Tubman went to recuperate at Emily Howland's home in Sherwood.[56] Howland found her "pleasant and bright, and entertaining with her accounts of adventure in Camp and forest leading her fellow bondmen to freedom."[57] Tubman may have been consciously deflecting suspicion away from herself by redirecting her hostess's attention with tales of heroism and glory. Tubman's insertion of the "ghost" stories into her narrative of the events in the woods, juxtaposed with her retelling of her Underground Railroad stories to Howland, may have been a clever survival strategy to protect herself and her family.[58] Ultimately Tubman may have played, willingly or not, into existing racialized expectations of the superstitious black woman, thereby providing herself with ample protection from voices that may have been searching for a clearer explanation of the mysterious sequence of events. Fortunately for Tubman, Shimer bore the brunt of the negative fallout from the ordeal; this indicates the complex layers of behavior and relationships Tubman had to negotiate in order to survive every day.

The motivations for Tubman's involvement in this curious situation are clear. Constantly struggling for money, her needs overcame sound judgment, putting herself and her brother at great risk of not only criminal charges but also local humiliation. That they avoided both is a testament to the community's willingness to overlook Tubman's failings in this regard; her neediness was obvious and no surprise to anyone in Auburn, and that she could be so foolish as to be duped by con men reinforced the racist views that many held regarding uneducated African Americans. Nevertheless, Tubman's friends stood by her.[59]

Little is known of Tubman's activities throughout the rest of the 1870s and early 1880s. She continued to operate her farm with Nelson; in 1875 they raised potatoes, vegetables, and a few apples, made butter, and sold eggs, chickens, and perhaps a few pigs. They also continued to operate the brickyard.[60] An economic depression during the early to mid-1870s created difficult times for farmers and laborers such as Tubman, Davis, and her brothers.[61] John Stewart worked for D. M. Osborne & Co., Eliza Wright Osborne's husband's farm equipment manufacturing company, as a teamster.[62] John owned his own team of horses, but he also worked for the Osbornes privately, plowing, grading, and "grubbing" their garden during the spring, summer, and fall.[63] John's sons, John Henry and Moses, probably worked as laborers in the local manufacturing companies.

Tubman's home remained a refuge for those in need. In 1874 Harriet and Nelson adopted a baby girl named Gertie, raising her in their home as their own daughter. Gertie Davis represents a different side to the Nelson and Harriet relationship—they were committed to each other as a family, and with Gertie they could fulfill a long-neglected aspect of Tubman's life as a woman, that of being a mother to her own daughter.[64] Gertie joined an already very crowded household; along with her mother, Tubman welcomed four other boarders, including Sarah Parker, a seventy-five-year-old blind widow who may have been a longtime family friend or relative from Maryland.

In October 1880 Harriet Tubman's mother, Rit, died.[65] Rit had lived nearly a century. Born enslaved, she had experienced firsthand many of the terrors of slavery. She died a free woman, surrounded by family and friends, including children, grandchildren, and great-grandchildren, many of whom were building successful lives. By 1880 Tubman's extended family had grown considerably. Margaret Stewart had married Henry Lucas in 1873 at Central Presbyterian Church and settled into a home on Cornell Street.[66] Tubman's nephew William Henry Stewart Jr., her brother William's son, had moved to Auburn sometime before 1875 from Canada, and then married Emma Moseby in 1879. John Henry Stewart, Tubman's nephew, had married Eliza Smith, and by 1880 they had three children, Dora, five, Gertrude, three, and Clarence, one. Elijah Stewart had married, too, settling into the same close-knit black neighborhood as the other Stewart family members, with his wife, Georgia, and child, Esther.[67] Ann Marie Stewart Elliott, Tubman's great-niece, had died, though, leaving behind Thomas and their two daughters, Mary and Nellie.[68] Tubman's other friends, many of them refugees from slavery on the Eastern Shore or acquaintances from St. Catharines, were also adding to their own extended families, creating a strong and self-sustaining postemancipation black community whose roots could be traced to Tubman's early leadership.

At some point between 1882 and 1884 Tubman's wood-frame farmhouse in Auburn burned down, and "most of her interesting collection of letters from prominent Abolitionists and Union officers was destroyed."[69] Harriet, Nelson, and Gertie probably found shelter with her brother John, who was then living next door with his wife Millie and his son Moses, or with other relatives and friends in the Auburn community.[70] A brick residence was soon built over the ruins of the original home, possibly by the masons employed in the brickyards surrounding her property, who presumably installed the now missing Masonic symbol near the peak in the roof on the front face of the house.[71] Though Nelson was probably quite ill by this time with advanced tuberculosis, he and Harriet may have worked on the house as well, along with family and friends.[72]

The early 1880s brought more difficult times for Tubman. Her nephew John Henry Stewart died, leaving behind his wife, Eliza, and their three small children. Nelson's health continued to deteriorate, requiring more and more care and leaving the financial responsibilities of the household more fully on Tubman's shoulders. During the summer of 1884 Tubman experienced another tremendous financial blow: Her herd of hogs was dying from an unknown disease. On July 11 the *Evening Auburnian* reported that forty of Tubman's hogs had already died and that "she fears she will lose them all."[73] By this date Tubman was apparently using her farm as a "swine ranch." According to the *Auburnian*, Tubman had become "the chief garbage system in this city"; she collected garbage "at the back doors of Auburn," carted it back to her property, and fed it to her stock of hogs.[74] Hog cholera was ruled out as the source of the deaths, and Tubman surmised it was from poisoning. She told the newspaper that she suspected it was common household poisons, used to kill rats, bedbugs, and cockroaches, that had found its way into the garbage she collected. The poison had been "swept up" into the "slop pail or garbage bucket," which was then carted off by Tubman to her farm. The editors of the paper, though perhaps sympathetic to Tubman's plight, nevertheless found some humor in her crisis, adding that "the devastation of [Tubman's] hog herds is chargeable to that vernal nightmare—house cleaning."[75]

Tubman's own health also remained precarious; her headaches and TLE seizures continued to affect her. On January 29, 1884, Tubman visited Eliza Wright Osborne. Sick with a respiratory ailment, Tubman was in need of some medicine for her cough. But she was also deeply troubled by recent "mysterious dreams and thoughts that had come to her," Osborne later wrote to her daughter Emily Harris. In her letter, Osborne described what might have been a TLE seizure in progress while Tubman visited with her that morning. "While Harriet sat here," Osborne wrote, "she said she heard a harp playing . . . she seemed sensible enough. She said water and fire troubled her—she lately saw so many people drowning and some burning up."[76] Tubman "dreamed of the drowning" the week before, Osborne wrote, which coincided with a fatal maritime accident at that time. Evidently eager to validate Tubman's visions, Osborne showed Tubman a newspaper from the week before that reported the story of the fatal "wreck of the Columbia."[77] The steamer *City of Columbus* had run aground during a storm off Gay Head on Martha's Vineyard on January 18. Over one hundred passengers and crew were lost, including many women and children. Tubman "had not heard of it," Osborne wrote to Emily, adding to the mystery of Tubman's prescient visions. Later Sarah Bradford noted that at one time Tubman had a terrible dream, and in "great agitation [she] ran to the houses of her colored neighbors, exclaiming that 'a dreadful thing was happening somewhere, the ground was opening, and the houses were falling in, and the people being killed faster than they was in the war—faster than they was in the war.' "[78] At that time, "or near it," there was an earthquake in South America, "though why a vision of it should be sent to Harriet no one can divine."[79] On October 13, 1884, the *Auburn Daily Advertiser* reported that "a considerable amount of excitement" had been caused by Tubman, whose "reputation is national," when she was "seized with what is familiarly known as the 'power' and began shouting and singing" on the street outside the city jail.[80] She had just come from visiting her nephew, Moses Stewart, who was lodged in the jail on charges of petty larceny.[81] The sheriff brought Harriet back into the building, where a Dr. Hamlin settled her down.[82] The manifestations of her TLE seizures in a public place are a reminder of the often unexpected nature of the illness. In the absence of modern medical understanding, these stories offer an interesting perspective on how the community chose to accommodate and cope with her seizures. While a modern physician might attribute her seizures to physical causes, for Tubman herself, as well as for Osborne, Bradford, the sheriff, and most probably her family and friends, Tubman's powerful faith lay at the root of her outbursts, visions, sleeping spells, and voices.[83]

Tubman's deep religious faith inspired and awed many who knew her. The Rev. James E. Mason remembered meeting Tubman for the first time at the AME Zion Church in Auburn during the 1880s, when the church was still located on Washington Street. He noticed her sitting close to the front of the church, "with shoulders somewhat stooped, head bent forward," making her seem older than her sixty years. She stood up and started to "give testimony to God's goodness and long-suffering." Soon she was shouting, inspiring others to join in, Mason recalled, and "she possessed such endurance, vitality and magnetism that I inquired and was informed it was Harriet Tubman—the 'Moses of her people.' "[84] Others remembered how she incorporated scriptural quotations into her everyday conversation, testimony to her remarkable memory.[85]

While Tubman's spirituality is a staple of her iconography, Bradford and other observers ignored Tubman's intellectual life because it did not fit the carefully circumscribed notions of late-nineteenth-century literate womanhood.[86] At a time when literacy was a marker for class status and intelligence, many whites viewed Tubman's illiteracy as a liability. Fortunately for Tubman, her spirituality allowed her to claim respectability and authority. Yet even later biographers have downplayed attention to Tubman's intellectual life in deference to a highly mythologized tradition that stresses Tubman's spiritual life, verging on the supernatural.[87] The possibility of an intellectual tradition rooted

outside of literacy has been lost in the perpetual retelling of the Tubman myth.

By the 1880s Tubman's fame as an Underground Railroad agent and
Civil War warrior had faded significantly. Tubman had not been a constant fixture at suffrage or black rights conventions and meetings
around New England and New York throughout the 1870s and early
1880s.[88] A newer and younger group of activists were more often seen
at these conventions, many of them middle-class and highly literate, in
distinct contrast to Tubman. In addition, many of the old abolitionist
guard had passed away, including Lucretia Mott, Thomas Garrett, Wendell Phillips, William Lloyd Garrison, Jermain Loguen, Lewis Hayden,
Martha Coffin Wright, and Gerrit Smith, leaving Tubman with a
shrinking support system. A few new friends were ready to step in to
help her, however. Martha Coffin Wright's daughter Eliza Wright Osborne and the Garrison children buoyed Tubman when she needed it
the most, but the support was not the same as in prior years. With the
exception of a few local newspaper articles in the late 1860s and early
1870s that mentioned Tubman, Bradford's *Scenes* still remained the primary source for Tubman's life story. Its limited publication run of
twelve hundred copies, however, did not provide a wide enough circulation to keep Tubman's life story in current memory. Sarah Bradford
herself even noted in 1886 that the "facts" of Tubman's life were "all
unknown to the present generation."[89] Tubman had been, it seems,
quickly forgotten.

But her needs were tremendous by 1886; after rebuilding her home,
struggling with her own ill health and that of her husband, Nelson, and
still trying to support sick, homeless, and needy boarders in her home,
she finally turned to Bradford and asked her to reissue *Scenes*.[90] "Another necessity has arisen," Bradford wrote in the preface to the 1886
edition, "and she needs help again not for herself, but for certain helpless ones of her people."[91]

Called *Harriet, the Moses of Her People*, this new edition was issued at
a time when the nation was struggling through a period of reconciliation and reunification between North and South. Eager to heal the
bitter wounds still lingering from the Civil War and Reconstruction,

Americans longed for a unified nation with a unified past. A reimaging of the history of the antebellum period and the Civil War was seen as necessary for a history appropriate for this unity.[92] The desire for reconciliation and reunification demanded a history that softened the harsh reality of slavery. Increasingly disenfranchised throughout the South, African Americans stood helpless as their history and memories of slavery and the war were deliberately obscured. In this environment, then, the reprinting of Tubman's original narrative became problematic— a new version was necessary, a version more in tune with the new political reality of reunification. Bradford's new edition exemplified this re-creation of historical memory. Though in many ways a reprint of the first edition, it was a less demanding and less detailed biography with a milder and more stereotypical image of a former slave than the Harriet Tubman of the 1869 book.

By the end of the 1870s, the fate of Reconstruction was sealed; with the inauguration of Rutherford B. Hayes as president, support for the federal military occupation of the southern states and other negotiations collectively known as the Compromise of 1877 brought an end to the advancement of the freedmen's interests.[93] In its place, the subjugation of African Americans found renewed energy among both southern and northern whites. African American rights became "sacrificial offerings on the altar of reunion."[94] By the 1880s, the contest over the memory of the Civil War, and why it was fought, was dominated by white reconciliators and veterans, whose need to "celebrate a common American manhood" muted and ignored African American veterans' memories as well as the black community's struggle to maintain its own memory of slavery, the war, and Reconstruction.[95] The glory of the Lost Cause and mourning for the Old South overshadowed the brutality and exploitation that had defined slavery.

By the mid-1880s "Blue and Gray" soldier reunions were taking place, and a "deliberate negotiation of a mutually acceptable version of the sectional conflict" was under way, obscuring any contradictory memories or histories that challenged the new unified history.[96] Historian David Blight demonstrated the struggles of Frederick Douglass and W.E.B. Du Bois to "forge an African American countermemory."[97]

Douglass struggled to preserve and remember the "regenerative meaning of the Civil War" with emancipation at its center.[98] Du Bois, like
Douglass, believed that Americans suffered from historical amnesia,
which contributed to a master narrative that celebrated "a people of
progress," detached from oppression, poverty, and racial tension.[99]

For Frederick Douglass, historical memory was "not merely an en-
tity altered by the passage of time; it was the prize in a struggle between
rival versions of the past, a question of will, of power, of persuasion."[100]
Douglass understood that the question of who owns history is political,
intellectual, and emotional. The ability of those in power to shape and
reconstruct the memory of the Civil War demonstrated the tremendous implications of the powerful political agenda that sought to rebuild the nation as a whole, rooted in a common past.

The transformation of the memory of the Civil War exemplified
the power of mythmaking, and the ability to create a collective
memory of the event went a long way toward reunion. Forgetting
that emancipation was the "great result of the war" was the tragedy
of reconciliation.[101] For blacks, this transformation robbed them of a
culturally important historical moment. The Old South's cultural and
sentimental investment in slavery was also mythologized as part of
the Lost Cause, and served to deny African Americans a right to their
bitter memories of slavery, the glory of emancipation, and ultimately
a historical identity. The manipulative potential of this mythmaking
was profoundly destructive to African American claims to a past of
their own.

When Bradford's second biography of Tubman was issued, the
country was already deep into reconciliation. Much of the power of the
original biography's detail and blunt commentary about slavery were
muted in deference to a less hostile South. Bradford, for the first time,
includes "merry little darkies" on Tubman's master's plantation; she
also feels compelled to testify that "their love for their offspring is quite
equal to that of the 'superior race' " and that Tubman's family "seem to
be peculiarly intelligent, upright and religious people, and to have a
strong feeling of family affection. There may be many among the colored race like them; certainly all should not be judged by the idle, mis-

erable darkies who have swarmed about Washington and other cities since the War."[102]

Bradford's original attempt to confront the South's legacy of violence and oppression through the inclusion of the "Essay on Woman-Whipping" in *Scenes* was cast aside when the essay was eliminated from the second edition. Tubman's woodcut image in her Union garb and gun, featured prominently as the frontispiece to her 1869 biography, is gone. Several tales are altered and exaggerated for comic or dramatic effect. Bradford also uses more dialect when quoting Tubman, which is what white audiences had come to expect from an illiterate black woman, no matter how famous or accomplished she may have been.

In the first edition of *Scenes* Bradford quotes Tubman's description of her mixed emotions upon arriving in Philadelphia with simple directness:

"I had crossed the line. I was *free*; but there was no one to welcome me to the land of freedom. I was a stranger in a strange land; and my home, after all, was down in Maryland; because my father, my mother, my brothers, and sisters, and friends were there. But I was free, and *they* should be free. I would make a home in the North and bring them there, God helping me. Oh, how I prayed then," she said; "I said to de Lord, 'I'm gwine to hole stiddy on to *you*, an' I *know* you'll see me through.' "[103]

But when Bradford rewrote the biography, she changed this quote, embellishing and inserting more dialect:

"I had crossed de line of which I had so long been dreaming. I was free; but dere was no one to welcome me to de land of freedom, I was a stranger in a strange land, and my home after all was down in de old cabin quarter, wid de ole folks, and my brudders and sisters. But to dis solemn resolution I came; I was free, and dey should be free also; I would make a home for dem in de North, and de Lord helping me, I would bring dem all dere. Oh, how I prayed den, lying all alone on de cold, damp ground; 'Oh, dear Lord,' I said, 'I haint got no friend but *you*. Come to my help, Lord, for I'm in trouble!' "[104]

Bradford also rewrote the story of Joe Bailey, the runaway slave who had escaped from a master on the Eastern Shore who offered a $1,500 reward for Joe's capture. By 1886 Bradford has changed this to $2,000.[105] Instead of using the word "whipping" and "whipped" to describe the lashes Joe received at the hands of his cruel owner, the 1886 version referred only to "a good licking" and a "flogging."[106] She also eliminated the threat the master gave to Joe if he did not submit; the earlier version read, "[T]he first lesson my niggers have to learn is that I am *master*, and that they are not to resist or refuse to obey anything I tell 'em to do. So the first thing they've got to do, is to be whipped; if they resist, they got it all the harder; and so I'll go on, till I kill 'em, but they've got to give up at last, and learn that I'm master."[107] By 1886, the cruelty of the master is much reduced; "[T]he first lesson my niggers have to learn is that I am master and they belong to me, and are never to resist anything I order them to do. So I always begin by giving them a good licking."[108]

In the 1869 version, Bradford wrote that Harriet had "heard them read from one paper that the reward offered was $12,000," but that a recent article claimed *"forty thousand dollars* was not too great a reward for the Maryland slaveholders to offer for her."[109] By 1886, Bradford makes no mention of the $12,000, but claims, rather, that "a reward of $40,000 was offered by the slave-holders of the region from whence so many slaves had been spirited away, for the head of the woman who appeared so mysteriously, and enticed away their property. . . . Our sagacious heroine has been in the car . . . and has heard this advertisement, which was posted over her head, read by others of the passengers."[110]

Why did Bradford change these stories? There may be several reasons, the least of which was perhaps Bradford's own desire to rewrite what she had thought was an inadequate biography. Bradford had a second chance to insert more of her own style and personal vision into the story. In doing so, she omitted important details, added additional descriptive material for literary effect, and even sensationalized certain stories for dramatic purposes.[111]

Oddly, Sarah Bradford predicted the ultimate reformulation of Tubman's narrative and, ultimately, African American history and memory as well. In the closing pages of *Scenes in the Life of Harriet Tubman* she wrote, "[B]y the time the South has been overflowed and regenerated by a beneficent inundation of Northern 'carpet baggers,' with Yankee capital and enterprise, it will be forgotten that a race capable of the crimes referred to in the preceding story [*Scenes in the Life of Harriet Tubman*], ever existed."[112]

While in the second edition Bradford did not go so far as to portray Tubman's life in slavery with the nostalgic imagery of an Old South with its abundant plantation culture teeming with happy, helpful slaves and contented, genteel masters, she did privilege certain aspects of Tubman's life and reformulate her image of Tubman to suit a nation more disposed to conciliatory stories of slavery, the war, and its aftermath. Her modified version was the one that for generations of Americans, both white and black, would reconfigure the narrative of Harriet Tubman into a more usable past that suited a variety of racial, gender, and class ideologies, and it is this 1886 biography that has remained the reprint of choice.

In spite of its failings, *Harriet, the Moses of Her People* probably provided Harriet with a little more income to help with her ever-present need for money. It brought her back into the public sphere, a place she seems to have enjoyed. She traveled to Boston, where Franklin Sanborn saw to it that she sat for a new photograph, possibly to sell with copies of her new biography.[113] An article appeared in the *Boston Sunday Herald* announcing Tubman's presence in the city, drumming up interest in her new narrative.[114] Bradford did not take any payment for her authorship, but she did apparently take it upon herself to dole out funds when she thought Tubman needed it most. While this may have been exceedingly frustrating to Tubman, it may have been in her best interest; many people throughout the years expressed exasperation with Tubman's preference to give her money away to others rather than provide for her own needs. Tubman was hoping, it seems, to start a hospital to care for the sick and disabled. "Her own sands are nearly run," Bradford wrote of Tubman, "but she hopes, 'ere she goes home, to see this work, a hospital, well under way. Her last breath and her last efforts will be spent in the cause of those for whom she has already risked so much."[115] Over the next twenty years of her life, Tubman would remain more public-oriented, using the same strategies to raise money and awareness that had worked so well for her before and after the Civil War, and she would share considerably in the fashioning of her own historical image and legacy.

—

MOTHER TUBMAN,
THE BLACK JOAN OF ARC

WITH THE PUBLICATION OF A REVISED BIOGRAPHY OF HER LIFE, *Harriet, the Moses of Her People,* Tubman reentered the public sphere with renewed vigor, only this time through the haze of the reunification sentiment that now dominated the memory of slavery and the Civil War. Though the new biography still focused on her years in slavery, her liberation of herself and others, and her Civil War experiences, it was silent on her postwar life. Tubman's support of woman suffrage remained obscured, and her community activism and humanitarianism received only a brief acknowledgment in the book's introduction.

Tubman's new public activism now focused on woman suffrage. Though she had long been supportive of the movement for women's rights, Tubman's daily struggle for survival had forced her to step back from active participation in the movement since she had first spoken at a suffrage meeting in Boston in 1860.[1] After the Civil War she had been occupied with supporting relief efforts for the freedmen in the South and maintaining a household full of dependants in Auburn. By the mid-1880s, as an older and more feeble woman, showing the effects of decades

of poverty and hard labor, Tubman cut a striking image, in sharp coun-
terbalance to the middle-class white and black women who shared the
suffrage convention and meeting circuit throughout the 1880s and
1890s.

When interviewed at the turn of the century, Tubman acknowledged that she had been a member of "Miss Anthony's organization,"
the National Woman Suffrage Association (NWSA).[2] Tubman maintained friendships with old-guard abolitionists, themselves split between two rival suffrage organizations that had emerged when the
Fifteenth Amendment outlawed voting discrimination against African
American men but failed to provide the same for women.[3] Though
Tubman "considered [Frederick Douglass's] judgment on political matters to be the very best, and she followed him in forming her views,"
she may have differed with him on the amendment. Douglass broke
ranks with Anthony, Elizabeth Cady Stanton, and others during the immediate postwar period, arguing that black men needed the vote more
than women. Supported by many black and white woman suffragists,
including Francis Ellen Watkins Harper, Lucy Stone, and Anna Blackwell, founders of the American Woman Suffrage Association, Douglass
and other prominent male black rights activists successfully sustained
Republican efforts to pass the amendment.[4] Though he supported uni-
versal suffrage, Douglass campaigned hard for the amendment, and he
resented Anthony's and Stanton's criticism of what he called "a cause
not more sacred, [but] certainly more urgent, because it is life and death to
the long-enslaved people of this country; and this is: Negro suffrage . . .
considering that white men have been enfranchised always, and colored
men have not, the conduct of these white women, whose husbands, fathers and brothers are voters, does not seem generous."[5]

Tubman may have ultimately favored Anthony's NWSA because of
her commitment to an expanded women's rights platform, in which she
was supported by her longtime friends Lucretia Mott, Martha Wright,
and Eliza Wright Osborne, but it is likely that she reflected a minority
view within the black community.[6] For Tubman, who had led her
brothers out of slavery on the Eastern Shore, counseled John Brown,
and commanded raids and advised generals during the Civil War, the
thought that men should vote "for" her may have been too much.

Tubman frequently attended suffrage meetings in New York and Boston throughout the late 1880s, 1890s, and early 1900s, and she spoke as often as she could.[7] In March 1888 Tubman addressed a meeting of suffragists at the "Non-Partisan Society for political education for women," in Auburn.[8] Asked to speak of her heroic service "in freeing and helping to emancipate her down trodden and emancipated race," Tubman informed the group that she was there not "to teach them but rather to learn and be taught."[9] At nearly seventy years old, Tubman probably reaped some of the respect young reformers offered aged activists. She "spoke affectionately of her friends of the late war, most of whom have passed away." But she was forceful and to the point when she told her audience of the "brave and fearless deeds of women who sacrificed all for their country and moved in battle when bullets mowed down men." Those women, she told them, "were on the scene to administer to the injured, to bind up their wounds and tend them through weary months of suffering in the army hospitals. If those deeds do not place woman as man's equal, what do?"[10] The story of Tubman's heroic feats was a tale of a personal and yet collective experience of resistance and liberation that resonated for African Americans, but it also spoke to late-nineteenth-century middle-class white women eager for the vote, making Tubman an ideal emblem for woman suffrage.

During the 1880s, as Tubman was reemerging on the public stage, a new generation of activist women began moving into positions of leadership in the suffrage movement. Some of these younger leaders held views decidedly more racist than those of Anthony's generation. Political expediency and racialized gender expectations combined with these views to silence many African American suffragists and push them aside. For some aging former abolitionists, including Tubman, these younger women needed to be reminded of the moral victories of the preceding generation. During this changing of the guard, Tubman served to reify the abolitionists' glorious pasts and to demonstrate an obligation to give the vote to women, who in Tubman's words "had suffered enough for it."[11]

However, as the 1890s wore on, many middle-class white woman suffragists shied away from support for racial equality. Racism reared its ugly head, striking at the heart of the emerging struggles in the 1890s for control of the suffrage movement. For twenty years, efforts to re-unite the two factions of the national organizations, the National Woman Suffrage Association and the American Woman Suffrage Association, had proved fruitless. By 1891, however, the rift had been repaired enough for the two organizations to form the National American Woman Suffrage Association (NAWSA). Southern women, who up until that time had remained unorganized on the issue, began voicing racist concerns about giving the vote to black women. NAWSA modified its arguments to pacify the growing discontent emerging from the increasingly power-ful southern groups.[12] Harking back to Henry Blackwell's assurances to the legislatures of the southern states in 1867 that white supremacy could be maintained with woman suffrage, NAWSA adopted a set of reso-lutions in 1893 that reiterated this point.[13] They also began to concede to southern pressure to support an individual state's rights in matters of voting qualifications. For black women this was a painful reminder that powerful state interests that had already ensured the de facto disenfran-chisement of black men in much of the South would find support from some white women activists.

White racist attitudes created barriers between activists; the call for "sisterhood" rang false in the ears of many black women struggling with both race and gender inequality. As discrimination against African Americans within the movement came to a head in the 1890s, many disillusioned African American suffragists began forming their own so-cieties and organizations, establishing their own lecture circuits and propaganda campaigns, and issuing their own suffrage and racial uplift literature. Long excluded from many meetings, particularly in the South, African American women became an increasingly problematic presence for the national organization. Black female activists in turn challenged their political, economic, and social silence. In the mid-1890s Anna Julia Cooper, a black feminist and intellectual, recognized that much equal-rights rhetoric encompassed only middle-class white women. "The 'all' will inevitably stick in the throat of the Southern woman. She must be allowed, please, to except the 'darkey' from the 'all'; it is too bitter a pill with black people in it. You must get the Revised Version to put it, 'love all white people as brethren.' "[14]

Responding to the racism they confronted in the predominantly white NAWSA, black women founded the National Federation of Afro-American Women in Boston in 1895.[15] In July 1896 the federation joined forces with the National League of Colored Women in Washington, D.C., to create the National Association of Colored Women.[16] Harriet Tubman was a featured speaker at the group's first meeting in 1896. *The Woman's Era,* an African American women's newspaper popular from the 1890s, featured Tubman as the first in a series on "Eminent Women." A tribute to her, complete with a picture of her with a shotgun, was featured in the official "souvenir" issue that doubled as a program for the convention. Calling on "the rising generation" of African American women to "clasp hands with this noble mother of Israel!" the editors of the *Woman's Era* and leaders of the convention urged solidarity "in the benign presence of this great leader, in days and actions that caused strong men to quail, this almost unknown, almost unsung 'Black Joan of Arc.' The primary object of our Federation is to bring our women together, we owe it to our children to uncover from partial oblivion and unconscious indifference the great characters within our ranks. The fact that we know so little that is creditable and truly noble about our own people constitutes one of the saddest and most humiliating phases of Afro-American life."[17]

Introduced to the audience at the meeting as "Mother Tubman," Harriet told of her war activities, and with her beautiful voice she "penetrated every portion of the large auditorium" as she sang a "war melody."[18] She was later asked, as the oldest member attending the meeting, to introduce Ida B. Wells-Barnett's newborn, "Baby Barnett," to the audience, after which Harriet spoke on the topic of "More Homes for our Aged Ones."[19] Donations were made in support of Tubman's home or hospital in Auburn, and a collection was made to help defray the expenses "of Mother Harriet Tubman during her visit in Washington."[20]

In November of that same year, Susan B. Anthony led Harriet Tubman to the podium at a predominantly white suffrage convention in Rochester, New York. She was introduced as the "great Black liberator." Thunderous applause erupted from the audience. Tubman's appearance onstage was heralded as the high point of the three-day convention. "With her hand held in Miss Anthony's, she impressed one with the venerable dignity of her appearance," a reporter for the *Rochester Democrat and Chronicle* wrote. The reporter noted that although Tubman's clothing was "cheap" and her "face was black, old and wrinkled, and strongly marked with her race characteristics . . . through it all there shows an honesty and true benevolence of purpose which commanded respect."[21] It was probably here that Tubman spoke her most famous words: "I was the conductor on the Underground Railroad for eight years, and I can say what most conductors can't say—I never ran my train off the track and I never lost a passenger."[22] Tubman spoke as an "Underground Railroad operator and Union fighter . . . but it was as a suffragist that she came to the Rochester meeting."[23]

Though Tubman was enjoying renewed public acclaim by the mid-1890s, she had spent many years struggling with personal challenges, private pain, and financial setbacks. On October 18, 1888, Nelson Davis died at the age of forty-five, probably as a result of the ravages of tuberculosis.[24] Tubman's older brother John, seventy-seven, died the following year.[25] It was about this time that Harriet's younger brother William Henry, who had been living in Grantham, Ontario, left Canada and moved to Auburn to be near his older son, William Henry Stewart Jr., and Harriet. Though he lived with William Junior for a time on Garrow Street, he eventually moved in with Harriet on South Street. His other son, John Isaac, also joined his father and brother in Auburn, probably around 1890, after the death of John's Canadian wife, Helena. According to Harkless Bowley, John Isaac's wife, "an Indian girl," sent for Tubman when she lay dying after giving birth to a baby girl, and asked her to take the child and raise her. "Aunt Harriet promise [*sic*] her she would. She said now I die happy, and passed away."[26] Harriet, now seventy years old, brought the child, named Eva Katherine Helena Harriet, to Auburn to live with her and Eva's grandfather, William Henry. John Isaac, however, soon died of unknown causes at Tubman's home, leaving little Eva an orphan.[27] He was buried at Fort Hill cemetery next to Nelson Davis. Eva remained in the household with Tubman, one of the constantly changing arrays of residents in Tubman's home. Helen Tatlock, a friend and neighbor, recalled that Tubman "had a great number of young and old, black and white, all poorer than she. There were children that she brought up . . . also a blind woman."[28] Emma Telford later wrote, perhaps more dramatically, that Tubman's "doors have been open to the needy, the most utterly friendless and helpless of her race. The aged . . . the babe deserted, the demented, the epileptic, the blind, the paralyzed, the consumptive."[29]

Sarah Bradford recalled visiting Tubman one day in early 1901 and finding her "providing for five sick and injured ones. A blind woman came to her door, led by four little children—her husband had turned her out of his house."[30] The blind woman soon gave birth to a fifth child. Tatlock told Conrad that Tubman also "took care of an incorrigible white woman who . . . was frequently in local difficulties." This woman had a child and "had been in jail."[31] As Tubman aged, work became more difficult; she lived day to day by selling chickens and eggs, and sometimes a little milk. Her brother William contributed to the household finances, too, but donations of food and money from friends and relatives helped make ends meet.[32]

A Civil War pension would have helped her financial situation, and Harriet continued to press her claim for her war service as a nurse and a spy. In 1887 she petitioned Congress to release the file containing her application for back pay, with the intention, it seems, to reinstate her petition once again.[33] No action was taken, however, and after her husband's death, Tubman applied for a widow's pension under the Dependent Pension Act of 1890. Designed to provide benefits to any disabled war veterans or their widows and dependents, the new pension act greatly expanded the original pension plan, which provided compensation only to veterans suffering with disabilities directly related to war service.[34] Within a month of the enactment of the act in June 1890, Tubman filed her first claim; five years later, on October 16, 1895, she was finally granted an $8-per-month pension as the widow of Nelson Davis.[35] She received a lump-sum retroactive payment of approximately $500 in late October 1895, covering the sixty-odd months from the time she first applied for the widow's pension until it was finally approved.[36]

The lengthy process to obtain a widow's pension must have been frustrating for Tubman. Her right to Davis's pension would seem incontrovertible. But the bureaucratic process, which all widows had to negotiate, worked against African American soldiers and their dependents in ways that it did not for white applicants. In the case of Nelson Davis, as for many other former slaves who joined the Union army, his identity was at first difficult to ascertain in the military records because he had changed his name after the war from Nelson Charles to Nelson Davis. When Tubman first applied for the pension under the name Nelson Davis, it was denied because the claims office could not find a Nelson Davis on the muster rolls of the Eighth USCT. It took at least eighteen months before the mix-up was straightened out, and then it was another three years before all the supporting documentation, including sworn testimonies of relatives, friends, fellow soldiers from the Eighth USCT, and Auburn lawyers and other officials, was gathered to the satisfaction of the Pension Bureau. After it was determined that Nelson Charles, who had served with the Eighth USCT, was the same person as Nelson Davis, the bureau required Tubman to provide documentation of their marriage, obtain sworn testimony that her first husband, John Tubman, had died before she married Davis, and demonstrate her worthiness to receive the pension. The personal reputations of her witnesses, including family members William Henry and Margaret Stewart Lucas, friends such as Thornton Newton and Charles Peterson, and fellow soldiers Edgar J. Fryman and Dorsey Brainard, among others, also had to be verified, making the process expensive and time-consuming. The documentation seems excessive, but this bureaucratic process was typical, particularly for African American soldiers, whose identities were often difficult to ascertain.[37]

The process might have taken even longer had not New York congressman Sereno E. Payne begun pressuring the pension claims board. When Tubman was finally paid, in October 1895, Payne still viewed it as inadequate and a poor substitute for a pension in her own right and the official recognition of her service that would come with it. In December 1897 Payne introduced a bill to Congress "granting a pension to Harriet Tubman Davis, late a nurse in the United States Army," at the rate of $25 per month.[38] A petition was circulated around Auburn, supporting Payne and urging him to "bring up the matter again and press it to a final and successful termination."[39] Finally, in January 1899, a report on the bill was filed, supporting her claim for a $25-per-month pension. Objections were voiced, however, arguing that giving Tubman a $25-per-month pension as a nurse far exceeded pension payments to other Civil War nurses. A compromise was reached, and she was awarded $20 per month: $8 per month as the widow of Nelson Davis and $12 for her services as a nurse. This increase in monthly pension payments brought her closer in monetary terms to the $25 she sought, but it did not bring any further acknowledgment from the government for her military service as a scout and spy.[40] Some of Tubman's friends felt that Payne "might have pressed the matter more than he did."[41] By 1899, however, Tubman was nearly eighty years old, and Payne may have decided that, rather than fight in Congress to get official recognition for Tubman's service as a scout and a spy, it was better to get her paid immediately for her nursing services.

Throughout this period, Tubman was deeply ensconced in the spiritual and social world of the AME Zion Church in Auburn. For many black women of the late nineteenth century, the church served as not only a spiritual sanctuary but also a social and political haven where they could forge strong networks in support of racial, gender, economic, and educational advancement.[42] In 1891 the Thompson Memorial AME Zion Church moved from its location on Washington Street to a new church on Parker Street. Tubman apparently pledged $500 for its construction, though how she paid for it remains a mystery.[43] She stayed actively involved in community work, raising money and clothing for needy families. "I have been appointed by the first M.E. and the A.M.E. Churches of Auburn," Tubman told Mary Wright in a dictated letter, "to collect clothes for the destitute colored children and the things which you sent are very acceptable."[44] She had been trying unsuccessfully for years to open a home for destitute and elderly African Americans, but the lack of funds prevented this, though her house remained a refuge. Tubman "is as busy as ever going about doing good to every body—her house is filled with 'odds and ends' of society—and to many are outcast," Jane Kellogg wrote to Ednah Cheney in 1894.[45]

Tubman's dream of an institution dedicated to caring for poor and sick African Americans started to become a reality in the spring of 1896. A twenty-five-acre lot adjacent to her property in Fleming was put up

for auction. On the day of the auction Tubman "appeared with very little money," but was determined to have the land and the buildings she
would need to house her infirmary and shelter for the sick and homeless.[46] Tubman bid on it and, to everyone's surprise, won. "There was
all white folks but me there," she later told Bradford, "and there I was
like a blackberry in a pail of milk."[47] When the auction was over and
they called out for the high bidder, Tubman stepped forward, shouting
that "Harriet Tubman" had bought the property. Asked how she could
possibly pay for the land, she responded, "I'm going home to tell the
Lord Jesus all about it."[48]

Friends and supporters contributed $250, and she obtained a mort-
gage of $1,000.[49] Within months she convened a group of AME Zion
ministers with whom she was familiar, and incorporated her venture as
the Harriet Tubman Home, Inc.[50] Because of the substantial debt en-
cumbering the property, Tubman was unable to use the buildings as she
had hoped because she lacked the requisite funds to run them. So she
rented out the buildings and land and kept those who came to her for
care in her own home.[51]

Tubman set about fund-raising immediately. She sent a letter to
Mary Wright in Syracuse, requesting money to help her pay for another
edition of Bradford's *Harriet, the Moses of Her People.* She told Wright
that she could raise $50 of the $100 dollars needed to publish another
five hundred copies, but she hoped that Ednah Cheney, Frank Sanborn,
and others could help raise the additional fifty. "If they will help me get
the money they can hold the books until I can sell enough to pay them
back," she offered, noting that "Miss Cheney has done very well by me
and I do not wish to ask for money [but] if through her influence I can
get the friends to help me I shall be ever thankful. My home is incorper-
ated [*sic*] for an asylum for aged colored people that will hold the mortgage and I won't be trouble[d] now."[52] Lillie B. Chase Wyman wrote an
article about Tubman for *New England Magazine* in March 1896; another
in *The Chautauquan,* by Rosa Belle Holt, soon followed that. Both relied
heavily on Bradford's work, though both added material gleaned from
personal interviews with Tubman.[53] Both mention her poverty and the
numerous sick and impoverished African Americans she was caring for
in her own home, noting she "never begs" but received occasional aid

from neighbors and friends, and gently suggesting that Tubman could use more help.[54]

Despite her physical and financial limitations, Tubman continued to frequent suffrage meetings in New York, Boston, and Washington. She traveled to Boston often, not just to attend meetings but probably to visit family (Elijah Stewart had moved there around 1890), friends from Maryland, and her former abolitionist associates and their children.[55] Because she could neither read nor write, Tubman "paid no attention to time-tables." She would go to the train station in Auburn and "sit and wait for the first train that would take her easterly to Boston."[56]

In April 1897 the *Woman's Journal*, the white suffrage movement's official newspaper, reported several receptions in Tubman's honor in Boston, sponsored by former white abolitionists and current suffragists, including Ednah Cheney.[57] Yet Tubman, so celebrated and honored over the weeks following her arrival there, had to sell a cow in order to pay for her train ticket to Boston.[58] She was feted at the offices of William Lloyd Garrison Jr., who was offering the latest edition of her biography for sale.[59] Tubman also visited with Sanborn and the Garrison children, among others, and spoke at the Old South Meetinghouse on Washington Street along with other aging former antislavery warriors later that summer.[60] In August she met with Wilbur Siebert in Cambridge, where she was staying with Dr. Harriet Cobb. Siebert was compiling evidence for his lengthy volume on the Underground Railroad.[61] Though Tubman was "considerably aged and worn," he wrote, "her mind was still clear."[62] He noted that she would doze off at "frequent intervals" for a few minutes, then regain consciousness and carry on "without losing the thread of the conversation."[63] Tubman's fame even traveled overseas; Queen Victoria read Tubman's narrative and, being "pleased with it," sent Tubman a silver medal that commemorated Victoria's Diamond Jubilee in 1897.[64] Apparently the queen also invited Tubman to her birthday celebration, but Tubman regretted that she "didn't know enough to go," never mind that she could not have afforded it.[65]

The terrible headaches from her childhood head injury remained a constant in her life. Unable to cope with the pain any longer, Tubman endured brain surgery at Massachusetts General Hospital sometime in the late 1890s.[66] On a visit to Samuel Hopkins's home, he asked about her shaved head (probably beneath the scarf and hat she usually wore), and Tubman told him of the ordeal she had endured:

When I was in Boston I walked out one day, I saw a great big building, I asked a man what it was, and he said it was a hospital. So I went right in, and I saw a young man there, and I said, "Sir, are you a doctor?" and he said he was; then I said "Sir, do you think you could cut my head open?" . . . Then I told him the whole story, and how my head was giving me a powerful sight of trouble lately, with achin' and buzzin', so I couldn't get no sleep at night.

And he said "Lay right down on this here table," and I lay down.

"Didn't he give you anything to deaden the pain, Harriet?"

No sir; I just lay down like a lamb before the slaughter, and he sawed open my skull, and raised it up, and now it feels more comfortable.

"Did you suffer much?"

Yes, sir, it hurt, of course; but I got up and put on my bonnet and started to walk home, but my legs kind of give out under me, and they sent for a ambulance and sent me home.[67]

Samuel Hopkins's grandson, Samuel Hopkins Adams, later wrote that Harriet had refused anesthetic when it was offered. She preferred a bullet to bite on, she told him, like the Civil War soldiers she had held down during medical amputations during the war. "Harriet lay motionless as a log, mumbling prayers through teeth clenched on the bullet."[68]

Though Harriet remained quite active, she had become feeble, and at times visitors and friends feared she was close to death. In November 1899 Agnes Garrison, who was spending time in Auburn visiting with her aunt, Eliza Wright Osborne, encouraged Tubman to tell "stories of her youth which a stenographer took down as best she could," though it was "impossible to unravel the chronology."[69] Perhaps with an idea to publish another account of Tubman's life, Agnes and Eliza invited Tubman back to the Osbornes'. "We had another bout with Harriet. . . . she got warmed up to her narrative yesterday and acted out parts of it, crawling on the floor, gesticulating and singing one of the old songs in a curious, nasal, mournful voice."[70] According to Agnes, Tubman, nearly eighty, was then caring for three "adopted" children, "two half white . . . and one little boy is half Indian and half Spanish."[71]

In 1901 Bradford reissued *Harriet, the Moses of Her People,* adding twenty-one pages of additional biographical material. Some of this material may have come from notes taken at earlier dates, though Bradford wrote that she had recently spent time with Tubman, who relayed new stories that she included in this edition. This also made the book a little more substantial; Bradford was apparently criticized for charging $1 for the book, though she felt "it should be looked upon as charity."[72] Bradford had just visited with Harriet (probably May 1901) and found her "in deplorable condition, a pure wreck . . . & surrounded by a set of beggars who I fear *fleece* her of everything sent her." She told Sanborn that she would keep the money she got for Tubman and pay her bills as needed. She hoped Tubman could be placed in a home where she "would be well cared for . . . but she will not leave her beloved darkies."[73] Emily Howland made a great effort to sell the new edition of Harriet's narrative, noting in her diary the many copies she purchased for resale or as gifts for appreciative friends.[74]

Nevertheless, Tubman seems to have recovered enough to attend numerous suffrage, church, and community meetings in New York and Boston. In late November 1902, while both were attending a suffrage meeting at Eliza Wright Osborne's home in Auburn, Susan B. Anthony met again with Harriet; they had not seen each other for some time, perhaps since the earlier suffrage meeting in Rochester in 1896. Anthony would later write, "This most wonderful woman—*Harriet Tubman*— is still alive. . . . All of us were visiting at the Osborne's, a real love feast of the few that are left and here came *Harriet Tubman!*"[75]

The financial weight of her properties had long been overwhelming for Tubman. Her dreams of an independent infirmary and home for aged blacks faltered due to lack of funds, and she continued to care for people in her home. At the second meeting of the National Association of Colored Women, held in Chicago in August 1899, Tubman offered her twenty-five-acre property to the organization, hoping it would be able to carry on her vision for a home for African Americans. The organization thanked Tubman for her offer but declined to accept it because the property was encumbered by a mortgage.[76] At one point Tubman had to sell her cows to pay the taxes on the properties.[77] In 1902 she signed over the deed to the AME Zion Church, hoping that it could fulfill her dream of establishing a home for aged and sick people of color.

In early 1903 the transfer of the deed was deemed defective, and Tubman was asked to transfer title once again, but she refused. Apparently, perhaps due to her own misgivings and pressure from "white friends [who] were bitterly opposed to her deeding the property" to the church, Tubman was having second thoughts. Her white friends may have felt that, given her situation, she could have sold the property rather than give it away. But Tubman held fast to her vision for a home. She could not raise the money to properly operate the home, and she may have recognized that a larger institution such as the church was one of her few alternatives. She finally acquiesced and formally transferred the property to the AME Church on June 11, 1903.[78]

The church, as it turned out, had bigger plans for the property.[79] The church assumed the mortgage obligations on the property, which included a $371 payment to Harriet's brother, William Henry.[80] The church immediately set about raising funds to support the opening of an official home for the aged, with a future plan of establishing an industrial training school to teach African American girls domestic science.[81] Whether this was also part of Tubman's vision is not known; her dedication to establishing a hospital or infirmary, as well as a home for indigent people of color, never changed or wavered, so it is possible that this plan for an industrial school was not in keeping with Tubman's hopes. This was the era of Booker T. Washington's greatest influence among both blacks and whites concerned with African American education. During this time period, Washington, a former slave like Harriet, argued that vocational training for people of color was far more realistic and appropriate than a purely academic education. As one of the most prominent and powerful black men in the country, his vision permeated programs and institutions for African Americans across the country, and it seems Auburn and the AME Zion Church were no exception. Noting that the concept of an industrial school for girls was "particularly popular with the white people in this western part of the state," the church seemed to be gearing its fund-raising efforts toward the white community.[82] Not all African Americans agreed with this emphasis; W.E.B. Du Bois, a prominent black intellectual, argued against industrial training. He believed that postsecondary education was the key to success, particularly for the African American community. Tubman's opinions on this subject remain unknown, although years later Frances Smith, a friend of Tubman's and a matron at the home, recalled that Tubman was interested in "higher education."[83]

The Harriet Tubman Home for Aged and Infirm Negroes was not officially opened until 1908; the process of raising funds was slow. Tubman, in the meantime, became disillusioned by the administration of the home and "broke off active participation in its management.[84] She complained that "when I give the home over to Zion Church what you suppose they done? Why, they make a rule that nobody should come in without they have a hundred dollars. Now I wanted to make a rule that nobody should come in unless they didn't have no money at all."[85] Harriet reconciled with the board, however, but the entrance fee remained in effect.[86]

Throughout the early 1900s many articles about Tubman appeared in national and local newspapers, possibly as a direct result of the church's efforts to promote interest in the home and solicit funds for its operations. In 1907 an article about Harriet's life appeared in the *New York Herald*.[87] Quoting Samuel Hopkins's introductory note in Bradford's *Harriet*, the article equated Tubman to Joan of Arc: "there is not a trace in her countenance of intelligence or courage, but seldom has there been placed in any woman's hide a soul moved by a higher impulse, a purer benevolence, a more dauntless resolution, a more passionate love of freedom. This poor, ignorant, common looking black woman was fully capable of acting the part of Joan d'Arc."[88] This condescending imagery ignores Tubman's intellectual development and her evolving confidence in her own abilities, and demonstrates a failure to grasp the essence of Tubman. But it served a valuable purpose in that it probably elicited valuable funds from a white public comfortable with such paternalistic and racist images of black women and men. Heralding her great achievements, an article in the *New York Sun* claimed she was the "founder of the Underground Railroad," ratcheting up the iconography that would remain part of Tubman's image, albeit sorely inaccurate, until the present day. [89]

Some of the press attention brought unintended consequences. Tubman's public profile, now much higher, left her vulnerable to opportunists who may have seen her as an easy target. Tubman was robbed twice by individuals playing on her willingness to shelter anyone in need. In August or thereabouts in 1905, a man came to her house looking for shelter. She became frightened when she realized he had a gun, and stayed awake all night watching him. Her fears were realized when he demanded money from her; she had none and had to borrow $5 from a friend to pay him. "He scorned so small a sum," Tubman later told Emily Howland. Harriet must have confronted this scenario before; she was afraid to tell her brother William Henry that the robber was in the house.[90] Perhaps he had warned her to be more cautious about the characters she allowed into her home. This time she was lucky to have lost only $5. Her friend Emily Howland was not so lucky. The man found his way to Howland's home, telling her that Tubman had sent him with the understanding that Howland would help him. He told her he had fled lynchers in North Carolina who had killed his sisters and shot at him, leaving two bullets in his back. Two days later Howland discovered she had been duped by a "highway robber," to the tune of $585.[91] Once again, Tubman's reputation had been used to take advantage of some of her wealthier friends.

On balance, though, the public attention brought greater benefits than problems. More articles appeared locally over the following years, highlighting the black community's efforts to raise money to help refurbish and decorate the home with new furniture as well as raise money for basic operating expenses.[92] The home officially opened in June 1908; tours were given of the home's facilities, showing the beds, linens, and other supplies, which had been successfully procured through the efforts of the local black community. The celebration included a parade down South Street, a band concert, a reception, and a dance.[93] Representatives from central New York churches, local officials and board members, and representatives from the Empire State Federation of Women's Clubs of New York all attended. Tubman spoke a few words to the crowd: "I did not take up this work for my own benefit . . . but for those of my race who need help. The work is now well started and I know God will raise up others to take care of the future. All I ask for is united effort, for 'united we stand: divided we fall.' "[94] Against Tubman's wishes, however, residents were charged a $150 entrance fee to the home.[95] John C. Osborne was elected treasurer of the home's board of trustees, managing the funds coming into the home, thereby taking the financial responsibility for the institution out of Tubman's hands.[96]

In the meantime, Tubman remained a fixture at local and New York State suffrage meetings.[97] In 1905 Tubman traveled to Boston with her great-niece Alida Stewart to attend an opening reception for the Harriet Tubman Christian Temperance Union at Parker Memorial Hall.[98] The Boston Journal noted that she was "one of the great benefactors of her race . . . For a woman of so great an age she is remarkably erect, her voice is clear, her manner bright and her wit keen."[99] Almost eighty-five, Tubman could still captivate a crowd.

That fall Tubman attended a suffrage convention in Rochester, where she addressed the convention body "briefly."[100] In spite of the integrated meetings in New York and Boston, Tubman was forced to sleep in the train station the night before the convention because she had no place to go, although it was not entirely clear whether she had been refused lodging at local hotels because of her race or because she had no money.[101] Emily Howland and Susan B. Anthony were not sure, either; puzzled over why Tubman did not contact either of them to secure lodging, they assumed she was being too independent-minded.[102]

Tubman's health continued to decline. By 1910 or so she was wheelchair-bound. Her niece Alice Brickler later wrote that "Aunt Harriet had lost the use of her legs. She spent her time in a wheel chair and then finally was confined to her bed."[103] Brickler and her mother, Margaret Stewart Lucas, used to visit Tubman, bringing her "sweets, which she liked so well." During one visit young Alice wandered off into the field to pick flowers while her mother and Harriet talked. "Suddenly I became aware of something moving toward me through the grass," Brickler wrote Conrad years later.

> So smoothly did it glide and with so little noise. I was frightened! Then reason conquered fear and I knew it was Aunt Harriet, flat on her stomach and with only the use of her arms and serpentine movements of her body, gliding smoothly along. Mother helped her back to her chair and they laughed. Aunt Harriet then told me that that was the way she had gone by many a sentinel during the war. Seeing the swaying grass, she was mistaken for an animal or in the dim flicker of the camp fire, she appeared as a small shadow.[104]

By 1911, now nearly ninety, Tubman was forced to enter the Harriet Tubman Home. "The most noted 'conductor of the underground railroad,'" the New York Age reported in June, "was taken to the home last Thursday ill and penniless."[105] Several more articles appeared in various newspapers, asking for donations to help defray the costs of caring for her.[106] Florence Carter, the wife of the local AME Zion minister, recalled that Eliza Wright Osborne and Jane Seward "helped her get to the hospital," where Frances Smith remembered she had a private room.[107] Through the efforts of Mary Talbert, the Empire State Federation of Women's Clubs also helped raise funds for Tubman's care,[108] and family and friends also took on some of the financial responsibilities.[109] The following year, while Tubman continued to become more weak and frail in the home, her brother William Henry and William Henry's daughter-in-law Emma died after lingering illnesses of their own.[110]

On March 10, 1913, at the age of ninety-one, Harriet Tubman died of pneumonia. Gathered by her side for a final religious service were the Rev. E.U.A. Brooks and the Rev. Charles A. Smith, who had known Tubman during the war when he was a soldier with the Fifty-fourth Massachusetts in South Carolina; Smith's wife, Frances; Martha Ridgeway, Tubman's nurse; Eliza E. Peterson, of the Women's Christian Temperance Union of Texas; and Tubman's two great-nephews, Charles and Clarence Stewart.[111] Before lapsing into a coma, Tubman supposedly told those around her, "I go away to prepare a place for you, that where I am you also may be."[112]

On the morning of March 13 several hundred Auburnians and dignitaries from out of town attended a service held at the Tubman Home. Later that afternoon her body was taken to Thompson Memorial AME Zion Church on Parker Street, where hundreds more came to view her body and pay their last respects. A final service at the church was followed by eulogies offered by various church and local dignitaries. All of them spoke of Tubman's accomplishments, noting that she exemplified morality and righteousness and that her fight for freedom and justice dominated her "heroic life."[113] Mary Talbert recalled her last visit with Tubman, about a month before her death. Tubman grasped her hand as she was about to leave, urging her to "tell the women to stand together for God will never forsaken us," a message, perhaps, to the larger women's rights community to overcome their racial differences in pursuit of a common goal.[114]

The medal given to her by Queen Victoria was placed in the casket, and in her hands was a crucifix; her casket was draped in an American flag.[115] She was buried at Fort Hill cemetery, next to her brother William Henry, William Henry Jr., and Emma Stewart. Two small pine trees, planted for William Henry Jr., and Emma Stewart remained the only markers for the graves.

Fund-raising began nearly immediately to raise money for a memorial to Tubman's memory.[116] An elaborate ceremony was planned; a bronze tablet, "a token of the love and esteem of the people of Auburn," was manufactured and paid for through contributions gathered from Auburn's black and white community, and Booker T. Washington was invited as the guest speaker. On June 12, 1914, the tablet was unveiled by young Alice Lucas (Brickler) during a ceremony at the Auditorium Theater. It was later placed on the county courthouse building in Auburn, "in recognition of her unselfish devotion to the cause of humanity."[117] The bronze tablet, bearing the likeness of Tubman in her later years, was inscribed with the following:

In Memory of Harriet Tubman.
Born a slave in Maryland about 1821.
Died in Auburn, N.Y. March 10th, 1913.
Called the "Moses" of her people during the Civil War,
with rare courage, she led over
three hundred Negroes up from slavery to freedom,
and rendered invaluable service as nurse and spy.

With implicit trust in God, she braved every danger and
overcame every obstacle; withal she possessed extraordinary
foresight and judgment so that she truthfully said—

"On my Underground Railroad I nebber run my train off
de track and I nebber lost a passenger."

THIS TABLET ERECTED BY THE CITIZENS OF AUBURN, 1914.[118]

The following year, through the efforts of friends and family and Mary Talbert of the Empire State Federation of Women's Clubs, a monument, designed by Mrs. Jackson Stewart of New York, was placed on Tubman's grave.[119] In spite of the problems Tubman had had obtaining a U.S. government pension for her active service during the Civil War, "the last rites [were] of a semi-military character when the Relief Corps of the Charles H. Stewart Post, G.A.R." conducted the closing services.[120]

IN THE YEARS following Tubman's death, the black community maintained Tubman's memory, mostly in segregated classrooms and in literature on black heroes and heroines. Her narrative, now shortened and simplified, became part of a usable past for African Americans.[121] Highly fictionalized accounts of her life began to appear in the 1930s and 1940s in works for children and young adults that sought to catch the wave of renewed interest in the Underground Railroad sweeping the nation at that time.[122]

During the 1930s the American communist movement began to use Tubman as a feminist icon, in recruitment literature aimed at women and the black community.[123] Featured in a small pamphlet published and circulated by the Workers Library Publishers, Tubman's brief biographical sketch hailed her as one of the most "courageous women that ever lived." The Communist Party reminded its readers, though, that while the slaves were struggling with freedom "from chattel bondage, a labor movement was growing up in America dedicated to the freedom of industrial slaves."[124] Once again, Tubman was appropriated as a "malleable icon," suitable for consumption by a variety of audiences.[125]

Earl Conrad, a former Teamsters Union organizer in Harlem, a communist sympathizer, and New York correspondent for the *Chicago Defender*, began researching a full-length biography of Tubman in 1938. For five years Conrad struggled to overcome racist attitudes toward his work. More than one librarian and archivist ignored or rejected his requests for help. Interviewees often thwarted his efforts to seek out the truth. Publishers turned down his manuscript time and time again. Finally, Associated Publishers, a newly founded African American press in Washington, D.C., agreed to publish Conrad's biography of Tubman.

Conrad's work is remarkably well researched and documented. Fortunate to be able to interview individuals who knew Tubman when she was alive, Conrad documented many lost and forgotten stories of Tubman's life. But he was hindered by the lack of available manuscript and archival material relating to Tubman, much of which had not been deposited in libraries and archives. He perpetuated some of Bradford's exaggerations as well—for example, repeating the erroneous numbers of trips to the South and slaves rescued.[126] He highlighted Tubman's military career (both with John Brown and the Civil War) and her suffrage activism, both struggles that were appealing to someone with his views.

The record of Tubman's work for woman suffrage perhaps provides the best example of Conrad's effort to counteract the erasure of African American history. After Tubman's death, the memory of her active participation in the suffrage movement became obscured, as did most African American women's presence in the suffrage campaigns. As Conrad researched his biography, he faced an uphill battle to record her suffrage activism; she was not well known for her struggle on behalf of women's rights. He contacted Carrie Chapman Catt, the former suffragist who had assumed the presidency of the unified National American Woman Suffrage Association after Susan B. Anthony stepped down in 1900 and who is credited with driving the movement to success in 1920 with the passage of the Nineteenth Amendment. Though in her eighties at the time of their correspondence, Catt was still an active reformer. In response to an inquiry by Conrad about her recollections of Tubman at various suffrage meetings, Catt denied knowing anything about Tubman. "There was a time, just after the Civil War," she wrote, "when the question of the rights of men and women and of Negroes brought forth much discussion, separately and collectively. During that period, I think it was possible that the leaders in the Women's Rights Movement . . . urged clever and unusual colored women to come to their conventions and to speak there. . . . In my time colored women did come to meetings occasionally. . . . The suffrage conventions always opened their doors hospitably to the colored race from the first to the last." Moreover, she argued, Tubman could "not have been interested or thought much of women's rights and she certainly would not have been interested in the suffrage."[127] Catt maintained that Tubman was an unimportant figure and argued that if she had been important, she would have been immortalized, much like Sojourner Truth. Catt's utter disregard for Tubman's life history is striking, and her careless assessment of the contributions of African American women to the suffrage movement presaged the reception Tubman's biography would continue to receive for several more decades.

When Conrad completed his manuscript on Tubman and decided to submit it to a literary fellowship competition in December 1939, he sent a copy of a prospectus to Catt and asked her to send a letter of support for his work to the competition committee. "I had hesitated about [submitting it to the competition]," he wrote her, "as I felt that the subject matter, concerning as it does a Negro woman, might meet with a discouraging reception."[128] In January 1940 Catt responded that she had not read the prospectus, and though she does not mention it, she clearly did not write a letter of support. Her next letter was particularly harsh and critical. "I take it that this [manuscript] may not, necessarily, be printed," she wrote, but if it ever is, or anything like it, I will ask you to *leave out my name*, because, to tell the truth, I had never heard of Harriet Tubman when you first wrote me . . . She did not assist the suffragists or the woman suffrage movement at any time. It was they who were attempting to assist her. That much I know from the nature of things and to make Harriet Tubman a leader in the woman suffrage movement and in all other good movements is quite wrong. There was no leadership on the part of the colored people at that time and there is very little even now.[129]

One week later Conrad fired off a fiery retort. "I am . . . amazed, even stunned, at your impressions of Negro leadership, or rather, as you say, their lack of it, and I naturally feel that you have dismissed a remarkable woman, together with a whole people."[130] Conrad argued point by point for the unparalleled contributions of African Americans to the nation, and called Catt's prejudice out into the open.

[T]he province of Negro leadership and Negro contribution is one of the largest and least explored in American historiography. . . . Here you have circumnavigated a globe which Magellan has as yet conquered with a brush of your pen. . . . Something of that task is the job I have undertaken with Harriet Tubman, and I see in her a symbol of all that has been "from the nature of things" sustained in disfranchisement, even unto this day.

Yours for the enfranchisement of all peoples, Earl Conrad.[131]

Catt grudgingly responded that she was still not convinced of Tubman's leadership qualities. She conceded that New York suffragists such as Anthony recognized Tubman as "unusual," though she did not see this herself. She closed with a final summation: "I do not wish to be understood as opposed to the fame of Harriet Tubman. I only say that I am not yet convinced."[132]

Catt was not the only white person to devalue Tubman's accomplishments. Originally titled "General Tubman," Conrad's biography met with significant resistance from publishers. Random House balked at her being compared to Joan of Arc. Simon and Schuster called it a "freak subject." One editor asked Conrad why he was wasting his time on this topic. A few noted that Tubman was a "colorful character," yet they would not add her story to their lists. Harper & Brothers called it "a bit strong meat for us"—rather ironic given that they had just published Richard Wright's Native Son in 1940. John Day Company turned Conrad down because they already had one "feminist subject" on their list. Alfred Knopf said the market for such a topic was limited, and "furthermore your book suffers somewhat from the inflation of the factual material beyond reasonable bounds." Ironically, given the current plethora of children's biographies of Tubman, Julian Messner rejected it as a possible children's book. "I don't think the life of Harriet Tubman is for children," the reader wrote. "Now, I'm for blood and thunder, murders and revolutions, and life in general, but I must admit that beatings and whippings and throwing weights at negroes' heads makes me wince and feel bad. And I doubt if to the children she is [an] important enough person to justify taking them through it. . . . I do think you are right about having a negro as a subject. Why not Carver . . . or James Weldon Johnson?" International Publishers did agree to publish a small pamphlet, and other communist and socialist newspapers and magazines published a few articles.[133] Conrad's biography, Harriet Tubman, was finally published under the leadership of Carter G. Woodson at Associated Publishers in 1943.[134]

In June 1944 the U.S. Maritime Commission named a Liberty ship in honor of Tubman. The SS Harriet Tubman was the first Liberty ship, out of thousands, to be named for a black woman, and only one of eleven named for an African American. The National Council of Negro Women formally requested the naming of the ship in honor of her, and the Maritime Commission granted the request in the spring of 1944.[135] It was possibly a direct result of renewed attention to Tubman's life with the publication of Conrad's biography the previous year that influenced the decision to name a ship for her. The Auburn Citizen Advertiser noted that Conrad was "partially responsible for the fact that the ship" would bear Tubman's name, "because he brought her to general public attention" with his new biography.[136]

On June 3, the SS Harriet Tubman was launched from its berth at the New England Shipbuilding Company in South Portland, Maine. Eva

Stewart Northrup, Tubman's grandniece, christened the ship during the ceremony, which was attended by Tubman relatives from across the country.[137] The National Council of Negro Women sponsored a war bond drive with the slogan "Buy a Harriet Tubman War Bond for Freedom."[138]

Conrad's book met with immediate, though limited, success, and it laid the foundation for fictionalized young-adult biographies of Tubman that emerged during the late 1940s and 1950s, including Dorothy Sterling's *Freedom Train: The Story of Harriet Tubman*, and Ann Petry's *Harriet Tubman, Conductor on the Underground Railroad*.[139] Both of these works, and those that followed, used fictitious characters and situations, expanding and perpetuating the mythical story of a runaway slave. These books, however, helped secure Tubman's place in the pantheon of American heroes, first as an African American icon and then later as a feminist symbol. The 1960s brought renewed attention to black history and historical figures, and by the 1980s Tubman's life story became a staple of mainstream juvenile literature. Still, racial and gender proscriptions have muted and reconfigured Tubman's place in the collective memory, making her suitable for children's biographies but not as a subject of serious historical inquiry. Though the myth has served the varied cultural needs of black and white Americans over time, the obscurity in which the details of her life have remained until now is a deeply troubling reflection of the racial, class, and gender dynamics of our nation. Though Harriet Tubman's life is the material of legend, it is more remarkable in its truth than fiction—the essence of a real American hero.

Ross–Stewart Family Tree

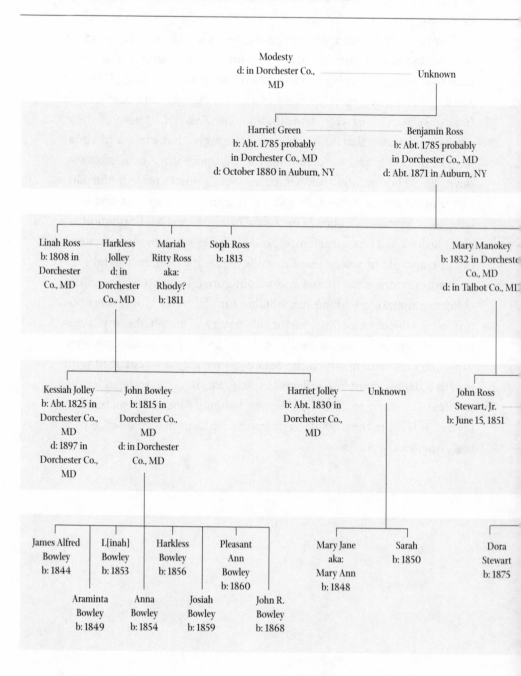

Modesty
d: in Dorchester Co.,
MD
——————— Unknown

Harriet Green
b: Abt. 1785 probably
in Dorchester Co., MD
d: October 1880 in Auburn, NY
——————— Benjamin Ross
b: Abt. 1785 probably
in Dorchester Co., MD
d: Abt. 1871 in Auburn, NY

Linah Ross
b: 1808 in
Dorchester
Co., MD
——— Harkless
Jolley
d: in
Dorchester
Co., MD

Mariah
Ritty Ross
aka:
Rhody?
b: 1811

Soph Ross
b: 1813

Mary Manokey
b: 1832 in Dorcheste
Co., MD
d: in Talbot Co., ML

Kessiah Jolley
b: Abt. 1825 in
Dorchester Co.,
MD
d: 1897 in
Dorchester Co.,
MD
——— John Bowley
b: 1815 in
Dorchester Co.,
MD
d: in Dorchester
Co., MD

Harriet Jolley
b: Abt. 1830 in
Dorchester Co.,
MD
——— Unknown

John Ross
Stewart, Jr.
b: June 15, 1851

James Alfred
Bowley
b: 1844

L[inah]
Bowley
b: 1853

Harkless
Bowley
b: 1856

Pleasant
Ann
Bowley
b: 1860

Mary Jane
aka:
Mary Ann
b: 1848

Sarah
b: 1850

Dora
Stewart
b: 1875

Araminta
Bowley
b: 1849

Anna
Bowley
b: 1854

Josiah
Bowley
b: 1859

John R.
Bowley
b: 1868

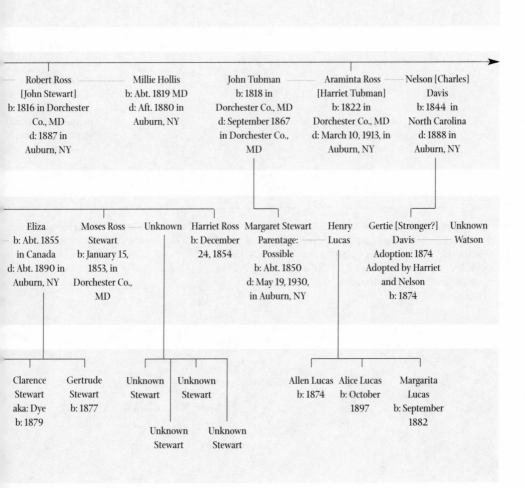

Robert Ross
[John Stewart]
b: 1816 in Dorchester
Co., MD
d: 1887 in
Auburn, NY

Millie Hollis
b: Abt. 1819 MD
d: Aft. 1880 in
Auburn, NY

John Tubman
b: 1818 in
Dorchester Co., MD
d: September 1867
in Dorchester Co.,
MD

Araminta Ross
[Harriet Tubman]
b: 1822 in
Dorchester Co., MD
d: March 10, 1913, in
Auburn, NY

Nelson [Charles]
Davis
b: 1844 in
North Carolina
d: 1888 in
Auburn, NY

Eliza
b: Abt. 1855
in Canada
d: Abt. 1890 in
Auburn, NY

Moses Ross
Stewart
b: January 15,
1853, in
Dorchester Co.,
MD

Unknown

Harriet Ross
b: December
24, 1854

Margaret Stewart
Parentage:
Possible
b: Abt. 1850
d: May 19, 1930,
in Auburn, NY

Henry
Lucas

Gertie [Stronger?]
Davis
Adoption: 1874
Adopted by Harriet
and Nelson
b: 1874

Unknown
Watson

Clarence
Stewart
aka: Dye
b: 1879

Gertrude
Stewart
b: 1877

Unknown
Stewart

Unknown
Stewart

Unknown
Stewart

Unknown
Stewart

Allen Lucas
b: 1874

Alice Lucas
b: October
1897

Margarita
Lucas
b: September
1882

Ross–Stewart Family Tree continued

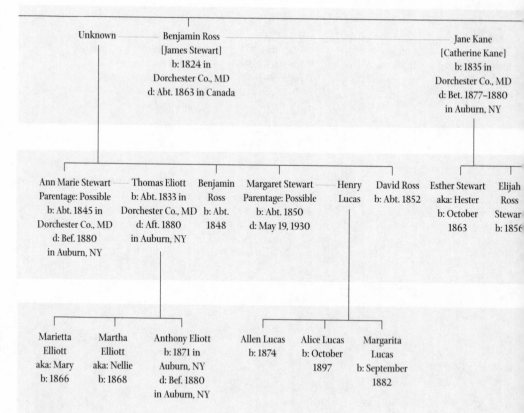

Unknown —— Benjamin Ross
[James Stewart]
b: 1824 in
Dorchester Co., MD
d: Abt. 1863 in Canada

—— Jane Kane
[Catherine Kane]
b: 1835 in
Dorchester Co., MD
d: Bet. 1877–1880
in Auburn, NY

Ann Marie Stewart
Parentage: Possible
b: Abt. 1845 in
Dorchester Co., MD
d: Bef. 1880
in Auburn, NY

Thomas Eliott
b: Abt. 1833 in
Dorchester Co., MD
d: Aft. 1880
in Auburn, NY

Benjamin
Ross
b: Abt.
1848

Margaret Stewart
Parentage: Possible
b: Abt. 1850
d: May 19, 1930

Henry
Lucas

David Ross
b: Abt. 1852

Esther Stewart
aka: Hester
b: October
1863

Elijah
Ross
Stewart
b: 1856

Marietta
Elliott
aka: Mary
b: 1866

Martha
Elliott
aka: Nellie
b: 1868

Anthony Eliott
b: 1871 in
Auburn, NY
d: Bef. 1880
in Auburn, NY

Allen Lucas
b: 1874

Alice Lucas
b: October
1897

Margarita
Lucas
b: September
1882

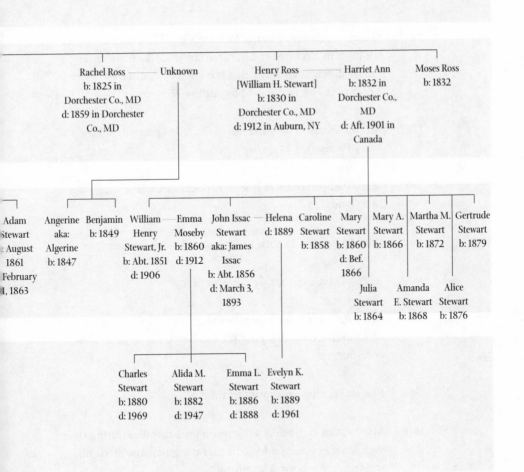

Rachel Ross
b: 1825 in
Dorchester Co., MD
d: 1859 in Dorchester
Co., MD

Unknown

Henry Ross
[William H. Stewart]
b: 1830 in
Dorchester Co., MD
d: 1912 in Auburn, NY

Harriet Ann
b: 1832 in
Dorchester Co.,
MD
d: Aft. 1901 in
Canada

Moses Ross
b: 1832

Adam
Stewart
: August
1861
February
1, 1863

Angerine
aka:
Algerine
b: 1847

Benjamin
b: 1849

William
Henry
Stewart, Jr.
b: Abt. 1851
d: 1906

Emma
Moseby
b: 1860
d: 1912

John Issac
Stewart
aka: James
Issac
b: Abt. 1856
d: March 3,
1893

Helena
d: 1889

Caroline
Stewart
b: 1858

Mary
Stewart
b: 1860
d: Bef.
1866

Mary A.
Stewart
b: 1866

Martha M.
Stewart
b: 1872

Gertrude
Stewart
b: 1879

Julia
Stewart
b: 1864

Amanda
E. Stewart
b: 1868

Alice
Stewart
b: 1876

Charles
Stewart
b: 1880
d: 1969

Alida M.
Stewart
b: 1882
d: 1947

Emma L.
Stewart
b: 1886
d: 1888

Evelyn K.
Stewart
b: 1889
d: 1961

Harriet Tubman
CHRONOLOGY

1785–1790   Harriet Tubman's parents, Ben Ross and Harriet "Rit" Green, are born in Dorchester County, Maryland. Both are enslaved, but by different masters. Ben is owned by Anthony Thompson; Rit is enslaved by Atthow Pattison.

1797   Atthow Pattison dies and leaves Rit to his granddaughter, Mary Pattison.

1800   Mary Pattison marries Joseph Brodess of Bucktown, Maryland.

1801   Edward Brodess is born to Mary and Joseph Brodess.

1802   Joseph Brodess probably dies this year.

1803   Mary Pattison Brodess marries widower Anthony Thompson of Church Creek, bringing Rit and Ben into the same slave community.

1808   Ben and Rit marry about this time.

1810   Mary Pattison Brodess Thompson probably dies during this year, leaving young Edward under the guardianship of his stepfather, Anthony Thompson.

1822   Araminta "Minty" Ross, later known as Harriet Tubman, is born, probably in February or early March on Anthony Thompson's plantation in the Peters Neck district, south of Tobacco Stick (now known as Madison), near the Blackwater River.

1823–1824   Edward Brodess moves to his ancestral property on Greenbriar Road in Bucktown. He marries Eliza Ann Keene in March 1824. They have eight children over the next twenty years.

1828–1835   Young Araminta is hired out by Brodess to various other masters, some cruel and negligent.

1834–1836   Araminta is struck on the head by an iron weight, which nearly kills her. She suffers from serious side effects from this injury for the rest of her life.

1836   Anthony Thompson dies.

1836–1842   Tubman is hired out to John T. Stewart of Tobacco Stick [Madison].

1840   Ben Ross is given his freedom through a provision in Anthony Thompson's will.

1844   Araminta probably marries freeman John Tubman in this year. She took the name Harriet at this time.

1847–1849   Harriet Tubman hires herself out to Dr. Anthony C. Thompson, Anthony Thompson's son.

1849   Edward Brodess dies in March, leaving his widow Eliza encumbered with debt. Harriet Tubman runs away from slavery sometime during the late fall after hearing she might be sold.

1850   The Fugitive Slave Act is passed. Tubman conducts her first rescue mission by helping her niece, Kessiah, and Kessiah's two children escape.

1851–1852   Tubman assists several other individuals escape enslavement on the Eastern Shore, including her brother Moses. When she returns to Dorchester County in the fall of 1851 to bring her husband, John, to Philadelphia with her, he refuses to go. He has remarried and moved on with his life.

1854   Tubman finally succeeds in rescuing her three other brothers on Christmas Day, bringing them to freedom in Philadelphia and then St. Catharines, Ontario, Canada. By now Harriet has attracted the attention of abolitionists and Underground Railroad operators Thomas Garrett, William Still, Lucretia Mott, and others.

1855–1860   Tubman makes several more trips to the Eastern Shore of Maryland, trying to bring away her sister and her sister's children. Though she was unsuccessful, she did bring away other friends and relatives, many of whom settled in Canada. Altogether, Tubman brought to freedom about seventy individuals in approximately thirteen trips.

1857   Tubman brings away her aged parents from Caroline County, Maryland, when she learns her father was at risk of arrest for aiding slaves to run away.

1858   Harriet Tubman meets John Brown at her home on North Street in St. Catharines, Ontario, Canada.

1859   John Brown's Virginia raid ends in failure in October. Tubman purchases a home and seven acres of land from William H. Seward, President Lincoln's future secretary of state, in Fleming, New York, in May. It is during this year that Tubman becomes more publicly active, particularly in Boston where she gives many lectures as a heroic Underground Railroad operator.

1860   Tubman is involved in the dramatic rescue of fugitive slave Charles Nalle in Troy, New York, freeing him from the custody of U.S. marshals charged with returning him to his Virginia enslaver under the Fugitive Slave Act of 1850.

1861   The Civil War starts with the firing on Fort Sumter in Charleston Harbor, South Carolina, in April.

1862–1865   Tubman begins her work as a cook, nurse, laundress, teacher, scout, and spy for the Union forces stationed in the Hilton Head district of South Carolina.

1863   Under the command of Colonel James Montgomery, Tubman becomes the first woman to lead an armed raid. On June 2, she leads Montgomery's forces up the Combahee River, where they rout rebel forces, free over 700 slaves, and burn buildings, crops, and stockpiles of munitions and food.

1865   The Civil War ends, and President Lincoln is assassinated in April. Tubman is hired to provide nursing service to wounded soldiers at Fortress Monroe in Hampton, Virginia. On her way home to New York, she is violently thrown from a passenger train by a racist conductor, and is severely injured.

1867   John Tubman dies.

1869   Sarah Bradford publishes her first biography called, *Scenes in the Life of Harriet Tubman*. Tubman marries Nelson Davis at Central Presbyterian Church in Auburn.

1871   Ben Ross, Tubman's father, probably dies this year.

1873   Tubman is involved in a mysterious "Gold Swindle."

1880   Rit dies. Tubman continues to farm her seven-acre property and run a small brick-making business with Davis.

1886   Sarah Bradford publishes her second biography of Tubman, *Harriet Tubman: The Moses of Her People*.

1888   Nelson Davis dies of tuberculosis.

1890s   Tubman becomes more actively involved in the suffrage movement, attending both black and white suffrage conventions.

1896   Tubman purchases the twenty-five-acre parcel next to her
        property to establish a home and hospital for indigent, aged,
        and sick African Americans.

1903   Tubman transfers ownership of the twenty-five-acre property
        to the AME Zion Church.

1908   The Harriet Tubman Home is opened by the AME Zion
        Church.

1913   Tubman dies on March 10 and is buried next to her brother at
        Fort Hill Cemetery in Auburn, New York.

$\mathcal{N} o t e s$

—

Note: Throughout *Bound for the Promised Land*, I have normalized the plantation dialect used by previous biographers when quoting Harriet Tubman. I am unsure of the accuracy of the recordings of her particular speech patterns, but I have placed the original text in these notes for readers interested in the original wording.

—K.C.L.

Introduction

1. Franklin Sanborn, "Harriet Tubman," *The Commonwealth,* Boston, July 17, 1863.

2. Ednah Dow Littlehale Cheney, "Moses," *Freedmen's Record,* March 1865.

3. Sarah H. Bradford, *Scenes in the Life of Harriet Tubman* (Auburn, N.Y.: W. J. Moses, 1869); William Still, *The Underground Railroad* (1871; reprint, Chicago: Johnson Publishing Company, 1970). There are only three true biographies for adults: Sarah Bradford's short biography, *Scenes,* published in 1869; her revised edition, published in 1886, entitled *Harriet, the Moses of Her People*; and a biography by Earl Conrad called *Harriet Tubman,* published in 1943. There are several motion pictures or documentaries, over forty juvenile biographies, and one adult novel, the majority of which are fictionalized histories. Most of these books and other items relied on Bradford and Conrad, either directly or indirectly, as primary source materials. The last significant contribution remains Conrad's work in 1943.

4. Michael Frisch, "American History and the Structures of Collective Memory: A Modest Exercise in Empirical Iconography," *The Journal of American History* 75, no. 4 (1989): 1139.

5. Edward Brodess in Account with Anthony Thompson His Guardian for the Years 1821 and 1822, *Edward Brodess vs. Anthony Thompson,* Eastern Shore Court of Appeals, 1823–1828, Maryland State Archives (hereafter MDSA); Benjamin Drew, *The Refugee: A North-Side View of Slavery* (1855; reprint, Tilden G. Edelstein, ed., Reading, Mass.: Addison-Wesley Publishing Co., 1969); Thompson Deposition, Equity Papers 249, Dorchester County Circuit Court, MDSA; advertisement by Eliza Ann Brodess, *Cambridge Democrat,* Cambridge, Md., October 3, 1849. Anthony Thompson's account record in *Brodess vs. Thompson* lists a payment to a midwife on March 15, 1822. Eliza Brodess's reward notice, October 1849, lists Tubman as twenty-seven years old. Dr. Anthony Thompson thought Tubman was born during this time period, too. See also Sanborn, "Harriet Tubman," *The Commonwealth,* Boston, July 17, 1863. Tubman's mother's name is assumed to be Harriet, but she is called variously "Rit" and "Rittia."

6. Numerous accounts of her speeches during the summer of 1859, in addition to private letters written by friends and associates at the time, reveal the consistency of these numbers. Tubman made at least one and maybe two more trips between the summer of 1859 and the end of 1860. See Franklin Sanborn to Friend [Thomas W. Higginson], May 30, 1859, Anti-Slavery Collection, Boston Public Library; Lucy Osgood to Lydia Maria Child, June 2, 1859, Lydia Maria Child Papers, Anti-Slavery Collection Microform, Card #1110, Cornell University Libraries, Ithaca, N.Y.

7. Frank C. Drake, "The Moses of Her People. Amazing Life Work of Harriet Tubman," *New York Herald*, Sept. 22, 1907.

8. David W. Blight, *Race and Reunion: The Civil War in American Memory* (Cambridge, Mass.: Harvard University Press, 2001), 231–37.

Chapter 1

1. Barbara Jeanne Fields, *Slavery and Freedom on the Middle Ground* (New Haven: Yale University Press, 1985). This census figure reveals only a portion of the runaways for that year. Slave owners often expected their runaways to return of their own accord or to be returned forcibly, resulting in under-reporting of the actual number of runaways. Eliza Brodess, for instance, did not report Harriet as a runaway in the 1850 slave census.

2. Michel Sobel, *The World They Made Together, Black and White Values in Eighteenth-Century Virginia* (Princeton: Princeton University Press, 1987).

3. Hulbert Footner, *Rivers of the Eastern Shore* (New York: Farrar & Rinehart, 1944), 170–204.

4. Ibid., 135–51. See also John R. Wennersten, *Maryland's Eastern Shore: A Journey in Place and Time* (Centreville, Md.: Tidewater Publishers, 1992), 119–21. The Nanticoke derives its name from that of the native people who populated the Eastern Shore when white Europeans landed here in the early seventeenth century. By the mid-eighteenth century, most native Nanticokes had died off as a result of disease and conflict with white settlers, and most of the survivors had been turned out of their land or had sold whatever rights they claimed to the land and moved west. Some Nanticokes and blacks, free and enslaved, intermarried, creating a marginalized yet distinct creole community in Dorchester County that persisted into the nineteenth century. Local names such as Menoke, Manokey, Clash, and other Nanticoke names still persist in Dorchester County.

5. See Ira Berlin, *Slaves Without Masters: The Free Negro in the Antebellum South* (New York: The New Press, 1874); Jeffrey R. Brackett, *The Negro in Maryland: A Study of the Institution of Slavery* (1889; reprint, 1969, New York: Negro Universities Press, 1969); Robert J. Brugger, *Maryland, A Middle Temperament, 1634–1980* (Baltimore: The Johns Hopkins University Press, 1988).

6. The majority of Dorchester County assessment and court records—including wills, trial, tax, and court proceedings—from colonial times to 1852 were lost forever. Few records survived the fire; those that did were supplemented by copies, requested at the time by local white officials seeking to reestablish record keeping. Most of these included the rerecording of wills, land transactions, and various other deeds and sales records. The documents that do survive, in combination with historical scholarship on African American family life under slavery and in freedom, histories of the Eastern Shore of Maryland, and extensive genealogical research into both black and white families, provide a strong foundation upon which to build a vivid picture of Tubman's life in Dorchester County.

7. Will of Atthow Pattison, Est. #0-35-E, Dorchester County courthouse, Registrar of Wills, Cambridge, Md. The presumed site of Atthow Pattison's dwelling is directly east, across the Little Blackwater River from the Blackwater Wildlife Refuge Office on Key Wallace Drive.

8. Though tobacco production on the Eastern Shore was witnessing a permanent decline in favor of grain, fruit, and timber production, tobacco was still an important commodity.

9. Will of Atthow Pattison.

10. Ibid.

11. Equity Papers 249. Atthow Pattison's will became the foundation for a contentious court battle during the 1850s, one that, thankfully for historians, created a lengthy court record that still exists in the Dorchester County courthouse. This court record remains one of the most important pieces of evidence providing clues as to Tubman's ancestry and her family's status under slavery.

12. Brackett, *Negro in Maryland*, 149–50.

13. For more information regarding the transformation of Maryland's agricultural practices and its attendent effects of slavery, see Brugger, *Maryland*; Fields, *Slavery*; T. Stephen Whitman, *The Price of Freedom. Slavery and Manumission in Baltimore and Early National Maryland* (Lexington, Ky.: The University Press of Kentucky, 1997).

14. Brackett, *Negro in Maryland*, 55–57.

15. Christopher Phillips, *Freedom's Port: The African American Community of Baltimore, 1790–1860* (Chicago: University of Illinois Press, 1997), 38–42; Whitman, *Price*, 66–68; Brugger, *Maryland*, 168–70; Wennersten, *Maryland's Eastern Shore*, 120–21.

16. Brackett, *Negro in Maryland*, 149–53.

17. When Pattison died in 1797, the wording of his will still met the requirements of the amended law of 1796, apparently securing the manumission of Rit and her children when they reached the age of forty-five. However, because Pattison did not specifically say what his wishes were with respect to these slaves once they reached forty-five, the intent of the will remained legally ambiguous. As we shall see in a later chapter, this oversight on the part of Pattison (or his lawyer) would leave the issue of liberty for Rit and her children, including Tubman, in legal limbo, even if his *intention* was that they be free once they attained the age of forty-five.

18. Whitman, *Price*, 67.

19. 1776 Colonial Census.

20. Bureau of the Census, *United States Federal Census*, 1790, Dorchester County, Md.

21. Thompson Deposition, 1853. Dr. Anthony C. Thompson, Anthony Thompson's son, who was a little boy when Mary Pattison Brodess married his father and brought Rit to their household, later recalled that "he knew Modesty, the mother of Rit and she belonged to Elizabeth Pattison [Mary Pattison's mother]." Modesty may have been manumitted at a later date, before her death, though there is no surviving documentation to support such an assumption.

22. Will of Atthow Pattison.

23. What became of Suke and Bess is unknown, though more detailed research in the chattel and land records of the time period may reveal the fates of these two women and their children.

24. Bill of Sale, 25 H.D. 395, Dorchester County Chattel Records, MDSA, 1809. Samuel Keene, son of Henry Keene. The naming patterns strongly suggest, then, that these slave women, Minty and Ritty, were related to Harriet Tubman's mother Rit, perhaps an aunt or a sister, and that the Pattison slaves constituted a close-knit family group. Rit would later name two of her daughters after these two slaves.

25. Bureau of the Census, *United States Federal Census*, 1800, Dorchester County, Md.

26. The tract of land he inherited from his father did not contain the family homestead; that piece of property was devised to his older brother and heir apparent, Edward Brodess. This land was subsequently sold by Edward (uncle to Tubman's owner, young Edward Brodess) to Clement Waters in 1803. Dorchester County Land Records, MDSA, 1803.

27. Debra Smith Moxey, *Great Choptank Parish Records* (Cambridge, Md.: Dorchester County Historical and Genealogical Society, n.d.).

28. Having inherited several hundred acres in the early 1780s from his father in the Church Creek and Whitehaven area, Thompson's own plantation sat upon the Big Blackwater River in central Dorchester County, "northside of the northwest branch of the Blackwater River," south of Church Creek (also, and more specifically, south of Woolford, then known as Loomtown, and Tobacco Stick, now known as Madison). Calvin W. Mowbray and Mary I. Mowbray, *The Early Settlers of Dorchester County and Their Lands* (1981; reprint, Westminster, Md.: Willow Bend Books, 2000), 2:54.

29. *Brodess vs. Thompson*. These slaves are probably Sam, Frederick, and Shadrach. The name of the fourth is unknown.

30. This date is estimated based on testimony given by the Rev. Dr. Anthony C. Thompson in October

1853 that Rit's eldest daughter, Linah, was approximately forty-five years of age. I have used the term "married" to recognize the known and documented committed relationship Rit Green and Ben Ross shared until their deaths in the latter part of the nineteenth century. See Thompson Deposition, 1853.

31. List of Anthony Thompson's Negroes, 1839, Levin Richardson Collection, 1758–1865, MS 1405, Maryland Historical Society, Baltimore, Md. This list of slaves was created in 1839 subsequent to the death of Anthony Thompson Sr. and served as a guide to Dr. Anthony C. Thompson and his brother, Dr. Absalom Thompson, for the distribution of the estate's forty-three slaves. Next to each slave's name Thompson listed that slave's time left to serve, as well as notes on the slave's "Relations." Next to Ben Ross's name (first name on the list and the slave with the least amount of time to serve as of January 1839) Thompson notes: "Wife and Children belonging to Edward Brodess." No documentation survives showing that Anthony Thompson purchased or sold any of his slaves.

32. Thompson Deposition, 1853.

33. Lorena Walsh, "The Chesapeake Slave Trade: Regional Patterns, African Origins, and Some Implications," *William and Mary Quarterly* LVIII, no. 1 (2001); David Eltis, "The Volume and Structure of the Transatlantic Slave Trade: A Reassessment," *William and Mary Quarterly* LVIII, no. 1 (2001): 148.

34. Sanborn, "Harriet Tubman." Sanborn would later write that she was "one degree removed from the wolds [sic] of Africa, her grandfather being an imported African of a chieftan family." Franklin B. Sanborn, "The Late Araminta Davis: Better Known as 'Moses' or 'Harriet Tubman,'" Franklin B. Sanborn Papers, box 1, folder 5, American Antiquarian Society, Worcester, Mass.

35. Frank C. Drake, "The Moses of Her People. Amazing Life Work of Harriet Tubman," *New York Herald*, Sept. 22, 1907.

36. Ann Fitzhugh, "Harriet Tubman," *American Review*, August 1912. 420. Miller is the granddaughter of Gerrit Smith, antislavery activist, Underground Railroad stationmaster, John Brown supporter, and friend of Tubman's from Peterboro, New York. There is no other documentation suggesting that Rit's father was a white man. The identity of the white man remains unknown; Atthow Pattison seems a logical choice, or it could have been a man named Green. However, this is indirect contrast to Sanborn's much earlier assertion that Tubman "has not a drop of white blood in her veins." See Sanborn, "Harriet Tubman."

37. Thompson Deposition, 1853. Interestingly, the name Modesty is very uncommon on the Eastern Shore as a name for either white or black women. The name Modesty here should not be confused with the much more common "Modeste" found throughout Louisiana as a name for slaves and French white women alike. The name Modesty is found in Puritan records during the seventeenth and eighteenth centuries. Only one other Modesty, a black slave, has been located in the Dorchester County census records, manumission records, or chattel records from 1790 to 1860. See Pattison, Gourney Crow, to William Henson, Dorchester County Chattel Records, Maryland State Archives.

38. March Ross, a slave, and possibly Simon Ross, a free man.

39. Michael A. Gomez, *Exchanging Our Country Marks: The Transformation of African Identities in the Colonial and Antebellum South.* (Chapel Hill: The University of North Carolina Press, 1998), 107.

40. Ibid., 109–11.

41. Ibid., 105.

42. Ivor Wilks, *Forests of Gold: Essays on the Akan and the Kingdom of the Asante* (Athens: Ohio University Press, 1993), 41–72. See also Gomez, *Exchanging*, 105–13. Gomez expands upon this scholarship, using T. C. McCaskie's work on the Asante. See T. C. McCaskie, *State and Society in Pre-Colonial Asante* (Cambridge: Cambridge University Press, 1995).

43. Gomez, *Exchanging*, 110.

44. Ibid., 112.

45. Ibid., 113.

46. David Eltis, Stephen D. Behrendt, David Richardson, and Herbert S. Klein, eds., *The Trans-Atlantic Slave Trade: A Database on CD-ROM* (Cambridge: Cambridge University Press, 1999). "Debate centers on

such issues as the composition of the peoples captured in the slave trade, the degree of random or concentrated redistribution in the Americas, the accuracy of the ethnic labels employed by slave traders and New World planters, and whether enslaved Africans" were cognizant of cultural similarities or ethnic bonds. See Walsh, "Chesapeake," 140–42.

47. Walsh, "Chesapeake," 148.

48. Ibid., 152.

49. Ibid., 168–69.

50. See Certificates of Freedom, Dorchester County Circuit Court Records, MDSA, and U.S. Census records 1800–1840.

51. Joseph B. Seth and Mary W. Seth, *Recollections of a Long Life on the Eastern Shore* (Easton, Md.: Press of the *Star-Democrat*, 1926), 31. Seth had erroneously construed that Suck was not a real name. "She could give no name, except a sound, like suck, so she was known as 'Suck' all her days." Seth may not have recognized her African name as such.

52. Berlin, *Slaves Without Masters*, 45–48.

53. See Kay Najiyyah McElvey, "Early Black Dorchester, 1776–1870: A History of the Struggle of African Americans in Dorchester County, Maryland, to Be Free to Make Their Own Choices," Ph.D. Dissertation, University of Maryland, 1991. See also U.S. Census data 1790, 1800, 1810; and Fields, *Slavery*, 8–13.

54. See Debra Smith Moxey, "Thompson Land Records," Dorchester County Historical Society, Vertical Files, Dorchester County Public Library, Cambridge, Md. D. F. Thompson, "The Thompson Family in Dorchester County and Maryland," *Democrat and News*, Cambridge, Md., Jan. 7, 1910; D. F. Thompson, "The Thompsons in Dorchester," *Democrat and News*, Cambridge, Md., Jan. 28, 1910; McElvey, "Early Black." From 1790 to 1800, the county witnessed an outmigration of residents, from 10,015 to 9,415, though by 1810 it had rebounded to 10,415, where it would remain for the next forty years. Anthony Thompson's brother Thomas, for instance, sold the majority of his landholdings, furniture, and other property throughout the 1780s and early 1790s in preparation for a move to North Carolina. In 1803 Joseph Brodess's brother, Edward, sold all of his property and set out for Mississippi with several other family members.

55. "Special Court, July 1805," *Dorchester County Criminal Court Docket, 1791–1805*, ed. Deborah Smith Moxey (privately printed, 1986), 1:52.

56. Christopher George, *Terror on the Chesapeake: The War of 1812 on the Bay* (Shippensburg, Pa.: White Mane Books, 2000), 68–69.

57. Brugger, *Maryland*, 196–99.

58. Bureau of the Census, *United States Federal Census*, 1810. Thompson is listed as "Anthony Thomas." This household includes one male under ten years old, who is assumed to be Edward Brodess. There are three other males, ages sixteen to twenty-six, who are probably Thompson's sons, Edward, Anthony, and Absalom. There is one female under ten years of age. The identity of this child is unknown; she may be Thompson's niece Barsheba, whom he identifies in his will in 1836. In 1810 Thompson petitioned the Orphans Court, and in 1811 he was awarded guardianship of Edward Brodess, thus legally assuming responsibility for maintaining Edward's inheritance and feeding and clothing him, as well as providing for his education. Dorchester County Short Judgments, 1818–1827, Dorchester County Court Records, MDSA, 157.

59. See Thompson Deposition, 1853; advertisement by Eliza Ann Brodess, *Cambridge Democrat*, Cambridge, Md., October 3, 1849; Emma P. Telford, "Harriet: The Modern Moses of Heroism and Visions," Cayuga County Museum, Auburn, N.Y., c. 1905.

Chapter 2

1. "Edward Brodess in Account with Anthony Thompson His Guardian for the Years 1821 and 1822," *Edward Brodess vs. Anthony Thompson*, MDSA. Harriet Tubman was born, "as near as she can remember,

in 1820 or in 1821, in Dorchester County, on the Eastern shore of Maryland, and not far from the town of Cambridge." Sarah H. Bradford, *Scenes in the Life of Harriet Tubman* (Auburn, N.Y.: W. J. Moses, 1869). See also Eliza Ann Brodess, "Three Hundred Dollars Reward," *Cambridge Democrat*, Cambridge, Md., October 3, 1849. Brodess identifies Harriet as twenty-seven years old.

2. According to the 1865 Fleming, New York, census, Rit is noted as having nine children. This contradicts Franklin Sanborn in his early article on Tubman (in *The Commonwealth*, July 17, 1863). Sanborn states that Tubman "has ten brothers and sisters"; thus Rit would have had eleven children. This discrepancy could be the result of Tubman referring to close kin as "sister" or "brother." Based on my research, it appears that Rit did indeed have nine children, and also cared for two grandchildren. These two grandchildren, Kessiah and Harriet, were very likely the daughters of one of Tubman's sisters, either Linah or Soph, both of whom had been sold. These two granddaughters were very close in age to Tubman, and so she may have considered them to be more like sisters.

3. Frederick Douglass, *Narrative of the Life of Frederick Douglass, an American Slave. Written by Himself,* ed. Benjamin Quarles (1845; reprint, Cambridge, Mass.: The Belknap Press, 1971), 23.

4. Bucktown is the site of the plantation where Edward Brodess farmed and lived from approximately 1823 to 1849. Bureau of the Census, *United States Federal Census,* 1830, Dorchester County, Maryland.

5. *Edward Brodess vs. Anthony Thompson,* Eastern Shore Court of Appeals, 1823–1828. *Brodess vs. Thompson,* 1–4. The court records refer to Brodess as "Edward Brodess Junior late of Dorchester County yeoman." This implies that Brodess is not living in Dorchester County at the time. Perhaps he is away at school, or living in Talbot County with Dr. Anthony C. Thompson, his stepbrother. He could also have been living with relatives in Mississippi or another territory or state. The record remains unclear as to Brodess's whereabouts until 1824.

6. Ibid.

7. Ibid.

8. Ibid.

9. Edward Brodess in Account with Anthony Thompson his Guardian for the years 1821 and 1822, Ibid.

10. Ibid. Thompson charged a total of $7.63 for Rit's care.

11. Ibid.

12. Polish Mills Deposition, Equity Papers 249, MDSA.

13. Emma P. Telford, "Harriet: The Modern Moses of Heroism and Visions," Cayuga County Museum, Auburn, N.Y., c. 1905, 3: "[I]n the eastern shore of Maryland Dorchester County is where I was borned. Du fust ting I member, was lyin' in de cradle. Youse seen dese trees dat ar hollow. Take a big tree, cut it down, put a bode in each and, make a cradle of it a' call is a 'gum. Ise member lyin in dat yar, when de young ladies in de big house whar my mother wukked, come down, cotch me up in de air befo' I could walk." Harkless Bowley, the son of Tubman's niece, Kessiah Bowley, claimed in 1939 that Tubman was born in "Bucktown Dorchester County . . . the property of Edward Brodas." Harkless Bowley to Conrad, August 8, 1939, Harkless Bowley Letters, Earl Conrad/Harriet Tubman Collection, New York Public Library, Schomburg Center for Research in Black Culture. Harkless is the only person to identify Bucktown as Tubman's birthplace. After the Civil War, Harkless Bowley lived with Harriet in Auburn, New York, for about two years. His family was in the process of moving from Chatham, Ontario, Canada, where they had fled with Harriet's help in 1850, back to Dorchester County. Resettling in Dorchester County, the Bowleys sought to reestablish their familial and community connections throughout the county. Harkless became a teacher in the local school system. Living near Bucktown, he would have met Edward Brodess's surviving children, several of whom continued to live on the family plantation in Bucktown. He would have been intimately familiar with the landscape where Tubman and his own family, particularly his mother, Kessiah, had been enslaved. No other evidence suggests that Tubman was actually born at Bucktown, and it seems quite possible that Harkless assumed this because he

knew the Brodesses and their plantation. In contrast, Harkless never met Anthony Thompson or Thompson's children, so it is unlikely he would not have associated their plantation with Harriet.

14. Bureau of the Census, *United States Federal Census*, 1820, Dorchester County, Md.

15. Affidavit of Harriet Davis, Original Pension Files, Nelson Davis, Pension no. 449,592, 1894, National Archives, College Park, Md.

16. B. Jean Woolston, comp., *Marriage References, Circuit Court, Dorchester County, Maryland. 1780–1867* (Cambridge, Md.: Weir Neck Publications, 1995).

17. Bureau of the Census, *United States Federal Census*, 1830.

18. Edward Brodess to Dempsey P. Kane, July 1825, vol. Liber 9 ER 624 p. 625, Dorchester County Land Records, MDSA.

19. Ibid.

20. The Pattisons would later identify Mariah Ritty as one of Rit's children, the only people to do so. It is likely her early sale resulted in the lack of knowledge on the part of Brodess's neighbors and friends as to her existence.

21. See pages 296–99 for the Ross family tree. Equity Papers 249, MDSA; Thompson Deposition, Equity Papers 249, MDSA; Assessment Record, 1852–1864, Dorchester County Board of County Commissioners, MDSA. During the early summer of 1849, Atthow Pattison's heirs filed suit against Edward Brodess's estate, asserting their rightful ownership of Rit and some of her children. They claimed that Brodess had violated the terms of his grandfather's will by maintaining possession of Rit after she was forty-five years old. In a complicated legal complaint, the Pattisons argued that they were entitled to an ownership interest in Rit because Atthow Pattison had only specified that she remain with Mary Pattison Brodess until she turned forty-five, when, they argued, ownership of Rit should have reverted back to the Pattison estate. In October 1853 Dr. Anthony C. Thompson, Anthony Thompson's son, testified in the lawsuit that he "always understood that said Rit was the mother of Linah, Soph, Robert, Ben, Harry, Minty, and Mose," or seven children in all. Dr. Thompson's deposition for the Pattison lawsuit over ownership of Rit, filed in 1853, remains perhaps the most accurate, though not necessarily complete, record of Tubman's siblings. A young boy when Rit and her mistress, Mary Pattison Brodess joined his father's household in 1803, Dr. Thompson knew much about Rit and her children. The Pattisons, through whom Rit had originally come to Brodess, were also in a particularly important position to have knowledge of Rit's offspring. Indeed, the heirs of Elizabeth Pattison and her son Gourney Crow Pattison, the initiator of the lawsuit, owned slaves who were related to Rit, and therefore would more than likely have known her family status; living in the same neighborhood, they had ample opportunity to observe Rit and her children. While the Pattisons had an economic interest in the outcome of the lawsuit, Thompson had little to gain, other than perhaps advancing a long-simmering feud between the Brodesses and the Thompsons.

According to Thompson's testimony, Linah was born sometime around 1808, and Robert was born around 1816. Minty, he believed, was born about 1821, and her younger brother, Ben, was born around 1823, with Henry or Harry following sometime around 1825, and Moses "at least 18 or 19 years of age." I believe that the transcriber of the deposition made a mistake and wrote "28" for Harry or Henry instead of "23." See Thompson Deposition, 1853. All other records indicate Henry was born around 1829–1830. Thompson's testimony excludes any mention of Soph's age; either it was omitted accidentally when transcribed into the court records, or Thompson neglected to say. The Pattisons thought that Rit had eleven children, including Soph, who was "about 40" years old in 1853, indicating she may have been born around 1813. They agreed with Thompson's assessment of Linah's and Robert's ages, but they claimed the existence of other daughters, "Mariah Ritty aged about 42," born about 1811; Rachel, supposedly thirty-eight years old; and Mary, born about 1822. Thompson may not have remembered Mariah or Rachel; Mariah grew up during the years when Dr. Anthony C. Thompson would have been out of his father's household. Mariah was later sold, but Rachel was actually born at around 1825 in Bucktown, far from Anthony Thompson's plantation and far removed from Dr. Thompson's social and economic world. And Mary was actually a granddaughter, possibly also known as Kessiah, Linah's daughter. The Pattisons believed Henry was about twenty-eight (born about 1825), the same age they claimed Moses to be. The Pattisons thought that Minty was about thirty-four (which would have placed her birth around 1819), her brother Robert about thirty-six, and Ben about thirty-two. They also claimed a Harriet, age unknown, who was probably a granddaughter, another child of Linah's. Numerous witnesses testified, and most agreed that the ages given by Thompson were within an acceptable range. Brodess's neighbor Polish Mills recalled that he knew Rit "and her son Moses, he hired the said Rit with her two children Hannah [Henry] and Moses from Edward Brodess in the year 1833 for their victuals and clothes, the said Rit and her children came to his house in the month of May in the same year, Moses her youngest was then sucking at the breast, he might have been one year old, or older, or somewhat younger, Hannah [Henry] her next child was quite small, and could run about, there was probably a year and a half or two years between them. Moses could not walk, but crawl about." Another deponent, John Scott, agreed as to Moses's age, though gave little other information. See Equity Papers 249, 1852–1855, Dorchester County Circuit Court, MDSA. The Pattisons claimed many of the children to be older than the ages claimed by other deponents; they may have simply hoped that by increasing the ages of the slaves they were improving their chances for claiming their labor once they reached the age of forty-five. The Dorchester County Assessors Field Book for 1852 lists Eliza Brodess as the mistress of six slaves. Harriet Tubman and her brother Moses had already run away by then, according to the record, leaving behind Harry [Henry], age twenty; Ben, age twenty-three; Bob, age thirty-five; Rachel, age twenty-seven; and two minor children, Angerine, five, and Ben, three. See Assessors Field Book, 1852–1864, Dorchester County Board of County Commissioners, MDSA.

22. Emma P. Telford, "Harriet: The Modern Moses of Heroism and Visions," Cayuga County Museum, Auburn, N.Y., c. 1905: "When I was fo' or five years ole, my mother cooked up to the big house an' lef me to take care ob de baby an' my little brudder. I use ter be in a hurry fer her to go, so's I could play de baby was a pig in a bag, an' hole him up by de bottom ob his dress. I had a nice frolic wid dat baby, swingin' him all 'roun, his fee in de dress an' his little head an arms techin de flo', cause Ise too small to hole him higher. It was late nights for my mother's git home, an' when he'd get worryin' I'd cut a fat chunk ob pork an' toast it on de coals an' put it in his mouf. One night he went to sleep wid dat hangin' out, an when my mother come home she thought I'd done kill him. I nussed dat er' baby till he was so big I couldn't tote him any mo,' " There is also the possibility that Harriet cared for a sister's child, unidentified. The ages here do not match exactly. We cannot be sure of the accuracy of the Telford interview. It is likely that Tubman cared for Ben, her "little brother," and either Rachel, misidentified as a boy, or Henry, who was born much later, making Tubman seven or eight when he was born. Or perhaps the child was her niece Kessiah, born about 1825.

23. Bradford, Scenes, 75.

24. Geoffrey M. Footner, Tidewater Triumph: The Development and Worldwide Success of the Chesapeake Pilot Schooner (Centreville, Md.: Tidewater Publishers, 1998), 136.

25. Howard I. Chapelle, The Search for Speed Under Sail, 1700–1855 (New York: W. W. Norton & Company, 1967), 299.

26. Ibid., 299–303. See also Quentin and Ann Jensen Snediker, Chesapeake Bay Schooners (Centreville, Md.: Tidewater Publishers, 1992), 33–35.

27. Laws Made and Passed by the General Assembly of the State of Maryland, vol. 3182, chapter CXI, 6th Jan. 1810, Archives of Maryland, MDSA, 712.

28. Thompson could access this canal by way of the Big Blackwater River, or through White Marsh Road, which ran north to Tobacco Stick from the Big Blackwater River just to the east of Thompson's property.

29. Laws Made and Passed by the General Assembly of the State of Maryland, vol. 540, Chapter LIV, 3rd Feb. 1830, Archives of Maryland, MDSA.

30. Laws Made and Passed by the General Assembly of the State of Maryland, vol. 192, chapter CXXIX, 28th Jan. 1814, Archives of Maryland, MDSA, 1529.

31. Freedmen's Bureau Bank Records, Church of Latter-Day Saints, Salt Lake City: 2000.

32. Robert J. Brugger, *Maryland, A Middle Temperament, 1634–1980* (Baltimore: The Johns Hopkins University Press, 1988), esp. 206–15.

33. Levin Stewart to Sundry Negroes, Dorchester County Court, Court Papers,1797–1851, MDSA. See also Elaine McGill, transcr., *Certificates of Freedom, Dorchester County Court 1806–1864* (privately printed, 2001). This is a transcription of the actual Certificates of Freedom Record Book, 1806–1864, for Dorchester County, held at the Maryland State Archives.

34. Gwendolyn Midlo Hall's research into slave names indicates that Binah was an African name, Muslim in origin and generally found on the West Coast of Africa.

35. John Seward to Sundry Negroes, January 15, 1817, Dorchester County Court, Court Papers, 1743–1849, MDSA.

36. Census, 1810 and 1820, Dorchester County, Md.

37. Last Will and Testament of Anthony Thompson, Register of Wills, Dorchester County courthouse, Estate no. 0-65-C, Cambridge, Md.: "ten acres of land for and during his life time, peaceable to remain to be laid out to his house binding with the road on the west side with the privilege of cutting timber on any part of my land for the support of the same."

38. Will of Anthony Thompson.

39. Census, 1820, Dorchester County, Md. Four slaves, two women and two men, were between the ages of fourteen and twenty-six; five more male slaves were between twenty-six and forty-five, as were seven of the female slaves.

40. "List of Anthony Thompson's Negroes, 1839," Levin Richardson Collection, MS1405, Maryland Historical Society, Baltimore, Md.

41. Two of Anthony Thompson's sons became doctors. As a young man of seventeen in 1810, Anthony C. Thompson probably left Dorchester soon thereafter to pursue higher education in Annapolis, Baltimore, or Philadelphia. Eventually earning a medical degree from the University of Maryland, he returned to the Eastern Shore in 1815, setting up his business as the first doctor in St. Michaels in neighboring Talbot County. See Oswald Tilghman, *History of Talbot County Maryland, 1661–1861* (Baltimore: Williams & Wilkins Company, 1915), 2:397. Within the year he had married a local woman, Martha B. Kersey, and by 1818 he had moved to his mother-in-law's estate, called Mary's Delight (or, as it would be known later, Webley) after the death of the mother-in-law's second husband, Captain Thomas Frazier. Thompson would remain on this property, assisting in its management until his mother-in-law died in 1825. See F. Edward Wright and Irma Harper, *Maryland Eastern Shore Newspaper Abstracts: Northern Counties, 1825–1829*, vol. 5 (Westminster, Md.: Willow Bend Books, 2000). Dr. Anthony C. Thompson's brother Absalom Thompson earned his medical degree from Harvard University in 1825. He returned to the Eastern Shore and married Martha Kersey's sister, Eliza. Absalom's first wife, Anne Gurney, died around 1821, leaving behind an infant son, Absalom C. C. Thompson. Dr. Absalom Thomson and his new bride moved into her mother's estate at Webley in 1825 when Dr. Anthony C. Thompson and his wife, Mary, moved back to Dorchester County.

42. "List of Anthony Thompson's Negroes, 1839."

43. When Anthony Thompson died in 1836, his son Dr. Anthony C. Thompson, Absalom's brother, became executor of his father's estate. He was assigned the responsibility of manumitting and devising to the heirs Thompson's forty-three slaves. At the outset it appears that the two brothers attempted to accommodate family relationships, with Absalom maintaining under his control those slaves with ties to Talbot County, or who were perhaps already working for him.

44. Sarah H. Bradford, *Harriet, the Moses of Her People* (New York: Geo. R. Lockwood & Sons, 1886); Bradford, *Scenes*, 15.

45. "Cash," *Cambridge Chronicle*, Cambridge, Md., December 25, 1830.

46. Notice, *Cambridge Chronicle*, Cambridge, Md., August 30, 1828.

47. Debra Smith Moxey, "Chattel Records." James W. Hanes to James Cox, Mar. 6, 1829. *Dorchester County Genealogical Magazine* XV, no. 2 (1995): 8.

48. Advertisement, *Cambridge Chronicle*, Cambridge, Md., January 9, 1836. See also Frederick Bancroft, *Slave Trading in the Old South* (Columbia: University of South Carolina Press, 1996), 39–44.

49. Dorchester County Court, Chattel Records, 1827–1833, MDSA.

50. Moxey, "Chattel Records." Peter Lowber to James Baldock, Nov. 25, 1829. *Dorchester County Genealogical Magazine* XVI, no. 5 (1997): 4.

51. Ibid.; Debra Smith Moxey, "Chattel Records." Peter Lowber to George W. Bates, March 23, 1830; and Peter Lowber to Winder C. Dingle, April 19, 1830. *Dorchester County Genealogical Magazine* XVII, no. 1 (1997): 7.

52. Bancroft, *Slave Trading in the Old South*, esp. 30. For additional scholarship on the slave trade, see Walter Johnson, *Soul by Soul: Life Inside the Antebellum Slave Market* (Cambridge: Harvard University Press, 1999); and Hugh Thomas, *The Slave Trade. The Story of the Atlantic Slave Trade: 1440–1870* (New York: Touchstone, 1997).

53. Debra Smith Moxey and Deanna Marshall, "Patty Cannon Story," *Dorchester County Genealogical Magazine* XVI, no. 4 (1994): 3. See also George Alfred Townsend, *The Entailed Hat or Patty Cannon's Times. A Romance* (Cambridge, Md.: Tidewater Publishers, 1955).

54. See *Brodess vs. Thompson*. There are numerous entries for purchases of items for Brodess that appear to be inconsistent with the life of a farmer.

55. Bradford, *Harriet* (1886), 15.

56. Thompson Deposition, 1853.

57. Mills Deposition, 1853.

58. Baltimore slave records for the period were destroyed during the 1970s.

59. John W. Blassingame, ed., *Slave Testimony: Two Centuries of Letters, Speeches, Interviews, and Autobiographies* (Baton Rouge: Louisiana State University Press, 1977), 414–16. The "class leader" may have been Dr. Anthony C. Thompson, who by this time had been ordained a minister in the Methodist Church, a "church leader." This person could have been a number of other local ministers, however.

60. Ibid.

61. Ibid.

Chapter 3

1. Ednah Dow Littlehale Cheney, "Moses," *Freedmen's Record*, March 1865.

2. Sarah H. Bradford, *Scenes in the Life of Harriet Tubman* (Auburn, N.Y.: W. J. Moses, 1869), 9.

3. William Still, *The Underground Railroad* (Chicago: Johnson Publishing Company, Inc., 1970), 307.

4. Interviews with John Seward (Robert Ross) and James Seward (Ben Ross), in Benjamin Drew, *The Refugee: A North-Side View of Slavery* (1855; reprint, Tilden G. Edelstein, ed., Reading, Mass.: Addison-Wesley Publishing Co., 1969), 27.

5. Marie Jenkins Schwartz, *Born in Bondage: Growing up Enslaved in the Antebellum South* (Cambridge: Harvard University Press, 2000), 158.

6. Brenda E. Stevenson, *Life in Black and White: Family and Community in the Slave South* (New York: Oxford University Press, 1996), 184.

7. Still, *Underground Railroad*.

8. Testimony of Polish Mills, Equity Papers 249, MDSA.

9. Bradford, *Scenes*, 73. An examination of the 1830 census indicates that Cook lived perhaps two or three miles from the Brodess plantation, next door to Brodess's cousin and uncle, both named Gourney Crow Pattison. Bradford wrote that Cook's farm was "ten miles distant." The difference in distance could be a faulty childhood memory, or perhaps Bradford mistook "two" for "ten" when she interviewed Tubman. There are numerous occasions where she has made similar errors. In the census, Cook is listed as the head of a household of seven slaves and four whites. This includes two male slaves under the age of ten, one between ten and twenty-four, and one between fifty-five and one hundred years old, and four female slaves, including one under ten, one between ten and twenty-four, one between twenty-four and thirty-six, and one between thirty-six and fifty-five. Cook's own family included one white woman between twenty and thirty and two boys under the age of five. It appears that Cook rented this property. He could have been an overseer for Thomas J. H. Eccleston, a very wealthy landowner in that area.

10. Emma P. Telford, "Harriet: The Modern Moses of Heroism and Visions," Cayuga County Museum, Auburn, N.Y., c. 1905, 4. "When we got dere," Tubman recalled, "day was at table eatin' supper. I' neber eat in de house where de white people wuz, an' I was shamed to stan' up and eat befo' dem."

11. Ibid. "I was as fond of milk as any young shote. But all de time I was dere I stuck to it, dat I didn't drink sweet milk."

12. Bradford, *Scenes*; Franklin Sanborn, "Harriet Tubman," *The Commonwealth*, Boston, July 17, 1863. Sanborn's article actually appears verbatim in both of Bradford's biographies. Valued for their pelts, muskrats were trapped also for their meat. See Frank R. Smith, *Muskrat Investigations in Dorchester County, Md, 1930–1934* (Washington, D.C.: United States Department of Agriculture, 1938).

13. Telford, "Harriet," 4. "I useter sleep' on de flo' in front ob de fireplace an' dar I'd lie an' cry an' cry. I useter tink all the time ef I could only git home an' git in my mudder's bed, an' de funny part of dat was, she nebber had a bade in her life. Nuffin but a board box nailed up agin de wall an' straw laid on it."

14. Bradford, *Scenes*, 73–74.

15. Telford, "Harriet," 4. "[L]ike de boy on de Swanee Ribber, 'no place lake my ole cabin home.' Whenever you saw a chile wasser homesick dan I wuz, you see a bad one."

16. Bradford, *Scenes*, 10–11.

17. Ibid. According to Sarah Bradford, however, this was Tubman's first experience away from home.

18. Bradford, *Scenes*, 11–12.

19. Whether "Miss Susan" and "Miss Emily" are fictitious names or the actual names of the women in Bradford's version of Tubman's first experience away from home is not known. Efforts to identify Susan and Emily have proved frustrating. While there are many such sister combinations in Dorchester County, additional research indicates that a couple of possibilities are more likely than others. One of the more intriguing possibilities includes Susan and Amelia Keene, who are related to Eliza Ann Keene Brodess. Amelia was married to Charles Tubman in 1816. Charles Tubman lived next door to Eliza Keene's parents. The other possibility is Susan Dawson Thompson, Dr. Anthony Thompson's second wife, and her sister Emily, though this seems less likely.

20. Bradford, *Scenes*, 13. "An dat baby was allus in my lap 'capt when it was asleep, or its mother was feedin' it."

21. Ibid.

22. Samuel Hopkins Adams, *Grandfather Stories* (New York: Random House, 1947), 274.

23. Sarah H. Bradford, *Harriet, the Moses of Her People* (New York: J. J. Little & Co., 1901). There is an additional chapter added to this edition of Bradford's 1886 biography, entitled "Some Additional Incidents in the Life of 'Harriet.'" Here, Bradford includes new stories as told by Tubman that were not included in the earlier biographies. "An dat sugar, right by me, did look so nice, an' my Missus's back was turned to me while she was fightin' wid her husband, so I jes put my fingers in de sugar bowl to take one lump, an maybe she heard me, an' she turned and saw me. De nex' minute she had de raw hide

down; I give one jump out of de do', and I saw dey came after me, but I jes' flew, and dey didn't catch me. I run, an' run, an' run, I passed many a house, but I didn't dar' to stop, for dey all knew my Missus an' dey would send me back." 135–36.

24. Bradford, *Harriet* (1901), 137. "I was so starved I knowed I'd got to go back to my Missus, I hadn't got no whar else to go, but I knowed what was comin."

25. Harkless Bowley to Earl Conrad, August 8, 1939, Earl Conrad/Harriet Tubman Collection, New York Public Library, Schomburg Center for Research in Black Culture. New York.

26. Ibid.

27. James Cook appears in Franklin Sanborn's autobiographical essay in *The Commonwealth* as Tubman's first experience away from home. Sarah Bradford focuses exclusively on "Miss Susan" and her sister Emily in her Tubman biography, but she also included Sanborn's article from *The Commonwealth* in its entirety in her book; therefore, confusingly, both stories are presented in Bradford's books as Tubman's first experience being hired away. Emma Telford, another early biographer, mentions no names in connection with Tubman's first time away from home, only that she was hired to become a weaver. Telford, "Harriet."

28. Bradford, *Scenes*, 13.

29. Equity Papers 394.

30. "Aunt Harriet Was Very Old," *Auburn Daily Advertiser*, Auburn, N.Y., March 12, 1913.

31. John P. Pratt, "Spectacular Meteor Shower Might Repeat," *Meridian Magazine*, October 15, 1999.

32. Meteor Shower, Samuel Harrison Collection, MS 432, box 4, Maryland Historical Society, Baltimore.

33. "Aunt Harriet Was Very Old." This meteoric event was the result of debris shed by the comet Tempel-Tuttle. Normally occurring every thirty-three years, the meteor "storm" caused by the passing of this comet near the earth in 1833 was by far the most spectacular. According to Samuel Harrison of Talbot County, "superstition attached a disastrous meaning to this appearance. The end of the world was thought to be drawing near." He also wrote that he was "under the impression that religious awe was the feeling inspired in most minds at the time." See Meteor Shower, Samuel Harrison Collection.

34. The identity of this temporary master is not known. This event probably happened sometime between 1834 and 1836.

35. Telford, "Harriet," 5. "My hair had nebber been combed an it stood out like a bushel basket, an' when I'd git through eatin' I'd wipe de grease' off my fingers' on my hair an' I spect dat ar hair saved my life."

36. There may have been at least two stores located at this crossroads, in addition to a blacksmith shop. An old former store of unknown date still stands at the crossroads, facing Greenbrier Road, on property now owned by the Meredith family. Architectural historians have been unable to determine the exact age of the building, though it is suspected that parts of it date from the mid-nineteenth century, and perhaps earlier. The interior, though dated to perhaps after the Civil War period, is probably reminiscent of dry goods stores of the antebellum period. Barnett's property was also located near Pritchett Meredith's farm in Bucktown.

37. Franklin Sanborn wrote that the slaveholder's name was Barrett, but census records confirm this person is more than likely Thomas Barnett. The names of the defiant slave boy and the irate overseer remain unknown. Thomas Barnett leased a large piece of property in Bucktown. Thomas Barnett's father, Thomas senior, was a successful planter, owning a large tract of property just east and southeast of the Brodesses' plantation, near the Bucktown crossroads. Thomas Barnett Jr. married Eliza Pitt in 1833 and later owned a plantation on the road from Airey's to Bucktown, perhaps a mile and a half east and north of the Brodess property.

38. Sanborn, "Harriet Tubman"; see also Bradford, *Scenes*, 74.

39. Telford, "Harriet," 6. "I had a shoulder shawl' ob de mistis' ober my haid an' when I got to do sto' I was shamed to go in, an' said de' oberseer raisin' up his arm to throw an iron weight at one o de slaves an' dat wuz de las' I knew . . . broke my skull and cut a piece ob dat shawl clean off and druv it into my

haid. Dey carried me to de house all bleedin an' faintin. I had no baid, no place to lie down on at all, an' dey lay me on de seat ob de loom, an' I stayed dere all dat day an' nex' . . . I went to wuk again an' dere I wukked wid de blood an' sweat rollin' down my face till I couldn't see."

40. Bradford, *Scenes*, 13–14.

41. Franklin B. Sanborn, "The Late Araminta Davis: Better Known as 'Moses' or 'Harriet Tubman,' " Franklin B. Sanborn Papers, box 1, folder 5, American Antiquarian Society, Worcester, Mass.

42. Sanborn, "Harriet Tubman"; see also Bradford, *Scenes*, 75.

43. Bradford, *Scenes*, 13.

44. Cheney, "Moses"; see also Sanborn, "Harriet Tubman." Franklin Sanborn, Sarah Bradford, and countless other abolitionists, suffragists, family, friends, and acquaintances noted the effects of this injury years later.

45. Earl Conrad Papers, Bourke Memorial Library, Cayuga Community College, Auburn, N.Y.; Wilbur Siebert to Earl Conrad, September 4, 1939, Earl Conrad / Harriet Tubman Collection, New York Public Library, Schomburg Center for Research in Black Culture.

46. Temporal lobe epilepsy is a complex and varied disease of the brain. Not all instances of TLE are precipitated by a brain injury, though often this is the case. There is a significant body of literature devoted to the study and treatment of TLE. Most of it is covered in medical and clinical journals for physicians and researchers, but a small body of research extends the knowledge gleaned from these reports and studies to the fields of history and social studies. Some scholars are now looking at the possibilities that some of history's great leaders and artists have suffered from this disease. Based on my research in clinical journals and research reports, Tubman exhibited a large number of symptoms associated with TLE. In particular, epilepsy patients sometimes develop an unusually profound reaction and interest in religion, in addition to other more visual and auditory symptoms. See the following for brief discussions of TLE diagnoses and symptoms: M. Ohtsu, H. Oguni, Y. Awaya, and M. Osawa, "[Clinical study on epileptic aura in children with temporal lobe epilepsy]," *No To Hattasu* 33, no. 5 (2001); Jamie Talan, "Religion: Is It All in Your Head?," *Psychology Today*, March / April 1998; Sharon and Anne Underwood Begley, "Religion and the Brain," *Newsweek*, May 7, 2001, 50; Vernon M. Neppe, "Possible Temporal Lobe Symptoms," Pacific Neuropsychiatric Institute, 1997, at http://www.pni.org/neuropsychiatry/seizures/ptls.html; Richard Restak, "Complex Partial Seizures Present Diagnostic Challenge," *Psychiatric Times*, September 1995; J. Bancaud, F. Brunet-Bourgin, P. Chauvel, and E. Halgren, "Anatomical Origin of Déjà-Vu and Vivid 'Memories' in Human Temporal Lobe Epilepsy," *Brain* 117, no. 1 (1994): 71–90.

47. Cheney, "Moses." See also John W. Blassingame, ed., *Slave Testimony: Two Centuries of Letters, Speeches, Interviews, and Autobiographies* (Baton Rouge: Louisiana State University Press, 1977), 457–65.

48. Sanborn, "Harriet Tubman."

49. Ibid. See also Bradford, *Scenes*, 79–80.

50. Bradford, *Scenes*, 56. Sarah Bradford noted that she could have written much of the "dreams and visions," but she had "thought best not to insert anything which, with any, might bring discredit upon the story."

51. Still, *Underground Railroad*, 411.

52. Frederick Douglass, *Life and Times of Frederick Douglass* (1882; reprint, Scituate, Mass.: Digital Scanning, Inc., 2001), 133.

53. Bradford, *Scenes*, 108–9.

54. Ibid.

55. Albert J. Raboteau, "The Black Experience in American Evangelicalism," in Timothy E. Fulop and Albert J. Raboteau, ed., *African-American Religion: Interpretive Essays in History and Culture* (New York: Routledge, 1997), 94.

56. This church is also known as Bucktown United Methodist Church.

57. Bradford, *Scenes*, 49.

58. For in-depth discussions of African American religious life, see Albert J. Raboteau, *Slave Religion: The "Invisible Institution" in the Antebellum South* (New York: Oxford University Press, 1980); Albert J. Raboteau, *A Fire in the Bones: Reflections on African American Religious History* (Boston: Beacon Press, 1995); Timothy E. Fulop and Albert J. Raboteau, eds., *African-American Religion: Interpretive Essays in History and Culture* (New York: Routledge, 1997); Lawrence Levine, *Black Culture and Black Consciousness: Afro American Folk Thought from Slavery to Freedom* (New York: Oxford University Press, 1977); Mechal Sobel, *The World They Made Together: Black and White Values in Eighteenth Century Virginia* (Princeton: Princeton University Press, 1987); Sylvia Frey, *Water from the Rock: Black Resistance in a Revolutionary Age* (Princeton, N.J.: Princeton University Press, 1991); Sylvia Frey and Betty Wood, *Come Shouting to Zion: African American Protestantism in the American South and British Caribbean to 1830* (Chapel Hill: University of North Carolina Press, 1998); Nell Painter, *Sojourner Truth: A Life, a Symbol* (New York: W. W. Norton & Company, 1996); Eugene D. Genovese, *Roll, Jordon, Roll: The World the Slaves Made* (New York: Vintage Books, 1976); Milton C. Sernett, ed., *African American Religious History: A Documentary Witness* (Durham, N.C.: Duke University Press, 1999); Charles Joyner, *Down by the Riverside: A South Carolina Slave Community* (Chicago: University of Illinois Press, 1984), 141–71; Jon Butler, *Awash in a Sea of Faith: Christianizing the American People* (Cambridge: Harvard University Press, 1990), 129–63, 225–56; and Christine Leigh Heyrman, *Southern Cross: The Beginnings of the Bible Belt* (Chapel Hill: University of North Carolina Press, 1997).

59. Lawrence W. Levine, "Slave Songs and Slave Consciousness," in Timothy E. Fulop and Albert J. Raboteau, eds., *African-American Religion: Interpretive Essays in History and Culture* (New York: Routledge, 1997), 78.

60. Ibid.

61. Levine, *Black Culture*, 81. Levine and other historians have discussed the process by which existing cultural and spiritual belief systems from West Africa coexisted or interacted with evangelical Protestantism and European Christianity in the slave quarters, where, Levine argues, neither "slaves nor their African forebears ever drew modernity's clear line between the sacred and the secular. Their spirituals indicate clearly that there *were* alternatives open to them—alternatives which they themselves fashioned out of the fusion of their African heritage and their new religion" (73).

62. Bradford, *Harriet* (1886), 75–76.

63. Moira Ferguson, ed., *Nine Black Women: An Anthology of Nineteenth-Century Writers from the United States, Canada, Bermuda, and the Caribbean* (New York: Routledge, 1998), 145.

64. Ibid.

65. Bradford, *Harriet* (1886), 61.

66. *Six Women's Slave Narratives*, Schomburg Library of Nineteenth-Century Black Women Writers (Oxford: Oxford University Press, 1988); *Spritual Narratives*, Schomburg Library of Nineteenth-Century Black Women Writers (Oxford: Oxford University Press, 1988); William L. Andrews, *To Tell a Free Story: The First Century of Afro-American Autobiography, 1760–1865* (Urbana: University of Illinois Press, 1986); *Sisters of the Spirit: Three Black Women's Autobiographies of the Nineteenth Century*, ed. William L. Andrews (Bloomington: Indiana University Press, 1986); Mary Grimley and Carol Hurd Green Mason, ed., *Journeys: Autobiographical Writings by Women* (Boston: G. K. Hall & Co., 1979); Ferguson, ed., *Nine Black Women;* Frances Smith Foster, *Written by Herself: Literary Production by African American Women, 1746–1892* (Bloomington: Indiana University Press, 1993); Carla L. Peterson, *"Doers of the Word": African American Women Speakers and Writers in the North, 1830–1880* (New Brunswick, N.J.: Rutgers University Press, 1995).

67. Peter Randolph, *Slave Cabin in the Pulpit* (Boston, 1893).

68. Maria Stewart, "Productions of Mrs. Maria W. Stewart," in *Spiritual Narratives*, Schomburg Library of Nineteenth-Century Black Women Writers (New York: Oxford University Press, 1988), 76–77.

69. *Sisters of the Spirit*, 1.

70. Ibid., 91.

71. Ibid.

72. Ibid., 92.

73. Ibid.

74. Jarena Lee, "Religious Experience and Spiritual Journal of Mrs. Jarena Lee, Giving an Account of Her Call to Preach the Gospel," in *Spritual Narratives*, Schomburg Library of Nineteenth-Century Black Women Writers (New York: Oxford University Press, 1987), 37.

75. Ibid., 41.

76. Ibid.

77. Ibid., 36–37.

78. Ibid., 90.

79. Notice, *Cambridge Chronicle*, Cambidge, Md., August 30, 1828, 4.

80. Blassingame, ed., *Slave Testimony*, 423–26.

81. Notice of reward, *Cambridge Chronicle*, Cambridge, Md., September 8, 1828, 3.

82. *The Confessions of Nat Turner and Related Documents*, ed. Kenneth S. Greenberg (New York: Bedford Books, 1996), 26.

83. Execution of Henny, in Cambridge, in 1831, Dorchester County Historical Society, Vertical Files, Dorchester County Public Library, Cambridge, Md.

84. Dorchester County, Certificates of Freedom, Dorchester County Circuit Court Records, MDSA; Chattel Records, Dorchester County Court Records, Maryland State Archives, Annapolis.

85. In 1831 there were 54 such manumissions and requests for freedom papers, up from 36 the year before. In 1832, however, the number increased dramatically to 119.

86. Jeffrey R. Brackett, *The Negro in Maryland: A Study of the Institution of Slavery* (1889; reprint, New York: Negro Universities Press, 1969), 199.

87. Ethiop, "The Early Days of the Underground Railroad," *Anglo African Magazine*, October 1859, 323.

88. Ibid., 321–24.

89. Kay Najiyyah McElvey, "Early Black Dorchester, 1776–1870: A History of the Struggle of African Americans in Dorchester County, Maryland, to Be Free to Make Their Own Choices," Ph.D. dissertation, University of Maryland, 1991, 270.

90. A. W. Wayman, *My Recollections of African M.E. Ministers, or Forty Years Experience in the African Methodist Church* (Philadelphia: A.M.E. Book Rooms, 1881), 7–11.

91. Cheney, "Moses," 34.

92. Still, *Underground Railroad*, 306.

93. Thompson Deposition, Equity Papers 249, MDSA.

94. Benjamin Drew, *The Refugee: A North-Side View of Slavery* (1855; reprint, Tilden G. Edelstein, ed., Reading, Mass.: Addison-Wesley Publishing Co., 1969), 20. Tubman told an audience in Brooklyn, N.Y., in 1865 that she received no education, "nor did she receive any 'brought-en up,' 'she came up." See "Mrs. Harriet Tubman, the Colored Nurse and Scout—the Bridge Street African M.E. Church Last Evening," *The Brooklyn Eagle*, October 23, 1865.

95. Drew, *The Refugee*, 20.

Chapter 4

1. Where Rit was living at this time is not known. Two locations seem to be the most likely possibilities. Rit may have been living in Bucktown at the time of Harriet's injury, possibly living at the Brodess farm, after having served a year under the control of Polish Mills, a local Bucktown farmer in 1833, or she could have been hired out again to another master in the immediate area. Rit also could have been hired out to Anthony Thompson, though during the early 1830s Brodess and Thompson may have still

been on unfriendly terms, thereby precluding any sort of hiring arrangement for Rit between the two men. Bucktown seems to be the most likely location for Tubman's recovery under the watchful eye of her mother.

2. Franklin Sanborn, "Harriet Tubman," *The Commonwealth*, Boston, July 17, 1863.

3. Now known as Madison.

4. Levin Stewart to Sundry Negroes, Dorchester County Court Papers, 1797–1851, MDSA. Levin also had a son named John Trevalian Stewart, and he was ten years older than his cousin, John T. Stewart, Joseph's son. John Trevalian returned to Dorchester County after his father died in 1826. Choosing to live with his uncle Joseph at first, John Trevalian then moved with his brother, Joseph, to land he purchased from his uncle, Joseph, at Henry's Crossroads in Vienna on the Nanticoke River, where they operated a store and mercantile business together.

5. Levin Stewart died in Georgetown in 1825, but his body was returned to Dorchester County and interred in the cemetery at Old Trinity Church at Church Creek.

6. James A. Stewart, "Valuable Plantation for Sale," *Cambridge Chronicle*, Cambridge, Md., July 13, 1844.

7. Statement of Mrs. William Tatlock, Earl Conrad/Harriet Tubman Collection, New York Public Library, Schomburg Center for Research in Black Culture.

8. Frank C. Drake, "The Moses of Her People. Amazing Life Work of Harriet Tubman," *New York Herald*, New York, Sept. 22, 1907.

9. Sanborn, "Harriet Tubman"; Sarah H. Bradford, *Scenes in the Life of Harriet Tubman* (Auburn, N.Y.: W. J. Moses, 1869), 75.

10. Sanborn, "Harriet Tubman."

11. Drake, "The Moses of Her People."

12. Jacqueline Jones, *Labor of Love, Labor of Sorrow: Black Women, Work, and the Family from Slavery to the Present* (New York: Vintage Books, 1986), 27.

13. Ibid., esp. Chapter 1. For another excellent examination of female slave life see Deborah Gray White, *Ar'n't I a Woman? Female Slaves in the Plantation South* (New York: W. W. Norton & Company, 1987).

14. Jones, *Labor*, 25–29.

15. For a look at recent research into the lives and labors of southern white mistresses and their relationship to their slaves, see Marli Weiner, *Mistresses and Slaves: Plantation Women in South Carolina* (Chicago: University of Illinois Press, 1998); Catherine Clinton, *The Plantation Mistress: Woman's World in the Old South* (New York: Pantheon Books, 1982); Elizabeth Fox-Genovese, *Within the Plantation Household: Black and White Women of the Old South* (Chapel Hill: The University of North Carolina Press, 988); Brenda E. Stevenson, *Life in Black and White: Family and Community in the Slave South* (New York: Oxford University Press, 1996); and Stephanie McCurry, *Masters of Small Worlds: Yeoman Households, Gender Relations, and Political Culture of the Antebellum South Carolina Low Country* (New York: Oxford University Press, 1995); Orville Vernon Burton, *In My Father's House There Are Many Mansions: Family and Community in Edgefield, South Carolina* (Chapel Hill: University of North Carolina Press, 1985); and J. William Harris, *Plain Folk and Gentry in a Slave Society. White Liberty and Black Slavery in Augusta's Hinterlands* (Baton Rouge: Louisiana State University Press, 1998).

16. During the early 1830 Brodess would have had, assuming he had not sold any of the male slaves he had inherited or those born to Rit, at least four male slaves, possibly more, who were old enough to labor productively in the fields: Sam, Frederick, Shadrach, and Robert. Ben, who was about eight in 1830, would have been somewhat useful in the fields. The possible female slaves at this time were Rit, Linah, and Soph. Mariah Ritty had presumably been sold, and Harriet was still under ten years of age. Daughters of Linah and Soph would also have been too young to contribute to the fields or household production, though even at five, Linah's daughter Kessiah could have helped around the house, as Harriet had been required to do at around the same age.

17. Cheney, "Moses," p. 35.

18. Sanborn, "Harriet Tubman"; Bradford, *Scenes*, 75.

19. Sanborn, "Harriet Tubman."

20. This community is quite evident as demonstrated by an examination of the U.S. Census, 1820–1870, for the area centered on White Marsh, Harrisville, Oldfield, and Buttons Neck Roads, south of Tobacco Stick (Madison), Woolford, and Church Creek to the Blackwater River.

21. Julius Sherrard Scott III, "The Common Wind: Currents of Afro-American Communication in the Era of the Haitian Revolution," Ph.D. dissertation, Duke University, 1986; Joseph B. Seth and Mary W. Seth, *Recollections of a Long Life on the Eastern Shore* (Easton, Md.: Press of the Star-Democrat, 1926), 9.

22. Scott, "Common Wind," 9.

23. Sale announcement, *Cambridge Chronicle*, Cambridge, Md. Lists property purchased by Joseph Stewart from Dr. A. C. Thompson as "Thompson's Range," "Westphalia," "Chamber's Chance," and "Thompson's Desire," for a total of approximately 420 acres.

24. Walter E. Huelle, *Footnotes to Dorchester History* (Cambridge, Md.: Tidewater Publishers, 1969), 63.

25. David S. Cecelski, *The Waterman's Song: Slavery and Freedom in Maritime North Carolina* (Chapel Hill: The University of North Carolina Press, 2001).

26. William S. Pettigrew to James C. Johnson, as quoted in Cecelski, *Waterman's Song*. 104.

27. For further discussion of canal building in North Carolina, see Cecelski, *Waterman's Song*.

28. While no account books or records remain for the company, these area landowners probably provided the slave labor required to build the canal.

29. Harriet Bowley, daughter of Binah Bowley, married David Linthicum.

30. The Bowley brothers, Major, John, and Richard, and their cousin Simon Bowley were freed by Stewart during the 1840s. Held in bondage by Joseph Stewart, they were trained in a variety of skills related to shipbuilding. Once free, these Bowley men hired themselves out as ship's carpenters, eventually building at least one ship in partnership with Joseph Stewart's son, John T. Stewart. Major Bowley to John Bowley, Richard Bowley, John T. Stewart, Chattel Records, MdHR 19626-1. loc 1/4/4/44, MDSA. Major Bowley sold an interest in "Vessel, now on the stocks at Steam Mill Wharf in Cambridge." The "Sandy Hill shipyard," near Cambridge, was owned by John T. Stewart. See also Huelle, *Footnotes*, 63.

31. Rit moved back to the Peters Neck area and lived with Ben for an undetermined period of time, probably from about 1836 to the mid-1840s. See Bureau of the Census, *United States Federal Census*, 1840, Dorchester County, Md.

32. Bradford, *Scenes*, 15.

33. For a discussion of slave and free marriage, see Thomas E. Will, "Weddings on Contested Grounds: Slave Marriage in the Antebellum South," *Historian* 62, no. 1 (1999): See also Barbara Jeanne Fields, *Slavery and Freedom on the Middle Ground* (New Haven: Yale University Press, 1985), 25–33. John Tubman's role in Harriet's escape and his subsequent marriage to a free black woman will be addressed in another chapter.

34. Certificates of Freedom, Dorchester County Circuit Court Records, January 4, 1850, MDSA. "Negro man John Tubman aged about 32 years, 5 feet 9½ inches high, dark mulatto complexion, with a small scar on back of left hand, also one other at the top of calf of left leg, was Born free and raised in Dorchester County. Identified by James Smith, S.C. [Slaughter Creek]." John Tubman's mother was most definitely a free woman, otherwise he could not have been born free. Another possibility, though more remote, for John's parents would be Tryphena and Planer Tubman. See also Elaine McGill, transcr., *Certificates of Freedom, Dorchester County Court 1806–1864* (privately printed, 2001), 59, 66, 76, 79, and for John Tubman, 84. After Harriet Tubman ran away, she claimed that a relative, Tom Tubman, participated in her rescues. He may have been one of John Tubman's free brothers. See Siebert, Interview with Harriet Tubman, in "The Underground Railroad: Manuscript Materials Collected by Professor Siebert," Houghton Library, Harvard University, Cambridge, Mass. The 1840 census shows a John Tubman, head of a free black household, in the Parsons Creek district several dwellings from Ben

Ross, Harriet's father. Nestled in the midst of a small free black settlement, this John Tubman, who is between fifty-five and a hundred years old, also had a woman of the same age in his house, along with two females age ten to twenty-four, two males under ten, and one twenty-four to thirty-five years of age. It is not known whether Harriet's husband, John Tubman, is in this household, as this older Tubman could be John's uncle. It seems likely, however, that young John Tubman could have been living here or close by, placing him in close proximity to Harriet.

35. See Franklin B. Sanborn, "The Late Araminta Davis: Better Known as 'Moses' or 'Harriet Tubman,' " Franklin B. Sanborn Papers, box 1, folder 5, American Antiquarian Society, Worcester, Mass.

36. For an excellent discussion of Maryland's particular circumstances relating to free black labor, see Fields, *Slavery*, and Berlin, *Slaves*.

37. Sanborn, "Harriet Tubman." See also Sanborn, "The Late Araminta Davis."

38. Sanborn, "Harriet Tubman"; Bradford, *Scenes*, 75.

39. Sanborn, "The Late Araminta Davis." According to Sanborn, after Harriet married John Tubman she left her parents' home and moved in with him, even though they "had different masters." See also the U.S. Census for 1840. Ben Ross is listed in the Dorchester County Census, Parsons Creek District, p. 5. In his household there are six free blacks: one male under ten years, two males between ten and twenty-four, one male between thirty-six and fifty-five, one female between twenty-four and thirty-five, and one female between thirty-six and fifty-five. While all these people are shown as free, they may in fact not be. This error was made in several instances in this census year. The older man is most certainly Ben; the older woman is probably Rit. The youngest child may be Moses, and the other three may be Ben and Rit's children, perhaps Henry and Ben and Harriet or one of her older sisters, Linah or Soph. Henry and Ben may have been working for Stewart as well. Edward Brodess is listed in the census, p. 12, with only three slaves on his property, one male between ten and twenty-four and two females between ten and twenty-four. Oral tradition also suggests that Harriet and John Tubman lived together at one point near or on the current Malone's Church property on White Marsh Road (personal communication with John Creighton, referring to his interview with elder Walter Ross in Madison in the mid-1980s). This church was built in 1864 on land deeded to the black community in 1862.

40. The fates of Sam, Frederick, and Shadrach, slaves owned by Edward's father, Joseph, and mentioned in Anthony Thompson's guardian's account book for 1821 and 1822, are unknown. As with Linah and Soph, perhaps Brodess also sold them out of the state to distant relatives or to a trader for sale to the Deep South.

41. Bill of complaint, May 12, 1852, for reference to the sale of Linah and her child, see Equity Papers 249, MDSA. At least two other children were left behind: Kessiah Jolley Bowley and possibly her sister Harriet. Whether they were the children of Linah or Soph is not known, though it seems likely that Kessiah was the child of Linah, and perhaps Harriet might have been the child of Soph, though no records have surfaced to indicate this to be true.

42. "Interview with James Seward," in Benjamin Drew, *The Refugee: A North-Side View of Slavery* (1855; reprint, Tilden G. Edelstein, ed., Reading, Mass.: Addison-Wesley Publishing Co., 1969), 27–28.

43. Testimony of Polish Mills, Equity Papers 249, MDSA. No record of the sale of Linah or Soph has been found either in the Dorchester, Talbot, or Caroline County records. Even if Brodess had sold them to relatives then living in Mississippi, Alabama, or Georgia, the transaction would have been illegal. Ben, Rit, and their son Henry all thought Linah and Soph had been sold to Georgia. See "Henry Stewart" in John W. Blassingame, ed., *Slave Testimony: Two Centuries of Letters, Speeches, Interviews, and Autobiographies* (Baton Rouge: Louisiana State University Press, 1977), 414, and "James Seward," in Drew, *The Refugee*, 27–28. Also, in December 1842 the sheriff of Dorchester County, William B. Dail, under order from the Dorchester County Court, ordered a sale of the majority of Brodess's assets, including approximately 270 acres of land, his home, several farm animals, and one slave, "Ben, 19 years old." See the *Cambridge Chronicle*, Cambridge, Md., December 24, 1842. Edward

Brodess and his cousin Richard Pattison were being sued. Brodess did not lose his property at this time, presumably because the suit was dropped and/or payment was made to satisfy the litigants in the case. This may coincide with the sale of Linah, who was probably being held in the local jail with her brother Henry as surety for Brodess's unpaid debts.

44. Sanborn, "The Late Araminta Davis." John D. Parker had probably been hired as an overseer by Anthony Thompson during the 1830s. An aging Thompson, with hundreds of acres of agricultural lands and vast tracts of timber in addition to well over thirty slaves, probably needed the assistance of someone younger to manage his property and slaves. Though Ben Ross was considered a supervisor or foreman for Thompson's timber business, Thompson's large landholdings and large slave population probably required the employ of a professional overseer. When Thompson died in 1836, John D. Parker apparently remained on the property, continuing to manage the plantation operations for Dr. Anthony C. Thompson and his brother Dr. Absalom Thompson. John D. Parker purchased some of Thompson's property from the estate in 1837, and then several more parcels of the Thompson property from the heirs of Joseph Stewart (who had purchased large parcels of Thompson's property in 1837) during the late 1840s. He also began acquiring slaves of his own. Parker continued to farm this property over the next couple of decades, and he probably continued to employ many of the former slaves and free blacks who worked on Thompson's property, much as Joseph Stewart did when he purchased parts of Anthony Thompson's plantation. Parker would remain intimately connected to the extended Ross family and other free and enslaved black families in this area throughout the 1840s, 1850s, and 1860s.

45. Drake, "The Moses of Her People." In fact, when Harriet was required to "draw a loaded stone boat," she was probably using a sleigh of sorts called a stone boat, which was used to haul hay and other agricultural produce in the fields. A stone boat could also be a flat-bottomed canal boat, used to transport goods through shallow, narrow canals. Alternatively, the only known stone in Dorchester County would have been ballast from the holds of ships.

46. W. Jeffrey Bolster, *Black Jacks: African American Seamen in the Age of Sail* (Cambridge, Mass.: Harvard University Press, 1997), 39–41.

47. He would have needed a Certificate of Freedom once he was freed, however, if he were to travel to Baltimore. Though no such recorded certificate has been found for Ben, this does not preclude the existence of one. He was a familiar face to workers on the waterfront in Dorchester County and probably the waterfront in Baltimore, and he may have been able to safely travel back and forth without being challenged by white authorities. There is no evidence, though, to support this possibility.

48. See Bolster, *Black Jacks;* David S. Cecelski, *The Waterman's Song: Slavery and Freedom in Maritime North Carolina* (Chapel Hill: The University of North Carolina Press, 2001); and Julius Sherrard Scott III, "The Common Wind: Currents of Afro-American Communication in the Era of the Haitian Revolution," Ph.D. dissertation, Duke University, 1986.

49. See Scott, "Common Wind."

50. Ibid., 18. See also Fields, *Slavery.*

51. "William Cornish. Interviewed, 1863, Canada," in John W. Blassingame, ed., *Slave Testimony: Two Centuries of Letters, Speeches, Interviews, and Autobiographies* (Baton Rouge: Louisiana State University Press, 1977). William was a foreman much like Ben Ross. Cornish had long been eager to run away, but his close familial and community relationships made him hesitate to flee when he had opportunities. However, Thomas Dail died in May 1853, throwing the estate into turmoil. William had always understood that he would be set free, but the will did not provide for his manumission. William took matters into his own hands and ran away in 1856. Ben Ross and his family would have known William Cornish and his family.

52. See Scott, "Common Wind"; Bolster, *Black Jacks;* Cecelski, *Waterman's Song.*

53. Thompson's sons Anthony C. Thompson and Absalom Thompson were the major beneficiaries of

his estate. Thompson also gifted property to a William W. Thompson (relationship unknown), and money to his niece Barsheba Thompson (parentage unknown). There is some speculation that William may have been an illegitimate son and Barsheba a granddaughter, possibly the daughter of another son, Edward, who may have died.

54. Last Will and Testament of Anthony Thompson, Register of Wills, Dorchester County courthouse, Estate no. 0-65-C, Cambridge, Md. See also "List of Anthony Thompson's Negroes, 1839"; and McGill, transcr., *Certificates of Freedom.*

55. Ibid.

56. McGill, transcr., *Certificates of Freedom;* and also, for example, "Anthony C. Thompson to Sundry Negroes," Dorchester County Chattel Records 1851–1860, MDSA.

57. No sale of a slave owned by Anthony Thompson during his lifetime has been found.

58. Thompson provided for Ben's freedom five years after Thompson's death. Anthony Thompson died in 1836, and therefore Ben would have been freed in 1841.

59. Will of Anthony Thompson.

60. Interestingly, Anthony Thompson's son, Dr. Absalom Thompson, manumitted most of his slaves in his own last will and testament, written a month before his death in October 1842. Through staggered manumission schedules, Absalom arranged for the eventual freedom of most of his enslaved labor, as his father had done before him. Absalom also bequeathed a home and money to Elizabeth More, a black woman who was probably Thompson's mistress, and he also provided for "a suitable English Education" for Mary Ann and James, More's (and possibly Thompson's) children. What became of Elizabeth More and her children is unknown. See Last Will and Testament of Absalom Thompson, Talbot County Register of Wills, C1925, 1-43-4-27, MDSA, 241–45.

61. Will of Anthony Thompson. According to the 1840 census, Jerry Manokey and Polly were between the ages of fifty-five and one hundred. Their youngest daughters, Mary (about eight years old) and Susan (about ten years old), are listed in this household. They are definitely not free, as Dr. Thompson sells Susan on April 22, 1847, to William V. M. Edmundson for $200. Anthony C. Thompson to Wm. V. M. Edmundson, Chattel Records, WJ2, I C691, MDSA. Tragically, Edmundson sold Susan to Margaret Tindle, the wife of a slave trader. Miles Tindle was taken to court for selling Susan out of the state illegally. See Dorchester County Circuit Court Docket, April 1851, Appearance #7. Once Thompson had sold Susan the first time, he lost any control he had over her fate. While he may not have anticipated Susan's eventual sale to a trader, one does wonder why he sold her in the first place.

62. Will of Anthony Thompson.

63. Thompson did not, however, bequeath ownership of the land to Jerry Manokey and Ben Ross, as he did with his own sons. The land was only available to them during their lifetimes, no longer. It is very unclear how this arrangement worked once Thompson's land was sold off to other parties after his death. Joseph Stewart, for instance, purchased several parcels of Thompson's property at Peters Neck in 1837. The deed specifically mentions "old Ben's house" as part of the description of the property, but it makes no reference to allowing Ben to continue living on the property and cutting timber for his own use. See Deed. According to the 1840 U.S. census for Dorchester County, Ben Ross and Jerry Manokey are both listed as living in the same area as Thompson's former plantation, surrounded by other free black households, some of which were also listed in the 1830 U.S. census.

64. The reason for this is unclear. Thompson was very specific about his manumissions. Ben was to be free five years after Thompson's death, which would have placed his liberation sometime during 1841. But according to Dr. Anthony C. Thompson's records (Anthony Thompson's List of Slaves), Ben was to be manumitted in April in 1840.

65. Thompson's will specified that Dr. Anthony C. Thompson hire out the slaves "at the customary wagers [sic] of the county," giving one-third of the proceeds to Dr. Absalom Thompson.

66. See Samuel and Edward Harrington from James A. Stewart, Dorchester County Land Records,

69 3WJ 53, June 22, 1846, which details the sale of former Thompson property, including 192 acres "now occupied by Mr. Parker, down by old Ben's"; see also Samuel and Edward Harrington from James A. Stewart, 69 3WJ 492.

67. See Anthony Thompson's List of Slaves. Maria and Isaac Bailey eventually had eight children and lived in the Bucktown area. The small sum of $10 is quite puzzling, even if Aaron was disabled and Maria unproductive. Ben could have possibly traded his tenancy rights to the ten acres Anthony Thompson had provided for him in his will for Maria and Aaron's freedom. Dr. Thompson and Absalom C. C. Thompson were eager to divest themselves of their inherited lands—this may have been an incentive to Ben to give up his rights to a small part of it. The very same day that Ben purchased Maria and Aaron from Dr. Thompson, he manumitted them. See Dorchester County Chattel Records, Ben Ross from Anthony C. Thompson, June 18, 1842, 519.

68. Bureau of the Census, *United States Federal Census,* 1850, Dorchester County, Md.

69. See Anthony Thompson's List of Slaves.

70. William Still, *The Underground Railroad* (1871; reprint, Chicago: Johnson Publishing Company, 1970), 411.

71. See Bureau of the Census, *U.S. Federal Census,* 1850, Caroline County, Md. Edward Thompson, age twenty, is listed with twenty-one male slaves working in the timbering operation, and in his household there are seven white males, five of whom are "sailors." Edward also had three adult female slaves and three juvenile male slaves at his residence.

72. This property in Cambridge, fourteen and a half acres on the outskirts of Cambridge on Pine Street, also had two slave houses on the property. See 1850 U.S. census, Dorchester County; Assessment Record, Dorchester County Board of County Commissioners, MDSA. The records of where Dr. Thompson's slave women were living have not been found; therefore, we do not know where they lived.

73. For instance, see the *Cambridge Chronicle* for Thompson's advertisements for Thompson's Vegetable Worm Syrup and Thompson's Vegetable Anti-bilious Pills throughout the 1830s and 1840s. On May 1, 1847, Dr. Thompson notified his clients that he was no longer practicing medicine in Cambridge. Thompson was obviously turning his attention to his growing Poplar Neck timber and agricultural venture.

74. See *Cambridge Chronicle.*

75. According to Frank Sanborn, "Harriet Tubman," Harriet spent her last two years in slavery with Dr. Thompson. The 1850 U.S. Census for Caroline County indicates that the great majority of Thompson slaves living and working at Poplar Neck are men. Where his female slaves were living and working remains a mystery. Tubman could have been working for Thompson at his Caroline County property, and her husband John could have been working for Thompson as well, but no records exist to confirm such a possibility.

76. Or, alternatively, Brodess refused to sell any of his slaves to Thompson because of an ongoing feud.

77. Bradford, *Scenes,* 14.

78. Ibid., 14 " 'Pears like I prayed all de time,' said Harriet; 'bout my work, everywhere, I prayed an' I groaned to de Lord. When I went to de horse-trough to wash my face, I took up de water in my han' an' I said, 'Oh Lord, wash me, make me clean!' Den I take up something to wipe my face, an' I say, 'Oh Lord, wipe away all my sin!' When I took de broom and began to sweep, I groaned, 'Oh Lord, wha'-soebber sin dere be in my heart, sweep it out, Lord, clar an' clean!' "

79. Ibid., 14–15. "I prayed all night long for master, till the first of March; an' all the time he was bringing people to look at me, an' trying to sell me. Den we heard dat some of us was gwine to be sole to go wid de chain-gang down to de cotton an' rice fields, and dey said I was gwine, an' my brudders, an' sisters. Den I changed my prayer. Fust of March I began to pray, 'Oh Lord, if you ant nebber gwine to change dat man's heart, kill him, Lord, an' take him out ob de way.' "

80. Ibid., 15. "Nex' ting I heard old master was dead, an' he died jus' as he libed. Oh, then, it 'peared like I'd give all de world full ob gold, if I had it, to bring dat poor soul back. But I couldn't pray for him no longer."

81. Dorchester County Orphans Court, Orphans Court Records, vol. T.H.H. 1, Cambridge, Md., 150.

82. Estate Papers of Edward Brodess, #0–482, Dorchester County Register of Wills, Cambridge, Md.

83. John W. Blassingame, ed., *Slave Testimony: Two Centuries of Letters, Speeches, Interviews, and Auto-biographies* (Baton Rouge: Louisiana State University Press, 1977), 415–16. Sarah Bradford wrote that they only believed that they were not to be sold out of the State of Maryland; *Scenes*, 15. Who informed them of this, or more important, how they came to believe this is not known, as Brodess's last will and testament burned in the county courthouse fire in 1852.

84. Blassingame, ed., *Slave Testimony*. See also Sarah H. Bradford, *Harriet, the Moses of Her People* (New York: Geo. R. Lockwood & Sons, 1886): "The word passed through the cabins that another owner was coming in, and that none of the slaves were to be sold out of the State. This assurance satisfied the others, but it did not satisfy Harriet" (25).

85. Bradford, *Scenes*, 107–8. "Twenty-three years ago, in Maryland, I paid a lawyer $5 to look up the will of my mother's first master. He looked back sixty years, and said it was time to give up. I told him to go back furder. He went back sixty-five years, and there he found the will—giving the girl Ritty to his grand-daughter (Mary Patterson), to serve her and her offspring till she was forty-five years of age. This grand-daughter died soon after, unmarried; and as there was no provision for Ritty, in case of her death, she was actually emancipated at that time. But no one informed her of the fact, and she and her dear children remained in bondage." Written in 1791, and probated in 1797 when Pattison died, the will devised multiple acres of Dorchester County land, livestock, furniture, and slaves to his surviving children and grandchildren. Will of Atthow Pattison, Est. #0-35-E, Dorchester County courthouse, Registrar of Wills, Cambridge, Md.

86. Will of Atthow Pattison.

87. Dr. Anthony C. Thompson speculated that Rit probably gave birth to her last child, Moses, after she had turned forty-five, making Moses freeborn. See Thompson Deposition, Equity Papers 249, MDSA.

88. Slaveowners could petition the court to allow such transactions, though there is no record of Brodess applying for a waiver of this law. Only the sale of one of these children, Rhody or Mariah Ritty, was recorded. See Edward Brodess to Dempsey P. Kane, vol. Liber 9 ER 624, July 1825, p. 625, Dorchester County Land Records, MDSA. See also Jeffrey R. Brackett, *The Negro in Maryland. A Study of the Institution of Slavery* (1889; reprint, New York: Negro Universities Press, 1969), 61. In 1796 Maryland passed a law making it illegal for "anyone who might transport, knowingly, from the State, and sell as a slave for life, any black entitled to freedom at any age" (60).

89. According to Maryland laws, passed in 1790, slaveholders were allowed to manumit their slaves by will with no restrictions as to when the will had to be written. Prior to this date, slaveholders could not manumit slaves by will unless the will was written at least three months prior to the testator's death. In 1796 the law was amended to reduce the age at which slaves could be manumitted, from age fifty to forty-five. Atthow Pattison's will satisfied all those legal requirements; he died six years after he wrote his will, and provided for manumission at age forty-five, thereby precluding any question as to the legality of his last will and testament. See Brackett, *Negro in Maryland*, 151–53.

90. Elizabeth Pattison's children were Gourney Crow Pattison, James Pattison, Elizabeth, Mary, and Achsah.

91. Orphans Court Records, Dorchester County Orphans Court, July-August 1849, T.H.H. 1, Dorchester County Registrar of Wills, Cambridge, Md., 162–65. The real motivations for this legal action remain shrouded in mystery. The value of Rit's labor was inconsequential, as was the value of the labor of any of her children who were then forty-five years old or older. Why pursue this legal battle in court, at considerable cost to both parties? Gourney Crow Pattison was in fact living in Baltimore at this time; he had sold most of his inherited land and moved to Baltimore ten years earlier. Why did

he return to Dorchester County to press this small claim? There may be several possibilities. A long-standing feud with Brodess may have forced this issue, particularly after Edward died and Eliza was preparing to sell several of Rit's children. But the "residue" that would have been generated from Rit's labor, divided among the many heirs then at law in 1849, would have meant very, very small sums to each individual, which would seem even more inconsequential when factoring in the enormous legal fees generated by the lawsuit and the ensuing work to untangle the specific shares each heir was enti-tled to. A second possibility is that James A. Stewart, one of Dorchester County's most prominent lawyers and a legislator, may have initiated this lawsuit on behalf of Gourney Crow Pattison and the other Pattison heirs for political or personal reasons of his own. Brodess was not a rich man, nor even a middle-class one, and it is likely he and Stewart did not even travel in the same social circles. Was there a personal issue between them of some sort? We may never know. In 1852, however, when the lawsuit continued its path through the courts, James A. Stewart bought the rights and title to Rit and her chil-dren from the Pattison heirs for a paltry $105—indicating perhaps some confidence the court would find in his client's favor. It would seem, then, that this issue was becoming personal. What would Stew-art want with an aged slave woman? This will be discussed further later in this chapter.

92. At the time of Edward Brodess's death, his surviving children were John E., age twenty-two; Joseph, twenty; William Richard, eighteen; Charles, fifteen; Benjamin B., thirteen; Thomas J., eleven; Mary Ann Elizabeth, nine; and Henrietta Mariah, six.

93. Orphans Court Records, Dorchester County Orphans Court, July-August 1849, T.H.H. 1, Dor-chester County Registrar of Wills, Cambridge, Md., 150.

94. Equity Papers 394, Dorchester County Circuit Court, MDSA. In 1855 Eliza Brodess filed suit against John Mills, claiming that he had failed in his responsibility as administrator of her deceased husband's estate, and that he had withheld money obtained through selling various slaves owned by her. Be-cause both Mills and Eliza Brodess died during the next couple of years, their estates continued the court fight. In 1859 Mills's brother, Polish, responded in court that Eliza had been indebted to John for $1,000, of which $230 to $240 plus interest was still owed Mills's estate.

95. Announcement by Elizabeth Brodess about "Negro for Sale," *Cambridge Democrat*, Cambridge, Md., June 27, 1849.

96. Ibid.

97. Announcement by Jonathan Mills about "Negro for Sale," *Cambridge Democrat*, Cambridge, Md., Sept. 5, 1849.

98. Ibid.

99. Orphans Court Records, Dorchester County Orphans Court, September 17, 1849, T.H.H. 1, Dor-chester County Registrar of Wills, Cambridge, Md., 172.

100. Kessiah Jolley was married to John Bowley, who had been manumitted by Levin Stewart's heirs several years earlier. Kessiah's father was Harkless Jolley, who was enslaved by Ann Stapleford Mar-tin Grieves. Grieves also owned the wives of Bill Banks and Isaac Kiah, both Thompson slaves. Linah is most likely Kessiah's mother. One of Kessiah's daughters may have been named Linah, and she named one son Harkless. See 1861 Canadian Census, Chatham, Ontario. See also Last Will and Testa-ment of Kessiah Bowley, April 30, 1888, Registrar of Wills, Dorchester County courthouse, Cam-bridge, Md.

101. Orphans Court Records, Dorchester County Orphans Court, September 17, 1849, T.H.H. 1, Dor-chester County Registrar of Wills, Cambridge, Md., 172.

102. Ibid., October 24, 1849, 177.

103. Major Bowley to John Bowley, Richard Bowley, John T. Stewart. Straw Mile Wharf was owned by John T. Stewart. 62–63.

104. Orphans Court Records, Dorchester County Orphans Court, October 24, 1849, T.H.H. 1, Dor-chester County Registrar of Wills, Cambridge, Md., 177. No documentation exists detailing this Har-riet's relationship to the Ross family. However, because Soph left two children behind when she was

sold, and this Harriet was sold until she reached the age of forty-five, it seems likely that she is the granddaughter of Ben and Rit. Eliza Brodess's own slaves, which she brought from her family (the Keenes), were all slaves for life.

105. Thomas Willis from John Mills and Eliza Brodess, Liber WJ no. 3, p. 259, MDSA. The name of the child has changed, although there it is the same person. This occurred quite often in local and county court records—in the recording and transcription process names and other details were often changed, particularly when slaves were involved.

106. William O. Cooper and Samuel Dunnock from Eliza Brodess, Liber WJ, no. 3, p. 286, MDSA. She sold Dawes to William Cooper and Samuel Dunnock for $300. Dawes Keene was most likely one of the slaves Eliza was given or inherited from her father, John Keene. Though a member of Tubman's extended household, he was more than likely not a blood relative.

107. There is no record of a court order authorizing the sale of "Minty," as Tubman was then known, by the Brodesses.

108. Notice of reward placed by Eliza Ann Brodess, *Cambridge Democrat*, Cambridge, Md., October 3, 1849. Interestingly, the advertisement was placed sixteen days after Harriet and her brothers ran away.

109. Ibid.

110. Ibid. Interestingly, Brodess requested that the advertisement be copied to the Wilmington, Delaware, newspaper, showing knowledge of a known route out of slavery from the Eastern Shore.

111. Bradford, *Scenes*, 16; Interview with Helen W. Tatlock [Mrs. William Tatlock], Earl Conrad/ Harriet Tubman Collection, New York Public Library, Schomburg Center for Research in Black Culture. Bradford wrote that Harriet left first with three of her brothers; Tatlock told Conrad that she recalled Tubman telling her she fled first with two of her brothers. The runaway advertisement confirms Tatlock's version of the story.

112. Bradford, *Scenes*, 16.

113. Ben's marital status is unknown, although he may have been the father of two young boys, Ben and David Ross, whose mother remains unidentified. John D. Parker from Benjamin Ross, Dorchester County Chattel Records 1851–1860, MDSA; John D. Parker from David Ross, Dorchester County Chattel Records, MDSA. Robert's wife was Mary Manokey, and she was enslaved by Dr. Anthony Thompson. Henry's wife was Harriet Ann (last name undetermined); her status as a slave or free woman is unknown.

114. Sanborn, "The Late Araminta Davis."

115. Tatlock interview.

116. Sanborn, "Harriet Tubman." See also as printed in Bradford, *Scenes*, 76; and Tatlock interview.

117. Tatlock interview.

118. The location on the Choptank River was ideally suited to Thompson's plans; he could ship out timber from the mouth of Marshy Creek, where there appears to have been a wharf, providing Thompson with the ability to export his timber once it had been felled and cut into boards, staves, and shingles. Living with Thompson's son Edward, in the "big house," were six white sailors, one black laborer, three female slaves, and three male children, also slaves. Edward also controlled more than twenty-one male slaves who were then timbering Thompson's land. These men probably lived and worked in the interior of the Thompson property, in small tents and cabins, in the area of present-day Haverford Camp Road in the Marshy Creek area.

119. Announcement by Jonathan Mills about "Negro for Sale," *Cambridge Democrat*, Cambridge, Md., Sept. 5, 1849.

120. Dr. Anthony C. Thompson was also a Methodist minister, and he may have had a small church built on his property in Caroline County (or it may have already been there when he purchased the property) for the convenience of preaching to his enslaved people.

121. Kenneth Carroll, *Quakerism on the Eastern Shore* (Baltimore: Maryland Historical Society, 1970), 132–38.

122. Ibid.

123. U.S. Census, 1850, Dorchester County, Maryland, District 1, p. 429. Thompson also owned a 450-acre farm in the area of Cordtown, slightly east of Cambridge. It is believed that Thompson did not live at this farm, but rather rented it out or had a hired manager run it.

124. William T. Kelley, "Underground R. R. Reminiscences [April 2, 1898]," *Friends' Intelligencer,* April 2, 1898, 238. Noted Quaker abolitionist Francis Corchran and his family, for instance, left Dorchester County during the 1830s and 1840s to live in Baltimore, where antislavery opinions were more actively, though cautiously, expressed.

125. Tatlock interview.

126. The exact identity or relationship of Mary to Tubman is not clear. It is not known whether this Mary is the same Mary who was living in Ben and Rit's house on Dr. Thompson's property at Poplar Neck in 1850, or another member of Thompson's slave community. Without knowing her age, it may not be possible to know who this Mary is.

127. Bradford, *Scenes,* 17–19.

128. In 1865, Edna Cheney described Tubman as singing her farewell song as "she passed through the street." The use of the word *street* may have some significance, although we may never know. It is likely that the use of the word *street* implies a well-traveled and probably cobblestoned lane in a city such as Cambridge, as opposed to the dirt roads and paths in a more remote area such as Poplar Neck, or it may be that Cheney used the word without any thought to its implications. Unfortunately, the majority of Thompson's female slaves are unaccounted for in the 1850 census, so we cannot be sure as to where Tubman would have most likely been living. It is not known where John Tubman was living at this time, or whether Harriet was living with or near him at the time she fled, although according to Bradford, Harriet's husband "did his best to betray her, and bring her back after she escaped." Bradford, *Scenes,* 15. John Tubman could have hired himself out to Dr. Thompson in Caroline County as well. One final clue may rest with Bradford. She wrote in the her first Tubman biography that when Harriet returned to the Eastern Shore to bring away her brothers during Christmas 1854 and New Year's 1855, they hid in the corn crib near Ben and Rit's cabin at Dr. Thompson's Poplar Neck farm; "Harriet had not seen her mother there for six years." Bradford, *Scenes,* 60. This would approximately coincide with her running away in the fall of 1849.

129. Cheney, "Moses," 35.

130. Tatlock interview. The identities of these people remain unknown. Tatlock told Earl Conrad that Tubman told her the name of the first woman who helped her, but that she had, unfortunately, forgotten it.

131. Kelley, "Underground R. R. Reminiscences," 238, 265. Jacob Leverton was sued for aiding a young slave woman who had run from her master after he beat her. This young woman fled north, and Jacob was immediately suspected. He "lost two farms" settling the lawsuit against him. See also Carroll, *Quakerism.* Tubman may also have been helped by Jonah Kelley and his family, who were then living in Preston, Caroline County.

132. Debra Smith Moxey, *Newspaper Abstracts from the American Eagle and Cambridge Chronicle 1846–1857* (Cambridge, Md.: Debra Smith Moxey, 1995). See page 47 for Jacob Leverton's death; see also Kelley, "Underground R. R. Reminiscences," 265; and Carroll, *Quakerism,* 142.

133. Mary Elizabeth Leverton was "disowned" by the local Quaker meeting in 1850 for several reasons. She was lax in her attendance at the Friends meetings, she married a non-Quaker, and when she moved from the area they struck her from their membership lists. Mary Elizabeth and Anthony Thompson moved to Anne Arundel County in early 1850, where Anthony became a merchant, though they did return within a couple of years to Dorchester County. See U.S. Census, 1850, Anne Arundel County, Md.

134. Bradford, *Scenes,* 19. "When I found I had crossed dat *line,*" she said, "I looked at my hands to see if I was de same pusson. There was such a glory ober ebery ting; de sun came like gold through the trees, and ober the fields, and I felt like I was in Heaben."

Chapter 5

1. Barbara Jeanne Fields, *Slavery and Freedom on the Middle Ground* (New Haven: Yale University Press, 1985), 16–17. There may be several reasons for the understatement of fugitives. Many slaveholders expected to find their runaway slaves, or assumed that the slaves would return of their own volition. Eliza Brodess, for instance, did not report any slaves as fugitives in the 1850 census. Also, many slaveholders knew that any indication that slaves were not happy was an indictment of the system of slavery itself and reflected badly on the slaveholders' own contention that slavery was a benevolent and beneficial system for the slaves themselves.

2. *Cambridge Chronicle*, Cambridge, Md. January 2, 1847, 3.

3. Ibid. September 4, 1847, 2.

4. "Runaways," *Easton Star*, Easton, Md., August 14, 1849.

5. "A Stampede," *Easton Star*, Easton, Md., October 24, 1849.

6. "Cost of Trial," *Baltimore Sun*, Baltimore, Md., December 7, 1849.

7. There is a significant historiography on the Underground Railroad (URR), though much of it reflects the many myths and mysteries perpetuated over the past 150 years. Oral traditions have dominated the history of the URR, particularly those of white Quakers and other white participants (real and imagined) in the system. Black participation has, until fairly recently, been mostly ignored. There are several reasons for this: Many white participants viewed their participation as heroic and worthy of public commendation, while many black participants viewed it as a community obligation. Many URR operatives in the slave states were free blacks and slaves, thereby precluding any acknowledgement of their participation before the Civil War, and even after—the fear of reprisals was great (the same could be said of southern white agents, too). Black participation in the North was rarely documented—in a racist and white-dominated world, blacks rarely had the opportunity to tell their histories or record them for the general public. There are exceptions. A particularly important and classic volume is *The Underground Railroad* (Philadelphia: Porter and Coates, 1872) by William Still, who documented not only his own important role in Philadelphia's URR network but also many other black agents' roles in the functioning and success of its operations. Numerous escape narratives speak of those nameless black people who helped their freedom-bound brothers and sisters north, including those by Frederick Douglass, Harriet Tubman, Harriet Jacobs, William Wells Brown, William and Ellen Craft, and others like them. R. C. Smedley wrote extensively on the URR network in Chester and its border counties in Pennsylvania in *The History of The Underground Railroad in Chester and Neighboring Counties of Pennsylvania* (Lancaster, Pa.: Office of the Journal, 1883). Focusing primarily on the white participants, Smedley ignored some of the important black partners active on this route to freedom. At the end of the nineteenth century, Wilbur Siebert, a professor of history at Ohio State University, and later at Harvard, wrote his classic contribution to the historiography of the Underground Railroad in *The Underground Railroad from Slavery to Freedom* (New York: Macmillan, 1898). Siebert interviewed and corresponded with many aging abolitionists and URR operators, and members of their families, and conducted extensive research into the operations of the system throughout the country. Though Siebert did uncover and acknowledge the participation of blacks as operatives in the network to freedom, their numbers pale in comparison to the legions of white people he identified. Siebert also misidentifies some black individuals as white. Throughout this whole period, postemancipation through the turn of the twentieth century, aging abolitionists wrote their memoirs and reminiscences, documenting their own roles in the antislavery movement and the URR, often obscuring the contributions of their black coworkers. Larry Gara, in *The Liberty Line: The Legend of the Underground Railroad* (Lexington: University of Kentucky Press, 1961), questioned the Quaker- and white-abolitionist-dominated histories, arguing that slaves themselves were far more responsible for taking their own liberty successfully; they often depended on white help after they reached the North. Gara argued that not all abolitionists were interested in help-

ing freedom seekers and that runaways were often left to their own devices to secure shelter and food even after they made their way to a free state. To a far greater degree than any other scholarship on the URR, his work credits black communities in the North with helping runaway slaves, but his sweeping dismissal of the numbers of runaways claimed to have fled to freedom on the URR, his dismissal of the idea that the URR was organized and efficient, and his assertion that the reminiscences of abolitionists were faulty and not reliable overshadowed his other contributions to the study of the URR. James A. McGowan wrote about the life of white Quaker abolitionist Thomas Garrett in *Station Master on the Underground Railroad: The Life and Letters of Thomas Garrett* (Moylan, Pa.: Whimsie Press, 1977), highlighting the important role Thomas Garrett played on the URR. McGowan reveals that, in spite of his own reservations about Garrett's claims to have assisted 2,700 slaves over a forty-year period, the documentary evidence supports Garrett's place in the pantheon of great URR operators. Garrett could not have been such a successful URR operator without the organizational and financial support he received from the region's vast URR network, which included many nameless agents, black and white. Benjamin Quarles's work *Black Abolitionists* (New York: Oxford University Press, 1969) expanded the scholarship on black participation, not only as URR operators but also as antislavery activists and founders of numerous black political, humanitarian, educational, and economic organizations and institutions vital to the survival of black communities and their sheltered runaways. Charles Blockson's contributions to the study of the URR have challenged the dominant white-centered model and have expanded our knowledge of the multitudes of forgotten narratives of runaway slaves and free black helpers who populated the URR, from Louisiana to Canada (see Charles L. Blockson, *The Underground Railroad: Dramatic Firsthand Accounts of Daring Escapes to Freedom* [New York: Berkley Books, 1987]). Many regional studies are being conducted by scholars and local researchers who are methodically piecing together URR stories, separating fact from fiction and discovering previously hidden and obscured histories of important participants on the road to freedom. Judith Wellman has done extensive work on the URR in central New York; Milton Sernett's *North Star Country* (Syracuse: Syracuse University Press, 2002) also focuses on the extensive abolitionist and URR networks in this region, highlighting the important synergies of an unusual group of whites and blacks working to end slavery and help runaway slaves find safety and security in New York and Canada. In her study of New Bedford, Massachusetts' fugitive slave and abolitionist community, *The Fugitive's Gibraltar: Escaping Slaves and Abolitionism in New Bedford, Massachusetts* (Amherst: University of Massachusetts Press, 2001), Kathryn Grover highlights many of the region's heretofore lost and obscured histories. One of the most recent and important regional studies, *Just Over the Line: Chester County and the Underground Railroad* (West Chester, Pa.: Chester County Historical Society, 2002), by William Kashatus, covers much of the URR route activity and activists with whom Harriet Tubman was most intimately involved in Pennsylvania. The opening of the Underground Railroad Museum in Cincinnati, Ohio, in 2004 will certainly spawn more detailed and continuing research on the operations of the URR.

8. John Hope Franklin and Loren Schweninger, *Runaway Slaves: Rebels on the Plantation* (New York: Oxford University Press, 1999), 149–81.

9. Sarah H. Bradford, *Scenes in the Life of Harriet Tubman* (Auburn, N.Y.: W. J. Moses, 1869), 20.

10. Ibid., 20–22; see also Ednah Dow Littlehale Cheney, "Moses," *Freedmen's Record,* March 1865, 35.

11. "Siebert interview with Harriet Tubman," in "The Underground Railroad: Manuscript Materials Collected by Professor Siebert, Ohio University," vol. 40, Houghton Library, Harvard University, Cambridge, Mass. Although Siebert indicated that Harriet referred to Tom as her "cousin," Tom was in fact John Tubman's brother and thus was Harriet's brother-in-law.

12. Louis Diggs, Baltimore City Directories, 1835–1860.

13. Mills Deposition, Equity Papers 249, MDSA.

14. Harkless Bowley to Earl Conrad, August 8, 1939, Harkless Bowley Letters, Earl Conrad/Harriet Tubman Collection, New York Public Library, Schomburg Center for Research in Black Culture. New York.

15. Ibid. See also Equity Papers 394, Dorchester County Circuit Court, MDSA. A log canoe was a common sailboat on the Chesapeake. It was generally constructed of three to five hollowed-out logs strapped together and fitted with a sail and a keel. Special thanks to Frank Newton, skipjack of the *Nathan of Dorchester*, and Harold Ruark, master ship modeler of Dorchester County, for explaining this type of vessel and its importance to travel throughout the Chesapeake.

16. Bellevue on the Tred Avon River in Talbot County is one such possibility.

17. Harkless Bowley to Earl Conrad, August 8, 1939. See also Franklin Sanborn, "Harriet Tubman," *The Commonwealth*, Boston, July 17, 1863. "In December, 1850, she had visited Baltimore and brought away her sister and two children, who had come up from Cambridge, in a boat, under the charge of her sister's husband, a free black." Sanborn was confused as to the exact relationship between Harriet and Kessiah, which was complicated by Harriet and Kessiah calling each other "sister." James A. Bowley, however, wrote in a letter sometime in 1868 that he was one of Tubman's "first passengers from the house of bondage." James A. Bowley to "Aunt" (Harriet Tubman), 1868, Harriet Tubman Collection. Harriet Tubman Home Museum. Auburn, N.Y.

18. Emma P. Telford, "Harriet: The Modern Moses of Heroism and Visions," Cayuga County Museum, Auburn, N.Y., c. 1905.

19. Cheney, "Moses," 35.

20. Her name may have been Caroline Jones, but the record remains unclear.

21. Cheney, "Moses," 35.

22. Ibid.

23. Sanborn, "Harriet Tubman"; Bradford, *Scenes*, 77.

24. Linda R. Monk, *The Words We Live By: Your Annotated Guide to the Constitution* (New York: Hyperion, 2003); C. Peter Ripley, ed., *The Black Abolitionist Papers* (Chapel Hill: University of North Carolina Press, 1991), vol. IV.

25. In 1851, in Christiana, Pennsylvania, a slave owner from Maryland and his son attempted to retrieve one of their runaway slaves. Black and white neighbors rioted, killing the father and wounding the son. Though some forty individuals were indicted for obstruction of federal law under the Fugitive Slave Act's terms, they were all acquitted. See also Ripley, ed., *Black Abolitionist Papers*, vol. IV, for information on various fugitive slave cases and rescues, including the Christiana riot.

26. Ripley, ed., *Black Abolitionist Papers*, II:9–10.

27. Sanborn, "Harriet Tubman." It is not clear which brother this was. This "brother" and his wife Sanborn mentions is not identified—he may be a fictive brother, a half brother, or some other relative. Or Sanborn could simply be mistaken. Sanborn may have been referring to John Bowley, Kessiah's husband, as Tubman referred to Kessiah as her sister. It could have been Moses and a wife, too. It is most likely that this person is actually not a blood brother but rather a fictive kin brother or some other male relative she referred to as her brother. We do know, however, that Moses ran away shortly after Tubman did, and that her three other known brothers, Robert, Ben, and Henry, ran away at Christmastime 1854. See Thompson Deposition, Equity Papers 249, MDSA.

28. By the fall of 1851 Tubman had brought away Kessiah, James and Araminta Bowley, her brother Moses and two unidentified men, and an unidentified number when she returned to Dorchester County for the first time in the fall of 1851. These individuals, taken collectively, and including Kessiah's husband, John, could have been the eleven fugitives Tubman brought to Canada in December. See Sanborn, "Harriet Tubman," and Bradford, *Scenes*, 77.

29. Frederick Douglass, *Life and Times of Frederick Douglass* (1882; reprint, Scituate, Mass.: Digital Scanning, Inc., 2001), 329–30.

30. Frederick Douglass, *Narrative of the Life of Frederick Douglass, an American Slave. Written by Himself*, ed. Benjamin Quarles (1845; reprint, Cambridge, Mass.: The Belknap Press, 1971), 101–2.

31. Ibid.

32. Ibid., 330. For detailed accounts of the the operations of the Underground Railroad in New York, see Sernett, *North Star Country*.

33. "Siebert interview with Harriet Tubman," in "The Underground Railroad: Manuscript Materials Collected by Professor Siebert," Houghton Library, Harvard University, Cambridge, Mass.

34. Ibid.

35. Douglass is known to have written specifically about Tubman only once. In a letter to Tubman, written at the request of Sarah Bradford for her first biography of Tubman in 1868, *Scenes in the Life of Harriet Tubman*, Douglass praised Tubman's many virtues and courageous acts. In one other surviving letter Douglass mentions Tubman but refers to her as a "colored woman, who escaped from slavery eight years ago, has made several returns at great risk, and has brought out, since obtaining her freedom, fifty others from the house of bondage. She has been spending a short time with us since the holidays." Letter to the Irish Ladies' Anti-Slavery Association, January 8, 1858, in *Frederick Douglass: Selected Speeches and Writings*, ed. Philip S. Foner (Chicago: Lawrence Hill Books, 1999), 600–1.

36. Douglass, *Narrative*, 57. This was in 1834. See Dickson J. Preston, *Young Frederick Douglass. The Maryland Years* (Baltimore: The Johns Hopkins University Press, 1980).

37. Douglass, *Narrative*, 77. This was in 1835–36. See also Preston, *Young Frederick Douglass*.

38. Douglass, *Narrative*.

39. See this exchange reprinted in Frederick Douglass, *My Bondage and My Freedom* (1855; reprint, New York: Dover Publications, Inc., 1969). See also Frederick Douglass, "Falsehood Refuted," *The North Star*, Rochester, N.Y., Oct. 13, 1848. Douglass reminded Thompson of the days they passed each other on the road near their homes at Bayside in Talbot County, "You remember when I used to meet you on the road to St. Michael's or near Mr. Covey's lane gate, I hardly dared lift my head, and look up at you. If I should meet you now . . . you would see a great change in me!" The exchange of letters first started with A. C. C. Thompson's letter to the *Delaware Republican*, early November 1845, which was reprinted in the *Liberator*, December 12, 1845, followed by a response by Douglass on February 20, 1846, and February 27, 1846; see also the *National Anti-Slavery Standard*, November 25, 1845, and the *Albany Patriot*, December 31, 1845. See also Preston, *Young Frederick Douglass*, 170–72; and Patricia J. Ferreira, "Frederick Douglass in Ireland: The Dublin Edition of His *Narrative*," *New Hibernia Review 5*, no. 1 (2001). In a very strange twist of fate, A. C. C. Thompson also ended up in New Bedford, Massachusetts, in 1841, to which Frederick Douglass had moved when he escaped slavery in 1838. Fortunately, Douglass had left the area earlier that summer, or they could have happened upon each other on the docks in New Bedford's busy waterfront. In early October 1841, twenty-year-old A. C. C. Thompson went to Baltimore with the express purpose of transacting some business for his father, Dr. Absalom Thompson. But the younger Thompson absconded with the $500 his father had entrusted to him, and made his way to New Bedford, where on November 11 he sailed out of Fair Haven on the whaling ship *Cadmus*, seeking adventure. Thompson got plenty of adventure when the ship foundered in the South Pacific, leaving the crew stranded on Tahiti for months. Dr. Absalom Thompson, however, had no idea what had become of his son, and he died one year later not knowing if his son was dead or alive. (See "A Mysterious Disappearance," *Delaware Republican*, Wilmington, October 8, 1841. I am indebted to Pat Lewis for bringing this article to my attention.) A. C. C. Thompson returned home in early 1843, many months after his father died. See Dickson J. Preston, "The Tale of Absalom Christopher Columbus Americus Vespucious Thompson," *The Banner*, Cambridge, Md., August 28, 1978; and A. C. C. Thompson, "The Log of a Talbot Seaman. Being a True Account of the Whaling Voyage and Shipwreck of the Author, Absalom Thompson, Born and Raised at 'Mary's Delight' in Bay Side," *Star Democrat*, Easton, Md., April 3, 10, 17, 24, and May 1, 1915.

40. See newspaper exchange in the *Liberator*, December 12, 1845, and February 20, 27, 1846. Thompson's support of Auld is quite weak in comparison to the other slaveholders who write in defending the characters of Auld, Covey, and others Douglass accuses of cruelty in his *Narrative*. In *Life and Times of*

Frederick Douglass, Douglass's later autobiography, he struggles with a more moderate view of Auld's treatment of him. See Douglass, *Life and Times of Frederick Douglass*. William McFeely argues that Douglass and Auld's relationship was far more complex than either of them acknowledged. See William S. McFeeley, *Frederick Douglass* (New York: W. W. Norton & Company, 1991), 294–95.

41. There are other links between the lives of these two famous former slaves from Dorchester County. Later, when Tubman helped her brothers and others run away in 1854, two of the men took aliases that coincidently figure into the lives of Douglass and these men. One runaway slave, John Chase, took the name Daniel Lloyd; the white Daniel Lloyd was the son of Edward Lloyd of Talbot County; as young boys, Douglass was Daniel's playmate, and Douglass would later remember him fondly. Douglass credited Lloyd with teaching him "good diction" in addition to sharing food, protecting him from bullies on the plantation, and keeping him informed of the activities in the big house. See Preston, *Young Frederick Douglass*. Another member of Tubman's party in 1854 was Peter Jackson, who took the alias Tench Tilghman, the name of a prominent and powerful land and slave owner in Talbot county. Although these slaves lived in Dorchester County, they chose names of prominent white men in the neighboring county, indicating a strong familiarity and relationship with people and places there.

For information about Isaac and Maria Bailey, see Debra Moxey, Dorchester County Historical Society, Vertical Files; U.S. Census, 1850.

42. Sanborn, "Harriet Tubman."

43. Ibid.

44. Ibid. The identities of these freedom seekers is not yet known.

45. "Progress in Maryland," *The National Era*, Washington, D.C., August 12, 1852; C. Christopher Brown, "Maryland's First Political Convention by and for Its Colored People," *Maryland Historical Society Magazine* 88, no. 3 (1993).

46. Announcements were made weekly in the Dorchester County newspapers for months for individuals to come forward with copies of their legal documents so that they could be reinscribed into courthouse files. "$1000 REWARD, BY THE AUTHORITY OF THE COUNTY COMMISSIONERS FOR DORCHESTER COUNTY will pay one thousand dollars reward to any individual or individuals, who may give information as may lead to the apprehension and conviction of the Incendiary or Incendiaries, who fired the court House on the 9th inst." *Cambridge Chronicle*, Cambridge, Md., May 22, 1852, 4.

47. Dorchester County Orphans Court Records, "T.H.H. 1," Register of Wills, Cambridge, Md., May 12, 1852.

48. Equity Papers 249, MDSA.

49. The bulk of this material forms another part of the crucial documentation relating to Harriet Tubman's family; Equity Papers 249, and a subsequent complaint filed by Eliza Brodess against her co-administrator, John Mills, Equity Papers 394, form the foundation of much of what is now known about Harriet Tubman and her family and the white families who claimed ownership of them.

50. Stewart paid Willis $312.50 for Harriet. See James A. Stewart from Thomas Willis, Chattel Records, Liber FJH, no. 2, p. 11, MDSA. When Stewart bought Harriet, he already held over forty slaves; half were women. Harriet was twenty years old at the time. See also Assessors Field Book, 1852–1864. Dorchester County Board of County Commissioners, 26–27. Harriet's fate is unknown. Stewart sent the majority of his slaves to labor on his plantations in Texas in 1855, including Harriet. Willis, however, kept the two little girls, Mary and Sarah, although who cared for them in his household is a mystery, as he owned no other slaves. See Assessors Field Book 1852, 165. In 1860, Willis sold Mary.

51. John Brown was a grandson of Elizabeth Pattison, and Achsah was Elizabeth's daughter, which accounts for the different amounts Stewart paid for their respective interests in Rit. James A. Stewart from John Brown, Chattel Records, Liber FJH, no. 2, pp. 25–26, MDSA; James A. Stewart from Achsah Pattison, Chattel Records, Liber FJH, no. 2, p. 55, MDSA.

52. Interestingly, Eliza Brodess did not claim Rit as her slave in the 1852 tax assessment record. This may be because she believed Rit was entitled to her freedom, or she had already sold Rit to Ben— though that was not recorded until 1855. This will be discussed further in the next chapter.

53. James Freeman Clark, *Anti-Slavery Days* (1883; reprint, Westport, Conn.: Negro Universities Press, 1970), 81.

54. Tubman helped rescued individuals from Baltimore, and probably Delaware, too.

55. Cheney, "Moses," 35–36.

56. Julius Sherrard Scott III, "The Common Wind: Currents of Afro-American Communication in the Era of the Haitian Revolution," Ph.D. dissertation, Duke University, 1986, 24–25. See also Franklin and Schweninger, *Runaway Slaves.*

57. Cheney, "Moses." Cheney says that Tubman chose a meeting place "eight or ten miles distant." Cheney does not indicate from where; whether she was referring to the Brodess plantation, one of the Thompson properties, or a variety of other places is not known. Nevertheless, Cheney did write that Tubman did not return to the plantation herself (p. 36).

58. Joseph D. Thomas and Marsha McCabe, eds., *Spinner: People and Culture in Southeastern Massachusetts* (New Bedford, Mass.: Spinner Publications, Inc., 1988), IV:66–67.

59. Cheney, "Moses," 36.

60. Clark, *Anti-Slavery Days,* 81.

61. Thomas and McCabe, eds., *Spinner,* IV:67. Henry Carrol is not listed in Still's book or Journal C. This may be an alias, thereby making it difficult to identify whom this man is. The Carroll name is one of the most prominent white names on the Eastern Shore, including that of Thomas King Carroll of Dorchester County and a former governor of Maryland.

62. Bradford, *Scenes,* 25.

63. Emily Howland Diary, October 4, 1873, Florence W. Hazzard Papers, Collection #2516–2, Division of Rare and Manuscript Collections, Carl A. Kroch Library, Cornell University, Ithaca, N.Y.

64. Ibid. While Tubman is not quoted by Howland as saying the bridge was in Delaware, this is the most likely place. In fact, Thomas Garrett wrote in a letter that there had been rumors of trouble in the form of harassment of blacks in Wilmington by gangs of Irish men. Tubman was right to be frightened; the animosity between blacks and Irish workers was already well established by the 1850s in most cities where large numbers of Irish had settled. Competition over jobs created many tense confrontations and bad feelings on both sides; Irish laborers, though discriminated against by native-born whites as well, felt some superiority to blacks. It did not take long for European immigrants to acculturate the antiblack and racist attitudes of native-born Anglo-Americans. For more on this topic, see Iver Bernstein, *The New York City Draft Riots* (New York: Oxford University Press, 1990); David R. Roediger, *The Wages of Whiteness: Race and the Making of the American Working Class* (New York: Verso, 1991).

65. Cheney, "Moses," 36.

66. Ibid.

67. "New York," in "The Underground Railroad: Manuscript Materials Collected by Professor Siebert," Houghton Library, Harvard University, Cambridge, Mass.; "When Men Were Sold. The Underground Railroad in Bucks County," *The Bucks County Intelligencer,* March 31, 1898.

68. William Still, *The Underground Railroad* (1871; reprint, Chicago: Johnson Publishing Company, Inc., 1970), 34–38. See also Thomas Garrett to Mary Edmondson, March 29, 1857, in McGowan, *Station Master,* 139–43; Thomas Garrett to William Still, March 28, 1857, in McGowan, *Station Master,* 96.

69. Account Book, 2:20, Rochester Ladies' Anti-Slavery Society Records, William L. Clements Library, University of Michigan, Ann Arbor.

70. There is a growing body of literature on runaway slaves in addition to work on the Underground Railroad. See Gerald W. Mullin, *Flight and Rebellion: Slave Resistance in Eighteenth Century Virginia* (New York: Oxford University Press, 1972); and Franklin and Schweninger, *Runaway Slaves.*

71. *Vigilance Committee of Boston Account Book,* July 19, 1858, p. 53, from "Massachusetts," in "The Under-

ground Railroad: Manuscript Materials Collected by Professor Siebert," Houghton Library, Harvard University, Cambridge, Mass.

Chapter 6

1. John W. Blassingame, ed., *Slave Testimony: Two Centuries of Letters, Speeches, Interviews, and Autobiographies* (Baton Rouge: Louisiana State University Press, 1977), 415.

2. Ibid. The identity of the white friend is unknown. It could have been Dr. Thompson, John T. Stewart, or another wealthy man who could afford the approximately $1,200 to $1,500 for the three brothers. According to testimony given by Dr. A. C. Thompson in 1853, Thompson hired "three of them, two boys and a girl, for which he paid $120.00 per year; he has now Robert in his possession for which he pays $55.00 per year." Thompson Deposition, Equity Papers 249.

3. Blassingame, ed., *Slave Testimony*, 416. Henry Stewart told his interviewer that the white man told them, "Boys, I can't buy you. If you can get away, get away."

4. Ibid.

5. Journal C of Station 2 of the Underground Railroad (Philadelphia, Agent William Still), August 28, 1854, Pennsylvania Abolition Society, reel 32, Historical Society of Pennsylvania, Philadelphia.

6. Samuel Harrington, notice of $250 reward, *The Cambridge Democrat*, Cambridge, Md., June 17, 1854.

7. Journal C. The entry indicates "July 29 [with "3rd" crossed out]/55" but it seems to be from June 29, 1854, due to its placement in the journal between June 20 and July 3, 1854, and because Harrington's advertisement for the recapture of Johnson appeared on June 17, 1854. It is not known whether Still used the familial expression "sister Harriet" to mean a blood kinswoman of Tubman or a more fictive use. While it is entirely possible that Ben Ross fathered children by another woman, little evidence has surfaced to date to suggest this possibility. However, the likelihood that Tubman and Winnibar are related, either as sister and brother or some other kin relationship, should not be discounted. According to Harrington's reward notice, Winnibar was twenty-seven years old in 1854, placing his birth sometime around 1827, which coincides with the period of separation between Ben and Rit due to Edward Brodess's removal to Bucktown.

8. Journal C. Johnson had been staying with Luke Goines, a member of the Vigilance Committee in Philadelphia. See also Massachusetts People of Color Census, 1865, New Bedford, Bristol County; 1860 U.S. Census, New Bedford, Bristol County, Massachusetts. On July 7, 1866, William Johnson (also called Winnibar or Winory) posted a notice in the *Christian Recorder* (Philadelphia) seeking information "of Charlotte and Ellen Johnson, who formerly belonged to one Samuel Harrington in a town called Tobacco Stick, Maryland. They were sold out of the State in 1854. Any information of their whereabouts will be gratefully received by their brother, Winory Johnson, No. 14 Cedar Street, New Bedford, Massachusetts."

9. Sam Green Sr. had been manumitted in 1832, and Catherine was freed on February 4, 1842, when Sam purchased her from Ezekiel Richardson. Both of their children, Sam junior and his sister, Sarah, remained enslaved, however. See Elaine McGill, transcr., *Certificates of Freedom, Dorchester County Court 1806–1864* (privately printed, 2001).

10. Journal C, August 28, 1854. See also Charles L. Blockson, *The Underground Railroad: Dramatic First-hand Accounts of Daring Escapes to Freedom* (New York: Berkley Books, 1987), 212–13, for information on the Bustills' large and successful family. For more information on Samuel Green Jr., see Richard Albert Blondo, "In Search of Samuel Green," *The Archivists' Bulldog*, April 30, 1990; on Sam Green Sr., see Richard Albert Blondo, "Samuel Green: A Black Life in Antebellum Maryland," master's thesis, University of Maryland, 1988.

11. Sam Green Jr. to Sam Green Sr., Sept. 10, 1854, in Blondo, "Samuel Green: A Black Life," 21. "I saw Harriet Caurishe in Philadelphia": this is assumed to be Harriet Tubman, possibly going by the name of Cornish.

12. Franklin Sanborn wrote that Tubman made another trip in the fall of 1852, bringing away nine runaways. Sanborn also suggests that this is about the time Tubman met Thomas Garrett. Franklin Sanborn, "Harriet Tubman," *The Commonwealth*, Boston, July 17, 1863. Tubman had already made four trips during 1850 and 1851 for a total of approximately twenty to twenty-two runaways. She brought another nine out in 1852. Thomas Garrett wrote in December 1855 that Harriet had made "four successful trips to the neighborhood she left, & brought away 17 of her brothers, sisters and friends." Thomas Garrett to Eliza Wigham, Wilmington, December 16, 1855, in James McGowan, *Station Master on the Underground Railroad* (Moylan, Pa.: The Whimsie Press, 1977), 123–26. It is not known whether she made any trips in 1853. In the spring of 1854, Tubman made another trip to Dorchester County, hoping to get away her brothers, and a sister and her children. She was unsuccessful, but she did bring away Winnibar Johnson, though it is not known whether she brought any others away at that time. She did, though, relay information to Samuel Green Jr. to help him effect his own escape in August 1854. She made a second trip in 1854, bringing away nine, including her brothers, that December. She made two more trips in 1855, bringing out one person each time for a total of two in 1855. Thomas Garrett may have been slightly off in his estimate of the numbers of runaways she had brought away between 1852 and 1855. So, in short, by December 1855, it can be assumed that she had brought away a total of approximately forty to forty-two freedom seekers.

13. James A. Bowley to "Aunt" (Harriet Tubman), 1868, Harriet Tubman Collection, Harriet Tubman Home Museum, Auburn, N.Y. It is not known which school Bowley attended. Martha Coffin Wright, a friend and supprter of Tubman's in Auburn, N.Y., met James Bowley in 1868, writing to her daughter, Ellen Wright Garrison, that Harriet worked "two years at a dollar a week & paid 50cts a wk for his board, & sent him to school." Martha Coffin Wright to Ellen Wright Garrison, December 22, 1869, Garrison Family Papers, box 39, f 1000, Sophia Smith Collection, Smith College, Northampton, Mass. Bowley may have attended the famous Lombard Street School for black children in Philadelphia.

14. Thomas Garrett is known to have discussed Tubman's rescue missions with Mott and Garrison in December 1856, and it is likely that they had known of Tubman for at least a year or two prior to this discussion. Mott, in fact, may have known of Tubman from the earliest days of Tubman's freedom— she may be one of the "white ladies" Tubman claimed she dreamed about and then met when she escaped to Philadelphia in 1849. See Garrett to Eliza Wigham, Dec. 27, 1856, in McGowan, *Station Master*, 134–37.

15. Lucretia "stood by them when there was no one else." See Martha Coffin Wright to Sisters, October 8, 1868, Garrison Family Papers, box 39, folder 996, Sophia Smith Collection, Smith College, Northampton, Mass.

16. For more information on this network of abolitionists and URR operators in Kennett Square, Pa., see William Kashatus, *Just over the Line: Chester County and the Underground Railroad* (West Chester, Pa.: Chester County Historical Society with Penn State University Press, 2002).

17. Aileen Kraditor, *Means and Ends in Abolitionism: Garrison and His Critics on Strategy and Tactics, 1834–1850* (New York: Pantheon Books, 1967), 62.

18. For further discussions of abolitionism and abolitionists, see Shirley J. Yee, *Black Women Abolitionists: A Study in Activism, 1828–1860* (Knoxville: University of Tennessee Press, 1989); Jean Fagan Yellin, *Women and Sisters: The Anti-Slavery Feminist in American Culture* (New Haven, Conn.: Yale University Press, 1989); Ronald Walters, *The Anti-Slavery Appeal: American Abolitionism After 1830* (Baltimore: Johns Hopkins University Press, 1976); Patricia Morton, ed., *Discovering Women in Slavery: Emancipating Perspectives on the American Past* (Athens: University of Georgia Press, 1996); Kraditor, *Means and Ends;* Margaret M. R. Kellow, "The Divided Mind of Anti-Slavery Feminism: Lydia Maria Child and the Construction of African American Womanhood," in Patricia Morton, ed., *Discovering Women in Slavery: Emancipating Perspectives on the American Past* (Athens: University of Georgia Press, 1996); Julie Roy Jeffrey, *The Great Silent Army of Abolitionism: Ordinary Women in the Antislavery Movement* (Chapel Hill: University of North Carolina Press, 1998); Debra Gold Hanson, "The Boston Female Anti-Slavery Society

and the Limits of Gender Politics," in Jean Fagan Yellin and John C. Van Horne, eds., *The Abolitionist Sisterhood: Women's Political Culture in Antebellum America* (Ithaca, N.Y.: Cornell University Press, 1994); Lawrence Friedman, *Gregarious Saints: Self and Community in American Abolitionism, 1830–1870* (New York: Cambridge University Press, 1982); Milton Sernett, *Abolition's Axe: Beriah Green, Oneida Institute and the Black Freedom Struggle* (Syracuse: Syracuse University Press, 1986); John Stauffer, *The Black Hearts of Men: Radical Abolitionists and the Transformation of Race* (Cambridge, Mass.: Harvard University Press, 2002); Henry Meyer, *All on Fire: William Lloyd Garrison and the Abolition of Slavery* (New York: St. Martin's Press, 1998); and C. Peter Ripley, ed., *The Black Abolitionist Papers*, 5 vols. (Chapel Hill: University of North Carolina Press, 1991).

19. Kellow, "Divided Mind." 108.

20. Yee, *Black Women*, 99.

21. Sarah H. Bradford, *Scenes in the Life of Harriet Tubman* (Auburn, N.Y.: W. J. Moses, 1869), 57. Jacob Jackson lived at Parsons Creek, west of Tobacco Stick, during part of the 1850s. At one point, however, he moved to the Buttons Neck area, south of Church Creek and west of Anthony Thompson's former plantation. Sarah Bradford is the main source of information for this escape story, which is supplemented by Benjamin Drew, *The Refugee: A North-Side View of Slavery* (1855; reprint, Tilden G. Edelstein, ed., Reading, Mass.: Addison-Wesley Publishing Co., 1969). See also Journal C.

22. He took in and adopted orphaned black children into his family, a practice he continued for over twenty years.

23. Bradford, *Scenes*, 57. Interestingly, the black spiritual "The Old Ship of Zion" supposedly has its roots in Anne Arundel County, Maryland, c. 1830–1840. If this is correct, then perhaps this particular phrase had specific regional importance, thereby increasing the likelihood that its message would be interpreted in a specific way. See Lucy McKim Garrison, William Francis Allen, and Charles Pickard Ware, *Slave Songs of the South* (New York: A. Simpson & Company, 1867), 102–3; see also A. S. Jenks, *The Chorus* (Philadelphia: A. S. Jenks, 1860), 167–70.

24. Bradford, *Scenes*, 58. How often Tubman communicated with Jackson to spread news and convey important instructions and information is not known.

25. Ibid. This refers to Poplar Neck. Tubman may have planned on meeting them in the Church Creek or Tobacco Stick area, possibly planning to sail up the Choptank River to Poplar Neck in Caroline County.

26. Bradford, *Scenes*, 59. Robert's wife was Mary Manokey, the slave of Dr. Anthony Thompson. See also Anthony C. Thompson to Sundry Negroes, Dorchester County Chattel Records, MDSA, and Anthony C. Thompson to Sarah Catherine Haddaway, Dorchester County Chattel Records, 1851–1860, MDSA.

27. Bradford, *Scenes*, 58–59.

28. Bradford, *Scenes*, 59 ("nebber waited for no one").

29. Journal C; William Still, *The Underground Railroad* (1871; reprint, Chicago: Johnson Publishing Company, Inc., 1970).

30. Interview with Mrs. James Seward (Stewart), in Drew, *The Refugee*, 28–29.

31. Ibid.

32. Ibid., 29. See also Bradford, *Scenes*, 63. This is probably near the Blackwater River, where Jones owned a farm not too far from Anthony Thompson's former plantation.

33. Journal C.

34. Bradford, *Scenes*, 61.

35. Ibid.

36. Ibid.

37. Ibid.

38. Ibid., 62.

39. Ibid., 61.

40. McGowan, *Station Master,* 48–69. Garrett had long been suspected of being an URR agent, but in 1848 he was caught aiding a family of slaves escape from their Maryland owners. Found guilty, Garrett lost and was fined $1,500. Defiant as ever, however, he announced to the court at his sentencing that he would never pass up the opportunity to assist a runaway slave. Interestingly, one of the presiding judges at the trial was Chief Justice Roger B. Taney, who would later deliver the landmark and very controversial Dred Scott decision in 1857. McGowan's latest research suggests that Garrett may have overstated the number of freedom seekers he directly aided.

41. Thomas Garrett to J. Miller McKim, December 29, 1854, in Still, *The Underground Railroad,* 305.

42. Drew, *The Refugee,* 29. No reward advertisement has been found for Robert, Ben, and Henry. Robert and Ben were assessed at $400 each and Henry was assessed at $250. See Assessors Field Book, Dorchester County Board of County Commissioners, MDSA.

43. George Ross's relationship to Tubman's family is unknown. It is likely, however, that they did travel with Tubman. In 1863 Henry told an interviewer that there were ten of them who came away together, which would have included George Ross, William Thompson, and one other unidentified individual. Blassingame, ed., *Slave Testimony;* Journal C, 143–46.

44. See Turpin Wright Certificate of Negroes, April 29, 1833, in Elaine McGill, transcr., *Maryland Chattel Records Dorchester County 1827–1833* (privately printed, 2002), 102. See also Harold B. Hancock and Madeline Dunn Hite, *Slavery, Steamboats and Railroads: The History of 19th Century Seaford* (Seaford, Del.: privately printed, 1981), 74–75.

45. See Journal C, May 25, 1854. Several of George Ross's and William Thompson's enslaved friends from Seaford, Delaware, had escaped earlier that May, following the same route to Wilmington and Philadelphia that Tubman probably used. James Edward Handy (alias Dennis Cannon) was owned by Samuel Laws of Seaford. Handy's wife and four children, who could not get away, were owned by Captain Hugh Martin of Seaford. Henry Delaney (alias Smart Stanley) was also owned by Captain Martin. James Henry Blackson (Blockson) fled from Charles Wright, Lewis N. Wright's brother, also residing in the greater Seaford area. Captain Hugh Martin was active in the slave trade, considered "a popular choice in the packet trade," shipping frequently for such large Baltimore–to–New Orleans traders as Hope Slater, Joseph Donovan, and Bernard Campbell. See Ralph Clayton, *Cash for Blood: The Baltimore to New Orleans Domestic Slave Trade* (Bowie, Md.: Heritage Books, Inc., 2002).

46. "Pennsylvania," "New York," in "The Underground Railroad: Manuscript Materials Collected by Professor Siebert," Houghton Library, Harvard University, Cambridge, Mass.

47. Vigilance Committee of Philadelphia, Accounts, Pennsylvania Abolition Society, reel 32, Historical Society of Pennsylvania, Philadelphia; Journal C.

48. Journal C, 143–46, December 29, 1854. See also Vigilance Committee Accounts, 379–80, December 29–31, 1854, and Still, *Underground Railroad,* 305–7. I prefer using the original Journal C records when possible, as it appears that Still made some errors transcribing the information from Journal C. I believe the more accurate document to be Journal C, as those were the notes Still recorded while the fugitives were standing before him. For a discussion of naming practices, see Herbert G. Gutman, *The Black Family in Slavery and Freedom* (New York: Vintage Books, 1976), 180–99, 230–56; John W. Blassingame, *The Slave Community: Plantation Life in the Antebellum South,* 2nd ed. (New York: Oxford University Press, 1979), 181–83.

49. Assessment Record, Dorchester County Board of County Commissioners, MDSA.

50. In William Still's Journal C, Still records these names as Daniel Floyd and Staunch Tilghman. John Campbell Henry owned John Chase. Whether these slaves had any blood relationship to either of these men is not known.

51. Journal C, 143–46; Vigilance Committee Accounts, 379–80. Robert, in fact, left behind three children, but in the haste of recording testimony, Still probably misrecorded Robert's response, as he definitely had three children, including newborn Harriet, when he left to go north. Henry told Still that his

wife, Harriet Ann, was to be known as Sophia Brown. This may have been in preparation of her chang-ing her name when she herself fled north, or else Still mixed up the testimony completely. When Henry settled in Canada, the census records indicate his wife's name as Harriet A., and they had two sons, William Henry Jr. and John. William Henry Jr. is consistently recorded as being born in the United States, while the Canadian records remain ambiguous as to John's birthplace, although he was probably born in Canada. Harriet Ann came north shortly after Henry fled with Tubman in 1854, although no record has been found of her escape with the children. In 1924 a Toronto newspaper reported that Tubman returned to Maryland soon after bringing her brother William Henry to Canada, and she brought away William Henry's wife and their child, William Henry Stewart Jr. See Fred G. Griffin, "Toronto Minister the Son of a Slave Knew 'Uncle Tom,' " *Toronto Star Weekly*, Toronto, Canada, January 19, 1924.

52. "Siebert interview with Harriet Tubman," in "The Underground Railroad: Manuscript Materials Collected by Professor Siebert," Houghton Library, Harvard University, Cambridge, Mass.; See also Frederick Douglass to Siebert, March 27, 1893, "New York," in Ibid.

53. Bureau of the Census, *United States Federal Census*, 1850, 1860, Rensselaer County, N.Y. Also see Let-ter to Sister Harriet Tubman, Nov. 1, 1859, Rochester Ladies' Anti-Slavery Society Papers, 1:19, William Clements Library, Ann Arbor, Mich., and Siebert Papers. According to the New York 1855 census (First Ward, Troy, Rensselaer County), William Bowley had been living there for fifteen years, John Hooper for eleven years. There are several other possible Eastern Shore, Maryland, families in this census, in-cluding William and John Meads and Edward and Leah Bishops, among others. In the 1860 federal cen-sus and then the New York State 1865 census for the same area, there are many more Maryland-born African Americans living in Troy and Albany.

54. Martin I. Townsend to Siebert, Sept. 4, 1896, and April 1, 1897, in "New York," Siebert Papers.

55. Martin I. Townsend to Siebert, Sept. 4, 1896, April 1, 1897, Sept. 7, 1898, and Sept. 14, 1898, in "New York," Siebert Papers.

56. Tubman may have been related to Hooper. According to Bradford, this person was a cousin. See Bradford, *Scenes*, 88. Tubman may have also stopped in Syracuse at this time, although she did not start using this stop until possibly the mid-1850s. See W. E. Abbott to Maria G. Porter, Nov. 29, 1856, Rochester Anti-Slavery Society Papers, 1:9, William Clements Library, Ann Arbor, Mich. See also Mar-tin I. Townsend to Siebert, Sept. 4, 1896; April 1, 1897; and Sept. 7, 14, 1898, in "New York," Siebert Papers.

57. Chatham was approximately thirty miles from Detroit, Michigan.

58. Bowley had been trained as a blacksmith and shipbuilder by the Stewarts in Dorchester County, Md.

59. Harkless Bowley to Earl Conrad, August 15, 1939, Earl Conrad/Harriet Tubman Collection, reel 1, box 3, folder d2, New York Public Library, Schomburg Center for Research in Black Culture. Harkless says he was born in 1858, but census records indicate he was born in 1856. Elijah Stewart was born in March 1856.

60. John Stewart worked first for Dr. Grimm. See Assessment Roll, St. Thomas Ward, St. Catharines, Archives of Ontario, 1855, 15. By 1860 John Stewart was a coachman for Dr. Mack. See Assessment Roll, St. George's Ward, St. Catharines, Archives of Ontario, 1860.

61. Interview with Henry Stewart, 1863, in Blassingame, ed., *Slave Testimony*, 416.

62. 1861, Ontario, Canada Census, St. Paul's Ward, District 5, Ontario, Canada, 1861.

63. Griffin, "Toronto Minister." "Harriet Tubman escaped in the first instance with two brothers to St. Catharines. She disappeared and as suddenly reappeared sometime later with her brother's wife and her little boy." This boy must be William Henry Stewart Jr., who was born in the United States. Ac-cording to William Still, when William Henry Stewart Sr. ran away, he left behind his wife, Harriet Ann, and two children. In the Canadian census, William Henry Stewart Jr. was the only child listed as being born in the United States.

64. There is one tantalizing possibility. On January 27, 1854, Dr. Anthony C. Thompson purchased a young slave named Moses Ross from a slave trader, Peter LeCompte. It is possible that Moses had been caught after he ran away in 1850 and was sold to a trader, who then sold Ross to Thompson. This is pure conjecture, however, as this Moses Ross's history and fate remains unknown. See Anthony C. Thompson from Peter G. LeCompte, January 27, 1854, Dorchester County Chattel Records, Maryland State Archives, Annapolis.

65. Bradford, *Scenes*, 62–63.

66. "Benjamin Ross Paid Eliza Brodess," Liber FJH no. 2, 163, MDSA. Interestingly, the bill of sale was not delivered to Ben until October 20, 1855. Perhaps it was then that Ben completed paying the $20 to Brodess. The transaction records Ben Ross as a resident of Dorchester County. It is possible he was living at one of Thompson's residences in Dorchester County, though it is likely it was just an oversight on the part of the court recorder. Ben and Rit appear to have lived at Poplar Neck in Caroline County from the late 1840s through 1857. I suspect that Ben had purchased Rit some years prior to June 1855 and that increased attention on his activities after his sons had run away forced him to make sure his "ownership" of Rit was secure.

67. The three young men had been valued at $1,150, out of a total estate value (based on assessment records) of $3,050. Assessors Field Book 1855.

68. Equity Papers 394, MDSA.

69. Ibid. The case continued on for the next four years, during which time both Eliza Brodess and John Mills died.

70. "The Terrors of Slavery!" *The National Era*, Washington, D.C., April 12, 1855.

71. See "Fears of Insurrection" and "The Wrath of the Fearful," *The National Era*, Washington, D.C., April 26, 1855.

72. Drew, *The Refugee*, 20, 27–29. Ironically, this is the surname of William Henry Seward, the governor of New York who would later become so instrumental in helping Tubman secure a home for herself and her family in Auburn.

73. "John Seward," in Drew, *The Refugee*, 27.

74. "James Seward. Brother of the Foregoing [John Seward]," in Drew, *The Refugee*, 27–28.

75. "Mrs. James Seward," in Drew, *The Refugee*, 28–29.

76. "Harriet Tubman," in Drew, *The Refugee*, 20.

77. Kitty Green applied for freedom papers on September 29, 1855, probably for the express purpose of traveling out of the state. Her husband, Samuel Green, had purchased Kitty from Ezekiel Richardson on February 4, 1842, and then Green manumitted her immediately. McGill, *Certificates of Freedom*, 95–96. The delegates from the cotton states were not identified in the proceedings of the convention, possibly for their own protection from reprisals back home. Franklin Turner, "Proceedings of the Colored National Convention," paper presented at the National Convention of the Colored People of the United States, Franklin Hall, Philadelphia, October 16–18, 1855 (National Standard Office, Salem, N.J., n.d.).

78. Kashatus, *Just over the Line*, 55. See also Passmore Williamson's Visitor's Book, Chester County Historical Society, West Chester, Pa.

79. See McGowan, *Station Master*, 31, 117–31, for more information on this symbiotic relationship between Garrett, Wigham, and Edmundson.

80. McGowan, *Station Master*. See also Assessors Field Book, 1852. Eliza Brodess is listed as owning Harry, age twenty, Ben, age twenty-three, Bob, age thirty-five, Rachel, age twenty-seven, Angeline, age five, and Ben, age three. Angeline is also variously listed as Algerine and Angerine.

81. Tubman interview [Siebert].

82. Thomas Garrett to Eliza Wigham, December 16, 1855, in McGowan, *Station Master*, 123–26.

83. Ednah Dow Littlehale Cheney, "Moses," *Freedmen's Record*, March 1865. "She was always a very re-

spectable looking [negro], not at all a poor fugitive." Tubman told Cheney she had to sell a silk dress to have enough money to bring her parents north.

84. Sarah H. Bradford, *Harriet, the Moses of Her People* (New York: Geo. R. Lockwood & Sons, 1886), 34–35. Harkless Bowley says this took place on the street in Cambridge. Harkless Bowley to Earl Conrad, August 8, 1939, Earl Conrad/Harriet Tubman Collection, New York Public Library, Schomburg Center for Research in Black Culture.

85. Emma P. Telford, "Harriet: The Modern Moses of Heroism and Visions," Cayuga County Museum, Auburn, N.Y., c. 1905, 11. "[B]ut he knew I couldn't read an so' didn't spect me, and 'de Lord save me dat time too."

86. Garrett to Wigham, Dec. 16, 1855, in Earl Conrad/Harriet Tubman Collection, New York Public Library, Schomburg Center for Research in Black Culture; McGowan, *Station Master,* 125.

87. See Still, *Underground Railroad,* 346; Journal C, 230; Vigilance Committee Accounts, 354; St. Catharines assessment rolls, 1861 Ontario census.

88. Garrett to William Still, Dec. 25, 1855, in Still, *Underground Railroad,* 661–62. Garrett claimed that Wilmer had forwarded twenty-five runaways in four months. Wilmer was owned by Eben Welch, a farmer in Kent County, near Georgetown Crossroads on the Sassafras River, a strategic path to upper Delaware and freedom in the North for Maryland runaways. Wilmer was apparently entitled to great liberties as a slave. He was freed in 1858 through a provision in Welch's will. Wilmer moved to Wilmington with his wife, Margaret, sometime prior to 1860 and was probably an active agent there, living two doors from Severn Johnson and others known to be URR operatives in that city.

89. Journal C, September 5, 1856, 288; Vigilance Committee Accounts, 330. William Cornish may have been related to Joseph, although Cornish is a very common name in Dorchester County. Interestingly, William and Joseph lived near each other in St. Catharines. Joseph continued an active ministry in Canada, while William worked as a laborer. See also William Cornish's interview with the American Freeedman's Inquiry Commission, 1863, in Blassingame, ed., *Slave Testimony,* 423–26.

90. Thomas Garrett to McKim and Still, May 11, 1856, in McGowan, *Station Master,* 93. See also R. C. Smedley, *History of the Underground Railroad in Chester and the Neighboring Counties of Pennsylvania* (Lancaster, Pa.: John A. Hiestand, 1883), 367; and Still, *Underground Railroad,* 402.

91. Charles Hubbard and William Creighton were tried in Dorchester County Circuit Court in April 1856 for "aiding and assisting" Levin Creighton, the slave of Pere North, to run away. See Debra Smith Moxey, *Dorchester County Genealogical Magazine* 15, no. 6 (1996), 21.

92. Journal C, May 16, 1856. See also Vigilance Committee Accounts, May 16, 1856. Still writes "Slycum" instead of Slacum. Slacum might have been Jerry Ennals Slacum, formerly a slave of Dr. Thompson, or alternatively Jerry and Jesse could have been related.

93. Anthony C. Thompson to Sundry Negroes, Dorchester County Chattel Records, MDSA.

94. Ibid. Also spelled Manoca.

95. Interestingly, Jesse Slycum, the runaway who arrived in William Still's office on May 16, 1856, just a few days after Tubman had come through with a party of fugitives, may have been related to the Slacums in Thompson's household, making the timing of Thompson's manumissions even more suspect.

96. Thompson, Anthony C. to V. M. Edmundson, Dorchester County Chattel Records, MDSA.

97. The manumissions became more important, though. In 1849 Thompson set new and reduced term limits for many of his slaves, and he continued to do this through the 1850s. But this seemingly benevolent act did not preclude Thompson from selling some of his slaves anyway.

98. In 1853 Thompson sold two young children, George, age nine, and Charlotte, age seven, to John D. Parker, the former overseer for his father's plantation at Peters Neck. It may have been a convenience sale for himself and for the children's mother, Sophia Brown, whom he manumitted the following June, and who may have been living there all along, hired out to John D. Parker. Or he could have sold

away her children without regard to her feelings. Nevertheless, they were children, and he sold them. See Anthony C. Thompson to John D. Parker, Dorchester County Chattel Records, MDSA. On another occasion, Thompson sold ten-year-old Sarah Jane Kiah and her twelve-year-old brother John Henry Kiah for $750. Anthony C. Thompson to Jesse Hubbard, Dorchester County Chattel Records, MDSA.

99. Still, *Underground Railroad*, 411. Ben and Rit would later tell an interviewer that Thompson "had reached out too far [and] several of his farms had slipped out of his hands," and that poor financial circumstances had led him to "make frequent sales" of slaves, thus reducing his "stock."

100. Thompson later sold Mary and her children to Sarah Catherine Haddaway. Anthony C. Thompson to Sarah Catherine Haddaway, Dorchester County Chattel Records, 1851–1860, MDSA.

101. Thomas Garrett to Eliza Wigham, September 12, 1856, in McGowan, *Station Master*, 127.

102. Sanborn, "Harriet Tubman." See also Bradford, *Scenes*, 80.

103. Bradford, *Scenes*, 50–51. Thomas Garrett to Sarah Bradford, June 1868 in Bradford, *Scenes*, 50–51. For the knocking out of the tooth, see Joseph D. Thomas and Marsha McCabe, ed., *Spinner: People and Culture in Southeastern Massachusetts* (New Bedford, Mass.: Spinner Publications, Inc., 1988), IV:66.

Chapter 7

1. Garrett to Eliza Wigham, September 12, 1856, in James McGowan, *Station Master on the Underground Railroad* (Moylan, Pa.: The Whimsie Press, 1977), 126–27.

2. One of these two children in Baltimore may have been Margaret Stewart, a young child Tubman would later leave with William Henry Seward's sister-in-law, Lizette Worden, to raise in the Seward household in Auburn, N.Y. This child and her relationship to Tubman will be discussed later. Garrett makes no further mention of the children, and Still has no record of Tubman arriving with any children during this time period.

3. Journal C of Station 2 of the Underground Railroad (Philadelphia, Agent William Still), September 28, 1856, Pennsylvania Abolition Society, reel 32, Historical Society of Pennsylvania, Philadelphia. See also William Still, *The Underground Railroad* (1871; reprint, Chicago: Johnson Publishing Company, Inc., 1970), p. 294. Francis Molock temporarily took the alias Thomas Jackson. He had been owned by James Waddell. Molock settled in one of the northernmost reaches of refugee settlement, in Owen Sound, Ontario, Canada. I am indebted to a relative of Molock's, Elaine McGill, for bringing this to my attention. Cyrus Mitchell, alias John Steel, had been owned by James K. Lewis. Joshua Handy, alias Hambleton Hambly, had been owned by Isaac Harris. Charles Dutton, alias William Robinson, had been owned by Mary Hurley, and Ephraim Hudson, alias John Spry, had been owned by John Campbell Henry. While most of these owners were from the Vienna area of Dorchester County, these slaves had been hired out to the Cambridge area, and thus were in contact and able to make secret plans to get away together.

4. When Tubman came through Garrett's home in May with a party of four men, Garrett wrote to Still, "I shall expect five more from the same neighborhood next trip." See Garrett to Still, May 11, 1856, in McGowan, *Station Master*, 93; see also Still, *Underground Railroad*, 402; and R. C. Smedley, *History of the Underground Railroad in Chester and the Neighboring Counties of Pennsylvania* (Lancaster, Pa.: John A. Hiestand, 1883), 367.

5. Garrett does not mention the name of this young woman in his letter to Eliza Wigham. Sarah Bradford, however, names Tilly in her second biography of Tubman. Though the escape sequences are slightly different, I have concluded they are one and the same, and have relied on Garrett's rendition of the escape because he wrote it the same day it was told to him by Tubman. While Garrett's purpose was to raise more money by telling Wigham the stories of the freedom seekers who came through his office, I believe Garrett can be viewed as trustworthy and accurate. Though he may have confused some facts on occasion, he is generally quite reliable, and based on independent documentary evidence

of other escapes described in his letters, Garrett's descriptions are very accurate. See Garrett to Wigham, October 24, 1856, in McGowan, *Station Master*, 129–31; and Sarah H. Bradford, *Harriet, the Moses of Her People* (New York: Geo. R. Lockwood & Sons, 1886), 57–59.

6. McGowan, *Station Master*, esp. 117–45.

7. Garrett to Wigham, October 24, 1856, in McGowan, *Station Master*, 129–31.

8. Ibid.

9. Ibid.

10. Bradford, *Harriet* (1886), 60. According to my estimates, this would have been her ninth trip, but by 1886, when Tubman relayed this story to Bradford, Tubman's exact memory of the event may have been vague as to which trip it was.

11. Garrett to Wigham, December 27, 1856, in McGowan, *Station Master*, 134–38.

12. Garrett to Wigham, October 24, 1856, in McGowan, *Station Master*, 129–31.

13. Garrett to Wigham, December 27, 1856, in McGowan, *Station Master*, 134–38.

14. Ibid. Garrett wrote in his letter to Wigham that Tubman was there for a sister and the sister's three children. Tubman's sister Rachel had two children, and her sister-in-law Mary Manokey had three children. I believe that Tubman may have been trying to get both sets of women and children away; however, by this date Mary Manokey was pregnant with the child of another man, Walter Wells, whom she later married. Their child was born sometime in December 1856 or January 1857. Therefore, it is unlikely that Mary was going to go north at this point with a newborn child who belonged to a man other than her first husband, Harriet's brother Robert Ross (John Stewart). Anthony Thompson sold Mary Manokey and her four children, John Henry, Moses, and Ritty Ross, and an unidentified baby with the surname Wells, to his daughter Sarah Catherine Haddaway in Talbot County on March 16, 1857. Anthony C. Thompson to Sarah Catherine Haddaway, Dorchester County Chattel Records, 1851–1860, MDSA. Tubman may not have been aware of Mary Ross's new circumstances. Therefore, I believe that Rachel is the last sister Tubman was trying to rescue.

15. William Hughlett owned Joe, and Bill had been hired out to him.

16. Journal C, November 26, 1856.

17. Sarah H. Bradford, *Scenes in the Life of Harriet Tubman* (Auburn, N.Y.: W. J. Moses, 1869), 29.

18. Eliza Manokey could have been related to the Manokeys enslaved by Thompson, and even enslaved by Thompson herself. She also could have been free. The circumstances of her life remain unknown.

19. Bradford, *Scenes*, 30–31.

20. Still, *Underground Railroad*, 279–81. See also Journal C, November 26, 1856. Still records her name as "Nokey." No record of a reward for Eliza Manokey has been found, and Still made no notes concerning her owner or her life under slavery. Eliza undoubtedly knew Tubman and her family, and she may have been related to Jerry and Polly Manokey. In fact, she may have been enslaved by Anthony Thompson when he died. A young woman named Eliza was "awarded" to Absalom Thompson in Talbot County as part of the administration of Anthony Thompson's estate. She was to be free in 1856. What became of that Eliza is unknown, though the Eliza Manokey who ran away with the Baileys and Peter Pennington supposedly arrived from Easton, Talbot County.

21. "Siebert interview with Harriet Tubman," in "The Underground Railroad: Manuscript Materials Collected by Professor Siebert," Houghton Library, Harvard University, Cambridge, Mass.

22. Ibid.

23. Thomas Garrett says nothing of a reward offered for Harriet's capture. Bradford, however, inserts into her narrative of this escape that a reward offer for $12,000 was posted for Tubman's capture. No reward notice for this sum, nor a notice for the capture of Tubman has ever been located. It seems likely that if such a reward was posted at this time, Garrett would have mentioned it, like he mentioned the rewards for the men.

24. Bradford, *Scenes*, 31.

25. Journal C, November 26, 1856.

26. Thomas Garrett to Joseph Dugdale, November 29, 1856, in McGowan, *Station Master*, 149.

27. W. E. Abbott to Maria G. Porter, November 29, 1856, 1:9, Rochester Ladies' Anti-Slavery Society Records, William L. Clements Library, University of Michigan, Ann Arbor. There are numerous places along the way from Syracuse to Rochester where Tubman and her friends could have found help. There were way stations in Skaneatles, Auburn, Weedsport, Port Byron, Geneva, Sherwood, and other places on the western route to Rochester.

28. Ibid.

29. Bradford, *Scenes*, 32–35.

30. Ibid., 35.

31. Ontario census, 1861, 1871, 1881. Also Lambton County Library, Sarnia, vertical file, "Peter Pennington." Peter established himself as a fish dealer, probably a similar profession to his work tasks while enslaved by Turpin Wright, who owned a fishery at Vienna, on the Nanticoke River, and at Secretary on the Choptank River, both in Dorchester County.

32. Semi Annual Report, Rev. Hiram Wilson, St. Catharines, Canada West, to Rev. Dr. Lathrop, Secretary for the Society for the Propagation of the Gospel, Peabody Essex Museum, Salem, Mass.

33. Sarah H. Bradford, *Harriet, the Moses of Her People* (New York: J. J. Little & Co., 1901), 142; William Wells Brown, *The Rising Son; or, the Antecedents and Advancement of the Colored Race* (1874; reprint, New York: Negro Universities Press, 1970), 536–39.

34. Brown, *Rising Son*, 538. "De whites can't catch Moses, kase you see she's born wid de charm. De Lord has given Moses de power."

35. McGowan, *Station Master*, 95; Still, *Underground Railroad*, 662.

36. McGowan, *Station Master*, 139–43.

37. George W. Putnam to Wilbur Siebert, Nov. 5, 1893, "Massachusetts," in "The Underground Railroad: Manuscript Materials Collected by Professor Siebert," Houghton Library, Harvard University, Cambridge, Mass. "She told me on one occasion when she was on her way South to meet by appointment *at a time* fixed a band of slaves to be brought out; she went to Loguen and asked for a little money for the purpose of enabling her to keep the appointment above named. But Loguen positively refused to let her have any, and Harriet told me that she *was obliged to go around Syracuse and seek some washing to do to obtain the money necessary for her expenses.*"

38. Bradford, *Scenes*, 109–10.

39. McGowan, *Station Master*, 139–43.

40. William Still identifies Henry Predeaux as "Predo," Denard Hughes as "Daniel" Hughes. See Still, *Underground Railroad*, 57–60. Still identifies James and Lavinia Woolfley on page 161. Their name may actually be "Woolford" or "Woolsey," though their exact identity has not been determined. Denard Hughes was also known as Denwood. Bill and Emily Kiah are identified in a runaway advertisement; see *American Eagle*, March 18, 1857, in Debra Smith Moxey, *Newspaper Abstracts from the American Eagle and Cambridge Chronicle 1846–1857* (Cambridge, Md., 1995).

41. Thomas Garrett to Samuel Rhodes, March 13, 1857, in McGowan, *Station Master*, 95.

42. William Brinkley to William Still, March 23, 1857, in Still, *Underground Railroad*, 60.

43. "Unsuccessful Attempt to Capture Fugitive Slaves," *New York Tribune*, New York, March 20, 1857.

44. Garrett to Edmondson, March 29, 1857, in McGowan, *Station Master*, 139–43.

45. Still, *Underground Railroad*, 58.

46. Garrett to Edmondson, March 29, 1857, in McGowan, *Station Master*, 139–43.

47. Still, *Underground Railroad*, 58.

48. Garrett to Edmondson, March 29, 1857, in McGowan, *Station Master*, 139–43.

49. Still, *Underground Railroad*, 58.

50. "Unsuccessful Attempt."

51. Ibid.

52. William Brinkley to William Still, March 23, 1857, in Still, *Underground Railroad*, 60. "We put them through, we have to carry them 19 mils and cum back the sam night wish maks 38 mils. It is tou much for our little horses. . . . We hav to go throw dover and smerney, the two wors places this sid of mary land lin."

53. Garrett to Mary Edmundson, March 29, 1857, in McGowan, *Station Master*, 141.

54. Pritchet Meridith, notice of reward of $600 for the return of Denard Hughes and Tom Elliot, March 11, 1857, published March 18 in the *Cambridge Democrat*.

55. Ibid. Meridith noted in his runaway advertisement for Elliott and Hughes that Elliott had a free uncle by the name of Moses Pinket living in Wilmington. Elliott and Hughes would not have been safe going to Pinket's; no doubt his residence was being watched. According to the 1850 U.S. Census for Wilmington, Moses Pinket was living in the household of Enoch Mortimer Bye, a Quaker merchant. Bye was intimately linked to Thomas Garrett through business and social contacts, and he had familial and business connections throughout Chester County and Philadelphia, Pennsylvania. Bye was probably active on the Underground Railroad, though as of this writing no documentation has surfaced to suggest this. Bye was related, through his mother, to Dr. Jacob Paxon, one of the more famous Underground Railroad operators in Norristown, Pennsylvania. Bye's wife, Phebe Pusey Passmore, also a Quaker, had strong antislavery and Underground Railroad connections in Pennsylvania and Delaware. By 1853, Pinket owned property in Wilmington. Perhaps his home there was an Underground Railroad stop. See McGowan, *Station Master*, 56; see also Smedley, *Underground Railroad*, and William Kashatus, *Just Over the Line: Chester County and the Underground Railroad* (West Chester, Pa.: Chester County Historical Society with Penn State University Press, 2002). On Pinket, personal communication with researcher John Creighton.

56. Garrett to Edmondson, March 29, 1857, in McGowan, *Station Master*, 139–43.

57. William Still records William and Emma "Chion" (Kiah) coming through his office in 1860. See Still, *Underground Railroad*, 543. They changed their last name to Williams, and they settled in Ontario for a few years before moving to Auburn, New York, to live near Harriet Tubman. See Ontario 1861 Census, St. Catharines; and Auburn, N.Y., 1865 census, where they are listed with their daughter Mary. In 1865 they are listed as servants in the household of Mrs. George Underwood, widow, who was a friend and supporter of Tubman.

58. Still, *Underground Railroad*, 160–61. Lavinia arrived in Still's office with another woman from Dorchester County named Ann Johnson. Ann's brother William, or Winnibar, had fled their owner, Samuel Harrington of Cambridge, in June 1854. After William had run away, Ann was sold to William Moore, of Bohemia Manor in Cecil County. The close proximity of this location to where Lavinia had been hiding probably accounts for the two women coming together. These sorts of connections point to a highly evolved and organized Underground Railroad network in this region.

59. Garrett to Edmondson, March 29, 1857, in McGowan, *Station Master*, 139–43.

60. Pritchet Meridith, notice of reward of $600 for the return of Denard Hughes and Tom Elliot, March 11, 1857, published March 18 in the *Cambridge Democrat*. William Still recorded their owner as "Richard" Meredith. Still, *Underground Railroad*, 58–59.

61. McGowan, *Station Master*, 59.

62. See note 57. The runaway notice posted in the *American Eagle*, March 18, 1857, noted that Emily was owned by Mrs. Ann E. Craig. Still recorded in his book that Emily, or Emma, was owned by "Bushong Blake," who was actually James Bushrod Lake. Ann Craig was Lake's mother-in-law. Craig died in 1862. In her will, written in 1849, she bequeathed Emily to her daughter, Louisa H. Lake, James's wife. The Kiahs' daughter, Mary, was bequeathed to William A. Lake, Louisa and James's son. See Leslie and Neil Keddie, *Dorchester County, Maryland, Wills. Liber Llk No. 1, November 1861–1868, Folios 209–428* (Salisbury, Md.: Family Tree Bookshop, n.d.), 6–7. For the runaway notice, see Moxey, *Abstracts*, 72.

63. Still, *Underground Railroad*, 57–58.

64. "A Negro Case," *Baltimore American*, Baltimore, Md., May 1, 1857.

65. *Baltimore American*, Baltimore, Md., April 21, 22, 23, 1857.

66. "Sam Green and Uncle Tom's Cabin," *Easton Gazette*, Easton, Md., August 28, 1858. See also Richard Albert Blondo, "Samuel Green: A Black Life in Antebellum Maryland," master's thesis, University of Maryland, 1988, 24.

67. "Sam Green and Uncle Tom's Cabin."

68. Samuel Green Jr. to Samuel Green Sr., September 10, 1854, in Blondo, "Samuel Green: A Black Life," 21–22. The actual quotes are: "plenty of friends plenty to eate plenty to drink," and "tell P. Jackson to come on Joseph Baley com on, Kom more."

69. "Sam Green and Uncle Tom's Cabin."

70. Ibid.

71. Ibid.

72. Ibid.

73. Prisoner # 5146 Samuel Green Free Negro, Maryland Penitentiary Records, Prisoner Records, MDSA. For a full account of the Rev. Sam Green's story, see Blondo, "Samuel Green: A Black Life." See also Still, *Underground Railroad*, 251–55.

74. Thomas Garrett to Mary Edmundson, August 11, 1857, in McGowan, *Station Master*, 143–45.

75. It is not clear whether Garrett has this part of the escape sequence correct, nor does he mention who this ninth person may have been. William Camper, a free black living in Bucktown, was arrested and convicted during the same court session in which Sam Green was being tried (April 1857). He was sentenced to four years in the state penitentiary for "stealing 94 cents, 1 bag and two handkerchiefs," a very stiff sentence for such a petty crime. It may have been a trumped-up charge used to circumvent trying him for aiding and abetting the Dover Eight to run away. William Camper, Free Negro, Maryland State Penitentiary Records, Prisoner Records. MDSA. Sarah Bradford wrote that the wife of the intended freedom seeker who turned back hoped to "curry favor with her master" and betrayed the plan to him. Bradford, *Scenes*, 48.

76. Thomas Garrett to Mary Edmundson, August 11, 1857, in McGowan, *Station Master*, 143–45. Bradford says that Ben had already been arrested, but Garrett makes no mention of this. I am taking Garrett's version of the event over Bradford's.

77. Robert W. Taylor, *Harriet Tubman: The Heroine in Ebony* (Boston: George E. Ellis, Printer, 1901), 9.

78. Thomas Garrett to Bradford, June 1868, in Bradford, *Scenes*, 52.

79. Still, *Underground Railroad*, 411. He also told Still that Dr. Thompson was "a spare built man, bald head, wearing a wig." Still did not differentiate between Brodess and Thompson when he wrote down Ben and Rit's story; he only mentions Dr. Thompson's name, and in his haste he may have conflated the two masters, neglecting to note that Brodess had once been Rit's owner and the one who had sold their daughters to Georgia.

80. Mrs. C. Bloss Webb to Wilbur Siebert, Sept. 7, 1896, "New York," in "The Underground Railroad: Manuscript Materials collected by Professor Siebert," Houghton Library, Harvard University, Cambridge, Mass.

81. Bradford, *Scenes*, 25. "At one time she collected and sent on a gang of thirty-nine fugitives in the care of others, as from some cause she was prevented from accompanying them."

82. Still, *Underground Railroad*, 100. Daniel Stanley was owned by Robert Callender, but Caroline and the children were owned by Samuel W. Le Compte, who was also the former enslaver of Joseph Cornish, who had run away in December of 1855. Nat Amby was held by John Muir, but Elizabeth Amby was owned by Alexander Bayley. Nat and Lizzie later settled in Auburn, New York, while the Stanleys settled in Canada. Caroline and one of the children, possibly an unidentified infant, did not survive long. They were not listed as part of the Stanley household in Ontario by 1861, and Daniel was listed as a widower.

83. "More Runaways," *Cambridge Democrat*, Oct. 28, 1857.

84. "Negro Stampede," *Cecil Whig*, Elkton, Md., October 31, 1857. The article says one of the owners was William D. Travers, but William was actually deceased. The Rev. Levi D. Travers was a nephew who had married one of William's daughters and therefore had inherited some of William's slaves. Mrs. Jane Cator may actually be Miss Jane Cator, the stepdaughter of Reuben Elliot Phillips. Phillips was married to Elizabeth Cator, Jane Cator's mother. Jane Cator's and Phillips's slaves, however, lived in the same household, although their ownership was separate.

85. Still, *Underground Railroad*, 88–89.

86. Ibid., 90–91.

87. Marshall Dutton was probably related to Charles Dutton, who had run away the previous fall.

88. Still, *Underground Railroad*, 87.

89. Garrett to Still, Nov. 17, 1857, in Still, *Underground Railroad*, 663. See also Brinkley to Still, June 13, 1858, 467.

90. Garrett to Still, Nov. 5, 1857, in Still, *Underground Railroad*, 663. See also Smedley, *Underground Railroad*, 276–77. Smedley reported that the Irish man was stabbed, not shot, and that he died later in Centreville.

91. Garrett to Still, October 31, 1857, in Still, *The Underground Railroad*, 100.

92. Smedley, *Underground Railroad*, 273–74, 276–77.

93. G. Lewis to William Still, Nov. 6, 1857, in Still, *Underground Railroad*, 101; see also E. Pennypacker to Still, Nov. 7, 1857, in Smedley, *Underground Railroad*, 365.

94. "St. Catharines," *New York Tribune*, November 23, 1857; "The Storm," *New York Tribune*, November 24, 1857.

95. Still, *Underground Railroad*, 99. James A. Stewart, William Goldsborough, Samuel Hambleton, Dr. Francis Phelps, and Dr. Horatio Grieves were some of the prominent slaveholders who convened the convention.

96. "Sam Green and Uncle Tom's Cabin." In this article on the imprisonment of Sam Green, the editor quotes an article from the *New Bedford Mercury*, which called Maryland "tyrannical" for sending Green to prison for possessing a copy of *Uncle Tom's Cabin*. Furthermore, the editor of the *Easton Gazette* suggested that the Eastern Shore slaveholders keep their business out of the newspapers, as such reporting was "injurous to the institution of slavery." See also "Abolitionists in Maryland," *The National Era*, Washington, D.C., November 25, 1858.

97. "Free Negroes," *Annapolis Gazette*, Annapolis, Md., March 18, 1858.

98. James A. Stewart, "Powers of the Government of the United States-Federal, State, and Territorial. Speech of Hon. James A. Stewart, of Maryland on African Slavery, Its Status-Natural, Moral, Social, Legal, and, Constitutional; and the Origin, Progress, Present Condition, and Future Diversity of the United States, Considered in Connection with African Slavery as a Part of Its Social System; with the Bearings of That Institution Upon the Interests of All Sections of the Union, and Upon the African Race," delivered in the House of Representatives, July 23, 1856, Congressional Globe Office, Washington, D.C.

99. "The Democratic Congressional Convention," *Easton Star*, Easton, Md., September 1, 1857.

100. See "Slave Laws of Maryland," *The National Era*, Washington, D.C., March 24, 1859; and "Political Intelligence," *The National Era*, Washington, D.C., June 30, 1859.

101. "Capture," *Easton Gazette*, Easton, Md., January 9, 1858.

102. Kenneth Carroll, *Quakerism on the Eastern Shore* (Baltimore: Maryland Historical Society, 1970), 143–44. See also William T. Kelley, "Underground R. R. Reminiscences," *Friends' Intelligencer*, April 2, 1898; and William T. Kelley, "Underground R. R. Reminiscences," *Friends' Intelligencer*, May 28, 1898. Daniel Hubbard apparently lost everything. A local farmer owned Hubbard's wife and children, but Daniel had been saving to buy their freedom. He had his own home and was employed as a ship carpenter, but had to leave everyone and everything behind when he fled with Arthur Leverton. Leverton's family sold

their home and joined him in Philadelphia immediately after the incident. They moved on to Indiana. Interestingly, Dr. Anthony C. Thompson's son, Anthony, who had married Arthur Leverton's sister, Mary, also moved to Indiana with the rest of his wife's family. She died there in 1859.

103. "Lynch Law in Maryland," *Liberator,* Boston, Mass., July 8, 1858. See also "[Bowers]," *Easton Gazette,* Easton, Md., July 3, 1858.

104. "Foul Outrage," *Liberator,* Boston, Mass., July 8, 1858.

105. "Suspicious," *The Public Monitor,* Easton, Md., July 8, 1858.

106. "Capture," *Cecil Whig,* Elkton, Md., August 7, 1858. Several of these slaves belonged to Reuben E. Phillips, who along with his stepdaughter Jane Cator had already lost seven of their slaves with the large party of twenty-eight that fled in October 1857. Jesse Perry was identified in a letter, Thomas Garrett to William Still, August 21, 1858. See McGowan, *Station Master,* 101–2; and Still, *Underground Railroad,* 497.

107. "Negroes Captured," *Easton Gazette,* Easton, Md., August 7, 1858; "Excitement at Cambridge," *New York Tribune,* New York, August 7, 1858. Hazlett broke out of jail shortly thereafter but was apprehended in East New Market. He was tried and convicted and sent to the Maryland Penitentiary for forty-four years. See "Escape and Recapture," *Easton Gazette,* Easton, Md., Otober 16, 1858, and "Trial of Hugh Hazlett," *Easton Gazette,* Easton, Md., November 20, 1858. See also Prisoner #5324 Hugh Hazlett, Maryland Penitentiary Records, Prisoner Records, MDSA. Hazlett was pardoned Dec. 21, 1864, after Maryland freed its slaves (Nov. 1, 1864.)

108. "Sam Green and Uncle Tom's Cabin."

109. Ibid. Hicks had been the Dorchester registrar of wills.

110. Ibid. Green would remain imprisoned until 1862, when Maryland's newly elected Governor, Francis Thompson King, pardoned Green and ordered him to leave the state. See Blondo, "Samuel Green: A Black Life," 63–72.

111. "Negro Stampede."

112. Ednah Dow Littlehale Cheney, "Moses," *Freedmen's Record,* March 1865.

113. Harriet Tubman is listed in the St. Catharines assessment roll (St. Paul's Ward), 1858. William Henry is listed in the St. Catharines assessment records (St. Paul's Ward) for 1856 at this same address. Brother John Stewart was listed in 1856 around the corner on Niagara St., in a building owned by the same landlord, Joseph Robinson. William Henry and a brother, possibly James, had rented land to try their hand at farming, probably around 1857–58, when Tubman returned to St. Catharines and took over the responsibility of taking care of their parents, Rit and Ben. Having failed at farming, William Henry returned to St. Catharines, and he is listed there in the 1861 census. He purchased six acres later that year in Grantham, Lincoln County, west of St. Catharines, and he remained there, with his family, for decades. See also John W. Blassingame, ed., *Slave Testimony: Two Centuries of Letters, Speeches, Interviews, and Autobiographies* (Baton Rouge: Louisiana State University Press, 1977), 416; and St. Catharines Census, 1861, District 5, p. 72.

114. Bradford, *Scenes,* 80.

Chapter 8

1. Interview with William Cornish, in John W. Blassingame, ed., *Slave Testimony: Two Centuries of Letters, Speeches, Interviews, and Autobiographies* (Baton Rouge: Louisiana State University Press, 1977), 423–26.

2. For detailed histories of black life in Canada, see Robin Winks, *Blacks in Canada: A History,* 2nd ed. (Montreal: McGill-Queen's University Press, 1997); Jason H. Silverman, *Unwelcome Guests: Canada West's Response to Fugitive Slaves, 1800–1865* (New York: Associated Faculty Press, Inc., 1985); Jonathan William Walton, "Blacks in Buxton and Chatham, Ontario, 1830–1890: Did the 49th Parallel Make a

Difference?" Ph.D. dissertation, Princeton University, 1979. See also work by Fred Landon, a professor at Western Ontario University in the early twentieth century, including articles on Canada's fugitive and black settlements in the *Journal of Negro History, Ontario History*, and in a variety of local historical society publications and records.

3. Seventh annual report, 1858, Rochester Ladies' Anti-Slavery Society Records, William L. Clements Library, University of Michigan. Ann Arbor.

4. Winks, *Blacks in Canada,* esp. 142–271. Some of the Eastern Shore's freedom seekers settled in other Ontario communities such as Sarnia, Chatham, and Owen Sound.

5. Ontario, Canada, census, 1861.

6. William Still, *The Underground Railroad* (1871; reprint, Chicago: Johnson Publishing Company, Inc., 1970), 92–93. Still transcribes Nat's name as "Ambie," though census records from Maryland indicate it is spelled "Amby." Nat inquired about Affey White, who lived on the waterfront in Baltimore, perhaps a clue to the long-distance maritime connections between Dorchester County and Baltimore. Many of the free black Ambys were involved in maritime trades, and several of the enslaved Ambys owned by John Muir and others were located in the Cooks Point region on the Choptank River in Dorchester County. A free Joseph Amby, age forty-nine and a seaman, was living in Baltimore in 1850; he was probably related to Nat and the two boys, Henry and Joseph, whom Nat refers to in his letter to Still. Living in Affey White's household in 1850 is Minty Bailey and her husband, Levin, a sailor. See Bureau of the Census, *United States Federal Census,* 1850, Baltimore, Md.

7. "New York," in "The Underground Railroad: Manuscript Materials Collected by Professor Siebert," Houghton Library, Harvard University, Cambridge, Mass. See Elbert Wixom, "The Underground Railway of the Lake Country of Western New York," thesis, Cornell University, June 1903 (located in this collection) for more detailed information on the URR route through the Finger Lakes region, which included Auburn and vicinity.

8. *Frederick Douglass: Selected Speeches and Writings,* ed. Philip S. Foner (Chicago: Lawrence Hill Books, 1999), 600–1. Douglass also wrote that Tubman possessed "great courage and shrewdness and may yet render even more important service to the Cause." This is one of only two surviving letters in which Douglass mentions Tubman.

9. The Secret Six were Gerrit Smith, Thomas Wentworth Higginson, Samuel Gridley Howe, Franklin B. Sanborn, George L. Stearns, and Theodore Parker. For secondary sources and more detail on John Brown and his plans for a raid into the south to liberate slaves, see Stephen B. Oates, *To Purge This Land with Blood* (Amherst: University of Massachusetts Press, 1984); Edward J. Renehan Jr., *The Secret Six: The True Tale of the Men Who Conspired with John Brown* (New York: Crown Publishers, 1995); W.E.B. Du Bois, *John Brown* (1909; reprint, New York: Modern Library Paperback, 2001). See also Franklin B. Sanborn, *Recollections of Seventy Years* (Boston: The Gorham Press, 1909). Also, for Frederick Douglass's role see William S. McFeeley, *Frederick Douglass* (New York: W. W. Norton & Company, 1991).

10. See Renehan, *Secret Six,* Oates, *Purge,* and Sanborn, *Recollections.*

11. Brown had traveled with Loguen to St. Catharines on April 5, 1858.

12. Several John Brown biographers have conflated Tubman's participation with Brown's scheme, her knowledge of Underground Railroad routes and border state territory, by claiming that she advised Brown on the terrain in that part of Virginia where he was planning his attack. There is no documentation, nor even circumstantial evidence, that Tubman did this. She was born and raised on the Eastern Shore of Maryland, limited her rescues to the Eastern Shore and Baltimore, and did not spend time in Virginia or western Maryland. More than likely, Tubman could solicit crucial information about slaveholders, geography, and other such reconnaissance information from Virginia fugitives known to her in Canada.

13. John Brown to John Brown Jr., April 8, 1858, in Franklin B. Sanborn, *The Life and Letters of John Brown* (Boston, 1885), 452.

14. Lillie B. Chase Wyman, "Harriet Tubman," *The New England Magazine*, March 1896, 117. See also Franklin Sanborn, "Harriet Tubman," *The Commonwealth*, Boston, July 17, 1863.

15. Sanborn, *Brown*, 452. Italics mine.

16. Sanborn, "Harriet Tubman." See also Sarah H. Bradford, *Scenes in the Life of Harriet Tubman* (Auburn, N.Y.: W. J. Moses, 1869), 82–83.

17. Wyman, "Tubman." 116.

18. Martha Coffin Wright to William Lloyd Garrison II, January 10, 1869, Garrison Family Papers, Sophia Smith Collection, Smith College, Northampton, Mass. According to Martha Coffin Wright, Tubman told her that "John Brown staid at her house in Canada, while he was there."

19. Renehan, *Secret Six*, 142–43.

20. Oates, *Purge*, 229.

21. Benjamin Drew, *The Refugee: A North-Side View of Slavery* (1855; reprint, Tilden G. Edelstein, ed., Reading, Mass.: Addison-Wesley Publishing Co., 1969). Interview with John Seward (Stewart), 27.

22. Brown to John Brown, Jr., April 8, 1858, in Sanborn, *Brown*, 452.

23. John Brown (Ingersoll) to William H. Day (St. Catharines), April 16, 1858, in John Brown/Boyd B. Stutler Collection, West Virginia Division of Culture and History/West Virginia Memory Project, Charleston; William H. Day (St. Catharines) to John Brown, April 17, 1858, in Dorothy Sterling, ed., *Speak out in Thunder Tones: Letters and Other Writings of Black Northerners, 1787–1865* (New York: Doubleday & Company, 1973), 274.

24. Sanborn, "Harriet Tubman." See also Wyman, "Tubman."

25. Diary, John Brown Note Books, 1838–1859, Ms. q. 1996, Boston Public Library. On April 14 Brown also paid Tubman $25 in gold for "G. Smith's Draft."

26. William Howard Day graduated from Oberlin College in 1847 and later received a D.D. from Livingston College. During the 1850s he worked as a reporter and editor for various newspapers in Ohio, and published his own newspaper, *The Aliened American*, from 1852 to 1855. He moved to Canada in 1857, setting up a shop in St. Catharines, where he printed Brown's pamphlet outlining the provisional constitution for his visionary free state. Working for the Freedman's Bureau after the Civil War, Day committed himself to establishing schools throughout the south for black children. He later became a minister in the AME Zion Church. Day remained a lifelong friend of Tubman's.

27. John Brown (Ingersoll) to William H. Day (St. Catharines), April 16, 1858, in John Brown/Boyd B. Stutler Collection, West Virginia Division of Culture and History/West Virginia Memory Project, Charleston.

28. Day wrote that Tubman had been put on the train by "Jackson." It is not known if this is Peter Jackson, who ran away with Harriet's brothers in 1854, some other fugitive from the Eastern Shore, or another friend. Day to Brown, April 17, 1858, in Sterling, ed., *Speak Out*, 274.

29. Ibid.

30. Day to Brown, May 3, 1858, in John Brown/Boyd B. Stutler Collection, West Virginia Division of Culture and History/West Virginia Memory Project, Charleston; Jermain Loguen to Brown, May 6, 1858, in Sterling, ed., *Speak Out*, 274–75.

31. Oates, *Purge*, 243–47.

32. Loguen to Brown, May 6, 1858, in Sterling, ed., *Speak Out*, 274–75.

33. Oates, *Purge*, 250–51.

34. Brown to Douglass, June 22, 1858, in John Brown/Boyd B. Stutler Collection, West Virginia Division of Culture and History/West Virginia Memory Project, Charleston.

35. Among his circle were Ralph Waldo Emerson, Bronson Alcott, Henry David Thoreau, John Greenleaf Whittier, Walt Whitman, Lydia Maria Child, and Oliver Wendell Holmes.

36. Franklin Sanborn to Friend (Thomas W. Higginson), May 30, 1859, Anti-Slavery Collection, Ms. E.5.1.53 pt. 1, Boston Public Library.

37. William Wells Brown remembered that Tubman had first come to Boston in 1854. See William Wells Brown, *The Rising Son; or, the Antecedents and Advancement of the Colored Race* (1874; reprint, New York: Negro Universities Press, 1970), 536–39. If this is true, she did not become widely known to the white antislavery community for some time. She may have visited Boston on occasion, seeking out friends who had run away from Dorchester County and who may have settled in larger cities and ports such as Boston and New Bedford. There is little evidence, however, that she spent any time in Boston prior to 1858, circulating among abolition's leaders.

38. Sanborn, "Harriet Tubman."

39. Ednah Dow Littlehale Cheney, "Moses," *Freedmen's Record*, March 1865.

40. Rebecca Green, "History of Harriet Tubman and Her Brick House," Cornell University, Ithaca, New York, 1998.

41. In May 1859, Seward also left for an extended tour of Europe, returning in the late fall.

42. Sanborn, "Harriet Tubman." See also Bradford, *Scenes*, 81. Seward was appointed secretary of state by Abraham Lincoln in 1860.

43. William H. Seward—Builder, Newspaper Scrapbook, Seward House Collection, Auburn, N.Y.

44. In fact, his support of immigrant rights negatively affected his campaign for the presidency.

45. Microfilm reels 192–93, Seward Papers, Harvard University, Cambridge. See also Green, "History of Harriet Tubman and Her Brick House."

46. Sanborn, "Harriet Tubman"; Bradford, *Scenes*, 81.

47. Edwin Morton to Frank Sanborn, June 1, 1859, in Sanborn, *Brown*, 468.

48. Wendell Phillips to Bradford, June 16, 1868, in Bradford, *Scenes*, 5.

49. Franklin Sanborn to Friend (Thomas W. Higginson), May 30, 1859, Anti-Slavery Collection, Ms. E.5.1.53 pt. 1, Boston Public Library.

50. Ibid. Mrs. Bartol was the wife of Cyrus Bartol, who was a Congregationalist-Unitarian minister at 17 Chestnut Street.

51. Lucy Osgood to Lydia Maria Child, June 2, 1859, Lydia Maria Child Papers, Anti-Slavery Collection Microform, Card #1110, Cornell University Libraries, Ithaca, N.Y. Ednah Cheney had requested that Bartol open her home "for a gathering of friends . . . who might be disposed to aid a real heroine." Osgood told Child that her neighbor, Mrs. Holman, informed her of Tubman's appearance.

52. Ibid.

53. Ibid. According to Tubman, William Lloyd Garrison gave her the name "Moses." See "Mrs. Harriet Tubman, the Colored Nurse and Scout—the Bridge Street African M.E. Church Last Evening," *The Brooklyn Eagle*, Brooklyn, N.Y., October 23, 1865.

54. Lucy Osgood to Lydia Maria Child, June 2, 1859, Lydia Maria Child Papers, Anti-Slavery Collection Microform, Card #1110, Cornell University Libraries, Ithaca, N.Y.

55. For an excellent source on Sojourner Truth's life and the challenges to her womanhood, see Nell Irvin Painter, *Sojourner Truth: A Life, a Symbol* (New York: W. W. Norton & Company, 1996).

56. Ibid., 178.

57. Thomas Garrett to Sarah Bradford, June 1868, in Bradford, *Scenes*, 49.

58. Cheney, "Moses."

59. *Letters and Journals of Thomas Wentworth Higginson, 1846–1906*, ed. Mary Thatcher Higginson (Boston: Houghton Mifflin Company, 1921), 81.

60. For an excellent analysis and discussion of Tubman's oral presentations and the resulting mediated texts written by white men and women, see Jean Humez, *Harriet Tubman: The Life and Life Stories* (Madison: University of Wisconsin Press, 2003).

61. Franklin Sanborn to Friend (T. W. Higginson), June 4, 1859, Anti-slavery Collection, Ms. E.5.1, pt. 1, p. 54, Boston Public Library.

62. Kenneth Walter Cameron, ed., *Young Reporter of Concord: A Checklist of F. B. Sanborn's Letters to Ben-*

jamin Smith Lyman, 1853–1867, with Extracts Emphasizing Life and Literary Events in the World of Emerson, Thoreau and Alcott (Hartford, Conn.: Transcendental Books, 1978), 17.

63. Franklin Sanborn to Friend (T. W. Higginson), June 4, 1859, Anti-slavery Collection, Ms. E.5.1, pt. 1, p. 54, Boston Public Library. See also Franklin B. Sanborn, "The Late Araminta Davis: Better Known as 'Moses' or 'Harriet Tubman,' " Franklin B. Sanborn Papers, box 1, folder 5, American Antiquarian Society, Worcester, Mass.

64. Maria Weston Chapman to Mrs. Arnold, June 4, 1859, Alma Lutz Collection, Schlesinger Library, Cambridge, Mass. Winnebar Johnson fled from Samuel Harrington in the summer of 1854. He later settled in New Bedford, taking the name William. See Johnson's notice looking for his sisters Charlotte and Eleanor in *Christian Recorder*, July 7, 1866. See also Samuel Harrington's notice regarding the running away of Winnibar Johnson, *The Cambridge Democrat*, Cambridge, Md., June 17, 1854.

65. Maria Weston Chapman to Mrs. Arnold, June 4, 1859, Alma Lutz Collection, Schlesinger Library, Cambridge, Mass.

66. Ibid.

67. Cheney, "Moses."

68. Higginson to L. Higginson, June 17, 1859, in *Letters and Journals of Thomas Wentworth Higginson, 1846–1906*, ed. Mary Thatcher Higginson (Boston: 1906), 81.

69. Ibid.

70. Ibid.

71. Lewis Hayden and John S. Rock were both members of Boston's Vigilance Committee and Underground Railroad operators.

72. James W. Yerrington, "The Fourth at Framingham," *The Liberator*, Boston, July 18, 1859. Yerrington noted that Tubman, "having first transformed herself from a chattel into a human being, had since transformed sixty other chattels into other human beings, by her own personal efforts."

73. Yerrington, "Fourth."

74. "Seward Papers," entry for July 6, 1859. See also Green, "History of Harriet Tubman and Her Brick House."

75. "The First of August Jubilees," *The Liberator*, Boston, August 26, 1859.

76. "New England Convention of Colored Citizens," *The Liberator*, Boston, August 26, 1859.

77. Ibid.

78. Tubman did make a quick trip to Auburn and St. Catharines during this period, probably stopping to visit with Douglass. See Rochester Ladies' Anti-Slavery Society Records, 8th Annual Report, 1859, Treasurer's entry for Harriet Tubman, $2.00, on August 3. On August 11, John Brown Jr. (alias John Smith) wrote to his father (alias J. Henrie) that Douglass suggested that Tubman, "whose services might prove valuable, had better be helped on." See John Smith to J. Henrie, August 11, 1859, in Sanborn, *Brown*, 536.

79. "Meetings in Boston," *The Liberator*, Boston, August 26, 1859.

80. Sanborn to John Brown, August 27, 1859, (held at the Pennsylvania Historical Society) in John Wheeler Clarkson, "An Annotated Checklist of the Letters of Franklin Benjamin Sanborn," Columbia University, 1971, 68. See also U.S. Senate, "Report of the Select Committee of the Senate Appointed to Inquire into the Late Invasion and Seizure of the Public Property at Harper's Ferry," Mason Committee, Washington, D.C., 1860.

81. Lewis Hayden to John Brown, September 16, 1859. This letter was published in the *New York Herald* after John Brown's failed raid on Harpers Ferry. It had been found among Brown's papers and was part of the evidence presented to the Mason Committee.

82. See also Franklin Sanborn to John Brown, September 23, 1859, *New York Herald*. Mason Report. Tubman later told Martha Coffin Wright that Brown "wanted her to go with him, in his expedition, but when he sent a message for her, she was not at home." Martha Coffin Wright to William Lloyd Garri-

son II, January 10, 1869, Garrison Family Papers, Sophia Smith Collection, Smith College, Northampton, Mass.

83. Dickson J. Preston, *Talbot County: A History* (Centreville, Md.: Tidewater Publishers, 1983), 205.

84. Oates, *Purge,* 290–302.

85. Sanborn, "Harriet Tubman." See also Bradford, *Scenes,* 83. Who Tubman was with is not clear, but Sanborn later wrote that "she was in New York at that time."

86. Sanborn, "Harriet Tubman."

87. Written by an amanuensis. I have not changed the wording, but I have added punctuation.

88. John Stewart to Harriet Tubman, Nov. 1, 1859, Rochester Ladies' Anti-Slavery Society, 1:19, William Clements Library, University of Michigan, Ann Arbor. It is unclear who "Brother John" is in this letter. The writer of the letter might have absentmindedly written "Brother John" in the third person, rather than maintaining a first-person narrative. John could have recently returned from a trip to Troy, N.Y., where their cousin John Hooper lived, and where several other Eastern Shore former slaves were also living. Or the reference could be to John Bowley, who may have traveled to Troy from his home in Chatham, Ontario, to visit friends and relatives there, including several Bowleys. Catherine Stewart, the wife of James Stewart, had at least two children, Elijah and Hester. Since there is no mention of James, it is unclear where he was at this time. William Henry was then living at the corner of Geneva and North Streets in St. Catharines, and the Bowleys were still living in Chatham.

89. Tubman did not make another payment until January 7, 1860, when she paid a total of $174.81 in interest and principal. See "Seward Papers"; Green, "History of Harriet Tubman and Her Brick House."

90. Cheney, "Moses."

91. Ibid.

92. Franklin Sanborn to Sarah Bradford, 1868, in Bradford, *Scenes,* 54.

93. See James M. McPherson, *Battle Cry of Freedom: The Civil War Era* (New York: Ballantine Books, 1988), 209–13.

94. Martha Coffin Wright to William Lloyd Garrison II, January 10, 1869, Garrison Family Papers, Sophia Smith Collection, Smith College, Northampton, Mass.

95. Oates, *Purge,* 359.

96. Franklin Sanborn to Friend, December 20, 1859, Anti-Slavery Collection, Ms. E.5.1 pt. 2, p. 141, Boston Public Library. Sanborn states that Tubman is at "83 Southac St." By the first of January 1860 she was back in Auburn, settling some of her debts with Seward.

97. Tubman and her family did not live in the house for most of 1860. See Bureau of the Census, *United States Federal Census,* 1860, Cayuga County, New York. They apparently returned to the house in late winter or early spring 1861. See Elijah R. Stewart, Citizenship Papers, October 23, 1888, United States Circuit Court, Boston. See also David Wright to Martha Coffin Wright, February 9, 1861, Garrison Family Papers, box 42. f. 1043, Sophia Smith Collection, Smith College, Northampton, Mass.; Martha Coffin Wright to Ellen Wright Garrison, December 30, 1860, Garrison Family Papers, box 36. f. 948, Sophia Smith Collection, Smith College, Northampton, Mass.; Martha Coffin Wright to Lucretia Coffin Mott, fragment—February 1861, Garrison Family Papers, box 37. f. 950, Sophia Smith Collection, Smith College, Northampton, Mass.; Martha Coffin Wright to Lucretia Coffin Mott, n.d. (early February 1861), Garrison Family Papers, box 37. f. 950, Sophia Smith Collection, Smith College, Northampton, Mass.

98. "A Fugitive Slave from Harper's Ferry at Auburn—Narrow Escape from a United States Marshall," *New York Herald,* January 21, 1860.

Chapter 9

1. Beriah Green to Samuel Campbell, March 19, 1860, Rochester Ladies' Anti-Slavery Collection, 1:22, William Clements Library, University of Michigan, Ann Arbor. Beriah Green, a radical abolitionist and

an early president of the Oneida Institute, an integrated "abolitionist" college in Whitesboro, N.Y., hosted a reception for Tubman on March 18, 1860. He sent her on to New York Mills, a few miles east of Whitesboro, near Utica, the following day. She also traveled to Syracuse, where the Rev. Samuel J. May, an antislavery colleague and friend of Gerrit Smith's, provided her with letters of introduction to antislavery supporters and societies in central New York. For an excellent biography of Green, see Milton Sernett, *Abolition's Axe: Beriah Green, Oneida Institute and the Black Freedom Struggle* (Syracuse, N.Y.: Syracuse University Press, 1986).

2. William "Jerry" Henry was an escaped slave who was captured by slave catchers in Syracuse, New York, on October 1, 1851. After a dramatic rescue by local abolitionists, Jerry was successfully taken to Canada and freedom. See Sernett, "North Star Country," 136–145.

3. Beriah Green to Samuel Campbell, March 19, 1860, Rochester Ladies' Anti-Slavery Collection, 1:22, William Clements Library, University of Michigan, Ann Arbor. Tubman may have been hiding in Troy as well. Two weeks earlier, Franklin Sanborn had been arrested in Concord, Massachusetts, for his refusal to testify before the Mason Commission. Though he was released and charges were eventually dropped, his arrest was upsetting to those who were intimate with Brown's plans. See Franklin B. Sanborn, *Recollections of Seventy Years* (Boston: The Gorham Press, 1909), 208–17.

4. Special thanks to Scott Christianson for information on Nalle and his rescue. Christianson is now working on a biography of Nalle. See also Sarah H. Bradford, *Scenes in the Life of Harriet Tubman* (Auburn, N.Y.: W. J. Moses, 1869), 88–103. Bradford includes in her narrative of the Nalle rescue a copy of an article from the *Troy Whig*, April 28, 1859, in addition to a statement sent to her about the rescue from Martin Townsend, who was at the time Nalle's attorney. Bradford also, it appears, quoted Tubman's recollections of the event. The *Troy Whig* article was also reprinted in *The Liberator*, May 4, 1860. See also "A 'Jerry Rescue' in Troy," *Troy Daily Times*, Troy, N.Y., April 27, 1859. This article, written within hours of the event, is very detailed and mentions the participation of a "venerable old colored woman," though they do not name Tubman; and A. J. Weise, *History of the City of Troy* (Troy, N.Y.: William H. Young, 1876), 176–78. For an anecdotal remembrance of Tubman's storytelling of this event, see Samuel Hopkins Adams, *Grandfather Stories* (New York: Random House, 1947), 275–77.

5. "A 'Jerry Rescue' in Troy."

6. Bureau of the Census, *United States Federal Census*, 1860, Troy, New York.

7. Bradford, *Scenes*, 88.

8. "A 'Jerry Rescue' in Troy."

9. Tubman is credited with yelling "fire" herself, or getting others to do it. "Harriet, now seeing the necessity for a tremendous effort for his rescue, sent out some little boys to cry *fire*. The bells rang, the crowd increased, till the whole street was a dense mass of people." See Bradford, *Scenes*, 89.

10. For a humorous account of this, see Adams, *Grandfather Stories*. 276.

11. Bradford, *Scenes*, 90. Bradford also suggests that Nalle was his master's brother. According to Nalle's lawyer, Martin Townsend, "Nalle is an octoroon," that is, he was what was considered at the time to be one-eighth black and seven-eighths white. See Bradford, *Scenes*, 100. The U.S. Census records and New York census records categorize Nalle as a mulatto. The *Troy Whig* reported that Nalle was "about thirty years of age, tall, quite light-complexioned, and good-looking." See "Fugitive Slave Rescue in Troy. Running Fight with the Officers—Recapture and Rescue," *Troy Whig*, April 28, 1860, as reprinted in *The Liberator*, Boston, May 4, 1860.

12. The antislavery press of the time made much of very light-skinned or seemingly "white" slaves, highlighting what William Wells Brown argued was "the best evidence of the degraded and immoral condition of the relation of master and slave in the United States." See William Wells Brown, *Clotel; or, the President's Daughter, a Narrative of Slave Life in the United States* (Salem, N.H.: Ayer Company, 1988), 55. For further readings on color consciousness, especially in the context of nineteenth-century literature, see John Ernest, *Resistance and Reformation in Nineteenth-Century African American Literature* (Jackson: University Press of Mississippi, 1995); Carla L. Peterson, *"Doers of the Word": African American Women Speak-*

ers and Writers in the North, 1830–1880 (New Brunswick, N.J.: Rutgers University Press, 1995); Jean Fagan Yellin, *The Intricate Knot: Black Figures in American Literature, 1776–1863* (New York: New York University Press, 1972); Jean Fagan Yellin, *Women and Sisters: The Anti-Slavery Feminist in American Culture* (New Haven, Conn.: Yale University Press, 1989); and Eric J. Sundquist, *To Wake the Nations: Race in the Making of American Literature* (Cambridge, Mass.: The Belknap Press of Harvard University Press, 1994).

13. "A 'Jerry Rescue' in Troy." See also Bradford, *Scenes*, 90–91.

14. "A 'Jerry Rescue' in Troy."

15. Ibid.

16. Ibid. Bradford wrote that Tubman's clothes were torn from her; Tubman's bonnet had been given to Nalle to disguise him.

17. Bradford, *Scenes*, 90.

18. Bradford, *Scenes*, 89.

19. Bradford, *Scenes*, 89. See also A 'Jerry Rescue' in Troy.

20. "A 'Jerry Rescue' in Troy."

21. Bradford, *Scenes*, 99; Ibid.

22. Bradford, *Scenes*, 102.

23. Adams, *Grandfather Stories*, 276. "I th'ow um acrost my shouldah like a bag o' meal and tote um away outen theyah."

24. "A 'Jerry Rescue' in Troy." Bradford modifies this story by stating, "A gentleman who was riding by with a fine horse, stopped to ask what the disturbance meant; and on hearing the story, his sympathies seemed to be thoroughly aroused; he sprang from his wagon, calling out, 'That is a blood-horse, drive him till he drops.' " See Bradford, *Scenes*, 91. Tubman, on the other hand, intimated to her audiences that she stole the horse from a passerby who "was a good judge of hawssflesh." See Adams, *Grandfather Stories*, 176.

25. Bradford, *Scenes*, 91, 100. Bradford says he was in Schenectady. See also "A 'Jerry Rescue' in Troy."

26. Bradford, *Scenes*, 103.

27. American Anti-Slavery Society, Executive Committee, *The Anti-Slavery History of the John Brown Year; Being the Twenty-Seventh Annual Report of the American Anti-Slavery Society* (New York: American Anti-Slavery Society, 1861), 61–62.

28. Ednah Dow Littlehale Cheney, "Moses," *Freedmen's Record*, March 1865. Martin Townsend, Nalle's lawyer, later remarked that Tubman "exposed herself to the fury of the sympathizers with slavery, without fear, and suffered their blows without flinching." Bradford, *Scenes*, 103.

29. Sanborn to Lyman, June 10–11, 1860 (held at Historical Society of Pennsylvania), in John Wheeler Clarkson, "An Annotated Checklist of the Letters of Franklin Benjamin Sanborn," Columbia University, 1971.

30. "Woman's Rights Convention," *The Liberator*, Boston, July 6, 1860.

31. Elizabeth Cady Stanton, Susan B. Anthony, and Matilda Joslyn Gage, eds., *The History of Woman Suffrage*, vol. 1, *1848–1861*, 2nd ed. (Rochester, N.Y.: Charles Mann, 1887), 276–77.

32. John Bell Robinson, *Pictures of Slavery and Anti-Slavery* (Philadelphia, 1863), 322–23. Robinson wrote this in 1860, but he published this in 1863.

33. Ibid., 324.

34. Daniel W. Crofts, "Seward, William Henry" at http://www.anb.org; American National Biography Online, February 2000.

35. "Seward Papers." See also Rebecca Green, "History of Harriet Tubman and Her Brick House," Cornell University, Ithaca, N.Y., 1998. On January 7, 1860, after Tubman had paid $170.89 to Seward, her debt had been reduced to $876.95; by the following December, after making no payments, Tubman owed Seward $968.46.

36. Harriet Tubman to Wendell Phillips, August 4, 1860, Wendell Phillips Papers, Houghton Library,

Harvard University, Cambridge. The identity of the person who wrote this letter for Tubman is unknown.

37. Ibid. Walcutt was also the person who sent Seward the first draft of $200 that Tubman paid on her mortgage in July, 1859. See "Seward Papers"; Green, "History of Harriet Tubman and Her Brick House" also, for a brief mention of Walcutt, see Henry Meyer, *All on Fire: William Lloyd Garrison and the Abolition of Slavery* (New York: St. Martin's Press, 1998), 533, 627.

38. Harriet Tubman to Wendell Phillips, August 4, 1860, Wendell Phillips Papers, Houghton Library, Harvard University, Cambridge.

39. William Still reports Stephen's name as "Ennets," though this is most certainly Ennals, a common Dorchester County name. There are no Ennets in Dorchester County. William Still, *The Underground Railroad* (1871; reprint, Chicago: Johnson Publishing Company, Inc., 1970), 554.

40. Ibid., 554–55.

41. Ibid.

42. According to the Dorchester County Assessment Records, Rachel was taken off the Brodess taxable property list in 1859. Only the two children, Angerine and Benjamin, remained. A local Auburn abolitionist, D. C. Collins, wrote to Franklin Sanborn on January 25, 1861, "We are much pleased that Harriet succeeded in assisting even a few of her suffering friends to escape from bondage, but her sister was not among the number, she having been released from her labors some time since by that friend of the poor slave, the Angel of Death." See D. C. Collins to Franklin Sanborn, January 25, 1861, Franklin B. Sanborn Papers, American Antiquarian Society, Worcester, Mass. See also Gerrit Smith to Franklin Sanborn, January 29, 1861, Franklin B. Sanborn Papers, Library of Congress, Washington, D.C. Smith wrote that Tubman "returned Christmas from another of her southern expeditions, bringing with her 7 slaves. But her sister, after whom she went was not among them. She died a little before Harriet reached her neighborhood."

43. Cheney, "Moses."

44. James Freeman Clark, *Anti-Slavery Days* (1883; reprint, Westport, Conn.: Negro Universities Press, 1970). Tubman apparently told Clark that "there were many people in the slave states, even slaveholders, who were willing to secret fugitives if paid enough for doing it" (81).

45. Sarah H. Bradford, *Harriet, the Moses of Her People* (New York: Geo. R. Lockwood & Sons, 1886), 91. This story does not appear in Bradford's first biography of Tubman, *Scenes in the Life of Harriet Tubman*. In her attempts to make the second biography a little fresher, Bradford added new details not mentioned in the first. Bradford knew Tubman and spent enough time with her over the years to support the conjecture that these additional stories and details came from Tubman herself. Bradford's accuracy remains inconsistent, however.

46. See Dorchester County Levy Book, Dorchester County Board of Commissioners, MDSA.

47. Still, *Underground Railroad*. Still wrote that Tubman "engaged to pilot them within reach of Wilmington, at least to Thomas Garret's" (555). Tubman usually traveled to Philadelphia and New York.

48. Ibid. Still identified Stephen's enslaver as "John Kaiger," and that of Maria and the children's as "Algier Pearcy." See also Assessment Record, Dorchester County Board of County Commissioners, MDSA. See District 4 for the various Cator families; and see also Will of Thomas E. Cator, in Leslie and Neil Keddie, *Dorchester County, Maryland Wills Liber T.H.H. I: September 1854–February 1857, Folios 340–448* (Salisbury, Md.: Family Tree Bookshops, 2002), 26.

49. Still, *Underground Railroad*, 555. See also Elaine McGill, transcr., *Robert Bell's Book of Slave Statistics 1864–1868* (privately printed, 2001).

50. Bradford, *Harriet* (1886), 53–55.

51. Ibid., 54–55.

52. Ibid., 55. Bradford says here that there were two babies, twins, whom she had "since seen well grown young women." It is unclear if the Ennals had one or two babies—Bradford often conflated sto-

ries, so we may never know exactly which trip this was. Given the timing, however, and that Tubman did not make additional trips after the fall of 1857 to the Eastern Shore (until the fall of 1860), it is likely she was out of touch with all the ramifications of heightened security on the Eastern Shore when she did return at the end of 1860.

53. Bradford, *Harriet* (1886), 56.

54. Ibid., 57.

55. Ibid.

56. Martha Coffin Wright to Ellen Wright Garrison, December 30, 1860, Garrison Family Papers, box 36, f. 948, Sophia Smith Collection, Smith College, Northampton, Mass.

57. Bradford, *Harriet* (1886), 35.

58. Martha Coffin Wright to Ellen Wright Garrison, December 30, 1860, Garrison Family Papers, box 36, f. 948, Sophia Smith Collection, Smith College, Northampton, Mass. I have made some editorial adjustments to this letter for easier reading: ". . . went out foraging, and sometimes cd. not get back till dark, fearing she wd. be followed—Then if they had crept further in, & she couldn't find them, she wd. whistle, or sing certain hymns & they wd answer."

59. Bradford, *Harriet* (1886), 36–37. See also Bradford, *Scenes,* 26.

60. Bradford, *Scenes,* 27.

61. Bradford, *Harriet* (1886), 37–38.

62. Still, *Underground Railroad,* 554–55. While at Garrett's house, another runaway from Baltimore, a young woman "in a delicate state," arrived. See also James McGowan, *Station Master on the Underground Railroad* (Moylan, Pa.: The Whimsie Press, 1977), 107–8. In his book, *The Underground Railroad,* Still apologized for his brief commentary and lack of details on Tubman's "last" rescue mission. The "capture of John Brown's papers and letters, with names and plans in full, admonished us that such papers and correspondence as had been preserved concerning the Underground Rail Road," were vulnerable to discovery and exposure, putting the operation at too great a risk. In fact, Still and his partner McKim had taken the precaution at the time of Brown's trial to hide some of the Vigilance Committee's journals and correspondence in a nearby cemetery. Afterward, Still "omitted some of the most important particulars in the escapes and narratives of fugitives," and often the "records were kept simply on loose slips of paper" (555).

63. Still, *Underground Railroad,* 555; McGowan, *Station Master,* 108.

64. Martha Coffin Wright to Ellen Wright Garrison, December 30, 1860, Garrison Family Papers, box 36, f. 948, Sophia Smith Collection, Smith College, Northampton, Mass.

65. D. C. Collins to Franklin Sanborn, January 25, 1861, Franklin B. Sanborn Papers, American Antiquarian Society, Worcester, Mass. Collins reported that Tubman had not been seen for "two or three weeks—but she is so very erratic in her movements."

66. Gerrit Smith to Franklin Sanborn, January 29, 1861, Franklin B. Sanborn Papers, Library of Congress, Washington, D.C.

67. Ibid.

68. James B. Clark, "An Hour with Harriet Tubman," in *Christophe: A Tragedy in Prose of Imperial Haiti,* ed. William Edgar Easton (Los Angeles: Grafton Publishing Company, 1911). The Gerrit home was quite large and impressive, much like a southern plantation. John Stauffer describes in his work on black abolitionists that Smith's home reminded Frederick Douglass of the great plantation of Edward Lloyd, of Talbot County, whose estate was one of the largest in Maryland. The Smith estate featured an impressive mansion, with many outbuildings and barns, and it also employed many African Americans, "artisans and servants along with field hands and farmhands," who had settled near the property over the many years the Smiths had lived there and provided land for black families. See John Stauffer, *The Black Hearts of Men: Radical Abolitionists and the Transformation of Race* (Cambridge, Mass.: Harvard University Press, 2002), 82–83.

69. Clark, "Hour with Harriet Tubman."

70. Ibid.

71. Martha Coffin Wright to Lucretia Coffin Mott, n.d. (early February 1861), Garrison Family Papers, box 37, f. 950, Sophia Smith Collection, Smith College, Northampton, Mass.

72. "New York," in "Underground Railroad: Manuscript Materials Collected by Professor Siebert," Houghton Library, Harvard University, Cambridge, Mass.; see Wixom "The Underground Railway," located in this collection for more detailed information, especially 31–34.

73. David Wright to Martha Coffin Wright, February 9, 1861, Garrison Family Papers, box 42, f. 1043, Sophia Smith Collection, Smith College, Northampton, Mass.

74. Wright's decision to send it to Hosmer may have also served as a quick way to warn other fugitives and antislavery activists in the area of the potential threat. See Martha Coffin Wright to Lucretia Coffin Mott, n.d. (early February 1861), Garrison Family Papers, box 37, f. 950, Sophia Smith Collection, Smith College, Northampton, Mass.

75. Ibid.

76. For more information on William Seward, see Glyndon G. Van Deusen, *William Henry Seward* (New York: Oxford University Press, 1967). See also Crofts, "Seward, William Henry." For more information on the sectional crisis of 1861, see James M. McPherson, *Battle Cry of Freedom: The Civil War Era* (New York: Ballantine Books, 1988).

77. Sanborn, "Harriet Tubman." See also Bradford, *Scenes*, 84.

78. Gerrit Smith to Franklin Sanborn, February 20, 1861, Franklin Sanborn Papers, Library of Congress, Washington, D.C. See also Martha Coffin Wright to Lucretia Coffin Mott, fragment—February 1861, Garrison Family Papers, box 37, f. 950, Sophia Smith Collection, Smith College, Northampton, Mass.

79. Martha Coffin Wright to Lucretia Coffin Mott, fragment—February 1861, Garrison Family Papers, box 37, f. 950, Sophia Smith Collection, Smith College, Northampton, Mass.

80. Sanborn, "Harriet Tubman." Smith returned to his home in Peterboro on February 20, leaving Tubman behind in Canada. Gerrit Smith to Franklin Sanborn, February 20, 1861, Franklin Sanborn Papers, Library of Congress, Washington, D.C.

81. Gerrit Smith to Franklin Sanborn, April 16, 1861, Franklin Sanborn Papers, Library of Congress, Washington, D.C.

82. Sarah H. Bradford, *Harriet, the Moses of Her People* (New York: J. J. Little & Co., 1901), 145.

83. Elijah R. Stewart, Citizenship Papers, October 23, 1888, United States Circuit Court, Boston. The papers indicate that Elijah came to New York in April 1861. It is not known whether James Stewart accompanied them or not. It is assumed he did so, though he must have died before 1865 (see State of New York, *New York State Census*, 1865, Cayuga County), after fathering two more children with Catherine; Adam, born c. Aug.–Sept. 1861, and Hester, born ca. Sept. 1863. Adam died on February 1, 1863. See Records of Central Presbyterian Church, Auburn, N.Y. See also 1865 N.Y. Census, Cayuga County. There is no record of James's death, although Catherine is listed as single in the 1865 census, and the widow of Andrew Winslow in the 1870 city directory. See Hitchcock & Smith, *Auburn Directory for 1870* (Auburn and Syracuse, N.Y.: Hitchcock & Smith Printers, 1870), 191. See also Bureau of the Census, *United States Federal Census*, 1870, Cayuga County, N.Y.

84. Bradford, *Harriet* (1901), 143.

85. See Auburn Daily Advertiser, *Auburn Daily Advertiser City Directory for 1862–63* (Auburn, N.Y.: Knapp & Peck, 1862), 183; Andrew Boyd, *Boyd's Auburn Directory, 1867–68* (Auburn, N.Y.: Andrew Boyd Publisher, 1867), 215.

86. Gerrit Smith to Franklin Sanborn, April 11, 1861, Franklin Sanborn Papers, Library of Congress, Washington, D.C. Gerrit wrote, "I do not know where Harriet is. Her mother visited us a few weeks ago."

87. See "Relief of Fugitives in Canada," *The Liberator*, Boston, October 25, 1861, and "Relief of Fugitives in Canada. An Association," *The Liberator*, Boston, December 20, 1861.

88. Wilkins's name was "Wilkinson," according to William Still. See Still, *Underground Railroad*. 453–67. The Ontario census, 1861, also lists him as Horatio Wilkinson, living in Grantham not far from William Henry Stewart, Tubman's brother. Wilkinson had been claimed by Thomas Hodson, of Dorchester County. The other men were Plymouth Cannon, who ran from Horsey's Crossroads in Sussex County, Delaware; Lemuel Mitchell; Josiah Mitchell; George Henry Ballard; and John Mitchell. Plymouth Cannon later settled in Auburn. George Ballard was related to Levin Parker, who had fled Dorchester County in October 1857. See Still, *Underground Railroad*; 466–67. Fletcher lived near Kit Anthony, and Anthony's fellow refugee from slavery, Joe Viney, in St. Paul's Ward in St. Catharines. See 1861 Canadian Census, St. Catharines, Ontario.

89. "Relief of Fugitives in Canada," and "Relief of Fugitives in Canada. An Association."

90. Still, *Underground Railroad*, 465.

91. Franklin Sanborn to Gerrit Smith, September 8, 1861, Gerrit Smith Papers, Syrcause University Library, Syracuse, N.Y.

92. Bradford, *Harriet* (1886), 92–93.

93. Ibid., 93.

94. McPherson, *Battle Cry*, 264–75.

95. Ibid., 284–88. See also Barbara Jeanne Fields, *Slavery and Freedom on the Middle Ground* (New Haven: Yale University Press, 1985), 92–100.

96. War Department, Records and Pension Office, *The War of the Rebellion: A Compilation of the Official Records of the Union and Confederate Armies* (Washington, D.C.: Government Printing Office, 1880), series 1, 2:593–95.

97. J. H. Bayne to General McClellan, March 12, 1862, citing a letter from F. A. Medley, January 21, 1862, Records of Asst. Commissioner for the State of S.C. Bureau of Refugees, Freedmen and Abandoned Lands, 1865–1870, 1.

98. Sanborn to Lyman, November 3, 1861, in Kenneth Walter Cameron, ed., *Young Reporter of Concord: A Checklist of F. B. Sanborn's Letters to Benjamin Smith Lyman, 1853–1867, with Extracts Emphasizing Life and Literary Events in the World of Emerson, Thoreau and Alcott* (Hartford, Conn.: Transcendental Books, 1978), 33. See also Fields, *Slavery*, 106–7, 110–13.

99. War Department, Records and Pension Office, *The War of the Rebellion*, series 3, 1:480–82. In September 1861, Thomas R. Stewart, brother of James A. Stewart, was arrested on suspicion of carrying supplies to rebels in Virginia. See Naval War Records Department, Office of Naval Records and Library United States, *The Official Records of the Union and Confederate Navies in the War of the Rebellion* (Washington, D.C.: Government Printing Office, 1896), series 1, 4:650–52.

100. McPherson, *Battle Cry*, 370–71.

101. Ibid., 354–55, 494–500.

102. Ibid., 496–500.

103. Ibid., 354–55. See also Ira Berlin et al., eds., *Freedom: A Documentary History of Emancipation 1861–1867*, series I, vol. 1, *The Destruction of Slavery* (Cambridge: Cambridge University Press, 1985), 70–75.

104. Berlin et al., eds., *Destruction of Slavery*, 22–23; see also McPherson, *Battle Cry*, 497–98.

105. Willie Lee Rose, *Rehearsal for Reconstruction: The Port Royal Experiment* (1964; reprint, Athens: The University of Georgia Press, 1999), 144–52; McPherson, *Battle Cry*, 499. See also Thomas O'Connor, *Civil War Boston: Home Front and Battlefield* (Boston: Northeastern University Press, 1997), 111.

106. McPherson, *Battle Cry*, 499; James M. McPherson, *The Struggle for Equality: Abolitionists and the Negro in the Civil War and Reconstruction* (Princeton, N.J.: Princeton University Press, 1964), 102–3; Rose, *Rehearsal*, 144–53.

107. Noah Andre Trudeau, *Like Men of War: Black Troops in the Civil War, 1862–1865* (Boston: Little, Brown & Company, 1998), 12.

108. War Department, Records and Pension Office, *The War of the Rebellion*, series 1, 6:218.

109. For an excellent study of this period of occupation of the Sea Islands and Port Royal, and efforts to educate, feed, and clothe newly liberated slaves and rebuild the area's farming operations, see Rose, *Rehearsal*.

110. Ibid., 35–44; O'Connor, *Civil War Boston*, 110–15; McPherson, *Struggle*, 158–64; Luther P. Jackson, "The Educational Efforts of the Freedmen's Bureau and Freedmen's Aid Societies in South Carolina, 1862–1872," *Journal of Negro History* 8, no. 1 (1923). Bostonians established the Boston Educational Commission, which soon became the New England Freedmen's Aid Society; New Yorkers established the New York National Freedmen's Relief Association; and Philadelphians created the Port Royal Relief Committee, later known as the Pennsylvania Freedmen's Relief Association. Jackson, "Freedmen's Aid," 6.

111. Sanborn, "Harriet Tubman." See also Bradford, *Scenes*, 85. Ednah Dow Cheney wrote that once the "war broke out, Harriet was very anxious to go to South Carolina to assist the contrabands." Cheney, "Moses," 37–38.

112. Interview with Helen W. Tatlock (Mrs. William Tatlock), Earl Conrad/Harriet Tubman Collection, New York Public Library, Schomberg Center for Research in Black Culture. Tatlock said: "During the war she had been opposed to some of the things Lincoln did; she had been prejudiced against him at first." See also Rosa Belle Holt, "A Heroine in Ebony," *The Chautauquan*, July 1896, 462.

113. Sanborn, "Harriet Tubman"; Bradford, *Scenes;* Sanborn, "The Late Araminta Davis: Better Known as 'Moses' or 'Harriet Tubman,' " Franklin B. Sanborn Papers, box 1, folder 5, American Antiquarian Society, Worcester, Mass.; and Bradford, *Scenes*, 6, 55, 85. Tubman lectured at various places, including the Twelfth Baptist Church in Boston, to help raise money for the Port Royal trip, but according to the *Liberator*, the donations were small. See "Harriet Tubman," *The Liberator,* Boston, February 21, 1862.

114. Cheney, "Moses," 38.

115. Martha Coffin Wright to Francis Wright, May 28, 1862, Garrison Family Papers, box 41, f. 1028.22, Sophia Smith Collection, Smith College, Northampton, Mass.

116. Personal communication with Peter Wisby, curator, William H. Seward House, Auburn, N.Y.

117. See Pam Greene, "Seward: Innkeeper on the Underground Railroad," *The Syracuse Newspapers: Cayuga Neighbors—Herald Journal,* Syracuse, N.Y., February 17, 2000.

118. Alice Lucas Brickler to Earl Conrad, July 19, 1939, Earl Conrad/Harriet Tubman Collection, New York Public Library, Schomburg Center for Research in Black Culture. For Carter's comments, see Earl Conrad, *General Harriet Tubman*, 2nd ed. (Washington, D.C.: Associated Publishers, Inc., 1990), 230 n. 13. "Mrs. Florence Carter, a close friend of Harriet Tubman in the closing period of Harriet's life, in a statement to the author, has verified the fact that the 'kidnapped' child remained throughout life a favorite of Harriet Tubman." Margaret Stewart married Henry Lucas in 1872 at the Central Presbyterian Church in Auburn.

119. Alice Lucas Brickler to Earl Conrad, July 19, 1939, Earl Conrad/Harriet Tubman Collection, New York Public Library, Schomburg Center for Research in Black Culture.

120. Ibid.

121. Ibid.

122. Ibid.

123. Ibid.

124. Ibid. Frances Seward died in June 1865, and Seward's daughter Fanny died in 1866. See Crofts, "Seward, William Henry." Lazette Worden remained a fixture in the Seward home, helping to oversee the domestic operations of the household. Margaret probably lived with Lazette in the Seward home and possibly at Worden's own home on Owasco Lake in Auburn. Margaret is also listed in the 1865 Fleming, New York, census in the Tubman household. According to Brickler, Margaret was often taken to Tubman's home for visits, and she may have been visiting, or even staying there temporarily when the census takers came by the house. The census was taken during the same period in which Francis Seward was dying, and William H. Seward and his son Frederick were still recovering from the near-

fatal attack they endured on the night of Lincoln's assassination, at the hands of Lewis Powell, one of John Wilkes Booth's co-conspirators. Margaret may have been sent to Tubman's home while the Seward house was in such turmoil.

125. John D. Parker from David Ross, May 25, 1857, Dorchester County Chattel Records, Maryland State Archives, Annapolis, Md., p. 275. John D. Parker, it will be recalled, was Anthony Thompson's overseer, who also purchased several hundred acres of Thompson property in the Peters Neck area. He was quite familiar with the Ross family. David and Benjamin's mother remains unidentified. The court record does not give her name.

126. Though the 1865 Fleming, N.Y., census indicates Margaret to be thirteen, all subsequent records indicate she was born around 1850. See 1880, 1892 (N.Y.), 1905 (N.Y.), 1920, and 1930 censuses.

127. Alice Lucas Brickler to Earl Conrad, July 19, 1939, Earl Conrad/Harriet Tubman Collection, New York Public Library, Schomburg Center for Research in Black Culture.

128. Thompson Deposition, Equity Papers 249, Dorchester County Court, Dorchester County courthouse, Cambridge, Md. Ben was hired out to Dr. Anthony C. Thompson at one point.

129. Bradford, *Harriet* (1886), 15.

130. "Foster Child of Harriet Tubman Dies," *Advertiser-Journal and Auburn Citizen*, Auburn, N.Y., May 19, 1930.

131. Alice Lucas Brickler to Earl Conrad, July 19, 1939, Earl Conrad/Harriet Tubman Collection, New York Public Library, Schomburg Center for Research in Black Culture.

132. Conrad, *General Tubman*, 230 n. 13. "Mrs. Carter verifies that this woman bore a marked resemblance to Harriet."

133. Unidentified newspaper article, Harriet Tubman Scrapbooks, Seymour Library, Auburn, N.Y.

134. In one letter to Conrad, Brickler says that her mother was the sister of Maria Elliot, and that Maria's daughter Mary Gaston (Gaskin) called Margaret "Aunt Maggie (much to my father's disgust)." What Brickler meant by her father being disgusted is unknown, although it may have meant he felt the relationship was not as Brickler imagined. There was so much tension in the family regarding Margaret that the resulting motivations and attitudes have perhaps forever clouded any hope of finding the true relationships.

135. Alice Lucas Brickler to Earl Conrad, July 19, 1939, Earl Conrad/Harriet Tubman Collection, New York Public Library, Schomburg Center for Research in Black Culture.

136. "To a Most Heroic Negress: Fitting Memorial of Harriet Tubman Davis Is Appropriately Displayed," *The Auburn Citizen*, Auburn, N.Y., June 14, 1914.

137. Mrs. E. S. Northrup to Earl Conrad, Earl Conrad/Harriet Tubman Collection, New York Public Library, Schomburg Center for Research in Black Culture. Eva was also known as Katy. According to her daughter, Mariline Northrup Wilkins, her name at birth was Katherine Evelyn Helena Harriet Stewart.

138. Ibid. Making sure that Conrad received her message clearly, Northrup reiterated her point: "Mrs. Brickler is in no way shape or manner a Kin of Harriet Tubman. Neither she nor her parents. . . . Since she is not rightfully a Kin she is eliminated from sharing any honors."

139. Earl Conrad to Alice Lucas Brickler, Earl Conrad/Harriet Tubman Collection, New York Public Library, Schomburg Center for Research in Black Culture.

140. Alice Lucas Brickler to Earl Conrad, April 23, 1940, Earl Conrad/Harriet Tubman Collection, New York Public Library, Schomburg Center for Research in Black Culture.

141. Ibid.

142. Alice Lucas Brickler to Earl Conrad, November 26, 1940, Earl Conrad/Harriet Tubman Collection, New York Public Library, Schomburg Center for Research in Black Culture.

143. Alice Lucas Brickler to Earl Conrad, April 23, 1940, Earl Conrad/Harriet Tubman Collection, New York Public Library, Schomburg Center for Research in Black Culture.

Chapter 10

1. Charles P. Wood, "Manuscript History Concerning the Pension Claim of Harriet Tubman," HR 55A-D1, Papers Accompanying the Claim of Harriet Tubman, Record Group 233, National Archives, Washington, D.C.

2. Emma P. Telford, "Harriet: The Modern Moses of Heroism and Visions," Cayuga County Museum, Auburn, N.Y., c. 1905, 15.

3. Wood, "Manuscript History."

4. Telford, "Harriet," 15. "Dey change dey programme an' wanted me to go down and 'stribute clothes to de contraban's who were comin' in to the Union lines night and day. Dey wouldn't let no colored people go down Souf den, unless dey went with some of the officers as a servant; so dey got a gentlemen from New York to take me as a servant. He was stoppin' at a big hotel on Broadway, an I went to de parlor an' dey sent for him an' he came down: but I didn't like dat man no how. He look at me an' said, 'well, I guess you're young enough. You go to the quarter master and tell him I sent you.' But I made up my mind dat I want goin wid dat man. He looked brave an' noble enough to be a gen'man if looks made one, a struttin' about; but I went out an' I aint seen de quarter master yit, nor him neither. So I jus' went on alone to Baltimore, an' General Hunter sent for me to go to Beaufort, an' de vessel dat was goin' dar didn't sail for two days, a waitin' for me till de Generals orders were fulfilled."

5. Tubman probably arrived just after Brigadier General Thomas W. Sherman was joined by Major General David Hunter, placing her there by late March 1862. See Willie Lee Rose, Rehearsal for Reconstruction: The Port Royal Experiment (1964; reprint, Athens: The University of Georgia Press, 1999), 144–45.

6. Ibid.

7. Telford, "Harriet," 16. See also James M. McPherson, Battle Cry of Freedom: The Civil War Era (New York: Ballantine Books, 1988), 483.

8. Wood, "Manuscript History." See also Ednah Dow Littlehale Cheney, "Moses," Freedmen's Record, March 1865. Susie King Taylor, a former slave who worked in the Union camps at Hilton Head, more specifically for the First South Carolina Volunteers, a black regiment led by Thomas W. Higginson, wrote that the black soldiers' wives, local to the area, "were obliged to support themselves and children by washing for the officers of the gunboats and the soldiers, and making cakes and pies which they sold to the boys in camp." See Susie King Taylor, A Black Woman's Civil War Memoirs: Reminiscences of My Life in Camp with the 33rd U.S. Colored Troops, Late 1st South Carolina Volunteers, ed. Patricia W. Romero (1902; reprint, Princeton, N.J.: Marcus Wiener Publishers, 1988), 42.

9. Wood, "Manuscript History."

10. Ibid. See also Sarah H. Bradford, Scenes in the Life of Harriet Tubman (Auburn, N.Y.: W. J. Moses, 1869), 37–38. Later, Tubman would lose some of the money she earned when it was stolen from her. See George Garrison to William Lloyd Garrison II, February 10, 1864, Garrison Family Papers, box 28, folder 790, Sophia Smith Collection, Smith College, Northampton, Mass. See also Benjamin Guterman, "Doing 'Good Brave Work': Harriet Tubman's Testimony at Beaufort, South Carolina," Prologue 42, no. 3 (2000): 163.

11. Franklin B. Sanborn, "The Late Araminta Davis: Better Known as 'Moses' or 'Harriet Tubman,' " Franklin B. Sanborn Papers, box 1, folder 5, American Antiquarian Society, Worcester, Mass. Through a friend of Sanborn's, Elbridge Gerry Dudley.

12. Rose, Rehearsal, 144–46. See also Noah Andre Trudeau, Like Men of War: Black Troops in the Civil War, 1862–1865 (Boston: Little, Brown & Company, 1998), 14–16.

13. Trudeau, Like Men of War, 14–17.

14. Rose, Rehearsal, 147–51; see also McPherson, Battle Cry, 499.

15. A fever often associated with malaria.

16. Lydia Maria Child to John G. Whittier, January 21, 1862, Lydia Maria Child Papers, Library of Congress, Washington, D.C. "Dey may send de flower of dair young men down South, to die ob de fever in de summer, and de agoo in de winter (Fur *tis* cold down dar, dough *tis* down South) Dey may send dem one year, two years, tree year, till dey *tired* ob sendin, or till dey use up all de young men. All no use! God's ahead ob massa Linkum. God won't let massa Linkum beat de South till he do *de right ting*. Massa linkum he great man, and I'se poor nigger; but di nigger can tell massa Linkum how to save de money and de young men. He do it by setting de niggers free. Spose dat was awfu' big snake down dar, on de floor. He bite you. Folks all skeered, cause you die. You send fur doctor to cut de bite; but snake he rolled up dar, and while doctor dwine it, he bite you *agin*. De doctor dug out *dat* bite; but while doctor dwine it, de snake he spring up and bite you agin; so he *keep* dwine, till you kill *him*. Dat's what massa Linkum oter know." Lydia Maria Child was a prominent Boston author and antislavery activist. She told John Greenleaf Whittier that Tubman enjoyed talking politics, and that "her uncouth utterance is wiser than the plans of politicians."

17. Bradford, *Scenes*, 38–39.

18. Rose, *Rehearsal*, 146–50.

19. Rose, *Rehearsal*, 185; see also Trudeau, *Like Men of War*, 17–19.

20. See also McPherson, *Battle Cry*, 502–5, 557–58. Also, James M. McPherson, *The Struggle for Equality: Abolitionists and the Negro in the Civil War and Reconstruction* (Princeton, N.J.: Princeton University Press, 1964), 111, 117–18. Lincoln also promised a plan for gradual emancipation in loyal states, too, at a later date.

21. Trudeau, *Like Men of War*, 18–19.

22. *The Complete Civil War Journal and Selected Letters of Thomas Wentworth Higginson*, ed. Christopher Looby (Chicago: The University of Chicago Press, 2000), 250.

23. Margaret E. Wagner, Gary W. Gallagher, and Paul Finkleman, eds., *The Library of Congress Civil War Desk Reference* (New York: Simon and Schuster, 2002), 638–51.

24. Rose, *Rehearsal*, 171–72. See also McPherson, *Battle Cry*, 487–88.

25. Henry K. Durant to Capt. Warfield, August 28, 1862, in Sarah H. Bradford, *Harriet, the Moses of Her People* (New York: Geo. R. Lockwood & Sons, 1886), 141.

26. Wagner, Gallagher, and Finkleman, eds., *Civil War Desk Reference*. 646.

27. *Journal of Charlotte Forten: A Free Negro in the Slave Era*, ed. Ray Allen Billington (New York: Collier Books, 1961), 180.

28. Bradford, *Harriet* (1886), 97.

29. Guterman, "Doing 'Good Brave Work,' " 163.

30. Diary entry, January 31, 1863, *Journal of Charlotte Forten*, 180. Forten turned to the Pennsylvania society when the Boston Education Commission wouldn't make a decision about allowing her to go. Forten traveled from her base on St. Helena's Island with Lizzie Hunn, the daughter of John Hunn, a Quaker abolitionist and Underground Railroad operator from Camden, Delaware. The Hunns met Forten on the boat coming from Philadelphia to Port Royal in October. They opened a store on St. Helena's Island, sponsored by the Pennsylvania Freedmen's Relief Association, which provided supplies to the newly freed slaves. *Journal of Charlotte Forten*, 32, 138, 188, 264. Though no documentary evidence exists, Tubman may have stopped at the Hunns' home, near Camden in Delaware, on one or more of her trips bringing runaway slaves out of the Eastern Shore.

31. Ibid., 180.

32. Ibid.

33. "The Celebration of the Emancipation of the Slaves of the South, on the 1st of January, 1863," *The Free South*, Beaufort, S.C., January 10, 1863.

34. Ibid.

35. Ibid.

36. "News from South Carolina. Negro Jubilee at Hilton Head," *The New York Herald*, New York, January 7, 1863; *The Journal of Charlotte Forten*, 172.

37. "Celebration of the Emancipation"; see also *The Journal of Charlotte Forten*, 172–73; *The Complete Civil War Journal and Selected Letters of Thomas Wentworth Higginson*, 76–78; Rose, *Rehearsal*, 196–97.

38. Rose, *Rehearsal*, 197. For descriptions of the great day at Camp Saxton, see *The Journal of Charlotte Forten*; *The Complete Civil War Journal and Selected Letters of Thomas Wentworth Higginson*; "Jubilee at Hilton Head"; "Celebration of the Emancipation."

39. Bradford, *Harriet* (1886), 93.

40. Wood, "Manuscript History."

41. Ibid.

42. Ibid. The list is signed Brigadier General Rufus Saxton, n.d.

43. Guterman, "Doing 'Good Brave Work,' " 165 n. 11.

44. Russell Duncan, ed., *Blue-Eyed Child of Fortune: The Civil War Letters of Colonel Robert Gould Shaw* (Athens: The University of Georgia Press, 1992), 337.

45. Rose, *Rehearsal*, 244. See also Trudeau, *Like Men of War*, 13–14. Montgomery was the commander of the Third Kansas Infantry at the start of the war; that unit was transferred to the Department of the South to become the foundation of Hunter's next black regiment, the Second South Carolina Volunteers.

46. Montgomery to Brigadier General Gilmore, July 6, 1863, Wood, "Manuscript History." "I wish to commend to your attention Mrs. Harriet Tubman a most remarkable woman, and valuable as a scout. I have been acquainted with her character and actions for several years."

47. William E. Connelley, *A Standard History of Kansas and Kansans* (Chicago: Lewis Publishing Company, 1918).

48. Trudeau, *Like Men of War*, 68.

49. See Taylor, *A Black Woman's Civil War Memoirs*.

50. Bradford, *Harriet* (1886), 140. Tubman may have accompanied Higginson on a successful raid up the St. Mary's River, on the border between Georgia and Florida, at the end of January 1863.

51. Guterman, "Doing 'Good Brave Work.' "

52. "Expedition up the Combahee," *The Port Royal New South*, Beaufort, S.C., June 6, 1863.

53. Telford, "Harriet." See also Bradford, *Scenes*, 39; Wood, "Manuscript History."

54. Telford, "Harriet."

55. Report of Col. James Montgomery, 2nd S.C. Colored Volunteers by Telegraph from Beaufort, June 3rd, 1863, to Major General D. Hunter, Records of Assistant Commissioner for the State of South Carolina Bureau of Refugees, Freedmen, and Abandoned Lands, 1865–1870, Beaufort, S.C. See also "Colonel Montgomery's Raid—the Rescued Black Chattels—a Black 'She Moses'—Her Wonderful Daring and Sagacity—the Black Regiments—Col. Higginson's Mistakes—Arrival of the 54th Massachusetts, &c., &c.," *The Wisconsin State Journal*, Madison, June 20, 1863; "Expedition up the Combahee."

56. Bradford, *Scenes*, 40–41; see also Telford, "Harriet."

57. "Raid Among the Rice Plantations," *Harper's Weekly*, New York, July 4, 1863.

58. "The Enemy Raid on the Banks of the Combahee," *The Charleston Mercury*, Carleston, S.C., June 4, 1863. The plantations of Dr. R. L. Baker, Oliver Middleton, Andrew Burnett, William Kirkland, Joshua Nicholls, James Paul, Charles Lowndes, and William C. Heyward were pillaged and destroyed.

59. "Enemy Raid"; see also "Expedition up the Combahee."

60. "Expedition up the Combahee."

61. Bradford, *Scenes*, 40.

62. "Expedition up the Combahee."; Bradford, *Scenes*, 40; "Enemy Raid."

63. "Enemy Raid."

64. Bradford, *Scenes*, 40.

65. Telford, "Harriet." "Some had white blankets on dere haids with dere things done up in 'em. . . . Some had bags on dere backs with pigs in dem; some had chickens tied by de laigs."

66. Bradford, *Scenes*, 40.

67. Telford, "Harriet." "[O]b de chillern ob Israel, comin' out ob Egypt."

68. Bradford, *Scenes*, 41.

69. Telford, "Harriet." Telford wrote, quoting Harriet, "Moses Garrison . . . come here an' speak a word ob consolation to your people."

70. Ibid. "Well dey wasn't my people any more dan dey was his'n,—only we was all Negroes—cos I didn't know any more about 'em dan he did. So I went when he called me on de gun boat, an dey 'on de shore. Dey didn't know any ting about me an' I didn't know what to say. I looked at 'em about two minutes, an' den I sung to 'em. Moses, you'll have to give 'em a song" (19). This was not the only time that Tubman tried to point out that the shade of one's skin did not make them all the same, nor did skin color transcend social and cultural differences within the black community. She told Sarah Bradford that when she was in South Carolina, she too had difficulty understanding some of the freedmen, and found some of their customs far different than ones she had grown up with. "Why, der language down dar in de far South is jus' as different from ours in Maryland, as you can think," said she. "Dey laughed when dey heard me talk, an' I could not understand dem, no how." She went on to describe a funeral service for a former slave, which seemed foreign to her (42–43).

71. Telford, "Harriet," 19; see also Bradford, *Scenes*, 41–42. Various reports give numbers that range from 725 to 840 contrabands. Montgomery wrote 725 (Montgomery Report, June 3, 1863); Tubman indicated 756 (Franklin Sanborn, "Harriet Tubman," *The Commonwealth*, Boston, July 17, 1863); the *Port Royal New South* published 727 ("Expedition up the Combahee"); the *Wisconsin State Journal* used the figure "near 800" ("Colonel Montgomery's Raid—the Rescued Black Chattels"); and Corporal James Henry Gooding, of the Massachusetts Fifty-fourth, wrote in his correspondence 840 (in *On the Altar of Freedom: A Black Soldier's Civil War Letters from the Front. Corporal James Henry Gooding*, ed. Virginia M. Adams (Amherst: University of Massachusetts Press, 1991), 28. Bradford recorded the song that Tubman sang that day (Bradford, *Scenes*): "Harriet lifted up her voice and sang:

> Of all the whole creation in the east or in the west,
> The glorious Yankee nation is the greatest and the best.
> Come along! Come along! don't be alarmed,
> Uncle Sam is rich enough to give you all a farm."

Emma Telford recorded a slightly different version forty years later (Telford, "Harriet," 19):

> Come from de East;
> Come from de West;
> Mong all de glorious nations
> Dis glorious one's de bes;
> Come 'long! Come 'long! Don't be alarmed,
> For Uncle Sam is rich enough
> To gave you all a farm.

72. "Extracts from the Journal of an Officer in the 54th Regt. Mass. Vols," *The Commonwealth*, Boston, June 26, 1863.

73. "Colonel Montgomery's Raid—the Rescued Black Chattels."

74. Ibid.

75. Ibid. The reporter incorrectly stated that Tubman was a former slave from Virginia, but he highlighted Tubman's activities, "effecting the escape of over 180 slaves" during "nine successful trips in different slave states."

76. Sanborn, "Harriet Tubman"; Bradford, *Scenes*, 86. See also Franklin B. Sanborn, "Harriet Tubman," *The Commonwealth*, Boston, July 10, 1863.

77. The actual number is unknown.

78. Telford, "Harriet."

79. *The Complete Civil War Journal and Selected Letters of Thomas Wentworth Higginson*, 288–89.

80. Duncan, ed., *Blue-Eyed Child*, 339, 356.

81. See *The Complete Civil War Journal and Selected Letters of Thomas Wentworth Higginson*; Tilden Edelstein, *Strange Enthusiasm: A Life of Thomas Wentworth Higginson* (New York: Atheneum, 1970), 286–87; and *Letters and Journals of Thomas Wentworth Higginson, 1846–1906*, ed. Mary Thatcher Higginson (Boston: Houghton Mifflin Company, 1921), 206–9.

82. Sanborn, "The Late Araminta Davis."

83. Guterman, "Doing 'Good Brave Work,' " 158–59.

84. As quoted in ibid., 159.

85. Ibid. Benjamin Guterman argues in this article on Webster's trial, that because of the nature of the abolitionist influence in the Port Royal district, efforts were directed at teaching the freedmen the basics of citizenship, which included the ability to testify in court and sit on juries.

86. Guterman, "Doing 'Good Brave Work,' " 159–60. The other black witnesses were Lucius Dobson, Nat Simmons, Isaac Blake, and Thomas Blake. It is not known if the Blakes or Simmons were related to Tubman's other trusted scouts, Mott Blake and Charles Simmons.

87. For full details of Tubman's testimony, see Guterman, "Doing 'Good Brave Work.' "

88. Ibid., 161.

89. Ibid.

90. Ibid., 159.

91. Duncan, ed., *Blue-Eyed Child*, 338–39.

92. Letter to Sanborn, written by an ameneusis, June 30, 1863, in Sanborn, "Harriet Tubman." See also Bradford, *Scenes*, 87.

93. Sanborn, "Harriet Tubman." See also Bradford, *Scenes*, 87.

94. Harriet Tubman to Franklin Sanborn, June 30, 1863, in Kenneth Walter Cameron, *Correspondence of Franklin Benjamin Sanborn the Transcendentalist* (Hartford, Conn.: Transcendental Books, 1982), 24. This part of the letter was not published in the *Commonwealth* article of July 17, 1863.

95. Sanborn, "Harriet Tubman."

96. Ibid.

97. Account book, entry for July 20, 1863, microfilm reels 192–93, Seward Papers. Harvard University, Cambridge. Another payment had been made the previous April 10, in the amount of $54.75.

98. Sanborn, "Harriet Tubman." See also Bradford, *Scenes*, 85–86.

99. Trudeau, *Like Men of War*, 80.

100. For a detailed description of the events leading up to the assault on Fort Wagner by the Fifty-fourth and other regiments, see Trudeau, *Like Men of War*, 71–90; Russell Duncan, *Where Death and Glory Meet: Colonel Robert Gould Shaw and the Fifty-Fourth Massachusetts Infantry* (Athens: The University of Georgia Press, 1999); Duncan, ed., *Blue-Eyed Child*; McPherson, *Battle Cry*, 686–87; Adams, ed., *Gooding*. 34–43.

101. Montgomery wrote a letter of introduction for her to General Gilmore on July 6, 1863, informing him of Tubman's talents as a spy and a scout. Countersigned by General Rufus Saxton, the letter further indicates Tubman's close association with officers at the highest levels of command in the Department of the South, and their direct knowledge of her accomplishments and skills. See Wood, "Manuscript History."

102. Robert W. Taylor, *Harriet Tubman: The Heroine in Ebony* (Boston: George E. Ellis, Printer, 1901), 13. See also Hidegard Hoyt Swift to Earl Conrad, September 8, 1939, Research Correspondence, Earl Conrad/Harriet Tubman Collection, reel 1, boxes 1 and 2, New York Public Library, Schomberg Center for Research in Black Culture. "She always stoutly maintained that she fed Col. Shaw his last meal etc. and that she was present at this time [of the battle]."

103. Trudeau, *Like Men of War*, 72; Duncan, *Where Death*, 66.

104. Albert Bushnell Hart, *Slavery and Abolition, 1831–1841, The American Nation: A History* (New York: Harper & Brothers Publishers, 1906), 16:209.

105. Trudeau, *Like Men of War*, 86.

106. "At Church of Zion. Body of Harriet Tubman Davis Will Lie in State," *Auburn Citizen*, Auburn, N.Y., March 12, 1913.

107. Bradford, *Scenes*, 37. "I'd go to de hospital, I would, early eb'ry mornin'. I'd get a big chunk of ice, I would, and put it in a basin, and fill it with water; den I'd take a sponge and begin. Fust man I'd come to, I'd thrash away de flies, an' dey'd rise, dey would, like bees roun' a hive. Den I'd begin to bathe der wounds, an' by de time I'd bathed off three or four, de fire and heat would have melted de ice and made de water warm, an' it would be as red as clar blood. Den I'd go an' git more ice, I would, an' by de time I got to de nex' ones, de flies would be roun' de fust ones, black an' thick as eber."

108. Trudeau, *Like Men of War*.

109. *Journal of Charlotte Forten*, 214–18. Forten herself left the area within a few weeks of the battle.

110. Rose, *Rehearsal*, 170–72. See also Nancy Scripture Garrison, *With Courage and Delicacy. Civil War on the Peninsula: Women and the U.S. Sanitary Commission* (Mason City, Iowa: Savas Publishing Company, 1999) for a description and discussion of the exhaustion and ill health Civil War nurses experienced.

111. "Deaths," "February 1, 1863. Adam Stuart. 17 months," Central Presbyterian Church Records, Central Presbyterian Church, Auburn, N.Y. See also New York Census, 1865, Town of Fleming.

112. See Auburn city directories.

113. Auburn Daily Advertiser, *Auburn Daily Advertiser City Directory for 1862–63* (Auburn, N.Y.: Knapp & Peck, 1862), 112.

114. John W. Blassingame, ed., *Slave Testimony: Two Centuries of Letters, Speeches, Interviews, and Autobiographies* (Baton Rouge: Louisiana State University Press, 1977). In his interview with the American Freedmen's Inquiry Commission, on or about November 8, 1863, Henry Stewart is quoted as mentioning his "sister (the one that is now here)." See also original manuscript interview, Samuel Gridley Howe, Canadian Testimony, American Freedmen's Inquiry Commission, Record Group 93, reel 201, National Archives, Washington, D.C., 1863. The interviews in St. Catherines appear to have taken place on November 8, 1863. Also, Mildred Myers places Emily Howland in Auburn in the late fall, either late October or early November, 1863, where she met Harriet Tubman while visiting Fanny Seward at the Seward house. Mildred D. Meyers, *Miss Emily: Emily Howland, Teacher of Freed Slaves, Suffragist, and Friend of Susan B. Anthony and Harriet Tubman* (Charlotte Harbor, Fla.: Tabby House, 1998), 63–64.

115. George Garrison to William Lloyd Garrison II, February 10, 1864, Garrison Family Papers, box 28, folder 790, Sophia Smith Collection, Smith College, Northampton, Mass.

116. Ibid.

117. Ibid.

118. Trudeau, *Like Men of War*, 135.

119. Bradford, *Scenes; A Woman Doctor's Civil War: Esther Hill Hawks' Diary*, ed. Gerald Schwartz (Columbia: University of South Carolina Press, 1984); George Garrison to William Lloyd Garrison II, February 10, 1864, Garrison Family Papers, box 28, folder 790, Sophia Smith Collection, Smith College, Northampton, Mass.; Telford, "Harriet."

120. Trudeau, *Like Men of War*, 137.

121. Ibid., 152.

122. Ibid., 150.

123. Ibid., 150.

124. See Bradford, *Scenes*; Wood, "Manuscript History." See also *A Woman Doctor's Civil War*, 79. Hawks mentions Tubman, "Moses," as being in the camp at Fernandina at the end of May 1864.

125. Telford, "Harriet," 16.

126. Ibid. ". . . dey was dying off like sheep. I dug some roots an' herbs an' made a tea for the doctor an'

the disease stopped on him. An' then he said, 'give it to de soldiers.' So I biled up a great biler' of roots and herbs, an' de General tailed a man to take two cans an' go roun' an' give it to all in de camp dat needed it, and it cured 'em." See also "Mrs. Harriet Tubman, the Colored Nurse and Scout—the Bridge Street African M.E. Church Last Evening," *The Brooklyn Eagle*, Brooklyn, N.Y., October 23, 1865.

127. Wood, "Manuscript History." This probably occurred sometime during 1863, as Tubman was reassigned to Folly Island in late November 1863.

128. Bradford, *Harriet* (1886), 139–40.

129. White soldiers also received bounties for reenlisting, whereas black soldiers did not. Rose, *Rehearsal*, 261–62; see also Duncan, *Where Death*, 105–6; T. C. McCaskie, *State and Society in Pre-Colonial Asante* (Cambridge: Cambridge University Press, 1995), 193–203; McPherson, *Struggle*, 212–20; Trudeau, *Like Men of War*, 91–93, 252–55.

130. Wendell Garrison to William Lloyd Garrison II, June 20, 1864, Garrison Family Papers, box 30, f. 852, Sophia Smith Collection, Smith College, Northampton, Mass.

131. Franklin Sanborn, "Harriet Tubman," *The Commonwealth*, Boston, August 12, 1864. Sanborn wrote that Tubman had "left Florida to come north in the latter part of June, and went from New York where she landed directly to the home of her aged parents in Auburn, whence she has come to this city."

132. Ibid.

133. Ibid.

134. Nell Irvin Painter, *Sojourner Truth: A Life, a Symbol* (New York: W. W. Norton & Company, 1996), 201. See also Earl Conrad, *General Harriet Tubman*, 2nd ed. (Washington, D.C.: Associated Publishers, Inc., 1990), 183.

135. Painter, *Truth*, 200–3.

136. Rosa Belle Holt, "A Heroine in Ebony," *The Chautauquan*, July, 1896, 462. Holt's article, which relied heavily on Bradford's work, was also based on "three long talks with Harriet Tubman" Holt conducted one within a month of writing the article. "I us'd to go see Missus Lincoln but I never wanted to see him [Lincoln]. You see we colored people didn't understand den he was our frien'. All we knew was dat de first colored troops from Massachusetts only got seven dollars a month, while de white regiment got fifteen. We didn't like dat. But now I know all 'bout it, an' I'se sorry I didn't go see Massa Lincoln and tank him" (461).

137. Ibid., 462.

138. Ibid. ". . . but he tole her [Truth] he had done nuffin' himself; he was only a servant of de country." Nell Painter shows, however, that the meeting between Truth and Lincoln was not so cordial, in spite of Truth's own description of the meeting. See Painter, *Truth*, 203–7.

139. Holt, "Heroine," 426.

140. On October 28 Tubman passed through Rochester, New York, probably to visit with Anna and Frederick Douglass, the Porters, and other friends living there, on her way to Canada. She received a $10 donation from the Rochester Ladies' Anti-Slavery Society for her work aiding freedmen in the South. Entry, October 28, 1864, Rochester Ladies' Anti-Slavery Society Records, William L. Clements Library, University of Michigan, Ann Arbor.

141. Gerrit Smith, November 22, 1864, in Bradford, *Harriet* (1886), 139. Two days later, the wife of General George W. Baird, who was also visiting the Smiths in Peterboro, wrote a testimonial for Tubman as well: "Harriet Tubman, a most excellent women, who has rendered faithful and good services to our army, not only in the hospital, but in various capacities, having been employed under Government at Hilton Head, and in Florida; and I commend her to the protection of all officers in whose department she may happen to be. She has been known and esteemed for years by the family of my uncle, Hon. Gerrit Smith, as a person of great rectitude and capabilities. Mrs. Gen A. Baird" (138). Tubman may have collected more testimonials and commendations at this time, but these are the only ones that have survived.

142. Pass, to Brig. General Van Vliet, from Louis H. Pelonge, Asst. Agt. Genl., March 20, 1865, Wash-

ington, D.C., Wood, "Manuscript History." Tubman was in Washington during the middle of February, visiting with William H. Seward, who loaned her $50. See entry, February 18, 1865, "Seward Papers."

143. "Committee on Teachers," *The Freedmen's Record* 1, no. 4 (1865): 55.

144. Cheney, "Moses."

145. Ibid.

146. "From Camp Wm. Penn," *The Christian Recorder,* Philadelphia, April 15, 1865.

147. Ibid.

148. Wood, "Manuscript History." The U.S. Sanitary Commission had been established in 1861 to provide humanitarian and nursing services and support to the Union Army during the Civil War. Wood does not identify who the Sanitary Commission workers were.

149. Ibid.

Chapter 11

1. Charles P. Wood, "Manuscript History Concerning the Pension Claim of Harriet Tubman," HR 55A-D1, Papers Accompanying the Claim of Harriet Tubman, Record Group 233, National Archives, Washington, D.C. Tubman had a friend write a letter to the *New York Independent* claiming that twenty to twenty-five black soldiers were dying per day in Hampton Hospital at Fort Monroe. This claim was denied by H. B. White, executive officer in charge of the hospital, in a letter to the *Independent*, stating that the total number of deaths for the month of June was "Whites, twenty-six (26); Colored, seventy (70); total, ninety-six (96)," or three per day. Regardless of the claims, it is clear by the numbers that black soldiers were dying at a rate 2.5 times greater than that of white soldiers, leaving us to wonder what sort of treatment the black soldiers were actually receiving. See "Hampton Hospital. Harriet Tubman's Statements Contradicted," *New York Independent*, New York, August 3, 1865. I am indebted to Jay Meredith for finding this article.

2. "Hampton Hospital. Harriet Tubman's Statements Contradicted."

3. Margaret E. Wagner, Gary W. Gallagher, and Paul Finkleman, ed., *The Library of Congress Civil War Desk Reference* (New York: Simon and Schuster, 2002), 654.

4. Manuscript History Concerning the Pension Claim of Harriet Tubman; Sarah H. Bradford, *Scenes in the Life of Harriet Tubman* (Auburn, N.Y.: W. J. Moses, 1869), 70. In Wood's manuscript, the words *nurse* and *matron* are capitalized, whereas in the Bradford work they are not. I am following Wood's transcription here, as he was working with original documents, and it is not clear whether Bradford also copied from original documents or used a copy of Wood's manuscript (he made several).

5. Wood, "Manuscript History"; Bradford, *Scenes*, 70.

6. Wood, "Manuscript History"; Letter, Seward to Hunter, July 25, 1865; in Bradford, *Scenes*, 65.

7. Debit entry, July 31, 1865, microfilm reels 192–93, Seward Papers, Harvard University, Cambridge; see also Rebecca Green, "History of Harriet Tubman and Her Brick House," Cornell University, Ithaca, N.Y., 1998.

8. Credit entry, August 9, 1865, microfilm reels 192–93, Seward Papers, Harvard University, Cambridge; see also Green, "History of Harriet Tubman and Her Brick House." Curiously, Hannah E. Stevenson, secretary, Commission on Teachers of the New England Freedman's Aid Society, wrote to Frances Seward on November 7, 1865, that they had not sent money to her since April. "Will you have the kindness to [write] me if you know anything of Harriet Tubman? It has been a long time since we have heard from her, & she has received no money since last April." Hannah E. Stevenson to Mrs. [Frances Miller] Seward, November 7, 1865, in Jean Humez, *Harriet Tubman: The Life and Life Stories* (Madison: University of Wisconsin Press, 2003), original letter in Harriet Tubman Home Museum, Auburn, N.Y.

9. Wood, "Manuscript History."

10. Ibid.

11. Lucretia Coffin Mott to Martha Coffin Wright, October 2, 1865, Garrison Family Papers, Sophia

Smith Collection, Smith College, Northampton, Mass. Thomas Mott, Lucretia's son, stopped by while Tubman was there, giving her $5 to help her on her way home.

12. Linda R. Monk, *The Words We Live By: Your Annotated Guide to the Constitution* (New York: Hyperion, 2003), 205. The amendment was passed in January 1865 but was not ratified until December 1865.

13. Eric Foner, *The Story of American Freedom* (New York: W. W. Norton & Company, 1998); Monk, *Words;* Eric Foner, *Reconstruction: America's Unfinished Revolution, 1863–1877* (New York: Harper & Row, Publishers, 1988), 66–67, 199–207.

14. Monk, *Words,* 213–15; Foner, *Reconstruction,* 251–61.

15. Foner, *Reconstruction,* 251–61.

16. Nell Irvin Painter, *Sojourner Truth: A Life, a Symbol* (New York: W. W. Norton & Company, 1996), 209–11. See also William S. McFeeley, *Frederick Douglass* (New York: W. W. Norton & Company, 1991), 92–93.

17. Bradford, *Scenes,* 46.

18. Martha Coffin Wright to Marianna Pelham Wright, November 7, 1865, Garrison Family Papers, Sophia Smith Collection, Smith College, Northampton, Massachusetts. "She told him she didn't thank anybody to call her cullud pusson." Bradford says she was thrown into the baggage car. Bradford, *Scenes,* 46.

19. Bradford, *Scenes,* p. 46.

20. Martha Coffin Wright to Marianna Pelham Wright, November 7, 1865. Martha Coffin Wright wrote this remarkable passage just after she had just received a visit from Tubman, who told Wright in detail the events on the train that night. The immediacy of Wright's description is far more moving than Bradford's account, written three years later. The powerful commentary by Tubman of her own sense of pride in her identity as a "black woman" and her impressions of the conductor's political affinity cast an interesting light on contemporary racial and social politics. During and after the Civil War, Northern sympathizers with the South were called "copperheads" by Unionists. Originally a term of derision used by Republicans against antiwar Democrats, during and after the Civil War it also came to symbolize the more conservative wings of the Democratic party. See James M. McPherson, *Battle Cry of Freedom: The Civil War Era* (New York: Ballantine Books, 1988), 494.

21. Bradford, *Scenes,* 46–47. See also Martha Coffin Wright to Marianna Pelham Wright, Nov. 7, 1865.

22. "Mrs. Harriet Tubman, the Colored Nurse and Scout—the Bridge Street African M.E. Church Last Evening," *The Brooklyn Eagle,* Brooklyn, N.Y., October 23, 1865.

23. Martha Coffin Wright to Marianna Pelham Wright, Nov. 7, 1865. According to Bradford, "the card the young man had given her was only a visiting card, and she did not know where to find him." Bradford, *Scenes,* 47.

24. 1865 Cayuga County, New York, Census, Town of Fleming.

25. According to Frank Sanborn in his *Commonwealth* article written in 1863, Tubman "had ten brothers and sisters, of whom three are now living, all at the North." The census record indicates that Rit was the mother of nine children, which have been accounted for in previous chapters. If three were still living, to the best of Tubman's knowledge at the time, at least two of them were John and William Henry. If James was still alive in 1863, then he could have been the third living sibling, but he probably was dead by the time the census was taken in 1865, when Catherine is listed as "single." Sarah Bradford wrote in 1868 that Catherine's husband had died in Canada (though she erroneously identified him as William Henry). See Bradford, *Scenes,* 63–64. Tubman's brother Moses, who ran away soon after Tubman did, has never been located. Rachel died in 1859. Because Tubman did not know where her older sisters were, she may have assumed that they had died after they were sold away from Maryland decades before. Thornton Newton was from Virginia and was probably a former soldier who had known Tubman during the war. Margaret Stewart, though she lived with the Sewards and Wordens, was probably temporarily staying at Tubman's home because the Sewards were in Washington, where William was recuperating from his attack, and mourning the death of Frances Seward, William's wife. Lazette Worden, Frances Seward's sister, was probably in Washington at this time, helping run the Seward household after the death of her sister, and helping to care for William.

26. See Andrew Boyd, *Boyd's Auburn Directory, 1865–66* (Auburn, N.Y.: Andrew Boyd Publisher, 1865), 183.

27. It should be recalled that Bill and Emily Kiah (Chion) ran away with the Dover Eight in March 1857. It appears that they stayed in the area while awaiting an opportunity to rescue their daughter, who was nine years old at the time and still enslaved. See William Still, *The Underground Railroad* (1871; reprint, Chicago: Johnson Publishing Company, 1970), 543.

28. Martha Coffin Wright to David Wright, April 2, 1866, Garrison Family Papers, Sophia Smith Collection, Smith College, Northampton, Mass.

29. Sarah H. Bradford, *Harriet, the Moses of Her People* (New York: J. J. Little & Co., 1901), 143.

30. Ibid., 144.

31. Ibid.

32. Ibid., 145.

33. Letter from Sallie Holley, *National Anti-Slavery Standard*, Washington, D.C., Nov. 30, 1867.

34. Martha Coffin Wright to Lucretia Coffin Mott, April 19, 1866, Garrison Family Papers, Sophia Smith Collection, Smith College, Northampton, Mass.

35. Ibid. Sarah Bradford also noted this reluctance to beg, even in times of greatest need. "Harriet's extreme delicacy in asking anything for herself" stood in sharp contrast to her willingness to ask for money to help support others.

36. Several letters written between Martha and David Wright and also between Martha and members of her family during April 1866 reveal concerted efforts on the part of the Wrights and others to force a settlement of sorts from the railroad. Martha had trouble tracking Tubman down to get the details—she had gone to Canada after William L. Garrison II's visit the first of April—and David Wright seemed unable to effect any sort of legal action against the company. See letters to and from Martha Coffin Wright, April 1866, Garrison Family Papers, Sophia Smith Collection, Smith College, Northampton, Mass. William Lloyd Garrison told his daughter-in-law, Ellen Wright Garrison, "that Conductor should be made to support her all her life," which Ellen agreed "would be poetical justice indeed." Ellen Wright Garrison to Martha Coffin Wright, April 26, 1866, Garrison Family Papers, Sophia Smith Collection, Smith College, Northampton, Mass.

37. Frances Ellen Watkins Harper, "We Are All Bound Up Together," in Philip S. Foner and Robert James Branham, eds., *Lift Every Voice: African American Oratory, 1787–1900* (Tuscaloosa: University of Alabama Press, 1998), 458–60. This speech was made at the Eleventh National Women's Rights Convention. At this convention, the first of its kind held after the end of the Civil War, the American Equal Rights Association was founded. After Harper's speech, the first Equal Rights Amendment was presented to the conference. See also Shirley Wilson Logan, *"We Are Coming": The Persuasive Discourse of Nineteenth-Century Black Women* (Carbondale: Southern Illinois University Press, 1999), 57–58.

38. Logan, *We Are Coming*, 58–59.

39. Harper, "We Are All Bound Up Together," 460.

40. Martha Coffin Wright to Ellen Wright Garrison, November 1, 1866, Garrison Family Papers, Sophia Smith Collection, Smith College, Northampton, Mass.

41. Lucretia Coffin Mott to Martha Coffin Wright, January 1, 1867, Garrison Family Papers, Sophia Smith Collection, Smith College, Northampton, Mass. The Auburn community was also mourning the loss of Fanny Seward, William Henry Seward's beloved daughter, who died in October 1866. Seward would find her death one of the most difficult trials of his life. Harriet, according to Bradford, had a premonition that Fanny Seward had died. In a dream, Tubman "saw a chariot in the air, going south, and empty, but soon it returned, and lying in it, cold and stiff, was the body of a young lady of whom Harriet was very fond, whose home was in Auburn, but who had gone to Washington with her father." Terrified by the dream, Tubman ran "to the house of her minister, crying out: 'Oh, Miss Fanny is dead!' and the news had just been received." See Daniel W. Crofts, *Seward, William Henry,* from the American National Biography site; also Bradford, *Harriet* (1901). The minister was probably the Rev. Henry Fowler, of the Central Presbyterian Church in Auburn.

42. Harkless Bowley to Earl Conrad, January 4, 1839, Harkless Bowley Letters, Earl Conrad/Harriet Tubman Collection, reel 1, New York Public Library, Schomburg Center for Research in Black Culture.

43. According to the 1870 U.S. Census, Dorchester County, Maryland, John and Kessiah Bowley had been in Maryland at least two years. Their youngest son, John R. Bowley, was two years old and was listed as born in Maryland.

44. 1861 Chatham, Ontario, Canada Census.

45. Martha Coffin Wright to Anna Mott Hopper and Patty Mott Lord, September 11, 1868, Garrison Family Papers, Sophia Smith Collection, Smith College, Northampton, Mass. Anna Mott Hopper and Patty Mott Lord were Lucretia Mott's daughters.

46. Harkless Bowley to Earl Conrad, August 24, 1839, Harkless Bowley Letters, Earl Conrad/Harriet Tubman Collection, New York Public Library, Schomburg Center for Research in Black Culture. Ben and Rit were too old to work. See also Harkless Bowley to Earl Conrad, Jan. 4, 1939, in the same collection. Harkless remembered vividly his great-grandparents Benjamin and Ritty Ross, particularly "Grandfather . . . walking the floor praising the Lord."

47. See Bureau of the Census, United States Federal Census, 1870, Dorchester County, Md.

48. Harkless Bowley to Earl Conrad, August 8, 1839, Harkless Bowley Letters, Earl Conrad/Harriet Tubman Collection, New York Public Library, Schomburg Center for Research in Black Culture.

49. Richard Paul Fuke, Imperfect Equality: African Americans and the Confines of White Racial Attitudes in Post-Emancipation Maryland (New York: Fordham University Press, 1999), 69–83, 88–106, 195–212. The transition from slavery to freedom had been difficult for blacks and whites, though blacks experienced a multitude of discriminatory and illegal practices, including violence, aimed at maintaining control over black advancement economically, politically, and socially.

50. Robert J. Brugger, Maryland, a Middle Temperament, 1634–1980 (Baltimore: The Johns Hopkins University Press, 1988), 302–10; Barbara Jeanne Fields, Slavery and Freedom on the Middle Ground (New Haven: Yale University Press, 1985), 124–32.

51. Indenture laws had long been on the books for the binding of whites and free blacks. In 1839, however, orphans courts were empowered to bind any free black child whose parents were deemed unfit to care for him or her. For a discussion of the phenomenon of indenturing and apprenticing black children in Maryland, see Fuke, Imperfect Equality, esp. Chapter 4; Jeffrey R. Brackett, The Negro in Maryland. A Study of the Institution of Slavery (1889; reprint, New York: Negro Universities Press, 1969), 218–24; Fields, Slavery, 137–42; and Anita Aidt Guy, Maryland's Persistent Pursuit to End Slavery, 1850–1864 (New York: Garland Publishing, Inc., 1997), 442–47.

52. See Fields, Slavery, 137–42.

53. Talbot County Indenture Records, Talbot County Orphans Court, November 15, 1864. See also R. B. Leonard, Bound to Serve: The Indentured Children in Talbot County, Maryland, 1794–1920 (St. Michaels, Md.: R. B. Leonard, 1983).

54. Anthony C. Thompson to Sarah Catherine Haddaway, March 16, 1857, Chattel Records, Dorchester County Court Records, Maryland State Archives, Annapolis. John Henry was seven, Moses was four, and Harriet (Ritty) was three years old in March 1857. Mary Ross had by this time given birth to another child, possibly the child of Wilson Wells, whom she later married and had more children with. Thompson had probably sent Mary and her children to live and work on the Haddaways' farm in 1855 or 1856, before formally selling them to his daughter, Sarah, in 1857.

55. Harkless Bowley to Earl Conrad, August 24, 1839, Harkless Bowley Letters, Earl Conrad/Harriet Tubman Collection, New York Public Library, Schomburg Center for Research in Black Culture.

56. On May 12, 1856, Dr. Anthony C. Thompson reduced Mary Manokey Ross's term of service, manumitting her when she turned thirty years old in 1861. He reduced the terms of service for approximately twenty-nine slaves on the same day, providing for their freedom when they individually reached the age of thirty years old. See Anthony C. Thompson to Sundry Negroes, May 12, 1856, Dorchester County Chattel Records, Maryland State Archives, Annapolis.

57. Mary gave birth to two children with the surname Wells before she was freed: an unidentified child born sometime in 1856 and another, Charles Wells, born in 1861. Mary and her children listed as security for a promissory note; see Thomas S. Haddaway and Sarah C. Haddaway to Alexander H. Seth and Charles W. Haddaway, August 3, 1858, Talbot County Court Records, Maryland State Archives, Annapolis. Note that John Henry, Moses, and Harriet are listed with the surname Ross, and the other two children under Wells. The Bowleys were definitely in Dorchester County by 1868, as their son, John R., was born in Maryland that year. See 1870 U.S. Census, Dorchester County, Md.

58. Black parents were nearly powerless to prevent indenturing of their children. In spite of their ability to support them or to teach their children trades, many black families found the local courts indifferent to their rights to their own children. See Fuke, *Imperfect Equality.* Mary Manokey Ross Wells, the boys' mother, may have objected to their going north, but there is no documentation of this.

59. Harkless Bowley to Earl Conrad, August 24, 1839, Harkless Bowley Letters, Earl Conrad/Harriet Tubman Collection, New York Public Library, Schomburg Center for Research in Black Culture.

60. Ibid. John Stewart apparently did not send for his daughter Harriet (Ritty) Ross. He may have decided that she should remain with her mother, or Mary may have insisted she remain with her. John had no relationship with his daughter before he ran away—she was born on Christmas Eve 1854, the night he ran away with his sister Harriet.

61. Harkless Bowley to Earl Conrad, August 24, 1839, Harkless Bowley Letters, Earl Conrad/Harriet Tubman Collection, New York Public Library, Schomburg Center for Research in Black Culture.

62. Bradford, *Scenes,* 111–112.

63. Ibid., 112.

64. Civil War Pension File, Harriet Tubman Davis, Widow of Nelson Charles [Nelson Davis], Original Pension no. 449,592, 1894, National Archives, College Park, Md.

65. Papers for Harriet Tubman Davis, Records of the U.S. House of Representatives, Record Group 233, National Archives, Washington, D.C.; see also Civil War Pension File, Harriet Tubman Davis. According to Tubman's testimony in her application for a widow's pension, Nelson's owner's name was Fred Charles, but his father's name was Milford Davis. Presumably this is why Nelson changed his name from Nelson Charles to Nelson Davis. See statement of Harriet Tubman Davis, November 10, 1894; see also statements of Edgar J. Fryman, November 9, 1894, in this file. Davis apparently ran away from his master sometime during or before 1861 and moved to Oneida County, New York (possibly Rome), a year or two before he enlisted in the army. See statement of Charles H. Peterson, January 7, 1895, and statement of Anna E. Thompson, June 19, 1894, in this file as well. Anna Thompson was the widow of Corporal Albert Thompson of the Eighth USCT. Thompson came from Scipio, in Cayuga County, New York, and he and his wife lived in Auburn from at least 1860. See 1850 and 1860 U.S. Censuses, Cayuga County, N.Y. The brickyard may have been that of Sylvester Ross. See Bureau of the Census, *United States Federal Census,* 1860; Census, 1870, Cayuga County, N.Y.

66. "Outrage in Talbot County. A Colored Man Murdered," *Baltimore News American,* Baltimore, October 7, 1867.

67. Foner, *Reconstruction,* 119–23. For Maryland, see Fields, *Slavery,* 142–49.

68. Foner, *Reconstruction,* 120.

69. Fields, *Slavery,* 149–51.

70. "Outrage in Talbot County."

71. "Letter from Cambridge. Trial of Robert Vincent," *Baltimore Sun,* Baltimore, December 17, 1867.

72. "Acquittal of Murderer," *The Baltimore American,* Baltimore, December 23, 1867. Tubman left behind his wife, Caroline, and four children, Thomas, Ann, William, and Alexander. See 1860 U.S. Census, Dorchester County, Md., and 1880 U.S. Census, Dorchester County, Md.

73. "Letter from Cambridge."

74. Letter from Sallie Holley, *National Anti-Slavery Standard,* Washington, D.C., Nov. 30, 1867.

75. Ibid.

76. See Martha Coffin Wright to Ellen Wright Garrison, September 6, 1867, Garrison Family Papers, Sophia Smith Collection, Smith College, Northampton, Mass. Tubman knew the children of her anti-slavery friends quite well, and apparently held great affection for them. In this letter, Martha Wright told her daughter Ellen, after Ellen had visited Auburn with her newborn baby, that "Harriet Tubman came on Wednesday to see you and the baby—she didn't hear of your call till the evening before, & was so disappointed that her eyes filled with tears—She never shed a tear in telling me of all her troubles. I comforted her with Wm's donation, & she seemed grateful, & sent her love to you & all enquiring friends—she said she wd see you yet—I wish I had thought to send for her while you were here." See also Martha Coffin Wright to Ellen Wright Garrison, March 22, 1868, Garrison Family Papers, Sophia Smith Collection, Smith College, Northampton, Mass.

77. Martha Coffin Wright to Ellen Wright Garrison, May 19, 1867, Garrison Family Papers, Sophia Smith Collection, Smith College, Northampton, Mass.

78. Martha Coffin Wright to William Pelham Wright, February 5, 1868, Garrison Family Papers, Sophia Smith Collection, Smith College, Northampton, Mass.

79. Ibid. See also the letters from Martha Coffin Wright to William Pelham Wright, January 19, February 5, February 9, and February 24, 1868, Garrison Family Papers, Sophia Smith Collection, Smith College, Northampton, Mass.

80. The Central Presbyterian Church was founded in 1861 under the pastorship of the Rev. Henry Fowler. Prof. Samuel Hopkins, Sarah Bradford's brother, helped the new congregation get started, after which Henry Fowler was elected pastor. In a dispute over slavery and the antislavery activism of Rev. Henry Fowler, approximately sixty to seventy members of the Second Presbyterian Society in Auburn seceded and formed the Central Presbyterian. Fowler, a fiery and "forcible advocate" of emancipation, was just the type of person Tubman was attracted to—a man who acted on his principles. D. Munson Osborne, Eliza Wright Osborne's husband, was among the church's first trustees. See Presbyterianism in Auburn, vertical file, Cayuga County Historian's Office, Auburn, N.Y. Sarah Bradford taught Sunday school here, and this is where she met Tubman's parents; see Bradford, Scenes, 3. "During a sojourn of some months in the city of Auburn, while the war was in progress, the writer used to see occasionally in her Sunday-school class the aged mother of Harriet, and also some of those girls who had been brought from the South by this remarkable woman. She also wrote letters for the old people to commanding officers at the South, making inquiries about Harriet, and received answers telling of her untiring devotion to our wounded and sick soldiers, and of her efficient aid in various ways to the cause of the Union." And in Sarah H. Bradford, Harriet, the Moses of Her People (New York: Geo. R. Lockwood & Sons, 1886), 129, "these old people, living out beyond the toll-gate, on the South Street road, Auburn, come in every Sunday—more than a mile—to the Central Church. To be sure, deep slumbers settle down upon them as soon as they are seated, which continue undisturbed till the congregation is dismissed; but they have done their best, and who can doubt that they receive a blessing. Immediately after this they go to class-meeting at the Methodist Church. Then they wait for a third service, and after that start out home again." Also, the deaths and marriages of family members are listed in Central Presbyterian's records.

81. See, for instance, Cousin Cicely [Sarah H. Bradford], Ups and Downs; or, Silver Lake Sketches (Auburn, N.Y.: Alden, Beardsley & Co., 1855).

82. Bradford would later publish a history of the town of Geneva, N.Y., and was often a contributor to magazines and newspapers. See James McGowan, "Harriet Tubman: According to Sarah Bradford," Harriet Tubman Journal 2, no. 1 (1994).

83. Martha Coffin Wright to Sisters, July 31, 1868, Garrison Family Papers, Sophia Smith Collection, Smith College, Northampton, Mass.

84. I am grateful to Jean Humez for sharing her research on John M. Bradford. John Bradford had an affair with another woman, which was exposed in late 1856 or early 1857, ruining his reputation. He soon abandoned Sarah and their six children and moved to Chicago, where he died in late 1860. See

also Sarah H. Bradford to William H. Seward, January 26, 1857, William H. Seward Papers, reel 54, no. 2100; and Humez, *Harriet Tubman*.

85. Wendell Phillips to Franklin B. Sanborn, c. June 1868, Franklin B. Sanborn Papers, Concord Free Public Library, Concord, Mass.; Franklin B. Sanborn to C. W. Slack, July 8, 1868, Anti-Slavery Collection, Rare Book and Manuscripts, Boston Public Library, Boston, Mass.

86. See Bradford, *Scenes*, for various testimonials. Not included in *Scenes* were letters from Lucretia Mott and James A. Bowley, Tubman's nephew. Why their letters were not included is not known, although their testimonies may have come too late to add to the short narrative. See James A. Bowley to Aunt [Harriet Tubman], 1868, Harriet Tubman Collection, Harriet Tubman Home Museum, Auburn, N.Y.; Martha Coffin Wright to Anna Mott Hopper and Patty Mott Lord, September 11, 1868, Garrison Family Papers, Sophia Smith Collection, Smith College, Northampton, Mass.; and Martha Coffin Wright to Sisters, October 8, 1868, Garrison Family Papers, Sophia Smith Collection, Smith College, Northampton, Mass.

87. Bradford, *Scenes*, 7–8. Oddly, Douglass never wrote about Tubman himself. He never mentions her in his autobiographies, and nothing has been located in any of his correspondence about her, save for the one letter written in 1859 (in Philip S. Foner, ed., *Frederick Douglass: Selected Speeches and Writings* [Chicago: Lawrence Hill Books, 1999, 600], which does not specifically name Tubman. It is puzzling that this prolific writer and lecturer, who sheltered Tubman and her family and friends in his home, never wrote about her activities.

88. For an excellent analysis of Bradford's qualifications to write Tubman's biography, see McGowan, "Harriet Tubman." Jim was one of the very first to systematically analyze Bradford's work, comparing *Scenes* to her later revised biography of Tubman, *Moses*, noting inconsistencies and inaccuracies with both versions. He also discovered that Bradford was not known as a careful and diligent researcher, and that she apparently conflated, manufactured, or ignored important information in at least one of her other books, specifically *The History of Geneva*.

89. Sarah H. Bradford to William H. Seward, August 17, 1868, William H. Seward Papers, reel 105, no. 4377. See also Bradford, *Scenes*, i: "The narrative was prepared on the eve of the author's departure for Europe, where she still remains." Bradford stayed in Europe for nine years before returning to Geneva, N.Y. See Louise Bradford Varnum to Earl Conrad, June 10, 1839, Research Correspondence, Earl Conrad/Harriet Tubman Collection, reel 1, boxes 1 and 2, New York Public Library, Schomburg Center for Research in Black Culture.

90. Bradford, *Scenes*, i.

91. Ibid., 3.

92. Ibid., 4.

93. Ibid.

94. Humez, *Harriet Tubman*. Humez points out that most of Tubman's biographers selectively edited and reformulated her stories to fit within the prescribed cultural norms of middle-class literary and social expectations. These mediated stories also fit within a range of acceptable slave narrative stories, at once horrible and redeeming, which ultimately comforted the white reader but did little to convey the inner truths of the slave experience.

95. McGowan, "Harriet Tubman."

96. Bradford, *Scenes*; McGowan, "Harriet Tubman." Both Milton Sernett in his forthcoming book on Tubman and Jean Humez in *Harriet Tubman* argue that "Essay on Woman-Whipping" was penned not by Bradford but by some other unidentified abolitionist. Though a powerful statement about violence in the South, it appears to be filler at the end of a very short book.

97. Account Record, Sales of *Scenes*, December 1, 1868–May 1, 1869. Harriet Tubman Collection, Harriet Tubman Home Museum. Auburn, N.Y.

98. Ellen Wright Garrison to Martha Coffin Wright, December 26, 1868, Garrison Family Papers, Sophia Smith Collection, Smith College, Northampton, Mass.

99. Martha Coffin Wright to Sisters, July 31, 1868, Garrison Family Papers, Sophia Smith Collection, Smith College, Northampton, Mass.

100. Martha Coffin Wright to William Lloyd Garrison II, January 10, 1869, Garrison Family Papers, Sophia Smith Collection, Smith College, Northampton, Mass.

101. Bradford, *Scenes*, 119–20.

102. Ibid., 122–24.

103. Subscription List, Harriet Tubman Collection, Harriet Tubman Home Museum, Auburn, N.Y. See also Martha Coffin Wright to Ellen Wright Garrison, September 24, 1868, Garrison Family Papers, Sophia Smith Collection, Smith College, Northampton, Mass.

104. Martha Coffin Wright to Anna Mott Hopper and Patty Mott Lord, September 11, 1868, Garrison Family Papers, Sophia Smith Collection, Smith College, Northampton, Mass., Sept. 11, 1868.

105. Ibid.

106. Bradford, *Scenes*, 112.

107. Ibid.

108. Martha Coffin Wright to Sisters, October 8, 1868, Garrison Family Papers, Sophia Smith Collection, Smith College, Northampton, Mass.

109. Ibid.

110. Martha Coffin Wright to Ellen Wright Garrison, December 16, 1868, Garrison Family Papers, Sophia Smith Collection, Smith College, Northampton, Mass.

111. Apparently W. J. Moses was not the first choice to publish Tubman's book. William Henry Wise approached Ticknor and Fields, a prominent Boston-based publisher, about publishing Tubman's narrative, but apparently they declined. Martha Wright noticed that on page 60 of *Scenes*, for instance, "sinner's flesh" was supposed to be "swine's flesh." Martha Coffin Wright to Ellen Wright Garrison, December 16, 1868, Garrison Family Papers, Sophia Smith Collection, Smith College, Northampton, Mass.

112. Ibid.

113. Ibid. Martha also managed to get six signatures for a "Suffrage Petition" while attending the fair.

114. See Account Record, Sales of *Scenes*, 1869. See also letters between Martha Wright and family members, winter and spring 1869, Garrison Family Papers, Sophia Smith Collection, Smith College, Northampton, Mass.

115. Account Record, Sales of *Scenes*, 1869.

116. Franklin B. Sanborn, "A Negro Heroine—Scenes in the Life of Harriet Tubman," in *Transcendental Youth and Age*, ed. Kenneth Walter Cameron (Hartford: Transcendental Books, 1981).

117. Ibid.

118. Ibid. See also mention in "Notice," *Freedmen's Record* 5, no. 1 (1869).

119. Account Record, Sales of *Scenes*, 1869.

120. See Green, "History of Harriet Tubman and Her Brick House."

121. Martha Coffin Wright to Ellen Wright Garrison, October 20, 1869, Garrison Family Papers, Sophia Smith Collection, Smith College, Northampton, Mass.

Chapter 12

1. Frank C. Drake, "The Moses of Her People. Amazing Life Work of Harriet Tubman," *New York Herald*, New York, Sept. 22, 1907.

2. Sarah H. Bradford, *Scenes in the Life of Harriet Tubman* (Auburn, New York: W. J. Moses, 1869), 7.

3. Manuscript History Concerning the Pension Claim of Harriet Tubman, HR 55A-D1, Papers Accompanying the Claim of Harriet Tubman, Record Group 233, National Archives, Washington, D.C.

4. For Services as Scout, Pay Claim, Jan. 31, 1865. Harriet Tubman Collection, Tubman Home Museum, Auburn, N.Y.

5. Scouts, Spies and Guides, Entries 31 and 36; and Secret Service Accounts, Entry 95, Records of the Provost Marshall General's Bureau (Civil War), Record Group 110, National Archives, Washington, D.C. I am indebted to Mike Musick at the National Archives for finding this information for me.

6. Mr. McDougall, House of Representatives of the United States, 43rd Congress, H.R. 2711; and Gerry W. Hazelton, House of Representatives of the United States, 43rd Congress, H.R. 3786.

7. Notice of Tubman-Davis wedding, *Auburn Morning News*, Auburn, N.Y., March 19, 1869.

8. See 1870 U.S. Census, Town of Fleming, Cayuga County, N.Y. William Hedgar is listed as owning a brick business in the same neighborhood. George Dale, another runaway from Maryland, worked in this brickyard, and also lived in Fleming with his family, not too far from Tubman's residence. It appears that several brick makers and masons lived in dwellings next to and near Tubman in Fleming.

9. Harkless Bowley to Earl Conrad, August 15, 1939, Harkless Bowley Letters, Earl Conrad/Harriet Tubman Collection, reel 1, box 3, folder d2, New York Public Library, Schomburg Center for Research in Black Culture.

10. Martha Coffin Wright to Ellen Wright Garrison, October 20, 1869, Garrison Family Papers, Sophia Smith Collection, Smith College, Northampton, Mass.

11. Interview with Helen W. Tatlock (Mrs. William Tatlock), Earl Conrad/Harriet Tubman Collection, New York Public Library, Schomburg Center for Research in Black Culture.

12. Ibid.

13. Alice Lucas Brickler to Earl Conrad, Sept. 6, 1939, Earl Conrad/Harriet Tubman Collection, New York Public Library, Schomburg Center for Research in Black Culture.

14. Statement of Mrs. Florence Carter, Earl Conrad/Harriet Tubman Collection, New York Public Library, Schomburg Center for Research in Black Culture.

15. Elliot G. Storke and Jas. H. Smith, *The History of Cayuga County* (Syracuse, N.Y.: D. Mason & Co., 1879), 211–12. The first minister of this church was Jacob Mowbry, also from Maryland. Other Marylanders included John Purnell and Jonathan Waire, who may have been former fugitive slaves as well.

16. Diary of Martha Coffin Wright, Garrison Family Papers, Sophia Smith Collection, Smith College, Northampton, Mass. (see entries for May 1870, for example). See also Harriet Tubman's tribute at Theodore Pomeroy's funeral, Obituary Scrapbook, Seward House Collection, Auburn, N.Y., c. March 25, 1905. Theodore Pomeroy was David Wright's law partner; he later became a U.S. congressman and then later mayor of Auburn. See Michael Cuddy Jr., *Hizzoners: A Brief Account of the Mayors of the City of Auburn* (Auburn, N.Y.: Jacobs Press, 1995), 19–21.

17. See entry for January 14, 1871, Diary of Martha Coffin Wright, Garrison Family Papers, Sophia Smith Collection, Smith College, Northampton, Mass.; and Sarah H. Bradford, *Harriet, the Moses of Her People* (New York: J. J. Little & Co., 1901), 144–45.

18. See, for example, 1870 U.S. Census, Auburn, N.Y., Cayuga County; see also Auburn city directories.

19. William Still, *The Underground Railroad* (1871; reprint, Chicago: Johnson Publishing Company, Inc., 1970), v–viii.

20. Ibid., 305.

21. Ibid., 306.

22. Ibid.

23. Philip S. Foner and Robert James Branham, eds., *Lift Every Voice: African American Oratory, 1787–1900* (Tuscaloosa: University of Alabama Press, 1998).

24. Still, *Underground Railroad*, 305.

25. Ibid., 797.

26. Ibid., 783. Still wrote several lengthy biographical sketches of white and black abolitionists and Underground Railroad agents. The omission of Tubman's history is a striking example of the complexities of gender and class within the postemancipation African American community.

27. Still also neglected to write about Frederick Douglass.

28. Martha Coffin Wright to Fanny Pelham Wright, November 29, 1871, Garrison Family Papers, Sophia Smith Collection, Smith College, Northampton, Mass. "I think Harriet Tubman's mother might as well have crossed to the shining shore, with her husband."

29. Rebecca Green, "History of Harriet Tubman and Her Brick House," Cornell University, Ithaca, N.Y. 1998.

30. Ibid.

31. "The Gold Swindle and the Greenback Robbery," Auburn Daily Bulletin, Auburn, N.Y., October 6, 1873.

32. Ibid.

33. Ibid.

34. Ibid.

35. Ibid.

36. Ibid.

37. Martha Coffin Wright to Ellen Wright Garrison, October 2, 1873, Garrison Family Papers, Sophia Smith Collection, Smith College, Northampton, Mass.

38. Ibid.

39. "Shimer's Career Is at an End," The Auburn Bulletin, Auburn, N.Y., October 8, 1896.

40. Ibid. Shimer was described as "industrious, miserly," and eccentric. He possessed "unflagging devotion to one object and that the accumulation of wealth—wealth above all else." He was not charitable, apparently, and he lived sparingly, spending "the small amount requisite for the purchase of the bare necessities of life." He was considered "a detriment to Auburn" by the time he died. As a landlord of many properties throughout Auburn, he was criticized for years for never repairing or keeping up his properties, instead leaving them to deteriorate into complete disrepair. Given the complexity of Shimer's relationship to the city by the time he died in 1896, one wonders what Wright's true motivations may have been in suggesting Shimer to Tubman.

41. Ibid.

42. "The Gold Swindle."

43. Ibid.

44. Ibid.

45. Ibid.

46. Ibid.

47. Ibid. Martha Coffin Wright speculated that Tubman had been chloroformed. See Martha Coffin Wright to Ellen Wright Garrison, October 9, 1873, Garrison Family Papers, Sophia Smith Collection, Smith College, Northampton, Mass.

48. "The Gold Swindle."

49. Martha Coffin Wright to Ellen Wright Garrison, October 2, 1873, Garrison Family Papers, Sophia Smith Collection, Smith College, Northampton, Mass.

50. "Shimer's Career Is at an End."

51. Ibid.; "The Gold Swindle"; also Martha Coffin Wright to Ellen Wright Garrison, October 9, 1873, Garrison Family Papers, Sophia Smith Collection, Smith College, Northampton, Mass.

52. "The Gold Swindle."

53. Ibid.

54. Ibid.

55. Ibid.

56. Ibid. See also Emily Howland diary entry, October 4, 1873, Florence W. Hazzard Papers, Collection #2516–2, Division of Rare and Manuscript Collections, Carl A. Kroch Library, Cornell University, Ithaca, N.Y.

57. "Howland Diary Entry, Oct. 4, 1873."

58. Jean Humez, Harriet Tubman: The Life and Life Stories (Madison: University of Wisconsin Press,

2003). Jean argues that this may have been a "rare view of Harriet Tubman adapting her Underground Railroad concealment skills," for "the clever trickster of the Underground Railroad days could undoubtedly resurface in an emergency."

59. See Martha Coffin Wright to Ellen Wright Garrison, October 2 and October 9, 1873, Garrison Family Papers, Sophia Smith Collection, Smith College, Northampton, Mass.; and fragment, Lucretia Coffin Mott to Martha Coffin Wright, October 1873, Garrison Family Papers, Sophia Smith Collection, Smith College, Northampton, Mass.

60. Andrew Boyd, *Boyd's Auburn City Directory, 1875–76* (Auburn, N.Y.: Andrew Boyd Publisher, 1875).

61. New York Census, 1875, Cayuga County, N.Y.

62. "The Gold Swindle."

63. Wage book, Osborne Family Papers, Syracuse University Library, Syracuse, N.Y.

64. Gertie is listed as adopted in Tubman's household in the New York 1875 census. In the 1880 federal census she is listed as Nelson and Harriet's daughter. Gertie eventually married a man named Watson around 1900. There is little documentary evidence of Gertie's life; if there is an actual adoption record, it is permanently closed per New York State laws.

65. Record of Current Events—Local Necrology, Collections of Cayuga County Historical Society, Auburn, N.Y., 8 1890.

66. Alice Lucas Brickler to Earl Conrad, July 19, 1939, Earl Conrad/Harriet Tubman Collection, New York Public Library, Schomburg Center for Research in Black Culture.

67. Or Edith.

68. See 1880 U.S. Census, Cayuga County, N.Y.; see also Auburn city directories for 1875–1880.

69. "Harriet Tubman," *Boston Sunday Herald*, Boston, October 31, 1886.

70. 1880 U.S. Census, Cayuga County, Town of Fleming, 4.

71. There is great confusion over this Masonic symbol. It supposedly contained the Masonic lodge number 741. No additional research has been done on this lodge or why the symbol would have been installed on Tubman's house. Green, "History of Harriet Tubman and Her Brick House." It is likely that given Tubman and Davis's own brick-making operation during the 1870s, and their close relationship to the other brick-making businesses in the area, the local masons, or brick makers, may have played a critical role in the building of the residence. The Masonic symbol may have been a tribute to them and their secret lodge. Thanks to Beth Crawford, Bonnie Ryan, and Doug Armstrong for informing me of the discovery of a burned layer surrounding the existing Tubman residence in Auburn, indicating the brick building was constructed on top of the original site of the frame structure.

72. No mortgage records have been located to indicate that Tubman borrowed money to rebuild the home, perhaps suggesting a community effort to rebuild and thereby reducing the financial obligation on Tubman.

73. "Harriet Tubman's Hogs," *The Evening Auburnian*, Auburn, N.Y., July 11, 1884.

74. Ibid.

75. Ibid. Interestingly, the subtitle to the article reads "Losses of Swine by the Lady Who Did Business with Mr. Shimer," indicating a long local memory of the gold swindle in 1873. The article concludes with the following comment: "No doubt Mr. Shimer will sympathize deeply with [Harriet's] losses, because she at one time is said to have caused him to be an object of public sympathy to the amount of $2,000 good money." The newspaper also noted that garbage was piling up in "Harriet's garden" because the hogs no longer ate the refuse. There is no mention in the article of the possibility that the hogs may have been poisoned deliberately, or that they may have died of some other disease.

76. Eliza Wright Osborne to Emily Osborne Harris, January 29, 1884, Osborne Family Papers, George Arents Research Library for Special Collections, Syracuse University, Syracuse, N.Y.

77. Ibid.

78. Bradford, *Harriet* (1901), 147–48: "a drefful t'ing was happenin' somewha', de ground was openin', an' de houses were fallin' in, and de people bein' killed faster 'n dey was in de wah—faster 'n dey was in de wah."

79. Ibid., 148.

80. "Considerable Amount of Excitement," *Auburn Daily Citizen*, Auburn, N.Y., October 13, 1884.

81. Moses Stewart, Cayuga County Court Records, Records Retention Center, Auburn, N.Y. Moses Stewart was convicted and sentenced to twenty days in jail and a fine of $10. He was released on October 29, 1884. The court record lists Moses as married and the father of four children. Moses disappears from Auburn public records near this date; the identities of his wife and children remain unknown.

82. "Considerable Amount of Excitement."

83. While it is not my intention to minimize Tubman's spirituality by reducing it to merely a manifestation of her illness, it is important to view the two, her illness and her spirituality, as perhaps symbiotic.

84. James E. Mason, in Edward U. A. Brooks. *Tribute to Harriet Tubman, the Modern Amazon* (Auburn, N.Y.: Tubman Home, 1914).

85. "To Aunt Harriet," *The Auburn Citizen*, Auburn, N.Y., March 13, 1913.

86. Hilary McD. Beckles, ed., *Taking Liberties: Enslaved Women and Antislavery in the Caribbean, Gender and Imperialism* (New York: Manchester University Press, 1998), 150. Beckles states: "women's behaviour is particularly vulnerable to the ideological charge that actions emanate from some place other than the cerebral."

87. "To Aunt Harriet."

88. Tubman probably attended local meetings in Auburn, Geneva, Seneca Falls, and other nearby towns.

89. Sarah H. Bradford, *Harriet, the Moses of Her People* (New York: Geo. R. Lockwood & Sons, 1886), 6.

90. Ibid.

91. Ibid., 7.

92. David Blight, " 'For Something Beyond the Battlefield': Frederick Douglass and the Struggle for the Memory of the Civil War," *Journal of American History* 75, no. 4 (1989): 1159. According to Blight, the "historical memory of any transforming or controversial event emerges from cultural and political competition, from the choice to confront the past and to debate and manipulate its meaning."

93. David W. Blight, *Race and Reunion: The Civil War in American Memory* (Cambridge, Mass.: Harvard University Press, 2001), 135–39.

94. Ibid., 139.

95. Ibid., 171–210, esp. 197–99.

96. Peter Novick, *That Noble Dream: The Objectivity Question and the American Historical Profession* (New York: Cambridge University Press, 1988), 74.

97. David W. Blight, "W.E.B. Du Bois and the Struggle for American Historical Memory," in Genevieve Fabre and Robert O'Mealley, eds., *History and Memory in African American Culture* (New York: Oxford University Press, 1994), 46.

98. Blight, " 'For Something Beyond the Battlefield,' " 1177.

99. Blight, "W.E.B. Du Bois," 48.

100. Blight, " 'For Something Beyond the Battlefield,' " 1159.

101. Ibid., 1163.

102. Bradford, *Harriet* (1886), 69.

103. Bradford, *Scenes*, 20.

104. Bradford, *Harriet* (1886), 31.

105. See Bradford, *Scenes*, 31–32: " 'Well,' said Mr. Oliver Johnson, 'I am glad to see the man whose head is worth fifteen hundred dollars.' At this Joe's heart sank." In Bradford, *Harriet* (1886), 46, however, she writes, "Mr. Oliver Johnson rose up and exclaimed, 'Well, Joe, I am glad to see the man who is worth $2,000 to his master.' At this Joe's heart sank."

106. See Bradford, *Scenes*, 29. " 'Now, Joe, strip and take a whipping!' " and "He stripped off his upper clothing, and took his whipping, without a word; but as he drew his clothes up over his torn and bleeding

back, he said, 'Dis is de last!' " Compare to Bradford, *Harriet* (1886), 28: " 'Now, Joe, strip, and take a licking' " and "He stripped off his clothing, and took his flogging without a word, but as he drew his shirt up over his torn and bleeding back, he said to himself: 'Dis is de first an' de last.' "

107. Bradford, *Scenes*, 28–29.

108. Bradford, *Harriet* (1886), 41.

109. Bradford, *Scenes*, 22–23.

110. Bradford, *Harriet* (1886), 33–34.

111. For more detail regarding Bradford's and other biographers' changes and dramatization of Tubman's life story, see James McGowan, *The Harriet Tubman Journal*, vols. 1–3 (1993–1995).

112. Bradford, *Scenes*, 129.

113. Franklin B. Sanborn to unknown, Nov. 1, 1886, John Brown/Boyd Stutler Collection, West Virginia Division of Culture and History/West Virginia Memory Project, Charleston.

114. "Harriet Tubman," *Boston Sunday Herald*, October 31, 1886.

115. Bradford, *Harriet* (1886), 7.

Chapter 13

1. Elizabeth Cady Stanton, Susan B. Anthony, and Matilda Joslyn Gage, eds., *The History of Woman Suffrage*, vol. 1, *1848–1861*, 2nd ed. (Rochester, N.Y.: Charles Mann, 1887), 276–77.

2. James B. Clark, "An Hour with Harriet Tubman," in *Christophe: A Tragedy in Prose of Imperial Haiti*, ed. William Edgar Easton (Los Angeles: Grafton Publishing Company, 1911).

3. For detailed discussions of the split in the woman suffrage campaign of the late 1860s over the Fourteenth and Fifteenth Amendments, see Rosalyn Terborg-Penn, *African American Women and the Struggle for the Vote, 1850–1920* (Bloomington: Indiana University Press, 1998); Aileen Kraditor, *The Ideas of the Woman Suffrage Movement, 1890–1920* (New York: W. W. Norton & Company, 1981); Ann D. Gordon with Bettye Collier-Thomas, eds., *African American Women and the Vote, 1837–1965* (Amherst: University of Massachusetts Press, 1997); Ellen Carol DuBois, ed., *Woman Suffrage and Women's Rights* (New York: New York University Press, 1998); Ellen Carol DuBois, *Feminism and Suffrage: The Emergence of an Independent Women's Movement in America, 1848–1869* (Ithaca: Cornell University Press, 1978).

4. Terborg-Penn, *African American Women*, 24–35; Kraditor, *Ideas of the Woman Suffrage Movement*, 166–67; William S. McFeeley, *Frederick Douglass* (New York: W. W. Norton & Company, 1991), 265–73.

5. *Frederick Douglass: Selected Speeches and Writings*, ed. Philip S. Foner (Chicago: Lawrence Hill Books, 1999). Quote from the *Anti-Slavery Reporter*, July 1, 1858 (page 600).

6. Clark, "An Hour with Harriet Tubman." Tubman and Anthony had been friends since the late 1850s or early 1860s. Anthony had sheltered Tubman and other fugitives in her home. See Susan Brownell Anthony, "Diary of Susan Brownell Anthony, 1861," in *The Life and Work of Susan B. Anthony: Including Public Addresses, Her Own Letters and Many from Her Contemporaries During Fifty Years*, ed. Ida Husted Harper (Indianapolis: Bowen-Merrill Company, 1898), 1:216.

7. Statement of Mrs. Florence Carter, Earl Conrad/Harriet Tubman Collection, New York Public Library, Schomburg Center for Research in Black Culture.

8. "The Suffragists. Proceedings of Their Meeting Held Yesterday," *Auburn Morning Dispatch*, Auburn, N.Y., March 15, 1888.

9. Ibid.

10. Ibid.

11. Clark, "An Hour With Harriet Tubman."

12. See Kraditor, *Ideas of the Woman Suffrage Movement*, esp. Chapter 7.

13. Aileen Kraditor, *Up From the Pedestal* (Chicago: Quadrangle Books, 1968), 253–63.

14. Anna Julia Cooper, *A Voice from the South* (1892; reprint, New York: Negro Universities Press, 1969), 100.

15. Terborg-Penn, *African American Women*, 61, 86–89.

16. Ibid., 88.

17. "Eminent Women," *The Woman's Era* (Boston) 3, no. 1 (1896): 8.

18. "Official Minutes of the National Federation of Afro-American Women Held in Washington, D.C., July 20, 21, 22, 1896," National Association of Colored Women's Clubs, Washington, D.C., 1902.

19. Ibid.

20. Ibid.

21. "The Fight for the Ballot," *Rochester Democrat and Chronicle,* Rochester, N.Y., Nov. 19, 1896.

22. Sarah H. Bradford, *Harriet, the Moses of Her People* (New York: J. J. Little & Co., 1901), 142–43. "Yes, ladies . . . I was de conductor ob de Underground Railroad for eight years, an' I can say what mos' conductors can't say—I nebber run my train off de track an' I nebber los' a passenger." Tubman was accompanied to the meeting by her "adopted daughter, whom she had rescued from death when a baby, and had brought up as her own." This daughter could be either Gertie Davis, who would have been about twenty-two years old, or Eva Katy Stewart, a great-grandniece, who would have been about seven years old at that time. Tubman had fallen asleep during the meeting, according to Bradford, and when she was called to the stage, the daughter called to her, "Mother! Mother! They are calling for you!" (142).

23. Earl Conrad, *General Harriet Tubman,* 2nd ed. (Washington, D.C.: The Associated Publishers, Inc., 1990), 214.

24. "Davis," *Cayuga County Independent,* Auburn, N.Y., October 18, 1888.

25. North Street Cemetery Records regarding John Stewart, Cayuga County Historian's Office, Auburn, N.Y.

26. Harkless Bowley to Earl Conrad, August 29, 1939, Harkless Bowley Letters, Earl Conrad/Harriet Tubman Collection, New York Public Library, Schomburg Center for Research in Black Culture. This child was Evelyn Katherine Helena Harriet Stewart Northrup.

27. "Stewart," *Auburn Daily Advertiser,* Auburn, N.Y., March 3, 1893. John died on March 2, 1893, at the age of forty.

28. Interview with Helen W. Tatlock (Mrs. William Tatlock), Earl Conrad/Harriet Tubman Collection, New York Public Library, Schomburg Center for Research in Black Culture.

29. Emma P. Telford, "Harriet: The Modern Moses of Heroism and Visions," Cayuga County Museum, Auburn, N.Y., c. 1905.

30. Bradford, *Harriet, 1901,* 151. Robert Taylor reported the same year that every visit he made to Harriet's home from the Tuskegee Institute, he found "strangers under her roof,—aged, maimed, blind, orphans . . . At this writing [sometime in 1901] she has under her 'vine and fig-tree' two friendless old women and two homeless orphans." See Robert W. Taylor, *Harriet Tubman: The Heroine in Ebony* (Boston: George E. Ellis, Printer, 1901), 15.

31. Tatlock interview.

32. Ibid.

33. U.S. House of Representatives, Harriet [Tubman] Davis, Widow of Nelson Charles, Alias Nelson Davis, Pension Claim, HR 55A-D1, Papers Accompanying the Claim of Harriet Tubman, Record Group 233, National Archives, Washington, D.C. Miscellaneous note, Jan. 24, 1887: "2nd Sess. 49th Cong. On motion of Mr. Levering leave was granted *Harriet Tubbman [sic]* to withdraw papers from the files of the HOPR. Record, 2nd Sess. 49th Cong., Vol. 18, pt. 1, page 954." Tubman also received some help from Philip Wright in Medford, Massachusetts, who apparently retrieved the files and sent them to her in Auburn. He encouraged her to have the claim petition taken up by her local representative. *"Nobody deserves a pension more than you,"* Wright wrote to her, *"and believe that if the matter were pursued by the proper person—the representative from your district in New York—you could get it."* Philip G. Wright to Harriet Tubman, November 24, 1887, in Donald R. Shaffer, " 'I Do Not Suppose That Uncle Sam Looks at the Skin': African Americans and the Civil War Pension System, 1865–1934," *Civil War History,* June 2000.

34. Shaffer, " 'I Do Not Suppose.' "

35. U.S. House of Representatives, Harriet [Tubman] Davis, Widow of Nelson Charles, Alias Nelson Davis, Pension Claim, HR 55A-D1, Papers Accompanying the Claim of Harriet Tubman.

36. Don Shaffer, in his work on African American Civil War pensioners, has discovered that while 84 percent of white widows who applied received pensions, only 61 percent of black widows did.

37. Shaffer, " 'I Do Not Suppose.' " Shaffer also describes many other problems with African American pension cases, including the high incidence of illiteracy, which hindered the application process, and the fact that many African American soldiers and their dependents had to hire lawyers and claim agents, some of whom were incompetent or used fraudulent practices. African American pensioners also often lacked necessary biographical documents, and tracking witnesses was often far more difficult and expensive. Ultimately, it was also racism that played a role in the final outcome of many cases that were denied.

38. U.S. House of Representatives, Tubman/Davis Pension File, H.R. 4982, 55th Congress, 3rd Session.

39. U.S. House of Representatives, Tubman/Davis Pension File, petition to Honorable Sereno E. Payne, House of Representatives, 28th district, State of New York.

40. U.S. House of Representatives, Tubman/Davis Pension File, 55th Congress, 3rd Session, Report no. 1619.

41. Tatlock interview.

42. For an excellent discussion of the role of churches in black women's lives and organizational activities, see Evelyn Brooks Higginbotham, *Righteous Discontent: The Black Women's Movement in the Black Baptist Church, 1880–1920* (Cambridge, Mass.: Harvard University Press, 1993). See also Darlene Clarke Hine and Kathleen Thompson, *A Shining Thread of Hope: The History of Black Women in America* (New York: Broadway Books, 1998), 184–86.

43. "Bills Menace Historic Church," *Syracuse Post Standard*, Syracuse, N.Y., January 28, 1982.

44. Harriet Tubman to Mary Wright, May 29, 1896, Ms.A.10.1 no. 90, Boston Public Library Rare Book Room.

45. Jane Kellogg for Harriet Tubman to Ednah Dow Cheney, April 9, 1894, Ms.A.10.1 no. 36, Boston Public Library Rare Book Room. See also Jane Kellogg to Ednah Dow Cheney, June 25, 1894, Ms.A.10.1 no. 37, Boston Public Library Rare Book Room. Kellogg indicated that Tubman was having trouble raising the requisite funds but that she "is not discouraged but is working along with that object still in view." Cheney quickly sent along $20.

46. The property contained approximately 25 acres, with two houses, one brick and one wood frame, both with ten rooms each, ample space for Tubman to operate a shelter and infirmary.

47. Bradford, *Harriet* (1901), 149–50.

48. Ibid., 150.

49. Ibid. See also Bonnie Carey Ryan and Douglas V. Armstrong, *Archaeology of John Brown Hall at the Harriet Tubman Home: Site Report* (Syracuse, N.Y.: Syracuse University Archaeological Research Report, 2000), 16; and James E. Mason and Edward U. A. Brooks, *Tribute to Harriet Tubman, the Modern Amazon* (Auburn, N.Y.: Tubman Home, 1914).

50. The directors were George E. Carter, James E. Mason, Henry J. Calles, Wesley A. Ely, and Charles A. Smith. See Harriet Tubman Home, Certificate of Incorporation, Cayuga County Clerk's Office, Auburn, N.Y. See also "New Corporations," *New York Times*, New York, April 5, 1896.

51. Mason and Brooks, *Tribute*.

52. Harriet Tubman to Mary Wright, May 29, 1896, Ms.A.10.1 no. 90, Boston Public Library Rare Book Room. Tubman apparently wanted to sell copies of the new edition at the "Methodist Centennial at New York" that fall (1896), but the book was not ready until the following spring.

53. Lillie B. Chase Wyman, "Harriet Tubman," *The New England Magazine*, March 1896; and Rosa Belle Holt, "A Heroine in Ebony," *The Chautauquan*, July 1896. Wyman, and possibly Holt, may have also received information about Tubman from Eliza Wright Osborne.

54. Holt, "A Heroine in Ebony."

55. Tatlock interview.

56. Ibid.

57. "Concerning Women," *The Woman's Journal*, Boston, April 17, 1897.

58. Helen Tufts Bailie Journal, 1886–1936, Helen Tufts Bailie Papers, Sophia Smith Collection, Smith College, Northampton, Mass.

59. Ibid. See also William Lloyd Garrison Jr., Scrapbooks vol. IX : The Anti-Slavery Struggle, Garrison Family Papers, Sophia Smith Collection, Smith College, Northampton, Mass.

60. Hannah Parker Kimball, "Christ in the Slums," *The New England Magazine*, July. 635.

61. Wilbur Henry Siebert, *The Underground Railroad from Slavery to Freedom* (New York: Macmillan Co., 1898).

62. "The Underground Railroad: Manuscript Materials Collected by Professor Siebert, Houghton Library, Harvard University, Cambridge, Mass.

63. Tubman interview, ibid.

64. Clark, "An Hour with Harriet Tubman."

65. Ibid. The letter "was worn to a shadow," Tubman told Clark. "It got lost, somehow or other. Then I gave the medal to my brother's daughter to keep." Queen Victoria also sent Tubman a fine lace shawl, now in the possession of a great-niece, Mariline Wilkins. See Rosemary Sadlier, *Tubman: Harriet Tubman and the Underground Railroad: Her Life in the United States and Canada* (Toronto: Umbrella Press, 1997), 65.

66. Bradford, *Harriet* (1901). "Harriet's friends will be glad to learn that she has lately been for some time in Boston, where a surgical operation was performed on her head" (151). Efforts to locate records of this surgery have been unsuccessful. Thanks to Jeffrey Meflin at the Massachusetts General Hospital Archives for researching this.

67. Bradford, *Harriet* (1901), 152–53. "When I was in Boston I walked out one day, an' I saw a great big buildin', an' I asked a man what it was, an' he said it was a hospital. So I went right in, an' I saw a young man dere, an' I said, 'Sir, are you a doctah?' an' he said he was; den I said 'Sir, do you t'ink you could cut my head open?' . . . Den I tol' him the whole story, an' how my head was givin' me a powerful sight of trouble lately, with achin' an' buzzin', so I couldn' get no sleep at night.

"An' he said 'Lay right down on dis yer table,' an' I lay down.

" 'Didn't he give you anything to deaden the pain, Harriet?'

"No sir; I jes' lay down like a lamb fo' de slaughter, an' he sawed open my skull, an' raised it up, an' now it feels more comfortable.

" 'Did you suffer much?'

"Yes, sir, it hurt, ob cose; but I got up an' put on my bonnet an' started to walk home, but legs kin' o' gin out under me, an' dey sont fer a ambulance an' sont me home."

68. See Samuel Hopkins Adams, *Grandfather Stories* (New York: Random House, 1947), 277.

69. Agnes Garrison to Ellen Wright Garrison, November 24, 1899, Garrison Family Papers, Sophia Smith Collection, Smith College, Northampton, Mass. Agnes is the daughter of Ellen Wright and William Lloyd Garrison II. Agnes also noted in her letter that Tubman "refused refreshments because it was Friday" and she "always fasts until 12 on that day—until the Lord comes down from de cross."

70. Agnes Garrison to Ellen Wright Garrison, November 26, 1899, Garrison Family Papers, Sophia Smith Collection, Smith College, Northampton, Mass. The transcript of these interviews has not been located. Though one of the children is most certainly her great-niece Eva Katy Stewart, the identities of the other children remain unknown.

71. Agnes Garrison to Ellen Wright Garrison, December 1, 1899, Garrison Family Papers, Sophia Smith Collection, Smith College, Northampton, Mass.

72. Sarah Bradford to Franklin Sanborn, May 11, 190(1?), in Jean Humez, *Harriet Tubman: The Life and Life Stories* (Madison: University of Wisconsin Press, 2003).

73. Ibid.

74. Emily Howland Diaries, Howland Family Papers, Friends Historical Library, Swarthmore College, Swarthmore, Penn. See entries for December 21–23, 1901; January 4, 1902.

75. Conrad, *General Tubman*, 216. Susan B. Anthony dated this January 1, 1903. Elizabeth Smith Miller (Gerrit Smith's daughter), Emily Howland, the Rev. Anna Howard Shaw, and Ellen Wright Garrison (daughter of Martha C. Wright and wife of William Lloyd Garrison Jr.) were all in attendance. Emily Howland also wrote in her diary of this gathering of aging suffragists at Osborne's home, noting that "Harriet said we should never all be there again together I tho't so I dreaded to turn away from the charmed group of [?] souls" (Howland Diaries, November 18, 1902). The juxtaposition of this meeting in Auburn, where Tubman and perhaps other women of color were in attendance, is striking when compared to the NAWSA national convention in New Orleans in March 1903. There Susan B. Anthony, along with Elizabeth Blackwell, Elizabeth Smith Miller, and Elizabeth Gilmer (who wrote under the pen name Dorothy Dix) left the segregated national suffrage convention to speak to the local black women's suffrage meeting at the Phyllis Wheatly Club, creating somewhat of a controversy. White Southern suffrage associations were not eager, nor willing in many cases, to call for suffrage for all women, preferring a racial restriction of some sort and often a property or literacy requirement that would have effectively disenfranchised most black women in the South. Ida Husted Harper, ed., *The History of Woman Suffrage* (New York: J. J. Little & Ives Co., 1922), V:60.

76. National Association of Colored Women, "Minutes of the Second Convention of the National Association of Colored Women. August 14th, 15th, and 16th, 1899," paper presented at the Second Convention of the National Association of Colored Women, Chicago, August 14–16, 1899.

77. "Tubman Home Dedicated," *Auburn Daily Advertiser*, Auburn, N.Y., June 23, 1908.

78. William J. Walls, "Twenty-Second Quadrennial Session, A.M.E. Zion General Conference, 1904," in *The African Methodist Episcopal Zion Church* (Charlotte, N.C.: A.M.E. Zion Publishing House, 1974).

79. Ibid. Though Tubman deeded the property to the church, she retained a life interest, with responsibility for taxes, insurance, and maintenance while collecting the rents until the current leases expired. No other details are known at this time. See Harriet Tubman Davis to the African Methodist Episcopal Zion Church of America, Deeds, Cayuga County Court Records, Cayuga County Registrar's Office, Auburn, N.Y.

80. Walls, "Twenty-Second Quadrennial Session."

81. Ibid.

82. Ibid.

83. Smith interview, Earl Conrad / Harriet Tubman Collection, microfilm, 2 reels, New York Public Library, Schomburg Center for Research in Black Culture.

84. "The Moses of Her People. Proposed Memorial to Harriet Tubman, a Negress," *The Sun*, New York, May 2, 1909.

85. Ibid. "When I geb de home over to Zion Chu'ch w'at you s'pose dey done? Why, dey make a rule dat nobody should come in 'dout dey have a hundred dollahs. Now I wanted to make a rule dat nobody should come in 'nless dey didn't have no money 't all."

86. Ibid.

87. Frank C. Drake, "The Moses of Her People. Amazing Life Work of Harriet Tubman," *New York Herald*, New York, Sept. 22, 1907. Frank Drake was married to Sarah Bradford's daughter, Emily.

88. Drake, "The Moses of Her People."

89. "The Moses of Her People. Proposed Memorial to Harriet Tubman, a Negress."

90. Howland Diaries, October 14–17, 1905.

91. Ibid.

92. "Dedication of Harriet Tubman Home," *Auburn Daily Advertiser*, Auburn, N.Y., June 24, 1908; "Tubman Home Open and Aged Harriet Was Central Figure of Celebration," *Auburn Citizen*, Auburn, N.Y., June 24, 1908.

93. "Tubman Home Open."

94. Ibid.

95. Ibid.

96. Ibid.

97. Tubman joined the meeting of the New York Suffrage Association when it met in Auburn in October 1904. Howland Diaries, October 19, 1904.

98. "Harriet Tubman at the Hub," *Auburn Daily Advertiser,* Auburn, N.Y., May 20, 1905.

99. Ibid.

100. "With the Suffragists," *Auburn Daily Advertiser,* Auburn, N.Y., Oct. 28, 1905.

101. Howland Diaries.

102. Mildred D. Meyers, *Miss Emily: Emily Howland, Teacher of Freed Slaves, Suffragist, and Friend of Susan B. Anthony and Harriet Tubman* (Charlotte Harbor, Florida: Tabby House, 1998), 209–10.

103. Alice Lucas Brickler to Earl Conrad, July 28, 1939, Earl Conrad/ Harriet Tubman Collection, New York Public Library, Schomburg Center for Research in Black Culture.

104. Ibid.

105. "Harriet Tubman Ill and Penniless. Noted Colored Woman Taken to Harriet Tubman Home Which She Founded," *New York Age,* New York, June 8, 1911.

106. "Moses of Her Race Ending Her Life in Home She Founded," *New York World,* New York, June 25, 1911; "When Slaves Were Spirited Underground to Canada," *New York Evening Sun,* New York, June 10, 1911.

107. Statement of Mrs. Florence Carter and Smith interview, Earl Conrad/Harriet Tubman Collection, New York Public Library, Schomburg Center for Research in Black Culture.

108. Humez, *Harriet Tubman.*

109. Private papers, Judith Bryant. Emma Stewart, the wife of William Henry Stewart Jr., incurred over $200 in hospital bills for Tubman.

110. Records of Fort Hill Cemetery, Auburn, N.Y.

111. "Death of Aunt Harriet, 'Moses of Her People,' " *Auburn Daily Advertiser,* Auburn, N.Y., March 11, 1913; "Harriet Tubman Is Dead," *Auburn Citizen,* Auburn, N.Y., March 11, 1913.

112. "Death of Aunt Harriet."

113. "A Race of Harriets Would Secure the Future of the Negro, Says Bishop Blackwell," *Auburn Citizen,* Auburn, N.Y., March 14, 1913.

114. "Mrs. Talbert's Tribute," *Auburn Citizen,* March 14, 1913, 5.

115. "Aunt Harriet's Funeral," *Auburn Daily Advertiser,* Auburn, N.Y., March 13, 1913.

116. "To the Colored Race. Mrs. Seward Was Always a True Friend, Declares This Negro," *Auburn Citizen,* Auburn, N.Y., Nov. 9, 1913.

117. "To a Most Heroic Negress. Fitting Memorial of Harriet Tubman Davis Is Appropriately Unveiled," *Auburn Citizen,* Auburn, N.Y., June 13, 1914.

118. "Program of the Unveiling of Bronze Tablet in Memory of Harriet Tubman," Harriet Tubman vertical file, Cayuga Museum, Auburn, N.Y.

119. "Proposes Monument over Tubman Grave," *Auburn Advertiser Journal,* Auburn, N.Y., June 15, 1914; "Unveil 'Tubman' Memorial," *Cleveland Advocate,* Cleveland, OH, July 17, 1915.

120. "A Race of Harriets."

121. Benjamin G. Brawley, *Women of Achievement. Written for the Fireside Schools of the Women's American Baptist Home Mission Society* (Chicago: Women's American Baptist Home Mission Society, 1919); Benjamin G. Brawley, *Negro Builders and Heroes* (Chapel Hill: University of North Carolina Press, 1937); Elizabeth Ross Haynes, *Unsung Heroes* (New York: DuBois and Dill, 1921); George F. Bragg, *Heroes of the Eastern Shore* (Baltimore: G. F. Bragg, 1939); George F. Bragg, *Men of Maryland* (Baltimore: Church Advocate Press, 1925); Thomas W. Burton, *History of the Underground Railroad, American Mysteries, and Daughters of Jerusalem* (Springfield, Ohio: Whyte Printing Co., 1925). See also Henrietta Buckmaster, *Let My People Go* (New York: Harper & Brothers, 1941).

122. David W. Blight, *Race and Reunion: The Civil War in American Memory* (Cambridge, Mass.: Harvard University Press, 2001), 231–37. See Hildegarde Hoyt Swift, *The Railroad to Freedom: A Story of the Civil War* (New York: Harcourt, Brace & World, Inc., 1932); Anne Parrish, *A Clouded Star* (New York: Harper & Brothers, 1948); Oscar Sherwin, " 'I'se Free 'fo' I Die,' " *The Negro History Bulletin*, June 1940.

123. Sasha Small, *Heroines* (New York: Workers Library Publishers, 1937).

124. Ibid., 20.

125. Blight, *Race and Reunion*, 332.

126. Conrad did his own accounting and came up with less than nineteen trips. But then, oddly, he decided to use Bradford's numbers instead. See James McGowan, "Harriet Tubman: According to Sarah Bradford," *Harriet Tubman Journal* 2, no. 1 (1994).

127. Carrie Chapman Catt to Earl Conrad, June 1, 1939, Earl Conrad/Harriet Tubman Collection, New York Public Library, Schomburg Center for Research in Black Culture.

128. Earl Conrad to Carrie Chapman Catt, December 20, 1939, Earl Conrad/Harriet Tubman Collection, New York Public Library, Schomburg Center for Research in Black Culture.

129. Carrie Chapman Catt to Earl Conrad, January 25, 1940, Earl Conrad/Harriet Tubman Collection, New York Public Library, Schomburg Center for Research in Black Culture.

130. Earl Conrad to Carrie Chapman Catt, February 3, 1940, Earl Conrad/Harriet Tubman Collection, New York Public Library, Schomburg Center for Research in Black Culture.

131. Earl Conrad to Carrie Chapman Catt, February 3, 1940, Earl Conrad/Harriet Tubman Collection, New York Public Library, Schomburg Center for Research in Black Culture.

132. Carrie Chapman Catt to Earl Conrad, February 17, 1940, Earl Conrad/Harriet Tubman Collection, New York Public Library, Schomburg Center for Research in Black Culture.

133. See Earl Conrad/Harriet Tubman Collection, reel 1, box 1, "Correspondence."

134. See Earl Conrad papers, Cayuga Community College, Bourke Memorial Library, Auburn, N.Y. See also Earl Conrad/Harriet Tubman Collection, New York Public Library, Schomburg Center for Research in Black Culture.

135. Mary McLeod Bethune to Mrs. Caroll Johnson, May 4, 1844, Bryant Family Scrapbook, private collection, Auburn, N.Y. See also Robert Bent, Research Correspondence, S.S. *Harriet Tubman*, Spring Point Museum. South Portland, Maine.

136. " 'Harriet Tubman,' New Liberty Ship, Launched in Maine," *Auburn Citizen Advertiser*, Auburn, N.Y., June 3, 1944.

137. See, "S.S. Tubman, New Liberty Ship, Slides Down Ways," *Chicago Defender*, Chicago, June 10, 1944; "S.S. Harriet Tubman, Named for Woman Abolitionists, Goes Down Ways at Portland, Maine," *Baltimore Afro-American*, Baltimore, June 6, 1944; and Toki Schalk, "A Dream Come True," *Baltimore Afro-American*, Baltimore, June 10, 1944. Alida Stewart Johnson and Thelma Frazier, both grandnieces, were matrons of honor. Twenty-two relatives attended the festivities, including members of the Bowley, Stewart, Keene, Cornish, Proctor, Thompson, Bryant, Brickler, and Wilkins families.

138. "S.S. Harriet Tubman, Named for Woman Abolitionists, Goes Down Ways."

139. Dorothy Sterling, *Freedom Train, the Story of Harriet Tubman* (New York: Doubleday, 1954); Ann Petry, *Harriet Tubman, Conductor on the Underground Railroad* (New York: Harper Collins, 1955).

INDEX

NB: Harriet Tubman is referred to as HT throughout this index.

ABOUT THE AUTHOR

KATE CLIFFORD LARSON has spent years researching the life and times of Harriet Tubman. She earned her doctorate in history at the University of New Hampshire. A graduate of Simmons College and Northeastern University, Larson has won numerous academic awards and fellowships in support of her work. She lives in Winchester, Massachusetts.